THE BEST OF
Outdoor Life

THE *Best* OF
Outdoor Life

Edited by
WILLIAM E. RAE

THE LYONS PRESS

First edition copyright © 1975, 1982, published by
Harper & Row as *A Treasury of OUTDOOR LIFE*

Second, updated edition copyright © 1987, published by
Outdoor Life Books as *A Treasury of OUTDOOR LIFE*

First Lyons Press Edition

Printed in the United States of America

10   9   8   7   6   5   4   3   2   1

The Library of Congress Cataloging-in-Publication Data
is available on file.

To my wife, Peg

Contents

Foreword

by Todd W. Smith

Editor in Chief
Outdoor Life

When founding editor J. A. McGuire launched OUTDOOR LIFE magazine in 1898, those who read his first editions did so by candlelight. Horse and wagon was still the most widely used mode of transportation, and indoor plumbing had yet to make its way into most homes. McGuire established his magazine not in a fancy New York high-rise, but in a small office just off Curtis Street in what today is downtown Denver.

In those days Denver was the gateway to the West—a wild and unbridled land filled with marauding bears and trout streams brimming with fish. Readers back East hungered for stories about the fabulous hunting and fishing opportunities to be found there. And McGuire was determined to satisfy their appetite—so much so, in fact, that he subtitled OUTDOOR LIFE "The Magazine of the West."

From his first editorial, McGuire's intentions were clear:

> *We propose to represent and reflect the interests of every devotee of outdoor life. . . . Reliability and accuracy in all things pertaining to outdoor life will be the cornerstone of our claim to popularity. . . . Our staff of contributors, as well as our editorial one, is composed of practical sportsmen, and their contributions will be veritable monographs on the topics and subjects treated. In short, we offer a sportsmen's magazine, conducted by sportsmen, in the interest of sportsmen . . .*

We'd call that a mission statement today, but in those simpler times it was merely one man's personal pledge to his readers. Yet from those roots sprang a magazine that has not only chronicled the news of the hunting and fishing world, but also, in many ways, created it.

I would define the best editors as those who have a clear vision of what their readers want, and the ability to deliver it. J. A. McGuire was that kind of man. He clearly understood the westward expansion of America and the riches of its outdoor environment, not only as subjects of great fascination to sportsmen, but also as resources in need of stewardship.

As OUTDOOR LIFE grew, he also saw the calamitous problems facing wildlife, which is why game conservation became such an important part of the magazine's foundation and purpose. McGuire personally crusaded for the protection of the grizzly bear and, likewise, made the need for waterfowl conservation a prominent cause of the day. In establishing the prestigious OUTDOOR LIFE Conservation Award, he surely helped build the magazine's reputation as the book of record where wildlife conservation is concerned—a reputation that the publication still enjoys today.

Most important, he set the framework for all the chief editors who followed by establishing a legacy of great storytelling that has entertained and informed OUTDOOR LIFE readers for more than 100 years. In the pages that follow, you'll find a compendium of some of the finest stories that have ever appeared in this magazine. William

E. (Bill) Rae compiled them originally some ten years after his retirement in 1973. The anthology was revised in 1982, and again now in 2001.

In my years as editor of OUTDOOR LIFE and other publications, I have come to believe that magazines are a bit like families; they take nurturing and time to build. Indeed, editors are a lot like fathers—offering a guiding hand to writers when it's needed, but always with a keen understanding of what their readers want. Though I did not know him personally, I believe Bill Rae was that kind of editor.

He certainly knew good writing talent when he saw it. More important, he understood how to develop it in those who had not yet made writing their profession. I have been told by many authors that Rae had a gift of being able to offer constructive criticism in such a way that they could go back to doing a rewrite feeling good about themselves and knowing that their stories would be stronger for it. Perhaps that is why Rae is remembered so fondly by so many of the writers who worked for him.

Jerry Gibbs, whom Rae hired in 1973 to succeed Joe Brooks as fishing editor, describes Rae as "a tyrant to work for in-house but a wonderful editor who helped writers make a story exactly the way he wanted it. He would spend hours with a guy that he thought had talent or a story that had possibilities. 'Do this,' he'd say, 'and I'll buy it.'"

Hunting editor Jim Zumbo says that "Bill Rae started most of us out on our writing careers. He told it like it was and how to make your stories better. In fact, Bill Rae was famous for writing nicer rejection letters than acceptance letters. He wasn't afraid to hurt someone's feelings to make him or her a better writer.

"Bill was also a firm believer in separation between editorial and ad sales. He didn't want any kind of influence from industry on copy. For example, you couldn't say you used a 'Flatfish' plug. It had to be a 'banana-shaped' plug. A 'Dardevle' became a 'red-and-white, spoon-shaped lure.'

"Bill was always looking for the gem in the rock pile. But he was a great editor who took the time."

Whitetail guru John Wootters speaks reverently of Rae, who purchased his first story in 1951. Wootters reminisces that "Bill Rae was the only editor I ever knew who never sent a rejection slip. If he didn't like a story, he would write me a page and a half about what he disliked about it. That taught me a lot about how to put together a story. He obviously cared about writers and went out of his way to work with them.

"My best memory of Bill concerns a Wyoming grayling story that I submitted to him at his office in 1961 on one of my yearly trips to New York. Bill glanced at the story, then reached into his desk drawer and pulled out a spiral notebook in which he kept the magazine's inventory. A third of the book was devoted to trout and grayling stories that he already had in inventory, but I noticed he didn't have many bass features.

"'Know anything about bass fishing?' he asked. I told him I'd have a manuscript on his desk by the end of the month. What this taught me is that it isn't just about having a good story that makes a sale, but knowing what an editor needs. . . . By the way, he bought the bass piece.

"On another occasion, I sent him my first deer article, about hunting whitetails in the thick Texas brush. The story had a lot to do with the personal tricks I used to work so close to the deer. I got this nice acceptance letter back from Bill, but the one sentence that still stands out to me is 'We like this piece because it has the ring of authority,' which goes to show that if you write about what you know about, you'll be all right.

"Bill Rae did not regard writers merely as sources, but rather as people who needed to be helped. He always made me feel welcome and important. And it was always a pleasure to do business with him.

"Coming out of World War II, the whole magazine industry was in transition. Bill Rae recognized this. What he did with OUTDOOR LIFE was show the rest of the industry what outdoor magazines would look like for the next few years by using more small illustrations, more color, and more live-game photos."

Jim Carmichel, who Rae hired to succeed Jack O'Connor as shooting editor, recalls that "Bill Rae was an old-school editor. He was quite austere, a Harvard graduate. His father had been an actor, and he came from a theatrical family. He used to delight in taking writers to the famous theatrical clubs in New York to hobnob with the Broadway stars.

"Bill Rae had a way of never saying what he wanted. But by the time he finished giving you that fish-eyed stare, you knew what he wanted. I was just a kid when I went up to see him on my first trip to New York. I met him in his office, but he never spoke and never changed expression. I finished making my pitch and finally said, 'Well, I guess it's time to leave.' Without uttering a word Bill gave me one of those 'Don't call us, we'll call you' expressions. Two years later he did call and invited me to come to work for OUTDOOR LIFE.

"The best advice he ever gave me was when he sent me on my first trip. 'Focus the camera and hold it still,' he said. And I've never forgotten that."

The original foreword to this anthology was written by Ben East, OUTDOOR LIFE's most famous adventure writer. East quoted Rae as saying, "An editor is a man who doesn't know exactly what he wants but recognizes it instantly." I don't believe that of Bill Rae. Given the great contributions he made to OUTDOOR LIFE during his tenure as editor in chief, I think he knew exactly what he was doing.

Interestingly, this was a man who was not born to hunting and fishing. He came to the outdoor sports rather later in life and picked up much of his outdoor experience once he became the magazine's chief editor. You get a glimpse of that when you read "Stag Line," the story of Rae's first elk hunting trip with renowned hunter Max Wilde and then editor-at-large Charlie Elliott. Yet Rae clearly had an eye for great outdoor stories, be they penned by famous names such as Zane Grey or those unsolicited diamonds in the rough that sometimes appear by writers who have but one good story in them.

Most of all, Bill Rae understood his readers emphatically. He had a great knack for creating balanced editorial packages that included all the elements that make OUTDOOR LIFE so popular: adventure, how-to, great destinations, conservation, and news.

What follows is truly a labor of love by Rae, who spent months pouring over every edition of OUTDOOR LIFE that had ever been published to choose its best stories. As editor-in-chief of OUTDOOR LIFE during its 100th anniversary, I know a little bit about what Rae went through in having to sort through a full century's worth of materials to glean the best. What you'll come away with in reading this anthology, however, is just how important OUTDOOR LIFE has been in chronicling the hunting and fishing sports, and how far we've come in preserving our wildlife resources.

When OUTDOOR LIFE began, the great buffalo herds of the West had been nearly exterminated. Many species of wild game from elk to antelope were on the brink of extinction due to overharvesting by market hunters. States east of the Mississippi had little wild game left at all. Witness today the vast populations of whitetail deer nationwide and the reintroduction of wild turkeys in virtually every state of the Union. Elk have been released in Kentucky and our waterfowl populations are at an all-time high. Grizzly numbers are clearly on the rise, as are populations of wild wolves in many western states.

Hunters and fishermen number some 29 million Americans and, thanks to stories like these, a whole new generation of outdoorsmen is beginning to discover the wonderful adventures that can only be had through hunting and fishing. Perhaps most important, the stories in *The Best of Outdoor Life* serve as a bridge between the generations—from Col. Townsend Whelen, OUTDOOR LIFE's first firearms editor, to present-day shooting editor Jim Carmichel; from angling editor Ray Bergman to fishing editor Jerry Gibbs.

If you're a longtime subscriber to OUTDOOR LIFE, I hope these stories will rekindle some fond memories. And for the new generation of readers who might not be familiar with some of these writers, may their stories provide a glimpse of the great outdoor adventures that lie waiting for you to discover just over the ridge or around the next bend in the river.

Introduction

When I retired in 1973, after having served as editor-in-chief of OUTDOOR LIFE Magazine for twenty-two years, it was seventy-five years old—and I was sixty-five. I was fourth in the line of editors begun in 1898 in Denver, Colorado by John A. McGuire, founder and first editor, who served in that capacity for thirty-one years. His son, Harry McGuire, took over when the magazine moved to Mt. Morris, Illinois, in 1929 and edited it for the next five years, although his father remained on the masthead variously as publisher, managing editor and, finally, associate editor.

At this point, 1934, Popular Science Publishing Co., Inc., purchased OUTDOOR LIFE and brought it to New York City, where Raymond J. Brown became the editor for the next sixteen years. I had the good fortune to succeed him and inherit the blue-ribbon staff he had put together, a group such as no other outdoor editor has ever had at his call, I'm sure.

Now I feel as though I have been editor for seventy-five years, because I have looked at, or read, everything my three predecessors put in the magazine in the years since 1898 as well as the material I selected during my tenure. It all adds up to something in excess of sixteen thousand stories and departments alone, out of which I have combed a fraction of one percent of the treasure, some of it stored in bound volumes for three-quarters of a century.

The best of OUTDOOR LIFE? Put it this way: it's probably as representative of what should be in a treasury of hunting, fishing and allied outdoor activities as is possible, considering all the facets of the subject. Think of all the animals to hunt between antelope and zebra, and all the ways and places to hunt them. Think of all the birds between Auerhahn and zenaida dove, and all the species of fish, and the ways to fish for them. And consider just this one aspect of method: do you use a rifle, a shotgun or a bow; a fly rod, a spinning rod or a casting rod?

John Mason Brown once quoted Charles Poore as saying one man's anthology is another man's doorstop. The cliché suits us better: one man's meat is another man's poison, especially if he is strictly a deer hunter and loathes, say, stumbling after coons in the dark. And if he is a snake hunter, he certainly will not settle for grunting, or fiddling, for worms, although "Worm-Fiddling Championship" (August 1973), by Frederick Behrnes, was an appealing story in itself.

No, each to his own taste, and I've tried to satisfy many tastes to make this anthology a reflection of OUTDOOR LIFE, the magazine. In my first wade through 75 years of writings I filled a notebook with 433 possible choices, any one of which would not be out of place in an anthology that professes to contain "the best of OUTDOOR LIFE," since under that standard one may collect the "best writing," the "most entertaining story," the "most instructive," the "most interesting," the "most unusual," and the "most significant."

But who had ever heard of a seven-volume bedside reader? Cutting the first harvest back to 180 stories involved many sacrifices, such as the hard-hitting articles on strip mining, channelization, pesticides, the use of locked gates and armed guards to bar public access to land in the West, the massive kill of wildlife by oil spills, the illegal taking of bighorn sheep in California and bears in Alaska, and the bootleg traffic in polar bear permits.

I had to pass over many topflight stories because of their length. For a number of years OUTDOOR LIFE ran a double-length story in each issue. We called them "longies," and their extra length—and payment—inspired high-grade writing. I have worked in a couple of examples, but there is no way to cram into even a volume of this size such book condensations as "Hunter," by J. A. Hunter, "Jungle Lore," by Jim Corbett, and "People of the Deer," by Farley Mowat, all published in sixteen-page bonus sections in the fall of 1957. I have not included any of the some forty Conservation Award stories because of length or changed circumstances.

Even so, I was still flying in the face of economic feasibility, sheer bulk, and considerations as yet unmentioned. What about covers, four-color paintings, the advertisements, other art and standing features that lend salt and sweet to a treasury like this? So—the last cut was with a cleaver and following the carnage it was a toss-up whether to put between covers the remains on the chopping block or what lay on the floor. Many of those old stories by now had become old friends.

Some have been omitted because one good story on a subject tends to cancel out another on the same subject. The reader will observe that field editors and department editors are often represented by multiple choices. The explanation is that these men have written literally hundreds of stories for the magazine, and were hired at the outset for their outstanding talents as writers, photographers and outdoorsmen. Many another fine story, by the way, has been excluded because its photos were an integral part of its message, and only a very limited number of photos can be used in a "reading" book of this kind.

Perhaps the strangest story of all goes back to the very first issue, published in January 1898 by Editor McGuire. To introduce it properly requires some historical background. John A. McGuire was born in Iowa in 1869 and moved with his parents to Denver when he was thirteen. At eighteen he became associated with an outdoor magazine (*Sports Afield*) as cycling editor and printer, and five years later started *Cycling West*, which he sold when he founded OUTDOOR LIFE with J. A. Ricker in 1898.

The first issue published in Denver had a press run of five thousand copies at ten cents each. In his opening editorial "concerning the publication of what we intend shall be a perfect sportsmen's magazine," McGuire went to the heart of the matter:

> We propose to represent and reflect the interests of every devotee of outdoor life and its attendant sports recreations, as well as those tradesmen who cater to and supply their demands.

This forthright statement was borne out in all fifty-four pages of this first issue's editorial content—except, curiously enough, in the lead story, "A Lost Soul," by Dan De Foe (no relation to the author of *Robinson Crusoe*). I want to summarize it.

The Lost Soul was Marie Cushman, "a tall handsome girl of sixteen, precociously developed, whose brown hair, blue eyes, and sprightly mien were admired by scores of the young gentry of the region (Missouri)."

She had eyes only for Clarence Woodruff, handsome but with little else except backbone. She had spirit. Her father had iron self-will. He forbade them to see one another. They planned to elope. The father sent her off to school in St. Louis, where she was virtually held prisoner for weeks. She planned an escape and "was so successful in executing it that while detectives searched the city for her, she was in the private car of a wealthy but lecherous railway magnate, speeding toward the city of Chicago."

Years pass. It is 1884 in Glenwood Springs, Colorado, with its "saloons, gambling houses, and *maisons de joie*." A covered wagon enters drawn by a span of large but bony horses. Driving it is Clarence Woodruff, and with him are his wife, two young daughters, and his dying mother. He is broke, there is no shelter in the town, and he needs work. As he pleads his case, one of the horses falls down in the last throes.

At this point "two young women of the demi-monde come by, one smoking a cigarette with evident relish." As she confronts this scene of misery, the taller one, with the brown hair and blue eyes, gasps: "Oh, my God!"

After tottering into the Palace saloon, where "she swallowed a full glass of brandy," she walked rapidly to the bank and instructed the clerk to arrange a credit of $100 for Clarence Woodruff and to make it known to him without revealing her identity. Clarence was stunned.

"Who done it?" he asked (honestly).

"A friend, and that is all I am at liberty to tell you," said the clerk.

His unknown benefactress departed immediately for Salt Lake City. Later, when Clarence went to the bank to pay back the sum, he was given a note left to him for the occasion. It read:

"Do not think of paying any part of the money, Clarence, for my whereabouts will be unknown to the bank and I shall never get it. Do not ask about me, or try to find me, or ever think of me again.

"I am lost. Good-bye, forever. *Marie*."

Fortunately for the future of OUTDOOR LIFE, at least as a sportsmen's magazine, we had no more of that, daring though it must have seemed for the times. In fact, the rest of that first issue hewed close to the line. Along with our first choice in this anthology, "A Moose Hunt in Alaska," by Dall DeWeese, the rest of the fifty-four pages was devoted to a rattlesnake story, a tiger hunt, fly fishing for trout on the Platte River, a scrimmage with a bear, a rabbit hunt, six pages to trap shooting, and thirteen pages, one quarter of the editorial content, to cycling.

This last, of course, derived from McGuire's interest in bicycling, both as an editor and an expert rider, but by 1903 the bicycle had just about vanished editorially as the automobile chugged in slowly, but relentlessly. There were twelve pages of advertisements in that first issue, most of them for bicycles, cameras and photographic supplies, and guns and ammunition, but there were also pianos, beer, typewriters and taxidermy, coal and carpets, English and Scottish woolens, candies, and, of course, this one: "Smoke D.W.C. 5¢ Cigars." Fishing tackle manufacturers were slow coming in.

The photography fascinated me. In a department of that name, its editor set forth this prospectus: "OUTDOOR LIFE aims to make its photographic department of interest and use to every camera owner from the boy who got a pocket Kodak day before yesterday to the veteran wielder of a lordly 15 X 12, and with this end in view each issue of the magazine will contain an editorial on some branch of our craft as well as contributed articles on the art and science of photography."

There were times in the early years when I felt the photography generally was superior to the stories. The December 1901 issue opened with a color photo of an elk, and several more color photos, "engraved for us in the three-color process by the U.S. Colortype Co. of Denver," were used as frontispieces in 1902. In June 1904 a series of eight game birds in "true colors" opened with a photo of a Wilson's Snipe. Extra prints were available for five cents apiece, or three for ten cents.

The Photography department did yeoman work from 1898 to 1906, and I feel that not until the Will Jacqmar-Fred McKinley-Pete Barrett cycle of stories in the last fifteen years did OUTDOOR LIFE make a comparable effort to teach readers how to take better wildlife pictures. The magazine did institute a photo contest in 1927 with a top prize of $25, but it wasn't the same.

From 1898 until 1917 the magazine's page size was 6½ by 9 inches, and for the first five years the pages were unnumbered. This was changed in 1903 when the editorial pages were numbered consecutively for the entire year and then for six months. It wasn't until 1910 that the ad pages got numbers. By July 1905 McGuire got around to the table of contents, moving it from the back to the front of the book and indicating the page numbers.

Periodically, he announced circulation figures. The December 1902 issue comprised 35,000 copies of 132 pages and, he said, "circulation now extends to every state in the Union and several foreign countries." Photos were used on the covers of the June 1903 ("Chicks") and July 1903 ("Beaver") issues. September 1903 (page 621) carries the first synopsis of The Game Laws of the United States. The December 1905 issue totaled 45,000 copies of 148 pages (new high) at fifteen cents—the first price increase.

(Incidentally, McGuire felt constrained to run an announcement in February explaining why OUTDOOR LIFE had to increase its price to fifteen cents "even though Munsey's, McClure's and other popular magazines can put out such elegant periodicals at 10¢.")

Being a senior citizen, I found extremely interesting—and sad—an advertisement in January 1905 announcing that OUTDOOR LIFE could be bought in combination with many now defunct magazines, such as *Pictorial Review, Leslie's Monthly, Pearson's, American Boy, Smart Set, Scribner's Magazine, Century Magazine, St. Nicholas,* and *North American Review.*

The next increase came in 1917 when OUTDOOR LIFE went to twenty cents and a "flat form," 8½ by 12 inches, slightly larger than its present size. It went up again, twenty-five cents in 1927 when it announced its consolidation with *Outdoor Recreation* (formerly *Outers*). The "big change" came in 1934 when Popular Science Publishing Co., Inc., purchased the magazine and brought it to New York City. A month after the purchase, the new owners dropped the price to fifteen cents and Raymond J. Brown became the editor. All in all, it was a good omen for what McGuire had taken pride in pointing to as "A Magazine of the West."

I have always had great respect for Ray Brown as an editor. Having come in on his heels, so to speak, I was surrounded with evidences of his exploits, the superb staff he had put together; the gallery of wildlife paintings by Francis Lee Jaques; the Conservation Pledge, originated as a public service in 1946 and presented to the nation in a public ceremony held in Washington, D.C., in February 1947, where Secretary of the Interior Krug delivered the acceptance speech; the enormous success experienced in having the pledge adopted in all corners of this country and Canada. The Pledge conception was a stroke of genius.

But until I undertook this project, John A. McGuire was not a great deal more to me than a large photograph of "our founder" in the lobby of the building on Fourth Avenue and later Lexington Avenue.

It's readily apparent now, however, that McGuire, too, was an astute editor. I think he really got his bearings when he published Teddy Roosevelt's lion hunt in two parts in April and May 1901 (reprinted in this volume). Before that there was a bit too much anonymity, suggesting fiction. A few by-lines illustrate the point: "By Tenderfoot," "By M. T. Gunne," "By Sobanichi" and "Marjorie." Or this ancient device: "S—— wanted to see the country. M—— was desirous of seeing the skeleton of a sheep." And one writer seemed to copy another in calling animals "his bearship," "his mooseship," etc. Finally, there was too much dialogue like this:

"Water rising?"

"Wuss'n that. Injuns! Look thar."

Only in much bigger doses.

From the start, OUTDOOR LIFE raised its voice in the cause of conservation and against game hogs, market hunters, and poor game management. McGuire introduced a monthly conservation department in February 1918 called: "Bulletin—American Game Protective Association." Several magazines carried it. That's undoubtedly why he substituted OUTDOOR LIFE's own department titled simply "Conservation" in 1927. It was under the guidance of an advisory board of distinguished conservationists.

The board was made up in large part of former winners of an OUTDOOR LIFE Award, established in 1923, which was presented to the citizen "who accomplishes the greatest good for the cause of conservation" in a given year. Among the recipients were Dr. William T. Hornaday, Arthur M. Hyde (later Secretary of Agriculture), Jack Miner, Aldo Leopold and J. N. "Ding" Darling, wildlife conservationists all.

For twenty years, McGuire himself carried on a campaign to outlaw steel bear traps, prohibit needlessly large dog packs in hunting bears, and establish closed seasons and bag limits in bear states. Many states adopted the model law.

As for the rest, the stories in this treasury attest to his abilities as an editor. He was quick to appreciate the significance for outdoorsmen of every new mode of travel, the safety bicycle, the automobile, the motorcycle sidecar, the camper, and, for a brief time, even gave departmental space to the airplane. Nor was he neglectful of the old modes, horse, foot, boat and canoe. Advertisers were quick to respond. The elder McGuire died in 1942.

Harry McGuire was only twenty-five when he became editor of OUTDOOR LIFE in 1929, the year it moved to Mt. Morris, Illinois. His father was now publisher and managing editor. Harry McGuire, a Notre Dame graduate, had studied playwriting under George Pierce Baker at his famous Yale '47 Workshop, and had several prizes for his plays to his credit. Over the next five years he wrote some strong editorials in support of conservation.

In 1931 he brought out, and dedicated to his father, *Tales of Rod and Gun* (Macmillan), a modest anthology of seventeen hunting and fishing stories selected by himself after having searched "the whole field of outdoor literature in America to find stories which came closest to his ideal." Only nine of the stories had appeared in OUTDOOR LIFE. The rest were from other sources.

It may prove something, possibly Charles Poore's evaluation of anthologies in general, that I have included in this treasury eighteen OUTDOOR LIFE stories from the John McGuire period, 1898–1931, alone (only one of which appeared in *Tales of Rod and Gun*), and omitted reluctantly several fine stories by writers who later became more closely identified with other outdoor magazines, omitted them not in pique, heaven forbid, but simply because there are too many other good stories by OUTDOOR LIFE "regulars" crying for inclusion.

As for myself, I'm proud of my twenty-two years as editor of OUTDOOR LIFE, the most enjoyable of all my working years (devoted exclusively to newspapers and magazines). Starting with Godfrey Hammond, the publishers were always understanding. I'm proud of the OUTDOOR LIFE Conservation Award I introduced in 1951. Its design was to make our conservation stories as readable as our adventure stories. It was awarded once a month on the basis of a story that told how some individual or organization had given meaning to the words of the

Pledge through a project in conservation. In later years it has been awarded on an annual basis.

I'm proud of the staff I inherited and the additions I made to it over the years. I'm proud of the Regional Insert, another first in the outdoor field. I'm proud of those circulation figures—1,840,000 copies a month. And I salute the writers who made this project possible.

I'd also like to express my warmest thanks to Margaret Noonan, Nereida Marks, Rose Badillo, Esther MacSwan, John Sill, Jeff Fitschen and Henry Gross for their aid in the preparation of this treasury.

WILLIAM E. RAE
Orleans, Mass. 1975

Introduction to the Second Edition

I must be the only man in the world who has read, or looked at, everything that has appeared in OUTDOOR LIFE magazine from the day it was founded in 1898 to December 1981. This came about when I was asked to add a dozen years to the First Edition of *A Treasury of Outdoor Life,"* which I had compiled shortly after my retirement as editor of the magazine a decade ago.

This Second Edition includes the best stories and illustrations right through the year 1981. In selecting the material I thought occasionally that the magazine had strayed off course, but it got back on track all right except for what I considered a curious imbalance in the use of photographs and paintings.

The photography was superb and there was no complaint on that score. There were also some exciting paintings by old friends such as Tom Beecham, Dave Blossom, John McDermott and Bob Cassell, but not nearly so many as one would expect. New names were few and far between, an exception being that of George Luther Schelling, who specializes in exciting underwater fish paintings.

Then I remembered that before my retirement some of our best illustrators had joined a movement to the West lured by rich rewards for Western art, by which is meant simply realist art with Western themes. Frank McCarthy, for example, five of whose paintings, dated 1964 to 1967, appear in this Treasury, is one of several stars of the school who started as professional illustrator in New York City.

Excellent photography has long been a mark of OUTDOOR LIFE, as well it should be. I need do no more than mention the superb photo-essays of John S. Crawford in the Sixties and Seventies, as well as the work of such people as Pete Barrett, Bill McRae and our own field editors.

The latter category really includes Erwin Bauer and his wife, Peggy, who moved from Ohio to Wyoming as freelancers, soon joined the staff of OUTDOOR LIFE and opened the way to a flood of wildlife photography. They already have published four books on the subject, especially of big game.

But good painting has always been an ingredient of the exciting outdoor magazine. There are things it can do that photography can't do. I'm thinking of the unpredictable close encounters between man and wild animal that leave no room for picture-taking.

It adds humor. For example we're pleased to see the beleaguered rabbit elude the hunters. Take a few moments to examine the paintings in this book and notice the many situations and encounters that are better portrayed by the artist than the photographer.

Having had a look ahead at some of the early issues of 1982, I'm happy to report that some new illustrators appear to be getting a chance.

As for the major ingredient of an anthology such as this, to wit, memorable stories, I had no trouble finding them. There were more yarns of outstanding quality than I could find room for in the pages allotted for new material, and once again I shall have to apologize to a lengthy list of writers for not being able to include their work.

WILLIAM E. RAE
Orleans, Mass. 1982

THE BEST OF
Outdoor Life

A Moose Hunt in Alaska

Dall DeWeese

January 1898

This was my favorite in the very first issue of OUTDOOR LIFE. Editor J. A. McGuire called author DeWeese "the greatest big-game hunter in the country." Born in Ohio, DeWeese moved to Colorado in 1883 at the age of twenty-six. There he became a fruit grower and "took a hunting trip every year." On another Alaska hunt the year after this one he killed four moose for mounting in "our national museum (Denver)." He said it was necessary to do this now "before this soon to be extinct animal follows the wake of the buffalo." Less accurate as a prophet than as a shooter. However, he was to hit the bull's-eye on another occasion when he knocked out a touring carnival boxer under four rounds for a sizeable purse.

[The following account is a letter written by Mr. DeWeese from Alaska to a coterie of sportsmen friends residing in his Colorado home, Canon City, relating the experiences of an Alaska hunt on which the largest moose ever recorded was killed. As the story is best told in the great hunter's simple language to his friends, we reprint it verbatim at his request.—Ed.]

Cook's Inlet, Head of Kusiloff River,
Moose Camp, Sept. 9, 1897

Consistent as I am with human nature, boys, I wanted one more moose and I don't believe you will say, "game hog," for you must remember that I am a long way from home and where these animals seem plenty and I am saving the skins and antlers to be mounted for my museum. Up to this time I could have killed two other moose with small heads (about 45 to 50 inches) and two cows and one calf moose, but I did not want them. After I secured my first bull it was then a good one or none. If you give this letter to our home paper and it should fall into the hands of some of the "would-be sportsmen," I will hear them yell "hog," but I should dread to see them have the opportunities for slaughter that I have been surrounded with on this trip.

The next day or two we looked up a better route through the timber to the lake and succeeded by following a well-worn bear trail which led in that direction. Mr. Berg still continued to pack my trophies to the lower camp and did not return that night, so I was alone in these far-away wilds some eighty miles from all but one living man, and he was twelve miles away. As night came on I had a good fire going in front of the "lean to" and sat down on some fir boughs. Had you been with me I know how you would have enjoyed your pipe and tobacco, but as I don't use it I sat there long into the night gazing into the fire; yes, all alone, high up on the rolling timbered table lands at the head of Kusiloff River, and my friend alone down at the lake. With lightning rapidity I recalled all your faces and reminiscences of our grand old times in former years, when I lived in Troy, and we made our camp fires on the Ausable, Manistee and Fife Lake Michigan; camps on the Au Plain, Menomonee and Spread Eagle Lake, Wisconsin; Swan River and head waters of the Mississippi in Minnesota; Devil's Lake, Dakota; camps on Black and White River, Arkansas (where we had those turkey roasts and duck bakes in our "clay ditch oven;") then, dear Jim, the camps on the Savogle and Marinuchi in New Brunswick; camps in Wyoming, Utah, Montana, Mexico and all the streams that head in the big game country of our Colorado from North Park south to head of the Bear, Williams, both forks of the White, the Grand, Eagle, Piney, Gunnison and southward to the San Juan. In the burning embers of my campfire, I could in my fancy see all your faces, and how gratifying to know that those of you who were with me were true sportsmen and never a thing occurred to mar the pleasure of our outing, for the good and bad side of man or woman will be revealed in camp. How I wished you all with me that night and tonight for I am having too much sport on this trip to enjoy it alone.

As my fire burned low I rolled up in my blankets and crawled under the "lean to" upon a caribou skin thrown on some spruce feathers, and then with a thought of the dear ones at home, what tomorrow's luck would be, and with weary body I was soon in dreamland. Daylight next morning found me preparing a hurried breakfast of moose steak, boiled rice, tor-te-os (fry pan bread) and tea. I ate heartily, for I intended to make in a new direction that day. I had a birch horn with me and had tried the "call" one evening for three hours without success and thought I would take it with me this morning. About 7 I tried the "call" more out of curiosity than otherwise; first, the "short call," then the "long call," and repeated several times. An hour passed and finally my patience was rewarded by a light crackling behind me. I listened—then a thud behind the alders. I then made a "low call" and soon his mooseship waded through the patch of alders and stood in open ground (other than the tall grass) not more than sixty yards from me. Oh, for a camera. He would swing his big head to and fro, sniffing the air; then lowering it with muzzle extended stood silently working his ears forward, then back. I had detected a slight puff of air and noticed it to be in his favor. Suddenly he raised his head high and sniffed loudly and slowly swung around and made for the low timber; not rapidly, but simply as if he had made a mistake. He was a big brute but his antlers were much inferior to those I had. My curiosity being satisfied, I again moved cautiously along much amused; how plainly I can recall his every move, and I want to tell you I don't like that kind of moose hunting. I was dressed for "still hunting," and as I moved silently along how little I dreamed that I would be rewarded in not killing this last animal by having in my path a much better specimen of moose than I had yet seen.

About 10, while still hunting through rolling ground with patches of spruce and tall grass, I sighted a cow lying down within eighty yards. I looked carefully, knowing the velvet was now off and a bull might be near, and after crawling a rod or so I saw the wide white blade of a bull between the trees close to the edge of the timber. I put my glasses on him to look at his horns but it seems he had sniffed me and a startled glance showed his big horns. The cow ran to my left— the bull to my right, quartering and a little down hill. My first ball caught him in the short ribs on the right side and stopped at the skin in front of the left shoulder; he stopped and swung around broadside. I sent another clean through him. He headed off again and I pitched another one into him. He again stopped broadside and coughed hard and when his great sides would heave I saw the blood spout from the wounds. I knew he was done for, and while he stood there with lowered head I ran around and below him as I had heard a terrible rolling through the tall grass (four feet high) below him, and thought it must be a bear making off. I could see nothing and returned to the moose expecting to find him down and dead; but imagine my surprise when on coming up a little raise I found myself within thirty yards of that great brute on his feet and coming toward me with his head lowered, shaking those massive antlers. I can't tell how I did it but as I afterwards found I sent a ball at his head which caught him in the brisket. Still he came and my next ball was better aimed and struck between the eyes.

That stopped him and he sank down upon his limbs but did not roll over. Boys, I am frank to acknowledge that I was startled. I am cold yet—never have I had even a grizzly give me such a feeling. As he came through that tall grass breathing the blood and tossing those wicked antlers, truly he looked like an old McCormick self-binder.

I was carrying my new Mannlicher that day and right there saw an advantage in smokeless powder as well as once more before the day closed. However, I have used the Winchester for twenty-four years; in fact, my first hunt for deer in Henry County, O., when but 16 years old, was with the old rim fire Henry rifle and when the King's model of 73 Winchester came out, I got that and have used all models since and had them made specially to fit me. I have now in camp my special made 40-70-330 metal patched soft-nose, black powder 86 model Winchester, which I have used for the past four years. I brought both my guns on this hunt for fear something might go wrong with one or the other. Boys, you wanted me to report on this Mannlicher and I must say that it is the most deadly gun I ever carried. Its great velocity of 2000 feet per second and its extreme flat trajectory makes it very desirable for long range shooting. At three to four hundred yards if held on the game the ball is into it almost the instant you touch the trigger. I was using the metal patch soft nose which will mushroom on flesh and the patch seems to be slightly cut with the lands of the barrel when fired and expands by the pressure of the soft nose when it strikes and then goes through the animal like a buzz-saw. The sheep when struck drop as limp as a rag, and the moose no matter in what part of the body he was struck seemed paralyzed from the first shot. Again, the gun is very light, which is a great advantage when you pack your loads on your back. You know I am not an agent for the Mannlicher works, but let honor fall where it is due. There is, however, an object to the close range between sights, for you must hold very carefully or you miss. This can be remedied by a peep on the rear of the hammer. I don't think they have any of these small calibres quite perfected; a few years more experiment will doubtless make a great improvement in them.

Well, there I stood by the side of my giant moose, without a camera or a friend with me to admire my prize. Oh, what a carcass. I had my steel tape with me and commenced his measurements and now give them to you as I put them down in my diary. Of course the first measurement was the spread of his antlers which is sixty-nine inches; length of beam, forty-eight inches; palmations fifteen inches; circumference of beam burr at head fourteen and one-half inches; circumference of beams at smallest place ten inches; antlers have thirty two points. His great body measured sixteen feet four inches from lip to point of rear hoof; seven feet eight inches from front hoof to top of nithers; girted eight feet nine inches, and six feet seven inches around the neck at shoulders; thirty-three and one-half inches from tip to tip of ears; ears seven inches wide and forty-four inches around the lips of the open mouth. What a match he will be when mounted for my big elk. Boys, I know that I hew close enough to the line of "true sportsmanship" not to be overcome by selfishness and will say that all points considered, size, massiveness, etc., I believe I have a world beater; but be this as it may I will be satisfied when I get it packed out and home. Some hunters saw the heads through the skull and then when being mounted by some they are given more spread; I know of a moose head whose spread was eight inches more when mounted than it was before it was sawed apart and an elk head that is seventeen inches more than it was naturally. I haven't a sawed head in my collection and would not take one as a gift for mounting. This method doesn't belong to true sportsmanship, and it makes the animal look very unnatural. They say it was necessary to saw them apart to get them out of the terrible country. I say that big game animal doesn't exist in such a country that makes it impossible to get the antlers out whole. I don't believe there has been game killed in a worse country of access than this. For many miles there is a mass of down timber, criss-crossed and covered with slippery moss, and intergrown with tall grass and bushes; then canons and ice cold streams to cross, but I intend to take those antlers down and out without sawing them if it takes all winter.

But back to the moose. It took me till 1 p.m. to dress him and I then started towards camp in the rain with the neck skin which was all I could carry, and content in mind that Alaska is the home of the largest moose in the world, and why not when this country affords such wonderful growth for food, and he lives to get age, which he must have to grow large horns; then his healthy condition does the rest.

About 3 in the afternoon, drenched, tired and hungry I was at the edge of the heavy spruce and thick willows six to ten feet in height and heard a cracking near me—thought 'twas a moose—then saw the willows shake near me, and stepping upon a rotten log and looking about, there, within twenty-five feet, on his hind legs, looking at me over the willows, stood one of those fighting Alaskan grizzlies. I had this neck skin of moose, shot pouch fashion, over my neck with left arm free; but in an instant I cocked my Mannlicher while bringing it in position and plugged him through the neck just under the head. He dropped and I stepped from the log that I could see better under the willows and sent another ball through his shoulders while he was roaring and fighting the willows and ground. I used lead and gave him another through the neck which settled him. I still kept the neck skin on, thinking to use it for a shield if he charged me. He had evidently scented the skin and was coming right after it. This was some sport. He is a monster, has claws four inches long, head twenty-two inches from nose to ears, measures ten feet seven inches stretch; foot eight by twelve inches and had a good coat of hair.

It took me till dark to skin him out and after it was off I could not lift it. I dragged it over the willows and left it and got in camp after dark thinking Alaska had bears of uncomfortable size and numbers for night travelling while alone.

As I approached camp I gave my usual shrill whistle and was answered by Mr. Berg through his gun barrel. Boys, how glad I was to hear it and when he came out to meet me, gave me a hearty hand shake and then relieved me of my heavy load. As I neared the fire how appetizing was the smell of his good supper already prepared, and I might add that my day's work without food had something to do with my appetite.

I was drenched to the skin and after a partial change of footgear we were soon drying, eating and talking of my "red letter day" which pleased my big hardy companion seemingly as much as myself; yet we knew that we had both taken great risks in being alone in these wilds.

This ended my hunt in Alaska. I have killed two specimens hard to duplicate, and of the class of animals of which I have had such a desire to add to my collection. I am more than pleased and wish all my hunting friends were here now, to take a look and a shake. Mr. Berg says they are more massive and heavier than the record head he killed two years ago which was mentioned in Forest and Stream, of March 6th, 1897.

It has been raining and snowing all day. We will now pack everything down to the lake and I will care for my heads and skins and work homeward as fast as possible, for truly I feel that I am well paid for my long and tiresome journey of 8,000 miles, round trip, on land and sea. I am compelled to travel 185 miles from here on foot and log canoe to reach the steamboat landing. It is now too dark to write and will finish at lower camp. We will make supper of moose steak, boiled rice, wild red currant sauce and tea.

CANON CITY, COLO.

My First Pneumatic

C. C. Hopkins

February 1898

It is interesting to note today, when the bicycle has once again achieved
tremendous popularity, that in its first four or five years, OUTDOOR LIFE
devoted a quarter of its editorial content and photos to bicycling, displayed a
sketch of a bike rider prominently on its covers, and carried many bicycle
ads for firms such as Columbia, Cleveland, and Racycle. In this issue,
the second, we learn that Editor McGuire was a well-known cycling journalist,
member of the Century Road Club, and founder of the magazine *Cycling
West*. Along with this story, this issue featured two hunting stories in which
bicycles figured, a cougar hunt and a camera hunt for elk. It's exhilarating to
read how the hunters sped down those Rocky Mountain grades. But how
did they get back?

*I doubt that anyone gets as keen enjoyment out of the now perfect wheels as I
did out of mine in the "early days."*

PNEUMATIC TIRES! What a thrill those words gave the wheelman only a
brief six or seven years ago. They were the subject of all subjects, discussed at
club rooms, on runs, and at all gatherings of wheelmen. We were all densely
ignorant on the subject, but naturally full of speculation and theory. The "light"
that had come out of the East (Ireland, this time), astonished us and aroused our
deepest curiosity. It was the dawn of a new era in the bicycle world.

But today! Universally used and generally comprehended, as common as any
article of merchandise, and millions of dollars invested in their manufacture and
distribution. The story of this rapid coming to the front is quite interesting, but
the subject now does not possess the charm of mystery and novelty that made the
first days of pneumatic tires so fascinating. And in those days, too, there were
curses deep and fervent, for in its swaddling clothes the first tire was not a thing
of unalloyed joy, but frequently a nuisance of the most provoking kind.

We all know that the bicycle, no matter of what type, did not become popular
with the masses until the advent of the pneumatic tire. The "safety" was a step in
the right direction from the high wheel. The "cushion" tire was only a makeshift
and an excuse and a very poor one too—having its little half-hold of the timid for
a brief period, then going deservedly to the wall before the giant pneumatic. The
"cushion" tire never was a rival of the pneumatic. It was, as before remarked, an
excuse, a "just as good," until the real article could be obtained. The securing of
one of the "real things" in the early days, however, was a much more difficult
matter than many today can comprehend.

First of all it had to be the "safety." Well do I remember my first favorable
impression towards that type of machine. In common with the majority of riders
of the high wheel, I had little respect for the "lowly, dirty and cumbersome
things" when they first appeared. But one day I chanced to be going in the same
direction as was "Sandy" Brown on his new safety. As a rider of the high "ordinary," Mr. Brown did not quite equal me. But that day, mounted on his safety,
he made it decidedly interesting for me, mounted on my high wheel—and I began
to think.

I soon owned a safety. It was a very heavy affair, as were all of the first ones. A couple of years later a man came to town with a bicycle weighing 32 pounds. He astonished us with his confidence or recklessness (we knew not which) by actually riding that "delicate thing" all over the streets. I soon liked a safety, but did not believe they would become popular, for the vibration in them, when shod with small tires, was something terrible—much worse than in the high wheel— and became unbearable in a ride of any considerable distance on anything but the smoothest of roads.

2:15! That was the first thing we ever heard about pneumatic-tired bicycles. An Irishman had ridden a mile in that remarkable time. It was hard—very hard —to believe; but we are a credulous people and we do like to ride fast. We would have to have those tires. The interest in them was keen. Every paper was scanned for news of the "balloon" tires. But to want one was not to get it, no matter how willing one might be to pay the price. I soon decided that I would have the first bicycle that I could obtain with pneumatic tires, and after a long, tedious wait, I was successful. The machine came, along with a letter, not of apology for the long delay, but of congratulations on our "success in securing one of coveted machines," and enclosing a bill for $160, the net wholesale price. Aside from the tires, the bicycle would not compare favorably with one of today costing one-third of that sum. But I got full measure, for the machine weighed, "stripped," 48 pounds.

At that time there was no "inside information" to be had about the new tire. You were either a believer or disbeliever in them, and as much was said against them as in their favor, while the desire to see one and "try it" was universal. I remember that I wrote to a well-known wheelman friend in an Eastern city for his private, honest, and confidential opinions, he having been fortunate enough to have ridden one of the first machines brought over. While he was a newspaper man and had his personal interests to guard (being in the trade), I felt that he told me much truth when he said he hardly dared to express an opinion either for or against pneumatics, as applied to bicycles. After my first short trial of the tires I understood much better why one would hesitate before giving them an unqualified recommendation. Too much was expected of them. One might naturally believe, from some of the exaggerated reports circulated in the papers, that a machine equipped with these tires would "run alone" and that anybody could ride a mile in 2:20 or better.

Finally, the long expected wheel arrived in Denver. On the day of its appearance the newspapers printed elaborate articles describing it (with illustrations), as in the following extract:

> The arrival of a pneumatic-tired safety marks an epoch in the cycling history of Denver. Long had our wheelmen waited for the sight of one, and great was the interest to inspect it when one finally made its appearance. The presence in town of such notables as President Harrison and John L. Sullivan did not detract one particle from the drawing powers of the new wonder, of which so much has been heard and so little seen. It is about one year since a pneumatic-tired wheel first made its appearance in Ireland. The sensation then created has been repeated everywhere upon the wheel's arrival. The principle is so different from anything else that it could but cause a commotion, not only among riders, but even with people who had scarcely given a thought to cycling. * * * The present wheel is the first to be received west of the Missouri River. The tires are two inches in width and as full of life (and air) as a football. The rubber is of the finest quality and is secured to the rim by means of specially woven and cemented canvas, which, however, does not come in contact with the ground. * * * The

advantages claimed for the pneumatic are speed, the reduction of vibration to the minimum, which naturally means comfort and ease of propulsion. It shows its superiority over solid tires in a greater degree where the road surface is uneven or loose and sandy. There is no sand so deep but that it can be ridden on a pneumatic tire. The rider has better control of a wheel thus shod. There is so little resistance to the tire that its wearing age is double or triple that of a solid tire, and in case of puncture is easily repaired.

Not such a bad prediction, after all, on a subject in which all were in the dark. Possibly exceptions might now be wisely taken to some of the above remarks, notably the sand riding and the ease (?) of repair. The first tires were not made to facilitate repair in case of puncture. Not only was there a fearful and complicated mass of canvas on outer case and rim, but the inner tube as well was incased in a sack, from which, when once extracted, it evinced a decided repugnance to return.

It was through Geo. E. Hannan, who was then branching out as a dealer on lower Sixteenth Street, that I was enabled to procure the bicycle. The people were so anxious to see a pneumatic that it was left on exhibition at this store during the daytime for nearly a month, and it was always surrounded by a crowd. Some of the remarks made would cause a smile nowadays. Many people were honestly of the opinion that the tire was made of snake's skin, owning to a peculiar color of the rubber. Some thought it the clumsiest affair they had ever seen. As a rule the machine was adversely criticized and condemned as a "fad" and passing fancy that could not possibly be practical, so wise are we in our ignorance. The late lamented Wilcox stubbornly opposed pneumatic tires for a long time and ridiculed them as a mass of "rubber, rags, and wind."

My pneumatic was treated very tenderly the first few days after its arrival in Denver. When not in use it was suspended from the floor in order to reduce the pressure in the tires. Advice as to the care of the tires was volunteered from all quarters. Every day, and many times a day, there were anxious inquiries by friends to know if the tires had been punctured. (What a bugbear "puncture" is to the tyro, even to this day!) Gradually I became bold and rode the machine everywhere at any time of day or night—and no trouble came! Wonderful! People began to have some faith in the new contrivance. My belief was honest and my enthusiasn unbounded. I went on every club run and I wanted to ride all the time. I attempted successfully trips that before were beyond the possibility of accomplishment.

On club runs we frequently started before daylight; when the roadway was at length clear to the sight the members would congratulate me that I had not met with a mishap, and, with a sigh of relief, would say: "You are all right now." In the club there were many who in speed and endurance far surpassed me, but I soon discovered that I had a decided advantage over them in mount, and they too finally realized it and fell in line. I recall our club "crack" receiving a new cushion-tired ordinary, "built special," with which for a brief spell he was much pleased. On our next club run he set out to "do" the pneumatic. The pace was hot (for an ordinary) and he rode himself out and actually bit the dust in less than an hour, falling in a faint from his wheel—and the pneumatic was there, with "not a hair turned."

I brought that wheel to the Pacific Coast a little later on, and for aught I know it is still doing service. The tires lasted about a year and were ridden several thousand miles. I sold the wheel in Stockton.

One night there was a commotion in the hotel where I stopped, the cause of which was a loud but muffled explosion. High and low did the inmates search, but without result, and the mystery was not solved until the following morning, when, on removing the bicycle from a closet, I discovered that one of the tires had collapsed. A piece of the inner tube as large as the palm of the hand lay on the floor. Gradually and unobserved the tire had been developing a "wart," and at last its pent up energies, chafing and expanding under the heat of a stuffy closet, asserted themselves. The first gun had been fired. Hostilities had commenced. Troublesome and tedious indeed was my first repair. However, I succeeded in making it ridable and continued to use it without difficulty for several months thereafter.

Much have the riders of modern tires and machines to be thankful for, but it is doubtful if they get the keen enjoyment out of their now perfect wheels and tires that I did during the first few months of the "early days" in which I owned my first pneumatic.

Duckville

Major Daniels

December 1900
January 1901

None of the some sixteen thousand OUTDOOR LIFE stories I have read in
preparing this anthology, not even those of the slaughter of the buffalo or the
extinction of the passenger pigeon, have had the impact upon me that this
one did. It was originally published in two parts in December 1900 and
January 1901 under the title "Tulies-Tulles," which escapes me but
presumably is a play on the word "tules." Anyway, the story shook me
because the duck could very well have followed the buffalo and the
passenger pigeon into limbo had this kind of shooting continued.

If you look at a large scale map of Utah you will see that, though it has no
outlet, there are three considerable rivers emptying into the Great Salt Lake on
its eastern side. Southernmost is the Jordon, of which I know little beyond that in
days gone by it and Utah Lake, through which it flows, used to provide some
shooting. North of this is the Uintah, of which I know nothing, and north of it
again is the Bear River, of which I have some knowledge. This Bear River rises
somewhere in northeastern Utah and, realizing early in life the advantages of
travel, journeys into Idaho to improve its mind. Once there it contracts the
common disease of travelers—homesickness—and, turning back again to its natal
State and after paying its respects to Bear Lake, hurries on to fulfill the serious
mission of its life. That is, it turns its attention to the duck shooter.

Shells to the number of 4,500 went by freight some days ahead of The Lady
and me. Guns to the number of four, shell cases and two trunks full of ducking
garments went with us on the train and were dumped off at Ogden late in the
night of October 9. Next morning, to the hotel came B.—with more guns and
more shell cases. Till train time we raided the defenseless city of Ogden for light
literature, tinned soups and a dozen other things we didn't need, and a little
before noon boarded the Southern Pacific. The diner was not open but we
unlocked it with a silver key, bolted a short order lunch and jumped off at Corinne, followed by a downpour of luggage that flooded the station platform knee-
deep. Thompson, who brings the lunch up every day to meet the train, organized
a rescue party. With the aid of every able-bodied man in sight he loaded us and
our dunnage on a wagon, hauled the whole outfit to the river, sorted us out and
put us in the launch and we were afloat.

Thompson steered and the scenery went by pretty rapidly, for the launch
makes eight miles an hour and the current is good for a couple more. With a
flying machine the distance from Corinne to Vince Davis' camp would not be
over ten miles across a country as flat as a polo field, but Bear River is as frisky
as a kitten chasing its tail and travels nearly thirty miles to get ten. You box the
compass a dozen times in two hours-and-a-half's voyage and you are sorry—at
any rate we were—when it's over. The eastern wall of mountains swings now to
the right, now to the left, now in front, now behind in a solemn saraband as the
river twists and turns.

The launch throbs us on and on and at last sweeps round, serious and stately
as any ocean liner, to the landing where the Lord of the Manor of Duckville,
Vince Davis himself, stands ready to welcome us.

Last year we found Davis' camp, the "Metropolis of the Marshes," as we called it, most comfortable, and since then he has made so many improvements that it is positively luxurious. Between the dining room, which with the kitchen, is a house by itself, and the "Club House," which has the general loafing room and bunk accommodations for as many as you please, Davis has built a row of six good-sized rooms, all opening on a board walk. The Lady and I moved our trunks and hand bags into No. 1 of "Palace Row," our guns, ammunition and etceteras into No. 2, which, when its bed had been moved out, made an excellent living room. And here, when B— had installed his belongings further down the Row, we three and Vince gathered and talked ducks.

Vince, as usual, took the Lady in his boat, while B— and I each engaged a market shooter to look after us, and our fleet of three double boats made quite a formidable naval demonstration as we dropped down the river.

The marsh about Davis' place was about nine inches above the river's surface and mostly bare mud, but when we passed No. 1 and No. 2 Overflows, branches, so to speak, of the river, about a mile down, which led south into a body of water known as South Lake, the mud sank almost to the water level and the first of the tule bull-rush and cat-tail beds appear. A mile below No. 2 Overflow is No. 3, leading west into the north end of West Lake, while what remains of the river a little below No. 3 Overflow becomes known as No. 4 and flows north into the North Lake.

I have made the very roughest sort of map to give some idea of the lay of the land, and in looking at this map several things should be borne in mind. Everything in the way of water except the river and the overflows should be considered mud from six inches to more than a foot deep, covered with a veneer of water nowhere more than three inches thick. From the mouth of No. 1 south through West Lake to water deep enough to float a boat is ten miles, and the water when you reach it is brackish. Everything figured on the map as land is dry mud east of Davis' house and nearly solid tules north, west and south.

In many places the tules along the lakes' shores are broken up into towheads, which, if they have much water around them, offer good stands. Sometimes these towheads attain the dignity of islands, as in the case of Slaughter Island, so named from some big bags made there in the distant past, and Lady's Island, which got its name from a killing made there last year by the Lady mentioned in this story.

Making a blind on a point or on a towhead is of course easy enough, but making a good "open" blind, a blind out in the lake, is an art to be learned in time but not easily. First a dozen willow bushes cut from along the river bank are stuck, bushy part up, in the mud in a circle some five feet across. Between these willows are stuck handfuls of rushes—I am presuming you have half a boat-load cut as you came through the overflow or taken from the nearest shore. The tops of the willows are then bent over and interwoven with each other and with the tule tops until, if all has gone well, you have a hide not to be blown down by every wandering breeze and sufficiently impervious to ducks' eyes without being so trim, so formal, so evidently a work of artifice as to arouse the ducks' suspicion. All this sounds easy; believe me it is hard, but nothing so hard as making mud balls or "muds," as we call them for short, the Duckville equivalent for decoys.

Last year, our first there, B— and I took out a huge trunk full of the real thing. Sibley hollow decoys, the prettiest shape and the most natural colors ever seen, but the weight of even a dozen of them was a handicap to a boat where every ounce counted in the mud, and the very mud itself furnished a substitute. You must remember that this mud is soft and that the water covering it is never more than a very few inches deep. Take then a curved spade and turn up a wad of mud about a foot long and four or five inches high above the water. Make a few score of these muds (I have seen Davis make over two hundred in less than half an hour) and go a hundred or two yards away and the effect is marvelously like a flock of ducks feeding. At any rate this is what the ducks think, and if they are in a mood to decoy, their credulity will lead them within easy gunshot.

It is not, you see, an easy shoot at its best, but with a pusher it is by no means beyond the powers of the ordinary man, though women of course must be stronger as well as keener than the average of their sex to thoroughly enjoy it. The Lady, who has been out both trips with me, is not phenomenally strong, but she is an old hand at duck shooting and keener than mustard. "Duckville?" said she, when I proposed this autumn's trip; "Of course I'll go. Why it's the finest shoot in the country."

The complete record of my 16 days' shoot would take too much space and be uninteresting in spots, for I had my lean days as well as my fat ones and no one, I fancy, cares to read of failure. So I will resort to my diary to relate only the high points. The shoot as a whole netted 1,152 ducks, an average of 72 and a fraction per day.

Thursday, October 11.—
The water is very much lower than last year and the ducks do not seem by any means so plentiful. We started at 8 a.m. B— put in on the west shore of the West Lake, about half way between mouth of overflow and Lady's Island. Vince took The Lady to a blind opposite the Lady's Island two-thirds of the way across the lake. I was in the same line about 300 yards east. Plenty of ducks wadded south of us, but the day was warm and still and even the teal refused to decoy at all. Nearly every duck seemed to fear a blind as a saint fears sin; they took the greatest pains to avoid even some empty blinds which lay between me and Lady's Island. Eight teal in all came properly to my muds and not so many came to The Lady. The rest of my shooting was well over 45 yards and from that on up to any distance. My bag was: Green wing teal 25, spoonbills 2, mallard 1, with at least 20 cripples and hard hit ducks.

Saturday, October 13, was calm and clear. I was high man with 45. There was a lovely flight up the middle of North Lake, but the birds were very shy and refused to decoy well. On the 14th, 15th and 16th we shot either in the neighborhood of Lady's Island or in the Slaughter Point country and without any unusually good results except that on the 16th B— got among the teal north of Lady's Island and made a fair killing.

Wednesday, October 17.—
B— and The Lady had not been able to plan for more than a week at Duckville and left this morning for Colorado. I had a go of sun cholera (or dysentery) last night and felt like 30 cents, but started out about 9:30. I had fair shooting at once in West Lake but two market hunters who went out ahead of me did so poorly that before long they moved way back among the towheads, a little north of west of me. Till sunset my shooting was at a few teal from the south and a lot of sprigs which came at me from the northwest—but most of them I fancy had come up the center of the lake from the south at sunset. I had two good teal flurries from the south and at dusk ducks of all sorts piled in from everywhere. If those two men had not been back of me I think I would have had a good run of big ducks, including mallards from the west. Total for the day: Canvas 1, mallard 4, sprigs 24, spoonbills 3, green wing teal 44.

Thursday, October 18.—
Vince and I made a late start and as a lot of shooters were moved toward the

West Lake by my making high bag there yesterday, we went out to No. 2 Overflow to a place two-thirds of the way across the South Lake.

We made a small blind and a huge lot of muds, anchoring the boat 300 yards north of us on the mud. Our first duck was a Gadwall about 11:15; then a teal, then two Gadwalls which I got with one barrel. Teal did not begin to come fast until nearly 2 p.m. and sprigs did not decoy well at any time, though there were lots of them about. The heaviest flight of teal came from the west and south between 3:30 and sunset and when we pulled up, about 6 o'clock, my pick-up was: Green wing teal 106, gadwall 5, sprig 5, spoonbill 1.

Saturday, October 20.—
Quinine was what I needed. This morning I got up weak but well enough to hold a gun. It was cloudy but with no signs of a storm and when Vince and I went out through No. 3 a brisk cold northwest wind was blowing. I shot a bluebill in the river which Vince and I considered meant new ducks in the country and we saw more ducks than usual everywhere in the West Lake. Our blind was on the outermost of a lot of towheads which almost fill a bay back of the island. We made a lot of new muds and while Vince was putting the boat in the rushes east of us, the flight began from the southeast over the marsh and from the southwest. The big ducks did not decoy very well but the teal came beautifully as long as the wind blew, which it did all day with few breaks. From noon till 4:30 my Purdey was never quite cold and often it was so hot I was glad I had a Heikes protector.

I opened up at a very hot gait and did better than two and a half for my first 150 shells. Then I had a rotten 25, then a brace up, then a 25 at big ducks a mile in the air, then a gradual falling off as I became tired, then a big brace just at the end. We knocked off at sunset; did a hard pickup (I lost 15 or 20 behind me in the marsh) and had a bad trip to the mouth of No. 3, as the wind had blown the water away and left the mud nearly bare. We were over an hour making the overflow. My total was: Green wing teal 98, sprig 48, gadwall 2, spoonbill 2, bluebill 1—151.

Sunday, October 21.—
It was a windless, dull day, cloudy but threatening sun. By 10:30 we were talking about the "off day" that must come now and then. Still, we agreed to make an easy trip anyway and shoot somewhere in the South Lake.

We both were perhaps the readier to do this as the glass showed us great wads of ducks all over the South Lake and especially at the southwest point. Anyway we went out through No. 2 and then west to the blind where I shot on Thursday. The ducks moved lazily down until there was a big wad on the point and another southwest of that in the West Lake and everything was ripe for someone to come out of No. 3 to shoot the northeast shore of West Lake and drive out ducks south to salt water—but no one came.

The ball opened with a bunch of teal which did the robin snipe act and gave me two from my left shoulder with the first barrel and two more from my right with the second. Then a long halt till 1:30 p.m., while odds that our bag would be under 25 found no takers. Then a very gentle breeze southwest and teal—in ones, in twos, in wads; teal, teal, teal, continuously. When the Purdey got so hot that the Heikes protector burnt me, I tried the Smith. When the Smith rose above boiling point I tried the Purdey, and sometimes I made both count. Teal from the west, from the south, from the north and sometimes from all three ways at once. Teal over the muds trying to light, teal going away behind, teal coming as far as the eye could see in front. Teal, teal, teal.

It was very much the hottest shoot I have ever seen, though not the easiest for the birds were mostly low, swift incomers.

Big ducks were about but not plentiful, nor would they decoy at all. Of them I got one sprig, a double of gadwall and two out of three passing canvasbacks, but one was a cripple and got away. The heaviest of the teal flight came between 2 and 4 p.m., after which the clouds cleared away and the wind fell. We had the cream of the positions. The next high bag to mine was 35, while my pickup was: Canvasback 1, sprig 1, gadwall 2, green wing teal 104.

Wednesday, October 24.—
Last night it rained off and on from 9:30 till morning, and after midnight blew hard from the northwest. At 9:30 when I started the rain had stopped and the clouds were breaking, but the wind held strong until we started out of No. 3 Overflow. Then it gradually died away to a flat calm, and down went our prospects of a big shoot. Even with the glasses we could see almost no ducks anywhere.

Vince and I had meant to go down in the vicinity of where I got 150 on the 20th and make a killing, but when the wind dropped, we shied at the labor of a long pull over the mud and began to canvass nearby easy places where we could resign ourselves to a languid forty or fifty-bird day. We were well on our way to the northwest corner when Vince's Mormon saints sent first a little zephyr, then a gentle breeze, then a good lusty twenty-knot wind with a body of it which promised permanence. Up went our hopes and away we pulled. We had not gone far when someone going down East Pass sent a cloud of ducks out southwest, nor gone much farther till we could see with the glasses that the whole south shore of West Lake, and especially where there were brakes and towheads, was simply swarming with birds. As the man in East Pass went farther down, thousands and thousands of ducks rose from in front of him and more yet flew from the tules between the Pass and West Lake. The east shore from a little south of Mud Point and the brakes sent up a very fog of ducks as we went south.

Never before, even here, have I seen so many birds in so small a compass, or birds so reluctant to move. We herded them before us and turned in to a brake some 500 yards north of the island back of which we shot on the 20th. The ducks settled down in a solid mass from just north of Lady's Island across to Slaughter Island and were joined by continual flocks from behind and east of us. Klondike contributed what amounted literally to many thousands (these birds must have moved of their own accord, as no one was down there) and the wind blew harder than ever. We selected a towhead open to the lake on the west and with plenty of clear water around it, so we might not lose too many ducks in the tules. Vince hurriedly turned up a few muds and then sat down in a boat drawn close in behind our towhead, for a steady stream of ducks was coming over us from the north, while I on my camp-stool among the rushes fired my first shot at half past eleven o'clock. By the time I had used up a box of shells, this southbound flight was practically ended, so the boat was pushed out of sight among the broken tule beds behind us, a low blind was built in the center of our towhead and I sat down on my shell-box, bolting my lunch, while Vince worked furiously at the upheaval of mud balls.

He had been at this work not over five minutes, and I was halfway through my second chunk of raisin bread, when the flight up from the south began. Into my blind tumbled my Mormon just as I spun out a teal in front of me and missed another twisting down wind behind, while the rest of the bunch of twenty tore out of range before I could bring my second gun to bear. A point of rushes a hundred yards southwest of us just cut off the sight of the island between which and the shore I fancy most of the flight came today as it did on the 20th, and helped to keep us out of sight without hiding our muds. Round this point the teal streamed like the water round the sharp river bend, almost as steadily, quite as confidently and with vastly greater speed.

At first there were few single ducks; from three to eight was the usual flock, with frequent bunches of from a dozen to fifty. They came low on the water (few were over a dozen yards high when they passed) and they paid no attention to us or to the blind, going in front, behind or squarely over us, as the spirit moved them. Some checked up as if about to light, and gave easy shots, but far the greater number seemed to put on extra steam when they were in range and near enough to accurately gauge the situation.

The wind was so strong that a straightaway shot across it needed two feet of allowance at thirty-five yards (for a straight incomer from the south, this meant holding almost that much to the right to center the bird) and the teal were coming at every known and seven or eight unknown angles. As I have already hinted, they were mostly in a nerve-racking rush to be elsewhere without loss of time and simply tore holes in the atmosphere getting there. Instantly a shot was fired, they lost their sense of direction. They kept up their speed, but some would soar as if they were climbing a ladder, others would jacksnipe as if they had taken lessons from a corkscrew, while the rest would do stunts to make you believe they were bred by Bullet Hawk out of Tumbler Pigeon, second dam St. Vitus' dance.

After ten minutes I made sure I was in for a very good shoot, and in less than half an hour it dawned on me that I should come to the bottom of my shell-case long before sundown, so I made a pious resolve not to waste ammunition on desperate chances, a resolve I am afraid I broke many times. The air was simply buzzing with little teals going every which way, and it was a terrible temptation to snap the first barrel at the first teal one saw over the gun, so as to get the second barrel in in time. Then there was not one occasion but twenty when both guns were empty and a dozen birds in range, with as many more coming up. These were the times when I longed for a pump gun with one hand and thanked heaven with the other that I didn't have one. Twice I climbed up into the blue empyrean and fired once seven shots and the other time nine for a total of no ducks, but on the whole shoot I held my usual shell average.

I took out 250 of The Lady's No. 2 loads, as I have been flinching badly the last two days, and 250 of my Ballistite new No. 3s. I fired her shells first, and though I missed a few birds for lack of the extra speed and power, I was glad I had taken them. If the whole 500 had been my No. 3s, I should have been pounded out of the box before 2 o'clock, for it was the fastest shoot I ever saw. The No. 2 shells were all gone by 1:30, and at exactly 3 p.m. I killed a teal with the last of the No. 3s, including eight shells which Vince had put in his pocket yesterday in case he came across a "crip" on the pickup—508 shells in three hours and a half (2.4 shells per minute) and the flight nearly as good as ever when I knocked off. I had fewer lost "crips" than usual and unloaded on the landing stage at Davis' house at 5:15. Green wing teal 176, sprig 10, spoonbill 2, mallard 1, bluebill 1—190 and a star spangled banner shoot.

The Roosevelt Lion Hunt

John B. Goff

Vice-President Roosevelt's Guide

April 1901

Theodore Roosevelt had already been elected running-mate of President William McKinley for the latter's second term when he made these hunts described by John B. Goff, his guide from January 12 to February 15, 1901 (inauguration at that time was March 4). When the stories appeared in OUTDOOR LIFE in April and May of that year, Roosevelt was serving as Vice-President of the United States and less than four months later became President following the assassination of McKinley. The huge cougar of 227 pounds shot by Roosevelt (Part 2) stood alone as the world record until it was tied at 15 12/16 points in 1954 and surpassed in 1964. In 1973 it dropped to third place in the *Records of North American Big Game*.

Part 1

Going after mountain lions with an ordinary hunter is the rarest of sport, but when in company with a man like Colonel Roosevelt it is the most exciting and enjoyable fun conceivable. In the first place, Colonel Roosevelt is a sportsman. The word is much abused—so much so, in fact, that in order to convey one's meaning many adjectives are often prefixed to show that the party referred to is not just a plain, every-day sportsman, but a higher type than the average. If there could be any more expressive word than sportsman I would use it, but I think not.

Colonel Roosevelt has roughed it among cowmen, has done his share of steer-roping, cow-punching, horseback riding and mountaineering; therefore he is a distinct Western type. He is as different from the average New Yorker who comes to Colorado to hunt as the sturdy pine is different from the delicate maple. Having ridden the ranges of Wyoming and the Dakotas for years, and having killed all the different kinds of big game of North America, with one or two exceptions, Colonel Roosevelt is at once the typical rider and hunter. He sits a horse as gracefully, whether it is galloping over down timber or over rocky ledges, as if the animal were on dress parade on the smooth streets of a city. He is a congenial companion on the hunt, always willing to share his part of the hardships, but never avaricious to accept his portion of the glory. He is always among the first to be in at the killing, for, being a reckless but sure rider, there is no one who can outdo him in getting over rough country to reach a desired goal. He is the last man to ask to pull for camp if there is any hope of getting game, and many an evening when we were riding the ridges together, or following the most inviting draws, have we scented game (and got it, too), after an ordinary hunter would have returned to camp, too tired after the day's hunt to explore further.

Hunting lions and hunting bear differ in at least one essential feature. In bear hunting you may see your quarry, and after traveling many miles allow him to slip away; but there is no escape for the lion or cat, once sighted by either the dogs or hunters. For a lion or cat will always tree, while a bear will lead his pursuers through rough country, over windfalls that impede the progress of horse and hound, and never stop until he is brought to bay. Even then he will sometimes get away, for the dogs may not be able to hold him until the hunters come up. If a fresh lion track is found it is, in modern slang, "all day with that lion," as his hide is almost sure to hang before the sun goes down.

I had at the disposal of the Roosevelt party, which included Dr. Gerald Webb and Phil B. Stewart, eighteen lion and bear dogs, and some of my best horses. I do not wish to be egotistic in quoting Colonel Roosevelt's verdict of the work of these dogs. He said he never saw their equal for tracking up and tackling game. He was also much impressed with the training that has taught them never to run a deer or elk. I have them so well trained now that they will pay no more attention to deer or elk than to cattle in a pasture.

The colonel was particularly amused at the behavior of one of the young dogs. I will first explain that in order to keep my pack replenished to counterbalance the dogs that die off or are killed while hunting (we had two killed on the hunt of which I write), I must keep up breeding nearly all the time, and therefore always have one or two young dogs to break in. This I do by placing them in the pack and chastising them severely when they disobey orders. I put a young pup in the pack one day when we started on our hunt, but as soon as he saw a bunch of deer he made off for them. When he came back I gave him a good slapping. It was not long before we again came across deer, when he put off after them in the same manner as before. I gave him another dose of the same medicine, and we watched his actions carefully after that. The next day we again came across deer, and while it seemed at first that he would make a dash for them, he hesitated, looked at me in a foolish way, and sneaked off toward the balance of the pack. This amused us all very much, but particularly Colonel Roosevelt, who prized that pup very highly after that, especially whenever the test came and he was able to overcome the temptation to give chase.

One thing that impressed the members of our party was the number of fresh deer carcasses encountered while riding for game. A number, some with a shoulder eaten away, the neck or other portion gone, were seen, and in most cases the evidence showed that they were killed by mountain lions. I wish here to refute a statement that has been made in print. A lion does not prowl in search of the young of deer to the exclusion of the older animals, but will kill either large or small when driven to it by hunger. The majestic buck, and lord of all the little bucks, is not immune from the ravages of these animals when they are out for meat.

We were especially favored with good weather conditions during the most of the five weeks that Colonel Roosevelt hunted with me. There was plenty of snow all the time, making tracking good, while at no time did the cold seriously interfere. Colorado certainly stood in with the weather man during that time, much to the disadvantage of "felis concolor."

I will say before commencing my account of the hunt proper that I started to keep a diary of the trip, but I lost my coat, in which it was placed, while riding after a lion between the Keystone ranch and the Matthews ranch. The coat was snagged off the saddle while we were going through some heavy, brushy timber, and not knowing within a mile or two where it was lost, I never went back to look for it. Therefore, the incidents here related are all from memory, and while the details in the main will be found to be accurate, yet any errors regarding minor facts will, I hope, be overlooked.

Colonel Roosevelt and party arrived at Meeker on the evening of January 11, and stopped at the Meeker hotel, the only first-class hotel in the town, run by a sportsman, Rube S. Ball. Here they remained one night, and on the morning of the 12th we mounted our horses and struck out for my ranch, which lies twelve miles northwest of Meeker, hunting en route. The colonel killed a lynx before we were far from Meeker, which added snap and enthusiasm to the trip right away at the very start. When within about three miles of the ranch the dogs picked up a fresh track of a bobcat, running it a mile or two, when it treed. It was no trick for Colonel Roosevelt to kill it when we came up.

We reached the ranch about sundown, and, after a supper prepared by Mrs. Goff (who, by the way, was our cook during the entire hunt), we sat around and swapped hunting experiences until it was time to retire.

On the morning of the 13th all hands arose early, and when the cobwebs had been wiped from our eyes we all felt happy at the prospects of a good day's hunt. We started for the Keystone ranch, fourteen miles from my place, and were fortunate in getting another cat. The dogs ran it in a hole in the rocks and pulled it out, finishing it about the time we came up. (The country over which we did most of the hunting on the trip is rough cedar ridges, dotted here and there with rocky ledges and sand hills. The altitude is about 5,500 feet, that of Meeker, 6,000). After killing one cat we cold-trailed a lion, but the track was too old, so it was abandoned, and we went direct to the Keystone ranch, arriving there shortly after dark. Here we were met by Mr. Wilson, the foreman, and Mr. Saby, an employee of four or five years' standing. After supper, and the usual ceremonies of exchanging jokes and yarns, we abandoned the homelike fireside for soft, warm beds, sleeping very soundly until morning.

On the morning of the 14th we commenced hunting below the Keystone ranch, where Colonel Roosevelt killed the first lion of the trip. The dogs picked up a fresh trail and soon his lionship treed. While on our way to the lion, we espied a cottontail rabbit under a tree, and Stewart immediately jumped from his horse and photographed the little animal, after crawling up to within six feet of it. Dr. Webb, who is a very congenial and entertaining young man, ventured to suggest —not having been able to think of anything more ludicrous—that we stop and eat lunch before tackling the lion. Judging by the noise that was being made by the dogs—we not as yet having come within sight of the quarry, but knowing from the sound of the dogs that it was treed—I believe that some of my "fighters" would have lost their voices if we had prolonged our approach longer. I will here say that to the hunter who has been used to killing bear and lion behind a pack of good dogs, there is nothing more musical to his ears than the chorus set up by them when they have the game at bay. It was on more than one occasion during our hunt almost impossible to make oneself heard within a radius of fifty feet of the dogs when a lion was treed, and during the pleasant but exciting intermission left for the taking of photos or the inspection of the animal before the fatal shot was fired.

I am diverging, however, from that lion which we had—in a tree. When we got to within thirty or forty yards of where the animal was located he jumped from the tree and ran about 150 yards, when the fighters (composed of two dogs, each of one-half bull and one-half shepherd extraction, and one dog one-half bloodhound, three in all) overtook the lion. They were having a rough-and-tumble fight, with the honors about even, when we came up. In order to save the dogs— for they were being bitten and scratched up horribly and it was too risky to shoot —the Colonel ran into the thick of the fight and stabbed the lion behind the foreleg. He aimed for the handiest part of the body exposed, although in his subsequent exploits of this nature he usually got the heart.

This act on the part of Colonel Roosevelt drew forth our heartiest admiration, and we considered him a hero at once. This is something that I would do myself in an emergency, but is a feature of lion hunting that I do not care to make a practice of. It is dangerous at best, for the lion could easily lift a paw and strike the hunter in the face, or catch him in the leg or arm with its teeth. It is usually kept too busy with the dogs to spring, even if, as would be rare, it were so inclined. There has been much very tiresome stuff written for the daily press about this stabbing work of the Governor's. Of course no sportsman has gulped it down without making due allowance for the idiots who framed it, or for the editors who passed on it; but, while I have killed over 300 lions myself, and have been among them for nearly twenty years, yet I would not care to tackle them in the off-hand, fearless manner the Colonel displayed on this trip.

We reached camp early on the evening of the fourteenth, for we all felt good over our success thus far. This lion we packed to camp, carcass and all, as we needed feed for the dogs. Their meat diet consisted entirely of lion and horse flesh, I having purchased three old horses for this purpose.

Good fortune and the weather continued to smile on us, and when these two combinations are met with on a hunting trip, glad, indeed, is the man who rides. The weather continued warm, and with plenty of snow on the ground, tracking was excellent.

On the 15th we hunted below the Keystone ranch, going across Ted's gulch. We ran onto the track of a cat, but it went into a hole in the ground and was lost. After a great deal of careful hunting we were unable to locate another fresh track of either cat or lion, so returned to camp empty-handed.

On the 16th we ran across a fresh lion track between Horse gulch and Willow gulch. He treed very quickly, when Dr. Webb killed him, after shooting him three times. The dogs had little difficulty in finishing him. Stewart was sick on this day, so did not accompany us. The Colonel and Dr. Webb never had more fun than on this day's hunt. Dr. Webb's witticisms and Colonel Roosevelt's hearty humor added much to the congeniality. This feeling, coupled with the success of the day's hunt, made the return to camp a march triumphant.

On January 17th we had a unique experience with a large lion. The dogs chased the animal into a hole in the ground. He was "smooth" enough to remain the greater part of the time at the entrance to the hole, where he fought the dogs to a stand-still. He had an advantage in position, as he was well protected from the rear, and dealt some telling blows to several of the dogs. There happened to be two exits to the cave, one on the side hill and another running at an angle from the top. Into the top hole one of my best fighters, Badly, went—a half bull and half shepherd. When the lion was afterward driven farther into the hole by the pack of dogs we heard some hard fighting going on, and as Badly never afterward reappeared, it is presumed that he was killed by the lion, which we afterward smoked. He was a cute old critter, for while the smoke was choking the last spark from his life, and the opening to fresh air was always in sight, yet he preferred a silent death to a chance of freedom which the path through the pack of howling dogs offered. He had tasted of the teeth of those dogs before, and with a rock for a pillow, sagebrush smoke for incense, and the deafening din and noise of the dogs as a funeral hymn, this monarch of many a conquest over deer and calves expired in silence. A blood-hound went into the hole and pulled him out far enough for us to reach him, when he was dragged out and skinned, the carcass being left, a custom followed with all but the first lion. This animal cut up the other dogs frightfully, but Dr. Webb—always on hand to render assistance, and one of the most valuable men around camp, or on the hunt, with whom I have ever traveled—gave all the medical attention to them that was possible, being compelled to sew up some bad cuts in two of the dogs.

Lion No. 4 was secured on the 20th. It was a yearling, which Stewart first photographed in the tree and afterward shot. Being very small, it was easily finished by the pack after it fell to the ground. I forgot to mention that three kittens belonging to one of the lions previously killed, were turned over to Mr. Stewart.

On January 25th business called Dr. Webb and Mr. Stewart home, but Colonel Roosevelt announced that he was having too good a time to leave for a while longer, so decided to remain. Up to this time we had secured seven lions and four or five cats, which was considered very good luck. It was with much regret that we bade our Colorado Springs friends good-bye. I will give the readers of OUT-DOOR LIFE a further account of Colonel Roosevelt's hunt in the May number. It will describe the killing of the largest lion it has ever been my good fortune to see.

May 1901

Conclusion

In my concluding chapter on Colonel Roosevelt's lion hunt, I will narrate some of the most noteworthy incidents of the last three weeks, or from January 26th to February 15th—it being that portion immediately following the departure of Dr. Webb and Mr. Stewart for home. During these three weeks I was Colonel Roosevelt's sole companion on the hunts, and I had an opportunity of becoming much better acquainted with him than during the first two weeks. We had by this time become so well acquainted that all stiffness and formality were eliminated from our manner toward each other, and we both took to the new condition of affairs as if we had been acquaintances for life. We were entering on that well-known epoch on a hunting trip, when the hunter forms an opinion of his fellow-man— either for better or worse—that is lasting. In my case it need not be said that my feeling toward Colonel Roosevelt grew warmer each day, until at the hour of his departure, I felt I was separating from some dear friend. So mote it be.

When Dr. Gerald Webb and Mr. Phil B. Stewart left on the 25th, we found that we had up to that time secured seven lions, of which Stewart got four (three of them being kittens), Dr. Webb one, and Colonel Roosevelt two. This was considered a very satisfactory score, and we thought that we would be lucky indeed if we would be able to duplicate it during the remainder of Colonel Roosevelt's stay. How well we succeeded in doing so the remainder of this article will show.

With hearts throbbing with wholesome emotion, and spirits as free and joyous as those of the birds, we mounted our horses on the morning of January 26th, for the ride to the Matthews ranch, eight miles from the Keystone, having had an invitation from the genial hosts of that place to spend some time with them. Here the Colonel's well-known ability to make himself comfortable and agreeable with new acquaintances under new conditions asserted itself, and many were the happy hours spent at this place. Zack, Bob and Clarence Matthews treated us royally, and formality soon gave way to jollity, humor and the display of a character of hunting oratory indigenous only to the hills. I took a snapshot of Colonel Roosevelt and Mrs. Matthews while out drinking a fresh draught of air one morning before breakfast. Neither of them was in society togs; but it was not long thereafter until Colonel Roosevelt was in the saddle, his horse dancing to the tune of the hounds' music. At the Matthews ranch we got two lions, and yet when we left there the hunting promised well.

One day a man came into camp and reported that a twelve-foot lion had been killed by one of the hunters roundabout. I would give $100 for a reproduction of the grin on Colonel Roosevelt's face as the story was related. He became interested at once, and handled that fellow without gloves. He first asked him if he believed such a story. The latter said he did, not having much experience in hunting. "Now, my dear fellow," said the Colonel, as he laid his hand on his shoulder in a fatherly way, "you go and tell the fellow who filled you with such nonsense that I will give him $5,000 if he will bring here to this ranch a lion twelve feet long. Do you not know that, taking for example the lions killed by our party, a lion that long would weigh in the neighborhood of 850 pounds, or as large as a fair-sized cow pony? The tail of a lion is usually about one-third the length of the body, so leaving off the tail the body and head would measure about eight feet long." We were all very much amused at the incident, but I must say that the man who brought in the news felt more like 30 cents than the bearer of important information to a distinguished sportsman.

From the Matthews ranch we went to fulfill a date at the Foreman ranch, owned and kept by Judge Foreman and his son. We remained there two days and two nights, during which time we killed one lion, getting it on the point of Colorow mountain, about twelve miles southeast of the Keystone ranch, and twenty miles west of Meeker. We were traveling along looking for signs when Jim, one of the dogs, dropped out. We heard him baying and knew he had struck a hot trail, so we went back to the place whence the noise proceeded. Soon the rest of the pack joined in the chase, and after about thirty minutes the dog had the animal treed. He was a magnificent lion and made a fine target as the Colonel drew his gun to his shoulder and gave him a dead shot. When he had crashed through the tree to the ground, the dogs were on him in a jiffy, and made quick work of him. It being late, we skinned our prize as quickly as possible and hurried to the ranch, where we were welcomed royally.

The following morning we were back to the Matthews ranch, remaining overnight, and then journeyed to the Keystone the following day. After planning to do considerable hunting about the latter ranch, we started out the following morning, keen and alert for the day's chase. Everything was favorable, and while it had been casually remarked by visitors that we had cleaned all the lions out of the country, yet we got two lions that day. The first of these jumped from the tree, the dogs catching him as he landed, and together they all went tumbling and fighting down the steep mountain side, now the lion on top and again the dogs. It was a great sight to see that animated ball of tangled legs, glittering teeth, and nerve-strung muscle and sinew, everyone of them fighting for his very life, while rolling down that steep grade.

Colonel Roosevelt was right after them with his knife ready for action, for it looked as if we might lose a dog or two at any minute. He soon got into a position for a center shot with the knife, and stooping among the fighting dogs plunged the blade to the heart.

While we were skinning this lion the dogs ran onto the trail of the second lion, and treed it before we had the first one skinned. After getting the hide off the first lion, we followed the direction whence came the baying of the dogs. Soon we reached the tree in which his lionship found protection from the dogs. Although he had been treed some time he didn't jump on our approach, but remained in his position until a dead shot from Colonel Roosevelt brought him down.

One day, while hunting out from the Keystone ranch, we bayed a very large lion in a crevice on the precipitous side of a rock ledge which extended from the point of the crevice, sheer down about sixty feet. The crevice was near the upper rim of the perpendicular wall of rock, and as we came up the lion was standing on this rim of rock over the crevice. It was dusk, and the light being poor, we could barely discern the faint outline of the animal. The Colonel prepared to shoot, although it was guesswork where he would hit. When he fired the lion disappeared and ran around in the crevice under the upper rim, just described. We looked around long and carefully before we discovered his whereabouts. Finally I leaned over the ledge and looked down as far as I could into the long crevice and thought I could see his ear. There happened to be a large rock standing loosely on the rim of the ledge weighing perhaps a couple of tons, and we saw at a glance that if it were possible for a man to be suspended out over this rock, head down, he might see further into the crevice, and thereby be able to detect the lion if there. The question which confronted us was, how was it to be done. Finally, Colonel Roosevelt stood still a minute, looked at me intently, and said: "Goff, we must have that lion if he is there. I'll tell you what I'll do. I will take my gun and crawl out over that rock, you holding me by the feet and allowing me to slide down far enough to see him. If I can see him I will get him."

And for once in my life my heart stood still for a while, so completely thunderstruck was I at the nerve of the man. There was a rock overhanging a precipice dropping off at least sixty feet, and at this time in the evening, with poor light, and both of us tired from the day's tramp, he proposed to practically suspend himself in the air, head downward with only a wall of rock against which to steady himself.

We prepared for the difficult and dangerous undertaking by his first climbing up on the rock, gun in hand, ready for work. When he had reached the summit of the rock, he then began to descend on the other side, and as he did so I caught hold of his feet, bracing myself against my side of the rock. From this on he underwent a sliding motion, controlled by my letting him out a little at a time until I heard the welcome:

"Far enough!"

At this point I steadied myself for a long wait, and realizing the preciousness of my burden, I held on for dear life. Finally I heard the Colonel say: "I see him!" and very shortly afterward heard the report of his 30-30 Winchester. At almost the same time I heard a rustling noise in the crevice, and soon there came the sound of a dull thud as the inanimate carcass of the lion fell to the bottom of the rocky abyss. I pulled the Colonel back, and after the strain on our nerves became relaxed he told me that although he wasn't able to draw a bead, owing to his position, yet he thought he had hit him in the head. We left him lie where he fell until next morning, when we skinned him and carried him into camp.

A short time after the incident above related, we received news that there were several lions on Juniper mountain, twelve miles north of the Keystone ranch. We decided immediately to start for Juniper, as I knew this to be a good lion country. On our way, and just as we had left the upper end of the Keystone ranch, we struck a lion trail. When I saw the tracks I told the Colonel that it was the largest lion we had yet found. The dogs had great difficulty in following the trail as it crossed over and over again trails that we had been on before, but after considerable cold-trailing and back-tracking, they managed eventually to tree him. When we came up he jumped from the tree and ran down under a ledge, the hounds in full cry after him. They soon had him at bay, so I turned the fighters loose. When they reached him they tackled immediately, and together they all rolled down the mountain for fifty feet. The lion broke loose from the pack and ran down the mountain side in plain view, affording what the colonel afterward said was one of the most novel and beautiful sights he had ever beheld. We soon had him treed, however, and when we came up it didn't take Colonel Roosevelt long to shoot him out. He fell over a ledge about fifty feet down, and when we reached the spot he was dead. We found on skinning him that he had been shot through the heart. It being too late to go to Juniper mountain that day, we repaired to the Keystone ranch, and prepared to make another start the following day.

But it seems we were destined never to reach Juniper, for on the second morning's start, while riding pretty lively about two miles from the ranch, and before we had left the field, I saw a lion-track crossing the road. I dismounted, and after a careful scrutiny of the tracks told Colonel Roosevelt that the lion which made the track was the largest in the country. Its paws measured six inches across. We set the dogs on the trail and ran him eight or nine miles—farther than any we had yet trailed. He persisted in crossing and recrossing many of the old trails of lions previously hunted, which bothered the dogs considerably. In the helter-skelter manner in which the dogs had to work, they got split up badly. Finally one of my oldest dogs, called very appropriately "Tree-em," treed the animal alone. Shortly after we got in sight of the tree a number of the other dogs joined their veteran companion, but before we had got fairly started up the side of the hill leading to the tree the lion jumped, ran down on a ledge and stopped to fight the dogs. One of the bull dogs ran in and took hold, making it so warm for the lion that he ran off and treed again. When we came up the Colonel shot him, breaking the spine. He was the liveliest spine-broken lion I ever before saw, but with a pack of dogs on him, the Colonel's liberal use of the knife and my clubbing him, we kept the monster from seriously hurting the dogs, and finally overcame him.

As he lay before us, the dogs panting in the background, I believe he formed part of the most magnificent picture I ever gazed on. He was the largest lion I ever saw, and I have killed hundreds. He weighed just 227 pounds, and to say that we both felt elated over our success hardly expresses our true feelings. It was not long before we had him skinned and were on our way to the ranch, where the tidings of our triumph were received with congratulations.

Colonel Roosevelt decided that the killing of a 227-pound lion was a pretty good way to end his Colorado hunt, especially in the further consideration of the fact that his time was about at an end. It was therefore decided to abandon the Juniper mountain trip and preparations were made for his departure for Meeker.

Accordingly, on February 15th, after bidding a cordial adieu to all, we left the Keystone ranch for Meeker, where we remained overnight. Colonel Roosevelt left Meeker the following morning for Rifle, where he took the train, Gates Kersburg accompanying him to Rifle in a light wagon.

In conclusion, I will only repeat what I have said before, namely, that the hunt with Colonel Roosevelt will always remain as one of the most pleasant memories of my life. His demeanor, his manliness, his generosity, his big noble heart, his simplicity—all combine to make him a companion in the field worthy the company of a king.

Trout-Casting in Washington

W. I. Agnew

May 1903

This is the first fishing story that I felt rated inclusion in this OUTDOOR LIFE anthology. Its style is in pleasant contrast to the staid, expository measures of so many of the magazine's early angling contributors. By comparison it sparkles and rollicks. Yet it was written seventy years ago.

Ten years ago (how time flies) the parties in this photograph were not tied down with either families or business as they are at present. Besides they all resided within easy access of the best fishing streams in the state of Washington. The writer and his wife lived at the capital, Olympia, and the other three couples at Montesano, forty miles west, on the Gray's Harbor branch of the Northern Pacific R. R. We were, and for that matter are yet, all fishing enthusiasts, although we do not revel as we used to in the greatest of all pastimes—casting the fly for the gamey cut-throat. Now all is different, except the streams. True, myself and wife are here, so are Bacon and his wife but Bud, the fat man, and Cora his wife, are at Shohomish, away north, and Ed Story and wife are in San Francisco. All have families of a greater or lesser size, and our joint trips have therefore vanished. The photo was taken after our very first trip, and though we made a dozen others, that one was the star trip of all.

Well, as I started to say, ten years ago next June, at the telephone request of the three couples living in Montesano, backed by the statement that trout were taking the fly greedily, my wife and I packed our camp outfit and boarded the Northern Pacific local to Montesano, where we found the others ready. With two wagons we struck back up the River Chehalis to a branch stream called Satsop, and thence up that stream to where it divided into three branches, Turner, Webber and East Fork, all about ten miles from Montesano. And let me say right now that these three streams have and do yield the largest and best fighting cut-throat trout I have yet discovered in my fishing trips. I have taken them as large as six and one-half pounds and sixteen inches in length. We left Montesano about the middle of the afternoon and after different experiences, all the way from bumping over skid roads, upsetting, nearly floating away while fording the river, etc., we made the camping place, Palmer's, a rancher at the mouths of the forks mentioned. We at once unloaded and dismissed the teams with directions to come for us in ten days, and then stripped off coats and went to work to fix up permanent camp. One big sleeping tent with partitions, a store tent and fly for table were in position with plenty of hay for beds, together with table, cupboard, etc., and ice house, all complete by dark; and then, with a hearty supper of bacon, eggs, etc., bed was in line. How we did snore until pandemonium broke loose all at once. Someone shot off a pistol, when simultaneously from the four corners of the tent rang out the campers' salute to the first night as four double-acting S. & W.'s cracked but five times each. How the ladies hallowed! They were sure we were attacked by Indians, cougars, bears and every old thing. After about a half hour of curtain lecture, we gradually dozed with the loving epithets of fools, idiots, etc., still humming in our ears.

About midnight one of the ladies awoke and in the semilight found the white transparency of the tent surrounding her with snores of all kinds and sorts, and with a yell she cast caution to the winds and in two seconds all four of them were hugging each other in the center of the tent, each and all emitting shrieks that would put a Sioux Indian to flight. Again quiet was restored, this time till daybreak.

We always made it a rule to get breakfast before waking the ladies in camp, so the breakfast call of "Get your coffee!" "Get your coffee!" always was sung out by the chief cook, Ed Bacon. And right well he deserved the position. I will back him as a camper against any man in the universe. Why, a camp fire and he are inseparable. Leave him alone ten minutes in the woods and he'll have one. I actually knew him to start one on a deer stand one day, preferring the fire he had to the deer he hadn't and didn't get.

That day we fished the East Fork, going up about three miles, and fishing it through to camp. We all fish, the ladies being good fly casters and handling six and one-half and seven-ounce rods and about forty-five feet to fifty feet of line as well as the best. No skirts for them, as you will see (and that's the only way to get fish). I'd like to see a skirted individual try to follow one of them in one of our mountain rivers like the Satsop. The half would not be told.

On this fork there are several good fishing strips all known by different names, viz., the Beaver-Dam, the Shale Run, the Canon, the Big Hole, at Comforts', the Big Bend, below Comforts', the Bluff, the Rapids, the Willow—all these running above camp. Below camp are the Webber Mouth, and the Moonlight Pools. All of these places yield big 'uns if you are there at the right time with the right fly and set it on the water right. I name these places because if you ever fish in these waters you will always be able to find the right places at once, as you will recognize them as soon as you see them. Besides, either Palmer or Comfort can tell you where they are.

But let me take you up stream, three miles by short cuts, to the Beaver-Dam; then come down with my wife and me. We strike the river, and isn't it a beauty about twenty-five yards across at the dam, and with a great deep swirling pool right below, with a shelving edge of soapstone rock on this side, while the water rushes down and then turns slowly back over by the other bank, where the sods and willows come down right to the edge. "Put on a black-body Royal Coachman and try it, Brownie," I say to my wife, and after a few casts to straighten the line (our lines have all been soaked overnight so not to delay and perhaps lose a good strike), she shoots the fly over to the opposite bank, and a dark shadow flashes out about three feet further down, churning the water into a swirl like a wheel as it dashes back. But, like the true fisherwoman she is, the cast is recovered lightly, quickly, and straight and true as a bullet it shoots out and up, and then sinks slowly and easily as a feather abou six inches back of where the shadow disappeared. Flash! A quick turn of the wrist and "scr-e-e-e-!"—the fight is on. A mad rush is made straight across to her very feet, then up stream, then down stream, the reel shrieking and the line fast paying out, now being reeled in, tension always the same, the little Bristol Steel six and one-half ounces standing right up to the work, till finally he seeks relief by sticking to the bottom, nose down, and refusing to budge. But Brownie is right after him and knows just what to do. A few little tips and out he charges like a mad bull, only to be met at every turn with the same steady even tension. "How will it end?" I say, as I stand and caution and advise as best I can, to be answered only by silence. It is skill against strength and activity. That trout could tear all that light tackle to mincemeat in a second if it was not delicately adjusted to every movement that he makes. But now, at the end of about thirty minutes' steady fish, the weakening begins; the tension is letting up; occasionally a black fin shows at the top of the rushing water, and I unhook the big landing net and drop down below him. As he is swung over the shallow bank, lying on his side, I slip it into the water and when right under and behind him the slack is given and it's all over. I take him to the bank and we stand and admire his shape, spots of golden sheen, red throat, black-green back, and then weigh him and find a five-pound prize. The cost of the trip has just been repaid a dozen times, and that hole at the dam is a memory; so down we go to the Shale Run, and it's up to me.

This pool is different. It is in a wider place in the river and the soapstone rock runs along like a table on both sides of the stream, with water about a foot deep running over it, while in the center a channel about twenty feet wide carries a rushing torrent about fifteen feet deep. It runs like this for about fifty yards, and then abruptly breaks off into one great pool about fifty yards across. As the main body of the water breaks out of the center run it strikes the deep pool, where the water is held back by the bluff and eddies off to both sides, but the greater portion curves back in a small whirlpool away over on the opposite side. The action of the water has cut away under a huge old fir that stood on that bank until it has fallen back into the woods and left a great yawning, foaming hole right where it once stood, with the roots still hanging down, forming a regular screen and a typical trout home where one big trout always camps and appropriates at least one of the many chambers of the castle under the water.

Carefully I let my line out, yard by yard, foot by foot, recovering my cast each time away down over the main body of the pool before I swing over to the home of the big trout I know is there. How do I know? My dear reader, did you ever cast a fly? Or—well, I have a "hunch." I measure the distance where I want to light and then gather my cast and without a breath send the fly right where I want it to go. It is a peacock-bodied governor. As it is about six inches above the water there seems to be a submarine volcanic eruption in the middle of the old fir roots, and a great green-red-and-gold body shoots into the air just under the fly and—tig! sting!—a hair too short, a slack line and a twigged trout that looked like a salmon. No use to try him again. That sting settled him for a few hours at least, and after a few careful casts to satisfy myself I was not mistaken, we move on, this time sorrowfully on my part. (Oh! he was a beauty. I made a trip every morning to the same place for six successive days, before I got him. But I got him. He was twenty-six inches long and weighed six and one-half pounds.)

But on we must go; so into the canon we wade. This is about one-half mile long and is a continuation of shale and soapstone, so that we walk side by side to assist each other over the slippery places. All through the canon the water for the most part is carried in a deep channel about fifty feet wide, while on either side the water spreads out about a foot deep for fifty feet. On either side in the center the action of the water has cut layers in the walls, so that innumerable average trout lie therein, and we catch quite a number on this stretch. We take none less than one pound in weight, releasing the others. I never saw a big trout in this place, but there are plenty such as I describe.

The next place is right at the foot of the canon where the waters from the gorge rush into the bottom land from a big hole all along the bank on one side. The high waters of each winter tear out the alder and maple along the clay banks and all along for two hundred yards the pool is twenty feet deep. In this place there are dozens of big trout, so we both strike out for a big one.

Right out in the center of the rapids lies a big rock, and I work my way over there and in front to gain the protection of the rock from the pressure of water, which is three feet deep and rushing like an express. Finally I succeed and commence operations. After a few preliminary casts I see a likely-looking place under the jam, and roll a cast away in and under and—"biff!" I get it. "Scream-m" goes the reel as foot after foot of line goes downstream. Brownie in the meantime has hooked a good one further down, but down goes my beauty until, when he breaks water, she thinks it her fish; and there we are with two big trout—I playing hers

25

and she mine, as we are led to believe. But soon we find that there is a letter **X** in the water made by the two lines, and then for a series of manipulations to land both, and not foul either on each other or the snags in the jam. Imagine the excitement. Well, you can't! You would have to be right there! There I am behind that rock, and dare not move, or downstream I go into a jam of twenty feet of water in front, with a big trout on. So all that can be done is for Brownie as quietly as possible to work downstream and away from me, with the danger of either or both fish jumping right over and around the other line. We finally get them separated and then I have the fight all clear. Did I say clear? Oh, no! There is the jam and the river boiling right into it, and a mad trout bound for under it. Give him the butt is the only thing, and give it I do until I fear everything will fly to pieces. But at last I turn him, and away goes one hundred and fifty feet of line with another rush. And so it goes for about three-quarters of an hour, until I have worked him close up and he is as still as a nail. But I am so stiff from bracing against the water I cannot move and dare not try to get him out as his dead weight would smash things. I dare not let Brownie go in to net him on account of the current and jam, and I am about to give up when all at once Ed Strong shows up and the trick is turned. And then another admiration society, and another five-pounder is in camp. We vote "enough for one day," and strike for camp to commence tomorrow where we left off today. A walk to camp while we pick up the other members of our party as we trudge along, each reporting with at least one big fish and we resolve there that we will not eat anything smaller than two-pound trout, so that we will always have good fishing. Soon we are in the Syringa grove, where we camp, and of course find Ed Bacon there with the camp fire ablaze and dinner on the road.

The catch of the morning is admired and we all turn in and help get dinner which consists of everything good, but above all fresh trout that is as hard as pork and sweet as sugar. Did you ever help eat a five-pound trout baked? If not, catch one and try it. If you get one don't keep it five or six days before trying. Bake him within an hour after you catch him and if you don't call in the physician your digestion is as good as mine.

After dinner we each relate our experiences of the morning, especially those of the trout we did not get, and plan how and where we can get these same individual fish during the afternoon. We speculate on the evening fishing at the moonlight pools, and different flies are ordered. Ed Bacon and his wife, Alice, make up a half dozen or so to suit the whim of all, and right here let me say that if any of you who read this want any particular fly just order a few from him. He manages the Olympia Arms Company's business at Olympia, Washington. And if you don't say that he or his wife—either one—ties the best flies you ever saw, I'll pay for the flies you get anytime you kick.

At 4 o'clock we gather our outfits together and strike out for the moonlight pools. We all can fish there at once, as there is plenty of room. It lasts about an hour. Just at dusk when the moon is right, how the big fellows will rise! It's a continual splash and scream. There is some one with a fish on all the time until dark, and then we wade back to camp, tired but happy. Thus we fish when we fish and lie around camp recounting exciting experiences with big fish until we know every big fish, or nearly so, in the different stretches of the different forks, until one noon a strange man is in camp when we come in, and when we get near enough we find it is our team. We had reached out limit, and although unwilling, we broke camp and commenced our journey home. The photo shown with this story was taken in Montesano in our creek outfits. On the next trip we educated Bud to use his light tackle on big trout, in one of the best fights I ever saw a trout put up.

The Quest of the Ptarmigan

Rex E. Beach

August 1903

Rex Beach, who spent several years in the Klondike, and made a fortune
from his novels and films, once told a friend that he had made his first real
money on a story written in longhand and sent to a sportsman's magazine.
For it, he received $20. This is the story. When Editor McGuire heard this,
he said he had wanted to pay $25, but his partner in publishing, J. A. Ricker,
had exclaimed, "My God, John! You don't want to bankrupt us, do you?
Fifteen ought to be plenty." "So we compromised on $20," related McGuire.
Contrast. In 1948, Beach, of whose novels fourteen were made into films
(*The Spoilers* four times), sold the rights to *Woman in Ambush* for
$100,000, at the time the highest price ever paid by Hollywood for an
unpublished manuscript. McGuire, a good picker, also got a lot for
his money. He ran "Ptarmigan" again in September 1927 at the height of
Beach's popularity.

Sell Keno? No—guess not. Need Money? Oh yes—but. No—you can't buy
him. That's a big price, I know, and I could buy lots of dog teams for that, but I
may as well tell you I would as soon sell my brother—my best friend, or, if I had
one, my wife. May be sentiment, but he saved my life, and no other man while he
lives shall ever curl the lash of a dog-whip across his shaggy back. He's not a dog
to me; he's my friend.

Want to hear about it?—Well—I don't mind. It's cold outside and nothing to
do. Better light up. It's mostly a story of a ptarmigan hunt. Kind of a peaceful
pastoral prelude, with merry guns cracking, ending up with a dash for life accompanied by a full fledged howling of the storm chorus under the baton of the spirit
of the North.

Did you ever have the meat hunger so strong in your vitals that you would
wake at night dreaming of the fried chicken that mother made, or could picture
the grill-marks on a broiled steak? Just in from the states, eh?

Well, after a continuous diet of bacon, ham and the poorly-embalmed beef that
made Chicago famous, the longing for something fresh becomes unbearable, so
when McMillan, another old timer, dropped in at the bunk house one night and
said that Nome River was "alive with ptarmigan" my partner Jack and I decided
to take the dog team and drive over for a day's sport—and a week's grub.

The heavy snows had driven the birds down from the mountains to the coast
where the willows were still uncovered. That was the year I had the great team,
considered the best on the coast; fifteen as fine dogs as ever stole a ham; kept me
broke, too, with dog-feed at 35 cents. Yes, that's the team we rescued the Cooper
party with, after the big storm. I brought two of the frozen men to a doctor
ninety-six miles in twelve hours, with Keno, here, in the lead. Good drive, eh?

Well, the next morning found us up, not bright and early, as daylight doesn't
come till about eight o'clock and isn't any too bright when it does get around, but
early nevertheless, and after a breakfast of oatmeal, bacon, evaporated potatoes
and "sour dough" flap jacks warranted to stick to your ribs for a week, I slipped
the harness over ten of the best dogs, and as the stars began to dim and fade we
heard the "swish-swish" of McMillan's twelve-foot skis as he came down the

27

creek. He looked ghostlike and unreal in his long white parka, or hooded shirt, with beard, mustache and eyebrows white from his frozen breath.

"How cold is it by your thermometer?" said he, "The 'quick' in ours is frozen up."

Our spirit thermometer registered 44 degrees below, but as there wasn't a breath of air stirring we anticipated a fairly comfortable day. My "malamoots" had shaken off their sleepiness and seated shivering on the snow with heads to the stars saddened the air with dismal complaints.

Jack took his seat in the bottom of the long basket-sled, behind McMillan. There was a crack of the whip and a "Mush boys" and as the dogs leaped into their collars we were whisked around the cabin and out onto the main trail at railroad speed. Then a word to old Keno here and the pack settled down to the even run which eats up distance and which well-trained dogs maintain for hours.

When we reached the bunch of willows at the mouth of Osborne Creek we slipped into the snowshoes and started back toward the foothills, keeping about a hundred yards apart.

I had been straining my eyes to detect some object on the monotonous expanse of white, when suddenly a spot of snow which I had scanned, broke up under my eyes into four animated, squawking snow-balls, which went whizzing in as many different directions. I wasn't sure on my snow shoes and missed with both barrels.

While the birds remained above the skyline they were readily visible, offering a splendid target, but as they settled lower they were merged into the whiteness of the snow and instantly disappeared.

I heard McMillan's 10-bore explode and concluded he was doing business in his usual way. Then a double from Jack, followed by a peculiarly easy and melodious flow of profanity, showing at least three years' continuous residence "north of 53," explained perfectly the result of his two shots.

Near me I noticed a black dot like a small shoe-button against the field of white, and straining my eyes until the tears came and froze on my cheeks, I detected the outlines of a bird. With shoes well under me I advanced on the enemy's right wing, as it were. This time when my bird rose I cut short his derisive squawk, and with my right barrel knocked the tail out of another which had followed, and saw him wabble off for a hundred yards before giving up the fight.

Again I heard the report of Jack's Parker, and then upon the still air there floated to me a bunch of the most earnest and sincerely heartfelt profanity that an active brain and facile tongue could master, interspersed with recurring prophesies as to the eventual destiny of the individual who invented smokeless powder, the corporation which made it, the store that sold it, and the infernal —— —— —— idiot who would attempt to use it in cold weather. I judged that he had attempted to use frozen nitro-powder and found that it would hardly clear the gun barrel of shot.

When I returned to the sled, the dogs were sleeping peacefully, curled up in the snow like round fur balls. While I straightened them out of the tangle of harness they had formed before lying down, Jack and McMillan cleaned the birds, distributing feathers and refuse impartially among the members of the team. The craving for fresh meat among the inner circles of the dogs is probably more acute than among us and certainly less often gratified.

Having put them in a good humor we were off again up the river in the direction our birds had gone. Jack had turned to ask me something when he interrupted himself to tell me that my nose was frozen. This particular feature is unduly prominent with me and its isolation from the base of supplies renders it "shy" on circulation, so that it grows chill and clammy in Indian summer and has been frozen stiff by Thanksgiving. These frost bites result in an exceedingly red-looking and painful member which later peels off like a boiled potato. After a few moments of vigorous rubbing and pinching I succeeded in restoring animation and thereafter by wrinkling my nose like a cow I could tell whether the circulation had "made good" or was laying off. If the part felt stiff and difficult to move, off would come the mittens and the osteopathy recommence, continuing until the organ became sensible to muscular control.

I had been sitting on the sled rail, engaged in working my nose up to a fever heat, when suddenly, with a jerk that nearly unseated me, the team leaped into a sharp run. Glancing ahead the cause was apparent in the shape of a big Arctic hare that had hopped from the deep snow in the willows to the bare ice of the river and was leisurely working the kinks out of his legs a short distance ahead of us.

The dogs quieted almost instantly, and with noses to the trail began to run madly, making our sled sing over the smooth ice, which allowed them a sure footing and offered no resistance to the sled. In fact, here lay the danger, for with the accelerated speed, our sled, striking the little inequalities of the ice surface, was veering wildly, sometimes sliding nearly broadside on. Striking an obstacle, with a string of sparks from the steel shoe, it would tilt on one runner, nearly hurling us headlong onto the ice, then back again to the other side.

To control a team with the smell of game in their nostrils is impossible, yet a spill on the ice at this rate of speed meant painful results, if not serious ones, while a runaway team would mean loss of outfit and a long trip home on foot.

The duties of the "chauffeur" of the team in addition to "dog punching" consists of preventing an upset, if possible, so bidding the boys keep their seats, I balanced my 200 pounds of avoirdupois on the upper rail of the sled, changing from side to side as it began its erratic flights. This method of shifting ballast was working admirably and we were enjoying our dizzy ride, when our pacemaker, thinking the excitement too tame, increased his speed, and turning abruptly, made for the willows on the river bank.

This particular curve was not graded for our rate of speed, and when the dogs turned the sled swung, skimming around broadside and striking an ice hummock upsetting with such violence as to hurl me flying through the air like a frog. I believe a parabola is the most beautiful curve in geometry, yet although I feel that the the one I described was geometrically perfect, its beauty did not appeal to me. Experience on a bicycle track, from the days of the high wheel onward, had taught me a valuable thing about falling, and I rejoiced in the knowledge that unlike a board track there were no splinters here.

I landed amid a rain of dead birds with the breath knocked out of me and a mental photograph of Jack and McMillan in positions absolutely defying the laws of nature. Mac was evidently attempting to rise at the critical moment, and with his long legs curled beneath him, had added to his momentum by jumping at random—so I caught a fleeting glimpse of a giant, red-headed Scotchman apparently seated at ease on the ice, but progressing with surprising rapidity in the direction we had been going. I had never before seen a practical demonstration of the Scotch game of "curling." I believe I would enjoy watching a game.

Jack's early training on the deck of a cattle pony asserted itself, and clinging tightly to the sled he was dragged up the bank through the snow, and into the bushes where the dogs, becoming entangled, came to a stop and awaited us with wagging tails, lolling tongues and an expression plainly saying: "We gave him the run of his life, didn't we?" We found Jack with pipe still clenched between his teeth, gingerly testing his knee caps.

"They were my only points of bearing for fifty yards," said he, "and if they weren't good, thick Missouri knee caps, they'd be looking like a glass of toothpicks, now."

An excited team will tie knots in its harness that would defy a sailor to unravel, so while the others gathered up the debris scattered across the river, I attempted to straighten out the tangle.

Busied in this way I suddenly became conscious of an ominous movement of the air which till now had been deathly still. Glancing north up the valley I saw that which caused me to snatch the struggling dogs out on the ice with a curse, and utter a cry of warning to my companions. The mountains, towering on either hand, had changed, and instead of standing clear-cut and white in the marble stillness, a dim haze had veiled the landscape while from the peaks flew gossamer streams of whirling snow, like thin smoke of many fires. As yet the air of the valley was scarcely stirring, but as we gazed, the twin walls of mountains gleaming miles northward up the valley were silently blotted out by the gray clouds of snow that swept down upon us. We were in the icy grip of the "Terror of the Northland," the sudden breath of the Arctic which sweeps south without warning over this desolate wilderness.

"We'll have to run before it," said Jack, as we hurriedly donned the fur "parkis" which till now had remained unused. "No living thing could face a wind in this cold."

As we threw the birds in the sled, a puff of snow whirled past, enveloping us in a stinging cloud of frost crystals, while the dogs whined uneasily and strained against the harness.

The storm did not break suddenly, nor did it sweep down upon us with the roar and violence of a hurricane, but rather with a darkening of the heavens there came a restless stirring of the air which rapidly quickened and brought with it a moaning flurry of snow. This writhed along the ground as though loathe to part from its drifts.

McMillan's hooded figure floated ahead of us, visible only above the waist, his long legs invisible in the swirling snow, which clinging close to the earth, hid the dogs from view and seemed to buoy us up on a drifting sea of white. Soon the familiar landscape faded out and we were hurried on through a thick, gray, biting atmosphere, trusting to our general sense of direction.

Given a good sleeping-bag, the proper course to pursue in an extremity of this kind is to free the dogs from the harness and seeking the shelter of the sled, crawl inside the bag and wait for the storm to abate. This is no beauty sleep which one enjoys inside a deerskin sack during the two or three days that a blizzard rages, but with sufficient food to sustain bodily heat, it is a safe resource.

Totally unprepared as we were, the anxiety I saw in Jack's countenance was mirrored in mine, but I thanked my stars for not having a little wife waiting for me back at the claim, as he had.

McMillan paused until we blew up to his side, and speaking through ice-burdened whiskers said, "Either my direction is wrong or the wind is changing. If we keep this course we'll be out on the ice of the Bering sea by night-fall."

"We don't need to complicate this pleasant situation by getting onto the ice-pack with an offshore gale," shouted Jack. "We'd better take the consensus of opinion and strike for the point we think is home."

The plain lying between the foothills and the ocean is devoid of vegetation and makes it extremely easy to wander out upon the ice-floe. Confused by the approaching darkness and the blinding snow, I feared for the result in such a case.

It seemed to our strained imaginations that we had travelled for hours before the early darkness, hastened by the gloom of the storm, settled upon us, and the dogs, wearied by constant plunging through soft snow and heavy with ice-matted coats, stopped, panting and exhausted.

There is no rest for man or beast on the frozen trail, and after cleaning the ice from their faces, with a cheering word to each, we forced them on.

When another hour had dragged itself by, the long, heavy dog whip was curling among them, and with hoarse cries of encouragement we plodded onward.

Suddenly with a shout Jack halted us. "We're out on the pack " said he, and stopping he dimly showed us the ragged point of an up-ended ice cake from which the snow had been blown.

With my sheath knife I chipped a piece off and the briny taste told me that we were indeed upon the ice of Bering Sea and perhaps headed for open water a few miles off shore. Fortunately we had not encountered a crevice, for had we done so nothing would have prevented our plunging into it, blinded and driven by the gale and with no question as to the result, for even though regaining the solid ice, the excessive cold would have instantly congealed our heavy clothes into icy armour impossible to bear.

Turning, we fought our way back again into the storm, but the dogs refused to face the cutting sleet. The heavy butt of the dog whip only produced whines of pain, so heading as closely to the wind as possible we changed our course back toward the shore.

I was faint from hunger and very tired. We had traveled for an endless time in this direction when McMillan staggered back to the sled and throwing himself upon it said, "I'm afraid I can't make it much farther. One of my skis is broken and I'm too far gone to travel without it."

Jack listlessly rubbed his cheeks with snow as he sank behind the sled.

"Fellows, my face has started to freeze," said he. "We might as well try to walk around till morning. We may go it till daylight if we keep moving and don't let each other go to sleep."

I was glad to yield to an overpowering desire to stop. Rest was what I wanted and a little doze. It seemed many days since I had slept, and a few moments' sleep now would fix me finely.

Too drowsy and exhausted to answer, I went forward to cut the harness from the dogs, thinking that they at least would sleep the storm out and return safely to the claim.

Immediately upon stopping every animal save one, had curled up and was sleeping in its tracks. "Keno," the leader, sat up and with quivering nostrils was casting the wind for a scent. Three winters on the trail with this shaggy veteran had taught me the significance of his every move and had bred absolute confidence in his instinct.

"He smells a camp!" I shouted, and fell to madly pulling, beating and kicking the weary brutes onto their feet. We yelled and coaxed and entreated, careful not to confuse the leader who, given his head, started rapidly into the very teeth of the storm, occasionally raising his nose to the wind.

Soon one of the big gray wheel-dogs whined eagerly and strained into the harness, and with a chorus of sharp cries the team broke into a run while we clung stubbornly to the sled and plunging heavily were dragged up over a bank where the blizzard howled down from the hills above, and tearing the hoods from our faces, froze our wet streaming hair. Then the dogs were suddenly swallowed up in a dark hole which pierced the depths of a large drift, and with a crash the sled struck the log forming one side of the entrance, throwing us partially into the low black tunnel of an "egloo."

Almost instantly a blaze of light appeared at the end of the passage as a door swung open disclosing the rough interior of a roadhouse, while a man's tall figure was silhouetted against the square of welcome brightness. A ravishing steam of hot cooking assailed our nostrils, and as he waded towards us through the struggling mass of smoking wolf-dogs he cried, "My God, strangers! Who hits the trail on a night like this?"

31

Red Letter Days
in British Columbia

Lieutenant Townsend Whelen

December 1906

"The late Colonel Townsend Whelen was a good friend of mine," wrote Jack O'Connor, for more than thirty years the titan of shooting editors. "I believe I have read almost everything of his that has been published, as I started reading his stuff back before World War I when I was a gun-struck adolescent and he was still only a lieutenant. I consider him one of the most sensible, honest and reliable gun writers ever to practice the rather doubtful trade in this country. He started hunting big game in the black powder days. . . . Almost everything he wrote made sense." To that I will add that this story, written nearly seventy years ago, is a milestone in modern writing about hunting. It's all here. Whelen was an expert in several departments of shooting in the Army, was a contributor and shooting editor for OUTDOOR LIFE well into the 1930s and later joined *Sports Afield*. He wrote many books.

In the month of July, 1901, my partner, Bill Andrews, and I were at a small Hudson Bay post in the northern part of British Columbia, outfitting for a long hunting and exploring trip in the wild country to the North. The official map showed this country as "unexplored," with one or two rivers shown by dotted lines. This map was the drawing card which had brought us thousands of miles by rail, stage and pack train to this out-of-the-way spot. By the big stove in the living room of the factor's house we listened to weird tales of this north country, of its enormous mountains and glaciers, its rivers and lakes and of the quantities of game and fish. The factor told us of three men who had tried to get through there in the Klondike rush several years before and had not been heard from yet. The trappers and Siwashes could tell us of trails which ran up either side of the Scumscum, the river on which the post stood, but no one knew what lay between that and the Yukon to the north.

We spent two days here outfitting and on the morning of the third said goodbye to the assembled population and started with our pack train up the east bank of the Scumscum. We were starting out to live and travel in an unknown wilderness for over six months, and our outfit may perhaps interest my readers: We had two saddle horses, four pack horses and a dog. A small tent formed one pack cover. We had ten heavy army blankets, which we used for saddle blankets while traveling, they being kept clean by using canvas sweat pads under them. We were able to pack 150 pounds of grub on each horse, divided up as nearly as I can remember as follows: One hundred and fifty pounds flour, 50 pounds sugar, 30 pounds beans, 10 pounds rice, 10 pounds dried apples, 20 pounds prunes, 30 pounds corn meal, 20 pounds oatmeal, 30 pounds potatoes, 10 pounds onions, 50 pounds bacon, 25 pounds salt, 1 pound pepper, 6 cans baking powder, 10 pounds soap, 10 pounds tobacco, 10 pounds tea, and a few little incidentals weighing probably 10 pounds. We took two extra sets of shoes for each horse, with tools for shoeing, 2 axes, 25 boxes of wax matches, a large can of gun oil, canton flannel for gun rags, 2 cleaning rods, a change of underclothes, 6 pairs of socks and 6 moccasins each, with buckskin for resoling, toilet articles, 100 yards of fishing line, 2 dozen fish hooks, an oil stove, awl, file, screw-driver, needles and thread, etc.

For cooking utensils we had 2 frying pans, 3 kettles to nest, 2 tin cups, 3 tin plates and a gold pan. We took 300 cartridges for each of our rifles. Bill carried a .38-55 Winchester, model '94, and I had my old .40-72 Winchester, model '95, which had proved too reliable to relinquish for a high-power small bore. Both rifles were equipped with Lyman sights and carefully sighted. As a precaution we each took along extra front sights, firing pins and main-springs, but did not have a chance to use them. I loaded the ammunition for both rifles myself, with black powder, smokeless priming, and lead bullets. Both rifles proved equal to every emergency.

Where the post stood the mountains were low and covered for the most part with sage brush, with here and there a grove of pines or quaking aspen. As our pack train wound its way up the narrow trail above the river bank we saw many Siwashes spearing salmon, a very familiar sight in that country. These gradually became fewer and fewer, then we passed a miner's cabin and a Siwash village with its little log huts and its hay fields, from which grass is cut for the winter consumption of the horses. Gradually all signs of civilization disappeared, the mountains rose higher and higher, the valley became a canon, and the roar of the river increased, until finally the narrowing trail wound around an outrageous corner with the river a thousand feet below, and looming up in front of us appeared a range of snow-capped mountains, and thus at last we were in the haven where we would be.

That night we camped on one of the little pine-covered benches above the canon. My, but it was good to get the smell of that everlasting sage out of our nostrils, and to take long whiffs of the balsam-ladened air! Sunset comes very late at this latitude in July, and it was an easy matter to wander up a little draw at nine in the evening and shoot the heads of three grouse. After supper it was mighty good to lie and smoke and listen to the tinkle of the horse bells as they fed on the luscious mountain grass. We were old campmates, Bill and I, and it took us back to many trips we had had before, which were, however, to be surpassed many times by this one. I can well remember how as a boy, when I first took to woods loafing, I used to brood over a little work which we all know so well, entitled, "Woodcraft," by that grand old man, "Nessmuk," and particularly that part where he relates about his eight-day tramp through the then virgin wilderness of Michigan. But here we were, starting out on a trip which was to take over half a year, during which time we were destined to cover over 1,500 miles of unexplored mountains, without the sight of a human face or an axe mark other than our own.

The next day after about an hour's travel, we passed the winter cabin of an old trapper, now deserted, but with the frames for stretching bear skins and boards for marten pelts lying around—betokening the owner's occupation. The dirt roof was entirely covered with the horns of deer and mountain sheep, and we longed to close our jaws on some good red venison. Here the man-made trails came to an end, and henceforth we used the game trails entirely. These intersect the country in every direction, being made by the deer, sheep and caribou in their migrations between the high and low altitudes. In some places they were hardly discernible, while in others we followed them for days, when they were as plainly marked as the bridle paths in a city park. A little further on we saw a whole family of goats sunning themselves on a high bluff across the river, and that night we dined on the ribs of a fat little spike buck which I shot in the park where we pitched our tent.

To chronicle all the events which occurred on that glorious trip would, I fear, tire my readers, so I will choose from the rich store certain ones which have made red-letter days in our lives. I can recollect but four days when we were unable to kill enough game or catch enough fish to keep the table well supplied, and as luck would have it, those four days came together, and we nearly starved. We had been camped for about a week in a broad wooded valley, having a glorious loaf after a hard struggle across a mountain pass, and were living on trout from a little stream alongside camp, and grouse which were in the pine woods by the thousands. Tiring of this diet we decided to take a little side trip and get a deer or two, taking only our three fattest horses and leaving the others behind to fatten up on the long grass in the valley, for they had become very poor owing to a week's work high up above timber line. The big game here was all high up in the mountains to escape the heat of the valley. So we started one morning, taking only a little tea, rice, three bannocks, our bedding and rifles, thinking that we would enjoy living on meat straight for a couple of days. We had along with us a black mongrel hound named Lion, belonging to Bill. He was a fine dog on grouse but prone to chase a deer once in a while.

About eight miles up the valley could be seen a high mountain of green serpentine rock and for many days we had been speculating on the many fine bucks which certainly lay in the little ravines around the base, so we chose this for our goal. We made the top of the mountain about three in the afternoon, and gazing down on the opposite side we saw a little lake with good horse feed around it and determined to camp there. About half way down we jumped a doe and as it stood on a little hummock Bill blazed away at it and undershot. This was too much for Lion, the hound, and he broke after the deer, making the mountainside ring with his baying for half an hour. Well, we hunted all the next day, and the next, and never saw a hair. That dog had chased the deer all out of the country with his barking.

By this time our little grub-stake of rice, bannocks and tea was exhausted, and, to make things worse, on the third night we had a terrific hail storm, the stones covering the ground three inches deep. Breakfast the next morning consisted of tea alone and we felt pretty glum as we started out, determining that if we did not find game that day we would pull up stakes for our big camp in the valley. About one o'clock I struck a fresh deer trail and had not followed it long before three or four others joined it, all traveling on a game trail which led up a valley. This valley headed up about six miles from our camp in three little ravines, each about four miles long. When I got to the junction of these ravines it was getting dark and I had to make for camp. Bill was there before me and had the fire going and some tea brewing, but nothing else. He had traveled about twenty miles that day and had not seen a thing. I can still see the disgusted look on his face when he found I had killed nothing. We drank our tea in silence, drew our belts tighter and went to bed.

The next morning we saddled up our horses and pulled out. We had not tasted food for about sixty hours and were feeling very faint and weak. I can remember what an effort it was to get into the saddle and how sick and weak I felt when old Baldy, my saddle horse, broke into a trot. Our way back led near the spot where I had left the deer trail the night before, and we determined to ride that way hoping that perhaps we might get a shot at them. Bill came first, then Loco, the pack horse, and I brought up the rear. As we were crossing one of the little ravines at the head of the main valley Loco bolted and Bill took after him to drive him back into the trail. I sat on my horse idly watching the race, when suddenly I saw a mouse-colored flash and then another and heard the thump, thump of cloven feet. Almost instantly the whole ravine seemed to be alive with deer. They were running in every direction. I leaped from my horse and cut loose at the nearest, which happened to be a doe. She fell over a log and I could see her tail waving in little circles and knew I had her. Then I turned on a big buck on the other side of the ravine and at the second shot he stumbled and rolled into the little stream. I heard Bill shooting off to the left and yelled to him that we had enough, and he soon joined me, saying he had a spike buck down. It was the work of but a few minutes to dress the deer and soon we had a little fire going and the three livers hanging in little strips around it. Right here we three, that is, Bill, the dog and myself, disposed of a liver apiece, and my! how easily and quickly it went—the first meat in over a week. Late that night we made our horse camp in the lower valley, having to walk all the way as our horses packed the meat. The next day was consumed entirely with jerking meat, cooking and eating. We consumed half the spike buck that day. When men do work such as we were doing their appetites are enormous, even without a fast of four days to sharpen them up.

One night I well remember after a particularly hard day with the pack train through a succession of wind-falls. We killed a porcupine just before camping and made it into a stew with rice, dough balls, onions and thick gravy, seasoned with curry. It filled the kettle to within an inch of the top and we ate the whole without stopping, whereat Bill remarked that it was enough for a whole boarding-house. According to the catalogue of Abercrombie and Fitch that kettle held eight quarts.

We made it the rule while our horses were in condition, to travel four days in the week, hunt two and rest one. Let me chronicle a day of traveling; it may interest some of you who have never traveled with a pack train. Arising at the first streak of dawn, one man cooked the breakfast while the other drove in the horses. These were allowed to graze free at every camping place, each horse having a cow bell around its neck, only Loco being hobbled, for he had a fashion of wandering off on an exploring expedition of his own and leading all the other horses with him. The horses were liable to be anywhere within two miles of camp, and it was necessary to get behind them to drive them in. Four miles over these mountains would be considered a pretty good day's work in the East. Out here it merely gave one an appetite for his breakfast. If you get behind a pack of well-trained horses they will usually walk right straight to camp, but on occasions I have walked, thrown stones and cussed from seven until twelve before I managed to get them in. Sometimes a bear will run off a pack of horses. This happened to us once and it took two days to track them to the head of a cañon, fifteen miles off, and then we had to break Loco all over again.

Breakfast and packing together would take an hour, so we seldom got started before seven o'clock. One of us rode first to pick out the trail, then followed the four pack horses and the man in the rear, whose duty it was to keep them in the trail and going along. Some days the trail was fine, running along the grassy south hillsides with fine views of the snowcapped ranges, rivers, lakes and glaciers; and on others it was one continual struggle over fallen logs, boulders, through ice-cold rivers, swifter than the Niagara rapids, and around bluffs so high that we could scarcely distinguish the outlines of the trees below. Suppose for a minute that you have the job of keeping the horses in the trail. You ride behind the last horse, lazily watching the train. You do not hurry them as they stop for an instant to catch at a whiff of bunch grass beside the trail. Two miles an hour is all the speed you can hope to make. Suddenly one horse will leave the trail enticed by some particularly green grass a little to one side, and leaning over in your saddle you pick up a stone and hurl it at the delinquent, and he falls into line again. Then everything goes well until suddenly one of the pack horses breaks off on a faint side trail going for all he is worth. You dig in your spurs and follow him down the mountain side over rocks and down timber until he comes to a stop half a mile below in a thicket of quaking aspen. You extricate him and drive him back. The next thing you know one of the horses starts to buck and you notice that his pack is turning; then everything starts at once. The pack slides between the horse's legs, he bucks all the harder, the frying pan comes loose, a side pack comes off and the other horses fly in every direction. Perhaps in an hour you have corralled the horses, repacked the cause of your troubles and are hitting the trail again. In another day's travel the trail may lead over down timber and big boulders and for eight solid hours you are whipping the horses to make them jump the obstructions, while your companion is pulling at the halters.

Rustling with a pack train is a soul-trying occupation. Where possible we always aimed to go into camp about three in the afternoon. Then the horses got a good feed before dark—they will not feed well at night—and we had plenty of time to make a comfortable camp and get a good supper. We seldom pitched our tent on these one-night camps unless the weather looked doubtful, preferring to make a bed of pine boughs near the fire. The blankets were laid on top of a couple of pack sheets and the tent over all.

For several days we had been traveling thus, looking for a pass across a long snow-capped mountain range which barred our way to the north. Finally we found a pass between two large peaks where we thought we could get through, so we started up. When we got up to timber-line the wind was blowing so hard that we could not sit on our horses. It would take up large stones the size of one's fist and hurl them down the mountain side. It swept by us cracking and roaring like a battery of rapid-fire guns. To cross was impossible, so we back-tracked a mile to a spot where a little creek crossed the trail, made camp and waited. It was three days before the wind went down enough to allow us to cross.

The mountain sheep had made a broad trail through the pass and it was easy to follow, being mostly over shale rock. That afternoon, descending the other side of the range, we camped just below timber line by a little lake of the most perfect emerald hue I have ever seen. The lake was about a mile long. At its head a large glacier extended way up towards the peaks. On the east was a wall of bright red rock, a thousand feet high, while to the west the hillside was covered with dwarf pine trees, some of them being not over a foot high and full-grown at that. Below our camp the little stream, the outlet of the lake, bounded down the hillside in a succession of waterfalls. A more beautiful picture I have yet to see. We stayed up late that night watching it in the light of the full moon and thanked our lucky stars that we were alive. It was very cold; we put on all the clothes we owned and turned in under seven blankets. The heavens seemed mighty near, indeed, and the stars crackled and almost exploded with the still silver mountains sparkling all around. We could hear the roar of the waterfalls below us and the bells of the horses on the hillside above. Our noses were very cold. Far off a coyote howled and so we went to sleep—and instantly it was morning.

I arose and washed in the lake. It was my turn to cook, but first of all I got my telescope and looked around for signs of game. Turning the glass to the top of the wooded hillside, I saw something white moving, and getting a steady position, I made it out to be the rump of a mountain sheep. Looking carefully I picked out four others. Then I called Bill. The sheep were mine by right of discovery, so we traded the cook detail and I took my rifle and belt, stripped to trousers, moccasins and shirt, and started out, going swiftly at first to warm up in the keen mountain air. I kept straight up the hillside until I got to the top and then started along the ridge toward the sheep. As I crossed a little rise I caught sight of them five hundred yards ahead, the band numbering about fifty. Some were feeding, others were bedded down in some shale. From here on it was all stalking, mostly crawling through the small trees and bushes which were hardly knee-high. Finally, getting within one hundred and fifty yards, I got a good, steady prone position between the bushes, and picking out the largest ram, I got the white Lyman sight nicely centered behind his shoulder and very carefully and gradually I pressed the trigger. The instant the gun went off I knew he was mine, for I could call the shot exactly. Instantly the sheep were on the move. They seemed to double up, bunch and then vanish. It was done so quickly that I doubt if I could have gotten in another shot even if I had wished it. The ram I had fired at was knocked completely off its feet, but picked himself up instantly and started off with the others; but after he had run about a hundred yards I saw his head drop and turning half a dozen somersaults, he rolled down the hill and I knew I had made a heart shot. His horns measured 16½ inches at the base, and the nose contained an enormous bump, probably caused in one of his fights for the supremacy of the herd.

I dressed the ram and then went for the horses. Bill, by this time, had everything packed up, so after going up the hill and loading the sheep on my saddle horse, we started down the range for a region where it was warmer and less strenuous and where the horse feed was better. That night we had mountain sheep ribs —the best meat that ever passed a human's mouth—and I had a head worth bringing home. A 16½-inch head is very rare in these days. I believe the record head measured about 19 inches. I remember distinctly, however, on another hunt in the Lillooet district of British Columbia, finding in the long grass of a valley the half-decayed head of an enormous ram. I measured the pith of the skull where the horn had been and it recorded 18 inches. The horn itself must have been at least 21 inches. The ram probably died of old age or was unable to get out of the high altitude when the snow came.

We journeyed on and on, having a glorious time in the freedom of the mountains. We were traveling in a circle, the diameter of which was about three hundred miles. One day we struck an enormous glacier and had to bend way off to the right to avoid it. For days as we travelled that glacier kept us company. It had its origin way up in a mass of peaks and perpetual snow, being fed from a dozen valleys. At least six moraines could be distinctly seen on its surface, and the air in its vicinity was decidedly cool. Where we first struck it it was probably six miles wide and I believe it was not a bit less than fifty miles long. We named it Chilco glacier, because it undoubtedly drained into a large lake of that name near the coast. At this point we were not over two hundred miles from the Pacific Ocean.

As the leaves on the aspen trees started to turn we gradually edged around and headed toward our starting point, going by another route, however, trusting to luck and the careful map we had been making to bring us out somewhere on the Scumscum river above the post. The days were getting short now and the nights very cold. We had to travel during almost all the daylight and our horses started to get poor. The shoes we had taken for them were used up by this time and we had to avoid as much as possible the rocky country. We travelled fast for a month until we struck the headwaters of the Scumscum; then knowing that we were practically safe from being snowed up in the mountain we made a permanent camp on a hillside where the horsefeed was good and started to hunt and tramp to our hearts' delight, while our horses filled up on the grass. We never killed any more game than we could use, which was about one animal every ten days. In this climate meat will keep for a month if protected from flies in the daytime and exposed to the night air after dark.

We were very proud of our permanent camp. The tent was pitched under a large pine tree in a thicket of willows and quaking aspen. All around it was built a windbreak of logs and pine boughs, leaving in front a yard, in the center of which was our camp fire. The windbreak went up six feet high and when a fire was going in front of the tent we were as warm as though in a cabin, no matter how hard the wind blew. Close beside the tent was a little spring, and a half a mile away was a lake full of trout from fifteen pounds down. We spent three days laying in a supply of firewood. Altogether it was the best camp I ever slept in. The hunting within tramping distance was splendid. We rarely hunted together, each preferring to go his own way. When we did not need meat we hunted varmints, and I brought in quite a number of prime coyote pelts and one wolf. One evening Bill staggered into camp with a big mountain lion over his shoulders. He just happened to run across it in a little pine thicket. That was the only one we saw on the whole trip, although their tracks were everywhere and we frequently heard their mutterings in the still evenings. The porcupines at this camp were unusually numerous. They would frequently get inside our wind break and had a great propensity for eating our soap. Lion, the hound, would not bother them; he had learned his lesson well. When they came around he would get an expression on his face as much as to say, "You give me a pain."

The nights were now very cold. It froze every night and we bedded ourselves down with lots of skins and used enormous logs on the fire so that it would keep going all night. We shot some marmots and made ourselves fur caps and gloves and patched up our outer garments with buckskin. And still the snow did not come.

One day while out hunting I saw a big goat on a bluff off to my right and determined to try to get him for his head, which appeared through my telescope to be an unusually good one. He was about half a mile off when I first spied him and the bluff extended several miles to the southwest like a great wall shutting off the view in that direction. I worked up to the foot of the bluffs and then along; climbing up several hundred feet I struck a shelf which appeared to run along the face at about the height I had seen the goat. It was ticklish work, for the shelf was covered with slide rock which I had to avoid disturbing, and then, too, in places it dwindled to a ledge barely three feet wide with about five hundred feet of nothing underneath. After about four hundred yards of this work I heard a rock fall above me and looking up saw the billy leaning over an outrageous corner looking at me. Aiming as nearly as I could straight up I let drive at the middle of the white mass. There was a grunt, a scramble and a lot of rocks, and then down came the goat, striking in between the cliff and a big boulder and not two feet from me. I fairly shivered for fear he would jump up and butt me off the ledge, but he only gave one quiver and lay still. The 330-grain bullet entering the stomach, had broken the spine and killed instantly. He was an old grandfather and had a splendid head, which I now treasure very highly. I took the head, skin, fat and some of the meat back to camp that night, having to pack it off the bluff in sections. The fat rendered out into three gold-pans full of lard. Goat-fat is excellent for frying and all through the trip it was a great saving on our bacon.

Then one night the snow came. We heard it gently tapping on the tent, and by morning there was three inches in our yard. The time had come only too soon to pull out, which we did about ten o'clock, bidding good-bye to our permanent camp with its comfortable windbreak, its fireplace, table and chairs. Below us the river ran through a canon and we had to cross quite a high mountain range to get through. As we ascended the snow got deeper and deeper. It was almost two feet deep on a level on top of the range. We had to go down a very steep hog-back, and here had trouble in plenty. The horses' feet balled up with snow and they were continually sliding. A pack horse slid down on top of my saddle horse and started him. I was on foot in front and they knocked me down and the three of us slid until stopped by a fallen tree. Such a mess I never saw. One horse was on top of another. The pack was loose and frozen ropes tangled up with everything. It took us half an hour to straighten up the mess and the frozen lash ropes cut our hands frightfully. My ankle had become slightly strained in the mix-up and for several days I suffered agonies with it. There was no stopping—we had to hit the trail hard or get snowed in. One day we stopped to hunt. Bill went out while I nursed my leg. He brought in a fine seven-point buck.

Speaking of the hunt he said: "I jumped the buck in a flat of down timber. He was going like mad about a hundred yards off when I first spied him. I threw up the old rifle and blazed away five times before he tumbled. Each time I pulled I was conscious that the sights looked just like that trademark of the Lyman sight showing the running deer and the sight. When I went over to look at the buck I had a nice little bunch of five shots right behind the shoulder. Those Lyman sights are surely the sights for a hunting rifle." Bill was one of the best shots on game I ever saw. One day I saw him cut the heads off of three grouse in trees while he sat in the saddle with his horse walking up hill. Both our rifles did mighty good work. The more I use a rifle the more I become convinced of the truth of the saying, "Beware of the man with one gun." Get a good rifle to suit you exactly. Fix the trigger pull and sights exactly as you wish them and then stick to that gun as long as it will shoot accurately and you will make few misses in the field.

Only too soon we drove our pack-train into the post. As we rode up two men were building a shack. One of them dropped a board and we nearly jumped out of our skins at the terrific noise. My! how loud everything sounded to our ears, accustomed only to the stillness of those grand mountains. We stayed at the post three days, disposing of our horses and boxing up our heads and skins, and then pulled out for civilization. Never again will such experiences come to us. The day of the wilderness hunter has gone for good. And so the hunt of our lives came to an end.

Camping with a Motor Car

A. Whiteman

December 1910

Now the automobile. First OUTDOOR LIFE ad, oddly, was for a steam
carriage, the Orient Victoriette (Dec. 1900). "Automobiling", a new
department, appeared in June 1901. An ad for Stevens-Duryea next (Jan.
1902, 15 hp., 3 speeds, reverse). Two stories that year: "An Auto Ride in
Colorado," by Editor McGuire (25 miles in 59½ mins.), and "Above
Timber Line in an Auto," by Webb Jay (400 miles, gas 20¢, "only"
45 minutes to change a tire). More ads: Winton, Wood, General, Baker,
Rambler, Oldsmobile, Toledo, The Pierce Great Arrow, Haynes-Apperson,
Cadillac ($800 to $4100), Ford ($950 to $2000) and Matheson. Then
(Jan. 1910), "An automobile within the reach of all, The Maxwell
Runabout—$600!" ("It sounds the knell of the horse and buggy.") And
also in 1910, honest to gas auto camping! Believe it.

In the summer of 1910 "touring fever" was epidemic throughout the United
States. The germ was imported from Europe a few years ago and each succeeding
summer has witnessed a growth of the infection. The fever usually starts as
"motoritis" and in the second or third stage develops into touring fever or an
irresistible desire to travel by motor car and see the country. The only successful
treatment is to start the patient on tour—preferably with a camping outfit.

If you have the fever, this treatment takes you anywhere—everywhere out into
the open. It is a game you can't play alone, and you wouldn't want to—a game
that includes your wife and family, your friends, too, if there is room. Unlike the
usual automobile stunts, it is not a way to burn money, but an enjoyable affair
that saves you money.

"An automobile camping trip" sounds formidable perhaps. Possibly you shudder at the recollection of some unfortunate camping experience. You can safely
forget it all, remembering that you didn't know how then, and let what follows
readjust your ideas.

Where to go—you are limited only by the quality of the roads and in no other
way. You may have read descriptions of hunting and fishing trips with the auto.
They are always fine, but tell but half of the story—they are discreetly silent
about the expense feature.

To get the most out of the trip, just open your Blue Book and find the road
from where you are to where you want to go. Start when the spirit moves you
and be it in New England, New York, Ohio, Indiana, Colorada, California or
Canada—you will have begun to enjoy life.

The constant worry to reach good hotels at noon or night, that has marred your
previous trips, is a thing of the past. Now, any fertile farming country will afford
good camping places and the best of fare. One can travel thirty miles per day, or
one hundred and fifty. If one doesn't like a nieghborhood, a day's run will change
the state and scenery. The auto contains everything wanted—beds, board and
shelter.

As to the matter of selecting your party, Stewart Edward White has given some
valuable hints in "The Forest." In any event, they must be congenial and blessed
with good dispositions. They need be neither strong nor robust—your trip isn't

going to be an endurance run and no more violent than you make it. Hardships won't be encountered, but the little party will get an awful lot of each other's society and this is the one element that requires careful handling—to see that it doesn't develop into a serious problem.

Chauffeurs, cooks and maids are all very well if you want the luxuries of life, but you miss half the fun of the trip if you take them along. If you must have servants, compromise on the chauffeur and let the rest go, especially if you can't see the poetry in changing a casing on the dusty road or struggling under a running-board on your back. It is really remarkable, however, how little of this there is to do if the car is given proper attention. An ounce of prevention is worth several pounds of cure. The manufacturers have done their part all right—many of the cars being built on honor to last.

The Ideal Party

The ideal party consists of two congenial couples. The women should know how to cook just a little and the men should understand the car, and the rest will take care of itself. When it comes to the car it pays to get a good one—this doesn't mean a big road locomotive—forty or fifty horsepower under the hood sounds and feels fine, but you haven't any earthly use for the power of so many horses and they will eat their heads off just as surely as though they were in your stables at home devouring oats.

The heavy six-cylinder car which slips up the hill so beautifully is all right then, but you pay dearly for the power on the level. Nine-tenths of the time a 20-30 will do just as well and it will take you anywhere you wish to go. Tires and gasolene cost money, and if that is an object, select a light car.

On the other hand, don't go to the extreme of trying to tour with a toy. The medium power, medium weight car is the right one, but it means get the very best of this kind—reliability is the keynote. For myself, the White gasolene touring car comes about as near being ideal as anything I have ever seen. But, any five-passenger car with a wheel base of 110 inches or thereabouts will carry you and all your impediments without a murmur. A large car isn't necessary for this purpose and the light car will require little special preparation for the trip.

Take along an extra casing or two, some inner tubes, Prest-o-lite air tubes, luggage carrier, tire trunk, tire chains, extra spark plugs and a complete set of curtains. Cut slots along each running board so you can run straps through. Some plastic cement to repair cuts in your casings will prevent trouble and everything else will be found in your tool-box already if you are a careful driver.

Camping Equipment

The equipment may be selected to suit individual requirements, but every article in the following list has been tried and tested. They will all pack on the car easily and will fill your every want. They are selected from a catalogue of camp equipment of a New York dealer in such supplies:

One Frazier canoe tent, 8¾ x 8¾. One A tent, 8x10. (The tents should have ground cloths attached, bobbinet fronts, windows, jointed poles and steel stakes.) Four folding campstools. Four folding cots (pneumatic mattresses will do just as well but they are very expensive). Blankets, Ponchos. Pneumatic pillows. Two or three waterproof duffle bags. Canvas water bottle. Folding water bucket. Folding water basin. Two hatchets. Clothes line. Aluminum cooking set (complete set of four packs inside the largest pail). Alcohol stove. Two quarts wood alcohol. Canned goods, bacon, in glass jars, condensed cream, coffee, sugar, etc. Refrigerator basket. Two Thermos bottles, in case. Two electric flash lights. Camera and tripod. Fishing tackle. Large assortment of straps. Several tarpaulins.

Personal baggage should be reduced as low as possible; two double suit cases will go on the luggage carrier nicely; two large duffle bags will ride in front of them, and it is well to have a combination camp and auto tool outfit, consisting of spade, hatchet and pick-axe, also coil of strong rope. It is surprising to see how easily all of this outfit can be stowed on the car. The picture on this page shows the outfit just as described in place ready for road work.

You have now been told how an automobile camping trip should be taken; it is usually easy to give such advice, but rather hard to follow it. This is the story of how the little trip was taken—where we took our own advice.

On a threatening day in July we pulled out of Cleveland in our 1911 White gasolene car, carrying with us the equipment I have described. The weight of the outfit was about 250 pounds, and none of the four passengers could exactly be called fairies. Its load, however, did not trouble the little car in the least, and almost with the smoothness of the flight of birds we crossed Summit and Stark counties into the beautiful Tuscarawas valley. Luncheon was eaten in a pleasant school house yard. At Massilon we took on ice for the refrigerator basket and refilled the Thermos bottles. Not far from Beach City we pitched our first tent in a fine open grove. Using a folding cot for a table and our four little steel camp-stools for dining-room chairs, we were soon enjoying a delicious supper in the cool evening air.

Next morning we were up with the sun. After a short time we were eating the best breakfast we ever ate, or was it our appetites and the environment? At least, four people voted it the best ham and eggs, bread, butter and coffee they had eaten in many a day, although it was prepared on an alcohol stove. The outfit shortly after was strapped to the machine and we were on the road. This day we followed the valley through Canal Dover, New Philadelphia, Coschocton and Dresden. The roads were good and we kept on our way with practically no slip. We lunched on the bank of the canal and at night camped in a field of new cut clover. Eggs and milk were purchased from the farmer, who gave us permission to sleep in his field, and we passed another very comfortable night.

The next day we sped through Zanesville and Newark, eating our noon-day meal at a Columbus hotel. Regardless of the quality of the meal, we vowed it would be the last luncheon in a hotel; that our future meals would be in the open, and we kept our vow. Thence on to Springfield along the National Highway, our next camp was pitched in a meadow some distance back from the road, where we were made welcome by the owner of the farm. It was as successful as the others, and the next day we spattered on through the mud of Dayton and Cincinnati, a heavy rainstorm having soaked the roads until they were a sea of mud. The streets in and out of the "Queen City" were torn up badly and the soaking from the heavy rains made them almost impassable. The climb out of the valley along Harrison Avenue was a nightmare of mud, unballasted tracks and holes of unknown depth. For miles we were compelled to use the low gear, but our sturdy car buzzed along until it seemed as though no cooling system ever devised could keep the engine from over-heating. Yet when we reached the good roads again at Cheviot and unscrewed the cap from the radiator not a drop of water had boiled away. As I said before, certainly some of the manufacturers are learning to build automobiles.

The rain was about over when we camped on a knoll overlooking the broad White Water valley, and the picture shows a view of the kitchen where a banquet was prepared that would make one leave home and mother.

We now crossed into Indiana and the fine gravel roads gave us ideal touring conditions. At Indianapolis we spent a hot sultry night in a hotel and decided that we would not again desert our cool tents and comfortable cots.

The next night we camped near a picturesque old church. At Rochester we learned of a fine lake, said to be full of fish, which was about three miles distant, and where on a clean wooded knoll, with a spring of cool water gushing out of a mossy bank just below, we spent two nights and a day in a perfect camp.

Our next run took us through South Bend and into Michigan, where we pitched our tents on Eagle Lake, in fully as pleasant a camping spot as that of the previous night. Here also it rained hard through the night, but not a drop came through to disturb our slumbers. The following afternoon as we were spinning along toward Ann Arbor, a violent thunderstorm came out of the west and struck us almost without warning. We quickly applied the curtains to the machine, ran into the nearest meadow and managed to get the tents up and well staked to the ground just as the storm burst. Supper was cooked in the A tent and eaten by lantern light.

Our next three camps were in Canada. The first, close to the shore of the Detroit River, where we bought a supper of frog's legs, fish and chicken. It was positively a dream. The next camp was in a shady school house yard some fifteen miles from London, and the last night under canvas was spent on a bluff overlooking Lake Ontario. It was the twelfth camp—not one of which could be considered uncomfortable nor unpleasant in any way. Everywhere we asked, we were given permission to camp, cheerfully, and we did not have a disagreeable experience on the whole trip.

The car behaved beautifully, the engine never missing an explosion nor misbehaving in any way. One puncture was the sum total of our tire troubles. Lucky, you say? Not altogether; we took care of our tires, using an air gauge, and stopped up every little cut in the casings with plastic cement. The odometer registered nearly 1,200 miles at the finish, and we had averaged a little better than seventeen miles per gallon of gasolene consumed.

If you will but follow our example and not forget the refrigerator basket, it will enable you to serve cantaloupe a la mode at noon or night; it will keep your butter and fruit cold and be useful in scores of ways.

One need only keep his eyes open for picturesque spots for noon-day stops. For example, one of them was on the north shore of Lake Erie, where we had a fine swim as well as a delightful luncheon in pleasant surroundings.

Above all things, enter into the spirit of the game; make friends wherever you go; do your full share of the work and do not undertake to cover too much distance every day.

After you have tried this game, you will never depend upon hotels again, and perhaps the most surprising feature of all will be the low expenses. You will find it difficult to spend money. For example, it costs us but one dollar to one dollar and a quarter per day to keep the car going and our meals rarely cost us two dollars and fifty cents per day for the crowd. When you consider that there were no transportation nor lodging bills to pay, it begins to dawn on one that this is just about the cheapest vacation to be devised.

The outdoor life is just the thing we all need. It will drive away bodily ills and in proportion to your capacity, you will enjoy every minute "on the pike."

Outdoor Life Ads, 1898–1909

Winchester

REPEATING SHOT GUNS

LOADED & EMPTY PAPER SHOT SHELLS AND SHOT GUN AMMUNITION

FREE. SEND NAME ON A POSTAL FOR 152 PAGE ILLUSTRATED CATALOGUE.

REPEATING AND SINGLE SHOT RIFLES IN ALL CALIBERS FROM .22 TO .50 METALLIC CARTRIDGES.

WINCHESTER REPEATING ARMS CO. NEW HAVEN CT.

POPE BARRELS DO THIS:

Shot at 200 yds. rest, .32 cal Full Size.

Lubricated Bullets. No Cleaning.

USE ONE AND IMPROVE YOUR SCORES.

Re-boring Rifles a Specialty.

H. M. Pope, 57 Ashley St., Hartford, Conn.

Newhouse Traps

THE STANDARD FOR OVER FIFTY YEARS. Used by all professional hunters and trappers, who find that THE BEST TRAP is the CHEAPEST.

Complete illustrated catalogue on application.

ONEIDA COMMUNITY, LTD., Kenwood, N. Y.

Hazard Smokeless

BLACK POWDER OR "BLUE RIBBON" BRAND SMOKELESS

"Blue Ribbon Brand"

HAZARD LEADS THE WORLD.

The Perfection of Nitro Powder . . . Is Safe, Reliable and Pleasant to Use Ask Your Dealer for it

S. C. MADDEN,
GEN'L AGENT,
DENVER, COLO.

DENVER AND RIO GRANDE RAILROAD

"SCENIC LINE OF THE WORLD"

DOUBLE DAILY TRAIN SERVICE

FAST TIME AND BEST ACCOMMODATIONS

FOR ALL POINTS IN COLORADO

UTAH AND THE PACIFIC COAST

Form 9.
E.T. JEFFERY PRES'T. & GEN'L MANAGER
A.S. HUGHES TRAFFIC MANAGER
S.K. HOOPER G.P. & T.A. DENVER

Marble's Safety Pocket Knife

We offer something better in the way of a hunting knife. Not merely better than the old unreliable kind, but far and away the BEST folding hunting knife made, equal in quality to our celebrated Ideal hunting knives, and one of the latest and best of the Marble Tricks.

It has a five-inch blade which folds into a four-inch handle. When the knife is open the blade locks so firmly that no mischance can cause it to close. It is as rigid as a one-piece knife. When it is closed it may be carried in the pocket or at the belt. It is not a ramshackle toy but a thoroughly dependable knife, which will never fail in the hour of need.

It is hand tested and hand made from the very best steel—tempered to stand the hard knocks of field service, beautifully finished and it bears the "MARBLE" guarantee of quality.

The price is $4.00. Get one from your dealer or direct from the makers. Send for catalogue "S."

MARBLE SAFETY AXE CO.,
Gladstone, Mich.

THE LITTLE SAVAGE

"Big Game Killer"

Hammerless
Smokeless
Six-Shooter

Write for..
1809 Catalogue S

Savage Arms Company
UTICA, N.Y.

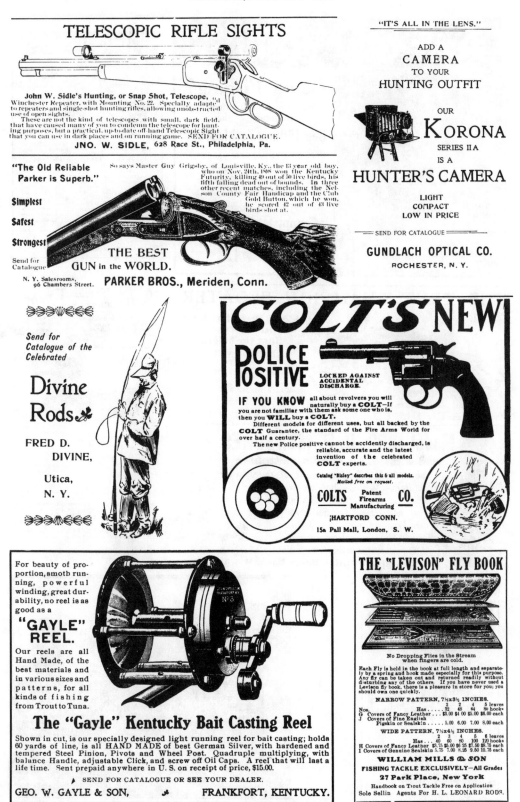

TELESCOPIC RIFLE SIGHTS

John W. Sidle's Hunting, or Snap Shot, Telescope, on Winchester Repeater, with Mounting No. 22. Specially adapted to repeaters and single-shot hunting rifles, allowing unobstructed use of open sights.

These are not the kind of telescopes with small, dark field, that have caused many of you to condemn the telescope for hunting purposes, but a practical, up-to-date off-hand Telescopic Sight that you can use in dark places and on running game. *SEND FOR CATALOGUE.*

JNO. W. SIDLE, 628 Race St., Philadelphia, Pa.

"IT'S ALL IN THE LENS."

ADD A

CAMERA

TO YOUR

HUNTING OUTFIT

OUR

KORONA

SERIES II A

IS A

HUNTER'S CAMERA

LIGHT
COMPACT
LOW IN PRICE

=== SEND FOR CATALOGUE ===

GUNDLACH OPTICAL CO.
ROCHESTER, N. Y.

"The Old Reliable Parker is Superb."

So says Master Guy Grigsby, of Louisville, Ky., the 13 year old boy, who on Nov. 24th, 1898 won the Kentucky Futurity, killing 49 out of 50 live birds, his fifth falling dead out of bounds. In three other recent matches, including the Nelson County Fair Handicap and the Club Gold Button, which he won, he scored 42 out of 43 live birds shot at.

Simplest

Safest

Strongest

Send for Catalogue

THE BEST GUN in the WORLD.

N. Y. Salesrooms, 96 Chambers Street.

PARKER BROS., Meriden, Conn.

Send for Catalogue of the Celebrated

Divine Rods

FRED D. DIVINE,

Utica, N. Y.

COLT'S NEW

POLICE POSITIVE

LOCKED AGAINST ACCIDENTAL DISCHARGE.

IF YOU KNOW all about revolvers you will naturally buy a **COLT**—If you are not familiar with them ask some one who is, then you **WILL** buy a **COLT.**

Different models for different uses, but all backed by the **COLT** Guarantee, the standard of the Fire Arms World for over half a century.

The new Police positive cannot be accidently discharged, is reliable, accurate and the latest invention of the celebrated **COLT** experts.

Catalog "Bisley" describes this & all models. *Mailed free on request.*

COLTS Patent Firearms Manufacturing CO.
HARTFORD CONN.
15a Pall Mall, London, S. W.

For beauty of proportion, smooth running, powerful winding, great durability, no reel is as good as a

"GAYLE" REEL.

Our reels are all Hand Made, of the best materials and in various sizes and patterns, for all kinds of fishing from Trout to Tuna.

The "Gayle" Kentucky Bait Casting Reel

Shown in cut, is our specially designed light running reel for bait casting; holds 60 yards of line, is all HAND MADE of best German Silver, with hardened and tempered Steel Pinion, Pivots and Wheel Post. Quadruple multiplying, with balance Handle, adjustable Click, and screw off Oil Caps. A reel that will last a life time. Sent prepaid anywhere in U. S. on receipt of price, $15.00.

➤ SEND FOR CATALOGUE OR SEE YOUR DEALER.

GEO. W. GAYLE & SON,   **FRANKFORT, KENTUCKY.**

THE "LEVISON" FLY BOOK

No Dropping Flies in the Stream when fingers are cold.

Each Fly is held in the book at full length and separately by a spring and hook made especially for this purpose. Any fly can be taken out and returned readily without disturbing any of the others. If you have never used a Levison fly book, there is a pleasure in store for you; you should own one quickly.

NARROW PATTERN, 7½x3½ INCHES.

	2	2	4	5 leaves
Nos.	Has 32	48	64	80 hooks
G Covers of Fancy Leather . . . $3.00	$4.00	$5.00	$6.00 each
J Covers of Fine English Pigskin or Sealskin . . . 5.00	6.00	7.00	8.00 each

WIDE PATTERN, 7½x4½ INCHES.

	2	3	4	6 leaves
Has 40	60	80	100	120 hooks
H Covers of Fancy Leather $3.75	$5.00	$6.25	$7.50	$8.75 each
I Covers of Genuine Sealskin 5.75	7.00	8.25	9.50	10.75 each

WILLIAM MILLS & SON

FISHING TACKLE EXCLUSIVELY—All Grades

27 Park Place, New York

Handbook on Trout Tackle Free on Application
Sole Selling Agents For H. L. LEONARD RODS.

A Record Grizzly Fight

James Bryce

August 1911

Early in 1899, E. O. Richmond of Durango, Colorado, visited OUTDOOR LIFE to chat with the editor of "in the Game Field." The editor reported the talk in his March 1899 department: "In his 23 years of 'roughing it,' Mr. Richmond, known among old-timers as 'the bear hunter of the Rockies,' has killed 202 bears. He scouts the idea of men being afraid of bears, and says there is no such thing in the annals of bear hunting as one of these animals taking after a hunter deliberately. 'Why a grizzly or any other kind of bear would as soon commit suicide as go after a foe in the shape of a man. They haven't the sense of combat to induce them to attack a man. The only time they'll do this is when they are injured and they come face to face with their conqueror.' " Wonder if Mr. Richmond was around in 1911 when this dreadful encounter was reported.

Of the many battles in the Yukon between man and grizzly there was probably never one more dreadful or closer to the death as far as the man was concerned than that which James M. Christie, now residing in Winnipeg, Manitoba, fought with one of that savage species at the headwaters of the Stewart River over two years ago. The terrific battle, the 8-mile tramp back to camp with his cheeks torn from ear to mouth, his lower jaw fractured in two places, and lying against his breast, his scalp thrown back like a cap, right cheek bone fractured, right arm broken in several places and covered with ugly wounds of more or less serious nature, while weakened and almost dead from loss of blood—these are things which Mr. Christie can look back to now with wonder that he survived them. And his heroic fight with death at the home of J. E. Ferrill, at Lansing Post, his trip to the Jubilee hospital from Dawson to Victoria, and his final recovery all bear evidence of the wonderful vitality of the man, gained in the healthy outdoor life of a trapper in the Northern wilds.

Mr. Christie left Carman for the North in the summer of '98, and prospected along the Stewart River for a time, taking to trapping when the winer set in, and learning the lore of the Northland like a book. At times he acted as guide for government parties, on one occasion meeting Agnes Deans Cameron's party far up the waters of the Mackenzie, and on another occasion making a geological survey across the unknown land from Dawson to Edmonton. At this time he met George Chrisfield, and they grubstaked and started north for the Rogue River, where they set up camp about 350 miles east of Dawson in the heart of the wilderness.

During the years up North Christie had learned many things about the silent places, but his experience with Bruin had inclined him to look upon him as an animal not to be feared. This was the view he held about the grizzly when about the middle of October he struck out over the light snow along the Rogue River to look up trapping possibilities. Before leaving camp he told Chrisfield, his partner, that he would be gone several days, and that if he did not return for a short period he was not to worry about him.

The first day out he shot a moose, and hid it in a ground cache, intending to call for it later. The next day he discovered a small lot of marten, and other furs, and concluded that he would move camp and gather them in. He then started for the home camp, and on the way back made a detour to visit the cache where he had left the moose carcass a few days before. On reaching the place he found the brush which he had piled upon it to keep the ravens off, pulled away and the meat all gone. Numerous wolf tracks were visible, and the huge track of a grizzly led from the spot straight across the river.

Christie started on the trail after Mr. Bruin, knowing from previous experience that the marauder would not be very far away. A few timber wolves were on the trail, and he fired at one, but missed. This, according to the trapper was the means later of saving his life, as he noticed after missing the wolf that his rifle which he had packed for some time through the scrub without using it had the sights improperly adjusted. He stopped at once and fixed them, and then proceeded on his way.

Continuing across the river and up the bank on the other side for a distance of 200 yards he struck into the thick scrub, but had not gone more than twenty feet when he heard the unmistakable grunt of an angry bear, and the animal loomed up shaggy and terrible through the scrub not more than thirty feet ahead of him, coming straight toward him. It was the work of a second to swing the rifle upon the oncoming monster, and pull the trigger. The bullet, which was a soft-nose .303, ranged the length of the animal's body, hitting him in the shoulder, but it did not stop his rush. Before the desperate trapper could fire another shot the beast was upon him with jaws wide open and spouting blood. Christie, however, managed to get in another shot, which struck the bear on the forehead, but failed to stop him. The hunter then jumped aside, but unluckily became entangled in the scrub, and fell with the bear on top of him. Then ensued a terrible fight.

The savage brute succeeded in closing its jaws on the hunter's head, and more through instinct than design, the latter managed to wedge his arm between and to free his head, but not before the bear had broken his jaw in two places, and almost ripped the entire scalp from his head. The arm, too, with which he had saved his head, was crushed and broken in two places, and the animal then sank his teeth in his victim's legs, but Christie with his arms free, fought desperately, and the wounds which the bear had sustained began to take effect. Finally he dropped dead within three feet of the desperately wounded man. The fight was over. It had not lasted more than a minute, but in that time the grizzly had done terrible damage.

When Christie arose from the fray and prepared to return to the camp eight miles away, he could see only out of one eye and that was continually filling with blood. His lower jaw was hanging upon his breast, one arm was hanging loose by his side, and he could hardly use his legs on account of the terrible pain from his wounds. He realized that his partner would not look for him for some days, and concluded that he simply must get back to camp or fall a prey to the wolves in the wilderness.

He stopped the flow of blood as best he could, fastening the torn scalp with a handkerchief and placing his coat over his head to keep the cold out. Then came the fight to reach camp.

"I'll never forget that tramp," said Christie, "and the hours of pain and misery which I experienced. The pain and loss of blood weakened me so that at times I staggered and reeled like a drunken man. I finally decided to make a detour of half a mile in order to reach a prospector's cabin which lay on the route to our camp. This cabin, by the way, had been built seven years before by four prospectors, two of whom were Winnipeggers, namely, Jack Patterson and Jack Baker, the former being the son of old Lieutenant Governor Patterson of Manitoba. There I decided to go and die if none came for me, and yet I hoped that my partner would come thither in search of me. However, on arriving there, I managed to write a note with my left hand, and decide to battle along to camp before my wounds stiffened.

"How I ever reached there will always be a mystery to me. However, I did manage to do so, and now almost blind, weak and bleeding from many wounds, and dragging my legs, which had become stiffened from my wounds, I staggered to the door.

"I must have swooned away, for on awaking I found Chrisfield working over me, he having followed the track of blood which I left back to the camp. He made me as comfortable as he could for the night and the next morning my whole body was stiff. We both realized that the only chance left of saving my life was to get me to a trading post called Lansing, about fifty miles away, and accordingly Chrisfield secured two dog teams and some Indian mushers, and, making one of the toboggans as comfortable as possible, placed me upon it. So the lonely procession started out over rough country and unbroken trails, every jolt or jar causing me excruciating agony. The snow was too deep to make good sledding, and the rough journey started some of my wounds bleeding again, even the bliss of unconsciousness being denied to me. So I lay hour after hour, waiting and praying sometimes for death to come and put an end to my sufferings.

"Lansing was reached at last. It was a stockade and a few buildings kept by a personal friend of mine named Ferrell. With the help of Mrs. Ferrell they washed my wounds with antiseptic solutions, stitched them up and set the broken bones as best they could. There I lay between life and death for two months, and after I had recovered sufficiently we started on the 250-mile tramp to Dawson and thence to Victoria, where at the Victoria hospital, under the care of Dr. O. M. Jones, I underwent several operations and had my jaw fixed properly, as it would not allow me to masticate my food."

Mr. Christie, who has spent over twelve years in the North, has crossed the country from Behring Sea to Edmonton overland with dog teams and snowshoes most of the way, and has had many adventures during his sojourn in the West. He has prospected and hunted over a vast territory, and has had many experiences, but the most exciting and terrible was that in which he tackled a grizzly on the headwaters of the Stewart River. Unable longer to stand the Northern climate on account of his hardships, Mr. Christie returned to Manitoba a short time ago and is now employed in the civil service of this province.

The Pursuit of the Elusive Forty

James Oliver Curwood

April 1913

James Oliver Curwood, like Rex Beach, was born in Michigan (1878) and, like him, became an immensely popular writer of fiction. After seven years of newspaper work he resigned to devote himself to literary pursuits and wrote twenty-six books of adventure in the North Woods between 1908 and his death from blood poisoning in 1927..He became a foremost authority on the northland and his novels of "God's Country," as he called it, include *The Courage of Captain Plum, Kazan, The Grizzly King, Nomads of the North, The Valley of Silent Men*, and *The Alaskan*. He spent several months each year in the wilds, and was an active worker for national wildlife and forest conservation.

We called the mountain paradise in which we found ourselves "Ptarmigan Plain," and made arrangements to camp there at once. This was in early October. During the preceding six or seven years I had hunted almost everything that could be called game in the Canadian wilderness. I had shot moose and caribou in the bush country; seals and walrus along Hudson's Bay; musk-ox on the barrens, and polar bear up on the Roes Welcome, where the Arctic ice crashes down into the big bay in the spring break-ups. But never had I found a game paradise like this that we entered in October. My companions were Jack Otto, of Fitzhugh, Alberta—the best known guide, packer, and grizzly bear hunter in the Canadian Rockies—and Dr. I. F. Burgin, of Delta, Colo. From Fitzhugh we hit out on a trail of our own north and west, beyond the Frazer. So far as was known, not even an Indian had been in that country for thirty years, and two days in from the end of the line of rail of the Grand Trunk Pacific we began to see big game, chiefly mountain goat and sheep. Five days in we struck a country of green and rolling valleys, where every slope was torn up by grizzlies in their burrowings for the little brown gophers. In this country we shot five grizzlies during the following seven days. On the evening of the day we entered Ptarmigan Plain we first saw the "Elusive Forty."

It was in the middle of the afternoon that we took off our saddles and relieved our pack-horses, and pitched camp. We were at the head of the big valley with towering, snow-covered mountains sweeping in a semi-circle to the left of us. Half a mile to our right was the other range. We had not stopped for dinner, so our "supper" was ready at 4 o'clock, just as the last of the sun was flooding the craggy side of the big mountain on our right. Otto was facing the sun-flooded mountain and was just about to bite into a chunk of hot bannock when he paused, and stared. Burgin and I turned to follow his gaze. Then we all faced the mountain.

I have seen a herd of 10,000 caribou sweeping across the barrens, but that herd was far less impressive than what we now saw on the mountainside, probably half a mile away, though the distance seemed less than half that. In one place the backbone of the mountain was free of snow, and glistened a reddish black in the glow of the sun. And slowly over that sombre ridge that split the sky far above the timber-line there filed a herd of mountain goats. They came Indian fashion, one after the other, their snow-white bodies showing like moving snowballs against the darkness of the mountain. One after another they continued to come, while we sat as motionless as rocks, and when the file ended Dr. Burgin had counted forty-one, and Otto and I forty. In a thin white line—never for a moment breaking the file—they moved along the bald cap of the summit, descended for a hundred yards down a precipitous slope of shale, and then followed a ledge along which, a few days later, we found it too venturesome for a man to travel. Before they disappeared we crept to our hunting glasses, and had a look at them at closer range. There were half a dozen magnificent heads in the bunch.

It was too late to think of stalking that night, so we rolled up in our sleeping bags, prepared to be on the hunt soon after dawn. We were a little late in our reckoning, and the sun was tinting the snow-covered peaks to the west when we finished breakfast and began the ascent of the mountain. We were sure that the goat feeding-ground was just over the range, and so we divided our force. I had hunted with various kinds of big game rifles, and had brought with me into the mountains two light .22 caliber Hi-Power Savage rifles. When climbing after goat and sheep every ounce additional weight soon begins to tell on one, and these guns, with the tremendous muzzle velocity of 2,800 and a fall of only six inches at 300 yards, I had found particularly effective. Dr. Burgin took one of these, and I the other. Otto carried a 303. We gave Burgin half an hour start, so that he would have time to swing well to the left. Otto set out fifteen minutes ahead of me, so that all of us began the ascent of the mountain at about the same time.

By my watch, it took me just one hour and fifteen minutes to reach the black cap over which the herd of goats had appeared the previous evening, and I was almost exhausted. But the sight that met my eyes when I crept above the last rocks of the ridge was ample reward for the strenuous work. Three or four hundred yards below, the mountain slope bulged out into a narrow plateau, free of rock, and with a velvety covering of grass. Within long rifle-range of me the herd was feeding. Fortunately, having the wind in my favor, I saw that it was possible, by making a detour, to bring myself almost on a level with the herd, at a shooting distance of 250 yards. It took me thirty minutes to accomplish my object, and then I realized that my first fire would turn the entire herd in Dr. Burgin's direction. So I picked out the best heads in the bunch through my hunting glass, and waited for Otto to have his chance, and begin firing. Meanwhile Otto was crouching behind a rock 400 yards from the herd, waiting for me to begin firing, as he knew that I must be very close to the game. I don't believe that for a moment the wind shifted, and yet, all at once, the herd took alarm, and the particular head that I had selected for my target came thirty yards nearer, and stood gazing straight in my direction. He was a little better than 200 yards away, and at my first shot he fell like a stone. It was about the first time I had ever seen a goat go down without a kick, for both goat and sheep will carry a lot of lead—a tough bull sheep standing next to a grizzly. I got another head before the herd was out of range. This was not because of good marksmanship, though running goats at 250 and 300 yards are not easy marks. I aimed at one of the big fellows, but the bullet went a few inches high, and struck a smaller fellow a few yards on the other side. Meanwhile Otto's .303 was cracking up the mountain, but nothing resulted, because of the long range. Otto and I both ran down into the little plain, and waited for Burgin to begin shooting. Very soon we heard the sharp crack of his .22 Hi-Power, and we began racing in his direction. Fifteen minutes later the doctor met us, panting and gesticulating.

"Where are they?" he gasped, the moment he met us.

He showed his astonishment, as he stared beyond us.

"The whole bunch came back toward you!" he exclaimed, in a second breath.

"I saw them not five minutes ago when they came over that bulge. Now—where in Gawd's name—"

We were all staring now. The goats had not taken to the mountainside, or they would have been plainly visible. We ran to the edge of the plain and looked down into the deeper valley beyond. There was nothing in sight. The entire herd had disappeared as completely as though the earth had opened and swallowed it. We climbed 100 yards down from the plain, and then returned more mystified than ever. Suddenly Otto gave an astonished cry, and pointed.

Over the bare summit which I had descended only a short time before, the last of the herd was disappearing.

"Now, what the devil do you think of that?" asked the M.D.

Otto grinned.

"They fooled you, Doc," he said. "Let's have a look at this bulge over here."

We found that the thirty-foot rise over which the doctor had seen the herd disappear was split in the middle by a narrow dip of five or six feet. The shrewd instinct of the goat leaders had told them that they were between two deadly fires, and instead of going down into the valley, which would have exposed them to further fire, they had swung up the dip and were among the big masses of rock not 100 yards away when the doctor rushed past them to meet us.

That's why I remember them as the "Elusive Forty."

Mushing in the Frozen North

Geo. F. Waugh

April 1913

This might seem an offbeat story today, but when Waugh wrote it in 1913 readers relished stories of the Far North, associated as it was indelibly in their minds with the Gold Rush in the Klondike. Writers like Jack London, Rex Beach and James Oliver Curwood kept their interest at high pitch with their books about the North Country. For example, London's *The Call of the Wild,* famous novel about Buck, the sled dog, had appeared only ten years earlier. And Waugh's advice was right on target, because the only means of travel during the long winter months in much of the North was by dog team. Now the snowmobile has virtually brought to a close the day of the working dog in the frozen North. Happily some adventurous souls still scorn the plane and the snowmobile to hunt by dog sled.

In these days when following the hardships of those who have striven, and those who are striving for honors in the frozen north, or the frozen south, the reader generally forms an entirely erroneous idea as to the amount of clothing necessary to keep the body warm and to prevent freezing. We picture them as traveling all bundled up in furs and skins, but this is impossible, unless the explorer has so many dogs that all he has to do is to sit on the sled and ride to the next cabin or roadhouse, but where there are no roadhouses and he is packing his own provisions, camping outfit, and dog feed, there is no room for him on the sled and he is likely to find himself the hardest-worked dog of the team.

He has to take the utmost care not to start perspiration, and the only safe way for him to win through is to keep uncomfortably cool; whenever he begins to feel warm it is a signal for him to remove some of his clothing or stop traveling. One scarcely ever hears of a person's losing life or limb, that is not in some way caused by getting the clothing damp—either by perspiring or by breaking through an overflow.

All properly-made clothing for extremely cold countries is made very large and adjusted so it can be readily removed. The fur parka is a garment made like a large hooded shirt coming to the knees, the edge of the hood having a ruff of wolverine, wolf or bear, to protect the face (wolverine being the best, as it is the only fur upon which the breath will not congeal), and is the most practical garment yet devised for Arctic work. This parka is made of reindeer summer skin (the winter skin sheds badly) or squirrel skin. It is worn with the fur outside and is lined with fur or some material which will allow it to slip on and off easily. The drill parka, which is used to break the wind, is made on the same model, only larger, as it, at times, is worn as the outermost garment of all. These fur parkas are seldom used by those who are experienced, when working on the trail; they are held in reserve until camp is reached, or until the trail is good and riding is possible; when pushing on the handle bars or running beside the sled, the parka would be too hot, and would cause perspiration to start.

As has already been stated, nearly every death from freezing is caused by getting too warm or wet, and not from excessive cold. One's clothing may become damp in many ways; by breaking through an overflow; by small particles of snow getting on the gloves and being melted by the heat of the body; by striking what

54

is called soft weather—a warm spell—(nearly every year in Alaska there occurs what is called a January thaw, when it is so warm for a few days that often the supply of frozen meat is lost) or by perspiring. Perspiration may start by having on excessive clothing, by working with the load, helping the dogs, or by the excitement that invariably follows when the explorer believes he is lost. Whenever the clothing is dampened by perspiration, or moisture of any kind, it requires constant heat to keep this moisture warm, and there is only one place from which to get it, and that is the body. The drawing away of heat gradually reduces the vitality as well as the temperature of the body and after a time chill sets in, energy becomes greatly impaired and to continue on the way seems not only impossible but futile. There is only one result and that is death—unless the traveler can get shelter, assistance, or a fire where he can get dry clothes.

When it comes to a test of what to do in life and death emergencies, it seems that the brains and education of the white man count for little. Although he has been told what experience has taught the Eskimo, in many cases he will not follow it. If an Eskimo or an Alaskan Indian is lost in a storm or blizzard, even if only a short distance from his cabin, he does not attempt to find his way, but gets into a snow drift, digs a hole if possible, kneels down, pulls the parka hood well over his head, turns his back to the storm, and stays there until the blizzard has passed; taking every precaution meanwhile to keep awake, and shiver himself warm whenever he commences to feel chilled. Shivering oneself warm is simply making use of nature's own provision. He will also carry a small article in his mitts, say a piece of wood or cork, that he will unconsciously play with and in that manner keep his hands warm. The white man does none of these things; he immediately begins to try to find his cabin, and being unable to do so, he gets nervous and excited; this causes him to sweat, and he finally rushes madly around, often even leaving his dogs if he has any. Eventually he comes exhausted and has to quit; then he tries to find shelter, and he may get into a snow drift, but his clothing by this time is all moist, his vitality is greatly reduced, and it is only a matter of a few hours until he perishes.

At St. Michaels, Alaska, last winter an Eskimo woman, carrying a small child, started to go from one cabin to another during a storm. She got lost and the storm turned into a blizzard, but as soon as she realized she was lost she dug a hole in the snow as best she could, knelt down, putting her back to the storm, pulled her parka hood over her head, drew her arms inside of the parka, cuddled her child against her breast and remained there until the blizzard was over, a matter of about twelve hours; then she found that she was only thirty yards from her cabin. Her greatest suffering was caused by her having been required to remain in the same position so long; the child was not harmed in the least. A white man named Desmond, who had spent several years in the North and who thought he knew all about the country, was caught in the same blizzard. He had a good fur parka with him and a fur robe on his sled, which latter was drawn by seven of the best Malamute dogs. Instead of rolling up in his robe and getting his dogs around him, he tried to find his way, became excited, lost his head, left his dogs and could not find them again; being a very large man, with a very powerful physique, he was able to keep going, and two days later he was found by natives wandering around near Pitmetalic, completely out of his head. His bare hands were dangling at his sides, frozen solid; in some manner he had gotten his right foot wet and that was also frozen. He was taken to St. Michaels, where everything was done to save his hands and feet, but without success, and it was necessary to amputate them. Desmond was well equipped to stand the blizzard and had he made proper use of his robe and dogs he could easily have weathered it, his chances being 100 per cent better than those of the Eskimo woman. Even after leaving his dogs, had he kept his head and drawn his hands inside of his parka, putting them under his armpits, he would not have lost them.

When a native is on the trail he never does any work; he loads his sled to its full capacity and then gets on and rides, letting his dogs do all the work. As he never exerts himself, the only chance of his getting warm would be in beating the dogs. Most white men are different, for when they see the dogs working, they are ashamed to ride so they generally remain off the sled, shoving on the handle bars and helping all they can, and before they are aware of it they have started to sweat and the result is easily foretold.

A year ago, a man with whom the writer was intimately associated, and who had spent two winters in Alaska, had occasion to make a trip from Nome to Teller, Alaska. A lady whose husband was in Teller wanted to visit him, and persuaded my friend to take her with him on the trip. On leaving Nome the lady was riding in the sled, the man mushing the dogs. He was wearing heavy fleece-lined underclothing, two flannel shirts, a heavy sweater, a reindeer parka lined with squirrel skin, which in reality makes it a double parka, and then a drill parka over all. For foot-gear, he had on four pair of heavy woolen socks, one pair of German socks, and a pair of winter mucklucks. It was not very cold, being in the vicinity of zero. He was dressed so heavily that while mushing the team, he was unconsciously perspiring. The trail was staked, besides running along the telephone line. In the afternoon they ran into a snow storm that the dogs did not want to face, and the man could scarcely make out the trail stakes. Having a woman with him, he was anxious to make Tishue roadhouse, and to get her out of the storm. His dogs laid down on him, and it was necessary for him to go ahead to break trail and then drag them after him. Within two miles of Tishue roadhouse he fell down exhausted, his vitality gone, and his clothing saturated with moisture. The woman tried to get him into the sled, but could not as he was a large man, weighing about 175 pounds; while she only weighed 107 pounds; the dogs would not go on so there was no chance of getting help. She took the robe off the sled, put it around him and asked for his knife to cut the tow line so as to get the dogs loose; she put them around him in order to give him the warmth from their bodies. He put his hand in his pocket but never withdrew it. During the entire night she walked in a circle around a telephone pole, at times supporting herself against it. In the morning she left the team, as they would not obey her, making her way towards the roadhouse. She walked backwards, as the storm blinded her so that she could not see the trail stakes when facing it. On reaching the roadhouse she could not make herself heard, and broke a window to wake the people. A relief party went out and brought in the body of the frozen man. With the exception of his parkas his clothing was frozen to his body, and it was necessary to cut the garments away. Had he worn ordinary all-wool underclothing, with a flannel shirt, and any kind of closely-woven trousers with footgear to match, saving the other garments until he was through traveling, he would not have lost his life. The writer often made fifty miles a day when the temperature was 30 degrees below zero, and, barring his gloves, fur mitts, headgear (toque with silk handkerchief tied over his nose) and his mucklucks, his clothing was no heavier than what is worn in the tropics. Garments worn next the body should be all wool or of fur. Fur, in the very far North, where one encounters the extreme cold, is worn next to the skin, and most garments are made without buttons. The wool carries the moisture away from the body to the outside and one's back will often look from the congealed sweat and steam as if it had been exposed in a storm.

Care of the hands and feet are of vital importance, especially the hands. If one freezes them while traveling alone, there is no hope, for one cannot start a fire, and even with one's fingers frost bitten one cannot light a match. On the trail one has to use one's hands a great deal, working with the load, adjusting harness, digging snowballs out of the dogs' feet so they will not go lame, and doing many other things; so it is necessary to wear gloves, as one could not do the work with fur mittens on, and besides the fur would be too hot and would start the hands to sweating. Fur mitts should always be where they can be easily reached. Gloves should be of the best wool, and the best glove is made in Scotland and is known as the McGeorge Scotch wool glove; there is nothing anywhere near its equal manufactured in this country. Small particles of snow constantly keep attaching themselves to the gloves and the first thing one notices is that the hands are commencing to freeze. The snow has worked through the glove until the heat from the hands has melted it. Soon the temperature of the hands is reduced and no more heat forthcoming, the gloves start to freeze and with them the hands. With the mucklucks, either winter or water, the native foot gear is the only article that will protect the feet; one's feet are practically sure to perspire, and the best thing to absorb this moisture is straw in the bottom of the mucklucks. The native straw (a coarse grass) is better than any other, and grows in abundance along the coast of Bering Sea. After a few lessons from the Eskimos one can acquire the art, to a certain degree, of properly preparing and arranging the straw. Besides absorbing the moisture, it forms a cushion which prevents bruising the soles of the feet or stubbing the toes while traveling over rough ice. On taking off one's mucklucks, before turning in, one will find the straw sopping wet, while the socks are nearly dry. One must put the straw out to freeze, and in the morning it is covered with little crystals of frozen perspiration. Rub it between the hands and it is ready for use again.

The overflows are encountered while traveling along the coast of Bering Sea or along the rivers. Those along the coast are caused by the tide coming in, and the water coming out along the shore where the ice had cracked when the tide went out. Along the rivers these overflows are mostly found during very cold weather. They are caused by the river freezing deep and the water pressure coming down the river, forcing the ice up and making breaks along the shore where the water comes out. When the snow is on the river the traveler often gets into slush a foot deep before he knows it. These overflows have claimed many victims, as whenever a man breaks through it means a dry garment and a fire as soon as possible, or a frozen foot. The most experienced men carry a change of clothing and several pairs of gloves on the top of the sled.

If you are riding on the sled and doing nothing but keeping warm, while someone else does the work, it is all right to put on all the clothes and fur mitts you want to; but if you are working with your team, you cannot do it. Always keep yourself uncomfortably cool; whenever you begin to feel comfortable, begin to remove some of your garments or quit work. Never get up a perspiration. If wind strikes one side of your body and makes you cold, fasten a drill parka or some other garment on that side to break the wind. If you were to put it on it would make the other side of your body too hot. Take care not to get your gloves damp, and if you do, change them immediately, and whenever your hands get cold, warm them, even if you have to stop and start a fire. Often when you think they are all right, your hands will be so cold you cannot strike a match; in that case put them under your armpits, next your body. A small mirror fastened to the cuff of your mitt is of great value, as then you can watch your face and tell when it starts to freeze. In the first stage it is easy to rub the frost out with the fur of your mitt. A silk handkerchief tied over the nose is the best protection for the face.

If lost in a storm or blizzard, stop, make camp if you have an outfit, or get in a snow drift, for you cannot find your way. Never, under any circumstances, leave your team. Nearly everyone going into a cold climate has the impression that a beard will protect the face, and therefore allows one to grow. Then he wonders why his face gets so cold and pains him. On feeling it he finds the beard is full of ice, a mat of ice having formed from the breath freezing on it. Without a beard there is nothing to catch the moisture.

The above observations may be of service to those who may be contemplating invading the Great White Silences, as they are based upon the actual experiences of the writer.

NOTE.—After reading the foregoing story the editor sent the manuscript on to one of our readers, L. L. Bales, of Seattle, Wash., merely for the pleasure we knew it would afford him in reading it, as he himself is an old musher of the North. In due time we received the manuscript back from Mr. Bales, together with the following note, which we reproduce for the interest it contains:

As to the article of Lieut. Waugh on "Mushing in the Frozen North," would say that I consider you fortunate indeed in having such an intelligent and truthful contributor on the above subject. It is correct in every detail, as I have "mushed" over the same ground many times myself. Every statement is correct. But as our mutual friend Chauncey Thomas would say: He should tell us "why" it is not advisable to leave the dog team under any circumstances. Native dogs raised by natives as a rule have a general dislike for a white man and will run away and leave him whenever they have a chance. They are continually on the lookout for the chance, and more especially so in a blizzard, and in lonely, isolated places the driver separated from his outfit is in great danger, and more than one good man has lost his life in this way.

In driving native-raised dogs I always have a rope tied to the sled and around my body, and to this precaution I owe my life. And again, if a driver who is alone should for any reason get any distance from his sled in a blinding blizzard, he is apt to become bewildered and lost, or the dogs become impatient and start off on their own account and run away from him.

A silk handkerchief over a man's face, leaving the eyes clear, is moistened with the breath, then becomes frozen and proves an excellent shield and protection for the nose and face. The warm breath inside of the kerchief does the trick.

L. L. BALES

Colorado Trails

Zane Grey

March 1918

Like many others of my generation, I used to believe it when I'd say of Zane Grey's westerns, "I've read everything he ever wrote," and I'd tick off titles that still make my blood run fast: *Riders of the Purple Sage, the Lone Star Ranger, The Vanishing American, Heritage of the Desert, the U. P. Trail,* etc. But now I know I haven't read all seventy-four of the novels Grey wrote (twenty appeared after his death in 1939). And that's not all I haven't read. In 1972, Prentice-Hall Inc. published a thick volume of Grey's "best hunting and fishing tales," selected and edited by George Reiger, called *Zane Grey: Outdoorsman,* on the 100th anniversary of his birth. In the introduction Reiger says the selections represent fewer than 100,000 words of the millions Grey wrote on the outdoors. Here are two parts of a four-part story, "Colorado Trails," that Zane Grey wrote for Outdoor Life.

Part 1

Riding and tramping trails would lose half their charm if the motive were only to hunt and to fish. It seems fair to warn the reader who longs to embark upon a bloody game hunt or a chronicle of fishing records that this is not that kind of a story. But it will be one of those who love horses and dogs, the long winding dim trails, the wild flowers and the dark still woods, the fragrance of spruce and the smell of campfire smoke. And as well for those who love to angle in brown lakes or rushing brooks or chase after the baying hounds or stalk the stag on his lonely heights.

Northwestern Colorado was my objective point this year, and after a memorable swordfish experience at Catalina Island I traveled to Denver, where I met my brother, R. C. It was through Mr. J. A. McGuire, editor of Outdoor Life, that I had engaged Scott Teague of Yampa to take care of us on this trip. All I had heard of Teague was that he was a bear-hunter of considerable experience. Mr. McGuire and Prof. Figgins of the Denver Museum of Natural History were exceedingly kind to us, and endeavored to make arrangements to get me a permit to shoot some specimens that were needed for the museum.

We left Denver on August 22 over the Moffat road and had a long wonderful ride through the mountains. The Rockies have a sweep, a limitless sweep, majestic and grand. For many miles we crossed no streams, and climbed and wound up barren slopes. Once across the divide, however, we descended into a country of black forests and green valleys. Yampa, a little hamlet with a past prosperity, lay in the wide valley of the Bear River. It was picturesque but idle, and a better name for it would have been Sleepy Hollow. The main and only street was very wide and dusty, bordered by old board walks and vacant stores. It seemed a deserted street of a deserted village. Teague, the guide, lived there. He assured me it was not quite as lively a place as in the early days when it was a stage center for an old and rich mining section. We stayed there at the one hotel for a whole day, most of which I spent sitting on the board walk. Whenever I chanced to look down the wide street it seemed always the same—deserted, But Yampa had the charm of being old and forgotten, and for that reason I would like to live there a while.

On August 23 we started in two buckboards for the foothills, some fifteen miles westward, where Teague's men were to meet us with saddle and pack horses. The ride was not interesting until the Flattop Mountains began to loom, and we saw the dark green slopes of spruce, rising to bare gray cliffs and domes, spotted with white banks of snow. And I felt the first cool breath of mountain air, exhilarating and sweet. From that moment I began to live.

We had left at 6:30. Teague, my guide, had been so rushed with his manifold tasks that I had scarcely seen him, let alone gotten acquainted with him. And on this ride he was far behind with our load of baggage. We arrived at the edge of the foothills about noon. It appeared to be the gate-way of a valley, with aspen groves and ragged jack-pines on the slopes, and a stream running down. Our driver called it the Stillwater. That struck me as strange, for the stream was in a great hurry. R. C. spied trout in it, and schools of Rocky Mountain whitefish. We wished for our tackle then and time to fish.

Teague's man, a young fellow called Virgil, met us here. He did not resemble the ancient Virgil in the least, but he did look as if he had walked right out of one of my romances of wild riders. So I took a liking to him at once.

But the bunch of horses he had corralled there did not at once excite any delight in me. Horses, of course, were the most important part of our outfit. And that moment of first seeing the horses that were to carry us on such long rides was an anxious and thrilling one. I have felt it many times, and it never grows any weaker from experience. I had seen many a scrubby lot of horses turn out well upon acquaintance, and some I have found hard to part with at the end of trips. Up to then, however, I had not seen a bear-hunter's horses; and I was much concerned by the fact that these were a sorry looking outfit, dusty, ragged, maneless, cut and bruised and crippled. Still, I reflected, they were bunched up so close that I could not tell much about them, and I decided to wait for Teague before I chose a horse for any one.

In an hour Teague trotted up to our resting place. Beside his own mount he had two white saddle horses, and nine pack-animals, heavily loaded. Teague was a sturdy rugged man with bronzed face and keen gray-blue eyes, very genial and humorous. Straightway I got the impression that he liked work.

"Let's organize," he said, briskly. "Have you picked the horses you're goin' to ride?"

Teague led from the midst of that dusty, kicking bunch, a rangy powerful horse, with four white feet, a white face and a noble head. He had escaped my eye. I felt thrillingly that here at least was one horse.

The rest of the horses were permanetly crippled or temporarily lame, and I had no choice, except to take the one it would be kindest to ride.

"He ain't much like your Silvermane or Black Star," said Teague, laughing.

"What do you know about them?" I asked, very much pleased at this from him.

"Well, Doctor, I know all about them," he replied. "I'll have you the best horse in this country in a few days. Fact is, I've brought him, an' he'll come with my cowboy Vern. . . . Now we're organized. Let's move."

We rode through a meadow along a spruce slope above which towered the great towering mountain. It was a zig-zag trail rough, boggy, and steep in places. The Stillwater meandered here, and little breaks on the water gave evidence of feeding trout. We had several miles of meadow, and then sheered off to the left up into the timber. It was a spruce forest, very still and fragrant. We climbed out up on a bench, and across a flat, up another bench, out of the timber into the patches of snow. Here snow could be felt in the air. Water was everywhere. I saw a fox, a badger, and another furry creature, too elusive to name. One more climb brought us to the top of the Flattop Pass, about 11,000 feet. The view back down the way we came was splendid, and led the eye to the distant sweeping ranges, dark and dim along the horizon. The Flattops were flat enough, but not very wide at this pass, and we were soon going down again into a green gulf of spruce, with ragged peaks lifting beyond. Here again I got the suggestion of limitless space. It took us an hour to ride down to Little Trapper's Lake, a small, clear, green sheet of water. The larger lake was farther down. It was big, irregular, and bordered by spruce forests, and shadowed by the lofty, gray peaks.

The camp was on the far side. The air appeared rather warm, and mosquitoes bothered us. However, they did not stay long. It was after sunset and I was too tired to have many impressions.

Our cook appeared to be a melancholy man. He had a deep, quavering voice, a long, drooping mustache and sad eyes. He was silent most of the time. The men called him Bill, and yelled when they spoke, for he was somewhat deaf. It did not take me long to discover that he was the best cook I had ever had in camp.

Our tent was pitched down the slope from the cook-tent and those of the men. We were too tired to sit round a campfire and talk. The stars were white and splendid, and they hung over the flat peaks like great beacon lights. The lake appeared to be inclosed on three sides by amphitheatre mountains, black with spruce up to the gray walls of rock. The night grew cold and very still. The bells on the horses tinkled distantly. There was a soft murmur of falling water. A lonesome coyote barked, and that thrilled me. Teague's dogs answered this prowler, and some of them had voices to make a hunter thrill. One, the bloodhound Cain, had a roar like a lion's. I had not gotten acquainted with the hounds, and I was thinking about them when I fell asleep.

Next morning I was up at 5:30. The air was cold and nipping. Frost shone on grass and sage. A red glow of sunrise gleamed on the tip of the mountain and slowly grew downward.

The cool handle of an axe felt good. I soon found, however, that I could not wield it long for lack of breath. The elevation was close to 10,000 feet and the air at that height was thin and rare. After each series of lusty strokes I had to rest. R. C., who could handle an axe as he used to swing a baseball bat, made fun of my efforts. Whereupon I relinquished the tool to him, which act resulted in his discomfiture.

After breakfast R. C. and I got out our tackles and rigged up fly-rods, and sallied forth to the lake with the same eagerness we had felt when we were boys going after chubs and sunfish. The lake glistened green in the sunlight and it lay like a gem at the foot of the magnificent, black slopes.

The water was full of little floating particles that Teague called wild rice. I thought the lake had begun to "work," a feature of all Eastern lakes during "dog-days." It did not look propitious for fishing, but Teague assured us otherwise. The outlet of this lake was the head of White River. We tried the outlet first, but trout were not rising there. Then we began wading and casting along a shallow bar of the lake. Teague had instructed us to cast, then drag the flies slowly across the surface of the water, in imitation of a swimming fly or bug. I tried this, and several times, when the leader was close to me and my rod far back, I had strikes. With my rod in that position I could not hook the trout. Then I cast my own way, letting the flies sink a little. To my surprise and dismay I had only a few strikes and could not hook the fish.

R. C., however, had better luck, and that wading right over the ground I had covered. To beat me at anything always gave him the most unaccountable, fiendish pleasure.

"These are educated trout," he said. "It takes a skillful fisherman to make them rise. Now, anybody can catch the big game of the sea, which is your forte. But here you are N. G. . . . . Watch me cast!"

Whereupon I watched him make a most atrocious cast. But the water boiled, and he hooked two good-sized trout at once. Quite speechless with envy and admiration, I watched him play them and eventually beach them. They were cut-throat trout, silvery-sided and spotted with the red slash along their gills that gave them their name. I did not catch any while wading, but from the bank I spied one, and dropping a fly in front of his nose I got him. R. C. caught four more, all about a pound in weight, and then he had a strike that broke his leader. He did not have another leader, and so we walked back to camp.

Wild flowers colored the open slopes leading down out of the forest. Golden rod, golden daisies, and blue-bells were quite plentiful and very pretty. Here I found my first columbine, the beautiful flower that is the emblem of Colorado. It was very large, white and blue in colors, and somewhat resembled the exquisite Sago lily of Arizona. Indian paint-brush thinly dotted the slopes and varied in color from red to pink and from white to yellow.

My favorite of all wild flowers—the purple aster—was there, too, on tall, nodding stems, with pale faces up to the light.

Another attraction of Trapper's Lake was the reflection of mountain and forest in the water. The effect was clear and beautiful, with both mountain and forest upside down, with patches of snow and trees under water.

The hounds bayed our approach to camp. We both made a great show about beginning the little camp tasks needful, but we did not last very long. The sun felt so good and it was so pleasant to lounge under a pine. One of the blessings of outdoor life was that a man could be like an Indian and do nothing. It occurred to me then that was a happy philosophy of life. So from rest I passed to dreams and from dreams to sleep.

In the afternoon R. C. and I went out again to try for trout. The lake appeared to be getting thicker with that floating muck and we could not raise a fish. Then we tried the outlet again. Here the current was swift. I found a place between two willow banks where trout were breaking on the surface. It took a long cast for me, but about every tenth attempt I would get a fly over the right place and raise a fish. They were small, but that did not detract from my gratification. The light on the water was just right for me to see the trout rise, and that was a beautiful sight as well as a distinct advantage. I had caught four when a shout from R. C. called me quickly down stream. I found him standing in the middle of a swift chute with his rod bent double and a long line out.

"Got a whale!" he yelled. "See him—down there—in that white water—see him flash red! . . . Go down there and land him for me. Hurry! He's got all the line!"

I ran below to an open place in the willows. Here the stream was shallow and very swift. In the white water I caught a flashing gleam of red. Then I saw the shine of the leader. But I could not reach it without wading in. When I did this the trout lunged out. He looked crimson and silver. I could have put my fist in his mouth.

"Grab the leader! Yank him out!" yelled R. C. in desperation. "There! He's got all the line."

"But it'd be better to wade down." I yelled back.

He shouted that the water was too deep and for me to save his fish. This was an awful predicament for me. I knew the instant I grasped the leader that the big trout would break it or pull free. The same situation, with different kinds of fish, had presented itself many times on my numberless fishing jaunts with R. C., and they all crowded to my mind. Nevertheless I had no choice. Plunging into my knees I frantically reached for the leader. The red trout made a surge. I missed him. R. C. yelled that something would break. That was no news to me. Another plunge brought me in touch with the leader. Then I assayed to lead the huge cut-throat ashore. He was heavy. But he was tired and that gave birth to hopes. Near the shore as I was about to lift him he woke up, swam round me twice, then ran between my legs.

When, a little later, R. C. came panting down stream I was sitting on the bank, all wet, with one knee skinned, and I was holding his broken leader in my hands. Strange, but true, he went into a rage! Blamed me for the loss of that big trout! Under such circumstances it was always best to maintain silence, and I did so as long as I could. After his paroxysm had spent itself and he had become somewhat near a rational being once more he asked me:

"Was he big?"

"Oh—a whale of a trout!" I replied.

"Humph!—Well, how big?"

Thereupon I enlarged upon the exceeding size and beauty of that trout. I made him out very much bigger than he actually looked to me, and I minutely described his beauty and wonderful, gaping mouth. R. C. groaned and that was my revenge.

We returned to camp early, and I took occasion to scrape acquaintance with the dogs. It was a strangely assorted pack—four airedales, one blood-hound and seven other hounds of mixed breeds. There were also three pup hounds, white and yellow, very pretty dogs, and like all pups were noisy and mischievous. They made friends easily. This applied also to one of the airedales, a dog recently presented to Teague by some estimable old lady who had called him Kaiser and made a pet of him. As might have been expected of a dog, even an airedale, with that name, he was no good. But he was cunning, very affectionate, and exceedingly funny. When he was approached he had a trick of standing up, holding up his forepaws in an appealing sort of way, with his head twisted in the most absurd manner. This was when he was chained—otherwise he would have been climbing up on whoever gave him the chance. He was the most jealous dog I ever saw. He could not be kept chained very long because he always freed himself. At meal time he would noiselessly slip behind some one and steal the first morsel he could snatch. Bill was always rapping Kaiser with pans or billets of firewood.

(to be continued)

Colorado Trails

Zane Grey

We have omitted Parts 2 and 3 of "Colorado Trails." Grey makes an interesting observation in Part 2 when they ride down the White River to fish. "We met fishermen, an automobile and a camp outfit," he wrote. "That was enough for me. Where an automobile can run, I do not belong." Part 3 tells of their journey toward bear country, near the Wyoming line, during which a fox and some ducks are bagged, deer are seen and bear signs are plentiful. The guide, Scott Teague, was a veteran bear and lion hunter and the author of a story for OUTDOOR LIFE in September 1913 called "Jaguar Hunting in Old Mexico." His puzzlement over Grey's ambivalent attitude toward hunting is not hard to understand. Yet, many a hunter feels that way: the pleasure and excitement are in the hunt, the chase itself, and they end at the touch of the trigger.

Conclusion

We spent many full days under the shadow of Whitley's Peak. After the middle of September the aspens colored and blazed to the touch of frost, and the mountain slopes were exceedingly beautiful. Against a background of grey sage the gold and red and purple aspen groves showed too much like exquisite paintings to be real. In the mornings the frost glistened thick and white on the grass; and after the gorgeous sunsets of gold over the violet-hazed ranges the air grew stingingly cold.

Bear-chasing with a pack of hounds has been severely criticised by many writers, and I was among them. I believed it a cowardly business, and that was why, if I chased bears with dogs, I wanted to chase the kind that could not be treed. But like many another, I did not know what I was writing about. I did not shoot a bear out of a tree and I would not do so, except in a case of hunger. All the same, leaving the tree out of consideration, bear-chasing with hounds is a tremendously exciting and hazardous game. My ideas about sport are changing. Hunting, in the sportsman's sense, is, biologically speaking, a cruel and degenerate business.

The more I hunt the more I become convinced of something wrong about the game. I am a different man when I get a gun in my hands. All is exciting, hot-pressed, red. Hunting is magnificent up to the moment the shot is fired. After that it is another matter. It is useless for sportsmen to tell me that they, in particular, hunt right, conserve the game, do not go beyond the limit, and all that sort of thing. I do not believe them and I never met the guide who did. A rifle is made to kill. When a man goes out with one he means to kill. He may keep within the law, but that is not the question. It is a question of spirit, and men who love to hunt are yielding to and always developing the old primitive instinct to kill. The meaning of the spirit of life is not clear to them. An argument may be advanced that, according to self-preservation and the survival of the fittest, if a man stops all strife, all fight, then he will retrograde. And that is to say if a man does not go to the wilds now and then, and work hard and live some semblance of the life of his progenitors, he will weaken. It seems that he will, but I am not prepared now to say whether or not that would be well. The Germans believe they are the fittest race to survive over all others—and that has made me a little sick of this Darwin business.

To return, however, to the fact that to ride after hounds on a wild chase is a dangerous and wonderfully exhilarating experience. I will relate a couple of instances, and I will leave it to my readers to judge whether or not it is a cowardly sport.

One afternoon a rancher visited our camp and informed us that he had surprised a big black bear eating the carcass of a dead cow.

"Good! We'll have a bear tomorrow night," declared Teague, in delight. "We'll get him even if the trail is a day old. But he'll come back tonight."

Early next morning the young rancher and three other boys rode into camp, saying they would like to go with us to see the fun. We were glad to have them, and we rode off through the frosted sage that crackled like brittle glass to the hoofs of the horses. Our guide led toward a branch of a park, and when we got within perhaps a quarter of a mile, Teague suggested that R. C. and I go ahead on the chance of surprising the bear again. It was owing to this suggestion that my brother and I were well ahead of the others. But we did not see any bear 'round the carcass of the cow. Old Jim and Sampson were close behind us, and when Jim got within forty yards of that carcass he put his nose up with a deep and ringing bay and shot by us like a streak. He never went near the dead cow! Sampson bayed like thunder and raced after Jim.

"They're off!" I yelled to R. C. "It's a hot scent! Come on!"

We spurred our horses and they broke across the open park to the edge of the woods. Jim and Sampson were running straight with noses high. I heard a string of yelps and bellows from our rear.

"Look back!" shouted R.C.

Teague and the cowboys were unleashing the rest of the pack. It surely was great to see them stretch out, yelping wildly. Like the wind they passed us. Jim and Sampson headed into the woods with deep bays. I was riding Teague's best horse for this sort of work and he understood the game and plainly enjoyed it. R. C.'s horse ran as fast in the woods as he did in the open. This frightened me, and I yelled for R. C. to be careful. I yelled to deaf ears. That is the first great risk—a rider is not going to be careful! We were right on top of Jim and Sampson with the pack clamoring mad music just behind.

The forest rang. Both horses hurdled logs, sometimes two at once. My old lion chases with Buffalo Jones had made me skillful in dodging branches and snags, and sliding knees back to avoid a knock from trees. For a mile the forest was comparatively open and here we had a grand and ringing run. I received two hard knocks, was unseated once, but held on; once I got a stinging crack in the face from a branch. R. C. added several more black and blue spots to his already spotted anatomy and he just missed, by an inch, a solid snag that would have broken him in two. The pack stretched out in wild staccato chorus, the little airedales literally screeching. Jim soon got out of our sight and then Sampson, but it was even more thrilling to follow by sound instead of sight. They led up a thick, steep slope. Here we got into trouble in the windfalls of timber and the pack drew away from us, up over the mountain.

We were half way up when we heard them jump the bear. The forest seemed full of strife, of bays and yelps. We heard them go down again to our right and as we turned we saw Teague and the others strung out along the edge of the park. They got far ahead of us. When we reached the bottom of the slope they were out of sight, but we could hear them yell. The hounds were working around on another slope, from which craggy rocks loomed above the timber. R. C.'s horse lunged across the park and appeared to be running away from mine. I was a little to the right, and when my horse got under way, full speed, we had the bad luck to plunge suddenly into soft ground. He went to his knees, and I sailed out of the saddle full twenty feet to alight all spread out, sliding like a plow. I did not seem to be hurt and when I got up my horse was coming; he appeared to be patient with me but he was in a hurry. Before we got across the wet place R. C. was out of sight and I concluded that instead of worrying about him I had better think about myself. Once on hard ground my horse fairly charged into the woods and we broke brush and branches as if they had been punk. It was again open forest, then a rocky slope, and then a flat ridge with aisles between the trees. Here I heard the melodious notes of Teague's hunting horns, and following that, the full course of the hounds. They had treed the bear. Coming into still more open forest, with rocks here and there, I made out R. C. far ahead, and soon caught glimpses of the other horses. Then, while riding full tilt, I spied a big black glistening bear high up in a pine a hundred yards or more distant.

Slowing down, I rode up to the circle of frenzied dogs and excited men. The boys were all jabbering at once. Teague was beaming. R. C. sat his horse and it struck me that he looked sorry for the bear. It had been a short and ringing chase.

"Fifteen minutes!" Teague exclaimed with a proud glance at Old Jim standing with forepaws on the pine.

All the time while I fooled around trying to photograph the treed bear R. C. sat there on his horse, looking upward.

"Well, gentlemen, better kill him," said Teague cheerfully. "If he gets rested he'll come down."

I suggested to R. C. that he do the shooting.

"Not much!" he exclaimed.

The bear really looked pretty perched up there. He was as round as a barrel, black as jet, and his fur shone in the gleams of sunlight. His tongue hung out and his plump sides heaved, showing what a quick, hard run he had made before being driven to the tree. What struck me most forcibly was the something about his face as he looked down at those devils of hounds. He was scared. He realized his peril. It was utterly impossible for me to see Teague's point of view.

"Go ahead and plug him," I replied to my brother. "Get it over."

"You do it," he said.

"No, I won't."

"Why not, I'd like to know?"

"Maybe we won't have so good a chance again—and I want you to get your bear," I replied.

"Why, it's like murder!" he protested.

"Oh, not so bad as that," I returned weakly. "We need the meat. We've not had any game meat, you know, except ducks and grouse."

"You won't do it?" he demanded, grimly.

"No, I refuse."

Meanwhile the young ranchers gazed at us with wide eyes, and the expression on Teague's honest, ruddy face would have been funny under other circumstances.

"That bear will come down an' mebbe kill one of my dogs," he protested.

"Well, he can come for all I care," I replied, positively and turned away.

I heard R. C. curse low under his breath. Then followed the spang of his .35 Remington. I wheeled in time to see the bear straining upward in terrible convulsion, his head pointed high with blood spurting from his nose. Slowly he swayed and fell with a heavy crash.

The next bear chase we had was entirely different medicine. Off in the ba under the White Slides, back of our camp, the hounds struck a fresh track and in an instant were out of sight. With the cowboy, Vern, setting the pace we plunged after them. It was rough country. Bogs, brooks, swales, rocky little parks, stretches of timber full of windfalls, groves of aspens so thick we could scarcely squeeze through—all these obstacles soon allowed the hounds to get far away. We came out into a large park, right under a mountain slope, and here we sat our horses listening to the chase. That trail led around the basin and back near to us, up the thick green slope, where high up near a ledge we heard the pack jump this bear. It sounded to us as if he had been roused out of a sleep.

"I'll bet it's one of the big grizzlies we've heard about," said Teague.

That was something to my taste. I have seen a few grizzlies. Riding to higher ground I kept close watch on the few open patches up on the slope. The chase led toward us for a while. Suddenly I saw a bear with frosted coat go lumbering across one of these openings.

"Silvertip! Silvertip!" I yelled at the top of my lungs. "I saw him!"

My call thrilled everybody. Vern spurred his horse and took to the right. Teague advised that we climb the slope. So we made for the timber. Once there we had to get off and climb on foot. It was steep, rough, very hard work. I had on chaps and spurs and soon was hot, laboring, and my heart began to hurt. We all had to rest. The baying of the hounds inspirited us now and then, but presently we lost it. Teague said they had gone over the ridge and as soon as we got up to the top we would hear them again. We struck an elk trail with fresh elk tracks in it. Teague said they were just ahead of us. I never climbed so hard and fast in my life and we were all tuckered out when we reached the top of the ridge. Then to our great disappointment we did not hear the hounds. Mounting, we rode along the crest of this wooded ridge towards the western end which was considerably higher. Once on a bare path of ground we saw where the grizzly had passed. The big round tracks, toeing in a little, made a chill go over me. No doubt of it's being a silvertip!

We climbed and rode to the high point, and coming out upon the summit of the mountain we all heard the deep, hoarse baying of the pack. They were in the canon down a bare grassy slope and over a wooded bench at our feet. Teague yelled as he spurred down. R. C. rode hard in his tracks.

But my horse was new to this bear chasing. He was mettlesome, did not want to do what I wanted, and when I jabbed the spurs into his flanks he nearly bucked me off. I was looking for a soft place to light when he quit. Long before I got down that open slope Teague and R. C. had disappeared. I had to follow their tracks. This I did at a gallop, but now and then I lost the tracks and had to haul in to find them. If I could have heard the hounds from there I would have gone on anyway. But once down in the jack-pines I could not hear either yell or bay. The pines were small, close together and tough. I hurt my hands, scratched my face, barked my knees. The horse had a habit of suddenly deciding to go the way he liked instead of the way I guided him, and when he plunged between saplings too close to permit both of us going through it was exceedingly hard on me. I was worked into a frenzy. Suppose R. C. would come face to face with that old grizzly and fail to kill him! That was the reason of my desperate hurry. I got a crack on the head that nearly blinded me. My horse grew hot and began to run in every little open space. He could scarcely be held in, and I, with the blood hot in me too, did not hold him hard enough.

It seemed miles across that wooded bench. But at last I reached another slope. Coming out upon a canon rim I heard R. C. and Teague yelling and the hounds fighting the grizzly. He was growling and threshing about far below. I had missed the tracks made by Teague and my brother and it was necessary to find them. That slope looked impassable. I rode back along the rim, then forward. Finally I found where the ground was plowed deep, and here I headed my horse. He had been used to smooth roads and he could not take these jumps. I went forward on his neck. But I hung on and spurred him hard. The mad spirit of that chase had gotten into him, too. All the time I could hear the fierce baying and yelping of the hounds, and occasionally I heard a savage bawl from the bear. I literally plunged, slid, broke a way down that mountain slope, riding all the time, before I discovered the footprints of Teague and R. C. They had walked, leading the horses. By this time I was so mad I would not get off. I rode him all the way down that steep slope of dense saplings, loose rock slides and earth and jumble of splintered cliff. That he did not break my neck and his own spoke the truth about that roan horse. Despite his inexperience he was great! We fell over one bank, but a thicket of aspens saved us from rolling. The avalanches slid from under us until I imagined that grizzly would be scared. Once as I stopped to listen I heard bear and pack farther down the canon—heard them above the roar of a rushing stream. Then they went on and I lost the sounds of fight. But R. C.'s clear, thrilling call floated up to me. Probably he was worried about me, too.

Then before I realized it I was at the foot of the slope, in a narrow canon bed full of rocks and trees, with the din of roaring water in my ears. I could hear nothing else. Tracks were everywhere, and when I came to the first place I was so thrilled that my hair seemed to rise on my head. The grizzly had plunged off a sandy bar into the water, and there he had fought the hounds. Signs of that battle were easy to read. I saw where his huge tracks, still wet, led up the opposite sandy bank.

Then, down stream, I did my most reckless and yet best riding. On level ground the horse was splendid. Once he leaped clear across the brook. Every plunge, every turn I expected to bring me upon my brother and Teague and that fighting pack. More than once I thought I heard the spang of the .35 and this made me urge the roan faster and faster.

The canon narrowed, the stream-bed deepened. I had to slow down to get through the trees and rocks. Suddenly I was overjoyed to ride pell-mell upon R. C. and Teague with half the panting hounds. The canon had grown too rough for the horses to go farther and it would have been useless for us to try on foot. As I dismounted, so sore and bruised I could hardly stand, old Jim came limping in to fall into the brook where he lapped and lapped thirstily. Teague threw up his hands. Old Jim's return meant an ended chase. The grizzly had eluded the hounds in that jumble of rocks below.

"Say, did you meet the bear?" queried Teague, eyeing me in astonishment and mirth.

Bloody, dirty, ragged and wringing wet with sweat, I must have been a sight. R. C., however, did not look so very immaculate, and when I saw he also was lame and scratched and black I felt better.

"Some chase, cull!" he said, in his cool, easy way.

Western Myths

Chauncey Thomas

October 1918

There has never been a department in OUTDOOR LIFE quite like "Campfire Talks," written by Chauncey Thomas from 1912 to 1919. Thomas, born in Denver in 1872, was a direct descendant of William Penn, and son of a newspaper editor. He worked on many newspapers in the country and several magazines in New York. He was associate editor of *McClure's* and *Smart Set*, and won acclaim as a writer (Rudyard Kipling said his "Snow Story" was America's best short story). He was a skilled hunter and cowboy. He returned to Colorado in 1912 to recover from a breakdown and started "Campfire Talks," in which he philosophized on everything except camping. He was the last man to talk with Buffalo Bill Cody. He admired the Indian and criticized Custer harshly. Ill again, he ended Talks, but kept on writing firearms for some years. He shot himself to death in 1941 and left a note: "Stroke—Agony."

It would be unfair to characterize history as fossilized fiction, which I have done in print, in these "Campfire Talks" and elsewhere, and also from the lecture platform, and then hide the truth about my own people, the Old Time Westerners, the men and women—and children, remember—of the frontier. Right today things are accepted practically the world over as historical truth that many of us who lived it know is fiction, pure and simple. And herein I will try to set down the simple truth of the American frontier as I knew it as a boy, and as my father and mother knew it before me; they themselves at that time mere boy and girl still in their early twenties, and both living in Colorado before there was an inch of iron rail in the state—before the railroads came. Each one entered Denver on the top of a Concord coach, and each of them in the '60s. I remember Leadville myself in 1878 and '9, and I saw Cripple Creek from its beginning to the present time. I remember the wild Indians of the plains, and the buffalo herds; the feather heads used to ride in a long scattered line down the centuries-old trail that is now one of the state automobile roads running out of Littleton—a suburb of Denver, practically—up along the prairie ridge to the southeast toward the Divide; and the wild herds, like a brown flood in a fog of dust, I recall, framed in a car window of the old Kansas Pacific. That was in '75 and '77, I believe. "There's an antelope," I eagerly informed a tired and dusty carload, to which my mother replied, "I guess it's your imagination . . ." "But my 'magination ain't white behind," I insisted, whereupon the car woke up, and voted that probably it was an antelope after all.

Now, I mention these things simply to qualify as a witness. And ever since I have followed keenly the history of the West, not only what little authentic written facts I have been able to unearth, but mostly the unwritten history of the Old Frontier—what actually was.

Here, for instance, is a sample of some of the ideas spread over the world today about the Early Days in the West: The badman, the cowboy, revolver shooting, Indians, gold mines, bears, women, ways of speech, gamblers, saloons and sundry other stock in trade of the movie screens and the so-called Western novel. The "Western novel" of today is just the old-fashioned dime-novel hair-raiser in a better binding. "Tiger Bill, the Terror of Tinhorn Gulch," is no more absurd than some of the plays, screens, books and short stories of alleged Western life by authors who have made big names and small fortunes by penning purely imaginary people and events that in themselves are, and always have been, impossible.

The other day Zane Grey wrote me and asked the actual truth about frontier revolver shots. I told him the truth. It is this: No man on the frontier could shoot either a revolver or rifle as well as our best experts of today. Right here in Denver, Colorado, we have perhaps the best revolver shots in the world. Men like C. M. McCutchen, who holds the world's record and the official gold and diamond medals given for shooting against not only the civilians but against every military shot in the armies and navies of seven nations. Colonel Cody, the world famous "Buffalo Bill," told me just before he died here in Denver, and I wrote the last interview of many thousand interviews he gave to the press, he told me himself that he never saw or knew of such revolver work on the frontier as is done by the best pistol shots of today. Other old timers, who tell the truth, say the same thing. Frontier men and women were more interested in postholes than bullet holes.

"Wild Bill," whose real name was James A. Hickok, was not a particularly quick, straight or fast revolver shot. I have shot with men who in their time have shot matches with "Wild Bill" and have had a practical means of gauging his shooting. It is said, however, that he could "fan" a revolver, which few men can do. Personally, neither McCutchen nor I have ever seen it done. We both believe "fanning" a six-gun to be a myth, and McCutchen was raised on the Texas plains and I grew up in the Colorado Rockies, both in frontier days. Hickok killed his men by shooting before they had decided to shoot, as he always had the law on his side, and those he killed did not. His skill lay in having the law on his side. Much of Cody's shooting with a revolver or rifle was really done with a shotgun; that is, a rifle bored out to take shot cartridges. He said so frankly in private, but the gaping circus crowds who knew not a gun from a broom took the really good shotgun work on horseback as rifle or revolver shooting. Buffalo Bill, by the way, never carried a gun except in the wilds; in civilization he went totally unarmed all his life.

Another, a life-long friend of mine, who came to Colorado as a prospector in 1859, never carried or owned a gun of any kind all his life. And he spent over forty years prospecting for gold in the Colorado Rockies, from 1859 on. My father was the pioneer editor of the Rockies and spent forty years lacking but a few days, in newspaper work in Denver, from 1866 down to 1904, and in all that time he never actually needed a gun and never saw a shooting scrap, never saw a man shot, cut or killed, nor any wild animal more dangerous than a black wolf that was boring a hole in the horizon. He was not a saloon loafer.

The popular idea of the Old West is that we lived on whiskey and gambled for a living—all of us. That all the women were dance-hall girls, and all the men were a cross between knights minus their stove-pipe clothes, and high-class criminals. Every horse was a broncho or "mustang" that bucked at the very smell of tanned leather—fancy plowing a quarter section with such a team. And we broke and seeded many a mile of sod in those days, for some of us—about ninety-nine per cent, to be more or less exact—preferred wheat to whiskey, and potatoes to poker. The Frontier had more plow horses than it had bucking bronchos.

But not even the wildest movie, short story or novel, either of the dime or dollar variety, thinks of having their terrible "Tiger Bill" invade a school room, shoot up a United States post office, monkey with the express company—usually the Wells-Fargo in those days—or even venture into the respectable streets of the town. They very properly confine his operations to the redlight sections, where, by the way he may still be found. The fire-snorting badman is a mythical joke.

Now, every mining camp, every cowboy-terrorized cattle town, in the West, from its first settlement right down to today, was, and is, 99 per cent school-house, hospital, postoffice, telegraph office, bank, railroad station, and all that. Occasionally a criminal or a drunken fool broke loose in those days, and he does just the same thing today, right in the same Western town, or in New York City or Paris.

The fact is there was not enough out of the ordinary on the Frontier to distin-guish it from the most staid portions of the East, so something had to be invented to tell the folks back home, when the brave traveler returned with his hair from the perils of the Wild West. That we had a thousand irrigation shovels to one bowie knife would have been a tale of common things, so he lied about it.

Even the danger from Indians was almost nothing to what was, and is, pic-tured. There are no actual records of the number of whites killed by Indians, but I doubt if there were over a few thousand, say from 1849 down till the Indian was a corralled creature, totally harmless. As near as I can estimate there must have been at least 500 English-speaking whites in what is today Colorado in the '40s, and as early as 1855 over 25,000 names had been signed to the register of white men, women and children passing West through Fort Kearney. Before Denver was founded, in 1859, probably over 100,000 whites had passed through various portions of Colorado, en route to California and Utah. Also as near as I can arrive at the actual facts, from old diaries and actual personal accounts, both in writing and verbally, it was practical for a man to walk from the Missouri river to almost any place he wished to go in the West along the great river bottoms, such as those of the Platte and the Snake and their branches, without carrying a blanket, a gun or a pound of food, and sleep and eat every night on the way at some ranch, or other more or less permanent settlement—and this was in 1855, if not earlier.

The people who were killed by the Indians usually had only themselves to blame for taking needless risks. In fact, so little was the danger, as a rule, that more were killed than if the danger had actually been greater. People settled on lone ranches, just one or two families, and single wagons crossed the plains, prac-tically unguarded, by many thousands, even in the "Indian Days." The stage coaches made regular time across the continent, only once or twice was regular communication stopped for a short time by Indians; and the famous Pony Express used lone riders along roads that the Indians knew they would travel, and at what hour they, the white riders, would pass a given spot, yet few of them were molested. An uncle of mine was one of them.

Such are the plain facts of the case, else the Pony Express and the stage lines could not have paid dividends. There were some individual adventures, sure enough, both from Indians and from white robbers, but such is the case today with an occasional express messenger on the most modern of railroads.

Men like Jim Baker, Godfrey, and all hundreds of others, maintained ranches and stopping places along the great trails for practically a life time, and long before Denver was founded, in 1859, and did it practically single-handed. It does not take much of a raid to overcome one family in a house, and as these men and places have become famous in Western history, one can easily draw a common-sense conclusion as to the amount of actual danger they were in from the Indians.

Bears and other wild animals have also served as convenient material for great raw tales by those who never saw a wild animal more dangerous than a rabbit. The fact is, we had no dangerous wild animals, even in the earliest days. Now and then a grizzly bear, wounded, would tackle a man, and so he will right today, but if he could get away the wise old grizzly made leaps for the skyline. As to killing a bear with a knife—if you hear any one tell that ancient yarn just put him down as a plain liar. No man ever killed a bear with a knife except "Windy Bill." I have heard all my life, from earliest boyhood up, of the man over in the next county who killed a grizzly as big as a load of hay and as ferocious as a mad elephant, and killed him with a knife—and a real honest-to-goodness "bowie knife" at that. Just carved his liver right out of him, and probably ate it raw. Bad man. Second cousin on his wife's side to the mild mannered chap who took a dozen scalps every morning before breakfast and had them boiled for dinner.

Yes, my own Uncle John, the famous Jack Sumner, Powell's scout on his first try at the Grand Canyon, and the first—or second?—white man to go through that awful gorge, told me, a wide-eyed urchin on the ranch, how he himself killed a bear, a grizzly, of course, with his trusty knife—but then Uncle John lied. He killed many a bear, and perhaps a few men, with a rifle, but nary a one with a knife. There is not an animal in the Rockies, and never has been, that, under half way right conditions, I would not tackle with my six-shooter, and a couple of horsemen can capture any of them alive with a rope.

The fact is, that many, if indeed not all, of the Old Timers had a sense of grave humor coupled to a lively imagination, and like the newspapers and writers, and other publishers of today, they told the public what it wanted to hear, regardless of the actual facts which reduce most things on earth to the ordinary commonplace of everyday existence. Many a cub, or nearly dead bear, made helpless and harmless by trap, dogs or rifle wounds, has been put out of its dying misery with a knife, perhaps, but not one live, vigorous, adult bear in fighting mood. So much for one of the dearest myths of the frontier, the bowie knife, the grizzly and ye hero. Vainer ones, in their mania for astonishment, get the Sinbad habit, but self-trapped in their boasting by contradictory statements, they soon betray themselves, and have to seek an ever new circle of gaping believers.

I was at a dinner in New York City one evening some years ago, fully arrayed in evening clothes, of course, or "my bald faced outfit," as I pleased to term it, just to amuse my Eastern friends, who knew that I came from the Old Frontier. At the table was a man who had just returned from the "Far West," and his tales were many. We let him go on, and his account of "those people out there" was quite well done. Finally, our hostess remarked innocently that I was born and raised in Colorado, whereupon he looked me over in alarm, and explained that I was certainly an exception. "Mr. Mackay was born and raised on the Comstock Lode," murmured the lady at the end of the table, and our fictionizing friend colored, and proceeded to explain that the editor of Success magazine was a Nevada exception. "Mr. Cosgrave, editor of Everybody's Magazine, was born and raised in California," suggested the hostess with suppressed delight. Mr. Cosgrave was, of course, another exception. "Henry M. Stanley was a reporter on the Rocky Mountain News with my father," I remarked, easily. Still another extraordinary exception from our sweating friend. "David H. Moffat, director in the Equitable Life Insurance Company," said Bob Mackay solemnly.

Then from all sides came a verbal volley: "C. B. Kountz of Kountz Brothers, Wall Street bankers; Senator Teller, Secretary of the Interior; Senator Charles S. Thomas; Judge Victor Elliott, whose decisions made the irrigation laws; and Judge Hallett, who fixed our mining laws; Bret Harte; Mark Twain; Irving Hale, the highest record in West Point; Pike; Fremont; Long; Powell; J. J. Hill; Warren of Wyoming, chairman of military affairs in the United States Senate; the Mackays; the Fairs; Frank Norris; Jack London; Rex Beach; Parkman; Deming; Eugene Field; Seibold, editor of the New York World; Hearst; Bryan; Leland Stanford; Corbett; Brigham Young; Frederick Remington; General Funston; Stewart Edward White; Colonel Dodge, who built the Union Pacific; Senator Clark; General Crook; General Sherman; Pullman invented the sleeping car in Colorado in 1860; Abraham Lincoln was on the Kansas frontier before the railroads."

It was too much for the returned traveler into the perils of the Rockies, where all the men ate with bowie knives and slept with their spurs on, and where every woman had a public nickname. Bombarded from right and left, he gulped, surrendered, and had to admit that he had traveled in perfect comfort and safety in electric lighted palace cars, had dined—not "chawed"—in the Brown Palace in Denver amid surroundings equal to things in Paris, London or New York. Also that he found comfort, safety, education and refinement in Cripple Creek and Leadville—two "Western mining camps"—and had not seen a gun or knife on his entire trip. He tried to crawl out of it under the cover of that prince of fools, the practical joker, but was pinned down.

"And another of our people, the Old Western type, sits tonight in the White House—Theodore Roosevelt," I added coolly. Then, lest we forget: "Jefferson, Jackson, Grant, Lincoln and Roosevelt, at least five of the great Presidents of the United States, came from the Frontier, from the Wild West of their day, remember; and many of our greatest men, especially in Revolutionary days, were born of frontier women, and were reared in frontier homes." But the Liar was silent.

Outdoor Life Ads, 1910–1920

THE FISH THAT DIDN'T GET AWAY
that big one—landed him this time —thanks to this handy gaff. Spreads 7½ inches—length 18 inches. Holds fish from ½ to 20 pounds.

MARBLE'S CLINCHER GAFF
Is controlled by one hand: closes in a wink—hangs on like a bull terrier—can't mangle fish or pinch hands. Can be locked with points together. Far better than a landing net. Dealers or postpaid direct, $1.00. Catalog of 60 specialties for outers and sportsmen free.

Marble Arms & Mfg. Co.
571 Delta Ave.
Gladstone, Mich.

THE ONLY LAMP OF ITS KIND

The Carbide BRILLIANT

SEARCH LIGHT for Hunting, Trapping, Camping. Sold throughout the world for 18 years. Shines 300 to 600 feet. Single or Double Lens with darkening door. Four styles, $10.00 to $12.00. Sold by Hardware & Sporting Goods Dealers. If your dealer cannot supply you we will ship on receipt of price, postage paid.

Catalog free on request.

BRILLIANT SEARCH LIGHT MFG. CO.   529 So. Dearborn St, Dept. 4, Chicago, Ill.

CLEANED 'EM ALL

One Enthusiastic user of our Pork Rind Minnows says, "This hook, (Oriental Wiggler) caught and landed more muscallonge than three other kinds of trolling hooks used in a party of twenty-one fishermen on Plumb Lake, Wis."

Oriental Wiggler, $1.00. All red, all white or red and white. ½ or ⅝ oz.

This angler hails from Chicago where they are keen to recognize something better.

If you want to make those plug splashers turn green with envy, just take one of our lures, follow behind their boat, and pick up the fish they pass over.

Our Pork Rind Strips are necessary to the successful operation of these lures.

If your dealer is asleep at the switch, send in your remittance.

MANUFACTURED BY

AL. FOSS   1724 to 1736 Columbus Road   CLEVELAND - - OHIO

Little Egypt Wiggler, 75c. Weight ½ oz.

25c 12 pieces

Skidder, 75c.   Weight ½ oz.

Oil Your Traps With 3-in-One

MAKES them quicker on the trigger. Keeps rust away—in use or hanging up for summer.

Beats bait as a lure. This is fact—expert trappers say so. Don't scoff—pour a few drops of 3-in-One on the pans of your traps when making a "set" and see how mink, muskrat, fox and skunk come to it.

3-in-One oil

is a trapper's true friend—never be without it. Sold in sporting goods stores, hardware, drug and general stores: 1 oz., 10c; 3 oz., 25c; 8 oz. (½ pt), 50c. Also in Handy Oil Cans, just right for trappers' use, 3½ oz., 25c. If not with your dealer, we will send one of these cans by parcel post, full of 3-in-One for 30c.

FREE—Write for generous sample and Dictionary of uses.

Three-in-One Oil Co.
153 New St.,   New York

Two Guns in One—

Upper barrel (rifled) shoots .22; lower barrel (smooth bored) shoots .44 shot or ball. Lengths, 12,15 or 18 inches. Fits you for large and small game or inexpensive target practice. Stock folds up or detaches. Shoulder holster furnished. Sample Nitro-Solvent Oil for name sporting goods dealer. Send for catalog of Marble's 60 Outing Specialties.
MARBLE ARMS & MFG. CO., 571 Delta Ave., Gladstone, Mich.
Successor to Marble Safety Axe Co

MARBLE'S GAME GETTER GUN

A Perfect Weed Repeller

Something new, an absolute weedless trolling or casting affair. Can be used with any kind of lure. It not only keeps weeds off from the hooks, but off from the spoon or propeller as well. It glides through the weeds like a snake, and every strike is a sure catch. It has been in constant use for two years, before putting on the market. Money back if not satisfied. Send for it now. Postpaid 25c, or at your dealer. Send for circular.

The Brilliant Search Light Mfg. Co.
Dept. 4   Duluth, Minn., U. S. A.

MICHIGAN DOPE

THIS IS THE DOPE THAT KILLED FATHER
"LETS GET A MOVE ON US"

You probably have not tried MICHIGAN DOPE. This is the dope that will actually give you comfort while out fishing, hunting or camping. Send for circular.

Postpaid 1-oz. can, 25c.; 4-oz. can, 50c.

The Brilliant Search Light Mfg. Co.
Dept. 4   Duluth, Minn., U. S. A.

MARBLE'S GUN SIGHTS

Will Improve Your Shooting

The choice of a sight is as important as the choice of a gun. Marble's Sights combine the ideas and suggestions of many renowned marksmen. They will improve your shooting. If your dealer can't supply you, order direct. Send for catalog. The Marble line includes in addition, axes and knives of different design and finish, waterproof matchbox, compasses, fish gaff, anti rust ropes, nitro solvent oil, gun rods and cleaning implements.

Marble's Flexible Rear Sight

A universal favorite with both professional and amateur—truly a *perfect rear sight*. Stem is not rigid—held by strong spring in base: won't break when struck. Two discs furnished, $3.50.

Sheard Gold Bead Front Sight

Shows up well in dark timber and will not blur in bright light. For practically all rifles and revolvers. $1.65.

Standard Front Sight

Ivory or gold bead instantly reflects the faintest ray of light and makes early dawn or twilight shots most certain. 1-16, 3-32, ⅛ in. $1.10.

Improved Front Sight

Makes accurate shots possible at any range without stopping to adjust rear sight. Object aimed at can be seen over or under bead, choice of 1-16, 3-32, or ¼-in. ivory or gold bead, $1.10.

Adjustable Leaf Sight—May be used alone or in conjuction with peep rear sight, folding down leaf of adjustable when peep is being used—has two different sized notches. $1.10.

V-M Front Sight

Embodies a principle new to many shooters—you look directly at the object and shoot right where you aim; no guess work. Use with any rear sight, preferably Marble's Flexible Rear Sight. $1.65

MARBLE ARMS & MFG. CO.
571 Delta Ave.   GLADSTONE, MICH.

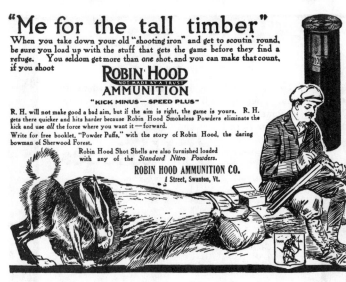
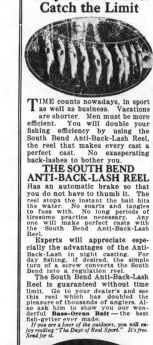

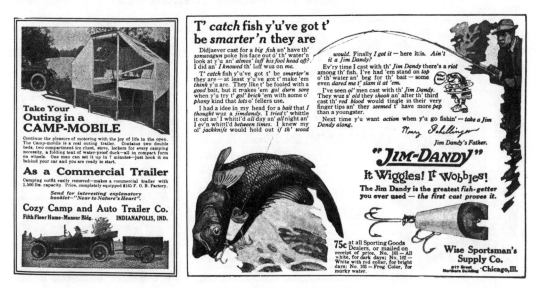

Northern Lives

Most of us who run and read do not require proof to know that the way of the musher is hard. The long Alaska winters alone, with none of the accompanying hardships, would insure that. Probably in no other country on the globe does the prospector and trapper encounter such heart-rending obstacles as in Alaska. A large number of these men whom you meet in that country—those whose lives are spent in the open—are going to get away from it "next fall." They need a larger stake, or they wish to finish just one task; then they intend to hike to the "outside"—as the States is called. But only a small percentage of those rosy dreams ever are realized, for before they know it something has happened that makes their exit from that land less likely than ever before. A bad fall in the glaciers, or a frozen and amputated foot, or hands, nose or ears may have been disfigured from freezing, with the result that they feel that they "belong" very well where they are.

A large number of the men of the Arctic wouldn't live anywhere else. They seem to have been seized with the lure of the Northland—which is there, all right, for those who like it, just as you find men who get fascinated with the desert, and who can't give it up—and once this spell is upon them, you might as well try to induce Mt. Shishaldin to shift positions as attempt to jar them loose from their enthrallment.

We are indebted to A. M. Bailey (an Alaskan of some years' experience) for complete detailed diaries kept by two "Sourdoughs" previous to their respective deaths in different localities of Alaska. In each of these cases they were alone and so far from civilization that, in their terribly weakened condition, neither of them could reach assistance. These diaries in their original shape covered a longer period of time and were in much more exhaustive form than that in which they are here published:

Note:—This is a correct copy of the diary left by one V. Swanson, known as the "Wildman of Dry Bay," whose body was found on the 18th of August, 1918, by Hardy Trefger and Fred Zastrow, trappers from Dry Bay:

1917

Oct. 28—Winter has come. Strong wind, two feet of snow.
Nov. 4—Shot one lynx.
    6—Made one pair of bearskin pants
    8—Sugar is all gone.
   13—Made two pair of moccasins.
   18—Finished one fur coat of bear, wolf and lynx.
   21—Finished one sleeping bag of bear, goat, blankets and canvas. Rain for several days.
   22—Left eye bothers me. Shot one goat.
   26—Shot one lynx while eating breakfast.
   27—Made one pair of bearpaw snowshoes.
Dec. 1—Getting bad. Cold for several days, river still open.
    4—River raised six feet in twenty-four hours
    6—Slush stiffening slowly, making ice

7—The wind is so strong that you can't stand upright. Snow getting deeper now.

15—Very cold and strong wind, impossible to be out without skin clothes.

19—Snowing, but still very cold. Can't travel. Very little grub; snow too deep and soft for hunting goats. Stomach balking at straight meat, especially lynx.

21—Shot a goat from the river.

25—Very cold. A good Christmas dinner. Snow getting hard.

26—Broke through the ice. Skin clothes saved the day.

31—Finished new roof on the house. One month cold weather straight. Stomach getting worse.

1918

Jan.   8—River open as far as can be seen. Health very poor.

12—Lynx moving down river one or two a night; no chance to catch them.

15—Goats moving out of reach. Using canoe on the river.

16—One lynx. Weather getting mild.

20—Rain today.

22—One lynx.

28—One goat; been cold for a few days.

Feb.   1—Cold weather nearly all month of January. Lynx robbed my meat cache up the river. Salt and tea but once a day. Gradually getting weaker.

5—Colder weather; feeling very bad. Just able to take care of myself.

10—Milder weather, feeling very bad. Heavy fall of snow.

15—Good weather continues; feeling some better.

24—More snow. Living on dry meat and tallow.

26—Shot one goat from the river.

Mar.   2—Shot one goat.

11—Starting for Dry Bay, believing the river open. Out about one hour, struck the ice; can't go either way; too weak to haul the canoe. Snow soft; no game here.

25—Trying to get to the house. River is frozen in places and rising. The sleigh now only three miles from there, but open river and perpendicular cliffs keep me from getting any farther. At present cannot find anything to eat here. Eyes are getting bad.

28—Eyes can't stand the sun at all. Finest kind of weather.

Apr.   1—Got to the house with what I could carry. Wolverines had been there eating my skins, robes and moccasins, old meat and also my goat skin door. They tried to run me last night; came through the stove-pipe hole, showing fight. Heavy fall of snow. Canoe and some traps down the river about five miles close to Indian grave mark. Camp about half-ways.

3—Still snowing. Cooking my last grub; no salt; no tea.

4—Shot one goat, using all but three of my shells. Can't see the sight at all.

7—Wolverines working on camp below, carrying away my things. Ate part of my bearskin pants. Packed the old .30-30 out into the brush. Eyes are getting worse again; don't even stand the snow.

10—Wolverines ate my bedding and one snowshoe. In the tent—getting shaky in the legs. A five-mile walk a big day's work.

12—Seen a fox track today. Birds are coming, too. Fine weather.

15—The no-salt diet hitting me pretty hard. Eyes are getting worse; in the bunk most of the time.

17—Rain yesterday and today.

20—Finest weather continues again; cooking the last grub; got to stay in the bunk most of the time; my legs won't carry me very far.

My eyes useless for hunting; the rest of my body also useless. I believe my time has come. My belongings—everything I got—I give to Jos. Pellerine of Dry Bay; if not alive to Paul Swartzkoph, Alsek River. April 22, 1918.

(signed)   V. Swanson

This is the statement of a man found dead in his cabin by Barry Trefger and myself on the 18th day of August, 1918.

(signed)   Fred Zastrow.

• • • •

Diary of Thomas A. O'Brien, who left Juneau, Alaska, Monday, August 25, 1919, and who was found dead in his cabin at Whiting River, Snettisham, Alaska, by Search Party on September 2, 1920.

Apr. 30—Baked bread. Stove up with rheumatism and a general breakdown.

May 1—Went out to river. Sicker than ever.

2—Rained all afternoon. My legs are going on the bum.

3—Snowed in night; rained and snowed all day. My left leg is all in; my teeth are all rattling and sore, and I am almost all in.

4—Legs not so bad, but still swollen and I have fever.

5—Rained mostly all day. I am the most helpless today I ever was to my recollection in all of my life. Just able to get a bucket of water by a desperate effort.

8—Sicker than h-ll all day; both legs on the bum.

11—In bed all day. Had some cold rice.

13—Built a fire and got breakfast; an awful job. Both legs are big, and pain awful.

15—Layed in bed all day; no sleep in the night; legs paining.

16—In bed all day and no sleep night or day. My gums are bad. Got up, but fell on the floor; out of my mind altogether. Started to fix the bed and had another; fell on my face, mashed my nose and side of my face.

17—Little better today: There's a chance now, I think; yesterday I gave it up.

19—Rained all night and part of day. Changed my cure; have eaten a small potato raw, pickles, and drank lemon extract and vinegar. Legs seem deader and itch a little.

21—Clear, strong wind. Laid in bed all day feeling a shade better. Ate raw potatoes, pickles, drank vinegar and extracts.

23—Seem to be mending, but not much change. So weak if I move now I faint.

25—I feel as if I will get better.

26—Got up, but fell in the door in a faint; I finally got up and made it to the bed, where I probably will be for good and all time.

27—Clear, cold. Started in on pickles and raisins. Got out Eagle milk; it seemed to hit the right spot, if it don't sour the stomach. Legs are larger and drawn up more.

28—Rested better in night. Will have to get out today to get water, and that will be h-ell. Got the water on the shelf at the door, and it almost got me. I am too far gone to ever get out of that door again. If something don't turn up I am a goner.

31—This is the day in the ending history of my life. I have tried once today to reach the door and failed. I did not faint, for I did not get far enough away from the bed. I must have water today or burst. I did not have strength enough to get water, so it's all off with me now, unless some stray bear hunter drops in on me.

June   2—Got sick and vomited, and still sick. Strained out three flasks of pickle brine. If I can live on that stuff I must be all right.

3—I have held down a piece of pickle and that is all. The stomach has refused to act all day. I can feel the end coming; if it would rain I might get water and help prolong life.

4—Another hard night. Vomited several times; can't touch milk at all. Lots weaker today.

5—No water yet. The storm is too light for any seepage. I have rallied a little today; the swelling in the legs are going down. If we get lots of rain there may still be another chance.

6—Rained in morning, not enough to do any good. This is the hardest night and day yet. I am still strong in the heart and mind.

7—Rained a little; put in a hard night and starting a hard day.

8—Almost the end.

9—Life is dying hard; the heart is strong.

The Case of the Elmwood Buck

Archibald Rutledge

January 1929

Archibald Rutledge, author of eighty books and Poet Laureate of South
Carolina since 1934, died at the age of ninety in 1973. He wrote for
OUTDOOR LIFE for forty-three years. This was his first story for us. His last,
"My Most Memorable Deer Hunt," ran in July 1971. In that story he said
he had killed 299 bucks in his time. "If that seems too many for one man,"
he said, "I remind you that South Carolina is a good deer state and that
some of its zones have the longest season in the U.S. (4½ months). A
hunter is allowed five bucks and I've hunted for seventy-eight years.
The shotgun and hounds are imperative in many parts of the South,
where the swamps are dense and stalking impossible. A rifle is dangerous
in the level woods. I have hunted in the mountains of Maryland and
Pennsylvania and readily understand why the rifle is the weapon to use
there, and why hounds would be out of place."

Though I have had the rare privilege of following the whitetail deer for a
period of more than thirty-five years, and though, as would be natural under such
circumstances, I have had some strange and startling experiences, none had perhaps the same dramatic interest as the case of the stag of Elmwood. This business
happened on the morning of Thursday, December 29, 1927, on the old plantation
that has been mentioned. It lies some 11 miles from the mouth of the Santee
River, in Carolina. Long deserted, it is a good place for deer—if a man can
stand the somewhat nerve-racking strain of hunting in dense thickets wherein, at
any moment, an old master will rip up under his feet. I used to enjoy greatly the
business of bouncing bucks from their beds, but I am beginning to feel the tension of such hunting. A stag so roused makes Lindbergh and other flight artists
look like the last rose of summer.

I shall tell this thing as simply as I can.

Five of us took up stands on the ancient avenue leading into Elmwood Plantation. The old roadway is still in good preservation, but the thickets have
encroached upon it, so that sweet-smelling bowers of smilax and jasmine overhang it. We stood a few paces in from the road where the woods were a bit
clearer. Two hundred yards ahead of us were dense thickets of pine and myrtle,
ideal country for deer to bed during the day. Yet it has been my experience, and
doubtless it has been shared by many another deer-hunter, that in the hunting
season old bucks will deliberately avoid dense cover. Of course, no man can lay
down rules about the behavior of intelligent wild things, imagining that a really
resourceful animal like a stag will always act in the same way. His very variabil-
ity is a part of his life-insurance. But I have found that old bucks prefer to lie on
the thin edges of thickets, in the tops of fallen trees in comparatively open woods,
or in low bushes or patches of broom-sedge. On a good many occasions, while
walking up deer, I have detected one lying down by seeing it crouch below the
short bushes or grasses that were not tall enough to conceal it as it lay in a natural position.

The case of this Elmwood stag illustrates this matter of a deer's lying down in
the open, and it also illustrates so many other wiles and characteristics of the

whitetail that I believe a detailed account of the whole business may be of some interest, especially to those who are as incurable deer-hunters as I am.

After posting my standers, I watched the negro drivers ride far down the avenue, chatting with that infectious humor characteristic of plantation negroes. As we were in the heart of the deer-country, all of us, I think, made too much noise; yet what difference did it make? Directly ahead of my stand, and right in the open, with no shelter save that afforded by the bare limbs of a little bush, at that very moment was lying the Elmwood stag.

Instead of going straight to my stand, I turned in somewhat to the left, going through a thin thicket of young pines. I took this route because we had left one stand uncovered, and I was supposed to straddle two. The forest was silent, hanging with dew, glistening. Fragrant airs moved softly. High overhead I could hear the dreamful mighty pines sighing mystically. My gun was loaded. I was stepping through the broomsedge cautiously. The place was just like one of those sparse thickets in which a sportsman in the North is likely to flush a ruffed grouse. But I had no premonition of the superb stag lying not 30 yards away, off to my right front. But for a few waving tufts of broomsedge, but for a tiny pine, for a paltry screen of a dry bush, he would have been in ridiculously plain sight. As I discovered later, he had no regular bed; he was lying on the bare damp ground. The day was so warm and still that, after a long night of roaming and browsing, he just luxuriated down by this old road—and here he intended staying unless he was actually kicked out of his "form."

I should have seen the buck before he got up; but I never expected anything so close to the road. My gaze was fixed farther away. Besides, he doubtless flattened himself when I got near. So crouched, if he did not move his antlers, he would be exceedingly hard to discern. At such a time, a buck will draw his feet up under him, take a regular stance for a start, meanwhile "grounding" his head until his lower jaw rests flat on the ground. Once when driving for a party of hunters I saw a buck in that position. Every time I whistled he would flatten his head to the earth; and after a moment or two he would raise it craftily to reconnoiter. He kept performing in this way until I was within easy gunshot of him.

The Elmwood buck must have felt that he was in something like a corner, for he surely had been aware of the general approach and also the separation of our hunting party. He must have had his fears confirmed when he saw me approaching on his left. He might have then sprung up and raced away from me. It seemed the obvious thing to do. But the principle of nearly all wild life strategy is the principle of doing the thing least expected by the pursuer. It is a game of wits. This stag lay still and let me not only approach but pass him—he all the while lying practically in the open. He was a big buck, too, full-antlered. As the time was about 8 o'clock in the morning. I am sure that the old stag could not have been couched more than an hour. It is safe therefore to suppose that he had hardly settled himself for the day. I was ready for a shot, for in such woods the hunter must continually be on the alert; but I saw and heard nothing. True, I was on the fringes of a thicket of young pines, and the dew sliding from their needles made a sibilant whisper in the broomsedge below; otherwise I might have seen the Elmwood stag as he roused himself.

It may be that I am making too much of this story and of all its incidents; yet, as I said before, it seems to illustrate almost perfectly many of the traits of behavior that we associate with the most popular of all American big game animals.

I had passed the stag perhaps 20 feet, he being at that time about 35 yards off to my right, and partly behind me. He must have crawled from his bed, gently insinuating himself up, elongating himself like a rabbit for a length or two. There was no semblance of the standard "rip"—a sound that has thrilled me in the wildwoods since the time of my first deer hunt, when I was 9 years old. What first attracted my attention to the buck was the sudden and amazing sight of him, caught out of the corner of my right eye. My vision was dramatically filled with this superb creature, now on the run dead away from me. I shall never forget how he seemed to prance, turning his head slightly so as to keep a weather-eye on what had startled him. At that moment he was just behind a very thin screen of bare bushes and several small pines, yet there was plenty of opening for a shot. One thing momentarily deterred me, even as I threw my gun up. He was headed straight for the stander next to me. Should I take a chance shot when the man below me on the road might get a perfect one? Little hesitancies of this kind often determine whether a man hits or misses—or perhaps does neither, but just does not shoot.

I had my gun on the Elmwood stag when he executed a master-maneuver, worthy of the ancient craft of the whitetail. In two great bounds he dodged artfully toward a dense thicket bordering the road, making these jumps sharply at right angles. In that final instant that remained for me to do some deciding, I knew that he would not now go near the next stander. I also knew that whatever my own intentions were, I must make them known at once. There was no time for more than one shot. I fired the choke barrel just as the stag took his last leap out of the broomgrass savanna toward the friendly darkness of the sheltering thicket. A hunter generally knows when his eye and gunsight and the game have coordinated rightly. It seemed to me that I was holding dead on the buck's shoulder.

Apparently I was right, for at the crack of the gun, much to my surprise (for the distance was not under 60 yards), the Elmwood stag went headlong. I saw him go down, but I could not see him on the ground.

Running forward through the sparse thicket, I came near where he had been when I shot. He was not there, but near the road I heard a terrific blundering such as is made by a deer that falls, gets up, and falls again. I listened carefully so as to determine by the nature of his struggle whether he would go far. Three times I heard him go down heavily. Then there was silence. I did not know but that he might be lying just across the road.

As soon as I came to where he first fell, I found spatters of blood, then a trail of it; I also could see where the old stag, in his heroic struggle, had fallen, risen again, blundered, yet somehow gone on. In the road and beyond it there were the same telltale signs of the wily and stubborn old creature's hardihood.

He was not lying within sight, nor yet within 200 yards of where he had first gone down. I therefore blew my horn, summoning the drivers and all the standers.

> They held a council standing
>   Before the river-gate;
> Short time there was ye well may guess
>   For musing or debate.

Thus it was with us. And I then made one of the master-blunders of my life as a hunter. As every word of this story is true, I must not fail to turn the spotlight on my own shortcoming. So confident was I that we could easily overhaul the wounded stag with the seven hounds with which we were hunting—for the whitetail in the South is seldom hunted without hounds—that I suggested that the pack be set to the slot at once. The amount of blood thrown out by the deer and the color of it led me to believe that the chase would be short and swift. Of course, I should have taken the standers a mile or so ahead and posted them in front of the oncoming circus parade. This I failed to do, and it was exceedingly dumb of me not to take this precaution.

As soon as we gave the hounds their heads, they went wild on the hot blood-trail. We followed fast; and I had fond visions of soon hearing them come to bay. It did not seem possible to me that a stag so thrown and so blundering could possibly go far. At a point about a quarter of a mile from where we started we came to an old ditch. Its sides were of clean white sand, and its bottom also, for it was empty. In this the buck had evidently lain down, for there was a pool of blood. Also, the old fellow had had much difficulty in negotiating the farther bank when he had again taken his feet. Over such a ditch he would usually have lithely sailed. Now he had the bank pawed down in his gallant effort. But he had gone on.

The dogs, the mounted riders, and certain standers who are younger than I distanced me. I kept pausing, not only to get my wind but also to listen to the hounds. They were having a great race. At last, in one of my pauses, I heard them divide. That was not so good. They had run into other deer; and in such a case it frequently happens that the hounds will take the wrong trail. I heard some of the dogs bearing far to the southward; others had turned due north, heading toward the creek. Fainter and fainter grew their voices, mingling at last with the soft music from the crests of the mighty pines. Fainter also grew my hope; and the antlers that my eye had coveted seemed farther away than I ever dreamed they could possibly be, after I had seen them go down in the broomsedge.

There were features about the horns that I had carefully noted, even in that fleeting dramatic moment when the stag had been in full sight; tall they were, and gray in color; and either because of foreshortening, or because of actual formation, the left antler looked considerably shorter than the right. He looked to me to be a heavy deer, with antlers not quite up to his size—but good horns of seven or eight points, and decidedly unusual in color and in conformation. Now, as the chiming hounds passed out of hearing, and as I could no longer hear the shouts of the following drivers, I wondered if I should ever see those antlers again. If I should, I felt sure of being able to identify them.

It was nearly an hour after the hounds had passed out of hearing before my crestfallen drivers and the chagrined standers returned. The stag had escaped. Some of the dogs had been recovered, but most of them had run off on other deer. I apologized to the assembled crowd for having botched the business; yet the chance had been small for a good shot. The Elmwood buck was gone.

Yet the interesting horns of this stag look down on me now as I write. About a month after I left the plantation, I had a letter from my negro head-driver somewhat to this effect:

"My Boss, you is had a good experience with the ole buck you shoot in Elmwood. He run to the Old Mill, turn to the Ocean, and come as far as Pinckney Run. My boy George hear his little dog barking at something about three days and one Sunday. But that is a fool no-account dog, and loves to bark at nothing. But when I hear the barking, I say to George, 'Son, come with me.' We find your buck. He been dead about five days, he been shoot bad. I send you the horns for 'member that day by."

Such is the tale of the Elmwood buck; not much of a story, perhaps; just one of those hunting yarns that sportsmen like to record. I might add that the run of the stag from where I shot to where he fell was about 2½ miles; but the route the fugitive evidently took would have caused him to double a great deal, so that he probably traveled more than 3 miles.

The Giant of the South Seas

Zane Grey

November 1930

Modern big-game fishermen look scornfully upon Zane Grey's western
novels while nominating his saltwater writings as classics. I refuse to
yield on the westerns. Grey was a saltwater giant, I agree, and this is a
thrilling tale. What he calls the giant Tahitian striped marlin here is today
called the Pacific blue marlin, the all-tackle record for which is 1,153 pounds.
So, even in settling for 1,040 pounds he was right up there even in those
pre-IGFA days.

Time is probably more generous and healing to an angler than to any other
individual. The wind, the sun, the open, the colors and smells, the loneliness of
the sea or the solitude of the stream work some kind of magic. In a few days my
disappointment at losing a wonderful fish was only a memory, another incident of
angling history.

On the 15th of last May, which was the seventh day of clear, hot, sunny
weather, I stayed in my camp near Tahiti, in the South Seas, to do some neglected writing, and let Cappy run out alone off the east end, where we had not
scouted for several weeks. He returned to report a rather choppy sea, but he had
raised two marlin, one of which was a good-sized fish that came for his bait three
times, to refuse it, no doubt because it was stale. Tuna, a small species, were
numerous, and there was some bonito showing.

"Same old story," averred the Captain (Captain Laurie Mitchell). "If I'd had
a fresh bait I'd have hooked that bird. A lunker, too. All of 500 pounds."

Just what had transpired in my mind I was not conscious of then. It all came
to me afterward, and it was that this game was long, and some day one of us
might capture a giant Tahitian marlin. We would go on trying.

That night the dry spell broke. The rain roared on the pandanus roof, most
welcome and dreamy of sounds. Morning disclosed dark, massed, broken clouds,
red-edged and purple-centered, with curtains of rain falling over the mountains.
This weather was something like March come back again for a day! Wondrous
South Seas!

I took down a couple of new feather gigs—silver-headed with blue eyes—just
for good luck. They worked. We caught five fine bonito in the lagoon, right off
the point where my cottage stands. Jimmy, one of my natives, held up five
fingers: "Five bonito. Good!" he ejaculated, which voiced all our sentiments.

Cappy had gone up the lagoon toward the second pass, and we tried to catch
him so as to give him a fresh bait. As usual, however, Cappy's natives were running the wheels off his launch, and we could not catch him. The second pass
looked sort of white and rough to me. Cappy went out, however, through a
smooth channel. Presently we saw a swell gather and rise, to close the channel
and mount to a great, curling, white-crested wave which broke all the way across.
Charley, who had the wheel, grinned up at me: "No good!" We turned inshore
and made for the third pass, some miles on, and got through that wide one without risk. Afterward Cappy told me his guide, Areiareia, knew exactly when to
run through the second pass.

We headed out. A few black noddies skimmed the dark sea, and a few scattered bonito broke the surface. As usual—when we had them—we put out a big bonito on my big tackle and an ordinary one on the other. As my medium tackle holds 1,000 yards of 39-thread Swastika line it will seem interesting to anglers to speak of it as medium. The big outfit held 1,500 yards of line—1,000 of 39-thread and 500 yards of 42 for backing; and this story will prove I needed Hardy rod and reel, and the great Swastika line.

Off the east end there was a brightness of white and blue, where the clouds broke, and in the west there were trade wind clouds of gold and pearl, but for the most part a gray canopy overspread mountain and sea. All along the saw-toothed front of this range inshore the peaks were obscured and the canyons filled with down-drooping veils of rain.

What a relief from late days of sun and wind and wave! This was the kind of sea I loved to fish. The boat ran easily over a dark, low, lumpy swell. The air was cool, and as I did not have on any shirt the fine mist felt pleasant to my skin. John Loef was at the wheel. Bob Carney sat up on top with Jimmy and Charley, learning to talk Tahitian. The teasers and heavy baits made a splashing, swishy sound that could be heard above the boil and gurgle of water from the propellers. We followed some low-skimming boobies for a while, and then headed for Captain M.'s boat, several miles farther out. A rain squall was obscuring the white, tumbling reef and slowly moving toward us. Peter Williams sat at my right, holding the line which had the larger bonito. He had both feet up on the gunwale. I noticed that the line on this reel was white and dry. I sat in the left chair, precisely as Peter, except that I had on two pairs of gloves with thumbstalls in them. I have cut, burned, and skinned my hands too often on a hard strike to go without gloves. They are a nuisance to wear all day, when the rest of you, almost, is getting pleasantly caressed by sun and wind, but they are absolutely necessary to an angler who knows what he is doing.

Peter (saltwater guide from New Zealand) and I were discussing plans for our great round-the-world trip next year, boats, camp equipment, and what not. And, although our gaze seldom strayed from the baits, the idea of raising a fish was the furthest from our minds. We were just fishing, putting in the few remaining hours of this Tahitian trip, and already given over to the hopes and anticipations of the new one. That is the comfortable way to make a trip endurable—to pass from the hard reality of the present to the ideal romance of the future.

Suddenly I heard a sounding, vicious thump of water. Peter's feet went up in the air.

"Ge-suss!" he bawled.

His reel screeched. Quick as thought, I leaned over to press my gloved hand on the whizzing spool of line. Just in time to save the reel from overrunning!

Out where Peter's bait had been showed a whirling, closing hole in the boiling white-green water. I saw a wide purple mass shooting away so close under the surface as to make the water look shallow. Peter fell out of the chair at the same instant I leaped up to straddle his rod. I had the situation in hand. My mind worked swiftly and coolly. It was an incredibly wonderful strike. The other boys piled back to the cockpit to help Peter get my other bait and the teasers in.

Before this was even started the fish ran out 200 yards of line, then, turning to the right, he tore off another hundred. All in a very few seconds! Then a white splash, high as a tree, shot up, out of which leaped the most magnificent of all the leaping fish I ever saw.

"Giant marlin!" screamed Peter. What had happened to me I did not know, but I was cold, keen, hard, tingling, motivated to think and do the right thing. This glorious fish made a leap of 30 feet at least, low and swift, which yet gave me time to gauge his enormous size and species. Here at last on the end of my line was the great Tahitian swordfish! He looked monstrous. He was pale, shiny gray in color, with broad stripes of purple. When he hit the water he sent up a splash like the flying surf on the reef.

By the time he was down I had the drag on and was winding the reel. Out he blazed again, faster, higher, longer, whirling the bonito round his head.

"Hook didn't catch!" yelled Peter, wildly. "It's on this side. He'll throw it."

I had instinctively come up mightily on the rod, winding with all speed, and I had felt the tremendous, solid pull. The big Pflueger hook had caught before that, however, and the bag in the line, coupled with his momentum, had set it.

"No, Peter! He's fast," I replied. Still I kept working like a windmill in a cyclone to get up the slack. The monster had circled in these two leaps. Again he burst out, a plunging leap which took him under a wall of rippling white spray. Next instant such a terrific jerk as I had never sustained nearly unseated me. He was away on his run.

"Take the wheel, Peter," I ordered, and released the drag. "Water! Somebody pour water on this reel! Quick!"

The white line melted, smoked, burned off the reel. I smelled the scorching. It burned through my gloves. John was swift to plunge a bucket overboard and douse reel, rod, and me with water. That, too, saved us.

"After him, Pete!" I called, piercingly. The engines roared, and the launch danced around to leap in the direction of the tight line.

"Full speed!" I added.

"Aye, sir," yelled Peter, who had been a sailor before he became a whaler and a fisherman.

Then we had our race. It was thriiling in the extreme, and, though brief, it was far too long for me. A thousand yards from us—over half a mile—he came up to pound and beat the water into a maelstrom.

"Slow up!" I sang out. We were bagging the line. Then I turned on the wheel drag and began to pump and reel as never before in all my life. How precious that big spool—that big reel handle! They fairly ate up the line. We got back 500 yards of the 1,000 out before he was off again. This time, quick as I was, it took all my strength to release the drag, for when a weight is pulling hard it releases with extreme difficulty. No more risk like that!

He beat us in another race, shorter, at the end of which, when he showed like a plunging elephant, he had out 750 yards of line.

"Too much—Peter!" I panted. "We must—get him closer! Go to it!"

So we ran down upon him. I worked as before, desperately, holding on my nerve, and, when I got 500 yards back again on the reel, I was completely winded, and the hot sweat poured off my naked arms and breast.

"He's sounding! Get my shirt—harness!"

Warily I let go with one hand and then with the other, as John and Jimmy helped me on with my shirt, and then with the leather harness. With that hooked on to my reel and the great strain transferred to my shoulders, I felt that I might not be torn asunder.

"All set. Let's go," I said, grimly. But he had gone down, which gave me a chance to get back my breath. Not long, however, did he remain down. I felt and saw the line rising.

"Keep him on the starboard quarter, Peter. Run up on him now. Bob, your chance for pictures!"

I was quick to grasp that the swordfish kept coming to our left, and repeatedly on that run I had Peter swerve in the same direction, so as to keep the line out on the quarter. Once we were almost in danger. But I saw it. I got back all but 100 yards of line. Close enough. He kept edging in ahead of us, and once we had to turn halfway to keep the stern toward him. But he quickly shot ahead again. He was fast, angry, heavy. How his tail pounded the leader. The short, powerful strokes vibrated all over me.

"Port—port, Peter," I yelled, and even then, so quick was the swordfish, that I missed seeing two leaps directly in front of the boat, as he curved ahead of us. But the uproar from Bob and the others was enough for me.

As the launch sheered around, however, I saw the third of that series of leaps —and if anything could have loosed my chained emotion on the instant, that unbelievably swift and savage plunge would have done so. But I was clamped. No more dreaming! No more bliss! I was there to think and act. And I did not even thrill.

By the same tactics the swordfish sped off a hundred yards of line, and by the same we recovered them and drew close to see him leap again, only 200 feet off our starboard, a little ahead, and of all the magnificent fish I have ever seen he excelled. His power to leap was beyond credence. Captain M.'s big fish, that broke off two years before, did not move like this one. True, he was larger. Nevertheless, this swordfish was so huge that when he came out in dazzling, swift flight, my crew went simply mad. This was the first time my natives had been flabbergasted. They were as excited, as carried away, as Bob and John. Peter, however, stuck at the wheel as if he were after a wounded whale which might any instant turn upon him. I did not need to warn Peter not to let that fish hit us. If he had he would have made splinters out of that launch. Many an anxious glance did I cast toward Cappy's boat, 2 or 3 miles distant. Why did he not come? The peril was too great for us to be alone at the mercy of that beautiful brute, if he charged us either by accident or design. But Captain could not locate us, owing to the misty atmosphere, and missed seeing this grand fish in action.

How sensitive I was to the strain on the line! A slight slackening directed all my faculties to ascertain the cause. The light at the moment was bad, and I had to peer closely to see the line. He had not slowed up, but he was curving back and to the left again—the cunning strategist!

"Port, Peter—port!" I commanded.

We sheered, but not enough. With the wheel hard over, one engine full speed ahead, the other in reverse, we wheeled like a top. But not swift enough for that Tahitian swordfish.

The line went under the bow.

"Reverse!" I called, sharply.

We pounded on the waves, slowly caught hold, slowed, started back. Then I ordered the clutches thrown out. It was a terrible moment, and took all my will not to yield to sudden blank panic.

When my line ceased to pay out, I felt that it had been caught on the keel. And as I was only human, I surrendered for an instant to agony. But no! That line was new, strong. The swordfish was slowing. I could yet avert catastrophe.

"Quick, Pete. Feels as if the line is caught," I cried, unhooking my harness from the reel.

Peter complied with my order. "Yes, by cripes! It's caught. Overboard, Jimmy! Jump in! Loose the line!"

The big Tahitian in a flash was out of his shirt and bending to dive.

"No! Hold on, Jimmy!" I yelled. Only a moment before I had seen sharks milling about. "Grab him, John!"

They held Jimmy back, and a second later I plunged my rod over the side into the water, so suddenly that the weight of it and the reel nearly carried me overboard.

"Hold me—or it's all—day!" I panted, and I thought that if my swordfish had fouled on keel or propellers I did not care if I did fall in.

"Let go my line, Peter," I said, making ready to extend the rod to the limit of my arms.

"I can feel him moving, sir," shouted Peter, excitedly. "By jingo! He's coming! It's free! It wasn't caught!"

That was such intense relief I could not recover my balance. They had to haul me back into the boat. I shook all over as one with the palsy, so violently that Peter had to help me get the rod in the rod socket of the chair. An instant later came the strong, electrifying pull on the line, the scream of the reel. Never such sweet music! He was away from the boat—on a tight line! The revulsion of feeling was so great that it propelled me instantaneously back into my former state of hard, cold, calculating, and critical judgment, and iron determination.

"Close shave, sir," said Peter, cheerily. "It was like when a whale turns on me, after I've struck him. We're all clear, sir, and after him again."

The gray pall of rain bore down on us. I was hot and wet with sweat, and asked for a raincoat to keep me from being chilled. Enveloped in this I went on with my absorbing toil. Blisters began to smart on my hands, especially one on the inside of the third finger of my right hand, certainly a queer place to raise one. But it bothered me, hampered me. Bob put on his rubber coat and, protecting his camera more than himself, sat out on the bow waiting.

My swordfish, with short, swift runs, took us 5 miles farther out, and then, welcome to see, brought us back, all this while without leaping, though he broke water on the surface a number of times. He never sounded after that first dive. The bane of an angler is a sounding fish, and here in Tahitian waters, where there is no bottom, it spells catastrophe. The marlin slowed up and took to milling, a sure sign of a rattled fish. Then he rose again, and it happened to be when the rain had ceased. He made one high, frantic jump about 200 yards ahead of us, and then threshed on the surface, sending the bloody spray high. All on board were quick to see that sign of weakening, of tragedy—blood.

Peter turned to say, coolly: "He's our meat, sir."

I did not allow any such idea to catch in my consciousness. Peter's words, like those of Bob and John, and the happy jargon of the Tahitians, had no effect upon me whatever.

It rained half an hour longer, during which we repeated several phases of the fight, except slower on the part of the marlin. In all he leaped fifteen times clear of the water. I did not attempt to keep track of his threshings.

After the rain passed I had them remove the rubber coat, which hampered me, and settled to a slower fight. About this time the natives again sighted sharks coming around the boat. I did not like this. Uncanny devils! They were the worst of these marvelous fishing waters. But Peter said: "They don't know what it's all about. They'll go away."

They did go away long enough to relieve me of dread, then they trooped back, lean, yellow-backed, white-finned wolves.

We ought to have a rifle," I said. "Sharks won't stay to be shot at, whether hit or not."

It developed that my swordfish had leaped too often and run too swiftly to make an extremely long fight. I had expected a perceptible weakening and recognized it. So did Peter, who smiled gladly. Then I taxed myself to the utmost and spared nothing. In another hour, which seemed only a few minutes, I had him whipped and coming. I could lead him. The slow strokes of his tail took no more line. Then he quit wagging.

"Clear for action, Pete. Give John the wheel. I see the end of the double line. There!"

I heaved and wound. With the end of the double line over my reel I screwed the drag up tight. The finish was in sight. Suddenly I felt tugs and jerks at my fish.

"Sharks!" I yelled, hauling away for dear life.

Everybody leaned over the gunwale. I saw a wide, sheery mass, greenish silver, crossed by purple bars. It moved. It weaved. But I could drag it easily.

"Manu! Manu!" shrilled the natives.

"Heave!" shouted Peter, as he peered down.

In a few more hauls I brought the swivel of the leader out of the water.

"By God! They're on him!" roared Peter, hauling on the leader. "Get the lance, boat hook, gaffs—anything. Fight them off!"

Suddenly Peter let go the leader and, jerking the big gaff from Jimmy, he lunged out. There was a single enormous roar of water and a sheeted splash. I saw a blue tail so wide I thought I was crazy. It threw a 6-foot yellow shark into the air!

"Rope his tail, Charley," yelled Peter. "Rest of you fight the tigers off."

I unhooked the harness and stood up to lean over the gunwales. A swordfish rolled on the surface, extending from forward of the cockpit to 2 yards or more beyond the end. His barred body was as large as that of an ox. And to it sharks were clinging, tearing, out on the small part near the tail. Charley looped the great tail, and that was a signal for the men to get into action.

One big shark had a hold just below the anal fin. How cruel, brutish, ferocious! Peter made a powerful stab at him. The big lance head went clear through his neck. He gulped and sank. Peter stabbed another underneath, and still another. Jimmy was tearing at sharks with the long-handled gaff, and when he hooked one he was nearly hauled overboard. Charley threshed with his rope; John did valiant work with the boat hook, and Bob frightened me by his daring fury, as he leaned far over to hack with the cleaver.

We keep these huge cleavers on board to use in case we are attacked by an octopus, which is not a far-fetched fear at all. It might happen. Bob is lean and long and powerful. Also he was mad. Whack! He slashed a shark that let go and appeared to slip up into the air.

"On the nose, Bob. Split his nose⁻ That's the weak spot on a shark," yelled Peter.

Next shot Bob cut deep into the round stub nose of this big, black shark—the only one of that color I saw—and it had the effect of dynamite. More sharks appeared under Bob, and I was scared so stiff I could not move.

"Take that! And that!" sang out Bob, in a kind of fierce ecstasy. "You will try to eat our swordfish—dirty, stinking pups! Aha! On your beak, huh! Zambesi! Wow, Pete, that sure is the place."

"Look out, Bob! For God's sake—look out!" I begged, frantically, after I saw a shark almost reach Bob's arm.

Peter swore at him. But there was no keeping Bob off those cannibals. Blood and water flew all over us. The smell of sharks in any case was not pleasant, and with them spouting blood, and my giant swordfish rolling in blood, the stench that arose was sickening. They appeared to come from all directions, especially from under the boat. Finally I had to get into the thick of it, armed only with a gaff handle minus the gaff. I did hit one a stunning welt over the nose, making him let go. If we had all had lances like the one Peter was using so effectively, we would have made short work of them. One jab from Peter either killed or disabled a shark. The crippled ones swam about belly up or lopsided, and stuck up their heads as if to get air. Of all the bloody messes I ever saw, that was the worst.

"Makes me remember—the war!" panted Peter, grimly.

And it was Peter who whipped the flock of ravenous sharks off. Chuck! went the heavy lance, and that was the end of another. My heart apparently had ceased to function. To capture that glorious fish, only to see it devoured before my eyes!

"Run ahead, Johnny, out of this bloody slaughter hole, so we can see," called Peter.

John ran forward a few rods into clear water. A few sharks followed, one of which did so to his death. The others grew wary, they swam around.

"We got 'em licked! Say, I had the wind up me," said Peter. "Who ever saw the like of that? The bloody devils!"

Bob took the lance from Peter, and stuck the most venturesome of the remaining sharks. It appeared then that we had the situation in hand again. My swordfish was still with us, his beautiful body bitten here and there, his tail amost severed, but not irreparably lacerated. All around the boat wounded sharks were lolling with fins out, sticking ugly heads up, to gulp and dive.

There came a let-down then, and we exchanged the natural elation we felt. The next thing was to see what was to be done with the monster, now we had him. I vowed we could do nothing but tow him to camp. But Peter made the attempt to lift him on the boat. All six of us, hauling on the ropes, could not get his back half out of the water. So we tied him fast and started campward.

Halfway in we espied Cappy's boat. He headed for us, no doubt attracted by all the flags the boys strung up. There was one, a red and blue flag that I had never flown. Jimmy tied this on his bamboo pole and tied that high on the mast. Cappy bore quickly down on us, and ran alongside, he and all of his crew vastly excited.

"What is it? Lamming big broadbill?" he yelled.

My fish did resemble a broadbill in his long, black beak, his widespread flukes, his purple color, shading so dark now that the broad bars showed indistinctly. Besides, he lay belly up.

"No, Cappy. He's a giant Tahitian striped marlin, one of the kind we've tried so hard to catch," I replied, happily.

"By gad! So he is. What a monster! I'm glad, old man. My word, I'm glad! I didn't tell you, but I was discouraged. Now we're sitting on top of the world again."

"Rather," replied Peter, for me. "We've got him, Captain, and he's some fish. But the damn sharks nearly beat us."

"So I see. They are bad. I saw a number. Well, I had a 400-pound swordie throw my hook at me, and I've raised two more, besides a sailfish. Fish out here again. Have you got any fresh bonito?"

We threw our bait into his boat and headed for camp again. Cappy waved, a fine, happy smile on his tanned face, and called: "He's a wolloper, old man. I'm sure glad."

"I owe it to you, Cap," I called after him.

We ran for the nearest pass, necessarily fairly slowly with all that weight on our stern. The boat listed half a foot and tried to run in a circle. It was about 1 o'clock, and the sky began to clear. Bob raved about what pictures he would take.

"Oh, boy, what a fish! If only Romer had been with us! I saw him hit the bait, and I nearly fell off the deck. I couldn't yell. Wasn't it a wonderful fight? Everything just right. I was scared when he tried to go under the boat."

"So was I, Bob," I replied, remembering that crucial moment.

"I wasn't," said Peter. "The other day when we had the boat out at Papeete I shaved all the rough places off her keel. So I felt safe. What puts the wind up me is the way these Tahitian swordfish can jump. Fast? My word! This fellow beat any small marlin I ever saw in my life."

I agreed with Peter and we discussed this startling and amazing power of the giant marlin. I put forward the conviction that the sole reason for their incredible speed and ferocity was that evolution, the struggle to survive, was magnified in these crystal-clear waters around Tahiti. We talked over every phase of the fight, and that which pleased me most was the old whaler's tribute:

"You were there, sir. That cool and quick! On the strike that dry line scared me stiff. But afterward I had no doubt of the result."

We were all wringing wet, and some of us as bloody as wet. I removed my wet clothes and gave myself a brisk rub. I could not stand erect, and my hands hurt —pangs I endured gratefully.

We arrived at the dock about 3 o'clock, to find all our camp folk and a hundred natives assembled to greet us. Up and down had sped the news of the flags waving.

I went ashore and waited impatiently to see the marlin hauled out on the sand. It took a dozen men, all wading, to drag him in. And when they at last got him under the tripod, I approached, knowing I was to have a shock and prepared for it.

But at that he surprised me in several ways. His color had grown darker and the bars showed only palely. Still they were there, and helped to identify him as one of the striped species. He was bigger than I had ever hoped for. And his body was long and round. This roundness appeared to be an extraordinary feature for a marlin spearfish. His bill was 3 feet long, not slender and rapier-like, as in the ordinary marlin, or short and bludgeon-like, as in the black marlin. It was about the same size all the way from tip to where it swelled into his snout, and slightly flattened on top—a superb and remarkable weapon. The fact that the great striped spearfish Captain Mitchell lost in 1928 had a long, curved bill, like a rhinoceros, did not deter me from pronouncing this of the same species. Right there I named this species, "Giant Tahitian Striped Marlin." Singularly, he had a small head, only a foot or more from where his beak broadened to his eye, which, however, was as large as that of a broadbill swordfish. There were two gill openings on each side, a feature I never observed before in any swordfish, the one toward the mouth being considerably smaller than the regular gill opening. From there his head sheered up to his humped back, out of which stood an enormous dorsal fin. He had a straight-under maxillary. The pectoral fins were large, wide, like wings, and dark in color. The fin-like appendages under the back of his lower jaw were only about 6 inches long and quite slender. In other spearfish these are long, and in sailfish sometimes exceed 2 feet and more. His body, for 8 feet, was as symmetrical and round as that of a good, big stallion. According to my deduction, it was a male fish. He carried this roundness back to his anal fin, and there further accuracy was impossible because the sharks had eaten away most of the flesh from these fins to his tail. On one side, too, they had torn out enough meat to fill a bushel basket. His tail was the most splendid of all the fish tails I ever observed. It was a perfect bent bow, slender, curved, dark purple in color, finely ribbed, and expressive of the tremendous speed and strength the fish had exhibited.

This tail had a spread of 5 feet 2 inches. His length was 14 feet 2 inches. His girth was 6 feet 9 inches. And his weight, as he was, 1,040 pounds.

Every drop of blood had been drained from his body, and this with at least 200 pounds of flesh the sharks took would have fetched his true and natural weight to 1,250 pounds. But I thought it best to have the record stand at the actual weight, without allowance for what he had lost. Nevertheless, despite my satisfaction and elation, as I looked up at this appalling shape, I could not help but remember the giant marlin Captain had lost in 1928, which we estimated at 22 or 23 feet, or the 20-foot one I had raised at Tautira, or the 28-foot one the natives had seen repeatedly alongside their canoes. And I thought of the prodigious leaps and astounding fleetness of this one I had caught. "My heaven!" I breathed. "What would a bigger one do?"

He Makes the Finest Rifle Barrels in the World

Edwin Teale

November 1934

It wasn't my good fortune to work with Edwin Way Teale when he was
contributing so many superb stories and photographs to OUTDOOR LIFE. I
came to the magazine too late for that, 1951, the year that *North with the
Spring*, first volume of his series *The American Seasons* appeared. I have
never read a review of any of the abundant writings of this author, naturalist,
and photographer that was anything but laudatory. It's always apparent to
the reader why he was awarded the John Burroughs Medal for
distinguished nature writing. I think readers will find this selection an
entertaining change of pace.

If you want to visit the place where the world's finest rifle barrels are made,
you have to climb four flights of fire-escape stairs zigzagging up the face of a red
brick warehouse in Jersey City, N. J. At the top, you knock at a begrimed door
bearing the faint letters: H. M. POPE.

Behind that door, for more than a quarter of a century, Harry Pope has been
turning out precision barrels that have made him famous. A dozen times they
have won in the Olympic Games. Again and again they have smashed world's
records. When Gustave Schweizer, not long ago, ran up the phenomenal record
of eighty-seven bulls-eyes at 1000 yeards in a Peekskill, N. Y., match, it was a
Pope barrel that directed the bullets at the distant target. When the five-man
American team captured the international rifle match at Milan, Italy, a few years
ago, defeating crack shots from Europe and South America, it relied upon Pope
barrels to carry it to victory.

Harry Pope never advertises. Yet, orders come from all over the United States,
from most of the countries of Europe, and from as far away as Australia, India,
and China. Wherever lovers of fine guns meet, the name Pope is familiar.

Several minutes pass after you knock. Then you hear the shuffling of feet, the
lock clicks, and the door opens. A stooped little man with a long white beard, a
black mechanic's cap perched on the back of his head, and two pairs of spectacles—a gold-rimmed over a silver-rimmed pair—resting on his nose, peers out
and invites you in. He is Harry Pope, an old-time craftsman in an age of mass
production.

Inside the shop, you follow him down a narrow lane between dust-covered
boxes, trunks, papers, yellowed magazines, toolkits, sheaves of rifle barrels, hogs-
heads of dusty gun stocks. A worn black leather couch is half buried under odds
and ends. A small table, piled high with papers, looks like a haycock, white at the
top and yellow toward the bottom. Pinned to it is a printed sign: "Don't lean
against this table. If these papers are spilled, there will be Hell to pay."

The only flat object in the room that is not loaded down is a single board.
Pope keeps it standing upright in a corner. Over two boxes, it forms an emergency table where he can lay his tools when working.

"You might think this is confusion," he says as you reach his workbench, almost hidden under odds and ends, "but what looks like order to other people looks like confusion to me. This room is like a filing cabinet. I can put my hands on anything in it, even if I haven't seen it for ten years. But if anybody moves something as much as three inches, it's as good as lost."

In the twenty-seven years he has been in the same building, he has washed his windows twice. He believes the accumulation of grime diffuses the light and enables him to see better. One of his windows he never will wash. It is covered with penciled notes. Half a dozen years ago, data he had placed on a scrap of paper blew out the window. Afterwards, he made it a rule to jot down important notes on the walls or window where they can't blow away.

Over his workbench hangs a sign, various words underlined in red. It reads:

"No delivery promised. Take your work when well done or take it elsewhere. When? If you must know when I will be through with your work, the answer is now. Take your work away. I don't want it. I have no way of knowing when. I work seventeen hours a day. Daily interruptions average 1½ hours. Dark weather sets me back still more. I'm human. I'm tired. I refuse longer to be worried by promises that circumstances do not allow me to keep."

The lower edge of the sign is smudged with greasy fingerprints, records of the many times he has jerked the pasteboard from the wall to hold before non-observant customers who persisted in knowing when. In fact, most of the guns that come in are now accepted with the express understanding that they will be fitted with new barrels when and if Pope ever gets time to do it. More orders are turned down than are accepted, yet between 200 and 300 guns are piled up ahead of him. At seventy-three, he is working seventeen hours a day and answering correspondence after ten o'clock at night. He makes barrels for pistols and revolvers when he has to. But what he wants to do is make rifle barrels.

After hours, when the warehouse is closed, customers who know the procedure stand on the street corner below and yell: "Pope! Hey, Pope!" until he paddles down and lets them in. Everybody in the neighborhood knows him and when you set up the shout they all join in until he pokes his head out the window four stories above. He never has had a telephone and he frequently brings a supply of food and sleeps in his shop until his grub gives out.

Not long ago, a man brought him a gun he wanted fixed. He found Pope bent over a vise filing on a piece of steel. When he started to explain what he wanted, he was told: "Don't talk to me now!" A little later, he broached the subject of his visit a second time. Pope shouted: "I said don't talk to me now!" By the time Pope laid down his file, the customer was packing up his things and muttering something about "a swell way to treat a customer."

It was an obvious statement. But, what the man did not know was that Pope had been working for two solid weeks making a special tool to rifle the barrel of an odd-caliber gun. He had filed it down to two ten-thousandths of an inch of its exact diameter and the light was just right for finishing it. If an interruption had made him file a hair's breadth beyond the mark, his whole two weeks' labor would have been lost.

All his rifling is done by hand. He judges what is going on inside the barrel by the feel and the sound of the cutting tools. To rifle out the inside of a .22-caliber barrel takes about seven hours. The cutter is fitted with a wedge and screwhead so the feed, or depth it cuts, can be varied from time to time. The steel shaving removed from the grooves at first is about 1/5000th of an inch thick. Later, when the end of the work is near and there is danger of cutting too far, less than 1/40,000 of an inch is removed during a "pass." It takes about 120 passes to cut each of the eight grooves within the barrel.

All his rifle barrels are drilled from solid stock, special oil-tempered fine-grain steel being employed. For fifteen years, he has been getting his steel from the same company after trying almost every kind on the market. Some batches of steel cut more easily than others and he has to "humor the stock." The worst steel he ever got came during the last days of the World War. It was so full of grit and cinders he had to sharpen a reamer fourteen times to get through one barrel. Ordinarily he can get through twelve on a single sharpening.

When he nears the end of a job, he pushes a bullet through the barrel and with a micrometer measures the exact depth of the grooves recorded on the lead. Sometimes it is two weeks before he is satisfied with a barrel he has produced. To him, they are almost like children and he will never do another job for a customer who abuses one through ignorance or neglect. On the other hand, he has made as many as nine barrels for a single individual who appreciated fine guns.

The high-pressure, smokeless ammunition and jacketed bullets used today are especially hard on the inside of barrels. Three or four thousand rounds is all they can stand. Owners of Pope barrels usually save them for important contests and practice with other rifles. In contrast, Pope has a .33-caliber black-powder rifle that has been fired 125,000 times and is still in almost as good condition as it was in 1892, when it was first made.

All told, Pope has turned out more than 8,000 hand-tooled barrels, fitting them on almost every make of gun produced in America and on many of those manufactured abroad. Most of the demand now is for .22- and .30-caliber barrels with only an occasional .32 or .38.

Thirty years ago, Pope records for off-hand shooting were almost as famous as Pope barrels. Once over a period of several days, he made 696 consecutive bulls-eyes at 200 yards and another time he placed fifty consecutive shots all within three and three fourths inches of dead center. His fifty-shot record, made shortly after the turn of the century, was 467. Today it is only 470. His hundred-shot record was 917. Today, the record is only 922.

But for a fluke during a match at Springfield, Mass., on March 2, 1903, Pope would still hold the world's record for 200 yards on the standard American target. He was putting bullet after bullet into the bulls-eye, when a spectator disturbed him by asking questions. He forgot to remove the false muzzle, a one-inch auxiliary barrel placed on the end of the gun to protect the real barrel when the bullet was rammed home, and did not see it when aiming through the telescope sight. The shot blew the false muzzle off and counted as a miss. In spite of this break in luck, he ran up a score of 467 for the fifty shots, was high man for the day, and advanced the existing record four points! Some time later, after his gun had cooled off and conditions had changed, he tried an extra shot just to see what his score might have been without the miss. He scored an eight. If that could have been added to his mark for the day, the total would have been 475, five points beyond the world's record in 1934!

As he tells you of these old-time matches, he fishes yellowed score cards from the inner pockets of an ancient wallet or digs into a pile of odds and ends like a squirrel finding a nut buried in a forest and brings forth a crumbling target riddled by his fire decades ago.

From time to time, as he talks, he lights a cigarette with a cigar lighter. But it is no ordinary lighter. It is a glass syrup jug a foot high filled with soaked cotton batting and having a flint wheel soldered to its top. One filling will last a year.

As long as he can remember, Pope has been interested in guns. He was born in 1861 at Walpole, N. H. By the time he was ten years old, he was running errands for a firm in Boston. Every noon he would duck up alleys from one sporting-goods store to another to gaze at the firearms in the windows. When he was twelve, he had one of the largest collections of free catalogs in the world. He wrote to European as well as American manufacturers for pamphlets and price lists.

In 1881 he graduated from the Massachusetts Institute of Technology with an engineering degree. For twenty-three years afterwards he was in the bicycle business, ending as superintendent of a plant at Hartford, Conn.

While he was turning out bicycles, he worked with guns on the side. At least twice a week, he used to get up at three o'clock in the morning, climb on his high-wheel bicycle, and pedal out to a target range, his muzzle-loader over one shoulder and a fish basket filled with ammunition and targets slung over the other. After shooting for two hours, he would pedal back uphill to town and be ready for work at seven.

When he traded in his .40-caliber Remington for a new .42-40 which had appeared on the market, he found himself confronted with a mystery which led him into making barrels of his own. His shooting dropped off as soon as he began to use the new gun. He blamed himself at first. Then he began making tests of various loads, bullets, and powders. He built a machine rest for the gun to take the human element out of the experiments. In the end, he discovered that the trouble lay in the pitch of the rifling. The twist was so slow it didn't spin the lead fast enough to keep the bullet traveling head-on. The slug was actually turning somersaults.

Working nights on an old foot lathe in his basement, he turned out his first gun barrel in 1884, and fitted it to the defective gun. His shooting scores not only equalled his old marks with the Remington but exceeded them. Some of his friends at the local gun club wanted barrels on their guns. Immediately, their scores jumped. The records made by the club attracted attention all over the country and letters of inquiry began coming in. In 1895, Pope took a few outside orders. In two weeks, he had enough to keep him busy nights for six months.

A few years later he headed for California. San Francisco was then the center of shooting interest in the United States. He set the opening day of his gun shop for the eighteenth of April, 1906. At five o'clock in the morning, the great earthquake and fire struck the city and wiped out his shop and everything it contained. Returning east, he settled down at 18 Morris Street, Jersey City, in the building he still occupies.

Only once in his half-century of handling guns has he had an accident. A friend asked him to fit a rifle barrel to one side of a double-barreled shotgun so he could hunt deer with the rifle side and ducks and small game with the shotgun side. Pope finished it just in time to catch a train for a week-end visit and hunting trip without being able to give it shop tests.

The next day, he took the curious combination gun out for a trial. On the first shot, the rifle side drove the firing pin back out of the gun almost with the speed of a bullet. Only the fact that it struck the stock a glancing blow and a cross grain deflected its course kept it from striking Pope squarely in the right eye. As it was, the spinning piece of steel, an inch long and a quarter of an inch thick, hit flat just above his left eyebrow, burying itself in the bone. After a surgeon extracted it, Pope went on with his hunting trip and bagged the first buck shot by the party.

It is just fifty years this spring since Pope made his first gun barrel. After half a century of machine-age progress in which most manufacturing has been turned over to automatic mechanisms, Pope remains a New England mechanic. Still using home-made tools, still employing time-worn methods, he is producing still, in his high-perched little workshop, gunbarrels that lead the world.

Are Posted Waters Free?

Ben East

July 1936

Ben East sold his first story in 1921, to *Outers' Recreation*, a magazine later absorbed by OUTDOOR LIFE. He's a life-long resident of Michigan (b. 1898), but has spent great spans of time traveling throughout the North American continent for the nearly one thousand stories and six books he has written. He was outdoor editor for Michigan's Booth Newspapers for twenty years until he became OUTDOOR LIFE's Midwest field editor in 1946. He was nurtured on a cane pole and a .22. He made the first color film of the Alaskan sea otter and won the Boone & Crockett Club's big-game photography contest in 1948 for a sequence of Alaska brown bears. He won membership in both the Explorers Club and the Adventurers Club for his lecturing, and he once spoke to seventy thousand persons in five evenings. His hard-hitting conservation articles have brought him many prestigious awards, including a citation by both houses of the Michigan legislature.

If you are a fisherman, living in Texas or Maine, California or Minnesota, chances are a hundred to one you never heard of Gideon Gerhardt, yet he rendered you a big service by going fishing one day in 1925. Gideon, wading Pine River in west Michigan, did not know he was embarking on one of the most momentous trout-fishing trips in history, or that, as he braced his legs against the rushing stream, he was about to make angling history, or that the day would come when anglers in Oregon and Florida and many points in between would have cause to thank him.

He had climbed over the three strands of barbed wire a short distance ·upstream, and passed warning signs that said, "No Fishing." He knew he trespassed in waters where he was not wanted. Still he firmly believed he had a right to fish those waters.

Considerable water has run over the clay ledges of the Pine since Gideon went fishing that morning in 1925. Many a creel of trout has been taken from the river, and the things that have happened as an outgrowth of Gideon Gerhardt's fishing trip should bring a flush of joy to the cheeks of anglers in every state, for on that May morning, Gideon Gerhardt, the Reed City merchant, was about to wrest a Magna Carta of fishing rights from the courts of state and nation, he was about to hew out a clear definition of how much right the public has in public waters.

The barbed wire that Gerhardt had clambered through, and the warning signs he had chosen to ignore, had been put up by Frank Collins, of Toledo, Ohio, a gentleman of wealth and very positive opinions. Among the opinions was one that anybody, when he purchased land along a trout river, was entitled to do all the fishing in the section of the river bordered by his land. Collins had acquired 120 acres of land on the Pine, where it flows through the cutover lands of Lake County, Mich., not far from the hamlet of Luther. He had strung barbed wire from shore to shore at the boundaries of his land, had erected signs, and was ready to enjoy his private fishing.

In doing these things, he overlooked two or three pertinent facts. Among them, was the fact that Pine River had been a public stream, open to use by all and sundry, since the days when it was famous for its grayling fishing, that it had been used repeatedly for log drives in the roaring days of lumbering, and that about four and a half million trout had been planted in it by the State Conservative Department, at the expense of the fishermen of Michigan.

Gideon Gerhardt knew these things. He had fished the Pine for twenty years, and he reasoned the river was still his to follow. And he followed it.

Collins acted promptly. He sued his unwanted guest for damages by trespass. The local justice ruled in Gerhardt's favor. Collins promptly appealed the case.

The Izaak Walton League was then in its early heyday in Michigan, and its Grand Rapids chapter included some of the state's most far-sighted sportsmen. It was plain to them that the issues involved were far bigger than the mere protection of Gerhardt against a minor judgment. If Collins won, they realized, the public could be shut out forever from trout rivers by the owners of the land on the banks. A vast majority of the stream frontage on every famous trout river of Michigan is privately owned. If the courts finally decided in favor of Frank Collins, it meant that, overnight, barriers could be strung and "No Trespassing" signs put up on the Pere Marquette, the Au Sable, the Boardman, and a host of others equally dear to fishermen.

The Grand Rapids chapter, therefore, stepped into the breach. Capable attorneys went to the aid of Gerhardt, providing him with a brilliant array of counsel as the battle went into circuit court. A jury again held him guiltless of trespass. Ignoring the verdict, however, the presiding judge entered a judgment of six cents —"nominal damages" under Michigan trespass law—in Collins' favor. This time it was Gerhardt, backed by the Izaak Walton League, who appealed to the State Supreme Court.

The Collins-Gerhardt case by then was famous in Michigan, one of the great public controversies of the decade. Every fisherman knew about it, and talked about, realizing that the future of his trout fishing hung on the outcome. It was the leading topic of conversation through the summer of 1926, discussed with equal fervor in cross-roads stores, and the directors' rooms of banks.

The case went to the State Supreme Court in April of that year, eleven months after Gerhardt incurred Collins's wrath. Not until December did the court render its decision. But the decision was a milestone on the long road to protect the rights of the public. The court held Gerhardt not guilty of trespass. He was fishing where he had a right to fish, the decision said, and, in assessing nominal damages, the lower-court had erred.

In addition to reversing the lower court, the supreme bench settled several other important issues. It decided that Pine River was navigable because it had been used for floating logs, and it pointed out that, under the ordinance of 1787, governing the old Northwest Territory, of which Michigan is part, the United States held in trust for the use of the people the waters of navigable rivers and the soil beneath them. When Michigan entered the Union, the court declared, she became vested with the same rights.

"The Pine River is navigable," the supreme court concluded. "In its waters, the people have the common right of fishing. So long as water flows and fish swim in Pine River, the people may fish at their pleasure in any part of the stream, subject only to regulations imposed by the State. In this right they are protected by a high, solemn, and perpetual trust which it is the duty of the state forever to maintain. Of course, in exercising this right, people cannot go upon the uplands of riparian owners, in order to gain access to the water."

The battle was won. The public had gained the right to fish in the public waters of Michigan. The highest court in the state had cleared Gideon Gerhardt of the charge that he had trespassed when he climbed through Collins's barbed wire barricade and ignored the "No Fishing" signs, continuing his way down a river that had for decades been a public highway.

But the victory was still confined to the State. It had no significance outside. What Gideon Gerhardt or anyone else could do in Pine River was not likely to have much bearing on what John Jones and his brother could do on the rivers, navigable or otherwise, of the other forty-seven states of the country. And there matters might have rested had it not been for the firmness of Collins's opinions, and his determination.

The Michigan Supreme Court had said that anglers had a right to wade or boat the Pine, but it had also said that those anglers had no right to step out upon the land owned by Collins, and it had said nothing about what he might, or might not, do to make it tough for fishermen who invaded his domain.

In the summer of 1925, considerable land on both banks of the Pine adjoining the Collins acres was acquired by the Ne-Bo-Shone Association, an Ohio corporation to which Collins belonged. In fact, enough land passed into the hands of this association to give it control of something like eight continuous miles of the river shore. Eight miles is a little too far for a day's fishing in waders. And, since anglers could enter the river above the Collins and Ne-Bo-Shone property but could not leave until they were below again, wading fishermen were effectively kept out.

Boating parties continued to run the river in quest of trout, however, and from those parties, indignant stories began to drift down state—stories of towering log jams, that grew bigger month by month, of armed guards, that kept pace along the bank with the canoe of fishermen in the river to make sure no one trespassed on the upland.

Other stories had it that the guards heaved stones into pools ahead of anglers; that lunches disappeared from canoes anchored in midstream while their occupants fished near by in waders; that cans of bait were filled with water; that canoes swamped if left unattended; that guards on horseback rode through pools ahead of anglers to foul them.

Irritating practices those, on a river held forever free by the highest court in the state. And, before the affair was finished, the stories were to be affirmed by sworn witnesses on the stand in a United States court.

In the fall of 1932 public indignation boiled over, and the Lake County Board of Supervisors was petitioned to clear the Pine of its log jams within the Ne-Bo-Shone property. Alfred Sellers, chief Ne-Bo-Shone guard, was by that time a member of the board of supervisors. The board took no action, and angry fishermen then appealed to Col. George Hogarth, Michigan's two-fisted, square-jawed director of conservation, to clear the Pine. In October, 1932, Hogarth wrote Collins and his associates a letter. It wasn't very long, but it was to the point.

"You are advised," Hogarth wrote, "that it is the desire of the Conservation Commission that you proceed at once to restore the navigability of Pine River. You are further advised that failure on your part to carry out this request by Nov. 15 will result in the Conservation Commission requesting the attorney general to institute proceedings to compel the removal of these obstructions."

Once more no delay marked the actions of Collins and his fellow members of the Ne-Bo-Shone Association. Because they resided in Ohio and the case involved Michigan officials and residents, there was a chance for them to go before a United States court, in the hope of doing what they had failed to do in Michigan courts. They seized the chance. Before Hogarth's deadline of November 15, arrived, they brought suit before Judge Fred M. Raymond, of the United States District Court for western Michigan, to restrain either state officials or private individuals from interfering with the obstructions in the Pine. Thus began the Ne-Bo-Shone case, which reopened and retried virtually every issue involved in the Collins-Gerhardt controversy, with one important difference. This time the fishermen of Michigan were battling in a federal court. Whatever the outcome now, it would affect anglers throughout the nation. No matter who won, the victory would determine what fishermen could or could not do in streams a thousand miles from the Pine.

The case was heard in August, 1933, without a jury. Witnesses repeated the stories about armed guards, of rocks and chunks of wood, thrown into pools ahead of anglers, of drowned bait and swamped canoes. Most frequently of all were repeated tales of the five towering jams of jagged logs and stumps that made the trip through the Ne-Bo-Shone lands a hazardous undertaking.

Fred A. Westerman, chief of the fisheries division of the State Conservation Department, told of the trout Michigan had planted in the Pine, beginning in 1874. Gray-haired lumberjacks recounted stories of half-forgot log drives down the river long before the turn of the present century to prove it was navigable. Ne-Bo-Shone witnesses contended the log jams had formed in the river of their own accord, and served as valuable fish shelters, although they admitted that many rolls of steel cable had been used to anchor the jams in place. And throughout the trial, Ne-Bo-Shone attorneys sought to show that Pine River was not navigable, and that the public therefore had no right in it.

While the trial was in progress, I ran the Pine by canoe, through the Ne-Bo-Shone property, to see the log jams for myself. They were there, all right, five of them, made fast to shore with steel cables. George Bradford, a Baldwin guide and a defendant in the case, took me on the river trip. A short distance within the Collins property, we encountered the first snag, a long piece of steel rail, lying on a shallow riffle, one end bedded in stones, the other just beneath the surface, ready to rip the guts out of any canoe unfortunate enough to strike it. Then the log jams began.

The first one wasn't bad. We got the canoe through with no great difficulty, taking to the river in our waders, and boosting the boat over the barrier. The second jam was a densely packed tangle of logs, stumps, and debris, filling the river from bank to bank, and rising six or eight feet above the water. Sharp spikes and knots in abundance made the carry over the uncertain footing of the logs a ticklish business.

Along the top of the third jam, we found a huge elm tree, felled and cabled in place untrimmed, an effective and wretched barrier to the passage of a canoe. The fourth was the highest and most jagged of the lot, rising ten to fifteen feet above the river, its top a jack-straw mass of logs and stumps. The fifth, like the first, was easier to get through. Two Ne-Bo-Shone guards followed us every foot of the way through the property, but they had no guns.

In February, 1934, Judge Raymond announced his decision. The Pine, he said, was navigable, the people of Michigan had a right to wade it or boat it for the purpose of taking fish, and the Ne-Bo-Shone jams must go.

"Throughout the centuries," Judge Raymond declared, "the oceans, lakes, rivers, and tributary streams have been highly useful to mankind, and, to a considerable degree, indispensable for fishing, travel and commerce. In modern times, not only are these resources used for various industrial enterprises, but, with the congestion and stress of urban life, has come necessity for rest and recreation. The utilitarian uses of the waters have been broadened or supplanted to meet these other important needs. With increasing private ownership of lands bordering lakes and streams, the average citizen finds it difficult or impossible to provide himself and his family with opportunities for rest and play. There should, in these conditions, be no narrowing of rights hitherto recognized. The citizen

102

ought not, for other than the most compelling reasons, be deprived of those blessings which nature's bounty has provided.

"It is difficult to see why the right to navigate should include, as an incident thereto, the right to take fish. Both rights arise from the fact that the waters are public. The rights coexist. Neither finds its source in the other."

In those history-making words, Judge Raymond wrote into his opinion the new concept that fishing may be fully as important as waterway navigation in the life of a people or the development of a region. Those who had followed the Collins-Gerhardt and Ne-Bo-Shone cases through their tortuous courses had maintained all along that it is vastly more important to Michigan today that the Pine can be used for fishing than that it was used for log driving fifty years ago. The days of logging are done in the region of the Pine. The days of fishing are close at hand.

Again the victory seemed won, but the trout fishermen of Michigan had learned not to be too hopeful. The mills of United States justice grind in no great haste. "What will Ne-Bo-Shone do next?" anglers asked as they tied flies, patched waders and made ready for the opening of the 1934 trout season.

Again they hadn't long to wait. Ne-Bo-Shone attorneys filed an appeal with the United States Circuit Court of Appeals at Cincinnati, and again the case entered a long period of delay. Not until January, 1936, did the court rule. Once more fishermen cheered when the front pages of Michigan newspapers carried the news that Judge Raymond had been upheld, that the Pine was still free.

One more avenue still is open. That is the United States Supreme Court. Trout fishermen are again wading the rivers of Michigan, again following the Pine through the Ne-Bo-Shone lands, again dragging their canoes over the five jams.

Whether Ne-Bo-Shone will attempt to go before the Supreme Court those who know are not telling. Whether that Court will accept the case for review no one knows. But it really begins to look as if the Pine belongs to the people of Michigan. And, if that be true, then other trout streams in other states, similar in nature, size, and history, have no owners but the people.

Babe's in the Woods

Bob Edge

March 1938

Babe Ruth, who died in 1948, was the greatest figure of the "Golden Age" of sports. It wasn't until this year, 40 years after his retirement from baseball in 1935, that his lifetime total of home runs, 714, was bettered by Hank Aaron. This roistering Yankee star loved to hunt and fish, but was a better hunter than fisherman and seldom missed a season. His companions were frequently sports writers like John Kieran, Bill Slocum, Sr. and the author of our story, Bob Edge. Edge was a native of New Jersey and nephew of the late Governor Walter E. Edge of that state. He was a radio and TV sports commentator, did play by play for the Brooklyn Dodgers and had a show on CBS called Clubhouse Quiz after World War II, in which he served as a lieutenant-commander in the Navy. He did much to promote the International Tuna Tournament at Wedgeport, Novia Scotia.

When the Babe's in the woods, he's the biggest thing there, and the moose, deer, and bears are no longer the star performers. He's always been that way ever since he broke into big-time baseball as a pitcher with the Boston Red Sox, years and years ago. As the Battering Bambino of the New York Yankees, Ruth took over the public, lock, stock, and barrel. He has seized the popular imagination and held it as has no other athlete of our time save, perhaps, Jack Dempsey. Three years out of baseball, the big man has lost nothing of his appeal as a public idol. He always put on a great show for the fans. Today he puts on just as great a show, even though his audience may consist of only three hunters and two guides, and the playing field is a wide stretch of Nova Scotian woods. I know because I was one of the three hunters with him in Nova Scotia last fall.

He arrived in the province with a bang. Bill Lovitt, owner of the camp where we were hunting, who met him at the steamer dock in Yarmouth, told me about it. The Babe was mobbed. He stopped traffic, and wherever he went the crowds went. His bulky shoulders towered above the swirling mob, a wide grin lighted his face, and perspiration streamed from him like water from a sluiced deck. Volleys of greetings crackled from all sides.

"Hello, Babe!"

"Hiya, Butch!" was always his answer.

We were to hear much of that "Hiya, Butch" the next few days. The big man's memory for names is not of the best, so he covers up by calling everybody "Butch." You come to expect it and like it. It's a part of the Babe. He's just a big kid. At forty-three, he has not yet grown up. It's doubtful if he ever will. It's that boyish, exuberant personality of his, together with extraordinary batting ability, that has made him such a grand newspaper figure and the idol of the public.

It was the Babe's first hunt in Nova Scotia, though he had killed deer in Virginia, and also hunts a lot farther South. The same eye that could follow the fastest ball to the plate and knock it out of the park is deadly when it looks over the sights of his .401 Winchester. He did some target shooting that first afternoon in camp—just to sight-in his rifle. He is a snap-shooter, as quick as lightning, and he can drill a tomato can at sixty yards.

At Bill's camp, forty miles from Yarmouth, the alarm clock clattered its summons at 4 o'clock the next morning, rousing the camp. While the fire crackled in the stove and the coffee boiled merrily, we finished our dressing, laced our boots, and examined the action of our guns. Breakfast was substantial if somewhat hurried. We were anxious to be off, the Babe in particular. Oblivious to sore muscles, hardly touching his breakfast, the big fellow was champing at the bit.

Outside the air was still, and the guide cautioned silence as we wound down the path to the lake. The guide had his birch calling horn, evidently planning to lure a moose from the forest. The Babe's presence made it necessary to use the bateau, so with Bill at the oars and the big fellow in the stern, they got away. Five minutes later, the rest of us—Jack Matthews, Hedley Doty, Louis Vacon, the French guide, and I—stepped into the canoe. The paddles bit deep. We were off for a hunt with Babe Ruth!

Presently the canoe scraped gently on the far shore. The Babe and Bill were waiting. We loaded our weapons, Louis swung the canoe to his shoulders, and, following him in single file, we made our way along a faint trail that was just becoming visible in the dawn. Just ahead of me was the Babe, walking with the characteristic little, mincing steps that all baseball fans remember. The mist wet his face, and left little globules of water on his hunting coat. The big fellow carries his weight well, for he is in excellent health, and his love of hunting and fishing, united with almost daily golf, keeps him in the open air, and in good condition.

Silence reigned over the forest, hung heavily with the mist. We traveled possibly a quarter of a mile before Louis signaled a halt, dropped the canoe easily to the ground, and, in whispers, directed Bill to take Jack and Hedley with him. The Babe and I were to remain with Louis.

Crouching on the edge of a bog, Louis put the birch horn to his lips, and emitted the plaintive, pleading call of the cow moose. The Babe grinned, patted the forearm of his rifle, and I eased the sling on mine, straining every nerve to catch the answering grunt of a bull—but none came. The sun rose in the east, scattering the mist, and we heard a crashing in the thicket. Again Louis gave the call, and once more we waited, but at last Louis straightened up and reached for the makings.

"Dere's beeg bull in dere somewhere, but he don' wan' to come out," grinned Louis. He shouldered the canoe. "We go," he said.

A short carry brought us to Wallabeck Lake where we joined the others. Two trips, on which the Babe did his share of the paddling, got us across, and presently we stood on the shores of the Point, a narrow strip between Wallabeck and Little Wallabeck Lakes. What a game country! It was there that Jack had downed his big buck early the first day and where I had the good fortune to get another nice head later the same afternoon.

Louis's first choice, based on wind direction, was a long cedar swamp, running down to the water's edge. Good, open ground on both sides, dotted with low clumps of alders and scattered rocks, made an ideal hunting spot. Louis sent Jack and Hedley down near the water, the Babe was posted atop a huge rock midway along the line, while I was assigned a stand to Babe's right. The Babe's rock afforded ideal cover, and he was making the most of it, crouched so that just the tip of his head showed. As I walked to my station, he turned and saw me. Reversing his hunting cap, catcher fashion, he grinned, spat a stream of tobacco juice, and shook one huge fist. I half expected him to bawl to an imaginary umpire, "Hey, why don't yuh call 'em right?" Fearing that anyone not a ball player might misunderstand his affectionate greeting, the full moon of his face beamed with a wide grin. For the Babe, in case you don't know it, is very considerate of others. Rarely do you find a man who has won such fame, who is so unaffected and unspoiled as the Bambino.

The guides dropped me off at the appointed place, and circled wide to enter the cedars. Presently I heard the familiar hollow sound of wood on wood as Louis and Bill beat short sticks on the cedar trunks. We call it "driving," but Nova Scotians have changed it to "running."

Nothing came my way, but as the "run" passed me, a single loud report broke the stillness to my left. Keeping quiet, I looked for signs of game but there were none, nor were there any more shots. After a decent interval, I ambled in the Babe's direction to find the rest of the party gathered around the big fellow, pumping his hand. The sweat was running down Babe's face, and he was grinning from ear to ear. Louis had his knife out. The Babe had downed a beautiful buck —an eight-snagger. One shot through the neck had done the trick.

"How's that, Butch?" yelled the Babe, dancing around and grabbing Louis. "Little bear hug, old-timer. Give Babe a little bear hug!"

Once more the Point had produced. The Babe had been in the woods less than twenty-four hours and had a buck!

With every one talking at once, it was some time before Louis got around to dressing Babe's deer, and considerably later when we finally dragged the animal to the canoe. Outdoor appetites demanded food, and the Babe clamored loudest of all for Louis to unstrap the pack. Over a meal of cold roast ham and strong, hot tea, the Babe grew jovial.

"That's a good game," Babe said. "When you make a hit, you don't have to run. How about driving us some moose?"

Lunch over, Louis took Babe's suggestion and said we'd hunt the upper end of the Point.

Taking the posts assigned by Louis, the Babe and Hedley sought cover behind a large rock that afforded an excellent view of the swamp. Placing me on a slight rise far to their right, Louis then sent Bill and Jack on a wide swing which brought them to a good stand on the left flank. Electing to run this one alone, Louis entered the swamp at the far end, and, in a short time, I heard the hollow sound of his beating. Suddenly a tremendous crashing came from the forest, and I made out the black bulk of a great animal. The noise stopped as quickly as it had begun, and, steadying myself, I could see clearly the outline of a moose, head lowered and turning from side to side as it suspiciously surveyed the scene. Slowly I raised my rifle, my pulse pounding. Then the rifle came down in disappointment. A turn of that massive head there at the edge of the swamp disclosed the fact that it belonged to a cow.

Even as I looked, crestfallen, the cow broke cover, and I saw that she was trailed by a calf. Glancing neither to right nor left, they came straight for me at a trot. As the wind was in my favor, and my concealment was good, I was afraid I might be run down. I stood up and shouted when they were within twenty yards. Startled, the cow fetched up standing, the calf following suit. The hair on their backs bristled, and, with a snort, they turned and trotted off directly for Babe and Hedley's hiding place. As true as the flight of an arrow, the big cow and the calf trotted for the Babe's rock. When the animals were within fifty feet of the hiding place, up popped the Babe. In his hands was a stout tree root held like a baseball bat. Never taking a backward step, the Babe waved his war club belligerently while Hedley followed the action with his movie camera. The cow and the calf swerved slightly and then disappeared over a ridge. We measured the distance later from rock to moose tracks and found it seventeen yards.

"That," panted the Babe as we surrounded him, "is enough for one day."

You couldn't blame the big fellow for feeling as he did. When we got back to camp a half hour before sunset, we had walked about fifteen miles, and the Babe had carried a heavy canoe for part of the way, but he was still full of energy and horseplay. Bill Lovitt's oxen, with which he carts in supplies to his camp, were feeding peacefully beneath the trees, and that gave the Babe an idea.

"I think I'll bulldog that steer," he said.

He stood looking at one of the oxen for a moment, then grabbed it by the horns. The ox tossed its head, but the Babe held on.

"Hold still a minute, won't yuh?" he begged. "I won't hurt."

He braced himself and so did the ox. The Babe got his great shoulders into it, and strained. So did the ox. The ox's eyes bulged, and looked wild. The Babe's eyes bulged, and looked wilder. The ox started to give a little, and the Babe put the last ounce of steam into it. With a bellow, the ox went over onto its side. As it scrambled to its feet, puzzled, the Babe wiped the sweat from his face.

"Just as I thought," he said. "All it takes is strength."

That night in camp, talk raged. The Babe loosened up, and told endless yarns of his days on the diamond, and of his hunting. He loves to hunt and used to own a hunting preserve on a farm in Sudbury, Mass., but sold it. He is fond of hunting quail in the Carolinas and Georgia, and makes many trips South. In spring and summer he likes to fish. In between, he plays thirty-six holes of golf every day. Those sports, with some radio work and personal appearances, keep him busy and happy. He enjoys life and lives it to the full. He wastes no time grieving over the fact that he's out of baseball, for he's having too good a time. Frank Stevens, caterer at New York's ball parks, and Howard Chandler Christy, the artist, are his favorite hunting companions, and they're together a lot. In his New York home, he has the walls lined with hunting trophies.

All of us were anxious for a shot at a moose. As we had only one more day left, Louis planned it with unusual care. Early in the morning we sighted a pair of big bucks that had lingered too long on the barrens. Doty blazed away. It was a nice, running shot, and, after we'd hung the meat, we worked our way for hours into a country that became wilder with every step. It was getting well toward noon when Louis called a halt, placed Hedley with me behind a clump of hackmatack and deployed the Babe, Jack, and Bill in a skirmish line to our right. We were in a big swamp, just the place for moose. Louis said he'd run the length of timber, and with that he left us.

Ten minutes passed and Hedley whispered, "Moose! Two bulls coming up ahead!" After a while, I could just make out, about 250 yards off, dark flanks and sun glinting on tremendous antler tips. Knowing that Louis was working toward the end of the swamp and that he should come out above the feeding bulls, I waited, figuring that, when he started them, they'd have to come down in front of us and that would give us all a chance. But I guessed wrong, and, before I could raise my rifle, the big animals slipped away. Louis had come out below them instead of above!

Did the boys ride me! "Hell," said the Babe, letting fly a huge stream of tobacco juice, "one muff doesn't mean the ball game." And then to Louis, "Come on, I want to have a look at that bear trap." The night before, Louis had told him of the trap in which an occasional bear was taken. It lay in the direction of home, so the Babe started off with Louis while Bill, Hedley, Jack and I chose a more roundabout way in the hope of stirring up something.

The sun was dropping rapidly behind the western ridges when we reached the canoe. Yet when we looked across the lake, we couldn't see a light in camp.

"That's funny," said Bill. "Babe and Louis ought to be in before this."

But just then we heard a muffled war whoop from our rear.

"That's the Babe," said Jack.

"Judas!" said Jack, "What do you suppose he's got now?"

"A bear, probably," chuckled Bill starting off in the direction of Babe's voice. We found the big fellow a quarter of a mile from the lake, sitting beside a small, black bear. Louis told the story of the bear.

He and the Babe had reached the roots and dead trees near the trap, and, rounding a big boulder, Louis spotted the bear about 300 yards ahead. It was fooling around the bait, but had not ventured too near. Then the Babe saw the bear, and grew excited, but Louis insisted that they circle around to get closer. When he thought they were close enough, he told the Babe to shoot. The big fellow raised his rifle, but as he did, his foot caught in a snag, and he fell sprawling. The bear started to leave, but the Babe kept shooting, and one of the shots dropped the bear.

It was a grand finale to a grand trip. The next day, when we bade good-by to Lovitt's camp and took the boat in Yarmouth, traffic again got twisted up. Then, while we were visiting in an office in Boston, the Babe, sweating as usual, went over to a window, and threw it up to get his lungs full of fresh air. Across the street was a large office building. In two seconds, some one in the building had recognized the Babe, and every window was filled with clerks, calling "Hello, Babe!" The Babe grinned broadly.

"Hiya, Butch!" he bellowed.

Whether the Babe's in the woods or in the city, he steals the show.

The Man with the Meat Dog

Wm. Cary Duncan

October 1938

How many dog editors write musical comedies? William Cary Duncan, who
edited OUTDOOR LIFE's department from 1935 to 1945, was the author or
co-author of twenty of them, some of them Broadway hits. A former teacher
of English and public speaking, he also wrote several books and worked
for a Hollywood film studio (Famous Players Lasky). In 1940 Twentieth
Century Fox bought the film rights to one of his books, *Golden Hoofs,*
on the career of Goldsmith Maid, a famous trotting mare. The same year
he came out with another book, *Dog Training Made Easy.* He was a
member of the board of directors of the American Kennel Club for more
than fifteen years and was president of the Irish Setter Club of America.
In addition to his dog department he wrote delightful feature stories for
OUTDOOR LIFE on his boyhood hunting around North Brookfield,
Massachusetts. The following is a typical feature story.

When that big-shot radio announcer with the vibrant voice dramatically
declares time marches on, the news isn't exactly startling. Many of us have suspected as much for quite a spell. But sometimes we forget to remember that,
while time is marching on, a lot of other things are marching off. Not only that;
they're leaving for good, passing out of the picture forever. This is especially true
in sections of the country settled centuries ago, like rural New England.

In that stern and rock-strewn land, barn raisings, corn huskings, quilting parties, and a score of similar merry-makings of other days are going or have already
gone.

When it comes to humans, not a few once-familiar types have been given the
gate, and had it latched and locked behind them.

Where is the dark-skinned foreigner with the big, brown dancing bear? What
has become of the old-time Uncle Tom's Cabin troupe? Who killed the King of
Dentists, whose gaudy, gilt wagon, copper crown, and royal-purple robe,
trimmed with cotton-batting ermine, used to make the gullible country urchin,
proud to be chosen as a "demonstrator," believe His Majesty's formidable-looking
forceps were really painless, only to learn too late the pangs that accompanied
removal of a perfectly sound molar or bicuspid.

What caused the final fade-out of the traveling fakir who performed miracles
of magic in the smoky light of a kerosene torch, and when the come-ons had con-
gregated in sufficient numbers, sold electric belts, the "electricity" consisting of,
red pepper concealed in little holes in the leather, cleverly covered with some thin
gauze?

But, interesting as these vanishing Americans were, none of them had greater
fascination for the boy born and brought up in the country, than the old-time
New England gunner, the market hunter with the meat dog. Admitting it's a good
thing he's got the gong, too, he was a real "character" just the same, and, as
such, deserves his modest little niche in the sporting Hall of Fame.

Measured by our modern yardsticks, he was no sportsman, but he was a
woodsman—and then some. In the little village where I was born, you could
count the local Nimrods on one hand. To add to his appeal to the country boy's

imagination, he was not only a rarity and something of a curiosity—he was a mystery as well.

A lone wolf, he rarely, if ever, ran with the pack. Hidden away on some lonely, back-country farm that was difficult to find in summer and almost inaccessible in winter, he almost never came to town. It was his "women folks" who drove to the village once a week to do the family trading. He stuck to the fields and forests where he belonged. Of the five local gunners that I recall, I never laid an eye on three until I was a man grown. To me, as a boy, all five were as legendary as Daniel Boone.

There was sound sense in their objections, not to say antipathy, to society in general, strangers in particular, and would-be gunners most of all. They knew that "pa'tridges" (ruffed grouse) were becoming scarcer and wilder every year, and consequently had no intention of allowing Tom, Dick, and Harry to learn where they could be found and how they could best be outwitted and shot. More important still, they didn't want a parcel of rank amateurs, in which class they considered even the most proficient of town-bred sportsmen, puttering around their pet preserves and interfering with their business.

This business was bagging birds, more birds and still more birds, for bag limits were unheard of in that era, and a game warden was known only as a more or less mythical character sometimes read about in books but never actually seen with the naked eye. Those old-fashioned gunners hunted for revenue only, knew their job, and stuck to it like a burdock to a bird dog. They belonged to no C. I. O. or A. F. of L., worked ten hours or more every day in the week except Sunday, and made every minute count. Silent and stealthy as Indians, they stole through the brush almost on a trot, like the Nipmucs and Narragansetts, who had hunted that same country before them, and a trace of whose blood many of them carried in their veins. It took a good, fast dog to work out the heavy cover they hunted and still keep ahead of the meat-mad marathoner who was the man behind the gun.

And they had good dogs, make no mistake about that. Native settlers and pointers, bred for generations for one purpose and only one, to bring home the bacon, they were no bench-show beauties. Hard as nails, with coarse heads and docked tails, and, in the hunting season, sparse and ragged as to coat and bony as a shad, you could count their every rib at twenty paces, and their backbones stood out like the teeth on a crosscut saw. Smart as steel traps, they were master mechanics at their trade and worked at it with no false motions and no fancy frills. No dropping to wing for those babies. They weren't even steady to shot; their masters didn't waste that much time. At the roar of the old 10-gauge, they were off like greyhounds from the box, back on the gallop with the bird, and, before you could say Jack Robinson, off again to locate the next victim.

On the rare occasions when they so far forgot themselves and their training as actually to chase, a charge of Number 7's at fifty or sixty yards, accurately deposited in Mr. Bird Dog's southern exposure and accompanied by a raucous "Hey, you blankety blank blank of a blank, you! Hey!" brought him back to normalcy with neatness and dispatch, and made him a model of obedient efficiency for the rest of the season.

Cruel? Possibly; though at that distance the shot only stung. A gun-shy dog the rest of his days? Not by a long shot—literally. In that brand of bird hounds, there was no such animal and never was. As for the gunner, he punished himself, as he punished his dog, without mercy. His day's work began before dawn and lasted until the deepening darkness made each booming discharge of black powder light the landscape like a Roman candle.

The kind of country he covered made gunning no cakewalk. If there is tougher grouse territory than that of central and northern New England, bring it on; it will be worth looking at. Rock-ribbed hillsides, slippery with pine needles and steep as a shed roof, thick with scrub pine, second-growth hard wood and tangled underbrush; wooded swamps that are dark at midday, treacherous with holding ooze and quaking bogs; sidehill pastures, grown up to birch and alder, where brier patches and thorn bushes clog the way and defy you to penetrate their depths. That's the sort of going those old-timers used to tramp all day long every day of a three months' open season, and thrive on it.

Could they shoot? Ask the city market man who bought their birds. All those murderers asked was the sudden silence of a tinkling bell, the whir of wings, six or eight square feet of open space in a tangle of tree tops, a frightened grouse to flash through it, and a dog with a choke-bore nose to find the bird after it fell. If they didn't get that six square feet, they shot from the hip, aiming by ear at the sound of a flush, and pocketed a good percentage of their prospects just the same.

One of the ilk, whom I'll call Lute Granger, complained to me one time about a new brand of shells he was shooting.

"I don't cotton to 'em," he grunted. "They's jest a leetle too quick fer me."

When I asked him what he meant by that, his answer, believe it or not, was this.

"Well, I'll tell yer, son; when I kill a bird that's quarterin' on me, I allus figgers to git him in his rear end, if I kin. With these here new-fangled shells I'm usin' now, I ain't leadin' 'em eny more'n I've allus done, but seems like I'm hittin' 'em jest a leetle too fer forrard and sort o' messin' 'em up, so's a shot or two's likely to git in folks' teeth when they's chewin' on the breast meat, an' that ain't no good for nobody."

Lute wasn't trying to be funny; he was that kind of shot, turned out a fancy article for his customers, and didn't want to ruin his reputation by selling inferior goods.

Lute's knowledge of the habitat and habits of the birds he hunted, like that of his colleagues in the craft, was amazing. I mean individual birds, not grouse in general. One morning, as he started out for the day's work, I listened as he told his wife where he could be found at any specified time during the day. His directions were about as follows:

"Listen, Lize, ef anybody wants me fer anythin' important, I'm strikin' in at the Needham cellar hole an' workin' them six birds that's in the sprouts as fer as the Gilboy place. Then I'm bearin' north—"

"I thought you said they was eight birds in them Needham sprouts," interrupted Mrs. Lute, busy with her doughnut dough.

"They was," Granger came back, a trifle irritably, "but Milt Bowen got two of 'em day before yesterday; so that makes six. Anyhow, I'm bearin' north from there up the Readin' run—they's four birds in them alders—an' comin' out through the Morse orchard to the Sykes place. Then I'm hittin' the big woods and follerin' through to the Oakham road. They's ten birds in them woods I'm sure of, like enough one or two more by now. They drops in there more or less all season when they's druv out o' somewheres else. They's ten anyway, 'cause I had 'em counted a week ago an' I ain't heard no shootin' in there sence."

So it went through the entire itinerary for the day. Lute had those wild grouse located and tabbed as accurately as a poultryman checks his chicks. Every day or two he made a recheck with other market gunners, subtracted the kills in each cover since his previous stock taking, and figured the balance on hand almost as accurately as a merchant or manufacturer.

It was the same with the habits of the birds in any given spot you might mention. I remember hunting a swamp we called "The Whaleback" (for what reason I never knew) with Lute and my son, for by that time I had become a more or less privileged character. Lute said there were four birds there, but we hunted it out pretty thoroughly and raised only three. So we went all through it again and, at the far corner, almost in the open, sure enough, out went that fourth bird, wild as a hawk. Lute hadn't a Chinaman's chance for a shot, but the old biddy came right over my head and I missed her clean with both barrels.

"Which way did she go?" called Lute, as he emerged from the depths of the swamp a minute or two later.

I had the bird nicely marked down and told him so.

"She swung up over that sidehill pasture," I explained, "turned sharp to the south, flew along parallel to the swamp for 300 yards or so and ducked back into it again right by that big white oak at the further end."

Lute listened carefully, without a trace of expression on his face. Then he turned to the east and pointed a gnarled forefinger toward the top of a wooded hill.

"See them two tall pines on the top o' that hill?"

I told him I did.

"All right, son. Want to know where that there bird is? We'll find her some-wheres near them two pines."

Needless to say, that's exactly where we did find her.

It was the same anywhere. No matter where flushed birds seemed to go, Lute knew where they actually went.

Many of those market gunners of the past had one-track minds that ran on narrow-gauge rails. At practically everything but hunting they were pretty hopeless specimens of manhood—bad farmers, poor providers, ignorant on most subjects, shiftless, and generally no good. Lute Granger was an exception so shining as to be not only unique, but almost unbelievable. I've known a good many gifted and intelligent men in my day, but I can honestly say Lute was, in my humble opinion, the most outstanding all-round man I've ever met.

A few years before he died, he lost his setter, Old Sam, by the dumb-rabies route. Before the dog became dangerous, Lute had him put out of the way by a neighboring farmer, for, as he confessed to me, he hadn't the heart to do the job himself.

"I couldn't kill a dog," he explained earnestly. "I reckon I could kill most anythin' else if I had to, but I couldn't kill a dog, an' I don't see how nobody kin."

As he told me about the affair, his voice was coolly unemotional as usual, but two or three big tears welled up into his eyes and rolled slowly down his weather-beaten cheeks. He had never shown any deep affection for Old Sam—the dog was apparently simply part of his equipment—but, when it came to a show-down, deep in his heart he loved the old dog just the same.

I'll never forget the last time I saw Lute alive. A friend and I were hunting down an alder run that ended at an old stone wall separating it from the heavy timber beyond. As we neared this wall, I heard a familiar voice calling my name. There sat Lute on a big dead log, his gun resting on the wall in position for a shot. I was astonished and a little troubled, for I knew he had had a stroke of paralysis only a month or so before, walked with a deal of difficulty, and couldn't raise his arm to his head, much less throw a gun to his shoulder.

When I passed the time of day and asked him sternly what he was doing out there in the brush with a gun when he should be in an easy chair in the kitchen, taking care of his health, he smiled a bit sheepishly and replied:

"I dunno. I'm gittin' kind o' crazy, I guess. I can't sling the ole gun to my shoulder no more, but I kin rest the barrel on a wall or a stump or somethin' I kin sight it with, and wait fer a bird some other feller has put up to come my way. I can't hit nothin', the way I am, I know that—but it don't do me no harm to imagine I kin; an' gosh a-mighty, Bill, I ain't lost my likin' fer seein' 'em fly!"

Maybe Lute's hunting meant more to him than the money he made selling birds; maybe it was something bigger and better than cold business, after all.

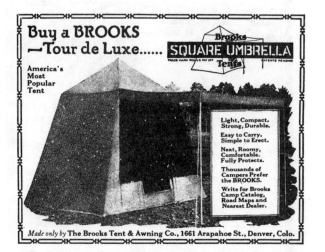

Buy a BROOKS
—Tour de Luxe......

Brooks SQUARE UMBRELLA Tents

TRADE MARK REG'S & PAT OFF   PATENTS PENDING

America's Most Popular Tent

Light, Compact. Strong, Durable.

Easy to Carry. Simple to Erect.

Neat, Roomy, Comfortable. Fully Protects.

Thousands of Campers Prefer the BROOKS.

Write for Brooks Camp Catalog, Road Maps and Nearest Dealer.

Made only by The Brooks Tent & Awning Co., 1661 Arapahoe St., Denver, Colo.

NO SPORT LIKE SKIING

Ski for fun, health and exhilaration. Enjoy winter's greatest sport on a pair of swift-moving

NORTHLAND SKIS

Best for novice or expert. Scientifically made for long wear and smooth running. Interesting booklet on skiing, free. Look for trade-mark.

NORTHLAND SKI MFG. CO.
8 Merriam Park
ST. PAUL, MINN.

CALIFORNIA ARCHERY TACKLE

The most complete line made in the U. S. A.

California By-Products Co.
2667 San Bruno Avenue
San Francisco
451 Eighth Avenue
New York

Ozark Ripley
Uses the Dardevle!

Ozark Ripley—expert angler, lecturer and noted writer in the sporting press—became a hearty convert to the Dardevle lures on a recent Canadian trip. Mr. Ripley writes:—

"In Quebec province the Dardevle Imp was used exclusively in the Black River for Small Mouth Bass. In the Ottawa River and adjacent lakes the Dardevle and Dardevlet were successful on Bass, Northern Pike and Wall-Eyes, and the True-Pickerel.

"On reaching the Nipigon, famous for its monster brook trout, the only lures used by my companion and me on this and nearby streams was the Dardevle Imp. This lure is particularly suited to the rapids of these streams, as it not only works wonderfully in the current but will stay under water, which most lures won't do. The Dardevle made many a pleasant day for me bait casting for these monster trout."

See these lures at your dealers. Send for catalog today. Don't be without them this next trip!

Dardevle's Imp
"The Little Devle"
2¼" long.
2-5 oz.
Price 75c

Osprey Lines
Guaranteed Waterproof Silk

Canadian Distributors:
Canada Needle & Fishing Tackle Co., Ltd.
76 West Wellington Street, Toronto

Lou J. Eppinger
"Outfitters of Sportsmen"
Dept. L. 131-135 Cadillac Square, Detroit, Mich.
"Gateway to Canadian Game Fish and Big Game"

Change from this
CROTCH SIGHT
to a
LYMAN
Aperture Rear Sight

See *all* of your target and *all* of the field. Give yourself a chance to make a clean shot. You get close to 100% sure shooting when you draw a Lyman ivory bead dead on the mark. Nothing to do but hold and pull the trigger.

Take your gun to your dealer's and get a Lyman front and rear sight. They are furnished for practically every gun made. If you prefer write us and we will be glad to help you.

The Lyman Gun Sight Corporation
85 West Street   Middlefield, Conn.

LYMAN SIGHTS

Send 10c for complete and useful catalog

The Bird Dog's Palace

COMFORTABLE, convenient and attractive. Clamps rigidly on the running-board of any car and does not touch the body. No holes to bore. The new clamp is adjustable to all running-boards, including the rounded edge with deep flange and take-up adjustment does away with anything hanging underneath.

Price $12.50 for the one-dog size and $15.00 for the two-dog size, suitable for large pointers or setters as well as other breeds. Also a De Luxe trunk rack model two-dog size priced at $20.00. Guaranteed to please. Immediate Shipment.

Mfd. by THE DWIGHT McBRIDE CO.
Golden City, Missouri.

Outing Comfort!

The Curtiss Aerocar with its sturdy airplane construction, exclusive pneumatic coupler, Pullman type upper and lower berths, large galley, generous closet space, roll screens, shades, radio, and leatherette finished interior is the most complete and beautiful vehicle built for camping, tours and outings. It is a veritable home on wheels — quiet, comfortable --- accommodates four people.   :   :   :

WRITE FOR ILLUSTRATED BOOKLET

CURTISS AEROCAR COMPANY, INC.
1050 SHARAZAD BLVD. OPA-LOCKA, FLA.
(SUBURB OF MIAMI)

1928 Will Be a "FROG YEAR"

The natural food of Bass is *Frogs*. Give them what they want and watch them strike.

Heddon FROG BAITS

Convenient—Efficient—Cleanly—Humane
as life-like as life itself. Choice of
Luny Frog—Little Luny—Spoon-y Frog
Also many of the famous fish-getting "Heddon Dowagiacs" are now made with Frog colorings. Be sure to put some Heddon Frog Baits in your tackle box. *Write for Catalog*

JAMES HEDDON'S SONS   Dowagiac, Mich.

Heddon Fishing
Genuine Dowagiac Tackle

At Last! a REAL Lighter WON'T BLOW OUT!

In strong wind. Safer, cheaper than matches. SURE FIRE cigarette lighter 3" high, one filling lasts a week—burns gasoline. Ideal for sportsmen. Makes splendid Christmas gift. Brass or nickel finish. Send fifty cent money order for one, $1.25 for 3, postpaid. Money back guarantee.
BOWERS MFG. CO., 624 W. Willard St., Kalamazoo, Michigan

OUTDOOR LIFE HUNTING SCALES

[Pat. by J. A. McGuire]

Why guess? Your friends will only smile when you tell them the *estimated* weight of that trophy. With a pair of OUTDOOR LIFE Hunting Scales in your knapsack you are prepared to give them the exact weight of the big game killed on your trip. *That* will be convincing. Made with two gradations; one side weighs up to 300 pounds when weight is suspended by large hook and ring; capacity of other side when using small hook and ring, 40 pounds. Strong enough for the big-game hunter, yet weighs only ¾ pound. With the hooks and rings folded the scales occupy a space the size of a sandwich.

Price $1 postpaid
(Formerly $2)

OUTDOOR LIFE BOOK SHOP
1824 Curtis Street   DENVER, COLO.

SPORTING SPANIELS

by John Stewart
50c postpaid

A book written by a practical shooting man, and applies to all breeds of spaniels. The first of its kind ever published in America devoted entirely to Spaniels. 35 years' experience breeding, breaking and shotting over spaniels.
OUTDOOR LIFE BOOK SHOP, Denver, Colo.

THE NUDIST

Official Publication, International Nudist Conference. Edited by Rev. Ilsley Boone

Devoted to nudism as a movement and philosophy of living. Health building thru sunbathing, diet and exercise. Endorsed by educators, writers, psychologists, doctors and many clergy. Beautifully printed and illustrated. 5 recent issues sent in plain wrapper for one dollar.

OUTDOOR PUBLISHING CORP.,
47 West 45th Street, N. Y. City

"THE ONLY SHOT THAT COUNTS IS THE SHOT THAT HITS."

Model 24 Autoloading Rifle (action open)

THE SNAPPIEST AUTOLOADING .22

You will be amazed at its speed in shooting. Just keep pulling the trigger as fast as you can work your finger and the automatic mechanism does the rest—ejects, reloads and fires. It talks so fast it stutters but it never misses.

Closer inspection will convince you that the Remington Model 24 Autoloader is just as amazing in simplicity of construction and beauty of line. It takes down in a second and will then fit in a suitcase. You can remove the breech block for cleaning without tools. And you can buy ammunition at any crossroads store.

The Model 24 is chambered either for the regular .22 shorts or for .22 long-rifle cartridges—not interchangeably. The magazine is in the stock and rifles chambered for shorts hold fifteen shots; those chambered for long-rifle hold ten.

Look at the Model 24 at your dealer's. Swing it up and get the "feel" that comes from perfect balance. See how easily and naturally it points. You'll know you want one.

Model 24a
Autoloading
Rifle (Standard Grade)
PRICE **$25.45**

REMINGTON ARMS COMPANY, INC.
25 Broadway (Established 1816) New York City

Remington

ARMS	AMMUNITION	CUTLERY
CASH REGISTERS		SERVICE MACHINES

C. 1928 R. A. Co.

The Comforts of *Home* on the Open Road

GET a Tourist Kitchenette—have tempting, appetizing meals—fresh meat, vegetables, fruit, cold salads, drinks, etc., anywhere, any time! It is a unit refrigerator, table cupboard and water-cooler. Separate compartments for all kinds of foods and supplies, ice, water, etc. All metal; sanitary; rattle-proof; dust-proof; rain-proof; odor-proof; antproof. Folds up on running board like a trunk. Easily detached and set up in camp or cabin.

Manufactured by
Tourist Supply Co.,
Inc., Los Angeles, Calif.
P.O. Box 216
Santa Monica, California

Dealers Everywhere—
Partial List of Distributors..

Adkins, Young & Allen Co.	Chicago, Ill.
Chas. G. Johnston	New York City
Fred S. Wilsey	Minneapolis, Minn.
Miller Auto Bed Mfg. Co.	Oakland, Cal.
Western Auto Supply Co.	Los Angeles
Brooks Tent & Awning Co.	Denver, Colo.
Harry J. Kaul	Salt Lake City, Utah
Walter H. Allen	Paris, Texas
Oklahoma City Tent & Awning Co.	Oklahoma City

TOURIST Kitchenette

ENJOY
Airubber Comfort this Season!

A good many people planning to tour or camp this season will avoid much discomfort by carrying Airubber conveniences with them. You should investigate and find out how Airubber can serve you when traveling and in camp.

We have a new free catalog which we shall be glad to send you upon request. In it you will find many suggestions for your comfort. Among the many Airubber innovations you should be especially interested in:

Airubber Bodifit Auto Cushion

This is a cushion, backrest or support for the head and shoulders—as you desire. May be adjusted to any position in the car. Lets you enjoy the longest trip in comfort. A few breaths inflate it. Made of durable rubberized fabric. Your choice of khaki at $4.00. Or corduroy in dark blue, beaver or auto smoke shades at $5.00.

Airubber Restesy Mattress

Makes for restful sleep because it is a yeielding cushion of air that fits the body, protecting it from cold and dampness. Deflated it occupies little space. The sections may be inflated and used as cushions for car, camp or canoe. At night easily joined together and makes the most comfortable bed you have ever slept on. Comes in several sizes and styles to fit cot, sleeping bag or car, and for one or two persons. Also shorter lengths for canoe or car. Prices range from $15.00 to $42.50. If your dealer hasn't this mattress, write telling us your requirements and giving dealer's name. We'll gladly advise style you should have and its cost.

Airubber Sleepesy Pillow

Makes for comfortable sleep because it supports the head in a natural position. Can be inflated with varying degrees of softness. Pocket size when deflated. Khaki cloth at $3.00. Fancy gingham patterns $2.50.

Airubber Sitesy Cushion

Keeps you comfortable through a long day in camp, at the office, driving or just riding. Guaranteed to keep its shape. Always cool and resilient. Two sizes. The 15-inch in khaki is $3.00; in corduroy and khaki it is $3.50, in which combination you may have your choice of dark blue, beaver or auto smoke shades. In the 17-inch the khaki is $4.00; the corduroy and khaki is $4.50 with your choice of dark blue, beaver or auto smoke shades.

Airubber Canoe Cushion

Makes canoe trips more enjoyable. Sit or kneel on it. Miles slip by as you paddle or fish. Yet you do not tire. An appreciated convenience for the passenger. Should canoe tip over it becomes a dependable life raft for every one in the canoe. A life line is attached for just this emergency. Also handy in boat or car. Made of durable rubberized khaki, size 12 by 34½ inches. Price $5.00.

If your dealer hasn't these Airubber conveniences, order direct and mention dealer's name. We ship upon receipt of check or M. O. Examine your purchases. Like them, keep them. If not, return for refund. You must be satisfied.

You will find these and many other conveniences in our new free catalog. Be sure to ask for it.

Airubber CORPORATION

474 West Superior St., Chicago, Ill.
67 N. Moore St., New York
70 King St., West, Toronto, Canada

Jobbers and Dealers Write for Particulars

Here's how to go Camping

Chenango Camp Trailer

will take you anywhere with all the comforts of home. You can camp where you please, entirely independent of the expense and inconvenience of hotels.

Easily converted in one minute, from a rugged trailer to a complete "house" on wheels. Two full sized double beds with springs and mattress; complete kitchen equipment and four large dust proof clothes lockers; nine foot head room; windows and doors with glass and screens. One owner has lived in it on the road for six years.

Write today for interesting printed matter.

CHENANGO EQUIPMENT MFG. CO.
3 Cortland St.   Norwich, N. Y.

$5 BIASCOPE

AMERICAN MADE FIELD GLASSES FOR YOU WHO

hunt, hike, fish, motor, camp or study birds. Great for movie, theatre or field sports. Makes everything look 6 times as big. Precise optical qualities. Fine finish. Leather case free.

POCKESCOPE

Compact telescope magnifies six times. Same finish and optical qualities as Biascope. Supplied with leather case. Both at your dealer or sent direct postpaid. Money back guarantee. Catalog free.

$2

Wollensak Optical Co.
849 Hudson Avenue
Rochester, New York

STICK 'EM UP

Regardless of strength or size defend yourself and friends against any foul attack, from bullies or by gun, knife or club. Subdue with ease persons much stronger than yourself. A complete course on approved American Police Jiu-Jitsu by internationally known police instructor. 151 illustrations with detailed instructions pocket and 13 knockout blows without using fists. Send One Dollar Full price, or C O D.

S. J. JORGENSEN
951 Maritime Building   Seattle, Washington

FOX'S "~~FLIP~~ " PUTTEES

Men have hiked all over the world in Fox's Puttees. Their double spirals of good English wool protect your legs. They give support without binding and leave the legs free to swing along easily. They are light in weight, but they wear well. You can roll them up into small space. They are handy and practical for active wearers everywhere. Buy a pair of Fox's and go tramping right. Look for Fox's tag on each puttee. Write for the name of the nearest dealer.

Regulation Heavy Weight........$4.00
Extra Fine Light Weight........ 4.50
Extra Fine Light Tan........... 5.00

THE MANLEY-JOHNSON CORP.
Sole Agents
Dept. O, 260 W. Broadway,
New York City

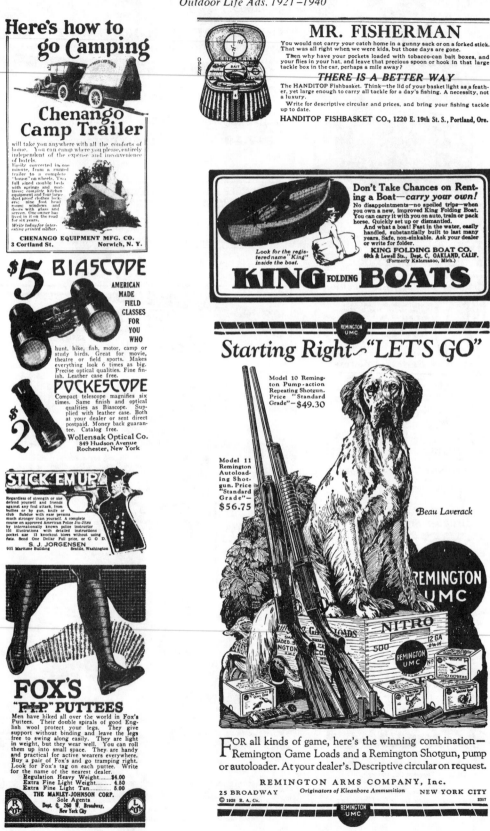

Pa'tridge Fever—Cause and Cure

Gordon MacQuarrie

January 1941

The late Gordon MacQuarrie, a Wisconsin native, left his job as managing editor of a Superior newspaper, to become outdoor editor of the *Milwaukee Journal,* and never looked back. Trouble with his writing is to decide what's best. It's all excellent, whether it be "Pickering Falls for the Brule" (about an angler "who quit his law practice on the Brule River in Wisconsin and resumed it on the Neversink in New York"); "How to Freeze to Death"; his story on wood ticks; an Alaska caribou hunt with guide Bud Branham, or a classic on pine knots that he wrote in lieu of a duck story he didn't get in the bitter cold of northern Wisconsin when he spent the whole time in a cabin burning pine knots to keep warm. His stuff was the editor's delight, and he could do anything. Oh, he did lament that he'd never become a good wing shot. Let's see.

With autumn, when the world is brown and the season hesitates between smoky Indian summer and leaden November, there comes to proper hunting men an urge to scuff their feet among the curling sweet fern and poke a load or two at pa'tridge.

Anyway he's pa'tridge here in Wisconsin. No Badger hillbilly would waste time wrapping his tongue around "ruffed grouse." And if you said "Bonasa unbellus," your man of the pa'tridge woods, from the blue Baraboo hills 300 miles north to Lake Superior's shore, would think you were swearing at him. No, your better class of pa'tridge hunters in Wisconsin refer to our gallant fantail as just plain old pa'tridge—"an 'dang it, neighbor, if you c'n ketch one toppin' the hardwood ye've earned 'im."

The will to go to a place where there are pa'tridge comes upon a man suddenly, inexplicably. It may happen in the midst of dense traffic. It may happen in the thick of a business conference. Your proper hunting man may have been quite complacent with the world and its things. And then, without a word of warning, as the cub reporter wrote when the cornice sell off the Masonic Temple, your proper hunting man becomes a mercuric creature of moods, soured on everything, especially hateful toward sweet old ladies and spaniel puppies.

Moneyed people in that frame of mind often make the mistake of winding up in one of those chromium offices where their unconscious selves are explored. Other kinds of people—pa'tridge hunters, for instance—people with a strong leaning toward sulphur and molasses and red-flannel underwear in season, know the remedy.

The remedy is walnut and steel, oiled leather, baggy canvas jacket, and the stinging smell of nitro hanging in the hazel brush.

Your proper hunting man standeth not upon the order of his going. And it makes no difference how far it is to The Place. He'll get there, and never give a hoot about the consequences. The only thing to do is to go, and let someone else worry about the storm windows, the World Series, or the state of the nation. The going is a very great part of it. It is the delicious prelude to the prime adventure of letting go with the right barrel on the first flushed bird.

I want you to know I had a nice day for it.

The country was exactly fine. Up through the fat, blacksoil counties of southern Wisconsin I drove. Up through the country of the vase-shaped elms, and the oaks like upturned bunches of grapes. Up and up—into the places north where the somber Puritan pines spotted the landscape, grew thicker and thicker and thicker, until finally the country was black with pines, and the elms and oaks were patchy interlopers.

I'd been tired for days, and that made it easier to loll back with a heavy foot and just panoram' right through Wisconsin from one end to the other. North up one long concrete carpet, west along another, then north once more onto the crooked fire lane, a highway in fact, a fire lane now only in name. The startled buck in his autumn sleekness leaping off the road. The lone, sinister cormorant on the rampike at the edge of the Chippewa flowage. The bouncing snowshoe rabbits, still brown. Up through the north of Wisconsin, in a warm, mellow world of gold and yellow and brown and red.

Toward the last of that drive I shifted often behind the wheel. A man has got to have a backbone to drive 360 miles fast; and how can you have a backbone after the auto-to-office and auto-to-home that we city folks go through day after day? You can't.

The fire lane ends, and the course is west again; west into the red, round setting sun, with a silty wake of sand and dust behind. West down the skinny, familiar road from the mail box, dodging the trees—and there is The Place.

The Place is in piny woods with a lemon-yellow log cabin in its center, a blue lake behind it for a back drop, a wisp of smoke from a cobblestone chimney, and a brown man in khaki trousers and a sagging, gray woolen vest waiting on the stoop for me.

The brown man was the president of the Old Duck Hunter's Association, Inc., a symbolic figure to all proper hunting men. Sometimes the president of an Old Duck Hunter's Association is a fellow named Joe, sometimes Jim, sometimes Louie. This one was Al, of the quizzical, challenging gleam in the eye and the much-chewed cigar and the traditional rainment of all the Als and Joes in pa'tridge time, right down to the khaki pants tucked into ten-inch boots, smooth on the bottoms from contact with pine needles.

"So you got here." He shook hands. "Where's the dog?"

Blazes! I'd forgotten it—him. The dog was to have been a shouldery setter with a back mask and a mantel-piece of trophies, whose owner had decided a day or two on pa'tridge was just what he needed, what with another field trial coming along.

"It's just like it always was," said Mister President. "I've got to do all the thinking for the association. Well, I'll show you pa'tridge without a dog. I'm glad you didn't bring him. It'd be too easy. Get out. Gimme that gun. Gimme that bag. Come on in. Sit down. Take off your shoes. Supper's almost ready. Shut up!"

God bless the presidents of the Old Duck Hunter's Associations, wherever they may be, and especially Al Peck.

He fiddled with things on a kitchen range that smelled of burning jack pine. He dropped one match on yellow birch bark beneath oaken logs, and the varished lemon-color cedar logs of the big room gave back the fireplace light. He relit his cigar, pushed back his chair from the spreading heat, and began:

"Boy, you've got an idea of what has been happening in your old stamping ground. Let's see, you've missed four pa'tridge seasons, and the last one was at the low point in the cycle. Since then your square-tailed friends have gone on a housekeeping rampage. There's pa'tridge in every hardwood clump I can find in southern Bayfield County. I'm not saying as many as in 1932—will you ever forget that?—but enough to prove to me that you are still a poorer wing-shot than me.

"Pa'tridge? It's a good thing the birds around here have had me to keep 'em stirred up. When the season opened two weeks ago they were so tame they wouldn't get out of the way of a car. But I learned 'em. Now I've got 'em trained so they get up thirty yards ahead of you and duck behind the first tree.

"Let's eat. What's that on your plate, did you say? God bless us, the boy has forgotten what roast pa'tridge tastes like!"

So it went. Until the owls began their lonely cries across the lake somewhere and the stars were bright and there was a rough woolen blanket under my chin and the waves on the lake shore went lap, lap, lap. . . .

Mister President was alive next morning at heaven knows what hour. It seemed only a moment before that I had closed my eyes. But there he was, yanking at the scarlet blanket and repeating such abysmal sounds as "Daylight in the swamps!"—the consequences of a well-spent youth in the logging camps of the North.

There was then a thing called breakfast, but which deserves a better name when it is eaten before a fireplace beating back the early morning chill. The Hon. President even had pancakes. Did you ever eat sour-cream pancakes, made by a master hand?

There was a beginning to pa'tridge hunting. The president of the Old Duck Hunters makes a rite of such a privilege. Everything must be just so—the season, the day, the company. He laced his boots a bit tighter, pulled on a baggy, stained hunting jacket, lit the familiar little crooked pipe and stood on the cabin stoop, 16 gauge under his arm—a full and proper and capable pa'tridge hunter if I ever saw one.

Now, this is not a bad pa'tridge country when the cycle is up. It's a sandy, piny country, with some surprising patches of hardwood here and there. And best of all for the pa'tridge hunter, it is interlaced with dozens and scores of trails—old tote roads and rights of way of lumbering days.

Mister President sniffed the air. It was good air to sniff, bracing, fragrant with pine and sweet fern and the honest, dewy smell of a bright October morning. He relit his pipe and mapped the plan of action:

"We can get into the car and drive down the Hayward road. Or we can push back in from Andy's and skirt that pothole lake. Or we can mooch down the back road and turn right into the Cathedral."

The Cathedral is a grove of stately Norway pines growing in a natural amphitheater perhaps a mile from the cabin. I have seldom walked into this enchanting place in autumn without flushing pa'tridge. The President knew my weakness for this place, so it was by a sort of mutual, unspoken meeting of minds that we started for it.

The way into it is little known, and God forbid that I should map it. (One time I spoke out in meeting about a certain mallard hole.) Many people supposedly familiar with the lake country roundabout have never been into it. Mister President had well named it the Cathedral that first day, years ago, when he had stumbled into it after fighting through the dense brush country almost surrounding it. There is a feeling of reverence in your proper hunting man in such a place. Reverence, and if he has been there before, vigilant alertness, for you never know when the brown one with the fantail will explode from the forest floor and go slanting off among the big boles.

Such mornings are not soon forgotten. The city was far, far away. The day was perfect. The President in the lead, we walked quietly out of the snaky, brushy trail into the open spaces beneath those big trees. We were in the pit of the

119

amphitheater of Norway pines. To our right the big sticks climbed the hill, and in front of us they were there too. To our left was the beginning of a swamp.

The President worked off to my left and signaled me to advance through the wood parallel with him. The silent solemnity was broken by the thunder of wings. A brown bomb, thirty yeards off, moving to my left, was heading for the swamp. Two shots and my double triggers were limp, and the bird had gained the dense spruce in safety.

The President spoke:

"Now you're gonna tell me you always did better on left-to-right shots. Well, if I'd had that shot I'd —"

A second buster climbed up and out, planing and twisting. With hardly a pause in his sermon, The President collected him and went on:

"— do it just like that!"

Modesty, to a president of the Old Duck Hunter's Association, is a becoming virtue only in children and setter pups.

Once through the grove, which I always leave with regret, we split, agreed to meet at noon in the cabin.

The brown woods tooks me in. The forest floor was moist below but dry and noisy above its mulch. Birds were flushing wild. The sun beat down. I saw a peculiar thing. A red squirrel, arguing with something, permitted me to come very close. I tried to reach out and touch him with my gun muzzle, and he scampered out of his tree and away. As he did so, a pa'tridge thundered up, not ten feet from me, and was gone in a grand, clattering parabola of flight before I could shoot.

The brown woods took me in again. The sun was climbing. There was a path, along the high bank of a water thoroughfare, where deer and fishermen and rabbits pass. From a dusting depression in the center of this path I took my first bird, a fantail that made the mistake of flying the thoroughfare. I collected.

Working along this high path I flushed several more far ahead. The path was too open. The birds were too wary. The President had "learned" them well. He had the pa'tridge in those woods ducking for cover at the first hint of danger. I could hear birds getting up as much as seventy and eighty yeards away.

It was as The President had said—almost as good as 1932.

There was a pa'tridge year that will live long in the memory of northern Wisconsin upland gunners. It was in 1933 when the plague hit. Had Wisconsin known in 1932 what it knows now about pa'tridge, you may be sure 1932, instead of having a short season, would have had a good long one.

The idea of collecting the crop before disease collects it is firmly planted in Wisconsin. The old idea was to save for the sake of saving—an idea that was a prostitution of sound conservation. It was the carrying of a good thing too far. Wisconsin knows better now.

Each year there is a meeting in Madison, where more than 200 sportsmen from 71 counties recommend to the state conservation department the hunting and fishing laws for the ensuing year. It is a unique and highly successful method of working out the laws, now being copied by other states, and proving with each passing year the soundness of the idea. At this meeting are the same sportsmen who, for four years, denied themselves and all others the right to hunt pa'tridge and prairie chicken, knowing the birds would have to be let alone to make a comeback—the same men who tote the grain bags through the winter drifts to feed the pheasants, while their argumentative opponents are writing letters to newspapers condemning all hunters as lustful killers. And they know the thing to do is collect the crop.

The buggy-whip brush beckoned me on—alders, small birches, and dense undergrowth close to the ground. It was obvious now I must get close for a shot. It was hard work, a continual fight with slapping brush. Of the shots I missed, of the shots I tried off balance, of the foot-tangling affection of that brush, any proper pa'tridge hunter could write many paragraphs.

After a half hour of it your jacket is open. In an hour you wish you'd left the jacket home and brought only a cord with which to tie the game, if any, to your belt. The sweat pours down. You get shots. You get tries at phantom wraiths blistering up and out. You send No. 7's on futile brush-busting errands through the whip switches at canny down-drifters. You accept mean, cutting slashes from springy branches. Your eyes are shut half the time, expecting a blow. You are mighty lucky to make feathers fly on one out of four offerings.

When it was over, I had only two birds to show Mister President back at the cabin at noon. Of course he had his limit of four—"Been here waiting for you an hour." I sluiced and doused from the waist up in cold pump water, partook of Mister President's noon repast, and then helped him buck up wood. All of the presidents of the Old Duck Hunters are alike in the respect that they can't sit still. He had enough wood for months.

It was late afternoon when he looked at the sun, dropped his saw, and said "come on." To the Cathedral again of course.

What a place was that grove in the slanting rays of the dropping sun! The trees seemed bigger. The shadows were blacker. The orange bark was brighter. There hung over it the sultry smoke of Indian summer. Insects buzzed in the sunny patches, and high in the Norway tops summer was still alive. But where we stood, the cool October night was beginning to gather among the big trees.

The President, without a gun, went to the top of the amphitheater, and sat on a log like a judge. He could see every move I made down below him.

I proceeded slowly, and for once luck was on my side, for the first one zoomed straight away. It flew down an open aisle among the big trunks, and the right barrel just couldn't miss it. But I was a little big deflated when I heard the voice of The President, from his spot on the hill: "Sissy! That pa'tridge committed suicide!"

Nevertheless he was my pa'tridge. One more now. One more to confute the President. I was almost through the grove when the second bird flushed, exactly like the first, straight away.

You know how those gift shots are. Nothing to it. Take it easy. Take all the time in the world. Be deliberate. Be cocksure. I think I even posed a little bit for the benefit of The President. I'd show him. I'd make him eat his words.

The crack of nitro in the Cathedral was thunderous. Once, twice I fired. Nothing happened. The pa'tridge vanished in the spruce swamp. I stood there in the pit of the grove, embarrassed to the ears, and heard the judgment from on high:

"Four feet closer and you'd have had him—maybe."

The pa'tridge day was over. We stood a minute looking down into that splendid grove. The spell of the place had hold of me. I told him that some day I wanted to stand right there where we were and let him drive a buck to me out of the spruce swamp. I told him I'd wait for the buck to emerge from the dark spruce, edge into the grove and perhaps offer me a running shot. And there I'd be —waiting.

Mister President studied the layout below. He studied the place where the last pa'tridge had vanished. Then he studied me and said:

"You might get him. Yessir, you might. But how about you doing the driving and me the shooting?"

Wild West Gunmen Were Not so Hot

Charles Askins, Jr.   July 1941

Since we're about to destroy some legendary paladins of the American West, we must quickly present the credentials of our author (and authority). Charles Askins, Jr. is the son of the late Maj. Charles Askins, a shooting editor for OUTDOOR LIFE for many years. At the time of this story, Charles Jr. (Col. Askins now) had won the national pistol championship, the national all-around championship and ranked No. 1, .22 caliber all-America pistol team. He had won state championships in Texas, Arizona, New Mexico and Oklahoma, and Southeastern, Southwestern and Northwestern regional championships. He had won a rapid-fire Olympic championship. And he was a former member of the U.S. Border Patrol. So, stand back, please, out of the line of fire.

"The Lily Belle Saloon was quiet with hushed expectancy, its silence broken only by the rasping voice of Wolf McSween. Big Wolf, sixgun, in hand, was taunting little Bucky Johns, fastest gunswoop of all the Big Bend. McSween teetered on his heels, the snout of his .45 describing little circles in the vicinity of Bucky's belt buckle.

" 'Why don' yah say yore skeered?" he demanded. 'We knows yah fer a yella dog. Beg, Tejino, 'cause I'm gonna cut yah down—now!' Screaming the words he threw the .45 forward.

"Bucky Johns in that death-stalking instant, moved. Moved with the lashing speed of a jungle cat. Spinning, his right fist flashed down and up, spitting fire. The blur of his shots became a staccato yammer. Then it was all over. With an agonizing scream big Wolf McSween clutched his wrist, blood spurting between his fingers. . . ."

How many times have you read tripe like that in the baker's dozen of Wild West pulp magazines which clutter our news stands? How many times have you read it in the supposedly authentic biographies of the gunfighters of the old West —Wild Bill Hickok, Billy the Kid, Bat Masterson, Wyatt Earp, and the rest? How many times have you seen it acted out for the movies by handsome gunmen who invariably flinch as their blank cartridges go off?

Countless times, I have no doubt. Matter of fact, the gunning fracas described above is mild indeed—generally the hero knocks half a dozen guns spinning. Western-story writers have a certain number of stock situations which they rotate for their gun-swinging valiants. Briefly they may be summed up as follows. 1. He rides down the trail, flips out the Old Equalizer, and dusts off a jack at 200 yards, not, please understand, killing the innocent rabbit, but neatly shooting him through both ears. 2. He dots the "i" in the sign over the Silver Dollar Saloon, remarking meanwhile that "some painter man was downright car'less 'bout his spellin'." 3. Later he knocks the gun out of the brother's, father's, or uncle's hand, when the brother, father, or uncle of the love interest (i.e. heroine) attempts to ventilate our hero (believing him to be the rustler king). 4. Finally, in the last paragraph, he tackles six gun-wolves all at one time, shooting three through their respective shoulders, two alongside the head, so that they are rendered instantly unconscious, and plugs the sixth and last—the real villain of the piece—plumb through the heart.

Glorifiers of our Men of the Draw, real and fictional, never feel they have done their hammer man justice until they have permitted him to perform half a dozen ballistically impossible gun stunts. Billy the Kid, First Gun Hand of New Mexico during the early '80s, whiled away many happy hours on the trail, it seems, by nonchalantly barking each fence post as he galloped past. Of course the chronicler blissfully ignored the fact that there were no fence posts along the trails in Lincoln County sixty years back. (N.B.: And damned few today!) Wes Hardin, Texas's brightest contribution to that shining galaxy of powder-burning immortals, used to draw his twin .41's, and fanning both simultaneously, ignite a dozen matches with as many bullets. This remarkable feat of gunning legerdemain has probably impressed me more deeply than any other, for the clever Mr. Hardin undoubtedly must have fanned the hammers with his teeth. Contemporary experts, as well as the less dexterous modern gun handlers, have found it necessary to hold the sixgun in one hand and fan the hammer with the other. Wes Hardin's scribe disdained to have his stalwart stoop to such petty conventionalities.

Clay Allison, dapper gambler and killer extraordinary, used to toss up the five of diamonds, thumb out a machine-gunlike burst of shots—and the pasteboard would float to earth, a ragged tear where each spot had been. Ben Thompson, Abilene gun wolf, with more notches on his old hawgleg than teeth in a buzz saw, shot a fellow's boot heels off while forcing him to dance, blasted the buttons off his pants, and laughed uproariously when the poor dude's breeches fell about his knees. Later Ben, who, if we may place any credence in his chroniclers, had a most subtle sense of humor, neatly clipped the ash from the Abilene mayor's cigar as he stood drinking in the Longhorn Saloon. When the mayor turned to protest, Ben upped his Old Convincer and bored a perfectly round hole in Hizzoner's ear exactly 45/100 of an inch in diameter.

Ah, but Wild Bill Hickok was the gunman extraordinary! Wild Bill, leadslinger without parallel. Wizard of the draw. Straight-shooting, fast-shooting Abilene marshal. Verily, the super triggerman in a day when there were only two classes of Westerners—the quick and the dead. Wild Bill, bless 'im, was colorful copy for ten million words of paperback fiction. Hickok has accomplished more with his magical sixes than Thor with his hammer, Zeus with his thunderbolts, and Darryl Zanuck with his entire corps of movie rewrite men.

To quote from Alsike's "Life of Wild Bill Hickok" ". . . he (Bill, of course) strode out of the Longhorn and noting that the street was filled with Texas men, all of whom were avowed enemies, Wild Bill thought to impress these fierce cowboys of the Texas pampas with his six-shooter skill. Forthwith he drew his long-barreled, cap-and-ball weapons and firing both revolvers so fast there was a steady stream of fire at the muzzles and the shots sounded so close together the reports could not be counted, emptied both weapons. His target was a sign hanging in front of the town's only blacksmith shop. 'Jim Cooley, Blacksmith' read the board above the swinging doors of the farrier's place. Wild Bill had fired his guns at the 'oo' in the name 'Cooley.' On inspection each 'o' was found to contain six bullet holes. Afterward, spectators paced the distance and found that it measured 187 long steps."

At 200 yards the modern .45 Colt bullet drops eleven feet. At 187 yards, or paces, as stepped by the witnesses of Hickok's little shooting lesson, the bullets would probably drop only about nine and one-half feet. So, you may see that while Wild William had been handed down to us as a pistoleer of remarkable versatility he was also an engineer of no mean accomplishment. On that memorable day in the streets of old Abilene, Bill whipped out his "cutters" and as he pointed 'em with that scintillating wizardy of his, he also instantly calculated the bullet drop for the range. Nine-and-one-half feet it was, and Bill, so far as I am concerned, on the basis of that little piece of shooting alone, makes some of our modern ballistics experts, who must plot for hours to figure a trajectory curve, look like the rankest amateurs.

What about all these entrancing yarns of the gun fighters of yesterday? How much of these grand Sagas of the Sixgun are we to accept as truth, what part pass over with a knowing smile? Isn't it possible the revolver wizardry of those super fighting men was a brand not seen among the effete target marksmen of today? Isn't it logical that those devil-men, grim gun hawks with a thousand enemies about them, practiced with such dogged persistence as to achieve a hammer skill which modern pistolmen have never attained?

Maybe—but I think not.

In the last ten years I've shot away something like 340,000 rounds of pistol ammunition. I'm betting that's more shells than all the leather slappers west of the Mississippi burned up among 'em! I fired those shells mostly at targets—but not altogether. In the last year, and at times before, I practiced constantly to master the hip-shooting technique of our Western immortals. Of the more than a third of a million bullets sped down the range by me, I expect a full 100,000 have gone into draw-and-fire practice. In the last decade, when I used up more than 30,000 hulls annually, I was lucky enough to win the national pistol championship, the national all-around championship and the .22 all-American No. 1 rating. Today 420 medals adorn my walls and I claim 117 cups and similar trophies won by me at one time or another. If a comparison is to be drawn between the shooting skill of our bygone trigger men and that of today's shooter, it may add some light to explain my success (or lack of it!) in attempting to duplicate the gunning feats accredited to those lead spillers who lived and died in the smoke of Colonel Colt's most famous invention.

To begin with, I got two .45 single-action sixguns. Made of infinitely better steel, bored to closer tolerances, fitted tightly at cylinder and joint, with good trigger pulls and improved sights, these modern counterparts were vastly superior to the best that the gun swingers of the old days could buy. Six-shooters in those days were made of inferior stuff, sloppily bored and rifled, the cylinders loosely pinned to the frame, chambers quite frequently drilled out of line, and the sights were an abomination. But the ammunition—whew! It was by long odds the worst part of the combination. I have before me a box of black-powder .45 loads purchased in Tombstone in 1889. This fodder shows a variance of eleven grains weight between individual bullets and a difference of 8.3 grains weight between powder charges. When Clay Allison pipped his cards, and Bill Hickok punctured his signboard, they must have had better hulls than these!

The old gunfighters never had been to the Camp Perry School of Marksmanship, so they did not know anything about sighting in a sixgun. They believed, like a lot of folks who buy new shooting irons today, that the factory makes 'em to hit dead center. When you attend the Camp Perry shooting school you learn better. The first .45 S.A. sixgun I bought, shot, I found, exactly level but four inches to the right; the second hit three and one-half inches high and four inches right. How in hell can I shoot the spots off cards and the gun out of an opponent's hand, as well as satisfactory plug signboards and otherwise be a bad man, with guns that shoot off center like that?

Maybe Wild Bill and Ben Thompson savvied more than I give 'em credit for. Maybe they adjusted their sights and got their powder burners to hitting true, but it is a fact that a lot of converted cap-and-ball sixguns in those days had a back sight which was also the hammer firing pin. I do not know how you'd move a notch like that to get in perfect zero on your target.

After sighting my guns in by bending the sights and filing down the back notch, I group-fired both at fifty yards with black-powder loads. This to get a definite line on the accuracy of the .45 single-action and the old, reliable 255-grain black-powder load. The first gun fired from a bench rest made a group size of 7.3 inches; the second ran 8.7 inches. At 200 yards my groups (multiplied by four) would mean the best I could do would be to hit a thirty-two-inch circle, approximately. Unfortunately Wild Bill's historian doesn't tell us the size of the "oo" in Blacksmith Cooley's name, as painted over the shop door, but somehow I have a feeling these letters did not measure thirty-two inches. I was somewhat discouraged by this and must confess that I did not even try to duplicate Hickok's 187-yard shooting feat. I'll grant he has me at the long range.

The next thing I did was to make a dummy. "Trigger McGook" I dubbed my stooge, and a right good make-believe man was he, what with his ready gun and fierce scowl. I stood Trigger up and put his sixgun in his hand. Then I had him do the road agent's spin, and just at that instant I decided to disarm him by the fiction-worn expedient of shooting the gun out of his hand. Now, .45 black-powder loads, which I was using are potent indeed. In fact, they pack more wallop than any smokeless load you can get. My bullet caught McGook's iron between barrel and cylinder. The gun came all to pieces, and the unfortunate part of the story must be related here. Various large chunks of the receiver, ejector-rod spring, spring housing, as well as the ricocheted bullet, penetrated McGook's paunch. He bled copiously of alfalfa, his life fluid.

Hell of a hero I'd make in one of those Wild West books if, intent on disarming the gal's brother by shooting his six out of his fist, I filled his belly full of assorted parts from the suddenly come-apart revolver! Evidently even in the heat of battle with my straw man, I should have selected a better aiming point than the junction of barrel and cylinder. I'll have to get acquainted with some of these Western writer chaps and find out where you hit the other man's iron so that it flies harmlessly behind the bar, and the owner isn't even bruised.

Trigger McGook eventually digested the ejector spring and other bits of steel, and was just as belligerent and ready to shoot it out as before. This time I gunned for his wrist. The distance was twenty-five feet, pretty long range for gun scrapping. My first shot, triggered from the hip after a fast gun snatch, hit McGook squarely in the chest. The second blast took him in the navel and the third connected with his elbow. Since Trigger was practically immortal, I blandly disregarded the highly probable lethal effects of that dose in the chest, followed by the hit in the belly, and congratulated myself on that damaging shot in the elbow. Of course, it had missed the wrist by a couple of inches, going high, and would never have done in the judgment of the rankest writer of Westerns, but I felt pretty good about it.

I think I should confess right here that I am an ardent Western-story fan. I digest 'em by the dozens. Not infrequently I find where the hero's Man Friday is being hanged by the villains of the piece. Invariably the hero gallops in and shoots the rope in two just before his pardner gasps his last. So it seemed to me I'd better try this with my man McGook. Forthwith I strung him up. Backing off on the paint horse about two pistol shots' distance, I galloped forward in best Hollywood style, jerked out the .45, and went to work. A brisk little wind was blowing and Trigger was swaying pretty badly. This had a wholly distressing effect on the rope. Undoubtedly a dancing lariat would prove no handicap to your real Western gun-pointer, but it proved damnably annoying to me. On the third shot I did manage to cut one strand of the rope. McGook's face was turning

black; I'd have to hurry. Wildly I whammed in the three other shots, missed—
and turned away leaving my pal to dance in the breeze.

Clay Allison, reputed killer of eighteen less-speedy hombres, tossed playing
cards into the air and while they floated and ducked above his head, knocked the
spots off 'em. Now, I have plenty of trouble puncturing pint-size tin cans in the
ozone, much less cards, so I wisely pinned my aces, deuces, and treys to a substantial backboard. I shot at these cards at twenty feet. Not, let me hasten to
assure you, by slap-bang, rapid fire from the hip, but by deliberate slow fire with
a carefully aimed gun. Altogether I shot away seventy-six black-powder loads. I
missed the spots on the cards twice. In all the shooting, however, I hit the spots
dead center only seven times. I nicked 'em, sure, but smack 'em plumb center I
did not. At that stunt old Guntwist Allison has me licked forty ways!

I tried shooting corks from whisky bottles and, when given plenty of time—say
four seconds a blast—I was deadly. I tried igniting matches at twenty feet, and
could break a match stick about every second shot. I never did get one to burn. I
snuffed candles, bounced empty cartridge hulls, and cut a string to which was
suspended a bottle. But all this stuff smacked more of the circus than the prairie
gun thrower, so I gave it up.

Billy the Kid got his lead-throwing practice by plinking fence posts, so why
shouldn't I? I saddled Snake and galloped alongside a row of narrow silhouette
targets at twenty yards. Six shots, six misses. H-m-m. Maybe the Kid edged over
a bit closer than that to his unresisting targets. Yep, that must be it; he was
closer to 'em. I got nearer. At fifty feet I thumbed out six shots as the horse
plunged by. Tally: one hit for the full cylinder. At thirty feet, and with Snake
running wide open, I smacked five of the six silhouettes. At twenty feet I got 'em
all.

Shooting two guns, I tried riding between the silhouettes, placed in parallel
rows facing each other and about twenty feet apart. This stunt invariably resulted
in fifty percent hits. If I watched the figures on the left I hit all of them. If I concentrated on the right-hand targets I smacked a bullet into each of them. But,
since I couldn't look in two directions at once, I'd always miss the targets on the
blind side.

I tried riding hell-for-leather at the silhouettes, wheeling abruptly at thirty feet,
and starting to shoot as I turned. This grandstand play netted exactly no hits at
all. I rode closer. At about a dozen feet, I could ventilate the figures with satisfactory regularity, but had they been men and not make-believe, they'd have drilled
me long before I reached them.

As I've said, I have fired upwards of 100,000 shots at man-shaped targets from
the hip. At distances up to forty feet hip shooting is dangerously lethal—of that I
am positive. Targets the size of a man can be plugged with a full cylinder of .45's
in around two-and-one-half seconds, and with practice it does not matter which
hand you use. Two guns fired together are not quite so accurate, but the gunner
can expect about ninety percent kill hits. But that forty feet, in my experience, is
extreme hip-shooting range. Half that distance is much more effective.

It is pure "toro" to say that the other fighter's gun can be shot out of his hand,
that his wrist can be punctured, or that he can be hit in the shoulder, ear, alongside the head, or in any other selected part of the body with a shot fired from the
hip in the heat of a kill-or-be-killed gun scrap. No man can do it, no man ever
has done it except by accident. Which doesn't mean that I will not highly enjoy
my next Western yarn in which the lightnin'-fast cowboy marshal sends six irons
spinning from as many fists with as many bullets. I'll eat it up, same as usual.

I've tried fanning the hammer, too, but with only one gun. (I'll leave fanning
two guns simultaneously to John Wesley Hardin.) With this style of shooting, at

six feet the shots are all kill hits, and you can get six shots off in less than two seconds. At distances beyond six feet fanning the hammer is nonsense—not that I do not think it is a silly, ineffectual gun stunt at any distance, for it is.

And that brings us down to the most romantic, colorful, and entrancing part of the whole story—the business of the quick draw. Ah, what glamour, what drama, what tension-packed moments have been built around the gun snatch! Haven't you read—a thousand times at least—where the hero told the villainous robber chieftain, "Go fer yer gun, Killer Floogel, I'm gonna salivate yah!" And then when he'd cajoled and pleaded with the craven gunman to draw he'd beat him to it. Well, Ike Akard and I stood face to face and practiced the draw with empty guns at least 100 times every day for a month. At the end of that time, so far as witnesses could tell, our hammers dropped exactly together. It did not matter whether we started with gun hand hanging at the side, with a grip on the gun butt, or with thumb hooked over the cartridge belt, we were always together. We'd have killed each other dead as hell at each exchange.

The old gun jiggers were popularly supposed to have swung their irons in quick-draw practice several hours daily—just as Ike and I did. Granted, then, that the fighters of yesterday were in good form all the time, it stands to reason that, if they stood up man to man and started for their sixes exactly together, they both died—just as Ike and I would have died had our guns been loaded.

I know a lot of gun slingers—not famous fellows like the old-timers who, since their demise, have had plenty of unofficial publicity agents to build 'em up—but buckos who have killed maybe six, maybe eight, or even as many as a dozen men. These gun wielders tell me that the quick draw is a minor item. When a man expects trouble, he takes his gun out before it starts and holds it ready in his hand. If the trouble develops suddenly, he distracts the other man's attention, and starts for his gun in plenty of time to get in the first shot without any race to see who clears leather first.

But of course you can't make a thrilling story out of that kind of stuff!

An Old Man Told Me

Geo. W. Heinold

July 1944

This is not only the first story George Heinold did for OUTDOOR LIFE, but
the first story he ever sold, and you might say he hit the bull's-eye, rang the
bell and dumped the pretty girl in the tank. First, it was chosen for the book
Best Sports Stories of 1944, and then condensed in *The Reader's Digest*.
(The *Digest* did this again with a raccoon story George wrote for the
Saturday Evening Post, "Burglar in the Treetops," later title story in a
Heinold book.) But let's stick with OUTDOOR LIFE. He became the saltwater
editor in September 1952, and has written well over three hundred pieces
for OUTDOOR LIFE alone since then. He had his schooling on commercial
fishing boats on Long Island Sound for seven years. George was born on a
Connecticut farm and was with the Madison police force for thirty years,
twenty of them as assistant police chief.

My objective was trout—lively speckled trout of a quarrelsome disposition! It
was a balmy day in late April. Springtime had garbed herself in such gorgeous
raiment that the very atmosphere would have put a poet beside himself in sheer
ecstasy; but I wasn't impressed because I never get poetical with an empty creel.

All forenoon long I had waded over slippery rocks and whipped early-season
bucktails and wet flies in vain; and I would have resorted to dunking night crawlers if I'd had them, but no trout big enough to stink up a pan appreciated my
efforts.

Weary and disgruntled, I leaned against the weather-beaten rails of a rustic old
river bridge and brooded over whom or what to blame. I finally came to the conclusion that it was a toss-up between the chap who started that propaganda about
fish biting best when the wind blows west, and the inadequacy of the State Board
of Fisheries and Game. . . . Sour grapes! They make a stout wine for a chap with
an empty creel, and they'll ferment forever.

The stream I had been fishing is one of those common to southern Connecticut. Its point of origin lies about twenty miles inland; it flows into Long Island
Sound. In the back-country region it runs rapidly through rugged, wild terrain, so
lavish with stands of hardwood and evergreen trees that it could serve for the
photographic background in an advertisement of the north country. As its course
approaches the Sound, however, the surrounding country flattens markedly and
the current slackens pace. At about the point where fresh water and tidewater
merge, the stream assumes a dull greenish appearance which thickens as it
approaches the delta.

The upper section of this stream is productive trout water, but the fishing
rights there are sewed up by a wealthy and exclusive sportsmen's association. I
confine my fishing to the extreme lower end of the stream.

The bridge where I stood is the approximate demarcation line between the
fresh and tidal waters. It marked the end of my journey downstream, for below
that bridge conditions were considered hopeless. Rumors about lunkers lurking in
the waters between bridge and Sound had circulated, but no angler of my
acquaintance put much stock in them. Those who had been gullible enough to

venture below reported conditions there as suitable for sinking eelpots, but hardly for wet flies.

As I stood, rod in hand, I heard a noisy old farm truck approaching. The driver, a gray-bearded patriarch of a farmer, upon discovering my presence, brought his ancient conveyance to a stop.

Another of these old-timers, I decided. He's going to ask what luck I've had. When I fess up, he'll bend my ear for half an hour, telling me all about the trout he used to catch in this stream when he was young. Oh, hum—too bad I wasn't born fifty years ago!

"Ketch any trouts, young fella?" he asked me, and I congratulated myself for my perceptive powers.

"Nope!" I answered. "Not even a rise. Guess I should have fished this stream fifty years ago."

That last remark had the earmarks of a rude dig, but the farmer didn't take it that way. Instead, he regarded me with humorous blue eyes. "You know, young fella," he said, "people these days don't know how to fish this here crick. Shucks, there's plenty of trouts left in it. Big fellas that'll go two pounds, mebbe three!"

I'm not accustomed to hearing men of his generation talk that way about the present time, and it left me momentarily speechless. When my blood pressure dropped a quarter of a point I replied, "You're not kidding, are you?"

Before answering, he spat through a hole in his windshield where a piece of glass was missing, and a spot near the steaming radiator sizzled momentarily. "Kiddin'?" he snorted. " 'Course I ain't kiddin'! Thet's the whole dern trouble with you younguns; you think everybody's kiddin' you. Why, I've told a dozen of you fellas how to ketch trouts in this here crick, but I ain't heard of any of you tryin' it!"

So that's how it is, I though to myself. He's raring to expound a theory—and I'll just have to humor him along. "Tell me how it's done," I requested aloud.

"Sure!" he said eagerly. "Fust of all, you hike down the crick a piece—mebbe a mile or so on an incomin' tide —"

That was too much for me to bear, for one becomes affectionately fond of one's own theories about where fish are to be found. I cut in on him good-naturedly. "Now listen, pop, that's tidewater down there—boggy and brackish. No trout live down there. I know fellows who have tried fishing there."

New Englanders of the old school aren't lightly rebuffed when they wish to make a point. "Is thet so?" the old gentleman flared, hopping out of his truck and pointing a forefinger at me. "Now you listen to me, sonny! There's only one reason why them fellas ain't caught trouts down there; they didn't go about it right. You'll never ketch trouts down there if you go stompin' along the bank swishin' flies an' plunkin' worms. Them trouts only feed on the incomin' tide, an' their feedin' grounds change with flood water. 'Tis a matter of locatin' where they're feedin', an' ketchin' them without 'rousin' their suspicions."

"But how can you locate them?" I asked, my curiosity mounting.

He chuckled. "My grandpappy told me how to do it!" he answered. "But supposin' I tell you?" he inquired suspiciously. "Are you goin' to laugh an' say 'Sure, sure,' like them other fellas I told?"

He had put me on a spot. His theory might prove laughable, but the prospect intrigued me. "No," I promised, "I won't laugh."

"Wal now, one thing more! Will you promise to try it out this very afternoon on the incomin' tide?"

That was really calling the turn—one of these all-or-nothing propositions. But what could I lose? "O.K., I promise," I told him.

My willingness evidently delighted the old man. His tone became confidential, his manner patronizing. "Thet's the spirit!" he beamed. "You c'mon to the farm with me. I'll tell you on the way up."

As we crawled over the half-mile run to his farm, and he unveiled his secret, it became increasingly apparent that I was one of those people Barnum referred to. But I had made a promise.

It seems that in bygone days many trout, salmon, and weakfish were taken in that salt-meadow stretch of the stream through employment of a forgotten technique. The old-time fishermen merely tossed bamboo poles six or eight feet long into the current, and let them drift by themselves upstream with the incoming tide. To each pole was fastened about ten feet of twine with a baited hook upon the other end dangling free in the water. Sooner or later the bait drifted over the feeding grounds of the fish. When it did, the fish would grab the bait and hook themselves.

The unregulated natural drift of the bait, and the fact that there were no fishermen there to arouse suspicion, did the trick. According to my informant, the old-timers used to set as many as a dozen such contrivances adrift. After the tide had reached its peak they would row upstream to retrive their rigs, plus a fine mess of fish.

The old gentleman was obviously sincere; but my mind was busy thinking up excuses. "Trouble is," I stalled, "I haven't any suitable gear for the purpose with me."

"Don't let thet worry you none, sonny!" my host said reassuringly. "I've got at least a dozen rigs all ready."

"But I haven't any bait."

"Thet also is of no account. Jest you take thet spade out to the manure pile. You'll find a can out there, too!"

In less than an hour we were climbing into the truck.

"I'll tote you down to your car," he said simply. "Tide's 'most right. Can't go along—too busy! But you let me know how you've fared when you bring back the gear."

I felt almost ashamed at my reluctance in the face of such hospitality. He made it seem that I was doing him a favor, instead of the other way around. But I still had my fingers crossed.

Back at my car, he issued final instructions: "Now you go right on down the road a piece, till you come to an old sand pit. Cut down to the crick, foller the path east from there, an' keep trottin' till you come to an old boat landin'. Throw your poles from thet landin'—one at a time and a couple minutes apart—an' then keep your eye on 'em till full tide. Then use thet rowboat tied up near there to fetch 'em back in."

A short time later I stood on the old boat landing and watched the tide flood upstream. Several times I glanced furtively about me to make certain there were no witnesses to what I was about to do. I felt like a senior deacon who had been asked to jitterbug; and, had there been anyone around, I couldn't have gone through with it.

Already I had decided against following one instruction: I wouldn't attach any hooks to the twine on my floating poles; instead, I'd tie the worms directly to the twine. Should I see the rigs bobble, as the farmer had predicted they would (though I doubted him), I would crawl within range and use my trout rod. Also, I wasn't too sure that the state laws permitted this unorthodox method of angling; but since I wasn't using hooks, the worst they could do was to hail me before an alienist.

What I dreaded most was meeting up with one of my friends; for, in that

130

event, I would never live down the fact that I was trying to catch trout with a Rube Goldberg contraption.

Eventually I threw three of the rigs into the stream, which at that point was about thirty-five feet wide. I was amazed at how well the rigs floated; the wood in them was thoroughly seasoned, and I imagine that the farmer had them hanging in his shed for a very long time. I hid the ones I didn't use, deciding that I would play dumb in case anyone should happen along and begin to ask questions. "Why, I was wondering what those sticks were doing out there myself!" I intended to exclaim in lamblike innocence.

Following at a safe distance on the bank, I now watched the poles voyage serenely upstream. Occasionally one would foul in grass or debris for a moment, but the incoming tide was stronger than one would suppose, and they continued upon their course.

One of the rigs was leading the others by about seventy-five feet when it approached a rather sharp bend in the stream. At that point something happened to it: one moment it was drifting peacefully, the next moment it began to tremble. Then it began to bob up and down so violently that ripples spread all over the surface of the water. Suddenly it tiled and dived for a brief moment; then it reappeared, acted as though it were trying to regain its bearings, and continued to drift upstream once more.

The sight amazed and excited me, but I was determined not to entertain false hopes. "Probably a big eel playing with it," I said to myself, but my pace quickened. I had my trout rod ready, silver-tinged bucktail and all; for hope springs eternal.

Mindful of the farmer's warning about the notorious shyness of these trout, I approached the bend cautiously and, when fairly close, completed the journey on my hands and knees. Hiding behind a big bowlder on the bank, I managed my first cast. After allowing the bucktail to sink almost to the bottom I began to retrieve, using the skip method. I had scarcely got my wrist action adjusted to the tempo of the proper rhythm, when wham! a big fish struck.

Having a fish strike so close to bottom, and so quickly, was a new and startling experience for me, and I would undoubtedly have missed hooking him if it hadn't been for his own ferocity in hitting the lure. In an instant I was on my feet, with my rod bent to a half circle and my line cutting through the water like a knife. From then on it seemed more like a tug of war than a battle with a trout. This fellow went places, all right; he was determined and powerful, but he seemed to insist upon hugging bottom. Could a young sand shark have ventured too far from his regular habitat? Of course that sounded fantastic, but so did my entire performance.

In due time—and who actually knows just how long he had played a fish?—my adversary grew weaker, but grudgingly! His resistance diminished, and there was less distance to his runs. I began to lead him toward the bank.

When he was netted and I was kneeling over him in awestruck wonder, I took stock of him. He was a genuine speckled brookie all of eighteen inches long. "These old-time farmers," I murmured penitently, "sure know what it is all about!"

Having eased my conscience thus, I once more turned my attention to the water and the rigs. The mates of the first pole had by this time passed the spot where I had made my catch; they were almost around the bend, and drifting smoothly. Even with proof in my creel that this method of locating feeding fish in tidewater was effective, I scarcely dared to hope for a repeat performance. But I put three more poles to floating.

And in the next hour, by employing practically the same methods that I had used in taking my first trout, I annexed five beautiful brookies running from sixteen to nineteen inches.

When it came time to call it a day, and a very fruitful day at that, I retrieved all the poles with the rowboat. As I wound the lines around them tenderly, I thought how much I owed to their kindly and wise owner, who had made my triumph possible. How to express my appreciation? How to make amends for having harbored all those doubts?

He was sitting in the doorway of his corncrib when I arrived at the farm.

"Look!" I cried elatedly, and I opened the creel and displayed the five big trout. "That method of yours certainly produced results!"

He gazed at the fish for a long time, like a man who can't believe his own eyes. Finally he scratched his head. "Wal—by gosh!" he exclaimed. "So it actually does work. Grandpa was right!"

I was growing accustomed to surprises, or at least I thought I was. Now it seemed as though I was starting all over again. "Do you mean to tell me that you didn't know?" I cried. "You've never tried those floating poles yourself?"

He looked sheepish. "Wal, no!" he replied. "You see, grandpa always did tell me that it would work, an' thet it worked fer him. But he used to spin sech yarns about fishin' thet I wasn't exactly sure. I always meant to git around to tryin' it, but somehow or other I kept puttin' it off."

The old man took another look at the fish, sighed, and shook his head.

"Guess I'll have to try it myself tomorrow!" he said.

The Kentucky Rifle

Fred R. Zepp

June 1948

In January 1948, OUTDOOR LIFE started a series of articles that told the exciting story of hunting and fishing in America. More than a year of research went into the project, of which this was the sixth article. "Nothing we have ever printed," said the editor, "has had an equal impact upon our readers." The author, Fred R. Zepp, was born on Long Island, New York, and early became interested in firearms and fishing. A graduate of the University of Pennsylvania, he worked for newspapers and press associations in widely scattered cities of the U.S. before becoming an associate editor of the magazine. In 1959, the Outdoor Life Book Division combined some of the yarns in this series with others by staff members in a single volume of fifteen stories under the title *The Story of American Hunting and Firearms*.

The first, and perhaps the most important, truly American firearm was the Kentucky rifle, a weapon which for more than a century was considered the world's best and chalked up records that still command respect. It was a picturesque arm—long, graceful, and accurate in both hunting and warfare—and its importance in opening large areas of the United States cannot be overestimated. Some authorities even say that a long-range hit by a Kentucky rifle may have won the American Revolution!

But before we go into that, let's take a closer look at the Kentucky rifle itself. In the first place, the name is misleading. The earliest models were made in Pennsylvania for pioneers, many of whom then pushed on into Kentucky—which included all the territory beyond the Cumberland Mountains. Subsequently these weapons were made in small shops as far west as St. Louis, along the Ohio River, and in what are now Pennsylvania, Tennessee, Virginia, the Carolinas—and Kentucky. But many men spoke of their Pennsylvania, not Kentucky, rifles and certain European firearms authorities still prefer to call them "American rifles." Then, too, quite a few of these pieces were not rifles but smoothbores, although the majority had either straight or spiral rifling.

Why was the Kentucky rifle such a success? Probably because here, for the first time, was a firearm that evolved in direct response to America's needs. Rifles brought over from Europe were of little value in the America wilderness. Loading was a slow, difficult job. The noise of hammering a tightfitting ball down the length of the barrel often scared off game or attracted scalp-hunting Indians. Construction was ugly and ungainly; trigger guards were bulky yet frail; sights were useless in dark forests or in any spot where accuracy was vital; calibers were large; and the rifles as a whole were heavy and unreliable. Little wonder that for many years the smoothbores reigned supreme.

That was the state of affairs in the 1720's when frontiersmen around Lancaster, Pa., began complaining to the newly arrived German and Swiss gunsmiths there. These immigrants were steeped in the traditions of their homelands, where they'd heard even the simple flintlock opposed because the smiths wanted to retain the more expensive wheellock firing mechanism. (The rugged flintlocks sent sparks flying into the flashpan when the trigger was pulled; the wheellock was a fragile spring mechanism which had to be wound in advance.)

It was in response to the demands of obstinate frontiersmen that the famous Kentucky model evolved. It hit its stride by about 1730 but underwent steady change for many years. Most rifles were built to the buyer's specifications or according to the maker's latest experiments, and the resulting new ideas were eagerly seized upon by competing smiths. For this reason, surviving examples show wide variations in detail.

No frontiersman wanted to carry a heavy weapon on his long treks in the wilderness. The weight was steadily reduced until the average Kentucky hunting rifle weighed between 9 and 10 pounds. (Those made for match shooting averaged about 19 pounds.) Similarly, using a large-caliber rifle meant that the lone pioneer had to carry a heavy load of bullets. So the caliber was reduced from the .65 and .70 common in Europe to about .45. The pound of lead that once yielded sixteen .70 bullets now gave forty-eight .45 balls—three times as many chances for fresh meat, or shots at hostile Indians.

Simultaneously the front sight was enlarged and the trigger guard strengthened while it was stripped of its old bulk. But probably the most distinctive change came in the barrel, which on previous rifles had been uniformly short and heavy.

Now it was lengthened, ranging in the early Kentucky models from 51 to 77 inches, or up to more than triple the length of the average big-game rifle of today. This meant that less powder was needed than before, because it burned cleaner. In the opinion of several authorities, this long barrel—which gave great accuracy at the same time that it deadened the noise of the firing—was the main factor in the success of the Kentucky rifle.

Coupled with this was the novel "patch" method of loading invented by some unsung genius. Thanks largely to this discovery, rifles could be reloaded in one fourth the time it took before, and eventually backwoodsmen were getting off their second shot in less than half a minute after the first.

To patch-load a rifle, you cast the lead-ball bullet in a mold 3/100 of an inch smaller than the actual caliber demanded. In loading, you slipped a piece of dressed buckskin or a bit of old felt hat, about the size of a 50-cent piece and well greased with tallow, under the ball as you held it over the muzzle. Then, when you rammed the ball down the barrel, the greased patch helped it slide along easily, doing away with practically all the old noisy hammering.

All these developments didn't come at once. They were spread over years, but if it were possible to describe a "typical" or composite Kentucky rifle it might be approximately like this:

Its 42-inch barrel, probably full octagon, gave the .45 caliber rifle an overall length of about 55 inches. The stock, which extended to the muzzle, was of curly maple or occasionally cherry—and, in the south, apple wood; the butt-plate crescent-shaped, instead of the old straight design. An eight-pointed brass star was sunk in the cheekpiece on the left side of the stock, while in the opposite side was cut a box, trimmed in brass, in which the greased patches were carried. The rifle's forty-four to fifty parts were handmade and not interchangeable. Many hunting models lacked decorations because these might reflect the sun and frighten game, but other Kentuckys made liberal use of brass on the side plates, buttplate, front sight, rod pipes or thimbles, and trigger guard, as well as on the patch box. Where brass was lacking, German silver or iron was substituted.

Although the early locks (firing mechanisms) were homemade, most of the later models were imported from Germany or England. The British usually supplied the flints, which sold for 2 cents each and were good for fifty shots.

To give a stock an artificial grain, the maker wound tarred string around and around the wood and burned it off. Soot and oil were rubbed in to stain the wood, and some stocks were treated with a special oil varnish. All in all, the Kentucky rifle—some models of which reportedly sold for $12 to $14 against $125 for a fancy European sporting smoothbore—was made to give lasting satisfaction.

However, exposure, rust, and the constant wear and tear of the split-hickory ramrod forced many owners to return their rifles to the smith for "freshing" or enlarging the caliber. This meant the hunter had to use larger patches or ream out his mold to cast bigger bullets. Still other worn rifles were refinished with smooth bores.

Although legend would have us believe that every frontiersman was a crack shot, and many of them doubtless were topnotchers, some users of the Kentucky rifle were away below par. That helps account for the popularity of Kentuckys with straight-cut rifling. These made good combination arms. They'd fire two lead balls at once, much as the smoothbore could, or even handle loads of BB to No. 4 shot. Yet they'd fire a single patch and ball accurately enough to bag big game. Some hunters even used mixed loads—a scattering of shot on top of a lead ball—when out for fox or turkey.

The Kentucky's flintlock firing mechanism and the bullet mold also had incidental uses. You could start a fire by placing a tiny wad of unspun flax in the flashpan and sprinkling it with powder. When you pulled the trigger, sparks fell on the wad and started it burning. Just drop this into a little pile of dry tinder, and presto—a fire!

Bullet molds were made of brass, stone, and even from old curling irons. They resembled pliers, with a hollow in one jaw to shape the bullet. Anglers of the day used them to cast weights for fish nets and seines.

Powderhorns were carved with scenes, family histories, and maps. They were often scraped so thin that the black powder showed through, giving the hunter a constant check on his supply. The average Kentucky rifleman's horn was some 11 inches in length and held up to 3/4 pound of powder. Much smaller was the primingpowder horn, which was carried in the pocket or in the hunting bag slung by a strap around his neck. This bag also contained a wire for cleaning the touchhole (through which the priming powder ignited the coarse powder and fired the rifle), flints, a few light tools, a bone needle for repairing ripped clothing, and extra bullets.

Plain open sights were preferred by the early hunters—some type of notch, say, for the rear with a post or a fin in front. Rear sights were placed on grooved slides, and horizontal adjustments were possible. Most frontiersmen sighted in their rifles to shoot a bit high at 50 yards. The ball reached its peak height between 50 and 100 yards; at 100 yards it registered a 3-inch drop.

Pinhead front sights—much like the modern bead sights—were standard for match shooting, but all sorts of rear sights, including peep sights, were used. Many marksmen swore by a long brass or iron tube, up to 5/8 inch in diameter and extending the full length of the barrel. It was possible to make horizontal adjustments on this because it was clamped at each end to a sliding base. A peekhole in the eyecup and a pinhead front sight, fixed slightly below point-blank range, completed the setup. Users claimed clearer definition of their targets—and some experts say that these were the sights Congress had in mind when it ordered the purchase of telescopes for use on rifles during the Revolution.

American pioneers who grew up with the Kentucky rifle in their hands were real riflemen. As hunters they were silent, swift, and deadly; as target shooters they were cool, self-confident, and accurate. And don't forget their womenfolk, some of whom could match their husbands shot for shot. The wife of one gunsmith was acknowledged to be better than any rifleman in the area. It was her job to test each rifle made by her husband. Other women won their laurels the hard way—by clean hits on charging redskins. And many a self-reliant frontiersman, who balked at resting a rifle barrel on a handy prop for an ordinary shot, was glad to support it on his wife's shoulder for a difficult long-range target.

To judge wind velocity, these men watched the fluttering of the leaves. They knew many little tricks, including a few that had been handed down for several generations. One of these, the practice of stalking big game while hidden beside a horse, had been used by archers in Europe hundreds of years before. Another was coaxing a bear from his hiding place in a big log by sneaking up silently and tapping at intervals on the wood. Pretty soon the nosy bruin would clamber out to investigate—just in time to be shot.

If his dog treed smaller game at night, the backwoodsman had no hesitation in climbing the tree and shaking the animal to the ground. If he wanted a change of diet, he could use his Kentucky rifle to shoot large fish! And to lure gobblers, he made a call from a turkey-wing bone.

A hunter needed all the practice he could get if he planned to enter a regular turkey shoot. Ranges depended on how much of the turkey was visible. If only the neck and head could be seen when the bird peered over a bulletproof plank, the range was shorter than if the entire bird was tied out in plain sight.

Many shooting matches were held in the woods, with squirrels as the targets; a natural form of competition, since nearly all these men shot bush-tails year in and year out. (Using a Kentucky rifle, a modern Tennessee gunsmith, William Walker, is said to have shot forty squirrels without a miss in a shooting match with a rival marksman.)

From Kentucky-rifle days come the picturesque stories about "barking" squirrels, a stunt which Daniel Boone is said to have been one of the first to perform. The trick was to hit the bark of the tree directly under the squirrel. When this was done properly, the bark was splintered and the squirrel, killed or stunned by the concussion, was sent flying head over heels through the air. Try it with your .22!

George Washington had learned the value of Kentucky riflemen in the French and Indian War. When the Revolution began, he urged the Continental Congress to put in a call for them. So it happens that the first troops raised by a central government on this continent were companies of straight-shooting backwoodsmen —and this might be called the beginning of the U.S. Army!

From the far fringes of the frontier the colorful, independent hunters flocked to their meeting places. One group of ninety-six men, recruited in Virginia by Daniel Morgan, marched 600 miles in 21 days to join the army facing the British at Cambridge, Mass. And some of these tough customers had walked 200 miles through the wilderness in order to enlist!

The bulk of the fighting in the Revolution was done with smoothbore muskets, so inaccurate that nineteen shots out of twenty would miss an 18-foot-square target at 350 yards. This performance was so poor that Benjamin Franklin urged the authorities to equip the Continental Army with bows and arrows.

Like every other improvement in arms, from the longbow to the atom bomb, the rifle was denounced as barbarous and uncivilized—by the side that didn't have it. After Bunker Hill, the British tried to alibi their heavy losses by charging that the Americans used rifles with slit bullets that broke in four parts when fired. As a matter of fact, the frontier riflemen hadn't arrived at the time of Bunker Hill; according to a writer of the time, the New England farmers who fought there were armed with muskets, mostly without bayonets. But he adds: "They are almost all marksmen, being accustomed to sporting of one kind or another from their youth."

Soon, however, the men with the Kentuckys were pouring northward, amazing townspeople with their marksmanship as well as with their outlandish garb and swaggering manners. Newspapers were filled with stories of their feats—many of which obviously gained in the telling. From Lancaster, Pa., a townsman wrote of seeing a man take a 5 x 7-inch piece of board and hold it between his knees while his brother put eight bullets through it in succession from a distance of 60 yards. Another chap offered to shoot an apple off a man's head at the same range, but the timid spectators declined to watch any such fool stunt.

After they joined the army at Cambridge, the backwoodsmen made life miserable for the British. Their specialty was picking off officers and sentries. Soon a Philadelphia printer was writing to a friend in London: "This province has raised 1,000 riflemen, the worst of whom will put a ball into a man's head at the distance of 150 to 200 yards. Therefore advise your officers who shall hereafter come out to America to settle their affairs in England before their departure."

British General Howe is said to have offered a large reward for the capture of a Kentucky rifleman. When one finally was taken, Howe sent him to London to show what the redcoats were up against. A few demonstrations of his skill brought British enlistments practically to zero!

The riflemen may have overdone their long-range shooting, however. Some American officers seemed to feel that by attempting too many "preposterious" shots the backwoodsmen were wasting ammunition and getting so many misses that it might lessen the wholesome respect the British had for them. So one outfit was given strict orders not to fire at any target more than 150 yards away.

The shot that may have won independence was fired by Daniel Murphy, a frontiersman with Morgan's outfit. At a critical moment in the Battle of Saratoga, according to the story, Murphy was ordered to pick off the British General Fraser, who was rallying the redcoats.

Fraser was standing with two aides on a hill 300 yards from Murphy's position. The backwoodsman calmly loaded, sighted his long-barreled Kentucky rifle, and fired. One of the aides fell. Murphy loaded and fired again—and missed. By this time Fraser knew he was being shot at, but his code of honor forced him to stay where he was. At the third shot he fell, dead. Some historians say that his death decided the battle, which in turn influenced the French to intervene and so made independence sure.

Just how good was the Kentucky rifle? Fortunately, we don't have to try to sift from fancy in the legends of frontier marksmanship. Modern firearms collectors have actually tried out the old flintlocks in hunting and target work, and have tested their ballistics by scientific methods.

The results of one of these tests are reported by Townsend Whelen in his book, *The American Rifle*. The arm was a Rosser flintlock made in Lancaster, Pa., in 1739. It fired a round ball of .32-inch diameter weighing 49 grains, with a charge of 22 grains of black powder. The test was made at the Remington-Union Metallic Cartridge Co. factory, and here's how the old gun showed up:

Muzzle velocity	1,483 foot seconds
Muzzle energy	239 foot pounds
Velocity at 100 yards	850 foot seconds
Energy at 100 yards	79 foot pounds
Velocity at 200 yards	617 foot seconds
Energy at 200 yards	41 foot pounds

According to Whelen, the best range for rifles of this type was about 60 yards. They were seldom used, he says, at more than 100 yards, and beyond 150 yards were not reliable. In power he classes them with the present-day .25 Stevens rimfire cartridge at short ranges.

A slightly more flattering picture was given in hunting and target tests made by

Capt. John G. W. Dillin, collector and authority on Kentucky rifles. In 1921 Dillin took a famous flintlock called "Old Killdeer" to a farm and had "a well-known off-hand rifleman" try it out.

The first targets were pigeons sitting on a high barn, 30 to 35 yards away. Two birds were killed in three shots. What is more, the rifleman called his shots: "High up, as I aimed above the center of the body." On the same trip, three starlings and a sparrow were hit at 15 to 40 yards—a total of six dead birds for eight shots, strictly offhand.

Another time, Dillin took "a good flintlock" to Ontario and tried it on wild ducks. Out of three shots at ducks swimming 150 yards away, he hit one bird squarely through the body, another in the wing. The miss was the first shot and was due to overestimating the drop of the bullet.

With Walter M. Cline, of Tennessee, Dillin tested three Kentucky rifles (a spiral-groove, a straight-cut, and a smoothbore) on standard silhouette targets the size of an average man. Out of ten shots at 300 yards, the spiral scored five hits, the straight-cut two, and the smoothbore one hit. Beyond 300 yards, Dillin reported, the percentage of hits was small.

While these cold figures demolish some of the tall stories of frontier legend, the fact remains that the Kentucky rifle was a great firearm for its day. Compared with the best sporting and military arms of the time, it represented nothing less than a revolution in its field.

Some flintlock Kentucky rifles are still in use today, mostly for target shooting by muzzle-loader enthusiasts, but for all practical purposes this famous arm faded from the picture about the year 1830.

Many specimens were refitted to handle percussion caps when these appeared. Calibers were reduced and barrels were shortened. However, men moving west found this rifle unsuited for use on horseback, and new weapons began to appear.

But still the Kentucky rifle lives in memory and tradition—a truly American, a truly great weapon, worthy of the men who used it.

Outdoor Life
Covers

Picking a cover subject for a magazine that will attract the greatest number of readers can be a frustrating game of chance. It wasn't a problem for OUTDOOR LIFE in 1898 when the first few covers were identical except for changing the date and table of contents. But then the notion took hold that the cover should help sell the magazine. After a few polite scenes ending with the 1906 tennis cover (No. 4), a double-fault if ever there was one, the editors came up with some pretty fair artists and OUTDOOR LIFE has stayed rough and ready ever since.

It has remained a cover illustrators' magazine. True, its covers as far back as June and July 1903 were black and white photos on colored backgrounds ("Chicks" and "Beaver"), and much later I tried to use three or four exceptional action photos every year, but otherwise paintings fared best. In July 1905 the magazine carried its first cover blurb: "Roosevelt Hunt Number." And when I retired we carried as many cover blurbs as a circus poster, but those exciting paintings still shone through.

My first art editor was Reg Hawley who liked what he called "happy" covers, and he got them from illustrators like J. F. Kernan, Keith Ward and Charles Dye. For all his humor Dye never slighted details and was greatly chagrined when several readers pointed out that one happy fisherman was holding up a big trout without the small adipose fin, especially since his rough sketch showed it plainly. Kernan, by the way, often used himself as model (No. 29).

Indeed, like so many of the illustrators represented in this small sample from more than nine hundred covers, Kernan knew his rods and guns from frequent use, but got his biggest kick out of painting the human side of hunting and fishing. Walter Haskell Hinton, who ranged the North American continent with rod and gun, pad and pencil, and camera, learned to ride when he had to be boosted into the saddle and to shoot when he couldn't hold the rifle himself.

Ralph Crosby Smith's interest in drawing and the outdoors dated back to the days he ran a trapline before school and drew pictures during it to the annoyance of his teachers. John Newton Howitt, a distinguished landscape artist, art teacher and illustrator, drew on a lifetime of hunting and fishing for his OUTDOOR LIFE covers.

Gordon Stevenson, noted portrait painter, trout fisherman and son-in-law of Edward R. Hewitt, famous angler and authority on trout, painted the extraordinary August 1942 cover (No. 31). The soldier's portrait is made up of sixteen scenes illustrating each form of activity indulged in by fishermen and hunters in the four seasons of the year.

Question was "How many scenes can you see?"

Bob Blinn succeeded Reg Hawley and became an art director any editor would count a blessing. Since Reg had done so handsomely by the happy hunter and fisherman, we felt we were simply doing variations on a theme, so we focussed on excitement, on confrontation between man and nature in all its wild manifestations, never forgetting, however, happiness in the form of leaping bass, salmon or trout.

It's noteworthy that at least four of the artists on whom Bob Blinn depended heavily for covers (all represented here) eventually gave up illustrating and became fine arts painters.

Bob Kuhn, probably the country's leading animal painter, got his start with OUTDOOR LIFE thirty-five years ago, now concentrates on painting African wildlife and exhibits in Texas.

Frank McCarthy, whose hobby is filming reenactments of Civil War battles, got his start doing society girl illustrations for slick magazines, switched to adventure, and now is a successful Western painter.

Tom Beecham, raised on a ranch and an avid hunter and fisherman, quit the field and is also doing Western paintings. His leaping grayling (No. 44) was one of OUTDOOR LIFE's bestselling covers in July, the "quiet" month.

Denver Gillen moved to Mexico, where he is a distinguished painter. I have a vivid recollection of a New York showing of his paintings of India.

On the other hand, there is David Blossom, son of an illustrator, who left advertising to become an illustrator, and George Giguere (No. 34) who was saved from a career as a mechanical engineer when his high-school drawing teacher hired him as assistant in free-hand drawing. His first commission was to illustrate a James Oliver Curwood serial of the Frozen North. That clinched it.

Among the several new covers appearing in the Second Edition of the Treasury is No. 56, October 1973 issue, a whitetail deer plus a curious figure at the bottom of the page over which, in small type, are these questions: Who is this man? What is he shooting? He is Bill McRae of Fairfield, Montana, a wildlife photographer who had done much work for OUTDOOR LIFE in the past dozen years, including this deer. He is armed with a 500mm lens and is wearing the white camouflage get-up he uses for winter photography.

Horseshoe Luck

E. C. Haase

December 1950

E. C. Haase's goat is still the world record today, twenty-five years later. A measure of his achievement is this excerpt from "Acrobat" (Aug. 1950) by Frank Golata, veteran British Columbia guide and frequent contributor to OUTDOOR LIFE: "It's many years since my introduction to the white goat of the Rockies and I have yet to see a mountain goat in good health lose his footing. Their natural habitat is usually the highest and roughest mountains in their district, and there they leap about and frolic like happy children in their own familiar playground. Apparently the goat thinks nothing of slipping, of broken bones or death from falling, and thus is able to concentrate on his footing. The average hunter, though, plagued with the constant fear of hurtling over the edge of the cliffs and lacking training, is no match for him."

The more you think about a project, sometimes, the more undecided and irresolute you become. At least it was that way with me when I was trying to make up my mind whether I'd go up to British Columbia on a hunt for a mountain goat.

I had good reason for wanting to go. For one thing, I had already collected excellent trophies of just about every other kind of North American big game. What I needed to make my trophy room complete was a good goat head. On top of that, I had just received my brand-new, custom-built .30/06 sporting rifle. After all, you don't lay out a nice wad of folding money just to fill space in the gun cabinet!

But I had my doubts. Goat hunting is, at best, a tough and unpredictable quest. You may get a good trophy or you may get a puny one. Or you may get none at all. It's hard work, too, for nature never intended man to claw his way up the precipitous, craggy peaks which are the home grounds of the beautiful white Rocky Mountain goat.

I was willing to tackle the hardships, of course. But there was always the possibility that the trip might turn out to be a fool's errand. Was the gamble worth the time and expense?

It dawned on me eventually that I'd never find out unless I tried. Luck might be on my side. Might be? Even now, as I look back, I'm dazed by the incredible good fortune that smiled on me as I clung to the wet, slippery surface of a high mountain ledge. . . .

I've been around quite a bit, so there's one thing I never leave to luck—my selection of a guide. That's why I shopped around before I decided on Allen Fletcher for the goat hunt. From all I could find out, he was a top-notch man. When I reached his ranch in Smithers, British Columbia, I was glad I'd been careful. He had A-1 animals and equipment, plus an air of quiet confidence that told me I had made the right pick.

We set out for the Babine Mountains at daybreak on September 15, 1949. As the packtrain plodded out of camp I cocked a weather eye at the sky. "You can't tell much what to expect," said Fletcher, reading my thoughts. "Weather's uncertain, this time of year. We've had a lot of rain lately."

141

That didn't sound too good but the die was cast. All day long we paralleled the banks of a rushing mountain stream, flashing with white water. We were following a primitive trail, Fletcher said, but I couldn't see any sign of it in the unbroken forest. It was a beautiful area, covered with virgin spruce, hemlock, and cedar. Occasionally, through a break in the trees, I'd get a glimpse of the mountains ahead.

But I didn't enjoy the scenery much at the start, for the going was rough. The first few times that my horse slipped on a wet, narrow ledge high over nothing at all I wished I'd never left home. But there must have been a goat somewhere in that horse's ancestry, for he always recovered his balance quickly, and after a while I began to relax a little. Sometimes we struck muddy stretches where our mounts sank to their knees. Other times we had to force our way through dense underbrush and the heavy moss that hung from the trees. We kept our rifles ready for action at all times. Fletcher explained that there were grizzly bears in the country, and we might suddenly come upon one blocking the trail.

But we met no bears. At dusk we halted among the stunted pines at timberline. In a grassy plot where the horses could graze, beside a cold-glacier-fed brook that would provide water for both men and animals, we unloaded Fletcher's pack horses, set up the tent, and soon were refreshed by the king of all perfumes—the aroma of frying bacon.

While we were sitting in front of the tent talking over the next day's plans, we heard something moving in the darkness at the edge of the pines. "Bear!" I thought, and reached for my rifle.

"Hi, neighbors," the bear said, breaking into view. "Saw your fire and thought I'd pay a sociable call. Name's Delong."

We introduced ourselves. I judged our caller to be a rugged seventy. His hands showed signs of heavy work, and he looked like a prospector, which he was. "Sinking a shaft for lead and silver over there." He nodded back toward the pines. "You men on a hunting trip?"

"Goats," Fletcher said.

The old prospector grinned. "You've come to the right place. Lots of them up in the mountains. Some big ones. But it'll be tough going. Dangerous, too, because the rocks haven't had a chance to dry in weeks."

I didn't suspect it then, but our visitor was destined to play a sort of offstage role at the climax of my hunt.

The ragged, dreary drumming of water beating against canvas awakened me next morning. Fletcher was already dressing. "No hunting today," he grumbled. "Too much rain and wind. Let's go fishing. Lots of trout in Two Bridge Lake. It's only a three-mile hike across that hunk of rock." He nodded toward a sizable ridge. . . .

Next morning we got up before daybreak. The rain had stopped, although the sky looked as if it could begin hurling water or snow anytime. There was considerable wind. "How about it?" I asked, remembering the prospector's remarks about wet rock.

"It'll be tough," Fletcher answered. "Whatever you say."

"Then let's go."

We ate a double-barreled breakfast, for we didn't want to be burdened with food packs during the climb. But we did put some candy bars into our pockets. I carried my new .30/06, while Fletcher toted my .375 H.&H. Magnum—just in case I found that I didn't feel completely at ease with the .30/06 and wanted to switch to the old reliable.

More than once, on the way up, I wondered whether it wouldn't have been wiser to have gone fishing again. The rocks were wet, and where they weren't wet they were dusted with snow. We tested almost every step before putting our full weight down. My arms ached from grabbing outcropping rock so that I could hoist myself up steep inclines or keep from tobogganing off ledges. I made slower progress than Fletcher; the flat country of western Ohio, where I live, doesn't offer much practice in mountain climbing. My rifle got in the way. The higher we climbed, the stronger the wind howled. A storm was developing, and hard snow began to sting my face.

I was beginning to think a candy bar would be a timely diversion when Fletcher, who was perhaps a city block ahead of me, stopped on a ledge to rest. While he waited for me to catch up, he unlimbered his glasses and studied the rocky landscape towering above and ahead. Apparently he saw nothing interesting, for he put down the binoculars, sat down on a wet rock, and got out his smoke-rolling equipment.

As I panted up to the ledge, he was trying to extract a cigarette paper from its little package. His damp fingers picked up two papers instead of one; and when he tried to push the extra one back into the package, the wind caught it and spiraled it upward toward the murky sky.

Idly we watched the cigarette paper do a flying-saucer act. It dived down and cruised at about our level along the mountain we'd been climbing. Suddenly Fletcher, whose eyes had been following its flight, grabbed my arm. "Look! There's a goat," he said, in a half whisper. "Right beyond the paper."

Then I saw a white spot against the dark rocks. I aimed my glasses at it, and when the image popped into focus I caught my breath. That big goat looked like the old man of the mountains! Altogether a specimen worth climbing for—and maybe in the record class.

I figured the billy to be about 300 yards away. He stood on a ledge a little to our left and about on our level. I dropped the glasses and was swinging my rifle up for a shot when the goat spotted us. He whirled, took a few steps the other way along the ledge, and disappeared below a rim of rock. I lowered the .30/06 and looked at Fletcher. He hadn't got that cigarette rolled yet. He stood up. "Let's go," he said. "But take it easy. These slippery rocks can throw you for a total loss."

Ahead of us was a sort of saddleback that ran along the top of the mountain, and we made our way to it. The saddle was as slick as a fresh watermelon seed and just as wet. The wind, carrying snow, tugged at us so badly that it was dangerous to stand; a gust could easily have sent us down the saddle and over the precipice. We crawled along on hands and knees. Soon we saw that we could not reach the goat's ledge, so we tried to parallel his course along the saddleback. Then we ran into a rock pinnacle that jutted up athwart the ridge like a horn. Attempts to by-pass it on right and left proved useless.

But then we noticed that the pinnacle had a little ledge somewhat above the level of the saddleback and jutting out into space. It was narrow, wet, and dangerous-looking. Fletcher didn't hesitate; he dug his fingernails and boot toes into the rough side of the pinnacle and clambered up to the ledge. In a few moments he turned, motioned to me, and said, "Out there's your goat!"

As I inched along the slippery ledge to Fletcher's side, the howling wind did its best to blow me off into space—space that dropped straight down for 300 feet. But I was thinking only of those ebony horns, not of danger. Fletcher pointed to the left and my eyes picked up the billy. He was making his way—without too much haste—along another narrow ledge. Now he was about 400 yards away.

What incredible luck I had that day! The ledge the goat was traveling on was shaped like a horseshoe. Already he had swung around its outer curve and was heading back on the far side. And although he was trying to escape from us, every step he took brought him nearer shooting range!

Carefully I edged into the prone position and brought the .30/06 up to my shoulder. When I put the scope on the goat I felt another surge of elation. This, undeniably, was a record-size head. The wind tugged at the rifle and I had trouble holding the crosshairs on the target. I squeezed off the first shot and a mushroom of rock dust puffed up below and to the right of the goat. The wind had fooled me. When that 220-grain bullet hit, the goat jumped straight up—as though powerful springs had been released in his feet. Then, back on all fours, he swung around, trying to spot his annoyers.

I felt a bit calmer now. Holding higher on the target, and trying to judge the wind more accurately, I squeezed the trigger again. The rock explosion was on the goat's level and closer to him, but still to the right. Again he leaped into the air, and again he tried to spot his enemies.

My third bullet went home. It took the goat in the left side of the neck and drove diagonally into the shoulder, breaking it. The billy didn't jump, this time, but tried to scramble over the rocks above the ledge. He couldn't make it, but lost his footing and started rolling down over the rock. Loose pieces followed him until I thought he was going to take the whole mountain along. But the avalanche petered out. After tumbling about 200 feet, he came to rest on a snowslide that summer heat had failed to melt.

"Nice shot," Fletcher said. "You can throw away the Magnum."

This broke the tension, and I took a deep breath. I had, at last, done something I'd always dreamed about—shot a bigger-than-average billy goat. But I didn't have my trophy yet, for it lay at the bottom of a little canyon that seemed about as accessible as a crater on the moon. I looked inquiringly at Fletcher. "Now what do we do?" I asked.

"We'll have to go down after it," he said. "Main problem will be to keep from going too fast."

We made our way back off the little ledge, and I watched while my guide crawled to a "chimney," a deep but narrow gash in the rock that extended downward in the general direction of the billy's snow bed. Bracing himself between the chimney's walls, Fletcher eased himself downward inch by inch, to the ledge—only to find that it led nowhere. Some ten feet away was another ledge, but between the two there was a drop of hundreds of feet. Fletcher looked up at me, shrugged, and then moved back as far as he could. He made a quick sprint and jumped, landed on the brink of the other ledge, looked for an instant as if he would topple backward into the chasm, and then threw himself forward on the wet, snow-spotted rock. I wiped the sweat from my forehead and called down. "I'm going to take the detour."

I used up an hour and a half edging along ledges, letting myself down, bear fashion, over steep slopes, and occasionally tobogganing on loose shale where a bad slip would have meant a roll of a couple of hundred yards. When I reached the goat, Fletcher was waiting. He looked pleased. "Best billy anyone ever got around here or I'll eat it, horns and all," he declared.

As we traced the bullet's path, it struck me that to hit a goat in the front while it was fleeing from me was slightly out of the ordinary. But by this time I was convinced that this was no ordinary goat anyway.

The sky must have been holding back just for us, for as soon as we reached camp the rain really let go. But that didn't keep us (including the prospector, who literally swam over to see how we had made out) from celebrating with the best banquet I ever attended. . . .

And that's how I got the world-record billy goat. Its horns surpass that of the old title holder, a billy taken in 1907 in the Cassiar Mountains of British Columbia. Here are the measurements of my goat (as contrasted with those of the older record, in parentheses):

Length of right horn, 12 inches (11¾); of left horn, 12 inches (12); circumference of right horn at base, 6½ inches (4¾); of left horn, 6½ inches (measurement of older horn not recorded).

Yes, that's how, with three shots, I got the world-record billy—plus two medals. The first medal, that of the Boone and Crockett Club, is for the first-prize Rocky Mountain goat in the club's 1949 competition. The second is the Sagamore Hill Medal, awarded by the family of Theodore Roosevelt for the outstanding big-game trophy of the year.

When the awards were presented to me, I couldn't help thinking, "I'm the fellow who hesitated because he thought a billy-goat head might look puny in his game room!"

Frozen Terror

Ben East

January 1951

When I began this project, I asked Ben East which of his OUTDOOR LIFE
stories he liked best, and then laughed at the absurdity of the question since
he had written hundreds of stories for the magazine. But without hesitation,
Ben said, *Frozen Terror*. It ran just one month before I became editor of
OUTDOOR LIFE, but I had already read it in preparation for my new job and
I wasn't to hear the last of it. By my count seven publications requested
permission to reprint it over the years. First time was in the 1952 edition of
Best Sports Stories, an anthology published annually by E. P. Dutton and
Company, and it was co-winner of the prize for the "best magazine story"
category. Then crème de la crème, it reappeared in 1964 in Dutton's
Best of the Best Sports Stories. Say it again Ben.

Tramping across the rock-strewn, snowy beach of Crane Island with two companions that bitter-cold winter morning, on his way to the rough shore ice and
the lake-trout grounds beyond, Lewis Sweet had no warning of what grim fate the
next seven days had in store for him, no intimation that before the week was up
his name would be on the lips of people and the front pages of newspapers across
the whole country. Nor did he guess that he was walking that Lake Michigan
beach for the last time on two good feet.

The date was Tuesday, January 22, 1929. There was nothing to hint that the
day would be any different from the many others Sweet had spent fishing through
the ice for lake trout, there on the submerged reefs off Crane Island.

He'd walk out to his lightproof shanty, kindle a fire of dry cedar in the tiny
stove, sit and dangle a wooden decoy in the clear green water beneath the ice,
hoping to lure a prowling trout within reach of his heavy seven-tined spear. If he
was lucky he'd take four or five good fish by midafternoon. Then he'd go back to
shore and drive the thirty miles to his home in the village of Alanson, Mich., in
time for supper.

It would be just another day of winter fishing, pleasant but uneventful.

The Crane Island fishing grounds lay west of Waugoshance Point, at the
extreme northwest tip of Michigan's mitten-shaped lower peninsula. The point is
a long, narrow tongue of sand, sparsely wooded, roadless and wild, running out
into the lake at the western end of the Straits of Mackinac, with Crane Island
marking land's end. Both the island and the point are unpeopled. On the open ice
of Lake Michigan, a mile offshore, Sweet and the other fishermen had their dark-
houses.

Fishing was slow that morning. It was close to noon before a trout slid into
sight under the ice hole where Sweet kept vigil. He maneuvered the wood
minnow away and eased his spear noiselessly through the water. Stalking his
decoy, the trout moved ahead a foot or two, deliberate and cautious. When it
came to rest directly beneath him, eyeing the slow-moving lure with a mixture of
hunger and wariness, he drove the spear down with a hard, sure thrust.

The steel handle was only eight or ten feet long, but it was attached to the roof
of the shanty by fifty feet of stout line. When Sweet felt the barbed tines jab into

146

the fish he let go the handle and the heavy spear carried the twisting trout swiftly down to the reef thirty feet below.

After the fish ceased struggling Sweet hauled it up on the line. When he opened the shanty door and backed out to disengage the trout, he noticed that the wind was rising and the air was full of snow. The day was turning blustery. Have to watch the ice on a day like that. Might break loose alongshore and go adrift. But the wind still blew from the west, onshore. So long as it stayed in that quarter there was no danger.

About an hour after he took the first trout the two men fishing near him quit their shanties and walked across the ice to his.

"We're going in, Lew," one of them hailed. "The wind is hauling around nor'east. It doesn't look good. Better come along."

Sweet stuck his head out the door of his shanty and squinted skyward. "Be all right for a spell, I guess," he said finally. "The ice'll hold unless it blows harder than this. I want one more fish."

He shut the door and they went on, leaving him there alone.

Thirty minutes later Sweet heard the sudden crunch and rumble of breaking ice off to the east. The grinding, groaning noise ran across the field like rolling thunder, and the darkhouse shook as if a distant train had passed.

Sweet had done enough winter fishing there to know the terrible portent of that sound. He flung open the shanty door, grabbed up his ax and the trout he had speared, and raced across the ice for the snow-clouded timber of Crane Island.

Halfway to the beach he saw what he dreaded, an ominous, narrow vein of black, zigzagging across the white field of ice.

When he reached the band of open water it was only ten feet across, but it widened perceptibly while he watched it, wondering whether he dared risk plunging in. Even as he wondered, he knew the chance was too great to take. He was a good swimmer, but the water would be numbingly cold, and he had to reckon, too, with the sucking undertow set up by 100,000 tons of ice driving lakeward with the wind. And even if he crossed the few yards of water successfully, he would have little hope of crawling up on the smooth shelf of ice on the far side.

He watched the black channel grow to twenty feet, to ninety. At last, when he could barely see across it through the swirling snowstorm, he turned and walked grimly back to his darkhouse.

He had a stove there, and enough firewood to last through the night. He wanted desperately to take shelter in the shanty but he knew beter. His only chance lay in remaining out in the open, watching the ice floe for possible cracks and breaks.

He turned his back resolutely on the darkhouse, moved to the center of the drifting floe, and began building a low wall of snow to break the force of the wind. It was slow work with no tool but his ax, and he hadn't been at it long when he heard a pistol-sharp report rip across the ice. He looked up to see his shanty settling into a yawning black crack. While he watched, the broken-off sheet of ice crunched and ground back against the main floe and the frail darkhouse went to pieces like something built of cardboard.

Half an hour later the two shanties of his companions were swallowed up in the same fashion, one after the other. Whatever happened now, his last hope of shelter was gone. Live or die, he'd have to see it through right in the open on the ice, with nothing between him and the wind save his snow wall. He went on building it.

He knew pretty well what he faced, but there was no way to figure his chances.

Unless the ice field grounded on either Hog or Garden Island, at a place where he could get to the beach, some sixty miles of open water lay ahead between him and the west shore of Lake Michigan. There was little chance the floe would hold together that long, with a winter gale churning the lake.

There was little chance, too, that the wind would stay steady in one quarter long enough to drive him straight across. It was blowing due west now but before morning it would likely go back to the northeast. By that time he'd be out in mid-lake if he were still alive, beyond Beaver and High and the other outlying islands. And there, with a northeast storm behind him, he could drift more than one hundred miles without sighting land.

Sweet resigned himself to the fact that, when buffeted by wind and pounding seas, even a sheet of ice three miles across and two feet thick can stay intact only so long.

In midafternoon hope welled up in him for a little while. His drift carried him down on Waugoshance Light, a lighthouse abandoned and dismantled long before, and it looked for a time as if he would ground against its foot. But currents shifted the direction of the ice field a couple of degrees and he went past only one hundred yards or so away.

Waugoshance was without fuel or food; no more than a broken crib of rock and concrete and a gaunt, windowless shell of rusted steel. But it was a pinpoint of land there in the vast gray lake. It meant escape from the icy water all around, it spelled survival for a few hours at least, and Sweet watched it with hungry eyes as his floe drifted past, almost within reach, and the squat red tower receded slowly in the storm.

By that time, although he had no way of knowing it, the search and rescue resources of an entire state were being marshaled in the hope of snatching him from the lake alive.

The two men who had fished with him that morning were still on Crane Island when the ice broke away. They had stayed on, concerned and uneasy, watching the weather, waiting for Sweet to come back to the beach. Through the snow-storm they had seen black water open offshore when the floe went adrift. They knew Sweet was still out there somewhere on the ice and they lost no more time. They piled into their car and raced for the hamlet of Cross Village, on the high bluffs of Sturgeon Bay ten miles to the south.

There was little the Cross Villagers or anybody else could do at the moment to help, but the word of Sweet's dramatic plight flashed south over the wires to downstate cities and on across the nation, and one of the most intense searches for a lost man in Michigan's history got under way.

The theme was an old one. Puny man pitted against the elements. A flyspeck of humanity out there alone, somewhere in an endless waste of ice and water, snow and gale, staving off death hour after hour—or waiting for it, numb and half frozen, with cold-begotten resignation. None heard the story unmoved. Millions sat at their own firesides that winter night, secure and warm and fed, and pitied and wondered about Lewis Sweet, drifting unsheltered in the bitter darkness.

The fast-falling snow prevented much action for the first twenty-four hours. But the storm blew itself out Wednesday forenoon, and the would-be rescuers went into action.

There was too much ice there in the north end of Lake Michigan for boats. The search had to be made from the air, and on foot along the shore of Waugoshance Point and around Crane Island, south into Sturgeon Bay and on the frozen beaches of the islands farther out.

Coast Guard crews and volunteers joined forces. Men walked the beaches for four days, clambering over rough hummocks of shore ice, watching for tracks, a thread of smoke, a dead fire, any sign at all that Sweet had made land. Other men scanned the ice fields and the outlying islands, Garden and Hog and Hat, from the air. Pilots plotted 2,000 square miles of lake and flew them systematically, one by one, searching for a black dot that would be a man huddled on a drifting floe.

Lewis Sweet, who on Monday of that week had hardly been known to anyone beyond the limits of his home town, was now an object of nation-wide concern. Men bought papers on the streets of cities 1,000 miles from Alanson, to learn what news there might be of the lost fisherman.

Little by little, hour by hour, hope ebbed among the searchers. No man could survive so long on the open ice. The time spun out—a day, then two days, three —and still the planes and foot parties found no trace of Sweet. By Friday night hope was dead. Life could not endure through so many hours of cold and storm without shelter, fire, or food. On Saturday, the last day of the search, those who remained in it looked only for a dark spot on the beach, a frozen body scoured bare of snow by the wind. At dusk the search was reluctantly abandoned.

Folks no longer wondered whether Lewis Sweet would be rescued, or how. Instead they wondered whether his body would be found on some lonely beach when spring came, or whether the place and manner of his dying would never be known.

But Sweet had not died.

Twice more before dark on Tuesday he believed for a little time that he was about to escape the lake. The first time he saw Hat Island looming up through the storm ahead, a timbered dot on a gray sea that smoked with snow. His floe seemed to be bearing directly down on it and he felt confident it would go aground on the shingly beach.

No one lived on Hat. He would find no cabin there. But there was plenty of dry wood for a fire and he had his big trout for food. He'd make out all right until the storm was over and he had no doubt that some way would be found to rescue him when the weather cleared. But even while he tasted in anticipation the immense relief of trading his drifting ice floe for solid ground, he realized that his course would take him clear of the island and he resigned himself once more to a night of drifting.

The next time it was Hog Island, much bigger but also without a house of any kind, that seemed to lie in his path. But again the wind and lake played their tricks and he was carried past, little more than a stone's throw from the beach. As if to tantalize him deliberately, a solitary gull, a holdover from the big flock that bred there in summer, flew out from the ice hummocks heaped along the shore, alighted for a few minutes on his floe, and then soared casually back to the island.

"That was the first time in my life I ever wished for wings!" Sweet told me afterward.

That night was pretty bad. The storm mounted to a raging blizzard. With the winter darkness coming down, the section of ice where Sweet had built his snow shelter broke away from the main field suddenly and without warning. He heard the splintering noise, saw the crack starting to widen in the dusk only a few yards away. He gathered up his fish and his precious ax and ran for a place where the pressure of the wind still held the two masses of ice together, grinding against each other. Even as he reached it the crevice opened ahead of him, but it was only a couple of feet wide and he jumped across to the temporary safety of the bigger floe.

Again he set to work to build a shelter with blocks of snow. When it was finished he lay down behind it to escape the bitter wind. But the cold was numbing, and after a few minutes he got to his feet and raced back and forth across the ice to get his blood going again, with the wind-driven snow cutting his face like a whiplash.

He spent the rest of the night that way—lying briefly behind his snow wall for shelter, then forcing himself to his feet once more to fight off the fatigue and drowsiness that he knew would finish him if he gave in to it.

He was out in the open lake now, and the storm had a chance to vent its full force on the ice field. Before midnight the field broke in two near him again, compelling him to abandon his snow shelter once more in order to stay with the main floe. Again he had the presence of mind to take his ax and the trout along. The same thing happened once more after that, sometime in the small hours of the morning.

Toward daybreak the cold grew even more intense. And now the storm played a cruel prank. The wind hauled around to the southwest, reversing the drift of the ice field and sending it back almost the way it had come, toward the distant north shore of Lake Michigan. In the darkness, however, Sweet was not immediately aware of the shift.

The huge floe—still some two miles across—went aground an hour before daybreak, without warning. There was a sudden crunching thunder of sound, and directly ahead of Sweet the edge of the ice rose out of the water, curled back upon itself like the nose of a giant toboggan, and came crashing down in an avalanche of two-ton blocks! The entire field shuddered and shook and seemed about to splinter into fragments, and Sweet ran for his life, away from the spot where it was thundering aground.

It took the field five or ten minutes to lose its momentum and come to rest. When the splintering, grinding noise finally subsided, Sweet went cautiously back to learn what had happened. He had no idea where he was or what obstacle the floe had encountered.

To his astonishment, he found that he had brought up at the foot of White Shoals Light, one of the loneliest lighthouses in Lake Michigan, rising from a concrete crib bedded on a submerged reef, more than a dozen miles from the nearest land. The floe, crashing against the heavy crib, had buckled and been sheared and piled up until it finally stopped moving.

Sweet was close to temporary safety at last. Just twenty-two feet away, up the vertical concrete face of the crib, lay shelter and fuel, food and survival. Only twenty-two feet, four times his own height. But it might as well have been twenty-two miles. For the entire crib above the waterline was incased in ice a foot thick, formed by freezing spray, and the steel ladder bedded in the concrete wall showed only as a bulge on the smooth, sheer face of the ice.

Sweet knew the ladder had to be there. He located it in the gray light of that stormy winter morning and went to work with his axe. He chopped away the ice as high as he could reach, standing on the floe, freeing the rungs one at a time. Then he stepped up on the first one, hung on with one hand, and went on chopping with the other, chipping and worrying at the flinty sheath that enclosed the rest of the ladder.

Three hours from the time he cut the first chip of ice away he was within three rungs of the top. Three steps, less than a yard—and he knew he wasn't going to make it.

His feet were wooden stumps on which he could no longer trust his weight. His hands had long since lost all feeling. They were so badly frozen that he had to look to make sure his fingers were hooked around a rung, and he could no longer keep a grip on the ax. He dropped it half a dozen times, clambering awkwardly down after it, mounting wearily up the rungs again. The first couple of times it wasn't so bad, but the climb got more and more difficult. The next time he dropped the ax he wouldn't be able to come back up the ladder. He took a few short, ineffectual strokes and the ax went clattering to the ice below. He climbed stiffly down and huddled on a block of ice to rest.

It's hard to give up and die of cold and hunger with food and warmth only twenty-odd feet overhead. Sweet didn't like the idea. In fact, he said afterward, he didn't even admit the possibility. There had to be some way to the top of that ice-coated crib, and he was bound he'd find it.

Hunched there on his block of ice, out of sight of land, with ice and water all around and the wind driving snow into his clothing at every buttonhole, the idea came to him. He could build a ramp of ice blocks up to the top of the crib!

The material lay waiting, piled up when the edge of the floe shattered against the base of the light. Some of the blocks were more than ten men could have moved but some were small enough for Sweet to lift. He went to work.

Three hours later he finished the job and dragged himself, more dead than alive, over the icy, treacherous lip of the crib.

Any man in normal surroundings and his right mind would have regarded Lewis Sweet's situation at that moment as pretty desperate. White Shoals Light had been closed weeks before, at the end of the navigation season. Sweet was on a deserted concrete island 100 feet square, in midlake, with frozen hands and feet, in the midst of a January blizzard—and no other living soul had the faintest inkling where he was or that he was alive. It wasn't exactly a rosy outlook, but in his fifty-odd years he had never known a more triumphant and happy minute!

The lighthouse crew had left the doors unlocked when they departed for the winter, save for a heavy screen that posed no barrier to a man with an ax. Inside the light, after his hours on the ice and his ordeal at the foot of the crib, the lost man found paradise.

Bacon, rice, dried fruit, flour, tea, and other supplies were there in abundance. There were three small kerosene stoves and plenty of fuel for them. There were matches. There was everything a man needed to live for days or weeks, or maybe until spring!

At the moment Sweet was too worn out to eat. He wanted only to rest and sleep. He cut the shoes off his frozen feet, thawed his hands and feet as best he could over one of the oil stoves, and fell into the nearest bed.

He slept nearly twenty-four hours. When he awakened Thursday morning he cooked the first meal he'd had since eating breakfast at home forty-eight hours before. It put new life into him, and he sat down to take careful stock of his situation.

The weather had cleared and he could see the timbered shore of the lake both to the north and south, beckoning, taunting him, a dozen miles away. Off to the southeast he could even see the low shape of Crane Island, where he had gone adrift. But between him and the land, in any direction, lay those miles of water all but covered over with fields of drifting ice.

From the tower of the light Lake Michigan was a curious patchwork of color. It looked like a vast white field veined and netted with gray-green. That network of darker color showed where constantly shifting channels separated the ice fields. Unless and until there came a still, cold night to close all that open water, Sweet must remain a prisoner here on his tiny concrete island.

At noon on Thursday, sitting beside his oil fire opening bloody blisters on his feet, Sweet heard the thrumming roar of a plane outside.

He knew it instinctively for a rescue craft sent out to search for him, and he bounded up on his crippled feet and rushed to a window.

But the windows were covered with heavy screen to protect them from wind and weather. No chance to wave or signal there. The door opening out on the crib, by which he had gained entrance to the light, was two or three flights below the living quarters. No time to get down there. There was a nearer exit in the lens room at the top of the tower, one flight up. He made for the stairs.

The pilot of the plane had gone out of his way to have a look at White Shoals on what he realized was a very slim chance. He didn't really hope to find any trace of the lost man there and he saw no reason to linger. He tipped his plane in a steep bank and roared once around the light, a couple of hundred feet above the lake. Then, seeing nothing but a jungle of ice and snow piled the length of the reef, he leveled off and headed for his home field for a fresh supply of gas to carry him out on another flight. He must have felt pretty bad about it when he heard the story afterward.

While the pilot made that one swift circle Lewis Sweet was hobbling up the flight of iron stairs as fast as his swollen, painful feet would carry him. But he was too late. When he reached the lens room and stepped out through the door the plane was far out over the lake, disappearing swiftly in the south.

Most men would have lost heart then and there but Sweet had been through too much to give up at that point. Back in the living quarters he sat down and went stoically on with the job of first aid to his feet.

"It doesn't hurt to freeze," he told me with a dry grin months later, "but it sure hurts to thaw out!"

Before the day was over another plane, or the same one on a return flight, roared over White Shoals. But the pilot didn't bother to circle that time and Sweet didn't even make the stairs. He watched helplessly from a screened window while the plane winged on, became a speck in the sky, and vanished.

Sweet was convinced then that if he got back to shore he'd have to do so on his own. It was plain that nobody guessed his whereabouts, or even considered the empty lighthouse a possibility.

After dark that night he tried to signal the distant mainland. There was no way for him to put the powerful beam of the light in operation, or he would almost certainly have attracted attention at that season. But he rigged a crude flare, a ball of oil-soaked waste on a length of wire, and went out on the balcony of the lens room and swung it back and forth, hoping its feeble red spark might be seen by someone on shore.

Twenty miles away, at the south end of Sturgeon Bay, he could see the friendly lights of Cross Village winking from their high bluff. How they must have mocked him!

On Friday morning he hung out signals on the chance that another plane might pass. But no one came near the light that day, and the hours went by uneventfully. Fresh blisters kept swelling up on his feet and he opened and drained them as fast as they appeared. He cooked and ate three good meals, and at nightfall he climbed back to the lens room, went outside in the bitter wind, and swung his oil-rag beacon again for a long time. He did that twice more in the course of the night, but nothing came of it.

The lake still held him a prisoner Saturday. That night, however, the wind fell, the night was starlit and still and very cold. When he awoke on Sunday morning there was no open water in sight. The leads and channels were covered with new ice as far as he could see, and his knowledge of the lake told him it was ice that would bear a man's weight.

Whether he would encounter open water before he reached shore there was no way to guess. Nor did it matter greatly. Sweet knew his time was running out. He feet were in terrible shape and he was sure the search for him had been given up by this time. This was his only chance and he'd have to gamble on it. In another day or two he wouldn't be able to travel. If he didn't get away from White Shoals today he'd never leave it alive.

How he was to cross the miles of ice on his crippled feet he wasn't sure. He'd have to take that as it came, one mile at a time.

His feet were too swollen for shoes, but he found plenty of heavy woolen socks in the lighthouse. He pulled on three or four pairs, and contrived to get into the heavy rubbers he had worn over his shoes when he was blown out into the lake on Tuesday.

When he climbed painfully down from the crib that crisp Sunday morning and started his slow trek over the ice toward Crane Island he took two items along, his ax and the frozen trout he had speared five days before. If he succeeded in reaching shore they meant fire and food. They had become symbols of his fierce, steadfast determination to stay alive. So long as he kept them with him he was able to believe he would not freeze or starve.

Now an odd thing happened, one of those ironic quirks that seem to be Destiny's special delight at such times. At the very hour when Sweet was climbing down from the lighthouse and moving off across the ice that morning, three of us were setting out from the headquarters of Wilderness State Park, on Big Stone Bay on the south shore of the Straits ten miles east of Crane Island, to have a final look for his body.

Floyd Brunson, superintendent of the park, George Laway, a fisherman living on Big Stone, and I had decided on one more last-hope search along the ice-fringed beach of Waugoshance Point.

We carried no binoculars that morning. We left them behind deliberately to eliminate useless weight, certain we would have no need for them. Had we had a pair along as we snowshoed to the shore and searched around the ice hummocks on the sandy beach, and had we trained the glasses a single time toward White Shoals Light—a far-off gray sliver rising out of the frozen lake—we could not possibly have failed to pick up the tiny black figure of a man crawling at snail's pace over the ice.

Had we spotted him by nightfall, we could have had him in a hospital, where by that time he so urgently needed to be and where he was fated to spend the next ten weeks while surgeons amputated all his fingers and toes and his frozen hands and feet slowly healed.

But the hospital was still two days away. Toward noon Brunson and Laway and I trudged back from our fruitless errand, never suspecting how close we had come to a dramatic rescue of the man who had been sought for five days in the greatest mass search that lonely country had ever seen.

Lewis Sweet crept on over the ice all that day. His progress was slow. Inside the heavy socks he could feel fresh blisters swelling on his feet. They puffed up until he literally rolled on them as he walked. Again and again he went ahead a few steps, sat down and rested, got up and drove himself doggedly on. At times he crawled on all fours.

He detoured around places where the new ice looked unsafe. Late in the afternoon he passed the end of Crane Island, at about the spot where he had gone adrift. Land was within reach at last and night was coming on, but he did not go ashore. He had set his sights on Cross Village as the nearest place where he would find humans, and he knew he could make better time on the open ice than along the rocky beach of Sturgeon Bay.

Late that day, Sweet believed afterward, his mind faltered for the first time. He seemed to be getting delirious, and found it hard to keep his course. At dark he stumbled into a deserted shanty on the shore of the bay, where fishermen sometimes spent a night. He was still seven miles short of his goal.

The shanty meant shelter for the night and in it he found firewood and a rusty stove, but no supplies except coffee and a can of frozen milk. He was still carrying his trout but he was too weak and ill now to thaw and cook it. With great effort he succeeded in making coffee. It braced him and he lay down on the bunk to sleep.

Before morning he was violently ill with cramps and nausea, perhaps from lack of food or from the frozen milk he had used with the coffee. At daybreak he tried to drive himself on toward Cross Village but he was too sick to stand. He lay helpless in the shanty all day Monday and through Monday night, eating nothing.

Tuesday morning he summoned the little strength remaining to him and started south once more, hobbling and crawling over the rough ice of Sturgeon Bay. It was quite a walk but he made it. Near noon of that day, almost a week to the hour from the time the wind had set him adrift on his ice floe, he stumbled up the steep bluff at Cross Village and called to a passing Indian for a hand.

Alone and unaided, Lewis Sweet had come home from the lake! When the Indian ran to him he put down two things he was carrying—a battered ax that had been dulled against the iron ladder of White Shoals Light, and a big lake trout frozen hard as granite.

I'm No Ted Williams

Charles Elliott

June 1951

Charlie Elliott beat me to OUTDOOR LIFE by a couple of months. He became Southern field editor in December 1950 and I became editor in February 1951. We came together in this, the first issue I scheduled. However, it wasn't my first contact with this top-flight writer. I bought a story from him in the mid-40s when he was director of the Georgia Game and Fish Commission and I was article editor of *Liberty Magazine*, and bought more from him when I was at *True*. Nevertheless, this was a milestone in a long and cherished association.

I can deposit a fly that weighs no more than thistledown on any square foot of a trout pool, or drop a plug through an opening at the base of a cypress, to entice the old bass there into a slashing strike. Once, after trailing a ram for two days along a high divide, I shot him just as he jumped for the protection of the rim-rock wall. And another time I stood in my tracks and broke the neck of a charging grizzly.

But never, either with a rod or with a gun, have I found a tougher challenge than the precise shot of the fly to a cruising bonefish.

A bonefish is, by no stretch of the imagination, a large or even a vicious creature. The world record on rod and reel is sixteen pounds. Yet I have seen strong men, who could flyrod a tarpon as big as an umpire without breaking a bead of sweat turn pale at the sight of an eight-pound bonefish moving at a walk through the water.

Joe Brooks, manager of the Metropolitan Miami Fishing Tournament, tried to explain it to me, and so did Ted Williams, one of baseball's immortals. It has something to do, they said, with the fact that in bonefishing a man must cast quickly and accurately to a specific target he can see, whereas in other kinds of fishing he's throwing blind, hoping for the best.

It combines both fishing and hunting where a man has to have eyes like an osprey, arms like the village blacksmith, and a shooting eye like Annie Oakley's —where wind and sun and a weed-and-limestone bottom conspire to help the fish instead of the angler.

"All you have to do," Ted explained, waving his hamlike paws at me, "is keep calm. Just don't get excited."

He was so serious that I wanted to laugh. Who could get excited about a fish in the ten-pound class? I'd had tarpon jump into the rowboat with me, and caught channel bass that could have flipped us over with a thrust of the tail. But I nodded solemnly and felt the powerful backbone of the plastic-impregnated rod Joe put in my hands. The big salmon reel on the butt end was equipped with a G-A-F line and 200 yards of backing.

"Why this?" I asked, putting my finger on the reel.

Joe grinned. "Wait till you hook one of those babies. You'll find out."

We were on the outer reefs between the broad Atlantic and the mangrove island flanking Key Largo. Bonefish come out of the deep water to feed on these shallow flats around the points and in the deep indentations of the bays. It is one of the most productive places on the upper Florida keys for bonefish.

"Sure you can handle that rod?" Ted asked.

I grunted a reply and shot out sixty feet behind the torpedo head to show him I was familiar with the technique of a heavy fly rod.

"If you'd add another forty feet to that, it wouldn't hurt," he said.

Everything must be right in order to see, hook, and land a bonefish. We had wiped the front section of the boat clean, to pile line in it. You don't have time to strip the nylon off the reel after you sight a fish in the water. The sun must be high. Early and late it throws shadows in the water, making a fish hard to locate.

Joe handed me a pair of glareproof sunglasses, which cut surface reflection and let the human eye penetrate into the green depths. And then they gave me my final instructions, as complicated as those a rookie gets before he goes up against a tricky hurler.

"A slow-action rod shoots line. Don't false-cast more than you have to. Drop the fly a foot or two in front of the fish; the shadow of the fly or the line across his head will flush him. Retrieve the fly slowly, in short jerks, then speed it up when the fish gets close. When he strikes, set the hook and feed the loose line through the guides with your fingers—don't allow it to foul—and then hold your rod tip high, letting him go to the end of his run against the six-pound drag. And look close. If you've never seen a bonefish, he's hard to spot at first."

Ted stepped up on the stern seat with his twelve-foot pushpole, forked on one end. Joe sat on the middle seat to instruct me and stay out of the way of any wild cast. I took the bow, an arrogant rookie with a what's-all-the-fuss-about attitude.

And I got more education in fishing that day than I've had before or since.

A shadow passed by, thirty feet off the bow of the boat. "There goes one!" I said.

Ted shook his head. "That's a barracuda. Look at his black tail. You've got to see them farther away than that."

"There's one over there to the right, then," I claimed, with a touch of triumph.

"A shark," Joe grunted. "He's too big and too black for a bonefish."

"Then what the hell does the critter look like?" I demanded.

"Maybe this will help you," Joe said. "Roughly speaking, his scientific name, Albula vulpes, means white fox. In the water he's a gray shadow, sheened over under certain conditions with a bluish or greenish cast. And he moves. A barracuda may lie motionless and a shark will cruise slowly in circles or curves. A bonefish is always going somewhere."

"There's one now!" Ted's voice crackled like a highvoltage wire. "Straight ahead of the boat, about eighty feet."

I strained my eyes until they bugged out.

"Now fifty feet," Ted snapped. "He's headed this way."

Still I saw nothing but rippling water and motionless bottom. He was thirty feet from the bateau when I finally did spot him, but by that time he'd seen us too, and turned off toward the rim of the flat that dipped into the Atlantic.

"At least," Joe said, "we know the flat's not barren today."

Twenty minutes later I got a bang as big as if I'd hit a triple when I sighted two bonefish seventy feet ahead of the boat. I'd never seen a bonefish, but I knew that's what they were. They were cutting from left to right in front of the bow.

I released the fly from my left hand and whipped a long line out toward the two fish, aiming at a point four feet in front of them, as if I were leading a slow dove in the air with a scattergun. The case was across wind, and I hadn't counted on that. The breeze caught my fly and shoved it to the water, directly over the head of the second fish. That was all. One moment I was looking at them. The next they were gone, leaving two threads of mud in their wake.

The water sizzled where Ted spat over the side of the boat. For a moment he seemed ready to bite an umpire. "Look sharp," he said, forcing a grin. "We'll see more."

Joe stood up on the seat behind me, braving the sharp barb of the Z nickel hook to furnish another pair of eyes. He spotted the next fish a hundred feet away and tried his best to point it out to me. I couldn't spot it.

"How in the hell can you catch 'm if you can't see 'm?" Ted asked explosively.

When we reached the first point that jutted out almost to the edge of the reef, I got my first shot at a bonefish. The sun was high now and behind us, and visibility was clearer than it had been all morning. The seagoing fox cruised around the point and came directly toward us. Joe pointed him out at fifty feet and I whipped out my line for action.

This time I was a little nervous myself. I was so involved in allowing for the wind, and wondering whether my line was correctly laid out in the bottom of the boat in case I did get a strike, that I forgot to even think about my backcast. The fly was too low. It caught the brim of Ted's hat and jerked it off into the water. The fish quickened his pace and swam on into the invisible depths.

"Here," I quavered, "somebody take this pole and show me how it's done."

Ted and Joe both stubbornly shook their heads.

"You're going to catch a bonefish if we have to kick it into the boat and fasten it to your fly," Ted said.

I was beginning to understand the jitters that come to every man on the bonefish flats. It wasn't as easy as I had planned. Not only did I fail to get the shot away, but every limestone ledge, every sand strip, began to look like a fish. Time after time I pointed—and Joe just shook his head.

"Don't worry. You'll know one when you see it."

We passed up half a dozen barracuda and at least as many sharks before I sighted another one of the white foxes. This one came from behind, on the downwind side of the boat. I saw him when I looked around to ask Joe a question and promptly forgot what I had planned to say. The fish, a big one, was boring like a torpedo through the water. I whipped out line and laid a perfect cast in front of him. My heart went into my throat and stayed there while he turned toward the fly. Ted was hissing, "Strip slower—strip slower—strip slower!" I had allowed the fly to sink, and just as the fish paused behind it I gave the lure an extra twitch. He hit it in a boil of water and I set the hook.

The leader cut through the brine and the line went out while I fed it through the guides. As the fish took off for the deep I pointed my rod tip high over my head as I had been instructed to do. The last loop shooting at the guides caught around the reel handle, which was turned to the front instead of away from the jumping nylon. The rod tip jerked downward—and the line went limp. The eight-foot leader had snapped like sewing thread.

Ted looked like he'd been caught stealing base. Joe sat down again. Nobody said a word, and my hands shook so violently that I had to pass the ragged end of the leader back to Joe and let him tie on another fly.

"Take the rod," I begged.

"You're gonna catch a fish," Ted yelled—and if they'd been listening, they could have heard him in Key Largo—"if we have to spend the winter out here."

All my confidence was gone. I was as weak as if I'd run the bases ten times around, and sweating just as much. I had to produce. We went for half an hour without spotting another fish, then one slipped under the bow of the boat and flushed before I saw him. My eyes felt as though they had been out on stems a foot long for a week. Joe sat dejected on the second seat.

At last I saw a fish cruising toward us out of the shadows of the mangroves. I knew he would pass fifty or sixty feet in front of the boat.

I had to make good this time. I didn't even point him out, but dropped the fly out of my cramped fingers, looked to the handle of my reel, checked the line in the bottom of the boat, remembered to allow for the wind, and shot a cast that fell two and a half feet in front of the fish. As he turned toward it I could feel my heart bumping against my ribs. The fish slowed up and I gave the fly a short jerk —and another—

I was watching the fly when it disappeared. I set the hook and raised the rod to straighten out the line before it reached the guides. But the braided nylon did not take off to sea. It went a dizzy circle around the bateau. Ted let out a yell that echoed back from the mangroves. Joe groaned. Then I saw the bonefish turn slowly and swim away. It was seconds before I realized what had happened. A barracuda had seen the fly and darted in ahead of the bonefish, snagging it out of his very teeth.

While I was trying to get him close enough to the beam to retrieve my hook, Ted sighted two huge bonefish lying between our boat and the island. Both were within easy casting distance. He threw his pushpole into the bateau, made a dive for the line, and almost went overboard. He caught the G-A-F on the 'cuda's next circle and with a vicious yank broke off the fly in its mouth. But the commotion had flushed the two bones out of the shallows. I reeled in line and sat down on the bow seat.

"I hate bonefish," I said. "I wouldn't catch one if either of you were starving."

"You couldn't catch one," Ted rumbled, "if it was in a goldfish bowl. But get back up there."

"I will when somebody proves to me it can be done,"I replied.

So we changed places. I went to the stern and Ted took the bow seat. Joe refused the rod.

"I'll try after you take one," he said to Ted.

Even though there is a trick to poling, I could handle the boat better than I had the bamboo, keeping the craft at an angle into the wind.

Ted's first fish was heading out to sea. The slugger made the finest cast I've ever seen for distance and accuracy, laying the line 110 feet into the stiff breeze and a foot away from the snout of the fish.The white fox saw the fly. He turned slowly, followed it for ten feet, then took it in a rush. Ted set the hook, pulled line from the floor of the boat, and let it into the guides. The end of the G-A-F shot through the tip and the squidding line followed, making the reel sing. The powerful drive of the bonefish carried him more than 700 feet against the six-pound drag on the reel before he came to the end of his run. Ted began to grind in line.

"Wouldn't it be easier," I suggested, "to strip it in?"

Joe snorted. "He'd have it tangled in a thousand knots on his next run."

Ted dragged his fish halfway to the boat before the finny motor cranked up and ran again, pulling out the squidding line to the last turn of the spool. Twenty minutes later Ted lifted his fish gently out of the water for weighing, then released it back into the brine. On Joe's hair-trigger scales it went an even ten pounds.

Joe took over the pushpole so that Ted could show me how to shoot line into the wind and explain the necessity of using a torpedo line and a slow-action rod. He was telling me that a bonefish will flush even at the shadow of the rod across the water, so the fewer the false casts the better, when Joe pointed out another fish.

Ted cast to it, hooked and caught it—as simply as that. It looked so easy that my own ears burned when I thought of the floundering I'd done.

After Ted's second fish he handed the bamboo to Joe and went back to his pushpole. From long practice in looking beneath the surface of the water, Joe could spot a fish at distances which were remarkable to me. And he could get his shot off as accurately as Ted.

He hadn't been on the casting seat ten minutes before a bonefish tried to run us down. Joe tensed, put his weight against the line, and dropped his lure where the fish couldn't miss it. He twitched the fly twice and the bone took it in a surge that brought him toward us so fast Joe had to strip ten yards of line to set the hook. When the fish was safely on, he handed the rod toward me.

"No," I said. "I'll catch my own."

"He's a small one," Joe insisted. "A five-pounder. I only want you to know how he feels. It's the first lesson."

I took the rod. The tip was jumping like it had tied into a winner of the K. Derby. The real sang in an off-key contralto, the line hissed like a pitful of cobras. Against the six-pound drag the bone ran out four fifths of the 700-foot line. He came to a halt and I cranked in the squidding thread. I cranked until I thought my elbows would jump out of their sockets. I got him halfway in and he ran again, to the end of the skinny squidding line.

A fly reel has no hidden ratios. When you turn the handle once, the spool turns once. I got the bonefish two thirds of the way back before he made his third bid for freedom. This time it was a relief to let him go. My arms felt as though they'd been pounded with a maul.

He didn't go far on his last trip. I was a little disappointed that he didn't drag out the line to its end and give me a longer breathing spell. I wound him in and Ted lifted him out of the water.

"I know one thing," I gasped. "I'm not man enough to catch a ten-pounder, if they grow in strength as they increase in size."

"If you don't learn to throw that line," Ted grunted, "you'll never have a chance at a ten-pounder."

The sun was at its zenith. The manner in which the bright light strikes the water makes high noon the best time for fishing, but we paused long enough to gulp down the ham sandwiches Cap'n Bill and Irene had made for us.

Even when those guys ate lunch, they talked bonefish. They compared flies and decided that any good bonefish fly has white in it, that a good lure is white and brown, or white and yellow. Joe confided that his favorite has red wrappings at the head, a gray hackle, yellow body, and white wings. He tied the pattern himself and it is now manufactured commercially.

We discussed other ways of fishing for bonefish than with a fly from a slow boat. That morning we'd passed two fishermen parked on the outer edge of the reef, fishing with casting rods and shrimp—stillfishing in much the way I angled for bullheads as a boy, but on the gently rolling ocean in the sunshine.

The most fascinating way to fish for bonefish is to wade along the flats at low tide, when the water is knee deep. In this way, as from a boat, the fish may be spotted either when they cruise along, watching for small minnows to dart out of the ragged bottom growth, or when they are tailing, with their heads in the rocks and grass, rooting out crabs and worms. Feeding in the sandy or muddy stretches, they throw up a cloud in the water. These "muds" indicate fish as definitely as his tail above the water, flashing silver in the sun.

When a man wades he's on his own, with no other eyes, no other hands, to help him. Then bonefishing takes on the aspects of big-game hunting, where you must find your quarry, approach cautiously to keep from spooking it, and make a perfect shot. In bonefishing, though, the shot is just the beginning of the fun.

"You don't see as many fish when you wade," Ted explained.

One thing that appealed to me is that when you go bonefishing you can spend as much or as little as you want. You can park your car along the edge of one of the many flats and wade out from shore. You can rent a bateau and a motor at almost any fishing camp, or you can pay up to sixty dollars a day for expert guides and services to insure your luck. Joe estimates that there are some 500 square miles of bonefish flats around the Florida Keys, and they're never crowded, though sometimes sixty fish a day are entered in the Metropolitan Miami Fishing Tournament. Best seasons of the year on the flats are from April through July and September through December.

Ted was casting an anxious eye at the sun, which still clung to high noon.

"Let's go—let's go," he said impatiently. "It'll be sundown and this game'll be called on account of darkness."

I took the bow again, laying out my line on the deck. I had learned to distinguish the black tail of the 'cuda from the dark, sinuous form of a shark. But the wind was blowing a little harder now, wrinkling the water's surface and making the fish more difficult to see. I felt like a guy standing at home plate with two outs, two strikes, and the bases loaded. If I fanned again I'd probably find myself on the bench for the remainder of the season.

Joe pointed to a couple of muds. "Looks hot in there," he said.

But by the time I had seen where the fish were mudding, they had slipped out from under the screen and were gone.

One nice bone came from behind and plowed beyond the longest cast before we saw him. And then I spotted one headed directly to the boat. Quickly I checked my stance and the lay of the line, estimated how far I'd have to lead him —allowing for the wind—and shot a fly that fell exactly in place. I didn't even have a chance to strip it in. The bonefish hit it with a thrust as savage as a peg to second and I hardly had time to drop the smoking line from my fingers. I cleared the screaming nylon through the guides and held the rod tip up. When the reel began to sing, Joe's sigh of relief was audible.

"He's a big one," Ted sang, "a big one! Boy, you sure hit that one on the nose!"

"Maybe he's a world record," Joe opined.

The line didn't even slow down. It smoked through the guides to the end of the backing and came to an abrupt and violent halt at the knot fastening it around the spool. The bamboo bucked in my hands and the line went limp. His last surging drive had carried the big fish far enough to break the eight-pound-test leader. I reeled in slowly, sick all the way to my toes. That had been in big fish. I'd hooked him fair and square, going through all the intricate process to—another error.

Joe's face was a mixture of disappointment that I'd fanned my big chance and relief that his bat in my hands was still intact. Ted made the kindest comment he could under the circumstances.

"Oh well," he said, "no man bats a thousand in the bonefish league."

A Double for the Captain

Allen Parsons

September 1951

P. Allen Parsons, before his death in 1963, was for more than thirty years
a writer for and Where-to-Go editor of OUTDOOR LIFE. He was also our
undisputed expert in all matters of hunting and fishing. Born in
Newburyport, Mass., where his ancestors settled in 1635, and graduated
from Wesleyan, he was truly a gentleman of the old school. He was an active
fisherman to the end, and his book, *The Complete Book of Fresh Water
Fishing,* appeared a few months before his death. When I took over as editor
in 1951, one of the first stories I scheduled was "A Double for the Captain."
I have never forgotten it. Nothing better reflects the kindness, the
generosity, the love of companionship, and of fun and people, that flowed
from the heart of "P.A."

The narrow road, which showed as a meandering line marked "unimproved"
on my map, didn't look at all inviting. But on a sudden whim I turned into it
from the busy highway. I wasn't gunning or fishing that day—just prospecting for
likely spots in that part of my state known as "South Jersey."

This particular section—just a few miles inland from New Jersey's famed
Atlantic beach resorts—is an almost unknown and somewhat mysterious area.
You pass mile upon mile of scrubpine and oak barrens. It's a wilderness in which
a stranger without a compass might easily get lost. Here and there you see traces
of once-thriving villages or the gaunt skeletons of long-abandoned mansions. Its
past is almost forgotten, its present unimportant, its future dubious. But it's a
land of deer and, to the east—along the "Shore"—of ducks.

The late-November morning was well along. I could hear the brown, dry
leaves rustling in the scrub trees whenever I'd pause to survey likely deer cross-
ings. One mile was much like another: sand and scrub trees. At long intervals I'd
see a house—little more than a shack. The gray sky, depressing landscape, and
general air of melancholy began to have their effect on my spirits.

Then I came to a wooden bridge that spanned a small river, perhaps thirty
feet wide. The water was the color of sherry wine, and the sandy bottom
streamed with long green weeds, all pointing downstream. The water was perhaps
four or five feet deep. Would there be bass or pickerel in there? Something to
think about, next season.

I parked near the bridge, took my package of lunch, and clambered down the
bank to a beached log. As I was about to sit down my eye glimpsed something
white, half hidden in a clump of bushes. I went over for a look. There it was—a
duck boat in good condition, turned upside down. Well, I thought, where there
are duck boats there are likely to be ducks.

Since I'd planned to make a long day of it I carried a generous lunch of six
sandwiches, two hard-boiled eggs, two big wedges of chocolate cake, fruit, and a
quart of hot coffee. I was spreading some of it out before me, as I sat on the log
when I heard a clump clump on the bridge.

I looked up just as a man leaned on the rail and gazed down on me. He was
well on in years, with a calm, weatherworn face and grizzled hair that straggled

from beneath an old cap. His peajacket was worn but snug, and he grasped a stout cane.

"Took me kinda by surprise, ye did," he said, chuckling. "Ain't used to strange faces. Like to see 'em, though!" he added hastily.

I laughed too, glad of company. "Come help me eat this lunch." I said. "It's too much for one man and I don't like to eat alone."

"Thanks," he replied. "Might be ye're hungrier'n ye think. Besides, ain't it a mite early for lunch?"

"It's noon, and it's never too early for lunch. Come on down."

He made his way off the bridge and eased down the bank, leaning heavily on the cane. Then he seated himself gingerly on the log.

"Roast beef or ham?" I asked, pointing to the sandwiches.

"Roast beef?" His eyes lighted. "I'm partial to that—long time since I et any. No butcher stores around here. I raise some hogs an' chickens. Smoke my own hams an' bacon. But a man kin git kinda sick of pork and chicken."

I put three beef sandwiches in front of him, together with a cup of coffee. Then we set to with a will. The bank sheltered us fairly well from the steady, chilling wind, but it was strengthening.

"A real blow's on the way," said my new friend. "Wind's nor'-nor'east."

"You a seafaring man?" I asked.

"Fisherman. Master of my own boat for thirty year. Sold her five year ago. Rheumatiz got me and the doc said no more salt water. Moved back in here to git away from the damp. Live in that white house just above here."

He cocked an eye at the somber gray clouds racing overhead. Four black ducks appeared out of nowhere, flying low. They swerved upstream.

"Strange to see blackies this far inland," I remarked. "They usually follow the tidal marshes."

"Ye ain't far from the ocean right now," he explained. "Those birds are headed for my pond. I planted wild oats in it some years ago and they took real good. Like to take a duck once in a while, durin' the season. It's a change from beef and pork. Used to be, anyway. Can't go gunnin' no more."

I was about to reply when a figure ran down the bank. I was startled, to put it mildly. The newcomer was a girl, but like no girl I was used to seeing. She was about fifteen and her features were strangely foreign. Her gaunt face accentuated high cheek-bones and black, shoe-button eyes. Everything about her was dark— her hair, her complexion. She clutched a man's rubber coat about her, and her legs were deep in boots that were five or six sizes too big.

"Well, Millie," said the captain evenly. "Was he lookin' for somethin'?"

She stared at him blankly for a second, then shrugged, and scrambled up the bank.

"She's a piney," the captain said after Millie had gone. "Sorta like a gypsy, only not a gypsy. Quite a few of 'em around here. Teacher feller told me once they been here since the Revolution. All sorts of blood mixed up in 'em, he said. White, colored, Indian, an'—let's see, now—yes, Hessian. Even A-rab. Git a sort of livin' by makin' baskets, ax handles, berry picking, an' such like. An' allus borryin'. Like as not she was here to borry my duck boat fer her old man, figgerin' I wouldn't be around to stop her."

"How do you get along with 'em?"

"Live an' let live. Allus borryin' a cup of sugar from me. Used to borry the cups, too, but never returned 'em. So now they gotta bring a cup or no sugar. Summertimes they'll send me a basket of berries, now and then. Last spring, one of 'em sent me a nice piece of meat—said it was mutton. I cooked it an' it turned out to be venison. I was madder'n scat—don't hold with illegal game killin'."

"How do they live?" I asked.

"In shacks. That gal lives with four other kids an' her mother an' father in one room. Minister says it ain't decent. Got a new one this year—minister, I mean. Sez he to me, 'Are ye a regular attendant?' 'That I be,' says I. 'Never missed an Easter or Christmas service in forty year.' Sez he, 'Is there anything in the text ye'd like to know more about?' Sez I, 'Know more? Yes; no more'n ten minutes!' "

I laughed appreciatively, then glanced at the sky. "The storm's really gathering," I said. "We'd better get going. I'll drop you off at your house."

"An' yourself too!" It was more than an invitation; it was a plea. "I have a drop of somethin' that'll warm us."

I was anxious now to get back to the highway before a rainstorm bogged the woods road. Yet I found I couldn't resist the invitation. Here, evidently, was a man who craved company. When we were in the car I said, "Get any ducks this year?"

"No," he said glumly, "nor will I. This rheumatiz has got my bones locked. I ain't spry enough to launch my boat, let alone swing a gun. My shootin' days are over."

As we climbed out of the car the far-off clamor of wild geese came to our ears. In the east a wavering wedge of the great birds was heading south. Then the rain struck, driven by a squall that lashed at us as we hurried (as fast as the old man could move) to his door. The captain's house, I saw at a quick glance, was a tidy cottage flanked by a barn and a little orchard of old apple trees. I dimly made out the hog pen and chicken house. And then the door was open and we stepped into the warmth.

The room I entered was kitchen, dining room, and living room, all in one. There were doors at each end of it, evidently leading to bedrooms. No welcoming voice was raised, so I surmised that the captain was either a widower or a bachelor. But no woman could have boasted a tidier home. A wood-burning stove gave out welcome heat. The table in the middle of the room was covered with a bright red cloth, the windows were curtained, and I noticed a little shelf of books. "Cozy" is a shopworn word, but it described that room.

A teakettle steamed lazily on the stove. The captain brewed some tea, spiked it with "a shot of apple," and we ate and relaxed. The drink soon kindled an inner glow.

"What did ye say yer name was?" the captain asked, between sips. I hadn't mentioned it but I told him now.

"Al," he said, "do ye ever shoot ducks?"

"Sometimes. But a lot of fools are spoiling the sport. No courtesy, no fair play. Last time out I had some ducks coming in to my stool. I'd waited hours for them. And what happened? A boob about 200 yards away blasted at them, out of range, and I lost my chance."

"Got a license and duck stamp?"

"In the car," I replied.

"Ah!" said the captain. "I kin rig ye out with waterproofs an' boots. Got a good shotgun an' shells. What say ye get some ducks at my pond—mebbe one for each of us. Ye'll not be bothered by other gunners; none ever come here."

The wind beat against the windows; now and then there was a clatter of hail. A vile day for humans, hence a good day for ducks. I was none too eager. But I knew that while the captain was extending an invitation he was also making a request. He wanted a change from chicken and pork, cooked in every known way.

"Fine!" I said.

He trotted out his "rig," and though the pants were too short the rubber boots closed the gap. He took an old singleshot 12 gauge hammer gun from a case,

163

then rummaged through a drawer. He muttered an exclamation and came up with just four shells. "All I got, dang it!" he said. "Didn't know I was so low. Kin ye do with so few?"

"I'll have to shoot straight. Any decoys?"

"Ye won't need 'em. Pond's narrer, and the ducks trade back an' forth in the wild oats I planted. Ye'll see. Bank on this side is about twelve foot high; 'twill give ye some shelter from the wind. Just pole the boat into them oats, hide yourself, an' ye'll git some shots. Ye can get into the pond on this side of the river, about a hundred yards up. Ye'll see sort of a cove, with a lot of tall rushes. Pole right through them for fifty feet, an' there ye be. Pole's under the boat."

Once in the boat I found the pond without difficulty, poled into the wild rice ("oats," the captain had called it), and bent the stalks over so they'd at least partially hide me. In getting in I flushed three blackies that had been feeding, but they were out of range before I could grab the gun.

Then I prepared to wait. Apparently the wind was too strong for the birds' liking, for no flocks came in, though now and then I'd see a duck working along the edge of the wild rice. I stared until my eyes blurred. Perhaps it was this concentration, or the steady whine of the wind, or the "shot of apple" in my tea. Whatever it was—I fell asleep. And that's quite a feat when you're hunched in a boat in a driving rain.

I awoke with a start. A gust of wind had yanked the rubber hood off my head, taking with it the captain's old red hunting cap. I had to salvage that. With one leg on the bottom of the boat, I started to put the other over the gunwale——

And two blackies, a drake and a hen, took off from the rice not more than ten feet from me! While I'd been dozing they'd come in to feed, quite oblivious of my presence. By the time I recovered my balance and got the gun up they were thirty yards away, flying close together and fighting the wind. I let go at the drake in the lead and, to my amazement, both ducks fell. Skill? It was the luckiest shot I ever made—and I've made a few.

I waded out and retrieved the birds. Now the rain was freezing and I'd had quite enough of it. As I walked back toward the house I saw the trees already sheathed in ice, with their branches creaking rustily in the wind. The captain was waiting for me and he opened the door the instant I put my foot on the steps.

"Well, here are your two birds, captain," I said, holding up the ducks. "And here are your three shells."

He stared at them as they lay in my hand. "Did ye git two birds with one shot?" he demanded.

"Oh," I said jokingly, "I figured that since you were low on ammunition——." Then I went on to explain how lucky I'd been.

"Damn this rheumatiz!" said the captain. "Why couldn't I been along to see that?"

The kitchen was filled with savory odors: ham frying in a skillet, biscuits baking, coffee boiling.

"Yer face is the color of a mackerel," declared my host. "Strip off them wet things an' I'll serve up supper. You can't go back home tonight—road'll be a glare of ice. I've made up yer bed. Glad to have ye. It gits lonesome here. . . . So you went an' got a double!"

I was glad enough to sit down near the fire, in the friendly yellow glow of the kerosene lamps.

"Getting a double for you, captain," I said, "was fun."

Coxe Reels HAVE GONE TO WAR

The experience of over 30 years in the production of precision made fishing reels is now utilized in the war production program of the United Nations.

This experience qualifies us for producing highly critical parts held to tolerance limits of two and three ten thousandths of an inch for various assemblies.

For the duration Bronson and Coxe reels will not be available unless your dealer has them in stock. Your present Bronson or Coxe reel will serve you well if given good care.

Buy more U. S. War Bonds-Stamps

J. A. Coxe Division
BRONSON REEL COMPANY
BRONSON, MICHIGAN

COXE REELS ARE NOT AVAILABLE UNTIL AFTER THE WAR

War workers! Take a tip... go fishing

When you've finished a tough week at the office or in the plant, and you feel as though you're worn out and on the ragged edge—on that day off, go fishing.

That's where you fishermen have the advantage over your non-fishing co-workers. You have a safety valve and a rest cure all in one. A day's fishing will go a long way toward getting rid of last week's jitters and putting you in good shape for the week to come.

If you have a good line, take care of it. And if you need a new line, see your dealer. He will have a limited supply of Gladding lines—perhaps not exactly the one you want, but you can rest assured that if it's a Gladding, it will give you outstanding performance and durability.

So let your favorite sport help you keep fit for the most important job ahead—the job of winning this war.

B. F. Gladding & Co., Inc., South Otselic, N.Y.
BUY BONDS NOW ★ ★ ★
for a real fishing trip later

GLADDING
INVINCIBLE · TRANS-LU-CENT · DONEGAL

America's New Light-weight Weapon
...with a Heavy-weight's Punch

THANK the United States Ordnance Department for this good news. They quickly realized that, in *this* war, our paratroops, and all other non-rifle bearing combat forces, needed a personal weapon that was lighter than the standard rifle... greater in fire-power, longer in range and faster in action than the automatic pistol.

Yesterday, no such weapon existed. Today, it is rapidly being made available to America's fighting men.

Here's the story. In record time Winchester *originated, engineered and developed* the U. S. Carbine, Caliber .30, M1. Gruelling tests in sand, rain and water—the toughest tests that Aberdeen Proving Grounds could devise—resulted in a unanimous verdict that this carbine as the best for this vital U. S. military job.

Operating on a simple principle that's entirely new to military arms, with 15 rounds in its magazine, the Winchester U. S. Carbine, Caliber .30, M1 packs a terrific wallop. It speeds its .30 caliber bullet 1900 feet per second...greatly increases offensive power.

Winchester is proud of this accomplishment...of originating and developing the U. S. Carbine, Caliber .30, M1...of manufacturing it in ever increasing quantities. We are mindful of the fact that it is Winchester *men*, not machines, that made it all possible. And that these same Winchester master craftsmen look forward to the coming peace when, once again, they can supply you with Winchester sporting arms and your favorite Winchester ammunition.

WINCHESTER REPEATING ARMS CO.
New Haven, Conn.
Division of WESTERN CARTRIDGE COMPANY

GARANDS, TOO!

Here again, Winchester craftsmanship is in the forefront of service to America. For we have long been on a 'round-the-clock production schedule of this famous rifle which won its spurs at Bataan and Wake Island.

"Everyday—with a Winchester Garand across his knees and a bolo to cut himself out of his harness if he fell into the water—he flew between Bataan and Corregidor..."
"The Heroic Defense of the Philippines"
—Reader's Digest, July 1942

WINCHESTER
"On Guard for America Since 1866"

SLEEPING BAGS *at FACTORY PRICES*

SAVE UP TO 40%

Why pay high retail prices for sleeping bags? Buy direct and save 40%! Highest quality FEATHER FILLED bag. Warm, water repellent, windproof. 100" Talon fastener with windflap. Roomy. Built for big men. Air mattress pocket. Side walls. 52" shelter half. Rolls compactly. A $45.00 value. Our price only $32.49. Warm WESTERN WOOL FILLED bags priced from $12.89. Shipped C.O.D. Write TODAY for FREE CATALOG. ALL BAGS MONEY-BACK GUARANTEED.

ALASKA SLEEPING BAG CO.
Dept. OL   312 S.W. Third Ave., Portland, Oregon

THE BEDROOM COMPANION

Outdoor Life Ads, 1941–1951

Here is a book of books guaranteed to make old men young and young men melt and to soften the hearts of the most sophisticated of maidens. It is a pulse-quickening, sparkling cornucopia of naughty fun and frolic. THE BEDROOM COMPANION will give you days and nights of unique entertainment.

THE BEDROOM COMPANION
or
A Cold Nights Entertainment

Being a Cure for Man's Neuroses
A SOP to his FRUSTRATIONS
A Nightcap of Forbidden Ballads
Discerning PICTURES
Scurrilous Essays
so far
A Steaming Bracer
for
THE FORGOTTEN MALE

ARDEN BOOK COMPANY
feet on Astor Place • New York • N. Y.

Only **1.98** Postpaid

Belongs on every man's personal bookshelf.

Walter Winchell Says:

"Gayer Than De Maupassant!"

The Wittiest, Raciest, chuckle-provoking collection of tasty tales, merry jingles, drawings and Art put together in one volume. **ACT QUICKLY, Gentlemen:** Rip off the coupon, mail it now and tickle your risibilities with the rare, riproaring gems and hilarious esquirish art.

LYMAN Sights

All for Service

Sportsmen can look forward to the day when Lyman service will again be devoted to them. In their interests, Lyman continues research to better its products, famous for over 65 years.

BUY
War Savings Stamps and Bonds

Latest Catalog 10c Folder Free

LYMAN GUN SIGHT CORP.
85-M West St.,
Middlefield, Conn.

THE COMPASS *Returns* to CHINA!

BATTLE COMPASSES TODAY!
AUTO
AVIATION
AND BOAT
COMPASSES TOMORROW

Whang-ti, Emperor of China in 2634 B.C., won the Battle of the Tchou-lou Plains because he improvised a compass and led his army through a fog. Today, 4500 years later, Sherrill Precision Compasses on U. S. Army vehicles are helping to defeat the Japs along China's Burma Road.

SHERRILL RESEARCH CORPORATION
PERU, INDIANA

N E
W S

SHERRILL COMPASS

HOLD HARD U. S. LINES!

Yes—hold hard

as you've always held —with amazing dependability and strength. Hold for bailer-outers, parachuting down from the skies, as you hold for baitcasters, plummeting plugs. Hold for fliers, floating down the airways, as you hold for fishermen fighting finny furies.

From Texas to Tunisia, Tennessee to Tokio, Boca Grande to Berlin, fishermen and fighters know that U. S. Lines and parachute cords can take it, stand up under it, and hold—hold hard always.

Many dealers still have U. S. Lines for sale—but should yours be sold out, you'll know why—Uncle Sam comes first. So let's all pitch in and help him hook and land Schickelgruber the shark, Mussolini the minnow, and Hirohitc the dogfish.

Meantime, to make every fishin' trip count more, send for copiously illustrated 68 page booklet "More Fun Fishin'" combined with "Fishermen's Kinks", all really inside fishing dope, Dep't L. U. S. Line Co., Westfield, Mass.

The right to walk in peace...

WE ARE fighting not only for the Four Great Freedoms, but for lots of smaller, more tangible things, too. For instance, we are fighting for the right to walk through peaceful, sunny fields with a dog and a gun, free of the shadow of war.

We're fighting for the right to enjoy the great American heritage of hunting . . . to watch a flight of greenheads whir out of the dawn.

We're fighting for *personal* peace, as well as peace between nations.

Here at Remington we are doing everything in our power to speed peace

through victory. We are grateful to be able to serve our country now that the country has had war forced upon it.

You, too, can serve by observing these conservation measures: wipe guns with an oily rag occasionally . . . store guns and ammunition in a cool, dry place . . . turn in empty shot shells and cartridge cases for brass salvage . . . and save furs, hides and down for war use.

And remember, after the war is won, Remington will be back to supply you again with its famous sporting guns and ammunition . . . in even finer quality

as the result of wartime research and experience. Remington Arms Company, Inc., Bridgeport, Conn.

The high quality and great quantity of Remington's production for the Armed Forces is shown by the fact that of the

eight large arms and ammunition plants operated by Remington, four have already been awarded the Army-Navy "E."

Remington
DU PONT

The Year the Pickerel Came

Don Holm

July 1952

Don Holm was born in Velva, North Dakota, where his father was the
village blacksmith. He grew up like Tom Sawyer, rafting on the Mouse
River, fishing and hunting, and earning money running a trap line. In the
Depression, he hitchhiked to Austin to enter the University of Texas. Moving
on to California, Oregon, Washington and Alaska, he worked variously in
mines, logging, construction, commercial fishing and shipyards until drafted
into the Navy. Post-war, he attended Portland State and Lewis and Clark
College in Oregon, teaching creative writing as a student-instructor.
Following ten years in advertising, public relations and sales promotion, he
returned to free-lancing and newspaper work. He has been with the
Oregonian for fifteen years, the last eight as wildlife editor. He has had ten
books published, including *The Complete Sourdough Cookbook* with his wife
Myrtle, and has won several awards for writing, photography and
conservation.

The town I came from was a wide spot in a narrow road in northcentral North
Dakota. The only relief from the monotonous prairie around it was a muddy,
meandering stream known locally as the Mouse River, a translation from the
French of its map name—the Souris. The Souris starts in Canada, loops lazily
down into Dakota for a hundred miles or so, then turns and goes back into
Canada as if it doesn't like the looks of what it's seen. The river and the mile-
wide valley through which it runs is a cool green ribbon in the dusty prairie.

Our little village was located at the southernmost point of the river's loop, and
my father was the village blacksmith—a native of Wisconsin who'd been raised
with a fishing pole rather than a hickory cane.

About a mile east of town was Downing's Creek, which started at some springs
six miles out on the prairie and came down into the valley through a swampy
coulee overgrown with diamond willow and cat-tails, which we kids used to collect for torches. At the railroad bridge over the creek the town had built a dam to
maintain the water table in the municipal wells near by. The pond, two or three
acres in extent, teemed with pike, pickerel, and perch. There were big ones in it,
too; you could see them by lying on the floor of an abandoned icehouse and
peering through its cracks into the clear, sun-lit water. There were even a few
muskellunge in the pond—one of them a giant lunker called "Krouse's Folly"
after an old bachelor who once hooked him and nearly got drowned for it.

Below the spillway, the creek meandered another half mile to the river, passing
through a farmyard, a cow pasture, and into the elm-and-oak woods along the
main stream. But below the dam the fishing wasn't very good. The creek was just
a trickle of water with a pool here and there beneath the low-hanging willow
limbs. You could catch a few small suckers and perch but I'd never known it to
contain enough water to support anything worth taking home to the cook except
frogs, whose legs made the most succulent dish anyone could imagine.

That summer of 1925, when I was a lanky, sensitive kid of seven or eight, with
crooked teeth and hair the color and texture of dried corn husks, I had grown

tired of most children's games, and was getting restless. Then one day in midsummer my father promised to take me fishing.

The rest of the week I helped him around the blacksmith shop, carrying water for the quench barrel and sweeping up horse droppings. By Saturday I had earned a quarter—enough to buy a bamboo pole, some fishline, and hooks at the general store.

Sunday afternoon, after my father had rested a bit from his seventy-hour week over the forge—a work week in those days lived up to the name—he took me out to Downing's Creek and showed me how to rig up my gear and where the fish were likely to hang out at different times of the day.

Everything was much simpler in those days. For bait we used worms, grasshoppers, crawfish, or frogs on No. 6 (or larger) long-shank hooks. We had no leaders and no reels—one merely tied the line securely to the end of the cane pole. Sometimes we used an artificial lure purchased at the hardware store; we called it a "spoon hook," and it was simply a treble hook equipped with red feathers and a red-and-black spoon-shaped spinner. We fished it by holding it in the current, when there was one, or by casting it out as far as the line would go and dragging it back just fast enough to turn the spinner. Sometimes we even jigged with the spoon hook, and you'd be surprised what a fish getter it was.

After teaching me the rudiments, spending a great deal of time impressing upon me the principles of sportsmanship, and cautioning me against wasteful "meat" fishing, my father wisely left me to discover for myself the joys of learning to outsmart fish. For the rest of the summer, up until the dog days, I spent every day out at Downing's Creek. But when the water turned bad and the leaves began to crisp up and change color the fishing was over for the year. It was like losing candy to have to put up the cane pole until the next spring.

That summer, I remember, was unusually hot and dry, and even before harvest time it was apparent that most of the crops were doomed. Rust had got into the wheat, and after that a plague of grasshoppers had gone through the country. And as if that weren't enough, the first snow came early, preventing threshing operations on a lot of the crops that were left.

My father's income was like an economic barometer of the immediate area. When the township prospered, he prospered; when the township was hard up, he was poverty-stricken. His income was entirely dependent upon the farmers' prosperity. Most of his work was done on credit, to be paid off when the crops were sold in the fall. That year few farmers paid their debts to the village blacksmith, and the other townspeople fared little better.

By Thanksgiving Day the snow lay two feet deep and the thermometer was 10 below. The town's normal activities had slowed to a crawl and already people were beginning to feel the pinch. A few, of course, were better fixed than others and able to tide themselves over, but most of the citizens had no reserves. Especially the village blacksmith. Austerity was a guest at our Thanksgiving table that year.

The usual Yuletide preparations did not start until less than a week before Christmas, and with holiday buying at a bare minimum merchants suffered even more. I remember we had a tree with candles on it and a few gifts charged at the store at the last minute. One of the gifts was a new, shiny casting reel. Naturally, I adored it, but I almost wished I hadn't been given it, for my impatience for spring to come was almost painful.

Then, just after New Year's, the weather went berserk. First it snowed steadily for several days, piling up waist-deep. Then the mercury thumped to the bottom and for the rest of the month never got above 30 below; sometimes it went to 40 and 45 below. About the middle of January a blizzard hit us. For days the wind swirled and howled around the house, whipping the snow into a blinding fog. With visibility less than twenty-five yards, it was practically suicide to get out of sight of a shelter. My father had to string a rope between the back stoop and the coal shed so we could tote in buckets of coal without getting lost.

The town was completely cut off from the outside world. For a week or more even the trains quit running. The schools shut down, and so did the churches, the movie house, and every other public establishment. The food situation became critical. Cattle caught outside shelters died in herds. People who kept cows in sheds were generally assured of milk and butter for the children, and those who didn't need the milk butchered the cows for their meat.

I don't remember many meals of beef, but I can still taste the breakfast cereal we ate daily. It consisted of raw wheat that Mr. Sears let me scrape from the empty bins at the near-by grain elevator. Even with cream and sugar, raw wheat still tastes just the way it sounds. Then there was the split-pea soup. This was the mainstay of every meal, and often the only dish. To this day I can't stand even the sight of pea soup.

I don't mean to say that people actually starved, but plenty of ribs would have shown if winter flannels had been removed. The thing that really affected everybody was a sense of dismal failure. A layer of black despair lay over the town as thick as the snowbanks.

But, like a child, I was not frightened or discouraged. In fact I scarcely noticed any hardship, except for our diet and having to stay in the house day after dreary day. The only thing I hated was the waiting; my impatience for spring to come and the ice to leave the rivers and creeks was nearly unbearable.

In the middle of February the temperature rose to 10 below—practically a heat wave—and life began to stir a little. But instead of feeling elated at having broken the back of winter, people acted as if each effort was the last surge of life before the spark flickered out. The winter had exhausted them spiritually as well as physically.

Farms were being offered for sale. Several town families were rumored to be getting ready to move to less rigorous parts. A number of bankruptcy petitions were filed. The atmosphere was one of hopelessness. None of this, of course, meant anything to me then. It was only in later years, looking back, that I fully understood. All I longed for then was spring and my first trip to Downing's Creek.

My wish came true shortly afterward, but not as I had anticipated. As though by a miracle, the temperature rose suddenly during the first week in March. The sun came out bright and hot each day, and the snow began to melt. Within a week the entire countryside was a swamp of dirty slush. Every hollow was a pond and water overran the gutters, clogging sewers and flooding basements. Citizens who had been bundled in mackinaws the week before now sweated outdoors in shirt sleeves. A warm, unseasonable chinook wind came up and whittled away at the snow on the hills, and still the temperature rose. The ice in the river began to crack and swell and the weekly paper carried an item about a farm lad who had broken through it and drowned in a creek.

Then it happened. One day my father came rushing home in midafternoon, his eyes alive with excitement.

"Fish! Pickerel!" he cried. "Thousands of them! Millions of them—running in Downing's Creek! Quick, get the wash tubs—pails—some gunny sacks!"

Almost incoherent in his eagerness, he managed to round up the family and the neighbors, and we hurried off with every container we could carry. The road toward Downing's Creek was already jammed with traffic: buggies, sleighs, wagons, even a couple of Model T's that had been stored for the winter. Everybody was as excited as we, and everybody was lugging pans, pails, sacks, and tubs.

When we reached Downing's Creek I saw that the ice had gone out and the lower creek, usually a trickle of water, was now a milky river held within its banks only by a thick jagged border of ice along each shore. Where the road crossed the creek I could look both ways and see people lining the banks or rushing toward the water. My father hastily staked a claim to a vacant spot above the bridge.

What I saw then almost sent my eyes popping out of my head. And my heart began to sink with foreboding.

Downing's Creek was literally alive with pickerel. As far as I could see in both directions the creek from bank to bank was jammed with frantic fish fighting their way upstream. They boiled and leaped and fought as if possessed by devils. The water rose and fell as they surged forward, and its surface seemed crowned from the pressure of their bodies. Hundreds were crushed before our eyes; others leaped high in death struggles and landed on the banks. The pickerel were so thick you could have laid a board on them and walked across. I was speechless with astonishment—and anxiety.

My family and our friends began dipping the pickerel out with milk pails and pouring them into tubs and sacks. By now the banks were lined solid with eager citizens, while others still swarmed toward the creek. Everybody had turned out —the banker, the teachers, the ministers, the merchants, the town marshal, the barber, the doctor, Mr. Sears who owned the grain elevator, farmers, the local fille de joie. And, for the first time in months, the pool halls disgorged their mob of pale-faced idlers.

Some citizens used nets and spears, others dipped with pails and wash tubs, or rigged up seines of grain sacking. Still others used pitchforks, rakes, hoes, or shovels, and a few waded right out into the icy water and scooped the pickerel up with their bare hands. There was even one blithe creature who stood silently on the bank dangling a baited hook and line. He was the only one who got skunked.

Aghast at such obscene, wasteful, drunken behavior by otherwise normal people, I hung back, refusing to take part in the carnage on my private fishing grounds.

For, frantic as the migrating pickerel were, the citizens were even more frantic in trying to hog the fish. Excitement rose to a fever pitch; a couple of fist fights broke out over squatters' rights, space on the bankside was being sold like footage at a gold strike, people who had already caught more fish than they could eat in a lifetime dickered with late comers, and containers were almost beyond price.

Once my father motioned me impatiently to get to work, but I clamped my lips tight and shook my head. He paused, looked up at me with a puzzled expression for a moment, then went back to work.

When my folks had filled half a dozen tubs and pails and the gunny sacks we'd brought, they began piling fish on the bare ground. They gave up only when sheer exhaustion forced them to.

While we waited for transportation back to town my father took my hand and we walked up to the dam. Here the slaughter was even worse. The pickerel had piled up at the spillway three feet deep and men with wagons were shoveling them up by the hundredweight. Water was running over the top of the dam in a mad flood, and this depressed me even more. I was sure the landlocked fish in the pond—my favorite fishing spot—were also being destroyed.

The pickerel run lasted all that day, all night, and part of the next day, with people dipping for fish around the clock. Torches and lanterns illuminated the entire length of the creek that night, and during the day wagonloads of fish lumbered to town.

Then the run was over. The freak warm spell broke and the temperature dropped to freezing. But strangely enough a change came over the townspeople. Their spirits were up, they forgot the despair of the past months, and they waited impatiently for spring and the planting of new crops. For the first time in months there was hope and optimism.

And there was fish to eat. Indeed, we had fish running out of our ears for weeks. We preserved our supply simply by stacking the pickerel on the back stoop in the freezing weather. When meat was needed it was convenient to step outside and chop off several pounds. Pickerel was sold over the counter at all the stores, and peddled from door to door—which was like carrying coals to Newcastle. The going price at the butcher shop was something like a penny a fish. But in spite of this bounty I stuck to pea soup.

There must have been game laws then, but we were an isolated backwoods community, and fish and game were always so plentiful that nobody paid much attention to licenses or seasons or daily limits. I suppose the pickerel run would have been classified as some sort of salvation anyway. At the time it certainly seemed like a miracle to the people who lived there, if not to me.

Along about April or May, when spring came to stay and the pickerel run was a sober memory, prospects for a good crop became so bright that people had almost forgotten the last year's failures and the rigors of the winter.

But they were saying that the fishing had been ruined forever in Downing's Creek by nature's wild spree. My father sadly agreed, and even Mr. Sears told me one day that all the fish in the pond above the dam, including Krouse's Folly, had escaped over the spillway.

I was heartbroken. By the time I was finally able to take my fishing gear—now equipped with a shiny casting reel—and hike out to the dam pond, I was about as sad as a boy can be—and with a well-developed grudge against human despoilers.

That first day's fishing confirmed all my fears. The water was back to normal, but dirty and stale-looking. I saw no fish jumping or ringing the surface, as I had so often during the summer before. And though I fished all day I got not even a nibble. Toward evening I trudged home, convinced that the townspeople were somehow responsible for my woe. I think I even blamed my father.

At the front gate I met the minister who lived next door. He was one of the few grown people I knew who seemed to remember what it was like to be a boy. Now he stopped me and asked how the fishing had been. I couldn't talk about it at first, but in his patient way he drew the story out of me and listened intently while I poured out my feelings on what was to me the most important thing in the world.

When I'd finished he didn't say anything at first but I could see he understood. Then he began to talk, not like a preacher, but as man to man. Nature, he said, sometimes acted in mysterious ways we did not understand, but there was always a reason for them. "It's natural and right for you to want to save your fishing pond," he said. "But it's even more natural and right for your father and me and other men to want to get food for our families. Some of the people acted foolish and greedy, but I imagine their consciences gave them a bad time afterward."

As for the pickerel run, he went on, the fish were destined to die, and it was providence that had sent them up Downing's Creek at a time when our people needed even a small miracle.

"And don't be discouraged about Downing's Creek," he said. "There were fish there before there was a town here, and there always will be. While the Lord taketh, He also giveth."

Those weren't his exact words, but I remember that suddenly I was immensely relieved and I went home with a new and wonderful feeling.

It turned out that the minister was right, too. The fishing wasn't ruined in my pond, nor had the fish escaped during the flood. When the water cleared up, later on that month, I had even better luck than I'd had the summer before. Maybe it was that shiny new reel. And along in July, when I was fishing through a hole in the icehouse, I became the second person in history to catch Krouse's Folly. I, too, lost him when the line caught in a wood sliver and broke. I hauled water for the quench barrel for a week to get money to buy a new spoon hook.

And that fall the farmers harvested the biggest bumper crop of hard spring wheat in years.

A Striper for the Consul

Harry R. Caldwell

September 1952

It was Roy Chapman Andrews, who hunted with him while on an expedition for the American Museum of Natural History, who first urged me to "go after" Harry Caldwell for a story. It led to a series of fine yarns for OUTDOOR LIFE. This was one. Caldwell was born in Cleveland in 1876, but grew up mostly in Tellico Plains, Tenn. Two of his brothers played major league baseball and Harry Caldwell had his chances, too, but instead became the shootingest missionary probably on record. General Thomas Holcomb of the U.S. Marine Corps, who also hunted with him in China, said of him once: "He is an amazing man, an effective missionary, a good amateur naturalist and the finest rifle shot I've ever seen." Caldwell killed forty-eight tigers in the forty-four years he served in China, eight or ten with a Savage .303, but then Savage sent him its .22-caliber High Power and he used that exclusively thereafter.

All around me was an undertow of terror. Not sudden fright or panic, but something deeper and more moving, like a river of human emotion. I saw it in the faces of the men and women I met in the villages and on the trails; it was in their speech and nervous eyes, as though they expected the monster to appear suddenly and snatch them out of my very presence into some horrible beyond. I talked to the county magistrate in Kutien about it.

"My records show that more than 250 of our people have been killed by this beast," he said. "The damage to livestock is appalling. It will bankrupt our province."

"But what is this terrible creature?" I asked. "The villagers talk of a saber-toothed monster that attacks and disappears with the speed of light. Some swear it's not even flesh and blood, but a phantom tiger begotten by devils."

The magistrate shook his head sadly. "Teacher," he said, "when you have lived long in this land, you will know that many of us are like children in our concept of the supernatural. I myself am at a loss to explain this evil which has fallen on our people."

Now, there are tigers in China, and vicious ones, but some of the stories he told me made my toenails curl. The man-killer, he said, terrified people not only by its ferocity but by its vast size. He told how it had taken a large heifer out of a pen behind a dwelling one night. When the farm people heard the commotion and went out to investigate, they saw a huge, misshapen beast pick up the heifer, jump straight upward into the starlit night, and disappear into the blackness. The pen was surrounded by a vertical embankment more than twelve feet high, and no tracks were found on the hard ground.

A couple of nights later, another family had just finished its evening meal. The men of the house were sitting around the table, smoking, and a child had fallen asleep with its head against a leg of the table. Everything was normal until something suddenly rushed through the door, upsetting the light and throwing the house into darkness and confusion. The table suddenly flew through the air into the courtyard and the monster left it there, with deep marks in the leg. The child had vanished.

175

Time and again men tending their herds or walking along the trails between the villages mysteriously disappeared forever, or were found later half devoured by the killer.

I was deeply concerned about all these horrible stories, but they really didn't hit home until they began to affect the work I'd come halfway around the world to do. The pastor of one of our local churches, Ling Siong-Daik, came to my house one evening for tea.

"It's disheartening, Caldwell," Ling said. "When we built the church, the response of the natives to our work seemed to indicate we'd make great strides. But then this unearthly creature appeared, killing native after native on their way to church. Our attendance has dropped off to nothing. Unless we end these murders I'm afraid we'll have to abandon the mission."

He could give me no description of the assassin. It struck with terrifying suddenness and was gone again into the night with its victims, and the conflicting reports of the natives made identification an impossibility. Here was something that threatened the very structure of the organization to which I belonged.

"No doubt," I said, more cheerfully than I felt, "we'll find some way to stop this thing. I'll do what I can to help."

I lay awake that night for a long time. Since I refused to subscribe to any belief in demon animals I had to accept the most likely explanation—that one or more man-killing tigers were wreaking havoc among the natives and their stock.

Knowing the probable answer and doing something about it were two different things. Obviously, the man-eater that was terrifying our church members must be hunted down and destroyed. I would undertake to do that, but I'd need help. So next day I went to see the British consul for the region, a bulbous fellow who, as far as I knew, had never been outside the city limits of Foochow during his tour of duty in China.

"Tigers in Fukien?" he snorted. "Only a missionary could dream up such a notion!"

"There has been a frightful loss of life in this province," I said, trying to hold my temper. "And from the widely scattered reports, there must be quite a population of the big cats. If you and the local government will give me a hand, I think we can dispose of the worst killers."

He snorted again.

"Tigers! I don't think you'd know the difference between a tiger and a civet cat if you met them both in the henhouse. No, His Majesty's Government won't help you with your hare-brained schemes."

I must have waited a full minute before replying.

"Mr. Price," I said, "I hope your teeth are good."

"Eh?" he grunted. "My teeth? Why?"

"Because," I said, "before long you're going to be eating some mighty tough words."

As I stood on the steps of the consulate, I murmured to myself, "Another challenge." I grinned wryly, for the stair steps of my life had been a series of challenges. Almost from the moment I first opened my eyes in Cleveland, Ohio, on a blustery March day in 1876, I'd spent my life—most of it around Tellico Plains, Tennessee—in bucking obstacles.

Even being in Foochow was the result of a challenge. As a young man I had a number of chances to get into professional baseball, but underneath I felt I was slated for more important work. I was sure of it when the call came for me to go to China as a missionary. This was one of the big dares that life had handed me.

And now a most important challenge had come in the form of a killer tiger— or tigers—and a sarcastic British consul. I had to win out, because to lose face in

China is bad. Not only would I have to produce tigers, but I'd have to produce them in a dramatic manner, that would convince the natives I was a man to hearken to.

I immediately wrote to my brother Will in New York, asking him to ship me the largest-caliber rifle he could find. But drawing on his experience as a deer and bear hunter in the Adirondacks, Will took it upon himself to fill my order with a .303 Savage, which, he decided, was heavy enough for any game, including the stripers.

Then the story of my appeal to the consul got into the papers, with the result that a group of German hunters came down from Shanghai to hunt the man-eaters. Those worthies obtained from the military authorities an armed guard to accompany them as they rode the mountain trails in sedan chairs, trying to find a tiger.

From what I heard of the expedition, they brought along more beer than ammunition and had a hilarious time of it. At any rate, they didn't kill a tiger, and went back to Shanghai grumbling about the damned missionary who had falsely reported big cats around Kutien.

At the annual mission conference in November, I sought and got an assignment to work at Kutien, far back in the mountains. I could have stayed in Foochow, but for several reasons I preferred the rural work. My rifle had arrived from America, and I hoped for a chance to use it. Besides serving as principal of a boy's school in Kutien, I traveled among the churches in two counties. And there wasn't any doubt about the presence of tigers. In many of the villages there was mourning among those who had lost a member of their family or their life's savings in livestock. And some of the tracks I saw, larger than dinner plates, and claw scratches on trees, higher than I could reach, were evidence that the lau-hu was the central figure in these tragedies.

There was no longer much talk about demons—the attacking cats were much too substantial. One had taken a cow almost out of a farmer's hands. He'd been eating his noonday meal when the big cat charged from a near-by thicket, killing the cow where it stood in the plow yoke, a few yards away.

Another tiger was disturbed in its bed by two deer hunters. The animal leaped at the man nearest him, seized him by the leg, and dragged him into the ravine below. Luckily the hunter succeeded in grasping a small tree, and the tiger released its hold, leaving the native almost paralyzed with pain and shock.

Wherever I went, people were discussing the killings in the hills adjacent to the villages and hamlets. There seemed not one but a hundred of the jungle cats that were taking a toll of human life, so I considered it a simple matter to fill that order for the consul, and incidentally make my job of bringing the Word to these people a thing of momentous import by giving them physical and moral aid, as well as spiritual help.

They needed it, too. In many ways that region, stretching vast distances along the rim of the East China and South China Seas, has been devastated by time. Ancient beyond recorded history, it's a poor land by western standards. For untold generations, men have sapped its soil until the yield became meager by even their own poor standards. The natives are impoverished to a degree that would be incredible to anyone not living with them day after day, year after year. They have few tools for agriculture, no adequate weapons for getting game or for defense against the larger animals.

Along the coast the hills are barren, but deeper in the interior of the province, both flora and fauna are lush and semitropical. The whole country was crudely terraced ages ago by a people who saw the life-giving soil slipping away into the streams. Succeeding generations gradually abandoned the bottom terraces which, with the ravines and hollow below them, reverted to the wild, growing heavy with thickets of low shrubs, bushes, ferns, and sword grass ten feet high—all interwoven with a network of tough rattan vines.

It is through these impenetrable thickets, nestling between the cultivated hills, that the tiger trails run, and from which the big cats stalk forth around dusk to wreak destruction on the villagers and their stock. Here on these trails I hoped to get my face-saving tiger, as well as help rid the country of some of its wanton killers. And although during the forty-four years I served as a Methodist missionary to the Chinese people, I bagged a total of forty-eight of the big cats, getting that striper for the consul stands out as one of the most dramatic moments of my life.

The hunt really started when I attempted to set up a mission in a certain community. But its elders would not even give me an audience. One attempt after another to soften them was blocked just when it seemed I'd be successful. I knew that the prejudice against me was not personal. It was the same prejudice the villagers had against all foreigners and their works. But disaster can level even prejudice. And disaster came to the community—in the shape of a man-killing tiger.

The elders of the clan appealed for help and I responded eagerly, carrying along my Bible as well as my rifle.

For several days I lived at the home of Ding, the elder who had extended the invitation. The first evening, as we sat at the table, the conversation centered around my rifle, with its little, sharp-pointed cartridges.

"Gun too small to kill the great cat," one of the elders stated.

"It packs a terrible blow," I replied. "Like hitting him with a stone it would take twenty men to lift."

"But our guns are larger," Ding said, "and they do not stop the charge of the lau-hu."

"Let me see yours," I requested.

He put an ancient 12 gauge fowling piece, bound together by wire, into my hands. It was the opportunity I had been waiting for. I explained in language as simple as I knew, the difference in the ballistics of the two guns, and from that point worked into the comparisons between their worship of idols and images and worship of the One God. They listened respectfully; the Chinese are most polite.

"If your gun proves to be as good as you say your religion is," one of the group finally said, "maybe you will be our great teacher. Let us first see what your gun does to the tiger."

Next day I borrowed a goat and two small kids, and placed the latter in a basket covered with cloth. With the basket, and the nanny, I worked my way into tiger territory on the rim of the village. Where two well-beaten cat trails crossed, I tied the goat securely to a stake and hid the basket of kids close by. Then I crouched in the tall grass to wait.

It's impossible to describe the sensations on a long vigil for a tiger. The imaginary stripers one hears and feels and smells in the dank recesses of a lair are worse than meeting a black-and-yellow killer face to face. A hunter never knows at what moment he may find himself stalked. It's dangerous to relax, even a little.

I had followed the first rule of a tiger hunt by staking out a goat in one of the well-worn trails. The big cats seldom attack through thick brush, but follow a pathway as stealthily as a tabby stalking field mice back at home. I had already scouted the trails of this particular area and knew I was safe unless I made some foolish blunder. If a cat came along his jungle beat to find the bleating kids buried in the dense grass behind me, he'd be within twenty yards of my blind before I saw him.

For more than two hours I sat perfectly still, alert to every movement and sound. Nothing broke the tense silence but the rasping call of a bamboo partridge. The tension was so great that the crawling of ants in the dry leaves sounded like the movement of some large animal through the brush.

There is no way to figure a tiger. I had about given up hope of glimpsing one that afternoon, when the head of a huge striper appeared in the overhanging grass, not more than fifteen yards away. He was moving toward the kids in the basket—intent, alert, and heedless of everything except the bleating of the baby goats. He was a magnificent brute, lithe and sleek, with the sinews rippling like corded cables under his saffron hide.

Realizing that if the tiger saw the movement of my arms and should turn on me he'd cover my carcass like a blanket before I could get my gun up, I very cautiously raised my rifle. At that moment, less than half a hundred yards behind the stalking tom, the edge of the jungle rang with the voices of children out gathering fuel.

The big cat paused and listened for a space. I could have put a bullet through him then, but I held my fire. If I only wounded him, he might crash back along the trail into the middle of the young fuel gatherers, leaving them mangled and broken at the ravine's rim. At that range I didn't see how I could miss, but I didn't dare take a chance.

With a great bound, the cat left his stalk and the sword grass swallowed him. Fearing that the killer might circle back and stalk the children, I jumped out of my blind and ran down the terrace to where I could guard them as they finished picking up sticks and dried grass roots and trudged back to the village.

The next day my cook, Da Da, joined me in the village. Da Da was my long and faithful companion during the years I traveled the back trails of China, and together we learned much about hunting the big cats.

"Master," he suggested, "we should make a study of all the trails around this and adjoining villages, so that when the killer strikes again, we will know his home territory as well as he."

I thought it was a good idea, so we set out to explore all the tangles and jungled ravines around the village. One amazing sign we found was on a lone pine tree standing beside the trail, high up on the mountain. The bark was slashed with fresh marks eleven feet above the ground, giving us some idea of the immense size of the cat. Other trees scattered around the bowl were similarly marked.

It was on this first exploratory trip that I came close to losing my scalp, and gleaned a grain of valuable experience that saved me half a dozen times while I was in the Far East.

I was walking ahead of Da Da, when my eye caught a movement in the brush on the hillside above the trail. I stopped in my tracks, swinging my rifle barrel around for instant action. Two voices—that of my cook and a strange one from the brush—reached me at the same time: "Don't move! Don't move!"

Then, as a native on the hillside scrambled down to where we stood, Da Da showed me a string stretched across the trail at the height of a man's hips.

"Tiger trap!" he said.

The hair-trigger string ran through the brush to a powerful crossbow that threw an arrow when it was tripped. The arrowhead was a steel dart, and just behind it was a cloth or string wrapping, soaked in potent poison that would drop a tiger within a few feet of the set.

Since the few guns in the villages were inadequate for bit game, this bow was about the only means the natives had for doing away with the man-eaters. But I found out that more humans than tigers were killed by trap crossbows. Never again did I travel the dense trails without a long brush of bamboo in my hand, feeling ahead for the string that would send a poisoned dart into my vitals.

Our job of exploration done, Da Da and I settled down to wait for a striper to show itself in one of the villages within the big bowl of mountains. And we didn't have long to relax. A few days later I heard an outcry from a settler's cottage across the creek followed by shouting among the women and children.

Fearing that the the tiger had caught another child, I caught up my rifle and tore down the trail toward the disturbance. I arrived out of breath to learn the victim was only a goat, but the frantic women pleaded with me to overtake and bring back the nanny, whose flesh was worth several dollars.

So I set out to pick up the tiger's trail—a well-defined one in the grass and tall ferns. The fresh marks in the vegetation led diagonally across the hill in the direction of the area where we had seen the marked pine trees, and I hurried as fast as I dared, hoping to overtake the animal when it stopped to feast on its kill before reaching the tangle of the ravine.

For half a mile I followed the trail. It zigzagged through every clump of bushes, and I approached each of them cautiously to keep from bumping heads with disaster. Since the tiger could pass through the brambles much faster than I, he gained a good lead.

I was disappointed that he did not halt in any cover but proceeded right through to a wide basin, densely covered with wild-grape vines and sword grass. I had no doubt that he was in this depression, devouring his goat, but it would have been much too dangerous to try to rout him out alone.

I went back to the village and organized a drive, assigning ten beaters, armed with pike staffs and guns with which to defend themselves, and with gongs and oil tins to make plenty of noise. They stormed into the ravine and I took my stand on an open ridge across which the animal would have to pass to reach his main lair.

The only position of vantage I could find was a wide, flat rock, over which the animal would come if he followed what the beaters assured me was the only trail out of the basin. I had two choices. If I stood on the rock, in the open, the killer would see me and dodge off into the brush before I could get a shot. If I hid behind the rock, he would approach much too close for comfort before I saw him at all.

Just as I took my place behind the boulder, the beaters shouted that they had found the remains of the goat. Seconds later I heard the tiger bounding along the ridge toward my rock. Then there was silence. The seconds turned into minutes as I waited, tight as stretched gut, but the animal did not appear. I figured he might have circled in the brush and was stalking me from behind, so I decided to climb, fast.

When I crawled up the surface of the rock, I saw for the first time that another trail branched off the one I was watching and angled toward the upper end of the basin. There was no doubt that the tiger had taken that pathway to escape and would cross the ridge somewhere above me. If I wanted a shot, I'd have to outrun him to where this branch trail crossed the ridge.

I had moved but a few yards when the killer appeared, not too far above me. He glared at me for a second, than swung quickly and put a pine tree between us. Behind this cover, he began to stalk me. Reaching the base of the pine, the huge striper laid back his ears and crouched for a spring. I threw up my rifle and fired squarely at his face. I couldn't understand how I missed at that distance, but I did and he whirled in the air, bounded once, and was gone. My bullet had struck the side of the tree, blowing out bark and splinters, and I was considerably annoyed at missing, even though I had stopped the charge under conditions that put all the odds in favor of the cat.

The next afternoon word came from a village beyond the big lair that the striped devil had just killed a small boy. Da Da and I hurried across the ridge and staked out a goat. We waited a few yards away, behind a bank of ferns.

It wasn't long before a tom came down the trail to the billy's bleating. As he crouched to spring, I put the .303 into action, but knew instantly that I hadn't hit him. One long, graceful bound carried him out of sight into the jungle.

Two misses in two days! That sort of thing could be serious if one of the big cats caught me in just the right position. Since I estimated that both bullets had hit more than a foot to the right, I rechecked my rifle sights as soon as I got back to the village. They were badly out of line. One of the natives admitted that he had hit the barrel against a wall when he picked up the rifle to look at it. He never knew that his carelessness might have cost me my life.

The tiger didn't show up again for several days. While we waited for him, a runner brought word that General Thomas Holcomb, of the U.S. Marines, was coming to my house for a visit, and I went off to meet him.

While I was gone, the striper was daring enough to invade a near-by settlement in broad daylight. One farmer had seen him duck into the thicket of an isolated ravine with a pig in his mighty maw. A group of villagers decided to rout him out. After making the proper overture to their gods, the men got word from their priest that the "big ruler god," whose frowning image sat in a temple under the hill, assured success if they wanted a skirmish with the wild tomcat.

Armed with pikes, poles, and guns loaded with slugs and rusty nails, a hundred men deployed themselves for the attack. They drove into the tangle, but the cat wasn't in a running mood. The foray lasted for almost an hour, during which time the hunters suffered more than the tiger. With masterful timing, the striper charged again and again, slashing right and left effectively, and with every roaring assault dampening the ardor of the would-be avengers.

The villagers, their enthusiasm stone cold at last, had retired from the fray, when a hunter from a neighboring hamlet arrived on the scene with a very much repaired double-barreled shotgun, loaded with slugs as long as a man's thumb. Followed by a number of friends, who went along to see the execution, he walked within twenty-five yards of the tiger before he saw it. The hunger fired two shots in rapid succession, one of them evidently creasing the big cat. He roared and charged, so frightening the hunter that the man fell helpless in his tracks.

The tiger swung and charged the nearest native, who was standing on a rise of ground overlooking an irrigation pool. The man tumbled backward and fell into the water, saving his life. The crazed cat then turned and charged a third farmer who stood on the terrace below. The man dropped to his knees and the cat passed clean over him, then turned and bounded into the fringe of sword grass that bordered his lair.

When General Holcomb came back with me next day, the villagers assured us that the striper was still in the tangle where they had last seen him. Tom and I spent the whole morning making a survey of the smaller ravines around the big lair, beating them out with the help of the natives. Satisfying ourselves that no tigers lurked on our flanks or at our rear, we tethered our goat on a barren terrace just before mid afternoon, withdrew some fifteen yards, and concealed ourselves in a clump of bushes.

Our first indication of a stalking jungle tom was the alarm call of a little bird, a bulbul, a few minutes after the goat began to bleat. I had already learned to note carefully the chirps of certain birds whose language always indicates a tiger on the move. Sentries stationed on all sides of a blind are a big help in dealing with an animal that drifts through the jungle as silently as a shadow!

By the disturbed notes of the birds, we followed our tiger along a hidden trail in front of us to a wild pear bush, which soon became literally full of the feathered sentinels, all of them scolding vigorously.

"From where he is now," I whispered, "he can see us."

"Will he charge?" Tom breathed.

"Be ready for anything," I warned.

For five minutes we both sat rigid, waiting for the big cat to spring suddenly out of the undergrowth into our faces. We had both begun to breathe again, when there was a sudden crash to our right. We both whirled, expecting a charge from that direction, but all we could see was grass weaving under the weight of a heavy body. While our attention was focused on this disturbance, there was another crash near the pear bush, accompanied by the cries of a struggling deer.

"Holy cow!" Holcomb gasped.

He jumped out of the blind, with me on his heels, and we sprinted to intercept the tiger before it could reach its lair. But we were not fast enough to get another glimpse of it. The tracks that we found—as plain as a story written in the earth —verified what we already suspected.

There had been two cats. The first—and from the size of his pads, he was the killer tom—had stalked within easy striking distance of the goat, then had seen us and crouched, probably trying to decide his next move. A second tiger, responding to the bleating of the goat, had approached along the upper line of terraces, and flushed a number of muntjac deer out of the grass. He sprang on one and spooked the others into the very jaws of the first striper. Both had made their kills within a few yards of us and slunk off into the recesses of the ravine, where we dared not follow.

A month after General Holcomb left, the killer renewed his predations with such terrifying results that the elders again sent word to me, requesting that I return to the village immediately. I canceled plans I had made to visit another community. Da Da was away and wouldn't return until late that afternoon. I didn't wait for him, but decided to start across the mountain, carrying the shotgun in order to kill a few pheasants for supper. I left word for Da Da to meet me at the village with my rifle, and walked across the hills to the elder's house, flushing and killing half a dozen cocks along the way.

I expected to find Da Da there when I arrived. Instead, I found excitement in the village. Only an hour before, the tiger had literally taken a goat out of a farmer's hands, while he tugged on the other end of its tether. The big cat hadn't harmed the man, but had bounded off with the billy.

I couldn't afford to let such an opportunity go by. Hoping that Da Da would show any minute, I prepared to go after the big cat without my rifle. Pouring the small pellets of bird shot out of a couple of shells, I melted them down and drained the molten lead into a hollow section of small bamboo. When the lead hardened again, I ripped the bamboo away, sawed the bright lead into slugs, and rounded off the corners by rubbing them together against rough stones. I reloaded the shells with these slugs.

Almost immediately after I had tethered my bait goat the tiger came, stalking alone one of the jungle trails to an abandoned terrace that rimmed his lair. In the edge of the brush, not more than fifty yards away, the animal suddenly stopped, as though he sensed something wrong.

For nearly an hour he sat there, too far away for an effective blow by the shotgun, repeatedly putting out his front foot like a huge tabby, as if to move forward, then drawing back again.

My exciting vigil came to an abrupt end. Suddenly the tiger left his seat and traversed a depression that flanked a barren acre between him and the goat. At the edge of the clearing he bounded forward, streaking across it to the terrace on the other side. Under cover, he made three great leaps that brought him to the foot of the very terrace where I was guarding the goat.

But when he settled for a spring, it was not at the goat but at me!

I had to act fast. Muttering a little prayer that the lead slugs would do the trick, I threw up the gun and blasted the striper full in the face. He sidestepped and crouched again, his yellow eyes burning into mine. I let him have the other barrel. He fell over backward and died on his side, kicking convulsively.

This tiger was a small male with a beautiful coat. I was examining it with some disappointment that it was not the killer I wanted to bring back in triumph to the consul, when the villagers swarmed up the hill, eager to see my kill. They hardly looked at the tiger, though, until every available drop of blood was sopped up with rags torn from clothing. Men and women alike fought for sprigs of blood-stained grass. From Ding, the elder, I learned that the blood of a tiger is highly prized for two purposes. A bit of bloody cloth is worn around the neck. of a child as a preventive against the evil spirits that are thought to cause measles and small pox. And a blood-soaked handkerchief waved in front of an attacking dog will supposedly turn its charge into a full retreat.

When I got to the village Da Da was there, and elated about the tiger I had taken. But since the villagers declared that the man-killer was still in the vicinity, we decided to stay long enough for one more try at it. I was beginning to fear that this was one challenge of my life that I might be unable to overcome. Two challenges, in fact—one from the villagers, who depended on me to rid their community of the killer, and the other from the consul who no doubt was still talking in his club at Foochow about missionaries who can't tell the difference between tigers and civet cats.

The next morning Da Da and I obtained a goat and tethered it where two trails crossed near a heavily timbered ravine. We had examined this jungle once before and I had a feeling that anyone looking for trouble in a striped coat could find it there. We backed a few yards away from our bait, to the foot of an abandoned terrace, and settled down to wait.

Although tigers seldom leave a well-traveled trail to plow through the jungle, there are exceptions, and one of them brought us a close call.

The first indication we had of the striper's presence was a guttural growl from somewhere very near. I shot a quick glance at Da Da. He was actually green with fear. The low growl rumbled along the ground again and I bounded to my feet. This time the big cat had approached our goat through a break in the waist-high grass, and was on the terrace above us, not more than a few yards away. He was crouched in the grass, either to hide or for the fatal spring.

I knew better than to try to run or dodge. That was something the big cat was accustomed to, and expected. In such a situation a fast, strong offensive was best. Without even weighing what the results might be, I scrambled up the retaining wall, with my gun in position to shoot at point-blank range. At the most critical moment my toe slipped and I sprawled over the rim of the terrace, right in the face of the crouching tiger. I believe I could have actually reached out and slapped him in the face.

I don't know what it was that cost the big cat his nerve. He'd probably never had a man dive headlong at him before and the sudden commotion may have been more than he could stand. It might have been the white man's smell, since Chinese scholars assured me it would often stop the charge of a tiger that hadn't been wounded. Whatever the reason was, he whirled and sprang into the dense bramble.

With no more than a battered knee from the fall, I tried to follow for a shot, but could not work myself into the right position for a sure poke with the rifle. When I returned to Da Da, we shifted to a new stand near the tethered goat and waited for a long time, but there was no further sight or sound of the tiger.

Bitterly disappointed over our continued failure to get this big cat, we arose to start back. In a dense clump of bramble above us, a lot of little birds were chirping excitedly. Picking up a brickbat from an old grave, I heaved it uphill into the thicket.

I was not only amazed but totally unprepared for the explosion that followed. I couldn't have got more violent action if I had tossed a hand grenade. The whole slope seemed to be covered with one huge tiger, charging down the hill toward us. The striper had gone off somewhere, worked himself up a good mad, and come back to stalk the two strange creatures that had spooked him.

Boiling down the slope, with his head almost touching the ground, the jungle tom did not look in the least like the lithe, nimble creature that he is on level ground or going uphill. Between bounds his back humped up and his legs looked too long.

At the crack of my rifle he bounded high into the air, turned completely over, and bounced against the earth, rolling almost to our feet. I backed off and waited, my rifle ready, but after a few minutes a last convulsive shudder told me the killer was dead.

This was the consul's tiger. After receiving the heart-felt thanks of the villagers, we traveled over the mountains that night to catch an early-morning launch for the river trip to Foochow.

Things could not have worked out better for us. The launch ran aground on a sandbar in the river, and stuck there for three hours until the incoming tide floated it off. All this time the tiger was on the open deck, bloating in the torrid sun. When we arrived in Foochow at noon, the proportions of the jungle tom were more like those of a well-fed horse than of a tiger.

The launch captain landed us at the busy customs jetty. My bearers picked up the cat and started ashore. People began swarming out of the tea hongs, custom-houses, and government buildings. I led the way, followed by eight men carrying the man-eater swung between poles. When we reached the top of the hill, near the Foochow Club, thousands of people were following us.

It was possible for only a couple of hundred of them to crowd into the mission compound at one time, so we let them through in groups to look at the tiger. I heard a violent rattling of the compound gate and saw the British consul peering through the uprights. I shouted to the gateman to let him in and he broke through the circle of onlookers with his elbows swinging. He looked down on the great cat, then walked completely around it.

"Mr. Caldwell," he said in awed tones, "I have lived in India and seen many Bengal tigers, but never one nearly as big as this."

"Do you call this a tiger?" I asked, feigning surprise.

"Do I——Why man, it's the biggest tiger in creation!"

"Just shows," I said, "how a man can be mistaken. I have always been under the impression that these things were civet cats. Back in the hills I have to chase them out of my chicken yard every morning. I thought I'd bring one along to Foochow to let you fellows see what they look like."

That did it. The consul stared at me for a moment, then shrugged his shoulders and elbowed his way through the crowd to the gate, which he slammed behind him.

Revenge may be wicked, but it sometimes has a sweet taste. And I date any success I may have had in China as a missionary from that moment on the slope, when I overcame one of the greatest challenges of my life.

Tale of the Minister's Dog

Arthur Grahame

September 1952

Arthur Grahame likes this best of the countless stories he did for OUTDOOR
LIFE as freelance, Eastern field editor and Washington correspondent for
thirty-five years. His fascinating career began in his native New Jersey with
the *Daily Advertiser* of Newark and the *Sunday Call*. He ran an auto
column, he says, when it was news if a car went twenty-five miles without
breaking down. In twelve years at Street & Smith he was managing editor of
Popular Magazine, "incubator" for *Saturday Evening Post* writers, and
conceived, and wrote for, *Sport Story*. He did his first story for *Popular
Science Monthly* in 1925, and when its owners bought OUTDOOR LIFE he
began his long association as Washington man and Eastern field editor. He
also wrote for *The Sportsman,* a "class" magazine (horse racing, polo, tennis,
golf, yachts) that came into OUTDOOR LIFE hands in 1936–37. If it was a
sport, Grahame played it, watched it or wrote about it.

When I was a cub reporter the paper I worked on had a rule that the opening
paragraph of each news story must answer these questions: who? where? when?
why?

The answers to those four questions I'm going to give in this story would have
got me cussed out by my old boss on the grounds of insufficiency. But here they
are:

Who? Two fishermen. One was a minister from Scotland, whose name I can't
tell you because I promised I wouldn't. I'll just call him The Minister. The other
was me—a guy who wanted to hook an Atlantic salmon.

Where? I promised the dominie I wouldn't tell that, either, because if I did it
would amount to the same as telling his name. But I can say it's a little river on
Cape Breton Island, Nova Scotia, that has a late run of salmon and is almost
never fished by anyone who doesn't live near by.

When? That's easy. Last September.

Why? Mostly a matter of opinion. I'd give half the credit to The Minister and
the other half to The Minister's Dog.

Now let's get to our fishing.

While I was tying a Jock Scott onto the end of my leader an old jingle came
into my head. Part of it goes:

> When the wind is in the south
> It blows the bait in the fish's mouth

The wind was in the south that Saturday morning, and I hoped it would blow
my fly into a salmon's mouth for I'd pretty well given up trying to get it there any
other way.

I'd been fishing Cape Breton rivers all week without even pricking a fish.
There were fresh-run salmon in most of them—blue-backed, silver-sided salmon
just in from the ocean—but I hadn't been able to coax a single strike.

I finished tying on the Jock Scott, waded into the river a step or two, flicked fly
and leader onto the water, and looked behind me to make sure I had clearance
for my backcast. As I did so I saw a man standing a couple of yards up the bank
watching me. He was middling tall, solid-looking, and had a face that was both

craggy and ruddy. He wore a threadbare canvas fishing coat over the vest and trousers of a dark suit, a white shirt with a starched collar, a dark necktie, rubber hip boots, and a stiff-looking gray felt hat. In the crook of his elbow he supported a long two-handed rod of a sort you seldom see any more on Nova Scotia rivers.

"It's a grrand day for fishing," he said when our eyes met. "What luck are you having?"

I told him. He pursed his lips sympathetically and stroked his chin. "I've not seen you before," he said. "I'm the minister here." He pointed down the valley to where a white steeple stood out against the dark spruce on a hillside. "There are few who fish here that I don't know."

I told him my name and where I live, and said that I was fishing his river on the tip a friend had given me over on the Margaree. "An American," he said. "You're welcome here. We Scots are verry grateful to you Americans for all you did for Scotland and all Britain, in the war and after."

He waded into the river, and with a seemingly careless flip of his rod sent his fly close to the far bank. "A fish was lying ten feet upstream from that spot in the dusk last evening," he told me. "Just below that swirl, which is caused by a covered rock. He may be there still. Just try him now."

Luckily I dropped my Jock Scott exactly where he'd told me to. Then I worked it across the current, picked it up, and cast again.

After I'd made half a dozen tries The Minister shook his head. "He may have run upstream in the night," he said placidly. "There's a pool at the head of the fast water. I'll take you to it."

Like most Cape Breton salmon rivers this one flows for most of its length through farmland. As we walked along the steep-sloping pastures he told me that he'd been in Canada three years, and formerly he'd been a minister in a little town in the Scottish Highlands. "And a salmon fisherman there?" I asked.

"Ay, since I was a lad," he said. "Like my father before me, who was a minister, too. It was from him I had this rod."

The pool he took me to is long and narrow. The current is swift at its head, slows to slick-surfaced swirling in the deepest parts, and quickens into a smooth glide before it spills over a lip of rock into a white-water riffle.

To know a salmon pool the way a good guide knows it you have to study it when the river is low and carry in your mind a relief map of its bed. You must know where the water deepens, where it is shallow, and the location of each submerged rock behind which a fish may lie. That's the way The Minister knew this pool. He made an opening in the curtain of brush that circled it and peered through. "There's a good fish lying just where the water dimples as the run comes into the deep pool, and there are three others where the tail sluice shallows," he told me.

I offered no more than token resistance to his suggestion that I fish down the pool first. My cast dropped the Jock Scott softly on the far side of the run. I was fishing a greased line, which kept the wet fly within an inch or two of the surface. I let the current carry it down close to where I hoped the fish was waiting, and then retrieved it cross-stream in foot-long draws.

The fly passed over the spot where The Minister said he'd seen the fish. The current carried it downstream. I followed the leader knot with my rod tip and fished the cast out into the straight. Then, at the instant I started to pick up the fly, there was a bulge on the water behind it. I lowered the rod tip a few inches to give more slack. There was a swirl and a fin broke water as the fish took the fly and turned away.

For a pulse-racing moment the line tightened. Then it went slack. The fish had spit out the fly.

"You moved him. He's a taker!" There was excitement in The Minister's calm voice. "Rest him a few minutes, then show him the same fly he came to, but a size or two smaller."

That advice must be as old as fly fishing for salmon, and sometimes it pays off. I tied on a No. 6 Jock Scott in place of my No. 4, made myself wait five minutes, and cast again.

Nothing happened. I put on a dry fly and floated it down the current. Again nothing happened.

One of the things I like about the greased-line method for salmon is the way you can alternate wet and dry fishing without having to change anything but your mind and your fly. I went back to a wet fly—this time my favorite No. 4 Black Dose. I fished it all the way down the pool, including the tail sluice.

Still no results.

I sat down on a rock and lighted a cigarette. "I'm licked," I said to The Minister. "My luck's out. I hope I haven't spoiled your chances."

He was standing half turned away from me and was tying on a fly. "Weel—" he said softly, then waded into the river and made a cast.

He hooked a fish at the spot where the run comes into the deep pool.

One of the things in this world really worth seeing is the sternly repressed excitement of a Scot playing a salmon. I sat back and watched. The Minister walked up the bank, planted his feet firmly, and took on the air of a man who intends to stay right where he is until he's finished his job. He didn't say a word, but the blood flooded up the back of his neck. His rod bent and line ripped off his reel as the fish tore down the pool on its first frenzied run.

That run ended with a spectacular leap, but The Minister's expression didn't change. He gave slack by lowering his rod until its tip was only inches above the water. Then, as the salmon splashed back into the pool, he raised the tip and cranked in a few turns of line. The fish took it back with another determined run, but the fish soon tired of fighting the resiliency of the long rod and the drag of the reel, and took to the air again. It jumped three times, but the second jump wasn't as high as the first, or the third as high as the second.

That visible loss of power was the tip-off. Almost gently, but firmly, The Minister began to reel in. The fish fought gallantly, but ten minutes after it had taken the fly it was in water so thin that its back was above the surface. In another minute it was on its side, dead beat, and so close to shore that The Minister was able to skid it up on the bank without using his gaff.

It had been an impressive demonstration of how a salmon should be played. "That was a pleasure to watch," I said, trying to keep the envy out of my voice.

Maybe I didn't succeed, or maybe The Minister just knew how I felt. "Ay," he said, "but it was you that I wanted to kill a salmon the day. Weel, now, there's a pool below the kirk that should have fish in it."

We went downriver, past his church and along a path to the first pool above tidewater.

That's where I first saw The Minister's Dog.

The pool proved to be exceptionally large for the size of the river. The current that runs through it is smooth, deep, and fast close to where the north bank of rock is high and steep. But it is in that deceptively smooth run that the salmon are most likely to be. In midstream the pool is very deep and there is little current. The only way to fish the run is to cast from the shallows close to the south bank.

The Minister propped his rod against a birch sapling, and I noticed that his leader was dangling. "You've lost your fly," I told him.

He looked at me, stroked his chin and shook his head. "No," he said slowly, "I've not lost it. I took it off."

I wondered why he seemed embarrassed. Then it occurred to me that I hadn't had a good look at the fly on which he'd taken his salmon. I remembered that when tying it on he'd half turned away from me, possibly because he didn't want me to see it.

I got out my box. "I guess I'd better switch from this Black Dose," I said. "What do you think I'd better try?"

He looked even more embarrassed. "Weel," he said after a while, "what fly to use is a question of personal judgment and conviction on which one mon's opinion is as good as another's."

"I'd rather trust your judgment than mine, especially on your own river," I told him. "What fly did you take your fish on?"

He stroked his chin again and shook his head. "That," he said, "I'll not tell you."

I was too taken aback by the abruptness of his reply to say anything. I couldn't figure out why a man should go out of his way to show a stranger where to fish, and then refuse to recommend a fly. My astonishment quickly turned to suspicion. What was The Minister covering up? I'd seen him tie some kind of fly on his leader before he made his strike-producing cast. Could he possibly have put a worm on that fly's hook? But even if he had, which I couldn't believe, he looked so miserable that I felt sorry for him. I put on a Silver Gray and made several casts, but got no response at all.

While I was still trying The Minister pulled a thick, old-fashioned gold watch out of his vest pocket, snapped it open, and pursed his lips. "I'm sorry I'll have to leave," he said gloomily. "What I sometimes fear is my sinful fondness for fishing has caused me to be derelict in my duty. My sermon for tomorrow morning is far from finished, and my discourse for the evening service is not even started."

I assured him that he had my sympathy and, skipping over our little unpleasantness about fly selection, thanked him for his kindness.

"Ay," he said, "but I wanted you to kill a salmon, this being your last day of fishing for the year."

"It should be," I told him. "I ought to be on my way home right now. But if I don't get a fish before dark I'm going to stay overnight, and have one more try tomorrow."

The Minister's face grew bleak. "I don't hold with fishing on the Sabbath," he said sternly.

That was a point I had no desire to argue with him, so I didn't say anything. He stood with his head down, frowning, and eyeing the toes of his boots. After a minute he looked up at me. "If you killed a fish the day," he asked, "you'd be off for home, and not fish tomorrow?"

"That's right," I told him.

"Then," he said slowly, "if I put you in the way of taking a fish, I'd save you from the sin of fishing on the Sabbath." He took his fly box out of his coat pocket, opened it, and picked out a fly which he pushed into my hand. "Take it, then," he said gruffly.

I looked at the fly. I'd never seen one just like it. "Why," I asked, "what fly is this?"

"Some call it the Garry," he told me, "but its rightful name is The Minister's Dog. I've killed many a good fish on it in our Scottish rivers, and I've found it equally effective in this one. I wanted to lend it to you long ago, but mon's inborn selfishness prevailed, for I feared you'd snag the barb off the hook on some rock. You see, it's the last Minister's Dog I have left of those I brought with me from Scotland, and I'm verry doubtful there's another one this side the Atlantic."

"Then I wouldn't think of borrowing it," I protested.

"Take it, I tell you," he urged. "There's a fish lying in the run, near the head of the pool. If you just swim The Minster's Dog down to him, you'll kill a salmon and start for home. Then I'll not have your sin of fishing on the Sabbath on my conscience."

He picked up his rod and went up the bank. When he got to the top he turned. "After you've killed your fish," he called, "you could stop at my house, across the road from the kirk, and give me back my fly."

No matter how it looks to a salmon, to the human eye The Minister's Dog is nothing out of the ordinary. It is a hair-wing fly—black body ribbed with silver, yellow upper and red lower wing, yellow tail, black hackle with a touch of turquoise in it. This specimen was tied on a No. 4 hook. Certainly there wasn't anything so remarkable about its looks to account for The Minister's almost fanatical faith in it. But somehow he'd inspired me with some of that faith.

Salmon fishing is full of contradictions, I know, but I've found that when you're fishing a wet fly over a spot where you believe a fish to be, your best chance of getting a strike is on your first cast. So you'd better make that first cast a good one.

I did. The Minister's Dog dropped on the fast water five yards upstream from where The Minister said there was a fish. The fly submerged and the current began to carry it rapidly downstream. Most of my greased line was floating on the slack water, and in an instant its resistance began to drag the fly across the run in an arc. Salmon aren't timid, but they aren't dumb either, and it's mighty seldom that they'll touch a fly that's acting unnaturally. I had to get rid of that drag—and fast.

I did it by roll-casting a downstream belly in the portion of the line that was floating on the pool. This is called "mending" a cast, and it's easier than it sounds. The "mend" floated a bulge of slack line below the fly, thus eliminating the drag, and allowed the fly to travel downstream at the speed of the current.

I followed it with my rod tip. The fly passed over the spot where the fish was supposed to be, and I thought I'd missed again. Then there was a swirl on the surface. I lowered my tip, stripped off a few feet of line, and let it run through the guides. The floating slack bellied downstream of the fly, and for a moment it floated with the current. For another moment it didn't move. Then it began to move upstream.

My tense nerves urged me to strike, but I waited. Then I swung my tip gently downstream—and felt my fish.

At the same moment the fish felt the prick of the hook, and its reaction was instantaneous and violent. It streaked down the run so fast that the line threw spray where it cut the water.

My rod bowed as the fish went down to the tail of the pool. Then he made a high, quivering leap. Close to twenty pounds, I guessed. He splashed back into the water and came up the run almost as swiftly as he'd gone down it. I reeled in the slack as fast as I could. When he was just across the pool from me he jumped again. Then he made a short dash downstream, stopped, came toward me, and went deep on the far side of the pool to sulk.

That put me in a spot. A salmon sulking in deep water is harder to move than a balky mule. I didn't dare use much force for fear I'd snap my light leader. I backed into shallower water, then worked slowly to the tail of the pool. The fish didn't move. Holding my rod parallel with the water, I put as much side strain on him as I dared.

That started him. He moved out into the run, swam fast upstream, and jumped again.

Now I was in a good position—downstream from my fish. By playing him carefully I kept him out of the pool and on the move. For the next ten minutes he made short dashes up and down the run, jumping half a dozen times. Then he began to tire. His runs became shorter, and I was able to work him toward me. After another five minutes I had him in the shallows at the tail of the pool.

When he was ten feet away he saw me and made another rush back into fast water. But he was dead tired, and soon I had him back in the shallows and was able to slip my tailer over him.

Seventeen pounds, my pocket scales said. . . .

The Minister's wife smiled but looked embarrassed when I stopped at his house. "He's writing his sermon, and told me he could see nobody," she said. "What with the fishing——" She shook her head.

"I just wanted to thank him, and return this fly he loaned me," I told her. "You might tell him——"

The Minister came to an open window and looked at me. He had his coat off and his spectacles on, and there was a fountain pen in his hand. "Did you kill a fish?" he demanded.

"I did," I said. "Seventeen pounds. On The Minister's Dog."

"Ay," he said, "it's a grrand fly, The Minister's Dog. They'll come to it when they'll give the go-by to all others."

As I got back into my car I wondered—would that fish have risen as eagerly to a Black Dose or a Durham Ranger as he had to The Minister's Dog? Or wouldn't he?

The Three Musketeers

F. H. ("Bert") Riggall

November 1952

A letter in What's on Your Mind, April 1965: "This will jolt a lot of people in the hunting world. The Willow Valley Trophy Club, Boone and Crockett Club representatives here, recently scored a Rocky Mountain bighorn head that should make No. 1 in the record book. (It did. Its score: 208⅛.) It was taken in 1911 by Fred Weiller in Blind Canyon, Alberta. Blind Canyon is about 45 miles south of Oyster Creek, where the bighorn now listed as No. 1 in the record book was killed by Martin Bovey in 1924. Bovey's bighorn scored 207 2/8. The new record head came into the possession of Clarence Baird of Twin Buttes, Ariz., when Mr. Weiller, his ranch partner, died. It was George Cairns, taxidermist, who urged Baird to have it measured— William Michalsky, Alberta, Canada," Well, jolt it did, but we still like the Bovey story better.

This is the strange story of Martin Bovey's bighorn sheep. It had its beginnings in 1917, when, for a spellbound moment, I gazed at three golden rams perched high on a cliff in the Canadian Rockies. It had its rousing climax thirty-five years later, in 1952. It's the story of a hunt for what I choose to call the Three Musketeers of Gould Dome.

Bovey caught up with the big ram in 1924. But another twenty-eight years were to pass before the significance of the long, curious hunt was fully understood and appreciated.

I've hunted bighorns since 1906, and taken out more sportsmen than I could readily add up. Up to 1916 the best of our Rocky Mountain hunting grounds was along the crest of the continental divide in an area south of Crowsnest Pass, Alberta. But then the area was set aside in national parks—Glacier Park in Montana and Waterton Lakes Park just over the border in Canada.

Now, years earlier I'd spent some time surveying coal claims in the wild region north of Crowsnest Pass and had been much impressed by the rugged High Rock Range, which separates Alberta from British Columbia. It looked like great sheep country, so I arranged with two old friends—Russell H. Bennett and Franklin M. Crosby, of Minneapolis—to hunt with me there in the fall of 1917. Since this involved a trek of perhaps 100 miles from my ranch at Pincher Creek, Alberta, not far from the Montana border, I put together a train of twenty packhorses and allowed three days for us to reach the southern end of our proposed hunting area. All went well and we made our first base camp late in September close to North Fork Pass.

It soon became evident that we were still too far south, so next day we moved on to the foot of a great rock fall near the head of Dutch Creek Valley, only a mile or so from the base of Tornado Peak, which looms 10,170 feet above sea level. There we put in two weeks of hunting and exploring. Bennett and Crosby each got a good sheep and a goat, and we saw many others.

Before we left, I had an experience with far-reaching consequences. I rode out of camp late one afternoon to search for two missing packhorses. I had a good notion where they'd gone—into a side draw formed by the cliffs of Gould Dome.

With my mind full of packhorse, I was nearing the end of the draw when I was startled by a sudden fall of rocks from a cliff.

Riding to a knoll, I turned my glasses onto the cliffs above. And there, in the bottom of a deep notch that looked like the V of a rifle sight, were three giant rams. The setting sun bathed them with its ruddy glow and they stood like statues of pure gold. All were giants, but the one in the middle was the largest ram I'd ever seen.

That sight alone was worth a thousand miles of travel. We'd filled our licenses, though, so there was nothing to do but file away the memory of the Three Musketeers for some future year.

I did not get back to the High Rock Range until 1920, when I took out two young men, already experienced hunters. They were Martin Bovey and Meridan Bennett, also of Minneapolis. Both were about to enter college. Bovey had gone out on his first big-game hunt with his father and me in 1916, at the age of 14, and had killed a goat. Now, after serving in the first World War, he wanted a bighorn ram. We established our base camp ten miles north of my 1917 camp.

We had just two weeks, for the boys had to start for college on September 15. I'd filled them in on my encounter with the Three Musketeers three years earlier, and they were determined to get at least one of the rams or die in the attempt. (That's no mere figure of speech. It's mighty easy to die if you miss your footing on the cliffs of the High Rocks!)

The first day out of camp we saw thirty-seven sheep, seven of them rams. But none was up to our exalted standards, so we were careful not to molest or frighten them. Every day for a week we saw other sheep, many of them excellent by most standards, but none of the stature of the Gould Dome rams. We'd sure set our sights high!

It was almost monotonous, this passing up of good heads, but our reward came at last on September 8. The sun was just rising when we poked our heads over the rimrock at the head of Oyster Creek. Earlier in the week we'd built a low stone wall there, behind which we could lie and examine the country beyond through chinks in the wall. I'd no sooner put my eye to one when I spotted twelve rams on the opposite hillside. Three or four were big ones with fine heads.

There was no way we could move toward them without being seen, however. So I glassed the country beyond them and made an even more important discovery—three really huge rams lying on the ledges of an ancient moraine. I got out my 35X spotting scope, and one glance through it convinced me that these were my old friends, the Three Musketeers.

We were all thrilled to the core, but we were worried, too, for the rams on the opposite hillside stood between us and the promised land. We considered the situation from every angle, and the answer always came out the same: Stay put until the twelve rams fed into a more favorable position. That went sorely against the grain, but there was nothing else we could do.

At 8 a.m., half an hour after we'd arrived at the rimrock, we cautiously withdrew downhill a bit. Every fifteen minutes or so one of us would crawl up to a spy hole in the rocks and check on the sheep. At 10 a.m. all the rams—including the Three Musketeers—were lying down, and the situation was as bad as ever. So there we stayed, feeling like so many fried oysters as the sun glared down on us, until 3:30 in the afternoon. Then the twelve rams began moving to the north to get out of the sun, and in a few minutes were out of sight. We were now free to move in on our trio.

The big three had fed down into some scattered bushes at timberline, then dropped below into terrain that was more favorable for stalking. The wind was all right too, and our hopes began to rise.

In coming down off our hill we had to pass a bull elk that was bedded down in some scrub brush. We were not interested in him, since the elk season wouldn't open for a month, but we certainly didn't want to spook him. So we slunk past like three well-kicked curs, our rifles ready in case he wanted to make an issue of things. Fortunately he was warm and comfortable, and only opened one eye sleepily as we passed.

We now headed for a little knoll, from whose top we hoped to locate the big fellows. To get to it we had to cross fifty yards of open mountainside, so I used a trick I've often employed in similar circumstances. Each member of the party simply cuts a balsam branch and holds it in front of him as he crawls slowly toward his objective.

We made it safely to the top of the knoll. Still shielded by the branches, we spotted our rams among some scrubby bushes 300 or so yards away. They were feeding steadily downward in our direction, so the boys got their rifles ready for action. Med Bennett was carrying a .30/06 with a Lyman 48 peep sight and gold-bead front sight. His 180-grain bullets traveled at 2,700 foot seconds' muzzle velocity. He got into his sling and adjusted it as tightly as he could. Martin had a .250/3000 Model 99-K Savage, Lyman peep and gold front sight, 100-grain Western open-point bullets, but no sling.

Med had won the toss for first shot, so he prepared to take a crack at the biggest ram as soon as it got within 200 yards. The three sheep advanced slowly and it looked as though they were indeed our meat. But you never know. They'd been feeding quietly for twenty minutes or so when one of them abruptly drew back and butted another a tremendous blow. Then both came together with a crack of horns that sounded like a rifle shot.

Like playful puppies, all three started to frolic, rushing downhill past us at forty miles an hour, and darting in and out of bushes. We were all so flabbergasted we couldn't get off a shot. Then, at the foot of the hill, they stopped dead about 200 yards away, facing uphill toward us—perfect targets.

Unfortunately Med had prepared himself for an uphill shot, and now, with the tight sling, he had to aim down a 45-degree slant. His bullet went low, and gravel flew up into the sheep's belly, stinging it like fifty bees. The ram reared and made for the timber, disappearing into it in a flash, followed by his pals. The belt of woods was about 100 yards wide, and the sheep got through it in an instant and then started across slide rock straight away from us and at 300 yards' range.

Med managed to get off another ineffective shot at the biggest ram before it disappeared around a curve in the cliff. Then he fired twice at the No. 2 sheep but failed to connect. His fifth and last bullet was directed at ram No. 3 just as it too was about to round the cliff. It crashed down among the boulders with a broken neck.

"Med!" I shouted. "You've got the little one!"

Well, it looked little in comparison with the others, but when we went up to examine it we were astounded at its head, of a size that few sheep hunters see in a lifetime and certainly in the record class. And we realized, with awe, that he was smaller than the two others!

Night fell when we were still miles from camp, and we spent hours skirting cliffs and feeling our way up and down hillsides. To complicate things, we were carrying a head that weighed about eighty pounds and we had only one flashlight, the size of a cigarette case. (In those days they didn't make the powerful flashlights we use now.) But we got to our horses around midnight and were back in camp at 1 a.m.

The next act of the drama occurred two years later. I was out with a party consisting of Sumner McKnight, Ted White, and R. B. ("Bunny") Rathbun, of

Minneapolis. (I've got a lot of friends in Minneapolis!) I took them to the same basin where Med Bennett had got his trophy. And on the first day's scout I located eight rams. They were about a mile away, and through the binoculars one of them seemed a buster—fully as large as Med's had been.

Next morning we got up before dawn and soon spotted the rams again. They were in a side gully and, with a little care, we managed to get within 350 yards of them. But we didn't dare attempt to move any closer until they fed down the gully and out of sight. When they did that, about noon, we moved in quickly and got in good position on the crest of a low butte at about 150 yards' range. None of my companions had done much rifle shooting previously, although they were crack bird shots. Anyway, in shooting from the prone they missed the rams by a wide margin. But when the sheep got into high and started to move away, the hunters jumped to their feet and knocked three of them down within five seconds! That's what wing-shooting does for you.

Sumner got the biggest ram, Ted and Bunny two smaller ones. When we measured the big fellow's horns they ran 43½ inches around the outside curve and had a girth at base of 16⅝ inches. This bettered Med's trophy by 1½ and ½ inches, respectively.

Obviously this was the second of the Three Musketeers. That left just one— the largest of them all.

I didn't get back to the Gould Dome area until 1924. This time I again took out Martin Bovey, and with him his brother Charlie. We were on sheep ground on opening day of the season and soon saw rams, but they were all small to medium, so we passed them up. Nothing less than the biggest of the Musketeers would satisfy us on this trip.

We carefully covered the areas north and south of what I'd come to call Med's Basin. But for a week the weather remained very hot, and we saw no sign of our quarry. Evidently the big rams were staying up near the snowy peaks. That was disheartening, for the Boveys had set a deadline for their departure. Martin, who'd transferred from Yale to the University of Minnesota after a winter of subarctic life as a trader in northern Manitoba, was about to start his senior year at college.

Our pessimism mounted as the days slipped by, for it seemed that the biggest Musketeer was likely to die a natural death, perhaps during the coming winter. Already he was of ripe old age, for the wild sheep seldom lives longer than from thirteen to fifteen years. Along about then they lose their incisor teeth and cannot graze properly, even in good pasture. Weakened, they fall prey to the wolves or coyotes.

We kept going. A change in the weather brought snowfall on the peaks, and like magic the sheep began to show up here and there. We had two days left, but there was still no sign of the big ram. I figured he wouldn't be far from Med's Basin, and probably was high up.

On September 12 we headed over the rimrock via High Notch and glassed the country thoroughly. At about 2 p.m., thanks to my 8X wide-angle Zeiss binoculars, I spotted something that might be the curve of a ram's horn against the sky at the peak of Mount O'Rourke, many hundreds of feet above our position. There was nothing to do but watch the "horn" closely.

With our backs settled firmly against rock we trained our glasses on it. Thirty minutes later we were rewarded by seeing a monster ram get to his feet and stretch. He looked huge, outlined against the clouds, and there was no doubt in my mind that here was the last of the Three Musketeers. He was about 9,000 feet above sea level.

After a good stretch and a long look around, he started briskly down the slope, evidently headed for good feeding ground.

We froze as still as mice when the cat's around, and he moved down to within 500 yards of us, then disappeared behind a wall of limestone. We scrambled to our feet and climbed the wall at top speed, with me a few yards in the lead. Near the top I slowed down and cautiously peeped over the rim. There was our ram, feeding, about 200 yards away, and with him about a dozen others.

There at last, after long years of hunting, was the noblest Musketeer of them all. Even now a puff of wind from the wrong direction could ruin our chances. And Martin Bovey, having once put his eyes on that breath-taking ram, could easily develop a severe case of buck fever. Apparently, though the fates had tested us enough. Martin calmly lined up the sights of his Savage .250/3000 on the ram's neck, just forward of the shoulder, and squeezed the trigger. The little 87-grain bullet sped on its way, staggering the ram. As it started to run, Bovey got off another shot, and the bighorn slumped to the ground, then rolled twenty feet down the slope and lay perfectly still. The first bullet, through the jugular, would have been fatal in a short time.

After that it was all anticlimax, as it always is after a long-drawn-out but successful hunt. I won't describe our yells of triumph save to say that they probably spooked every animal within fifty miles.

Out came the steel tape measure. In awe we read the figures for the outer curl of the horn—forty-six inches! And the girth—nearly seventeen!

A head to be proud of in any company. Jack O'Connor recently told me, "That was probably the best trophy ever taken on the North American continent —in the eyes of a lot of people anyway. After all, experienced hunters generally rate the bighorn ram as the finest of our trophies. And Bovey's—well, that was the best of the rams."

At the time, though, I only knew that this was the biggest ram I had ever seen.

Our work was cut out for us. We started to struggle down to camp, carrying the big head and cape. But night was coming on apace and I knew we'd have all we could do to reach camp. And after a few slips, in which we cheated death only by a whisker, we cached the head on top of a steep cliff and went on, reaching our base about midnight. I was up again at dawn and out after the trophy, which I retrieved and lugged back.

Well, often during the long stretch of years since 1924 I've reflected that that September day was the high point of my career as a hunter and outfitter. It was, too—for twenty-eight years after the hunt.

Then came a bigger thrill. One day early this year I got word that the Boone and Crockett Club had awarded first place among all American bighorn sheep to Martin Bovey's golden ram. It jumped from fourth place to first place under the club's improved rating system, displacing the former world record trophy taken by James Simpson in 1920. The explanation: the new system of scoring takes into consideration not just length of horn alone, but massiveness and symmetry as well.

When the club's committee on revision was at work a year or so ago, Grancel Fitz, one of its members, got in touch with Bovey, now a wildlife photographer, lecturer, and producer of industrial motion pictures. Mr. Fitz asked Bovey to bring the head from his home in Concord, Mass., to New York City for remeasurement. Since it's really Bovey's story, let him tell what happened in New York:

"My wife and I dined that evening with Mr. and Mrs. Fitz and Samuel B. Webb, the committee chairman. During dinner, either Mr. Fitz or Mr. Webb said he thought my ram might become the new No. 2 head.

"After dinner we drove to Mr. Fitz's home, with the head still in the trunk of my car. When we were going up in the elevator both men got their first close look at it, and both whistled. 'Well,' I thought, 'a fellow should look and whistle at even the No. 2 head.' But I wasn't prepared for what was coming.

"After the head had been measured and Mr. Fitz toted up the rating he said to his wife, 'Check my addition carefully, because if it's correct this is not the No. 2 head—but the head.'

"Have you ever held your breath while figures were being added? I have, when checking my bank account. But I never held it with quite the feeling of suspense I experienced now.

"When Mrs. Fitz said the addition was correct my first thought was to get an airmail letter off to Bert Riggall."

And that's the story of the last of the Three Musketeers.

Santiago and the Lady

Jack O'Connor

March 1953

Jack O'Connor wrote for OUTDOOR LIFE for forty years and was its gun
editor par excellence for nearly thirty-five. He was born in Tempe, Arizona,
and wrote a fine book about his boyhood there called *Horse and Buggy West*.
He received his MA from University of Missouri in 1927 and was a
newspaperman, novelist (*Conquest* and *Boomtown*) and professor of
journalism before joining OUTDOOR LIFE. He has hunted on four continents,
taken two grand slams of all four varieties of North American sheep, and
collected record-class trophies of the major animals of Alaska, Canada,
United States, Mexico, Iran, Africa and India. For all this he received the
Weatherby Big Game Trophy in 1957, awarded for outstanding
sportsmanship and achievement in big-game hunting. And he has written a
dozen books on hunting and shooting. Salud!

The first time Santiago Romero saw me I was on my elbows and knees, my
hind end up in the air, and I was blowing up an air mattress. I didn't get a good
look at him at the time, but my wife did. She said that his eyes almost popped out
of his head and that he turned pale—that is, if Santiago, who is largely Indian
and quite swarthy, could turn pale.

Anyway, said Eleanor, his skin became yellowish with faint green overtones.
For a moment she thought he was going to swoon and fall off his horse or clap
his spurs into the steed's side and get the heck out of there. Apparently he
thought he was seeing some strange ritual the gringos practice before they devour
innocent Mexican vaqueros. He spoke not a single word of English and had never
known an American.

Inadvertently I saved the day. I had heard the horses coming and was conscious out of the corner of my eye that one had a rider.

"Que tal, amigo?" I said between puffs. That's just about equivalent to "How
goes it, friend?"

The sound of his own language apparently served to reassure Santiago. He dismounted, bowed to my wife, and said, "I am called Santiago Romero."

My wife said she was called la Señora O'Connor and that her esposo who was
laboring on the bed was called Jack O'Connor.

"O-cone-nor," said Santiago.

"Call me Jack," I said.

"Djek," repeated Santiago.

"The same as Juanito in Spanish."

"Oh," he said brightening. "I then call you Juanito!"

We were in the process of making camp out in the Mexican desert perhaps
twenty miles as the crow flies from the Gulf of California. The spot was locally
known as the "tinajo," or tank. It consisted of a corral of gnarled mesquite, a
windmill, and a big tin water tank. In the corral was a watering trough which
range cattle used. Next to it was a mud hut in which lived the caretaker, his wife,
and five children. His sole duties were to shut off the windmill when the tank was
full and to shut off the tank when the watering trough was full; then to turn them
on again. He was paid fifty pesos a month—at that time about $10.

Our own camp was in an adobe hut on a little knoll overlooking the corral. Near it was another hut where hay was stored. I had made a deal back at the ranch for hay, horses, and Santiago.

"Drive on up to the tinajo," Epifanio, the ranch owner, had told me earlier that day. "You can camp in one building and you'll have hay and water right there. I'll send a boy up with some horses."

While we blew up our mattresses and laid out food and cooking gear, Santiago stood around watching. Without being asked, he went down to the trough and brought back a bucket of water, then rustled a couple of loads of firewood.

He seemed to sense when my chores were done. "Would you care to mount a horse and take a turn with me?" he asked. "Maybe we could see some deer."

By that time it was midafternoon, but I tied my scabbard on a saddle, stuck my old .270 rifle in it, and Santiago and I took off. It was late in December and a storm was brewing. Great white clouds with gray bellies were blowing in from the gulf on a chill wind, and when they passed over the sun the gray desert was suddenly drab and cold. As Santiago and I rode along we could see the long tracks of big desert mule deer and now and then the little heart-shaped tracks of white-tails. Occasionally we'd see where a herd of the little Southwestern pigs called javelinas had crossed our path, and we flushed a few coveys of Gambel's quail. Once we came over the crest of a hill in time to see a frightened white-tail doe running wildly through the cactus below us.

We'd made a long circle and were turning back toward camp when Santiago suddenly put up his hand. "Buros!" he said. He pointed across a wide valley to a hill thick with paloverde trees. I detected a movement, put my binoculars on it, and saw a long-eared mule-deer doe. Then I saw another, and another— in all about half a dozen. Since the rut was just beginning, the does were probably a harem, and the buck who had collected them should be around.

Then my hungry horse saw an appetizing ironwood branch above him. He reached up and yanked it off with a sharp crack. That did it. The does started to run, and out from behind a paloverde came a magnificent buck. He was in sight for only an instant as he cut over the low ridge to the left.

"Look at the buck! Look at those antlers!" muttered Santiago. "Let us go!"

He unbuckled his chaps, dropped them to the ground, and took off his spurs. Then away we went on foot, with me right behind him. How he knew exactly where the buck would head I'll never guess, but he did. We ran for a quarter of a mile, then pounded over a ridge. Immediately we saw a big doe come streaming by, not much more than fifty yards away. Right after her came the buck—big, dark, and fat—running with his nose up and his great antlers laid back.

I was, alas, in no condition to shoot after my sprint, but I managed somehow to get the wavering crosshairs behind the old macho's shoulder. I touched her off and the buck swapped ends. I shot again and he was down. The first 130-grain Silvertip had taken him high through the lungs and the second had broken both shoulders. The bullets went clear through.

I dressed the buck while Santiago went back to get the horses, and then it dawned on me that this desert buck not only had the best head—thirteen points —of any Mexican mule deer I had ever taken but that he was also the heaviest. When we got the four quarters to the locker they weighed 176 pounds. As he lay there he couldn't have weighed much less than 250. All in all, he was quite a buck.

"How big!" Santiago commented when he joined me with the horses. "Like a bull."

We got a riata on the big buck's antlers, threw it over a paloverde branch, and, with me hoisting and Santiago lifting, managed to get the enormous buck over

Santiago's saddle and tie him in place. Then Santiago seated himself on the buck and led the way in triumph back to camp.

When we jangled up my wife had a fire going, green beans heating, potatoes boiling, and a dozen quail browning in a big frying pan. Santiago turned to me "It is good," he said, "to bring along a woman to cook the meals, to wash the dishes, and to talk to."

"Yes," I said, "it is good. Women are useful."

Most poor Mexicans are not hearty eaters. They never have much more than enough to get by on and their capacity is small. Santiago, though, was an exception. He devoured the crisp brown quail, remarking that he'd had no idea the little birds were so good to eat, and savored the boiled potatoes like an epicure with a truffle. Papas, he told me, were a delicacy he had rarely eaten. The fluffy Dutch-oven biscuits, he said, were equal to his wife's tortillas, and the canned peaches were a delight. Ah, women! They were handy in a camp.

But the next morning Santiago did a double-take. Following my usual custom when on a trip with my wife, I crawled out of my sleeping bag, built a fire, and put coffee on. Then I fried bacon, scrambled eggs, made toast, and took my wife's breakfast in to her as she lay in the sack.

Poor Santiago was astounded. When I handed him his plate he was brooding so heavily he could hardly eat. Later, after he had brought in the horses, he drew me aside. "Tell me," he said, "in los Estados Unidos do all the wives lie abed in the mornings while the husbands arise and cook the food?"

"Yes," I assured him. "It is an old North American custom."

"In Mexico it is not," he told me with great definiteness.

But other surprises were in store for him.

"Put a saddle on a horse for la senora," I directed.

"For why?" he asked.

"La senora this day must shoot a buck."

He blinked, swallowed a couple of times, then went over and picked up blanket and saddle.

I'd discovered earlier that the extractor on my wife's .257 was broken, so now the only functioning firearms we had were my .270 and a 16 gauge shotgun. Poor Santiago was fit to be tied when he saw me putting my scabbard and rifle on Eleanor's saddle.

"For why, Juanito, you give the rifle to la senora and take none yourself?"

"We have but one that is effective," I told him.

"But when we see the buck he must receive a ball!"

"La senora," I assured him, "is a good shooter."

So we rode off, Santiago in the lead, followed closely by Eleanor, and with me tagging along at the end.

We headed for a chain of low, brushy hills where, in previous years, I had always found white-tail deer—venados, the Mexicans call them. The sandy soil of every valley was dimpled with white-tail tracks, but no deer did we see. I could tell, though, that they were moving out ahead of our noisy cavalcade.

Finally I said to Santiago, "It is good for you and la senora to ride to the saddle ahead, get off, and tie your horses. I shall make a circle and perhaps frighten the deer so that you shall see them."

"It is good," said Santiago.

I waited until they were within a couple of minutes of the saddle ahead, then turned my horse and rode down into a brushy little valley. I hadn't gone a quarter of a mile when I heard the brush pop and two bucks—an old one with a massive head and a younger one of frying size—ran up on the hillside not over seventy-five yards away and stopped to look at me.

"Boo!" I yelled.

Startled, the bucks took off—in the general direction of Santiago and Eleanor. A few moments later I heard a shot, then another. I rode around a point. I could see the two standing horses, but Eleanor and Santiago were not with them. Presently I saw them bending over a buck down in the little valley below.

I joined them, noted that it was the smaller of the two bucks, and heard Eleanor's story: The buck had run right into the trap (the big deer turned off), tearing by at about 200 yards. Eleanor swung the scope smoothly ahead of him and touched off her shot. The buck collapsed, hit squarely through the lungs. Then a desert gray fox, frightened by the racket, popped up clear across the valley, a good 300 yards away.

"Behold!" Santiago said, pointing. "Una zorra!"

Eleanor leveled down on the fox and knocked it for a loop.

Santiago was still goggle-eyed when I got there. "Ah," he told me, shaking his head, "a good shooter is la senora."

So we started back toward camp.

Since we had our deer and there was now no need for quiet, Eleanor, whose knowledge of Spanish is limited but who does not worry about it, held the following conversation with Santiago as we rode along:

"Grass is green!" said Eleanor.

"Si," agreed Santiago.

"Cows eat grass."

"Si."

"When they eat much grass they get fat."

"The truth," said Santiago.

"When cows are fat they are very good to eat."

"Ah, how good!" he agreed.

But I could see his thoughts were elsewhere, and when we got back to camp and Eleanor went into the shack to repair her make-up, he drew me aside.

"Tell me," he said, "in los Estados Unidos do many women shoot the rifle and kill the deer?"

"Ah yes," I assured him. "The North American women love to shoot. Many times they go to the mountains to hunt while the husbands remain in the home to care for the young."

"Can that be!" he gasped, shaking his head. "What a people!"

Presently we heard quail calling down by the water. One of the coveys that watered there was coming in. Eleanor, who dearly loves to shoot quail, came whipping out of the shack with her 16 under her arm, looking as glamorous as a dame can look in a wool shirt, cowboy boots, and a soiled pair of pants with a hole in the knee.

"Hear those quail?" she said. "I'm going down and shoot our supper."

"Why don't you go with la senora and pick up the corpses?" I suggested to Santiago. "While you do I shall remove the pelt from the buck."

"It is good." said Santiago.

I stood and watched. They weren't halfway down the hill when a bird buzzed off. Eleanor's gun came up. It went bang and the bird dropped. Santiago picked up the fluttering quail, then pointed to another scurrying along the ground about thirty yards away.

"Shoot!" I heard him shout. "Shoot before he flies."

Eleanor rushed in until the frightened quail took wing. She shot and it tumbled.

I went about the business of skinning the white-tail. While I worked, I could hear Eleanor's 16 gauge popping. Presently she and Santiago came back. In each hand the vaquero carried a cluster of quail.

"I got nine," Eleanor told me.

"Good going," I said.

Santiago had never seen any wing-shooting and I doubt that he'd ever seen a shotgun. "How good the shooter is la senora," he told me. "The quail it flies. Bang! It is dead. Another flies. Bang again!"

That night was New Year's Eve. We feasted on baked quail, broiled back-straps from the big buck, French-fried potatoes, and stewed tomatoes. For dessert Eleanor had whipped together a cherry pie and baked it in the Dutch oven. Then we toasted one another, friendship between the United States and Mexico, and anything else we could think of in a mild concoction of rum, sugar, water, and lemon juice. When the New Year came, we all hit the sack.

We packed up the next day to drive back across the border. Santiago had his horses ready for the ten-mile trek back to the ranch and he was wearing a jacket and a good pair of shoes I had given him. He had fifty pesos in his pocket. Yet he was forlorn.

"You go quickly," he said. "You should stay longer—two days, five days, a whole week. There are many deer and we could shoot them."

"But we must go," I told him. "In our house there is much to do."

"I have never seen a shooter like la senora," he said. "Bang, bang, bang—the deer, the fox, the quail. But it makes me sad to know that anyone so lovely has death in her heart. That should be only for the men!"

Mucha Trucha

Red Smith

April 1953

Walter "Red" Smith, sports columnist of the *New York Times,* made this trip for OUTDOOR LIFE when he was with the *N.Y. Herald Tribune*. Part 2 was mostly rain, but in it Red recounted a weird experience. He had never bothered carrying extra eye-glasses, but this time he thought it wise to have an extra pair in a jungle six thousand miles away. Nuf ced. He broke both pair within twelve hours and fished blind until his return to Santiago, where an oculist consented to grind a lens in two hours. On the plane Red parted the curtains to gaze on the Andes, caught his glasses and shattered them a third time. Said he, "My wife saw me groping off the plane at Idlewild. Over one eye was a cut. My sunburned ears were tattered, my peeling face scarred and blotchy. She thought I'd been mugged in Chilean."

When this fish took the lure, he did not explode in a geyser of white water. He did not rocket out of the water like a 12-inch projectile. He did not erupt, or detonate, or blast the lure, or attempt any of the other warlike measures commonly attributed to big fish in the literature of the outdoor magazines. Being intelligent, if not widely read, he tried to eat the lure.

Being also large and muscular and energetic, he approached his snack with enthusiasm. He jerked the reel handle out of my grasp and made it spin, removing tracts of hide from several knuckles. When the drag was set he came to the surface and leaped, just once. He came up pretty high and fell back on his side with a large splash.

He looked as long as a dishonest basketball player. I was scared. I had never seen a trout like this with my eyes open.

The fish dived. Our boat was drifting fast before a stiff wind but the trout wouldn't come along. He was like a spoiled boy digging his heels in the earth when a parent tries to drag him. There were spasms of jerking that made the reel go zzzzaatt . . . zzzzupp . . . zaazzuuuutt!

In the stern of the boat Capt. Warren Smith realized that the fish had found refuge in the weeds. Twice he started the outboard and steered upwind above the fish, and we tugged timidly at the line. When we freed it the trout came up obediently, tuckered out by his struggles down there in the broccoli.

He was a lusty rainbow of 12 pounds with shoulders like Max Baer's, magnificently colored, and splendidly deep, like Jane Russell. I killed him and helped eat him and I am still awed by him. I can't shake off a feeling that I made a meal off Tony Galento. To me, that trout lives as a symbol of fishing in the Chilean Andes.

I am a clumsy, enthusiastic leisure-time angler with little leisure. Because I grew up in the Middle West I am a fresh-water fisherman, dedicated to trout and bass. Until January, 1953, my biggest trout was a 2½ to 3-pounder, caught in the Laurentian Mountains of Quebec.

In the East we think of the Laurentians as near, yet it takes as long to reach them by car as to fly 6,000 miles to Chile. It was midafternoon and winter had a hammer lock on New York when the plane left Idlewild Airport. A little after midnight the Pan American-Grace Airways ship paused in sweltering Panama. Dawn came up somewhere around the equator, and that afternoon we were

202

having a tall, cool one beside the roof-top swimming pool of Santiago's Hotel Carrera, ogling the dolls in swim suits. It was January, and mid-summer.

Capt. Warren Smith is a big, bluff, ex-pilot for Panagra who flew up and down and back and forth across the cruel peaks of the Southern Hemisphere until they named him "King of the Andes." He lived in Chile sixteen years, seems to know every cop and hack driver and railroad porter in the country, and he goes back from Miami every year for at least a month of fishing.

He is part owner with a group of friends of a cache of outdoor gear—rowboat outboard motor, tent, sleeping bags, air mattresses, cooking utensils. He put in a half day loading this stuff onto an American-make pick-up truck that had been rented for us, complete with a blue-eyed Chilean driver named Herman (pronounced Airmon). A friend lent his camp boy, a swarthy, mustached Chileno named Hernan (Airnon). The four of us rattled out of town, were stopped at a traffic cop's barricade, and got a ticket. The cop had a whole pad of summonses already made out; he just filled in names, license numbers, and such misdemeanors as pleased his fancy when he made each pinch.

Our objective was Laguna del Maule, a lake such as you don't see more than once in a lifetime. You go 150 miles south from Santiago to the ancient city of Talca, turn left, and climb ninety miles to the Chilean-Argentine border. (Chile is a skinny sliver of a country on the Pacific but due south of New York, a couple of thousand miles deep and averaging around 100 miles wide.)

The "road," which is a euphemism with ruts, ends at the lake which perches a mile and a half high. There is nothing to the east save a wild, indescribably desolate scraggle of volcanic peaks crumbling into gray dust under the cold wind that blows eternally up the gorge of Rio Maule from the west. Dead Chilean volcanoes, their crests touched with snow in midsummer, crowd the lake shore. Immediately beyond them you see Argentina's mountains. This is a mountain pass, but high above timberline; there is not a tree, not a shrub, scarcely a blade of grass.

Like all Chilean waters, Lake Maule is matted with apancoras—small crawfish which look like miniature lobsters, dark on top and sort of shrimp-pink below. Apparently here are the tidbits trout have been looking for ever since Izaak Walton invented them. The fish smack their gills over the crustaceous canapes and grow to phenomenal size. All good Chilean fishing waters have produced trout weighing more than 20 pounds.

There are no native trout in Chile. There's a native fish called "trucha chilena" (Chilean trout), because it was considered a trout before rainbows were imported from the United States about 45 years ago, to be followed by German browns from Europe. Groping for a name, Chileans called the newcomers "trucha salmonidea."

The trucha chilena has the bronze back of a bass but the shape of a perch and there is nothing to recommend him except his succulent white flesh. Put a hook in his face and he behaves like a German infantryman; "Vateffer is the rules," he mumbles, and comes along quietly.

Fish can't commute between Lake Maule and the river which tumbles out of it toward the Pacific, because of a towering waterfall. There were, according to the tale, no trout in the lake until about a quarter-century ago when an old Englishman took some out of the river and trudged on foot up the mountains with the fish in milk cans slung over his horse's back. The size and villainy they have attained since then testify to the quality of their shellfish diet.

Well, Herman blessed himself as we set out from Santiago, muttered a small prayer when we finally got past the traffic cop's barricade, and we went clattering down through a lush valley of vineyards and eucalyptus trees with snow-capped Andes on the left and the lower coast range on the right.

Physically the country looks like southern California. Or, rather, this is how southern California would look if every movie company in Hollywood were on location filming epics of the soil. You keep passing bit players on horseback, swarthy vaqueros wearing pie-plate sombreros and brightly striped ponchos, which are vari-colored blankets with a hole in the middle for the head, giving the wearer the appearance of a bug in a rug.

There were laden burros, and oxcarts whose two wheels were solid disks, just cross sections of tree trunks. Two little kids swam naked in a muddy ditch beside the highway. Short-tailed hawks wheeled in the hot blue sky.

So a rear tire blew out. One look at Herman's gouged and blistered spares, and it was obvious this safari would hole up overnight in Talca while new tires were bargained for. So it was ordained.

In the morning while Herman haggled over tires, his passengers took a horse-drawn hansom to the city market and bought provisions from the ancient crones who squat on flagstones selling everything from big coils of seaweed (for making seaweed soup) to sections of old automobile tires (for making sandals). One purchase was eight kilos (about 17½ pounds) of sirloin, all meat and no bone, at 25¢ a pound.

"Maule?" said the hack driver when he learned where the expedition was bound. "Muy bonito rio."

It is that, a very pretty river. You go east from Talca for a while through a rich valley, then you start up a dirt trail and the river is below you. It is milky blue in the pools, foaming white in the rapids. The road is far above, a twisting shelf on the face of volcanic cliffs.

Houses grew fewer and poorer. They became shacks with thatched roofs and walls that were insubstantial tangles of crooked sticks and vines, live bamboo, and broom-corn stalks. The truck frightened flocks of tan-bodied, black-winged mountain doves. There was a roadside pond where a mamma duck gave swimming lessons to seven infinitesimal blobs of downy yellow. A pair of quail raced across the trail convoying a brood of tiny chicks. From the tail of a passing truck, grinning Chilenos brandished huge wine bottles aloft and toasted us, smiles gleaming white in olive faces.

The radiator of the pick-up boiled over. Herman stomped on the brakes, and nothing happened. Oh well, the altitude was only about 5,000 feet at that point and brakes weren't what you'd call vital. Every kilometer or so there was a mountain brook where water could be scooped up for the radiator. Thus, haltingly, timberline was reached.

Camp was pitched there among a sparse growth of chunky, small-leaved maitenes trees, the very last trees on the climb. While others did the work, I fished. Because the river was low—they're building a dam at the lake, and sometimes water in the stream is shut off—Capt. Smith suggested using a small spinner.

The trout were nuts about this metal dingus. One snatched it in a pool just above a succession of small falls, ran downstream, and vowed he'd smash the tackle of anybody who tried to bring him back up the rapids. A scrambling, stumbling pursuit ensued over boulders. The fish got loose, naturally.

Lots of fish were lost in a couple of hours. Eight or ten were landed and six kept for supper. They ran about 1½ pounds each and were displayed proudly to Capt. Smith, who started to snort, counted ten, and then said indulgently that they were nice trout. Capt. Smith is a tolerant man.

That evening Herman stood by the roadside stopping the few trucks going to and from the dam job above, seeking fluid for his bone-dry brakes. Nobody was carrying any, of course, but one Chilean genius said that although motor oil would ruin the brakes, wine could be used as a substitute because it contained alcohol.

Capt. Smith knew what contained more alcohol than wine. Out came the bottle of Scotch. Next morning the truck went buck-jumping up to the lake with a brake cylinder full of Scotch, the happiest car in Chile.

Herman, a teetotaler who loves his beat-up camioneta, had been unhappy about feeding it hooch. First time the bus topped a rise and pitched downward toward a precipice, he tried the tiddly brakes. They took hold like a lush clutching a lapel.

In twenty dizzying kilometers after that, Herman never stopped laughing.

On the long haul up from Talca we had seen maybe three or four fishermen in the river. Capt. Smith said their lures were "terribles" (tay-reeb' lace). Using a long cane pole cut from the woods, they wade the shallows and slowly, gently, work the current with a little flat metal minnow bristling with hooks. They catch fish.

Wet flies are effective in the river but there is no admiration in Chile for dry flies, perhaps because neither the trout nor the Chilenos see much insect life. Except for a lazy horsefly confined to a brief season on certain waters, there are no stinging bugs in the land—no mosquitoes or gnats or blackflies or midges or no-see-ums. Comparatively few hatches appear on the streams.

Obviously, a big wet fly in fast water looks like a minnow to a trout, until the hook bites back. Silver-bodied patterns are most highly regarded and the popular size is 1/0, the theory being that big flies grade out small fish.

Such as I am, I'm a fly fisherman but no purist like the companion Capt. Smith had on one trip. Somewhat like Sweet Alice, Ben Bolt, this guy wept with delight at the sight of a fly and trembled with horror at the thought of offering a spinner, spoon, or plug to a trout. "But," said the captain, "the sucker would tie a fly on a 6/0 hook big enough to land sharks."

Maybe on a calm day the trout of Lake Maule would rise for flies. Generally, though, they lie deep in a belt of weeds that circles the lake not far from the shore, munching apancoras and cultivating a venomous temper induced by the barren desolation around them. The accepted technique for striking up an acquaintance is to drift over the weed beds casting spoons or other gaudy hardware, much as one attracts a blonde with costume jewelry.

The idea of fishing trout with a casting rod gave me faint qualms, but when you're traveling you drink the wine of the country. When we hauled boat and outboard from the truck we took only plug rods aboard, rigging them with bronze-backed spoons of scarlet and orange that had been recommended in a Santiago sporting-goods shop. A fly-rod would have been useless, anyhow, in that day's fierce wind.

Even in the lee of a point or rocky island, the wind was stiff enough to stop a cast in mid-air while bird's nests burgeoned on the reel. On a cast downwind the drifting boat followed so swiftly you had to reel like crazy or be snagged in the weeds a few feet below the surface. We settled for cross-wind casts from bow and stern.

I was still trying to get the hang of this and picking out backlashes when Capt. Smith grunted. In the same instant there was a noise as of a troop of Boy Scouts in the old swimming hole. I looked, and I didn't believe it. I'm not sure I do now.

A Thing had the captain's spoon. It wasn't as big as a steam yacht or a beer truck or even a sea serpent, but it was angrier and much more agile than any of these. It was in and out of the water, and in and out, and around the boat from stern to beam and back again.

"No," I said. "That's not a trout."

"It is," the captain said. "Oops!" His reel was chattering.

At length The Thing came flopping aboard on a gaff, a beautiful brute, dark and silver with sunrise along the sides.

"He'll go about nine pounds," Capt. Smith said mildly. Then: "That first time you saw him jump," he said, "he wasn't on. He missed the spoon and came out of water and I let him have it again and he took it."

This was on the first drift below a small point. We were to learn that strikes would come only close to the shore or over the weed belt. Farther out, where a rocky bottom could be made out dimly through the rough, clear water, no fish were shopping for metal gewgaws.

The captain caught several more fish, slightly smaller than his first, before my inept casts aroused troutly attention. Then there was a shock of contact and a dark body that seemed monstrous to my incredulous eyes leaped once and departed without ceremony. I had not set the hook.

Now I locked up with another. He need not have been as big as Primo Carnera, but he jumped four times in dazzlingly swift succession, and every time he got up on his tail and shook his head he grew taller. On the fourth jump the leader parted. He went away with a faceful of hardware.

The captain was chuckling. "Oooh, he was provoked," he said. "I never saw a madder fish. That trout hates you."

I didn't care. I was laughing with joyous excitement. Those four shuddering leaps were what I had dreamt about, planning this trip at home. Several of my fingernails were broken. It was an untidy manicure, but well worth coming 6,000 miles to get. Losing the trout didn't matter. I didn't wish him dead.

The captain was right, though. In Maule the hatred is all on the side of the fish. They dislike people, they outnumber people, and sometimes they outweigh people.

Now a fish broke Capt. Smith's leader. Then I lost one the same way. We had started with eight spoons, and when trout had taken six of them by force it filtered through two slow minds that something must be wrong with the 15-pound-test nylon, bought new in Miami. The leaders all broke in the same place, not at a knot but in the middle of the loop at top or bottom.

Conceivably a couple of those fish were heavy enough to break leaders on their own, but not all of them. We saw one plainly when Capt. Smith brought it to the surface close to the boat. He wasn't being horsed in, and he wasn't big enough to snap a sound leader, but he dived and went off with the spoon.

With the two remaining spoons tied directly to the lines, no more lures were lost. We fished until midafternoon of this gusty, overcast day, then pulled up on the gritty shore for lunch. A small cliff of volcanic rock gave protection from the wind. It crumbled at the touch, pouring small avalanches into hip boots.

We were near the east end of the lake, some miles from the squalid construction camp at the dam site at the western outlet. We had seen one other boat with a fishing party. Otherwise there was no life save the ducks and geese and terns and grebes on the surface and the fish below. The loneliness of the scene lent it a kind of sullen majesty.

Wading and casting near the shore I saw what looked like an ostrich egg floating near me. I picked it up. It was a floating rock, for Pete's sake. Pumice.

Daylight lingers in summer at these altitudes but it was a dim day and we didn't fancy teetering down that skimpy ledge of road after dark at the mercy of Herman's rum-dum brakes. Consequently we didn't fish overlong after the late lunch.

Not every float across the weed beds brought a strike, but we were never long without evidence of the presence and malice of these fish. At length Capt. Smith said, "What do you say we try it once more and then call it a day?"

It was on that last drift that I was assaulted by the 12-pounder, our best of the day. He was what the Chilenos might call mucha trucha, but whether they put it just that way I wouldn't know. Chances are we caught about ten trout and lost as many more, counting those that made off with the spoons. We kept six, whose total weight must have been more than 40 pounds. We did not see one smaller than three or four pounds.

We were to meet a man later who told of a day when his party—I forgot how many rods—took 88 trout out of Maule, all between eight and 18 pounds. I was glad we could make no such boasts.

There is no creel limit in Chile. Since construction of the dam began the road has been "improved," I was told, so that cars sometimes bring several hundred fishermen to the lake on a week-end. The dam is supposed to raise the level of the lake about 17 feet. What all this may do to the fishing in the next few years, one can only guess.

Creeping, shuddering, hicupping down the face of precipices, we made timber-line in about an hour. Darkness had beaten us into that deep gorge. (Hernan, the camp boy, told Capt. Smith he was unhappy camping there; the crags crowded him like cell walls.)

Unhappy or not, he'd been busy. The dusty ground under the maitenes trees had been tidied. A campfire was burning, a lantern hung from the tent pole, and under it a folding table was set with the first course for dinner—big, blushing tomatoes stuffed with the minced pink flesh of rainbow trout. This was only the beginning. Scotch and the frothing red wine of Chile are versatile fluids.

Sometime in the black middle of that night a shout from Capt. Smith emptied the sleeping bags. It had started to rain. Gear had to be hauled under cover. Next morning it was still raining, and cold.

Delays in Santiago and on the road had cut one day off the fishing schedule. Now the weather ruled out plans for further experiments on the river. Between rain squalls, camp was struck and the truck overloaded.

The old pick-up shivered down the greasy trail through howling rains. At a carabinero station the soldier-cops said it was snowing that morning up at the lake. Once the truck had to stop because boulders had been washed onto the road from the cliffs above. We rolled them over the shoulder. They plunged out of sight, crashing faintly.

Back at Talca we parted. Capt. Smith and I would take a train to the lake-and-river country some 350 miles south. Herman, Hernan, and the six big fish turned north for Santiago and a freezer.

Departing, Herman said miserably, "I am sorry. My camioneta is not good enough." He needn't have apologized. Riding his truck, such as it was, was better than crawling to Maule on all fours over broken beer bottles, and that would not have been too high a price for such trout.

In this melting-pot nation of ours there are people who admire basketball, and people who vibrate with pleasure at a ballet, and people—hundreds of thousands of them—who consider a three-pound rainbow trout nobler, lovelier, and more desirable than Marilyn Monroe. For these latter, the sky-top waters of Laguna del Maule would be Shangri-La with knobs on it.

It is a long way to go, though, and any pilgrim undertaking the journey should not forget the grog. Snake bite is not a hazard in Chile, but you never can tell about hydraulic brakes.

I, Fisherman

George Tichenor

May 1953

This is one of the best stories I ever bought. George Tichenor, the author, was public relations man for a hat-makers' union in Danbury, Connecticut, but no dedicated fisherman could have painted a truer picture of a weekend at the Wright farm on the Willowemoc. I was there, one of the "boys" Tichenor mentions. The story never fails to recall vividly the many happy days I spent at the Wright farm with P.A. Parsons, Rod Ayers, George Gordon and other friends. Perhaps happily for this story, Bob Wright, Clarence's son, was away this particular weekend. Bob used a battered rod, automatic reel and almost nothing but a Royal Coachman hairwing (or bivisible). He once showed me his current chewed-up hairwing and said he'd caught at least sixty trout with it. It might have altered George's image of the "experts."

There's one thing I enjoy doing, and it's showing up the experts. And the second is like unto it—talking about it afterward. I belong to the school of "They Laughed When I Rose to Speak," or "They Little Knew When I Sat Down to the Piano." That's me. The natural genius with hook and line, for instance: Or at least I thought so . . . until I took up fishing.

It all started the day I dropped into OUTDOOR LIFE headquarters and got to talking with P. Allen Parsons, associate editor, about a bug I saw lying on his desk. He said it was a Fly, not to be swatted, and the more he talked about it the more intensity crept into his voice; I realized I was in the presence of a man in need of the fishermen's equivalent of Alcoholics Anonymous.

In three minutes he had me worked up too, and if he hadn't hidden that thing away one of us would have snapped at it. It occurred to me that artificial flies could be cheap substitute for live bait, and that fishing could be an inexpensive harmless sport. Yeah, that's what I thought, and I saw myself casually sending some friend a couple of king-size trophies, resting on a bed of glittering ice that would look just right in Tiffany's window. And I could hear the friend's wife saying, when they had recovered from their surprise, "Isn't that just like George? He does everything with such Natural Grace."

With the bashfulness of a sea lion at feeding time, I put myself in the way of an invitation to learn the ropes of fly fishing. P. A. paled but had the courage of a born sportsman. He said he'd take me along.

When I mentioned our date to Al Smoke, the accountant in our office, he was struck with admiration; you could have turned him over with a stick. For besides being fond of fishing, Al follows what P. A. says in print. I wanted Al to see how a beginner could make monkeys out of experts, so I cleared through channels and he became a third member of our party.

On a day late in May I arose at 5:30 to get the car, pick up Smoke, and hie to Livingston Manor, which is about 110 miles from New York City, and a fishing spot in the Catskills. Al, with his boodle, was lurking in the shadow of his apartment as I drove up. He hopped in, I gunned the accelerator, and we roared off, not too soon to hear one of his kids at the window: "There they go, mom; the jerk from the office is driving the get-away car."

In due time we arrived at Clarence Wright's place, which is up a narrow winding road, almost hidden (so as not to attract tourists), and country-folksy as a Currier and Ives print. It's one of those gingerbread American Gothic farmhouses, with a comforting clatter from the kitchen, an old dog lolling under a tree, and two black kittens popping in and out of boots against the wall.

Clarence, in short boots and a battered hat cocked on the side of his head, is as characteristically Yankee as a Winesap apple. He gave us a crisp welcome and a vigorous handshake. He and P.A. (who had just arrived) plunged into fish talk, and all of us wasted not a minute but pushed into boots and waders, stomping and strapping them on, anxious to get going before the stream dried up. My waders—borrowed from Al, who'd promised to provide other gear as well—looked like the rear end of a gray horse that had been skinned with a dull knife.

For the benefit of those who came in late, I'll pause to explain what we were after. Maybe, like myself, you've thought that fishing is just a matter of hook, line, and sinker. Or the way they did it in the mountains of Georgia where I grew up. They filled a demijohn with lye, inserted a cork loosely, and tossed it in a stream. The cork came out, soon there was a boom, and the fish came up.

Well, it's not so simple as that. In the circles where I'm now moving even the Marquis of Queensberry would have difficulty in observing all the rules.

I have learned that fishermen are graded according to the size of fish they catch. The lowest and most vulgar type (according to stream fishermen) are those who go in for tuna and other deep-sea stuff. As a trout man explained to me not long ago: "There's nothing to it. They bait a hook with meat"—here a special grimace of distaste—"and toss it over; the tuna grabs it and sounds. Then it's just like hauling coal up an elevator shaft."

Going higher in the piscatorial kingdom, there are those who fish for pickerel, pike, bass . . . and, at the top of the ladder . . . trout! But wait, I'm not finished. There are also grades of trout fishermen. There is the low criminal element that uses worms ("The sort who'd put a scorpion in a baby's crib," the man said). And there are spinners, wet-fly . . . and ultimately dry-fly men. P. A., of course, was strictly High Church.

All too soon, I was rigged out in the waders Al had lent me. They were Navy surplus, minus a diving helmet. The lead plates had been removed from the soles, and Al told me comfortingly this gave the feet a tendency to float. In addition to suspenders, there was a drawstring arrangement near my middle that worked like the mouth of a laundry bag. Below the waist I was well protected, but if a trout had leapt at me from above, I would have been done for.

I felt like the rear end of a stage horse, but Al kept piling stuff on me in a mournful manner. You see, he's an accountant and keeps track of everything. He finally announced, "You have about $75 worth of equipment on you," and I knew he'd be sorry to see me step into quicksand, disappearing inch by inch, dollar by dollar.

We moved off, Al very natty in high brown boots, P. A. and I slogging along in waders.

The Willowemoc, which we were going to fish, is a famous trout stream. It was hereabouts that Theodore Gordon introduced the dry fly to this country with a batch of imitation insects he got from England in 1890. Before then trout were caught the way you'd expect, with a w---m on a hook, or wet flies, and neither fish nor fishermen got neurotic about it. But brown trout, which also came over from England—in 1883, probably on a ship called the Mayfly—proved to be suckers for insects. Between Gordon's flies and the brown trout, a new era of the

Light Touch was born, with a whole new generation of fishermen to match. Watch P. A. in action, as I did, and you begin to get the idea.

P. A. approaches the stream with a thrust-forward gait, pipe jutting from his jaw. Let others think of the spring day and lissom lads and lassies; he knows there's man's work to be done.

In a quiet voice, so as not to alarm the pink-cheeked recruits who have never witnessed battle, he now discussed the Insect Situation with Al. They looked at the rushing water, which looked like plain water to me, and agreed that the shadfly hatch was past. May flies were due, but the water was just about right for a hatch of blue flies. But the temperature was only 38° F., and P. A. shook his head ominously. "Sixty to 65 would be just right." I gathered it would be difficult to connect with a fish, even on a pre-heated hook. But the sun was fine, and I was almost chuckling about what would happen to those poor unsuspecting trout when my fine Italian hand presented an offering.

P. A. took out his fly box and he and Al bent over it eagerly. To be frank—and not for publication—I told myself I'd as soon reach my hand into a busted horsehair sofa and pull out a bunch of stuffing. But I was mildly interested when P. A. selected a fly with long hackles made of deer hair, touched it up with water repellent from a bitty bottle, and then attached it to a nylon leader about as fine as the hair on your head. The line wasn't much thicker, and the split-bamboo rod was like a long switch.

P. A. moved out into the swirling water and began to shake out the line, not quite over his head, not quite sideways. (This part I can't explain. I watched it. It seemed as rhythmic and effortless as a bit of ballet dancing.) Slowly, then accelerando. The yellow line lengthened with each swish until it was about 40 feet long. Then P.A. "presented" the fly as though it were a live insect, alighting in a little pool and caught up by a swirl of water. The fly came floating down. Leader and line were invisible, without too much slack, pulled in by the quick fingers of a veteran as the lure drifted toward him. Then he raised it up and tried again, to the same spot . . . and again. Never a slop. Surely any trout down among the rocks, however doubtful that a hatch was on, would be convinced upon seeing four or five flies in succession alight, with nary a shadow of leader or line.

O.K., I said, I'll do the same. We were strung out about a quarter of a mile by now, for no fisherman likes anyone nudging his elbow. At a point below P. A., me and the waders slithered into the water, with a splash no larger than the launching of the U.S.S. Missouri. The cold came through instantly, swift water gripped my legs, the rocky bottom seemed to be greased—and my invaluable head began wobbling above my thrashing arms and shoulders. I'd have called the whole thing off, if someone had sent a breeches buoy my way, as they do in the newsreels of a stormy rescue at sea.

And now to cast my fly. I held the leader between two fingers, and the wind caught it. I lengthened the line so as to begin the swish, and the whole business slopped into the water. I picked it up and whirled it around my head—only it didn't whirl, it just clung damply to the pole. Could be I should have had a little back-yard practice, heaving a milkweed fluff into the wind with the help of a switch and a cobweb for a fishline.

I was standing there, with my banner marked Excelsior sadly drooping, when something happened with P.A. It happened in a wink, though you remember it all in slow motion. It was as though the rim of a rainbow came up out of the water, and a brownness followed, the end of P. A.'s line zigzagged through the water like a torpedo gone wild. Then that stopped too.

P. A. was reeling in his empty line. He shouted over the noise of water: "The fly was too big. He got the feather, but not the hook." Strange, but he didn't seem disappointed.

It made me feel uncomfortable. I didn't want my fish to get away—the one that was going to make Leviathan look like a guppy. And how would I handle it? I could see that juggling a greased pig would be relatively simple. I plowed upstream to where Al was working his spinner against the current. "What'll I do," I asked, "when a big fellow gets on the line?"

Looking me in the eye, he said seriously, "Only one thing to do. Stick your rod in the bank, reel him in, shinny up the pole, and choke him to death." Well, I thought, there'll be one answer to the scoffers.

Someone suddenly noticed it was 1 p.m. We marched back to the house, P. A. vigorously leading the way and I plopping along in the rear like a jalopy with flat tires. Tired and hungry . . . yet somehow the day was beautiful. Curious admission to make, for I don't usually recommend the raw, unpasteurized country air.

Meals at the Wrights' are hearty and substantial, with more coffee, more everything urged on you. Clarence usually stands in the doorway of the dining room, adding now and then to the table talk on the only subject that matters. Here's a sampling—the gist of a juicy bit of gossip—and I'm not saying who told the story, if it was told. I don't want trouble with the police, or with anglers either.

"Folks can be such liars, but what I'm telling you is true. Fellow named Burbank was one of the best fly tyers in these parts, very good for a man with a large thumb. His wife was always after him to earn a living, so finally he up and lit out to where he could find peace. But there was always the pull to come home; he recollected a big trout that he never was able to get.

"Well, one time he did come back, and found his wife had busted up all his gear. So he smacked her once or twice, I guess with a meat cleaver. Then he run her through the meat grinder that he used for hamburgers for the trout he was raising for stock; and he took his pole—what was left of it—and a few flies and went upstream. Right in that pool, by golly, he caught the fish on a first cast. It was a beaut . . . must have been 21 inches."

At this point a man put his fork down to interrupt: "What sort of fly was he using?"

The fame of local fly tyers gave me an idea. Privately after lunch, I inquired around for the name of a man who could supply a real killer. "None better," someone said, "than Garrett Rose. You'll find him down at the railroad crossing. He's a crossing tender." I got the car and went down. Mr. Rose in his little house by the side of the railroad is certainly the friend of man. He is a large, quiet-handed, philosophical sort who knows that (theoretically) trains must run, even though fish are biting. Growing cordial at the mere mention of flies, he brought out a box with some he'd tied himself.

And again, as that first time in P. A.'s office, enthusiasm was contagious. I wanted to buy one little jewel that caught my fancy, but Mr. Rose shook his head. For right now and in these waters, he recommended a less expensive Light Cahill.

I looked at my watch. I be a black-nose dace if we hadn't been chinning for half an hour. Absorbed as we were, anything could happen, and I visioned a locomotive on its side, steam still hissing, and headlines in the paper: TRANSCONTINENTAL EXPRESS WRECKED BY A FLY. Quickly I got a couple of Cahills and hurried away, relieved that the sun was quietly shining and rails smoothly bending into uneventful vistas.

These were to be my ace-up-the-sleeve. For the present, I thought I'd try my hand at spinning. The fellows were out on the stream when I got back, with the absorbed concentration that discourages questions. I helped myself to a reel of good stout line that would hold anything up to a shark, and tied a weighted streamer to the leader with the sort of knot that would look well on a Christmas package. I worked way up above the boys (which I don't think they minded at all). My first downstream cast, outfielder-style, would have brought any fish to the surface—if it had hit him in the head.

As I was reeling in the third cast, something happened. Yessir! There was that thrill every fisherman knows when a good rod loops and promises to hold and play whatever's there. In this case, there was more hold than play. "He's sulking," I thought, advancing to the kill.

I suggest that it's never good policy to turn your back to a rushing stream when wearing waders that are just itching to float. Suddenly my feet went up and I moved downstream faster than I could reel in, ice water poured into my pants, and I got all tangled in the line. (Later I was tempted to write the manufacturer a testimonial praising his product, from which neither fish nor man can free himself once he is hooked.)

I still had a thought for my catch, and with a relatively shallow dive I brought up the rock which had found my lure irresistible. It was a beautiful four-pounder, iron-gray and sort of disk-shaped. Then I came ashore, looking like a bloated Michelin Tire man, and poured myself out of the drink.

There was somebody upstream, watching me all the while. I suppose I had a guilty conscience (spinning in the company of fly fishermen) so I casually ambled up, ready to face the music and set my soul at peace. To my surprise, it turned out to be a little lady who could be anybody's grandmother. She had on hip boots and was casting a wet fly. "You ought to be home," I said, "bending over an apple pie."

"No," she said, "pies aren't biting today." And, looking over my wet and tangled gear, "What's that clothesline for?"

I allowed I planned to use it for a leash for any stray trout I could lay my hands on, and we got to talking. She told me about how far a trout can see (maybe 35 feet in clear water) and that I shouldn't hold a fly a couple of feet above the surface, expecting the fish to jump (as she had seen me do). "He'd sooner jump into a frying pan. From down below, your fly looks like a hawk, and it puts the fish down." She fished because it taught her about fish. She explained about casting across current, and showed me the special way of tying a leader to a fly (with six twists after the loop). And then I left, feeling chastened (partly due to wet clothes which always induces in me a mood of humility).

I rejoined the fellows in time to see P. A. taking in a trout, which he netted as deftly as a poached egg. I suspected now that my course in fishing would take more than six uneasy lessons, and although I still had my Cahill to try, I began to wonder whether I'd ever catch a fish, even with a worm.

I was relieved when the sun went down.

At the house there was a young fellow named Green who had caught seven trout that day. Al kidded him, suggesting that instead of driving back with his three buddies he ought to go by bus, where there'd be a lot more people who hadn't heard about his fish. The living room filled up. Wright's place was no mere hostelry but an open house for his friends, who come back year after year to spawn their lies. Pictures of many, with their catches, adorn the walls.

Roderick Ayer and his wife dropped in. Ayer is a hearty school superintendent, who never had a rod in his hand before coming here. He uses two wet flies on his line—a Dark Hendrickson above, a Light Cahill below—and he showed photos of a dozen gleaming trophies, laid out in a row.

My cup of bitterness was complete. I longed for sleep, but even that was to be denied me. In my fevered state I sensed an undercurrent of cross purposes between Clarence Wright and Roderick. The superintendent said that since he was moving to the Esopus (to take over a school system where the fishing is good) Clarence ought to let him have a whack at that 24-inch trout up at the pool—it was spoiled enough to be a pet and all but obstructed the stream.

Clarence said the fish was closer to 30 inches; Rod said "Let's see," and offered free of charge to bring him in before the night was over. Clarence shuddered visibly; it was like sending Billy the Kid, fully armed, to bring a young one home from school. Both Rod and Clarence have that glittering eye, and I felt that it boded no good' when Rod bantered that he might go out that night and fish those posted waters, and Clarence bantered right back that he'd shoot anybody he saw, and check afterward to see if it was a friend.

"Good night, all," I said, and soon was in bed and dreaming. I dreamt I was a captive in a creel, with a big cannibal trout forcing its way through the narrow slot. I woke suddenly and sat up in a cold sweat. An explosive noise had shattered the night. It sounded as though a tire—or a school superintendent—had been punctured. I fell back into troubled sleep, wondering how many pounds Roderick would go. He had been such a nice fellow, too.

Oddly enough, I woke in the morning feeling nimble as a minnow. And there was Roderick in the kitchen, having coffee with Mrs. Wright and still chaffing Clarence. Well, that left the big fish for me!

For some reason, however, I got not a bite that day. P. A. caught another trout, which I put down to veteran's luck, and Al had several strikes, but though I fished the pool where the fabulous monster lay, he rose not to riddle, song, or dance. I went down on my knees and offered my Light Cahill. No soap. It wouldn't have surprised me if the wily patriarch had attached a note to my hook: "Go back and learn at the beginning, bub!"

Well, I was learning something fundamental as I stood in the freezing water. The stream ran as clear as jellied glycerin and with a sound like drawn silk. P. A. caught another fish; I had no hope of catching any, and I didn't mind at all. It seemed enough to be there, dipping a rod, and with every care racing away with gurgle and bubble. The art of fishing is to make fishermen.

We also fished at dusk, all of us except P. A., who had sprained an ankle. The water was a sort of fish-scale whiteness, with circles starting here and there . . . and then it happened to me too. I felt a jerk on my arm as though someone had hit the funny bone, and the rod dipped and the line caught on a rock that moved.

What does it matter that the hook came up empty? I'd had a strike on a dry fly. I was on sufferance a member of the Peerless and Benevolent Order of Fly Fishermen. Like the golf dub who knocks off a 275-foot drive, I had something to go on, build on, go bankrupt on. If the old patriarch did it just for a laugh, I shared the laugh with him. My cup of happiness was overflowing . . . or at least my waders were.

Never Say Uncle

Fred Meyer Schroder
as told to Robert Easton

July 1953

Author Schroder's father was murdered before his birth in Charleston, S.C. He grew up on a California ranch, punched cattle in Sonora, Mexico, and took part in revolutions as far south as Chile. From 1893, he spent ten years sourdoughing gold strikes in Alaska, and went to London to sell Yukon gold stocks. He hunted sea otters in the Aleutians, prospected on foot for hardwood in Borneo, and shot tigers in India and Manchuria. He served as staff officer for Sun Yat-sen during the Chinese revolution of 1912, was instrumental in bringing about the Mongolian revolt from China, and took a one-thousand-camel caravan to Siberia with Red Cross supplies for prisoners of war. He acted as a secret agent for our State Department and was blinded by mustard gas while fighting Germans on the Russian side in World War I He was ninety-four when this story appeared.

It was no easier to grow up in the 1860's than in the 1950's, possibly harder. There were certain hazards. Horse thieves murdered my father before I was born. Mother had gone east so I could be born in the bed in Charleston, S. C., where my father and grandfather had been born. Word could have been sent to her by pony express but my uncle—her brother—saw fit to withhold it. So she did not know she was a widow till she got back to southern California eight months later.

My uncle—the Old Man—ran the ranch alone after my father's death. I was afraid of him. The horse thieves had given him the same buckshot-in-the-back treatment they had given dad, but he survived to become even more ornery than before.

He used to take me out shooting when I was still very small. "Get that squirrel!" he'd command. Maybe I hadn't seen the squirrel. I'd have to dismount and find it. Maybe it ducked into its hole before I could shoot. "Why didn't you shoot him before he ducked?" And if I hit in the belly instead of the head I got criticized for that, too. I was never good enough. I said I might do better if I had one of the new Winchester repeaters, but the Old Man snorted and kept me using the muzzleloader from George Washington's time.

After mother died things became worse. It was like being left alone with a bear. The Old Man was short and gruff and had chin whiskers. A six-shooter hung from his bedstead every night because the horse thieves still paid us visits. He was a deadly shot. "Keep both your eyes open!" he'd bellow at me, seeing me aim with one eye. Later I learned to keep them both open, pistol or rifle, hip or shoulder, either hand, and to knock a meadowlark out of the air. But still he wasn't satisfied.

The year that mother died, 1869, was the one when the transcontinental railroad linked us to the rest of the world. In the autumn the Indians came as usual to the ranch to gather pinon nuts and sweet oak on Cuyamaca Peak, and as usual one of the chiefs came to the house to ask permission of the Old Man. It was only a formality because the Old Man rented their reservation for pasturage for a rental of a steer a year, "a fiesta a year," and things were understood.

But this morning the chief, an ungainly, squat, and homely California Indian, had something to add. As he came up the walk between the rosebushes he pulled a brindle puppy from the pocket of his blue bib overalls and handed her to me. As soon as I took her she began to wiggle and lick at me.

"Ugh—lap dog, eh?" the Old Man commented.

We kept dogs galore around the place, mainly Southern fox-hounds to which the Old Man was partial, but no pets; he didn't believe in pets. So I'd never had a dog of my own. Now the chief by giving me one as much as said he had heard of mother's death and was sorry. I thanked him and set the dog down. She ran away among the rosebushes and tried to make friends with a hen and chicks, got soundly pecked, and came running back, tail between her legs.

"Likely won't have enough gumption to bite her own fleas," the Old Man said.

For the first time I could remember I stood up to him. "She's a good dog," I retorted. "She's got bull in her! Look at that short head and strong jaw."

"Bull in her? Sixty kinds of mongrel blood is what she's got. But no bull!"

"I'll call her Jip," I said defiantly, "and she'll make us a catch dog—won't you, Jip?"

"I know what she'll catch and you too, youngster, if you're both not careful. A boy's bad enough. A boy with a dog I can imagine! But I'm not going to, see? We'll give her a try. If she makes good she stays. If not, she goes."

He seldom failed to make himself clear. He was accurate with words as with everything. He had been educated as a surgeon at Heidelberg University in Germany, and he owned 2,000 books that he read far into the night, sitting by the fire, a pitcher of red mission wine at his elbow, bending that elbow more and more freely as the night wore on. He grew mellow as he smoked his huge meerschaum pipe and gave me puffs of it while I was still a baby, saying it was better than milk to grow on; he also gave me a pistol to cut my teeth on, a pistol always being handy. He didn't practice surgery regularly but answered the calls of neighbors in distress, and once went all the way to Kansas City to perform a single operation.

I stood in awe of him. He had owned nine leagues of land in Starr County, Texas. That in itself was enough to make a man awful: to have owned nine leagues of land. But when you added the buckshot in his back that had failed to kill him and just stirred around in there and riled him up, why, you had something truly terrible.

He relented enough to let Jip sleep on the porch. "But don't go to her if she cries," he warned. "There's no quicker way to spoil a pup."

Of course she cried. She was away from home and mother for the first time. She cried and cried. The Old Man bellowed back like a wild bull from his bed in the next room to mine. But I knew something of what it was to be alone and without a mother. After he'd grown quiet I slipped out of bed. I had to go through his room to get to her. I could see his chin whiskers protruding over the counterpane and the six-shooter hanging from the bedpost. If I startled him he'd shoot me sure.

I trembled as I slipped across the floor, careful to step on the lion and deer skins wherever possible, and at last reached the safety of the porch. As soon as I took Jip in my arms she quieted. Her little wet nose and warm tongue went all over me in the dark. In no time we were back to bed.

Next morning when the Old Man called I pretended to delay until he was dressed and gone. Then I whisked Jip from under the covers and outdoors.

Night after night the stratagem was repeated successfully. It made me feel mighty proud of myself. Not till long afterward did I discover that the Old Man was awake and watching me all the time.

Jip was my only playmate except for Indian children, so we became close friends. We had fun Sundays with the Indians catching wood rats. The rats were highly desirable for stews, being as clean and succulent as squirrels. The Indian bucks would climb upon the rats' huge nests—piles of sticks and rubbish as much as 10 feet high—and jab with long poles till the rats ran out. Then the squaws and kids and dogs, including Jip and me, went into action with sticks and clubs and bows and arrows. Our bows were willow, the bowstrings babiche trimmed to an even thickness. I grew pretty accurate with the reed arrows that had sagebrush tips hardened in the fire. They had quills of twisted hawk or chicken feathers, the twist giving them a revolving motion in flight.

I could kill rats and rabbits and bluejays at 20 yards but I worried lest Jip fail to find out what her teeth were for. I don't know how many times she was bitten around the nose and mouth before she finally learned. She thought the rats were there to play with. And the Old Man seemed to know at a distance, and to disapprove by the expression of the back of his head. A cold qualm of doubt would go through me.

Jip quickly learned the difference between a horse and a cow. She would heel the cows. The time came later when I could tell her to go into the brush after a wild steer and she'd go in and heel him out into the open, then grab him by the nose and hang there till hell froze or somebody came.

She grew fast. By the time she was a year old she looked grown.

My 11th birthday arrived and the Old Man announced it was time for me to grow up. He found me a horse that had never been ridden, and told me to ride it. Juan Meron and Joe Lopez, our top vaqueros, stood at either side as I climbed aboard. By some miracle I stayed there. I nearly pulled the bucking strap out by the roots but I stayed. Thereafter there was hope for me. I wasn't yet a man but I wasn't a boy any more. I was in that limbo called youth; and the Old Man said, one evening drinking wine, "You'll get you a lion one of these days, sir."

"I hope so," I replied.

"Hope he's a big one?"

"Yes, sir," I said.

I'd never faced up to anything more dangerous than a rattlesnake and that didn't count.

Fall came and brought the damp nights that hold scent well. There was that ring around the moon and the sycamores and maples turned yellow in the canyons. The wild pigeons came with a beat of wings that filled the air, and ate the acorns under the oaks. Then the Old Man took Jip to hunt with the grown dogs on the Peak. I could have gone; I was too nervous to. I lay all of that still, warm October morning in the barrel-stave hammock in the oak grove listening to Jip's trial: the cry of the hounds now strong, now faint. I wondered if they were singing her praises or disgrace. Toward noon she crept home alone. I knew the worst. I saw her avoid me and go into the kitchen door with the cats.

The Old Man came in raising Cain. "Cottontail rabbit thumped the ground a time or two and she was gone. I mean she wasn't there. I'd like to put a bullet through her."

"You'll do no such thing," I said, astonished at the boldness of my words. "She's my dog. You can't shoot her!"

"Oh, so-ho . . . !" I saw his startled expression.

"Give her another chance," I begged, and I'd never begged him for anything, not even to let up on the whippings. "She's the only playmate I've got."

It was a low trick: to recall my orphan state. But I did it for Jip's sake. The Old Man had adored my mother, his sister, and the way she was like a vinegar bottle bubbling over, galloping everywhere on the back of a stallion sidesaddle, as ladies did in those days, and the stallion kneeling for her to get on, as stallions did.

He choked up, turned gruff, and said he'd see about giving Jip another chance. He did, though, and this time it was in a chase after the wild pigs that had run upon the mountain since Spanish times. The hounds quickly brought a sow to bay and got good, sensible holds on her ears. But Jip, being the pup, walked up to the sow's face. She landed on the sow with all four feet and everything else. A sow's tushes aren't as long as a boar's but they rip like knives. For a while things looked bad for my Jip. Then she got the idea that the sow wasn't doing right by her. The bulldog in her began to show. Bristle by bristle it came, growl by growl. Long after the pig was dead she was still chewing its ear.

"Mighty hard on 'em after they're dead," the Old Man commented.

I could have killed him. I thought I had the bravest dog in the world.

"Any old dog can handle a pig," he said, "but wait till she meets a cat."

A week later she did meet a cat, a big, tufted-ear lynx that weighed 40 pounds, her weight. We ran him up a tree in the Rancho Viejo and shot the feet out from under him so he wouldn't rip the dogs too badly. But he still had plenty of teeth. That is how you make a dog. Jip joined in the rush. He fastened to her underlip. Oh, but she cried. She tried to back out and run home, to quit, to die, anything to get away, but he wouldn't let her. She had to stay and face it. After a while she got tired of facing it. She got mad. She squirmed around and, despite the way he had her, sunk her teeth into him. Then, tooth to tooth, eye to eye, they chewed it out.

Long after he was dead she was still chewing. The bulldog in her came out that day and never went back. She became a hot-trail dog. Her nose was never any good so she left the cold trails to the hounds, but as soon as their voices went up a notch she knew and was gone. Cats became her pet hate. Every time she smelled one she remembered what the lynx had done to her.

I was coming along. I could shoot almost on a par with the Old Man—either hand, pistol or rifle, hip or shoulder. I never did learn to snuff a candle placed inside a half-broken beer bottle by shooting through the nozzle end, but I learned to hit coins tossed in the air. Later I learned to hit them once and knock them on up and hit them again. The Old Man explained that my life might depend on my shooting, an explanation that was quite unnecessary seeing what had happened to my father and him.

So matters stood when one day he ordered, "Go up onto the mesa and get us a mess of quail for supper."

The mesa was three miles away and 1,500 feet up. When he said he didn't mean 15 or 20 quail; he meant half a sack. So I got the 12 gauge double-barreled hammer gun and some of the brass shot shells we loaded at home. I called Jip and Hec, a Southern foxhound, got my horse and sack, and started up the trail. The month was February, clear and warm, the grass green from the rains. The wild lilac brush was in bloom, so thickly in places that the fragrance almost made me sick.

We found quail feeding in the openings and Jip pointed them for me in her remarkable way, which consisted not in looking at the quail but at me. She'd freeze still and watch me till she saw that I saw the quail. We collected nearly half a sack while Hec was off scouting around. All of a sudden we heard his deep boe-woe. Immediately it went up a notch. Jip left.

"Golly," I said to myself, "Hec's hit a hot trail already!"

I threw the sack over the back of the saddle and galloped after them. The brush meant slow going but finally I located them in a water cut. I knew perfectly well what the situation was. I could hear it. It sounded pretty snarly. I could visualize it so well that I hesitated for a moment to go forward. But I did; I got off and crept up through the brush along the edge of the cut, to the place whence the noise was coming. And there, very carefully, I peeked over.

Fifteen feet below me, hemmed against the bank on my side by the dogs, was a male mountain lion.

He was crouching and facing them, pivoting back and forth, one paw cocked like a prizefighter's right hand, ready to let go. Meanwhile he told the world what he thought. Jip came too close. He let her have it. She sailed through the air and lit 10 yards away. I thought she must be dead but back she came, game as ever. That encouraged me. Instead of departing for home and help, as I had been tempted to do (my lifelong desire to kill a lion having suddenly weakened), I emptied both barrels of the shotgun into the lion's backside.

Of course, I never stopped to realize I was using only quail shot. The effect was much the same as if I'd shot him in the rear with hot pepper. He went straight into the air, clawing and squalling like a cat with firecrackers tied to its tail. When he came down he bowled over the dogs and departed down the cut in the direction of Mexico, with Jip and Hec hot behind.

I halfway hoped he'd never come back, and that they'd lose him completely. He had looked awful big, particularly when he went up in the air that way. Seemed he came nearly level with my face, a whole self-propelled mountain lion.

"Guess I'll have to get me a gun that will kill something!" I said aloud, gruffly, in the way one does when one is 12 to buck oneself up.

I jumped on the horse and piled off the mesa like an avalanche. I found that the farther I got away from the lion, the braver I got. I charged up to the cookhouse door and pitched the sack of quail at Cap'n Hulburd, the cook, who had been a Yankee banker and Union officer before he came to cook for us Rebels, and I don't think in all his broad experience he had ever seen a boy in such a rush. I felt now that I would like to kill my lion alone, as any man should.

I didn't explain. I grabbed my Winchester .44 saddle rifle, a repeater that was a recent present from the Old Man and as fine a thing as any boy in the land possessed. Then I charged back up the mountain as fast as I could.

I found that the nearer I got to the top, the more I was hoping the dogs had lost him. But no such luck. When I got on top I heard them far away. They'd stayed with him; I would have to do the same.

I tore through the brush at full speed. Sometimes just plain velocity helps in a case like that. The thick chaparral was thorny and dusty, and it scratched and choked me, and again the lilac was so sweet it nearly stifled me; but on I went, feeling like I don't know just what. And, sure enough, in one of the biggest, thorniest patches of brush and lilac, centered around a great, black, bushy live oak, I found them.

I couldn't see the lion but I could hear him. He was up in that bushy oak. And he left no doubt how he was feeling. He was mad. I could tell my quail shot was burning his rear end. The dogs were making a continuous row around the foot of the tree. Altogether there was a good deal of noise and excitement. I thought how fine it would be if I could shoot him from the saddle where I sat safe, but there was no chance of that. If I wanted him I'd have to go get him.

I started to get off, and then I reflected that I was only 12, a long way from home, and alone, and there was a wounded lion up in that tree. And then I started to get off again, and I reflected again. Finally I got off.

I slipped forward nervously through the lilacs. They were regular trees 10 and 12 feet high. I kept peering up, trying to locate him, not wanting to walk right underneath a wounded lion. But that was where I had walked to when I spotted him.

I saw immediately what my quail shot had done—it had inflated him! He looked positively enormous—twice as big as before. Of course I was now looking up at him, not down, and when you see a thing as big as that up in a tree, well,

Classic Covers

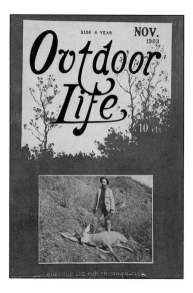

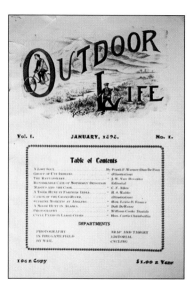

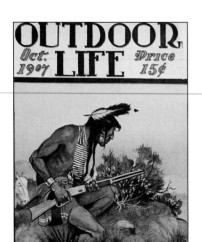

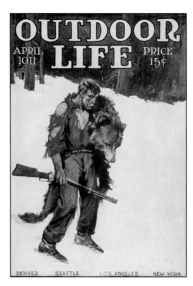

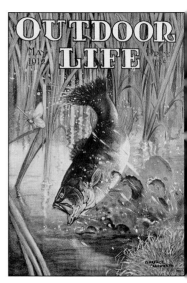

OUTDOOR LIFE
SEPT. 1916 PRICE 15¢

TED'S SAFARI (AN AFRICAN
LION HUNT), THIS ISSUE.
BY CHAS COTTAR.

OUTDOOR LIFE
MAY 1917 PRICE 15¢

Outdoor Life
DEC. 1918 PRICE 20¢

THE LIFE OF AN ELK BY S.N. LEEK

Outdoor Life
DEC. 1919 PRICE 20¢

WITH THE WILDFOWL OF BARNEGAT — F.A. WILLITS
IN THE REALM OF THE SOURDOUGH — J.A. McGUIRE

Outdoor Life
NOVEMBER 1920 PRICE 25¢

HUNTING IN THE FLORIDA CYPRESS SWAMPS — W.M. GARLINGTON
A MUSEUM COLLECTING TRIP TO THE NORTH — Dr. EDW. D. JONES

Outdoor Life
JULY 1921 PRICE 25¢

IN THE SELKIRKS OF THE CANADIAN ROCKIES — Gus Cook
SHEEP OF THE PINCATE — Edw J Ekman

Outdoor Life
APRIL 1922 20¢

Outdoor Life
MAY 1923 20¢

GAME PARADISE OF THE CANADIAN ROCKIES — J. Kipkes

Outdoor Life
JANUARY 1924 20¢

Outdoor Life
APRIL 1925
20¢

Outdoor Life
JANUARY 1927
20¢

In the Peace River Game Fields . . . . *Dr. C. J. Miller*
Where the Trout Leap in Main Street . . . . *Billy O'neal*

Outdoor Life
Feb. 1929
WITH WHICH IS COMBINED "OUTDOOR & RECREATION" 25¢

The Asiatic Story **BLUE TIGER** Begins This Month

Outdoor Life 25¢
October 1931
With which is combined
OUTDOOR & RECREATION

1931-32 Game Laws and Seven Hunting Stories

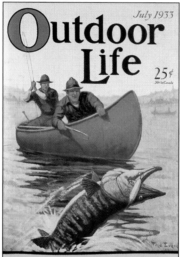

Outdoor Life
July 1933
25¢
50¢ in Canada

e Duck Battle in Utah, by Harry McGuire

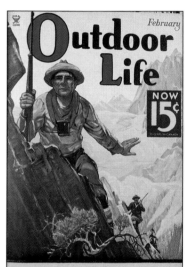

Outdoor Life
February
NOW 15¢
75 CENTS IN CANADA

FISHING · HUNTING · CAMPING · BOATS · DOGS

Outdoor Life
August
NOW 15¢

FISHING · HUNTING · CAMPING · BOATS · DOGS

Outdoor Life
April
15¢

1939 *Fishing Laws*

Outdoor Life
New!
8 PAGES OF GREAT OUTDOOR PHOTOS
15¢
JANUARY

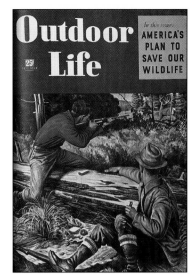

Outdoor Life

Conservation Pledge

I GIVE MY
PLEDGE AS AN AMERICAN
TO SAVE AND FAITHFULLY TO
DEFEND FROM WASTE THE
NATURAL RESOURCES OF
MY COUNTRY – ITS SOIL
AND MINERALS, ITS
FORESTS, WATERS,
AND WILDLIFE

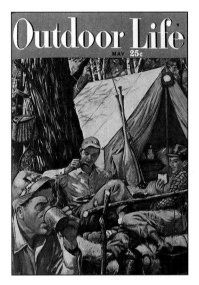

A PIONEER FANNIN HUNT by Jack O'Connor

HE MOST DANGEROUS HUNT OF ALL by Berry Brooks

No Job too
BIG for Sam

ING FISHING SPECIAL • MY MOST DANGEROUS HUNT p. 4

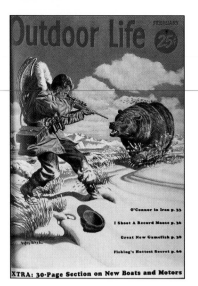

Outdoor Life

FEBRUARY 25¢

O'Connor in Iran p. 33

I Shoot A Record Moose p. 36

Great New Gamefish p. 38

Fishing's Hottest Secret p. 66

XTRA: 30-Page Section on New Boats and Motors

Outdoor Life

35¢ • JULY, 1957

Boom in Sports Trailers: What to look for in a camp on wheels page 32

The Grayling page 56

Five Best Bets for Bass page 25 | We Put Tags on Live Bears page 38

Outdoor Life

35¢ • NOVEMBER, 1958

Deer Hunting In North and South

O'Connor in Africa

How to Buy A Hunting Dog

Do Brown Bears Attack? see pp. 41

Outdoor Life

35¢ • FEBRUARY, 1959

I Shot The World's Biggest Bear

Winter Fish Lures

How Experts Shoot

FITZ IN INDIA
Trophy Expert Hunts First Tiger

Special Section
NEW BOATS AND MOTORS IN FULL COLOR

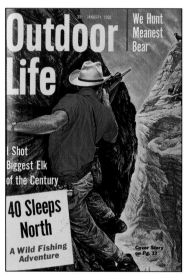

Outdoor Life

35¢ • JANUARY, 1960

We Hunt Meanest Bear

I Shot Biggest Elk of the Century

40 Sleeps North

A Wild Fishing Adventure

Cover Story on Pg. 33

Outdoor Life

35¢ • MAY, 1961

New Trout Area
FORBIDDEN LANDS

Best Fishing on West Coast

Big Game Series
POLAR BEAR

FOR MORE FISH
▸ Wade Right p. 48
▸ Know Bait p. 54
▸ Fly A Kite p. 56

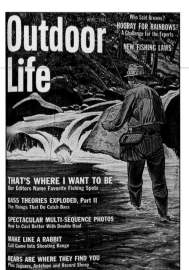

Outdoor Life

35¢ • APRIL, 1962

Who Said Browns?
HOORAY FOR RAINBOWS!
A Challenge for the Experts

NEW FISHING LAWS

THAT'S WHERE I WANT TO BE
Our Editors Name Favorite Fishing Spots

BASS THEORIES EXPLODED, Part II
The Things That Do Catch Bass

SPECTACULAR MULTI-SEQUENCE PHOTOS
How to Cast Better With Double Haul

MAKE LIKE A RABBIT
Call Game Into Shooting Range

BEARS ARE WHERE THEY FIND YOU
Plus Jaguars, Antelope and Record Sheep

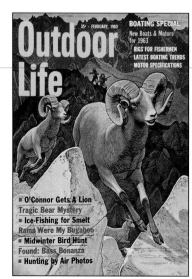

Outdoor Life

35¢ • FEBRUARY, 1963

BOATING SPECIAL
New Boats & Motors for 1963
RIGS FOR FISHERMEN
LATEST BOATING TRENDS
MOTOR SPECIFICATIONS

■ O'Connor Gets A Lion
Tragic Bear Mystery
■ Ice-Fishing for Smelt
Rams Were My Bugaboo
■ Midwinter Bird Hunt
Found: Bass Bonanza
■ Hunting by Air Photos

Outdoor Life

35¢ • MARCH, 1964

4 SPRING FISHING STORIES

NEW WAY TO SHOOT WOODCHUCKS

IDEA FOR OPENING DAY
Look Southward, Angler

AMAZING PHOTO STORIES
■ Headlong Bears
■ Savage Encounter

LOST FOR EIGHT DAYS

PLUS: Spring Turkey, Ducks

Outdoor Life

35¢ · SEPTEMBER, 1965

WE CAMPED IN RUSSIA
FOR BARGAIN HUNTERS
$25 Got My Goat
MAGIC FISHING MONTH
BACKPACK ADVENTURE
We Gamble on Poison
NEW HUNTING LAWS

30 Special Photos!
HOW TO SKIN A TROPHY
Step-By-Step In Color
HELL ON AN ISLAND
A Castaway's Ordeal
BLOOD IN HIS EYE
Murderous Moose Attack

Outdoor Life

35¢ · FEBRUARY, 1966

A DAY ON SNAKE MOUNTAIN
THE DEVIL JAGUAR
MOST NEGLECTED BIRD

MEANEST GAME?
HOT WINTER FISHING
1: North and 2: South
DEER FOR THE RECORD
Hot Line on Rabbits
ADVENTURE IN LATIN AMERICA

Outdoor Life

JANUARY, 1967 35¢

BONUS 1967 Boats and Motors
FISHERMAN ABROAD
AMAZING BEAR PHOTOS

THINGS TO READ AND DO NOW:
• Hare Hunting • Ice Fishing
• Crow Shooting • Quail Ditto
THE JAGUAR FOLLOWED US:
Record Deer; Fun Duck Hunt

Outdoor Life

FEBRUARY, 1968 35¢

Close Call for Moose

The Trouble with Grizzlies
Also: End of A Deer Jinx
The Postwar Cartridges
by Jack O'Connor
2 Ice-Fishing Stories
Plus: Fishing The Keys
What Do You Know About Guns? | Varmint Shoot

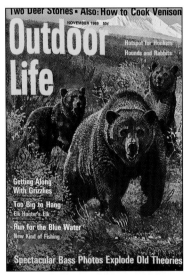

Outdoor Life

NOVEMBER 1969 50¢

Two Deer Stories • Also: How to Cook Venison
Hotspot for Honkers
Hounds and Rabbits

Getting Along With Grizzlies
Too Big to Hang
Elk Hunter's Elk
Run for the Blue Water
New Kind of Fishing
Spectacular Bass Photos Explode Old Theories

Outdoor Life

JANUARY 1970 60¢

by Jack O'Connor: Elephants on the Zambezi
1970 Motors & Boats

Best Antelope in 70 Years
Ice-Fishing Stories
Deer, Crows, Doves, Moose
More Olive Fredrickson Adventures: Bears!

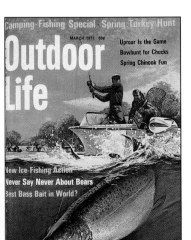

Outdoor Life

MARCH 1971 60¢

Camping-Fishing Special · Spring Turkey Hunt
Uproar Is the Game
Bowhunt for Chucks
Spring Chinook Fun

New Ice-Fishing Action
Never Say Never About Bears
Best Bass Bait in World?
Safaris in the Seventies Will Be Different

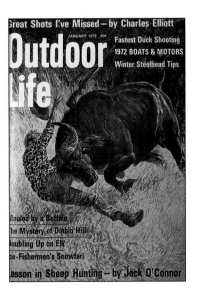

Outdoor Life

JANUARY 1972 60¢

Great Shots I've Missed — by Charles Elliott
Fastest Duck Shooting
1972 BOATS & MOTORS
Winter Steelhead Tips

Mauled by a Buffalo
The Mystery of Diablo Hill
Doubling Up on Elk
Ice-Fishermen's Snowfari
Lesson in Sheep Hunting — by Jack O'Connor

Outdoor Life

AUGUST 1972 60¢

SPORTSMEN'S FEAR: MUST THIS LAND DIE?
NEWS! 8 PAGES ON YOUR REGION

COVER: PERILS OF A HUNTING GUIDE
HERE COMES BASS BLITZ
THE BIG PIKE YOU CAN DRIVE TO
SHOW YOUR KIDS OUR GREAT OUTDOORS
REACHING HIGH FOR TROUT TREASURE
SALMON'S BRIGHT LIGHT; FIRST DOG UP

Outdoor Life

MAY 1974 50¢

NEWS
8 PAGES on Your Region
HOTSPOTS · PHOTOS · MAPS

COVER STORY
FLOAT TRIP TO BASS ADVENTURE
HOW TO CATCH SNOOK AND DRUM
YANKEE GOBBLERS

CARMICHEL BUCKS A HUNTING JINX
WE TAKE BREAM, TROUT, WALLEYES
MOSSYHORN MULE DEER

Outdoor Life

JANUARY 1975 60¢

Cover Story:
THE GRIZZLY SHOWDOWN

BASS AGAINST ODDS: HOW TO FIND PATTERN

DEER: BLACKPOWDER IN BONUS SEASON

DANGER: RAM HUNT ON THE ROCK WALL

SALMON SNAGGING THE BATTLE RAGES

EXCLUSIVE YELLOW SECTION
8 PAGES ON YOUR AREA

1976 BOATS & MOTORS

Outdoor Life

JANUARY 1976

COVER STORY
Photographing BEAR at close range
How to hunt FOX in winter
better ways to PANFISH from shore
flinch when you shoot? How to stop
super vacation idea for BASS now
Build your own pond
Venison recipes
experts tell their flycasting secrets

Outdoor Life

AUGUST 1977 · STILL ONLY 75¢

STEEL SHOT MAKES NOW!
FISHING'S hot
Arctic by canoe
hunter's guide stands
of the Amazing show
BASS

COVER
The colorful COUGAR — endangered by man, or new danger to man?

NEW YORK, PENNSYLVANIA, QUEBEC, MAINE
Guide to ice fishing

Outdoor Life

DECEMBER 1978 $1.00

LICENSE $ $ — DO WE GET OUR MONEY'S WORTH?

HUNTING
Deer ■ Quail ■ Squirrels
Foul-weather shooting

FISHING
Hot new rig ■ Update: Bass, Trout

TEST RESULTS...
radical plan to nab poachers

COVER STORY
The Great Horned Owl:
Nature's Flying Tiger

PENNSYLVANIA, CONNECTICUT, NEW YORK
• Upland Game • Hunting Preserves

Outdoor Life

OCTOBER 1979 $1.00

TOUGH SHOTS
Jim Carmichel and Fred Bear show how

FISHING
4-pound BREAM
Meanmouth BASS

New Facts on WOODCOCK

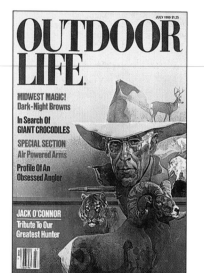

OUTDOOR LIFE

JULY 1980 $1.25

MIDWEST MAGIC!
Dark-Night Browns

In Search Of GIANT CROCODILES

SPECIAL SECTION
Air Powered Arms

Profile Of An Obsessed Angler

JACK O'CONNOR
Tribute To Our Greatest Hunter

How To Decoy Buck Deer Right To You!

OUTDOOR LIFE

JUNE 1981 · STILL ONLY $1.25

MIDWEST SPECIAL FEATURES
How And Where To Fish The New Lake-Trout Hotspot
Tricks That Take Big Muskies Quickly
How To Get More Crappie Now

How To Fish A Lake You Don't Know
Where You Find Big Fish In The Weeds

OUTDOOR LIFE

JANUARY 1982

MIDWEST EDITION

CARMICHEL: Hunt For A Giant Kodiak

World's Best Fishing Reels

Shocking Facts About Poaching

Icefishing Devils Lake

Ohio Grouse At New High

you can't believe it. I found that my rifle wasn't holding steady. The sights kept jumping every time I saw lion through them.

I intended to break his neck. I squeezed as I'd squeezed a thousand times. I heard my bullet hit. Next a body came hurtling down, but it wasn't a dead body!

Whether by accident or design, he jumped almost on top of me, crashing through the oak leaves and lilac branches like the whole sky falling, and I was trying to get another shell into the chamber but failing to, as he landed six feet away.

I saw the blood from the wound in his neck. Things happened very rapidly now but I couldn't move. He was bewildered just for an instant before coming to kill me, bewildered by the bullet, the fall, me.

In that instant I saw Jip take hold of his skinny tail. I saw him become aware of her and debate which to go for, her or me. Finally he chose her. He swung, and there was just room enough among the lilacs for him to swing and hit her with all his might. Dempsey in his prime never delivered a harder blow. Jip flew through the air. She'd be going yet, I think, but a lilac trunk stopped her with a thud. It knocked a yowl out of her. Hec was on the lion before he could get back to me. Then Jip flew at him again, streaming blood, minding it not at all.

About that time I got my gun working and put a bullet through the lion's head.

When all was over I saw stars, and the world went spinning in an aroma of sweet lilacs. . . . The faintness lasted only a minute. When I came to, Jip was nuzzling my face.

I rode proudly down the mountain, hoping to find the Old Man now and say offhand, like nothing at all, "Killed a lion on the mesa. Got time to come help me skin him?"

I met him riding up the trail at a trot. "What's all this rifle shooting?" He had an ear for rifle shooting.

"Just killed a lion——" I began, but before I finished it was flat. He was looking at me too hard.

"Couldn't you skin him out by yourself?"

Burning with shame, I followed him to where the lion lay. Then I saw with satisfaction that a serious look crossed his face. The carcass seemed about the size of a horse, stretched out there. The Old Man made the official examination. My quail shot had lodged between the outer hide and the thin inner skin. No wonder the lion had been mad. My bullet had penetrated the neck between the jugular and the bone, missing the spine by a fraction.

"What happened?" he asked.

I told him the story, briefly, dispiritedly.

"What's the matter, couldn't you break his neck?"

I said nothing. The whole day had long since gone sour.

"Some shot! Next time make that first shot count."

"Yes, sir."

"Make it your last one."

"Yes, sir."

"If it hadn't been for Jip you probably wouldn't be here."

"I know, sir."

He gave the dog a chuck for congratulation and a pat for her wounds, and then all at once he began to laugh. Softly and incredibly he laughed.

"Can't get over your warming him with that quail shot!"

I laughed, too. He had spoken as one man does to another, not as a man to a boy, not as the Old Man to me. I felt different. But I didn't know I had grown up.

Never Trust a Moose

Eric Collier

September 1953

Eric Collier wrote nearly forty stories for OUTDOOR LIFE. A great memory of my twenty-two years at the magazine was my association, mostly by mail, with Collier in Meldrum Creek, British Columbia, seventy-five miles from the nearest rail. A young Englishman, he went to Canada in 1919, married a quarter-blood Indian girl, Lillian, and settled on 150,000 acres of barren wilderness with a wagon, thirty dollars and their young son Veasy. For his heroic efforts in bringing the beavers back to Meldrum Creek he won the fifth OUTDOOR LIFE Conservation Award. We were rewarded with his marvelous stories of his adventures as pioneer, guide, hunter and trapper. In 1959, E. P. Dutton & Co. published his book, *Three Against the Wilderness*. My wife and I cherish the memory of the week Lily and Eric spent at our home on his first trip east of the Rockies in forty years.

I should have known better in the first place. I was hunting mule deer in a tongue of fir and lodge-pole pine forest that licks almost at the log walls of our home in the British Columbia wilderness where I farm beavers and muskrats in their natural habitat. A November moon was waning, and three inches of snow blanketed the kinnikinnick and blueberry vines. The wind was faintly from the arctic, the air tangy and crisp with a definite hint of more snow to come.

Now was the time I must go to work and stock our moss-chinked meat house against the hungry months ahead. In my country a deer killed in November stays frozen until the following April.

I found my buck—a three-pointer—bedded on the rim of a deep gulch, staring languidly into the westering sun, as bucks have been doing on late-November afternoons ever since there have been bucks. I shot him in his bed, dragged him out of the gulch, and gutted him. Then I put him beneath a fir tree to cool off. Next morning I'd come with a horse and pack him to the meat house.

Standing beside the steaming carcass, 30 yards from the rim of the gulch, I could neither see nor hear any movement below. True, a red squirrel shucked a cone from a fir tree, but squirrels don't count. Yet I had a sudden intuition that life was abroad down there in the bowels of the gulch, although why I don't know. But it was definitely there, and I bolted a cartridge into the breech of my .303 Ross, crouched back on my heels, and strained my ears and eyes.

A bull moose of full maturity weighs around 1,400 pounds on the hoof, and he may carry a rack of horns spreading 60 inches or better. It doesn't seem possible that so large an animal can move through timber as silently as a foraging lynx cat. But it can, and it does: a bull moose is often seen before it's heard.

Such was the case that afternoon. The horns came up out of the gulch first; a spread of 45 inches, I judged. Then the grotesque Roman nose, followed by the rest of the head. It was the kind of opportunity a trophy hunter dreams about but doesn't often get.

I wasn't interested in trophies, for I have yet to find horns that taste good in a stew. At the moment I wasn't even interested in moose. I don't like their meat, for I ate far too much of it during the gaunt years of the depression. And I'd left my camera at home.

It was a couple of seconds before horns, head, body and all four legs were up out of the gulch. Then, head high and nostrils testing the air, the bull moved stiffly toward me. That was odd, for he could see me crouching tensely by the body of the deer. By all rules of the game he should have wheeled and gone back into the gulch much more quickly than he'd left it. But he moved up to within 20 yards before he stopped and gazed at me intently, obviously unafraid. If I've ever seen mayhem in a bull moose's eyes, it was in his.

For 33 straight years my everyday life has been spent here, and these woods had to provide me not only with a living but with recreation to boot. After all, when you're 100-odd miles from the nearest electric light you wouldn't recognize Clark Gable if you met him along the trail.

Anyway I'd think twice before digging into my jeans for the price of a movie ticket. But I'll spend hours in the hush of the forest, crooning softly to a suspicious bull moose, inching up, camera ready to snap a picture if I can get within 15 to 20 feet before he takes off. That's my personal moose hunting. I do it with a rather poor camera but if you don't like an animal's meat or want a trophy why hunt him with a gun?

Sure, I guide moose hunters in the fall, but my job is to find the bull; they take over from there.

I've been within 15 to 20 feet of more moose than I can tell you about—and got photos of almost every one—but up to the time of this story I'd yet to shoot my first bull or cow in self-defense. Several had got snooty enough, for if you work around a moose any considerable time it soon sheds its instinctive fear and distrust and begins talking back. When that happens you start looking at your hole card.

When a cow or bull has fight on its mind, there's a lot in its expression that isn't altogether sweet. The ears flatten against the neck, the mane stands up, and the whites of the eyes show. Usually there's only a single soft grunt of warning, and then the animal moves forward and comes exceedingly fast. That's why I brought the .303 to my shoulder within a split second of the big bull's first show of truculence. Maybe I should have settled the business for good right then and there, and been spared the ordeal that was to come.

I know now that I'd have been forced to shoot if a yearling hadn't got into the act, because here was one moose that would kill or be killed. But the yearling temporarily solved the problem, paying a harsh price for doing so. I didn't know he was around until the bull suddenly pulled his eyes from me to stare questioningly and belligerently at something off in the timber.

I lowered my rifle and followed the line of this stare. At first I could see nothing except timber, but after another prolonged look I saw a yearling bull moving slowly toward the gulch. The little fellow wasn't doing any harm; just nipping the shoot of a red willow here, or rubbing his poor sprout of horns against a seedling fir there.

Feeding slowly toward us, he apparently didn't notice the big bull until he was within 30 yards of him. Then he tossed up his head and froze in his tracks. Somehow I wanted to yell, "Get the blazes out of here, you little fool, while the getting is good!" But it wouldn't have helped.

The yearling was oozing good nature, and it was as clear as the air you breathe that he just wanted to move up alongside the big bull and pass the time of day. As he started forward again I heard the big boy grunt. There was a weight of hidden warning in that grunt to anyone who understands moose talk. Again I was tempted to shoot but I couldn't make up my mind to. The old bull charged before I could decide.

Despite popular belief, a bull moose does far more fighting with his front feet than with his horns. True, the antlers are used extensively, and sometimes with fatal effect when the heat of the rut is on. But at any other time of year it is the front quarters that throw the most lethal blows.

That yearling was worse off than any babe in the woods. By the time he came awake to what it was all about the big bull was almost within striking range. Then the youngster did something you'll not often see a sensible moose do. He wheeled and broke into a gallop. And a galloping moose is about as graceful as a knock-kneed man in a sack race.

I didn't even see the first blow, it flicked out so fast. But I certainly heard it connect. Crack! A sickening crack, too—one that could be heard from one end of the gulch to the other. The youngster stumbled and almost went down. Crack! I saw it this time. It was like the flick of a swamp adder's head. And the little fellow was down in the snow.

That's when I roared in instinctive anger. The right-front foot of the big bull was raised for another blow, but at the sound of my voice it went stiffly back into the snow. The bull half turned, staring angrily at me. Thus the yearling got his one chance for a getaway, and he lost no time grabbing it. Limping badly—I'm sure his hip had been dislocated—he came up from the snow and lurched away into the sanctuary of the gulch.

The bull moose continued his belligerent appraisal of me for a moment. Then he blew his nostrils, scratched vigorously at his right ear with his hind foot, shook himself, and moved slowly off into the thickets.

"You cantankerous old bum! I yelled after him.

Old Cantankerous was as good a name as any for him, and he lived up to every syllable of it.

In my country moose browse the timbered ridges until the snow gets knee-deep, then come down to the beaver dams and pasture in the second-growth beaver cuttings. Usually this is not until Christmas or New Year, but that year mother nature showed the harsher side of her breasts, and by December 15 the snow was belly-deep to a calf, and the moose came drifting into the creek bottom. Old Cantankerous was among them.

I was kneeling down, building myself a mink set in the overflow of a beaver dam, and at first glance I didn't fully recognize him, although I knew I'd seen this bull somewhere before. He'd shed his horns, and that made a difference.

He was standing on the ice of the beaver pond 50 yards upstream, and had neither seen nor winded me. A beaver dam covered with sodden snow provides exceedingly treacherous footing, and my snowshoes were on the far side of it, 300 feet or so away. So was my Ross .303. When I finally recognized the bull, I cursed myself and began fruitlessly scheming how I could get across to the rifle without attracting his attention. But I decided it would be better to stay put until he moved off. I think I was scared of that bull.

I cautiously sank down behind the dam, wishing he'd go so I could finish my business. I wasn't looking for trouble that afternoon. After at least 15 minutes of indecision he smelled of the snow, belched, and veered up-pond toward a willow patch that would furnish his supper.

Christmas sulked in on a bloated full moon. Azure skies, and a wind out of the Yukon as sharp as porcupine needles. Spruce trees along the creek bottoms popping their useless protests. A little cross fox yapping on a mountaintop, beseeching the harsh land that had spawned him to give him food. Moose calves coming up from their beds in the snow at daybreak, with frosted hocks and ears; chickadees falling from the perches in the spruce thickets, little feathered bodies frozen solid while they roosted. Christmas, the birthday of our Lord; Christmas and 54 degrees below zero.

You don't trap mink, otters, or other fur bearers in weather like that; only the coyotes and timber wolves are abroad. And moose. Come rip-roaring chinook or searing arctic blizzard, moose must eat. The lower the mercury, the more browse they must consume lest the body heat be extinguished within them. No shed or den for them; just the overhang of a spruce tree for shelter, virgin snow for a bed.

For myself, hibernating over a pot-bellied stove soon becomes irksome. Two or three days of it is all my stomach can stand. Then, cold or no cold, I must busy myself with some outdoor chore. While the cold snap lasted, running the traplines would be a dreary, useless business. So, having mastered the somewhat tricky art of handling a camera with mittens, I went to stalking moose. And by moose I mean Old Cantankerous.

And that brought me to New Year's day. Thirty-six inches of snow, now, and warmer. Only 28 below. Gray, scurfy clouds scudding across the face of the sun; mink tracks again beginning to show in the seepage from the beaver dams. For that's another miracle of the beaver. No matter how bitter the cold, the water seeps through his dams and moves freely down the creek to keep its rendezvous with the river.

That afternoon the bull chewed his cud at the edge of a small meadow only half a mile from my cabin, and my mind was made up. I'd get a photograph. But now there was a nasty question that had to be solved. How could I handle camera and rifle at the same time? No matter how quick you are, it takes a second or two to drop the camera, unsling the gun, slip the safety, and bring the butt to your shoulder. A mature bull moose, murder in his eye, covers a deal of ground in just two or three seconds. I wasn't kidding myself; if Old Cantankerous were to charge, only powder and lead would stop him.

Had my son been at home the whole affair would have been simple. He'd cover the bull while I took the photo. But he wasn't with us. The previous fall he'd traded the loneliness of the wilderness for a three-year hitch in the Canadian army. That day there was only my wife.

I broached the matter quite casually. "I believe we could get a picture of Old Cantankerous this afternoon," I told her. She knew all about him by this time and was under no illusion as to what I meant by "getting a picture." It meant stalking to within 10 or 15 feet of the big bull.

"We?"

"If you'd like to handle the camera while I cover with the gun?" I said, a little tolerantly. Perhaps I was hoping she'd say, "You couldn't get me within 400 yards of that brute!" Then maybe I'd have scuttled the whole idea.

Instead, she began pulling on her overshoes in a very matter-of-fact way. Which is what I should have expected, for we came into the wilderness together determined to enjoy the sunshine and endure the storm. Why should I think she'd deny me when I asked that she share my adventures with a moose?

While she was piling on sweaters and mackinaw I got her snowshoes from a shed and pummeled the leather harness soft. Next we checked the box camera. It held four unused negatives. I took the .303 Ross down from its peg on the wall and fondled it briefly, for that old gun has been with me since 1922.

"Ready?" I asked my wife. She was set to go, all 115 pounds of her, and seemed impatient to get this bit of business over with. I stared thoughtfully at the five 220-grain soft-points in the palm of my hand and hoped I wouldn't have to use one. I dropped the cartridges into the magazine and stepped into my snowshoes. "O.K.," I said.

A smooth trapping trail took us within 100 yards of the meadow. The bull hadn't moved; he was still out in the open, 15 yards from the brush. He half turned in his tracks as we came into view, watching us with seeming indifference. The approach across the meadow wasn't easy, for here the snow was 36 inches deep. Our snowshoes sank into it for some eight or 10 inches, and each time we lifted a foot three pounds of snow came up on the webbing. "Think you can manage it?" I asked.

"I think so," my wife said.

With me breaking trail, we moved cautiously to within 30 yards of the bull. He looked as big as a mountain, and he was watching us with bold intentness. I stopped and slid a shell into the breech of the .303 and pulled the moosehide mitten from my right hand. Now there was just a thin woolen glove between my finger and the trigger. I stared at the old bull. As long as he stood with his ears well up and his mane down we had nothing to fear.

We slid forward another half-dozen snowshoe lengths. Now he was 20 yards from us, and still showing no sign of animosity. At this point my wife must slip around in front of me and take the lead, for the camera had to have a clear view. I stepped aside and let her pass.

We shuffled forward again and now there was only 15 yards between us and the bull. I stopped and breathed, "How does he look through the finder?"

"I'll try one but another five yards would be better."

Another five yards! That would put her within 10 yards of a bull moose packing as much danger as a case of ditching powder. I was beginning to experience a gnawing uneasiness.

"Unbuckle the heelstraps of your snowshoes," I suddenly told her. Free of the straps she could still move forward, but, in an emergency, could slip quickly out of the shoes and dodge. She unbuckled the straps and looked up at me. "O.K.," I said. "Another five yards—but not an inch closer."

We never made it. The words had hardly left my mouth when I heard the old bull grunt. Both his ears flattened back against his neck, his mane bristled over his withers, and his eyes rolled to show a bloodshot white.

I sucked in my breath. "Quick—shoot now!" I said.

The camera came up against her chest and she looked down into the finder just as the old bull charged. A scream forced itself from her lips. "You shoot!" she cried.

Even in the flick of time it took for the gun to jump to my shoulder, for my eye to look down the sights, he was almost on top of her. It had to be a brain shot; no other could possibly drop him before his front feet began pounding my wife to a pulp. A good many thoughts might have hammered at my brain in that moment. I might have been cursing myself for exposing her to this danger in the first place. I might have thought of the 100-mile trek with sleigh and team to a doctor.

But there was only one thought, and it was more of a prayer: that the .303 wouldn't miss. I held my fire deliberately since there would be no time to reload. Somehow I managed to keep the pressure off that trigger until he was 10 measured feet from her snowshoes. Then I held right between his eyes and tripped the trigger of the Ross. A brain shot, I'd said—it had to be a brain shot. And, thank God, a brain shot it was. He was dead when he hit the snow.

Slowly, almost reluctantly, my eyes rose to meet those of my wife. The fear that had been in her lingered in the tenseness of her face, the pallor of her cheeks, the dilated pupils of her eyes. And it was a fear of which she need never feel shame. To see Old Cantankerous standing and chewing his cud would tingle the roots of your hair; to see him charging was a vision of hell itself.

I looked down at his body, still quivering in death. My thoughts went back to the gulch and the yearling, to those other moose he had quarreled with as they approached his feeding spot. I thought of the long winter days ahead when I'd be away from home on some distant part of the trapline, and my wife there alone. True, I had killed a bull moose out of lawful season, and while game laws are necessary to the preservation of wildlife, there are isolated occasions when breaking them does far more good than harm.

My wife had rebuckled the heelstraps of her snowshoes and started toward me when a thought flashed through my mind. I held up my hand. "Wait," I said. "I want a photo of you right there where you were when he went down."

I moved forward, took the camera from her, and backed up a couple of snowshoe lengths. I was about to take the picture when she asked, "Did you wind it?"

"Wind it!" I almost shouted. And as the words sank in, I asked in amazement, "You mean there's a photo of him charging?"

"I think so," she said.

There are a good many things in the life of one who follows the forests and watersheds for a living that I cannot properly explain. How she was able to keep her eyes on the camera, hold the thing steady, and press the button when 1,400 pounds of rage was almost on top of her is one of them.

Lions Don't Come Easy

Jack O'Connor

November 1953

OUTDOOR LIFE was the first outdoor magazine to send its shooting editor on safari. In doing so it satisfied Jack O'Connor's lifelong ambition—and brought the magazine no fewer than fifteen stories from this one trip. The lion story was the first in the series. The second was "Africa's Top Trophy" (December 1953). It celebrated O'Connor's introduction to the greater kudu. On this safari he shot one of the largest kudu heads yet taken in East Africa by an American—54¼ inches. In 1959 he downed an even bigger one—60 inches. This story of a lion hunt is another of O'Connor's great hunting tales.

Practically everyone who has never hunted in Africa will assure you that there is nothing to getting a lion. All you have to do, they say, is drive around in a safari car for a few hours, looking over various samples of the king of beasts. Then, when you find the kind you want, one with a mane that exactly matches the pine paneling in the rumpus room, you just step out and give him the business.

Yet I have just finished eight days of dawn-to-dark hunting—and only this morning did I shoot my lion. Incidentally, I shot the 78th lion I saw—an average of almost 10 a day. There are still plenty of them in the best areas of British East Africa, but unless you are lucky you have to rustle to get a good one.

The three of us—H. W. (Herb) Klein, M. C. (Red) Earley, and I—first started to think about a lion hunt back in 1950, when we were chasing Dall sheep and grizzlies in the Yukon. Herb and Red, old friends of mine, like to hunt and shoot and fondle a firearm as much as I do. Both are husky Texas oil men, and they have hunted everything from Texas white-tail deer to Alaska brown bear. They are among the half-dozen hunters who have taken all varieties of North American wild sheep. When you've accomplished things like that, you have to begin to raise your sights a bit.

One night we were gabbing in our Yukon cooktent when Herb suddenly said, "What do you say we take a whirl at lions in Africa one of these days?"

"Sounds good to me!" Red grunted.

I said little, but all my life I had, like most American sportsmen, dreamed of the fabulous game country that is East Africa—of the great, black, truculent Cape buffalo; the fantastic wildebeest, which looks like a cross between a mule, a deer, and a buffalo; the leopard; the elephant; the many strange antelope. But most of all I had dreamed of someday knocking over a great-maned lion, the grandest of the cats, the epitome of all that is Africa.

The dream began to come true last fall, when OUTDOOR LIFE gave me the go-ahead on the trip. The three of us engaged the famous Nairobi outfitting firm of Ker & Downey Safaris, Ltd., and for months we were busy getting together rifles, ammunition, and photographic equipment, obtaining passports, and enduring injections for everything from cholera to housemaid's knee. Stories of the Mau Mau trouble gave us pause, but we discovered that the uprisings were confined to an area far from the hunting fields. Finally last June we met in New York and flew to Nairobi by way of London, Paris, Rome, and Khartoum in the Sudan.

Three and a half days out of Nairobi we were in our first hunting camp in northwestern Tanganyika with Don Ker and Myles Turner, white hunters, 26 native helpers—gunbearers, cooks, drivers—and two hunting cars and two big five-ton trucks. The camping equipment would knock your eye out. Nairobi outfitters cater to the carriage trade, and while we hunt we live in style.

As I write this, I am sitting at a portable typewriter in a clean, airy, and spacious dining tent. While I labor at one end of the table, Don Ker and Red Earley are playing blackjack at the other. Herb Klein has just come in with a zebra and a Thomson's gazelle. Hot and tired after stalking the zebra, he is taking a bath in a folding canvas tub while his personal boy stands by with the towels. This is astonishing luxury for an old desert rat like me, who on most of his trips has been his own guide, his own cook, and his own skinner.

The amount of game we've seen has been fantastic. I have hunted from Mexico to Alaska, but in the 12 days since we left Nairobi I have seen more game than ever before. Yesterday we saw at least 10,000 zebras. Beautiful little Thomson's gazelles hop around in the tall grass like so many fleas; we've surely seen over a million of them. And hundreds of giraffes and ostriches; thousands of topi, wildebeests, and goofy-looking kongoni.

Game of some sort is continually in sight. Here you see a herd of gazelles, over there you see a few water bucks among the trees. Beyond the hill a zebra barks like a cocky little dog, and a dainty dik-dik, an antelope no larger than a rabbit, scurries through the grass.

The same armchair hunter who tells you that catching your lion is easy, also tells you that Africa is hot. Of course it is. That's why, when an acquaintance back in the States advised me to take an eiderdown jacket for early-morning wear, I thought he was balmy. But I took it along—and it's the most useful garment I have. We've been camping at about 5,500 feet. Nights are so cool we sleep under two or three blankets. And in the morning my jacket is as welcome as it was in the Yukon.

But back to the lions. We made our first camp near a donga, or dry stream bed. Tents were being set up when Myles called to Herb and me. "Come here, pals," he said. "I want to show you something."

In the mud beside a near-by water hole were the big round pug marks of two lions. "A lion and a lioness," Myles told us. "Things look good!"

Actually they were even better than we had hoped.

After lunch we went out in the hunting cars, Myles with Herb and Red, and Don Ker taking me. We were not a mile from camp when Don suddenly put on the brakes. "See the lions?" he asked, lifting his binoculars to his eyes.

I jumped as if I had been shot, but I managed to follow the direction of his gaze. Across the donga, perhaps 150 yards away, and beneath a big thorn tree, were the silhouettes of a couple of lions. They looked just like the circus kind. Then my binoculars showed me lions all over the place—females, half-grown cubs, and a couple of young males with sprouting manes.

For whatever the reason, lions are not afraid of automobiles. Putting his four-wheel-drive hunting car into low, Don crossed the donga and in a moment we were up to our necks in lions. Those around the thorn tree posed like mamma, papa, and the children in an old-fashioned family portrait. More lions popped up out of the grass until there were 18 in all.

Breaking out my black-and-white still camera, I shot several pictures of them. Then I turned to color movies. One lithe and beautiful young lioness detached herself from the group, walked up to within a few feet of the car, and looked it over.

Reluctantly we drove away. This, I told myself, was going to be a cinch. I was even more convinced we were on the gravy train when we saw two more lionesses, shortly after. They were lying in the thin shade of a thorn tree right out on the hot, bright plain. One was devouring the carcass of a Thomson's gazelle she had killed, and when we drew up and stopped she nervously picked up the dead Tommy and trotted away until she found herself another tree. She didn't know what the strange mechanical monster was, but she wasn't going to share her Tommy with it, that was sure.

That same afternoon I shot my first African game—a Tommy for us dudes and the white hunters to gnaw on, and a topi for the help. Each was a one-shot kill with an 87-grain bullet from the .257 Weatherby Magnum, and each was made at around 200 yards.

I figured I'd really have something to tell Herb and Red when I got back. I had actually seen some real live lions with hair, long teeth, and big red mouths. I had also actually shot a couple of funny-looking un-American antelope. Would the boys be burning with envy?

But when Don and I drove up to camp my small accomplishments faded into nothing, for there was Red gloating over the carcass of a big blond lion, while the native boys whopped and hollered around him in triumph. Just as the debunkers had said; there's nothing to shooting a lion in Africa. You simply drive around until you see the one you want.

Actually, Red had done just about that. From a distance Myles had spotted a lion and lioness lying in the grass. Leaving the car half a mile away, the two men had made a long stalk, creeping along on their hands and knees through the tall grass until they were about 75 yards from the lions. Then Red eased himself up onto the convenient anthill, and when the lion raised its head above the grass he plugged it through the neck.

Easy? For him, yes. But Herb and I didn't shoot our lions the next day, nor the day after that. We didn't shoot any old he-lions on account of we didn't see any. We saw lady lions. We saw baby lions. We even saw young legal males which we passed up because they had small manes.

In East Africa, male antelope (which by all laws of logic should be called "bucks") are called "rams" if they are small and "bulls" if they are large, and the very feline male leopards and cheetahs are called "dogs." So Herb and I gagged up our reports to each other when we met at night. "Oh, the usual! Lots of ewe and lamb lions, but no old boar lions."

We went out at dawn, came in after dark. We covered country in the hunting cars. We glassed from the little rocky hills called kopjes and pronounced "copies." We explored dongas. We shot a few antelope to keep our help sleek and fat and our own bodies and souls together. But what we wanted was a lion apiece.

I got the first break. We moved part of the outfit a few miles from the place where Red had shot his lion and camped on a donga spotted with water holes every half mile or so. The area was very dry and the high grass had been cured by the sun. All around us was the fresh, clean, delicious smell of natural hay.

A little scouting soon showed that the lions in the area were concentrated along this donga. They had cover in the brush along the watercourse, pools in which to drink, and plentiful game close at hand. Every night we could hear their grunting, coughing roars as they hunted. Water bucks, Thomson's gazelles, topi, impalas—all came down to water and paid their toll to the great lurking cats.

There are various ways of getting lions. One is to cruise around in a hunting car until a shootable specimen is spotted and then to stalk him afoot. In both Kenya and Tanganyika the law says that no game may be shot from a car or within 200 yards of a car. So even if you spot a fine trophy lion you have to drive on at least 200 yards before you can get out and begin your stalk.

Another way is to hit fresh spoor, or tracks, follow the lion to his lair, boot him out, and take your shot at him. Still another is baiting. You shoot one of the commoner antelope and drag it behind an automobile to leave a blood-scent trail. Then you tie the bait animal securely in a tree so that a feeding lion cannot drag it off into the brush. Perhaps a shootable lion will be attracted to the bait, and still be there when you come around at daylight. But more often the bait has been devoured by other visitors—buzzards, Marabou storks, and hyenas. And when lions do come they are likely to be females and immature males that are not so wary of ambushes as the great maned lords of the jungle.

Don Ker elected to cruise in his hunting car, and we covered a beat along the donga, stopping now and then to glass our surroundings or to get out to look for sign. We saw lions every day—sometimes a lone and beautiful female shining like gold in the early-morning sun as she lay full of antelope, replete, and happy, enjoying the warmth after the chill of the night at almost 6,000 feet. Sometimes we'd see two or three females or young lions together. Now and then they'd be sunning themselves, but in the afternoon they'd either be lying in the tall grass or bedded down in the thin shade of a thorn tree.

There were big he-lions about, no doubt of it. We'd see their tracks by the water holes. At night we'd hear their rattling low-pitched grunts, their full-throated, deep-chested roars. But when we went out at dawn they had gone back to their brush retreats. But sometime, somewhere, we'd be bound to see a trophy lion.

Then it happened.

One morning, just as the first clean, bright rays of the sun shone on bush and grassland, the lookout boy—his head through a hole in the car top—whispered that magic word, "Simba!" Across the donga, about 200 yards away, seated majestically on a big flat rock, were two big males, with a black and a blond mane respectively. My heart almost jumped out of my throat.

Calmly Don Ker, that old pro, stopped the hunting car, lifted his 7 x 35 Bausch & Lomb binoculars to his eyes, and took a look at the lions. "They're both worth shooting," he said calmly.

He drove on and parked the car some 300 yards away. Then Mr. O'Connor's personal whammy took a hand.

"Give me my .300," I told the gunbearer in the back seat.

That Weatherby Magnum is one of my favorites, a rifle I have described in these pages. It's a short-barreled, scopesighted featherweight, so accurate it will keep five shots on a silver dollar at 200 yards.

So off we went. We dropped into the donga and presently came to a spot where I could shoot. The lions had become nervous. Apparently they had seen or heard us because when I sat down to shoot, they were on their feet.

The rifle was wobbling all over the place. My first shot at the black-maned lion got away from me. I missed, and off went the old boy into the bush. I worked the bolt rapidly, then swung over to the blond. This time the crosshairs settled down right behind his shoulder, and when I squeezed off the shot I expected old Leo africanus to drop. Instead he gave no sign of being hit, turned his big broad fanny to me, slowly walked off the rock, and disappeared.

The only thing that could have happened, I told myself, was that I'd given the trigger a terrific yank and jerked my shot high.

As we sneaked back to the car I was about as low as I have been in all my life. I had dreamed for 40 years of killing a great-maned lion. Two of them had been tossed into my lap—and I had flubbed the opportunity like an excited schoolboy missing his first buck. I crept along trying to hide my head in my jacket. The gunbearers wouldn't look at me, and until we got into the car Don said not a word.

Then he turned to me. "Don't feel badly," he said. "Lots of people have missed their first lion—and they have missed at a lot less than 100 yards."

I said nothing. There was nothing to say. So off we drove. Presently Don stopped the car.

"We'll have to try baiting now," he told me. "See that kongoni over there, about 300 yards away? I'd like to have you shoot it."

The kongoni is a big, horse-faced antelope with short, twisted, cowlike horns and a gallop like that of a spavined plowhorse. Nobody loves the poor kongoni. He exists in multitudes but he isn't much of a trophy, and his destiny seems to be lion food and lion bait. This one stood under a tree asleep on his feet and with his head down. He was about 300 yards away and the shot should not be difficult with my souped-up .300 Magnum.

I held onto the tree with my left hand, rested the foreend of the .300 over my wrist, put the crosshairs on the center of the kongoni's shoulder, and touched one off. Not a darned thing happened except that—far away, through an avenue in the trees—I saw dust kick up. I felt even lower. I worked the bolt, squeezed off another careful shot with exactly the same result.

"Way high!" Don said gloomily.

"I'll try a 220-grain bullet," I said. "It shoots a lot lower."

I fed one in, held as before, shot, and down went the kongoni.

A great light dawned on me. Carefully I examined my .300. The continual pounding of the hunting car over rough country had loosened the guard screws of the rifle so that it took three complete turns to tighten them. The scope mount was so loose that I could rattle it with my hand. I tried a shot at 100 yards, and the bullet landed to the right and a foot high. Even the three screws in the scope base were loose. I had to remove the scope to tighten them, and the .300, of course, was out of action until I could sight it in again. I didn't have a lion, but I did have an alibi.

In the rack in the hunting car was my .375 Magnum, a Model 70 Winchester restocked by Griffin & Howe and fitted with a Stith 2 3/4X scope on a Griffin & Howe mount. I took it out, tightened the guard screws, then shot twice with the 270-gr. bullet at a knot on a tree 100 paces away. One shot was in the middle of the knot, the other about one inch away. Here was my lion rifle.

I got another chance a couple of days later. We were cruising along early one morning when what should we behold about 200 yards away but two big blond lions strolling along as amiable-looking as two well-fed house cats, their big bellies—full of meat and water—swinging from side to side as they walked.

It would have been very easy to leap from the hunting car with cries of joy and to salivate those two big cats, but the Tanganyika game laws and the long arm of Don Ker's conscience would not permit. We cruised slowly between them, as if shooting lions was the last thing in the world we'd think of. I even thrust my camera out of the car and shot a picture of one.

But when we got about a quarter mile away we grabbed rifles, dived into the donga, and ran like the devil after the lions. When we got to the spot where they should be, we stuck our heads over the bank expecting to see them. No lions. Their tracks showed they had done eactly what we had done. As soon as they were out of sight they had run.

So we took up the spoor.

For five miles we followed it, with Don, the gunbearer Thomas, and a Wandorobo tracker doing most of the work. I must say with pride, though, that two or three times I found the spoor when it was lost.

It was noon. We were hot, weary, and thirsty when we saw a little Thomson's gazelle standing just out of a brush patch into which the tracks led, and gazing at something the way a bird looks at a snake.

"He sees the lions," Don hissed at me. "Get ready!"

So into the brush we crept. But the lions saw us first and we became aware of them as bouncing silhouettes fleeing through heavy brush about 75 yards away. I brought up the .375 and had the crosshairs swinging along the chest of a lion when Don shouted for me not to shoot. Like all white hunters he wants no part of a wounded lion in heavy brush.

We chased the cats about 300 yards and saw them again across an open flat just before they disappeared into another brush patch.

"Shoot if you think you can land one right!" Don yelled.

"Hell, I couldn't hit an elephant right now," I said, as I gasped for breath.

So back we turned, again defeated. We had now spooked four big-maned lions and we were really loused up.

The next day, not far from where we lost those two, Herb Klein polished off a big blond male, probably one of the two we had muffed. Don and I continued to see lady lions but no males.

So back we went to our first camp, where Red had shot his lion. We held a conference and decided to try two more days for my lion. Since Herb and Red had killed not only lions but leopards—something for which I had no license—it was time to move on to other territory for other game.

The next morning we saw a big pride of 18 lions, including two young maned males. The temptation to bop one was pretty strong. That afternoon we put out a kongoni bait and chopped in two a big eland which Herb had shot the day before.

It was gray dawn the second day when Don and I drove out in the hunting car to inspect our three baits. When we could see the first one Don said calmly, "There's something on the kongoni—a lioness, I believe." He lifted his glasses. "No, it's a lion."

My own binoculars went to my eyes. I saw a very respectable maned male, young but shootable and a better lion than most Americans come back from Africa with. "I'll settle for that baby," I said.

Don kept the glass to his eyes.

"We've got two more baits to look at," he told me, "and I'd hate to have you go back with a second-rate lion like that one."

"You wouldn't hate it half as much as I'd hate to go back without any lion," I told him. "My best friends wouldn't speak to me."

"Well, maybe he'll be here when we get back," he said.

"You're the doctor!"

Off we went. The second bait had not been touched, but when we got to the third we could see that a lion had been eating on it and below it in the dust were the big round tracks of a male.

We parked the car away from the kill and got out. "He hasn't been gone from the bait for more than a few minutes," Don whispered. "He's bound to be close by."

We had hardly gone 300 yards through the tall grass and thin brush when the Wandorobo boy whispered, "Simba!"

Now luck was with us. A bit less than a hundred yards from the lion was a big anthill that would give us cover from the stalk and a rest to shoot from. Slowly, quietly, hardly daring to breathe, we crept up on his nibs. I poked my head over the hill. There was the great lion. He was sitting in grass so tall that only his head and neck showed, nervously looking in the direction of his free meal, half of Herb's bull eland. His shaggy, majestic head and thick mane shone golden in the early-morning sun.

Cautiously I poked the big .375 over the top of the anthill. I rested the fore-end on my left hand and the crosshair in the scope came to rest rock-steady

231

against his burly neck. I squeezed the trigger so gradually that the rifle seemed to go off by itself.

As the 71.5 grains of No. 4064 powder exploded and drove the 270-grain soft-point bullet into the great cat's neck, all hell broke loose. Roaring like a fiend possessed, the lion tossed his great tawny body clear of the grass in his dying convulsions. I have heard many a wounded grizzly roar in his death agonies, and it's a blood-curdling sound, but I have never heard more racket than that big lion made.

We rushed forward for the finishing shots, and I was so excited that if Don hadn't restrained me, I think I would have tried to stab him to death with my pocketknife.

We stood over him. We gloated. We measured. We admired.

He was a beautiful lion. His great sandy body was as smooth and round as a sausage. His blond mane was heavy, shaggy, long. Don Ker told me he probably weighed 500 pounds, and was one of the largest lions he had seen in 27 years as a white hunter. From the tip of his nose to the last joint of his tail he was nine feet seven inches long as he lay there.

All in all, he was some lion, and of all the trophies I have taken, the only one that has given me a greater thrill was the first desert ram I stood over, almost a quarter of a century earlier and a half a world away.

Worth Two Shells

K. C. Randall

January 1954

Chuck shooting can be a lot of fun for the people doing it. They can sharpen their eyes for big game; they can add spice by stalking their prey through various stratagems; they can shoot at vast distances or close up with bow and arrow, and, of course, they can help the farmer. Still, it doesn't often make for entertaining reading. K. C. Randall has made good reading for OUTDOOR LIFE for years and does it here with chucks, too. I bought a long series of stories from him, but it wasn't until I began searching the back files that I learned his secret. In a March 1945 issue I learned he was a Michigan professor, teaching story writing, and an outdoor enthusiast with two setters, an arsenal of fine shotguns and rifles and a supply of fishing tackle. Put that all together and you have something worth two shells.

Coming out of the hollow we could see faintly the tall white outline of my Uncle Leon's house, the darker shadow of the barns. It was late June—a warm night, alive with the grass-scented stillness of the Massachusetts countryside, and with fireflies lighting the Granby meadows. Fred, the Morgan-strain buckskin horse, broke into a smart trot that rattled us up to the gate in the second-best buggy. Aunt Anna had let me drive, and I was glad to be arriving with such a flourish—glad, too, to see Uncle Leon, who had come out to welcome me and take care of Fred. I cramped the wheels before the granite carriage block, and Aunt Anna, a young woman then, stepped nimbly down and went inside.

"Hello," Uncle Leon said, looking up at me and smiling. "You hold Fred for a minute so he won't start for the barn."

He reached into the buggy box and pulled out my bag and the .22 rifle in its canvas case. "Looks like you were ready to do business on the chucks," he said. "Got plenty of bullets?"

"Two boxes of Long Rifles," I told him. "Think that will be enough?"

My uncle was always something of a joker in a dry Yankee way. "Let's see," he said slowly. Light from the lantern lit his strong-nosed, leathery face, and for an instant I caught the twinkle in his eyes. "Let's see," he said again. "Fifty to a box and about a hundred chucks in the high pastures. Yes, that should about do it, but it will take you the best part of the summer."

We stabled Fred and stepped into the dining room where, under a hanging lamp above the square table, Aunt Anna had set out two bowls of milk and a loaf of homemade bread. This eating of bread and milk just before retiring was a habit with my uncle during haying. The milk, ice cold from the milk house, tasted almost as good as ice cream. Eating with Uncle Leon, two men at table, I almost forgot I was only 12 and all dressed up and city pale. Tomorrow night, I told myself, I'd be wearing a blue shirt and overalls and by the end of August would be nearly as brown on arms and face as my uncle. He sat now, hunched over his bowl, a big man, lean and powerful in the shoulders, sharp eyes twinkling at me as he spoke again of the chucks. He wanted them hunted hard, he said, early mornings and late afternoons. That would be part of my job along with driving Fred on the rake and leading Ned to lift the hayfork.

And so next morning I was up and out at 4:30 and with the little rifle under my arm circled the barnyard and into the home pasture. It's usually good haying weather in New England around the Fourth, and already a red sun had lifted to sparkle on the dew. Pasture grass, close-cropped and cut by paths, felt soft and wet between my toes. Climbing the low hill where the windmill stood, I could look off into brightness across the meadow, a lighter green from the timothy stand, and mark the threadlike course of a little brook where some morning not long from now, I would fish for speckled trout.

But chuck hunting was now my business. I hurried on along an old, gray wall that separated hill pasture from the mowing. Over the next rise lay Stonewall Pond, so named because a wall ran through it. I had fished here for eels and bull-heads since I was eight, and shot frogs over a foot long with a Daisy air rifle. It was a temptation to linger along these inviting shores, but the fishing could come later—a showery day when haying came to a standstill. I had never ventured far beyond the pond. New territory lay ahead, the high pastures and my uncle's woodlots.

Crossing a rounded knoll I surprised my first chuck. He was a young one, not full grown and light brown in color. For an instant he sat up looking and then ran for his hole under the wall. I have said I surprised him; it would be more truthful to say he caught me napping. For I stood to watch him race over the turf with a speed astonishing in an animal so squat and short in the legs. He dived into the wall, or seemed to do just that, and I ran up to find the patch of sand that marked his doorway. Retreating to the knoll I lay on my stomach on the wet grass and trained the sights of the .22 on that patch of sand. I lay there trembling with chuck fever until the bell sounded for breakfast. Nothing happened. The chuck may have had his nose out investigating, but so close to the color of his doorway was he that I failed to see him.

Uncle Leon laughed when I told him about this first fiasco. "Chucks are smart," he said. "That was a young one, or you never would have seen him. An old one would have been holed up long before you came over the rise in plain sight."

"That's right," I said, crestfallen at my failure. "I should have stalked him like an Indian. I will next time, you bet."

"You say his hole is under the wall?" my uncle asked. "Then you should keep on the other side of that. Start a good 20 rods away and crawl until you get oppo-site the hole. Then peek over to see if he's out in the open. Get between him and his hole. Don't make a sound, for if you do he'll hear you. And come on him downwind."

"What's downwind?" I asked.

"The wind blowing from him to you," my uncle told me. "How's the gun shoot?" he asked.

"Right on the money," I said. I'd read this expression somewhere in a boy's magazine, and now I got it off.

"We'll try it after breakfast," Uncle Leon said.

I knew how busy he was at this time of year, neighbors coming this day to help mow the big stand, but Uncle Leon liked small boys and guns and never was in a hurry where they were concerned. We stepped out into the yard, and he fastened a white chip of birch wood to the chopping block.

"Stand back by the croquet set and center on that chip," he said.

"You shoot first," I said and handed him the gun.

It was my first rifle, a Stevens single-shot with lever action and an open sight. I'd shot it since Christmas at sparrows and tin cans until I knew the feel of it and was pretty good offhand. (Years later, searching mother's attic, I found the little gun stowed in a corner and still in its case, oiled and ready for use. But I had outgrown it; the short barrel and light stock felt like a toy in my hands. My uncle was as big a man as I grew up to be.)

Gravely, without a word, he took the gun and threw it to his shoulder with easy motion, firing so quickly he scarcely seemed to aim. The birch chip jumped from the block in two pieces, split cleanly in half. The Long Rifle slug had centered it.

Now it was my turn. I felt a little nervous, but I was used to the gun. I aimed a shade longer than my uncle at a second chip and split it with a shot a touch high of center.

"Good enough," he said. "We won't need to practice any more today. You go after that chuck at milking time and bring him home for supper. I'll make a bargain with you. Five cents for ammunition for every chuck or red squirrel you shoot. Or a shotgun shell and a chance to fire my old hammer gun. You're getting big enough to begin handling a shotgun."

I thought now of his fowling piece standing in the kitchen and the boxes of yellow shells in a drawer of the kitchen table. I had long admired them.

"I'll take the shells," I said quickly.

Perhaps my uncle's offer wasn't so magnificent as it had seemed at the time. That summer, hunting hard all through haying and corn cutting, I doubt if I took more than six chucks and perhaps twice that number of reds. It was a week before I had another chance at the young chuck I'd stumbled on that first morning, a lesson in patience well learned, for I stalked him every day crawling on hands and knees to get opposite his hole. When I peeped over, after this Indian-like approach, he wouldn't be there. But I persisted, and one afternoon, inching forward with the breeze just right, cooling my face, I peered over the wall some little distance from the hole and found him out feeding.

He might have been a deer or bear so intent was I on getting him. He raised up now and looked my way, and I froze still as the wall before me. And then he went back to nibbling the tender grass, moving slowly away from his doorway. A yard or two ahead was a window in the wall, two boulders set so that an opening showed between them. I edged toward this natural rest and cover for my shot, and, reaching it without a twig cracking, peeped through to see the chuck upright as a small brown post and looking straight at me.

I held my breath and never moved until he was on all fours again, and then I made ready to aim, bringing the barrel up, careful not to scrape it against stone. He was out perhaps 30 yards and now sat up again, not facing me but broadside. At the crack of the .22 he rolled and flopped. I scrambled across the wall, knees weak as jelly. The brown mound on the turf didn't move, and after that long uncertain instant making sure, I knew I had him.

Uncle Leon was milking when I rushed into the barn with this first trophy. He stood and inspected the kill.

"Got him close to the heart," he said. "Did your bullet stop him?"

"Yes," I said. "He went right down and didn't stir."

"Sometimes they'll run with the bullet," Uncle Leon said. "They're hard to knock down for keeps, especially with a light-caliber gun. The heart shot is good, but often it won't stop them in their tracks."

"Why not?" I asked.

"It's the same with deer and bear," my uncle said. "They'll travel unless you shoot for bone, the shoulder or spine. Break them down and they stay put. You try it on the next one."

In the month I shot four chucks, traveling far into the high pastures. I'd spot a fresh hole and stalk warily until I got a shot. Sometimes I'd surprise one, come upon him running, and at such times I wished the little rifle were a repeater. I remember one afternoon following a pasture wall to the south well beyond my uncle's line. It had been a hot, bright day but on this high table-land a cool breeze blew over stony slopes long since burned and withered. Yet even in late afternoon the gray slabs and boulders of the walls were like heated stove lids. In a far corner I came on a fresh hole larger than any I had seen, and crept away to where a flat stone formed a natural shield some 40 yards away—and waited.

I must have dropped off for a little in the sun, for when I woke and peeped over the barrier, there showed the head and shoulders of a gray old chuck, post-like above his doorway. He looked twice the size of any of the others. My heart thumped in my mouth as I twisted to bring up the .22. Losing him for an instant in this process of setting to aim, I found he'd vanished and for a time could scarce believe I'd seen him. That bearlike head, a hoary gray and big to me as a bushel basket, was gone like a sliding shadow. Again and again I came back into that high corner to stalk, but never caught him feeding, never had a shot unless he was the big one of the summer I took in the mowing a month later. He may have moved down to feed on the rowen.

Taking that biggest one brought a hard lesson from Uncle Leon. It was one to learn early, although at the time my pride was badly hurt. Haying was over and the meadow so clean and light green it was possible to see far and away toward the upper mowing any chuck that came in to feed. Uncle Leon and I stood in the barn doorway just before milking time.

"There's a big one just come into the white clover," he said.

I looked up the rise and saw a black speck against the green. For a time it was still as a stone. Then it moved.

"Could I try him with the shotgun?" I asked.

My uncle hesitated.

"Rifle's better for sitting game," he said.

"I know," I said. "I just thought maybe this once . . . "

"Go fetch it then," he said. "One shot won't hurt. I'd had in mind practice on wing-shooting, but you go ahead."

I'd fired the hammer gun three or four times under Uncle Leon's direction. It was a 12 gauge and packed a mule's kick. I couldn't do much with the swing, but boylike admired its heavy roar, felt like a man to be using a grown-up's gun. Never would I admit the sore shoulder it gave me.

"Fetch two of the yellow shells marked 1's," my uncle said. "You'll have to crawl up behind the wall. Don't load until you get placed for a shot."

So I crept up the rise, crawling the last few rods on hands and knees. The double-gun, harder to manage than the .22, grew heavy as I lifted it along; but at length I reached a spot opposite to where the chuck should be. When I peered through a chink in the wall, he sat directly out from me. I wished then I had the rifle.

In shooting with my uncle I'd gained some ability to estimate distances; the big chuck sitting erect in the stubble, his back to me, was a good 40 yards away, but close enough for my No. 1's, which were big shot, midway between the BB's and No. 2's common today. In my excitement at seeing him I didn't think long of this. He looked big as the chuck I'd tried for in the high pasture—a gray old veteran, a black streak down his back. I fumbled a single shell into the left barrel, put the sight high in line with his shoulders and squeezed off.

The heavy kick nearly bowled me over, but I bounced up to watch the chuck. It was down on all fours, but it didn't run. I scrambled across wall and ran up to him and he raised his head in a low hissing snarl; but he couldn't move his body.

And then I did a foolish thing. Swinging the heavy gun by the barrels I clipped him on the head until he didn't lift it. There was no doubt he was a big, old one —twice the weight of the largest I had taken. I examined him and found blood where a single lucky shot had hit the spine low down, paralyzing the hind-quarters.

Looking back toward the buildings, I wondered if Uncle Leon was still watch-ing, but he had started milking when I brought my prize into the barn. I came slowly down the alley not feeling as good somehow about this one as I had about the others. And I stood before Uncle Leon, gun in one hand, chuck in the other, a heavy load for a small boy.

"Got yourself a real good one this time," my uncle said. He straightened up from the stool and came across the gutter lifting the foaming pail. "Where'd you hit him?" he asked.

And then I blurted out my story.

"I saw you," Uncle Leon said. "You were so far up I couldn't be sure, but I heard only one shot. I'm glad you told me, Cal. Was the other barrel loaded?"

"No," I said. "The second shell was in my pocket. I'd forgot about it."

Uncle Leon said mildly: "I wouldn't ever, if I were you, swing a gun with the barrels pointing toward my middle. Might have a bad accident. Hard on the gun, too, using it as a club."

I didn't say anything. My throat felt all choked up and somehow the big chuck — a real prize—didn't mean anything to me any more.

My uncle put his hand on my shoulder. "I guess a big one like this is worth two shells," he said.

"You mean," I said at last, "I can still use your gun?"

"Don't see why not," he said. "A feller has to learn. Wouldn't be quite natural if he didn't make a mistake now and again. The big thing is to learn from them, grow to be careful. And never forget how important carefulness is when handling a gun—loaded or unloaded."

That's all that was said. It was enough to hold as long as I'll ever take the field. In all my hunting after that with Uncle Leon and Dale Mathews, his neigh-bor on the next farm, neither had occasion to remind me that a gun can't be taken lightly in the handling. Other summers, other falls, but none will ever dim the bright memory of the one I spent learning to hunt chucks for my Uncle Leon.

Lost for Forty Days

Robert J. Mullins
as told to Ben East

May 1954

I can't read this story without welling up inside. Ben East, represented
elsewhere in this volume, is a master hand with any story, but he has a
special talent for telling an ordeal story, and he has written, shared in writing
and ghosted more of them than I can recall in the twenty-two years I edited
OUTDOOR LIFE. I have a measure, though. The editors of the annual Dutton
anthology, *Best Sports Stories*, have chosen to reprint ten stories over the
years in which East had a hand in the writing. Six of the ten were ordeal
stories. The first one, "Frozen Terror," is in this volume, too. The following
is the story of seven ordinary men, strangers, unequipped for cold, having
rations for four days, thrown together by accident in the vastness of the
Canadian bush for forty days. Lost! I rate it above "Frozen Terror."

Vanstone and I lowered our net over the side of the crude raft and watched
anxiously as it sank through the choppy water. It wasn't much of a net—20 feet
of linen mesh, weighted at the bottom and with a row of floats along the top. So
far it had taken only one fish, a sucker less than a foot long. But to seven men
stranded in the bush country of northern Quebec it was a big link in the frail
chain holding off starvation and death. We had not had a full meal in six days.
Our chances of eating tomorrow depended on the net.

I had rigged a proper bridle for lifting it and attached a wooden buoy at the
end of a line to mark its location in the lake. We saw all the line we had tighten
under water, then the float went under . . . and kept going. Too late we realized
we'd overshot the drop-off on the lake bottom. The anchor weights were too
much for our buoy and the net was sinking in deep water.

We lunged for it in vain. Then we grabbed up the raft paddles, but before we
could even turn the cumbersome raft in the right direction the float was gone. We
hated to go ashore and tell the others what had happened. Our plight had been
bad before; now it was desperate.

The affair had begun simply enough, with no warning of what was ahead. The
seven of us were on a routine bush flight from Fort Chimo—a lonely Eskimo settlement and trading post on the arctic rim of Quebec almost at the northeast tip
of the continent—to Roberval on Lake St. John, 700 miles south.

Flying above poorly mapped country where the magnetic compass deviates as
much as 37° from true north, fighting shifting winds of gale strength, we strayed
off course and missed our refueling station, a pinpoint in half a million square
miles of uninhabited wilderness. Almost out of gas, we landed on a lonely lake,
confident we'd be found and on our way again within 24 hours. Forty days later
we were brought out—seven ragged, starving scarecrows of men—after an ordeal
that has, I think, no counterpart in the records of the bush.

It wasn't a hunting or fishing trip. If it had been we'd have been far better prepared. In late August of last year my 19-year-old crew man, Dick Everitt, and I
had flown the chartered Norseman, a single-engine pontoon plane, north from
Roberval to Chimo to bring out a group of mining men and prospectors before

freeze-up. On the evening of August 24, with wet snow pelting down, we were told we'd fly back to Roberval the next morning. A drilling boss had an abscessed face and needed medical attention. And since there was a waiting list of men whose summer work in the iron-rich area was finished and who were eager to get out of the arctic, we'd take a full load.

The morning of the 25th dawned clear and crisp. We ate a hurried breakfast of toast and coffee—we were to regret that light meal later—and gunned the Norseman off the water, loaded to capacity with seven men and their sleeping bags and gear.

There were a few drums of gas cached midway between Chimo and Roberval, at the weather station on Lake Nichicun. We'd have to stop there and take on fuel.

The flight was uneventful. I drove the Norseman south at a little better than 100 miles an hour, with the mixture leaned out, over a jumbled, crazy-quilt country of lakes and rivers, mountains and tundra and bog, much of it not mapped at all. Save for the tiny weather station on Nichicun there was no human habitation ahead until we neared Roberval.

Shortly after noon we flew over the sprawling watershed of the Fort George River, a chain of big lakes linked together like misshapen beads on a crooked string. I recognized it from my maps and began to look for Nichicun. But a high wind, shifting from west to east, had blown us off course and we by-passed Nichicun 35 miles to the west without sighting it. When we'd been in the air over four hours I realized we had missed our fueling station.

It's poor airmanship under those conditions to stay up until your fuel is gone, so I started looking for a lake free of rocks and islands and big enough to land on. Some miles to the west I spotted one that looked all right, and on the far shore I made out a tiny clearing. When we came over it I could see the remnants of a tent. We didn't have much gas left by then, so we sat down. It would be almost six weeks before we'd learn that we had landed on Lake Emmanuel, on an upper tributary of the Eastmain River. We named it Lake Aurora the second night, when the northern lights hung their flaring curtains of ghostly radiance across the sky.

When we taxied ashore we found the clearing had been made by Indians, likely Cree trappers. They'd built a shelter of log walls, and covered it with a tarp. But it had been at least a year, perhaps more, since anyone had used the place, and the walls were sagging and the tarp rotted and fallen in.

We felt no real concern at first. Somebody remarked, "Hell, it's only 2 o'clock. If they get a rescue party here quick we'll still make the night train at Roberval." Our plane was radio-equipped. Our signals would be heard, somebody would fly us gas, and that would end the mishap.

A chill of misgiving went through me later that afternoon, however, when I sat down and radioed out "mayday," the international aircraft distress signal, adding the call letters of the Norseman and a request for fuel. I could hear all kinds of traffic, but nobody answered my call, and I realized I wasn't getting through. But I still wasn't worried. Somebody would hear me tomorrow.

We put up our tent for overnight shelter, sorted our supplies, took inventory, and made ready for an emergency, more to keep us busy than because of a sense of danger.

We were fairly well equipped for a short stay. We had two boxes of emergency rations, a 9 x 9-foot wall tent, and a gun and a limited supply of ammunition, a casting rod with reel and half a dozen lures, a net, three axes and a crosscut saw, and a kit of pots, pans, and dishes. Odds and ends included a roll of fine copper wire, three smoke flares, two hand-held Very cartridges for night signaling, and a first-aid kit that contained bandages, a bottle of an antifainting drug, sulfa ointment for burns—and very little else.

The gun was a Savage over-and-under double, one barrel a .22 rifle, the other a .410 shotgun. We had a box of cartridges for the .22, plus a few loose ones. Ammo for the .410 consisted of a box of fine-shot shells and five slug loads.

The ration boxes contained enough food to last two men 14 days on an emergency footing. For seven men that meant a four-day supply. There was no sugar, no frying fat, very little salt, less than a pound each of tea and coffee, and only a little flour. The supplies were chiefly tinned meats and fruit juices, powdered milk, beans, and dehydrated soups and vegetables. There were also three packages of tobacco.

It didn't seem like much, but we didn't expect to be there four days. Everybody was hungry, so at supper time we treated ourselves to a light meal. It proved to be the best we'd have for many days to come. When our radio signals went unanswered the next day and the next, we tightened our belts and grimly settled down to trying to live off the land, eking the rations out, saving them for a final, last-ditch stand against starvation.

We were no hand-picked party of experts, chosen deliberately for desperate adventure. We were seven ordinary men, strangers thrown together by accident. I had known young Dick Everitt, my crew man, only a few days. The others I'd met that morning, and they were only slightly acquainted. Two were Europeans, totally unfamiliar with the country and situation in which they now found themselves. They were Dr. Rolphe Theinhaus, a geologist from Siegen, Germany, and Dr. Klaas Koeten, a Rotterdam, Netherlands, mining engineer. They had come to Canada in the summer and flown to Fort Chimo to investigate its iron deposits and mining properties for European interests.

Victor Abel of Senneterre, Quebec, was the sick man, with a huge lump on the side of his face. He was the only experienced bush man in the party except myself but was too ill to be of much help. The other two were Abel's helpers, Marc Levesque of Rimouski, Quebec, and young Ray Vanstone, a 20-year-old student from the University of Toronto who had been working that summer on topographical surveys.

We did not even have the bond of a common language. Levesque spoke only French, Vanstone and I only English, Theinhaus German and a few English words. Everitt spoke both English and French, Abel French, English, and Belgian. Koeten was the real linguist of the party, fluent in English, French, German, his native Dutch, and two or three other languages.

We were an oddly assorted crew to face danger, hardship, and suffering. That we survived at all was due, I think to the unquenchable will of man to live, however great the odds against him, and to the fact that from the start we put the welfare of all ahead of the welfare of any individual.

I'm a bush pilot with many thousand air hours behind me, part of them in the R.C.A.F. and the R.A.F., where I flew from 1939 until the end of the war, and a great deal of them over the remote districts of Alaska and Canada. I grew up in the town of Kenora at the north end of Lake of the Woods, where just about everybody hunts and fishes, and married a girl whose family runs two fishing camps. The bush was nothing new to me, and although this was the first time I had ever been forced down in it, stripped of my wings in a place where I could not get out, I knew what men have to do to stay alive in such a spot. Consequently, leadership of the party fell to me automatically.

We knew from the outset we could not walk out. The distances were too great, the country was too rough and laced with too much water. We had come down almost at the exact center of the great triangle of wilderness that lies north of the St. Lawrence River and east of Hudson Bay. Somewhere—probably less than 50 miles away—was the Nichicun weather station, but we did not know in which direction. The nearest settled country, around Lake St. John, was 300 miles to the south. Four hundred miles north was Fort Chimo; eastward 500 miles lay the scattered settlements along the Labrador coast. The remote trading posts on James Bay were 300 miles west. And all this is country that no man can travel without a canoe, since it's slashed by white-water rivers and pocked with sprawling lakes.

Whatever happened, we'd have to wait for rescue. There were two possibilities there. But one—the chance that the Indians who had built the camp might return —was too slim to pin hope on. Empty canoe racks indicated they had come and gone by water, but the absence of a cache—pails, sleds, or any other equipment —meant they'd abandoned the place permanently.

The other hope of rescue lay, of course, in the air search that we knew would be made even though our radio signals failed to get through. The difficulty there would be finding us with so much country to cover and nothing known of our location, so we set about doing what little we could to help.

First we built a raft of logs, fastening it with bolts from the Indian structure and lashing it with rope. Then we moved the Norseman out and anchored it in midlake, where it could be seen readily from the air. We cleared a place on a hill a mile or so behind camp, gathered dry wood and green branches, and set a fire ready to light, because a smoke column there could be seen for 20 miles. We kept a man on watch, ready to light the fire, from daylight to dusk until the strongest of us could no longer climb the hill. We also stood a fire watch in camp at night, taking turns, with a flare at hand ready for firing if a plane came over. The campfire never went out until, toward the end, we were too weak to stay up and tend it.

Everitt and Levesque paddled across the lake and tried vainly to set fire to the rain-soaked woods on the far shore. When that failed we attempted to burn an island in midlake, but it also was too wet. And every day or so as long as we had sufficient gas to run the plane's engine briefly and provide power, I pounded out an SOS call over and over, sending at varying hours when I knew R.C.A.F. stations would be listening. After each transmission I held my key down for 10 seconds to give ground stations and planes a chance to get a fix on our position. No reply ever came.

We had been down seven days when we heard the first aircraft, droning along behind a ridge to the west. I was out on the raft fishing. Back at camp the others set off a smoke bomb, but it did no good. Two days later, when Vanstone and I were on fire watch on the hill, we caught the drone of a plane early in the morning, and that time we saw it coming—due to pass within two or three miles of us. It was a bright day with broken, fleecy clouds. We waited until the plane was almost abreast of the hill and then touched off the second of our smoke bombs. But just as the orange smoke poured out, a cloud cut off the pilot's view! When he came out from behind it he was too far south to see us. I cursed that cloud like a personal enemy.

At least we knew they were looking for us. What we could not know was that we had triggered the biggest air search in the history of Canada. Our story was one to stir the sympathy of all who heard it. A little band of men down in the vast reaches of the bush—lost, cold, hungry, perhaps hurt, waiting prayerfully for help. All across Canada and the United States—even in Europe—newspapers speculated about us under black headlines. Back home in Kenora my wife and family kept a tireless vigil, never far from a radio, jumping each time the phone rang, never losing hope. And Canada threw everything into the search.

R.C.A.F. and private planes, even planes of the U.S.A.F., flew together, covering more than 200,000 square miles of wilderness, looking with dogged determination for a thread of smoke, a scar of broken timber on a mountainside, the wreckage of the Norseman, any sign of us at all. As many as 48 aircraft were in the air in one day, directed by the R.C.A.F. Search and Rescue Command. A total of 1,056 hours were flown, in transit and search. Radio operators sat glued to their sets day and night, now and then getting garbled signals that were never strong enough to supply a fix on our location. We were picked up often enough to prove we were alive, but never clearly enough to bring help. Planes equipped with special gadgets for tracking us down flew out of the base at Goose Bay night after night, in pea-soup fog and rain and snow, but they never heard us.

The day came finally, in the fourth week, when the last of our gas was gone and our radio was silenced. If we were found now it would be by accident.

Meantime things grew worse for us day by day. There is no true autumn in that savage land. Rain changes to snow, the ground freezes, and winter is at hand. That was happening now. The day we landed we had set up the tent in swarms of blackflies. Two days later they were gone, killed by the cold in a single night. We had no clothing fit for such weather. Theinhaus's outfit consisted of a business suit and a light cotton fishing suit. He sat for hours patiently sewing one inside the other for added warmth. Vanstone had no windbreaker and no hat and his boots were falling apart. Koeten's boots were poor. Everitt had one wool shirt and two pairs of light cotton pants, but no heavy coat. Among us we had three parkas and a leather jacket, no heavy underwear and not enough gloves to go around.

The weather stayed wet for days on end, with rain and sleet and snow. Our tent leaked and our sleeping bags were soaked night after night. There was hardly enough room in the tent for all, so at first two of us paddled out on the raft and slept aboard the plane. Two or three times the wind was so bad in the morning we couldn't make it back to shore. Twice Vanstone and I huddled in the plane all day and through a second night, without heat or food. But it didn't matter much; there was next to nothing to eat at camp, either.

As the weather grew worse we had to have heat in the tent, and I tackled the job of making a small tent stove from a ration box, using empty food cans for the door and draft, and to form a short length of pipe. It worked, and after that we all slept in the tent. It was crowded but at least we were warm.

There was no time to spare by day. Every minute was crowded with the search for food, as well as other necessary tasks. But from dark to daylight there was little to do but try to sleep, and that was hard in the cold and wet.

We had two or three crossword puzzle books and a couple of pocket-size reprints. Vanstone and the others fashioned a deck of cards from cigarette cartons. Evenings we passed the time with these few amusements, or sat around the fire for an hour or two, planning the things that needed to be done the next day or talking about homes and families.

"I was married seven years ago on the second of October," Koeten told us one night. "I hope I'm home by then."

We talked incessantly, too, about being found. Abel was reading a book about the search for the Franklin Expedition, lost in the arctic a century ago. That search failed, and we talked a lot about it. But toward the end we dropped the subject.

A few evenings we sang around the fire, Koeten and Theinhaus coming in with Dutch and German songs.

The endless, discouraging hunt for food began the second day and never stopped. We took one fish in the net before it was lost. Incidentally, we dragged for it many hours with a grapnel rigged from big fishhooks, but never found it. Just before we lost it we had caught a second fish, a nine-inch trout, on the casting rod. They were the only two fish we took. We cast along shore, around the islands, and from the raft until the reel wore out, but never got another strike. We had found a few dry fish heads, a year or two old, on a shelf in the Indian camp and they raised our hopes at first, but we soon concluded the fish had been carried there from another lake. Later those heads were boiled and eaten.

Three or four days of hunting convinced us there was no big game in the country—no moose, deer, caribou, even beaver. A few days after we landed, one of the men, bending over to do some work at the plane, lost our .410 slug loads out of his pocket into deep water. Had there been big game around that could have been a major tragedy. As it was, it didn't matter.

The first week wasn't too bad. We dipped sparingly into our little store of rations, and the third morning I had the good fortune to come on a flock of five spruce partridges, the fool hens of the north. I shot all five, and they provided us with the best meals we had since that first supper.

We hunted partridges constantly after that but they were scarce; we killed only about 30 in all. We made rabbit snares from copper wire and Levesque and Everitt tended them daily, but they were not very successful. In 40 days our total take of rabbits was five, one of which we got with the gun. The rabbits and partridges, the scanty allowances of tinned meat we doled out for ourselves, and two red squirrels we shot—scrawny little beasts that did not yield a spoonful of meat per man—made up the total meat supply for the seven of us while we were lost.

Vanstone and Everitt came up to the tent one day from a trip out to the plane. "We're getting lighter," Vanstone announced with a cheerful grin. "At first Dick and I couldn't ride that raft without getting our feet wet. Now it floats the two of us high and dry!"

We could see an old burn on a range of hills about three miles from camp. There would be blueberries there, so we sent parties to pick them, but the freezing weather quickly finished them. By the end of the second week our berrying parties were coming back from a whole day of patient search—tired, cold, drenched with rain—carrying no more than a cupful of frost-softened fruit. As the supply dwindled we added other berries—any kind we could find, red, black, or green. They were tasteless and they cooked to a pulpy mush, but they helped a little to fill the aching emptiness.

Sitting around the fire one night, Theinhaus made a quiet announcement. "The mushrooms we see in the woods look like those I have eaten in Europe," he said. "I'm going to try them. If they don't poison me we can all eat them." Next morning he gathered a mess and ate them, and a day later we added mushrooms to our skimpy menu.

After that our average meal consisted of berries and mushrooms boiled together, without sugar or salt. But they became harder to find as the weather grew colder, and many evenings there was only a spoonful for each man—never more than half a cupful. But each got his share, for if he was away hunting or on fire watch it was kept for him.

We got on one another's nerves and there were differences of opinion, of course. A few times tempers flared and we had minor arguments. But we never had a real quarrel.

On red-letter days there was a partridge or a rabbit to divide among us. We ground up the bones, head and all, even the beaks and feet of the grouse, washed the entrails, and added them to the pot. The meat was portioned out equally, a spoonful at a time. But we never drank the broth at the same meal. That was saved for breakfast.

Poor as our meals were, they became the one event we looked forward to each day. We were out of tobacco, reduced to smoking leaves and bark—even coffee grounds. There were two small cans of peaches in the rations. We opened one on the second Sunday, the other on the fourth. We got half a peach apiece, and nothing ever tasted better.

Abel had been lost in the bush twice before. The first time he walked for two weeks before he met a party of Indians. The second time was in winter and he was compelled to kill half his sled dogs for food before he was found. "But this is worse," he told us.

Koeten agreed. He had spent most of World War II in a Jap prison camp in the Dutch East Indies and he confessed he'd rather go through the whole four years again than take what we were enduring now.

As the weather worsened and mushrooms and berries got scarcer, I concluded we'd have to find a substitute for them or die of starvation before freeze-up. I had heard that caribou moss is edible and there was plenty of it on the hill behind camp. So on fire watch one day, I took the plunge.

There were two or three kinds of the moss, some greenish, some black, some gray. I know now that the latter is the true caribou moss. I tried the wrong kind first and almost died from it. My stomach was tied in knots for days. When I was better I tested the gray moss and it was all right, once we learned how to cook it. We boiled it to remove the acid, dried it in a pan until it was brittle, and crumbled it to a fine powder. After that we made more than one meal on a spoonful of powdered moss, and air-force doctors told us later that in all likelihood it saved our lives.

"You know what I dreamed last night?" Vanstone said one morning. "I dreamed about a harvest dinner, the kind we used to have on the farm. Chicken and potatoes and all the trimmings! Boy, oh boy!"

That day I used the last of our flour and a scanty supply of frozen berries to make a "blueberry pie." There was no sugar for it and the berries were not all blueberries, but it seemed to lift everybody's spirits.

Cramps and pain, dizziness and nausea grew worse and worse. Bit by bit we went down to gaunt, bearded skeletons. I learned later that I lost 51 pounds, dropping from 184 to 133. The others fared no better, each losing in proportion to his weight. Every exertion became an agony. Cutting firewood was fast getting to be beyond our strength, and even walking was an ordeal. We lay down more often, did the necessary camp chores in shorter shifts.

Abel walked to the edge of camp one morning to cut a small tree. He struck three or four feeble blows, then the ax slipped from his hands and fell to the ground. "I can't do it," he groaned as he turned back to the fire.

I knew from my experience in the R.C.A.F. that the search for us would be thorough and persistent. But I also knew that sooner or later it would have to be called off. In my own mind I had set 30 days as its extreme limit, and the blackest hours of all came for me when the 30 days were up and I figured we had been abandoned for dead—that if we got out now it would be on our own. There was only the slimmest chance of doing that, but it was a chance to which we clung with the desperation of men who knew that otherwise death was only a short time away.

We began to chink the log walls of the old Indian camp, readying it for a winter shelter, meaning to move the tent there on the first fair day. But no fair day came and we never finished the chinking. It was too much for us.

Abel was in the worst shape. We couldn't do anything for his infected face except bathe it with warm soda solution and give him a couple of bottles of aspirin from my personal kit. He was extremely weak now and had headaches almost constantly. I realized that he and one or two of the others could not live more than a few days and I found myself haunted by a new and morbid worry. As each man died, how would the survivors dispose of his body?

None of us had the strength for a decent job of burial in the frozen, rocky soil. If we weighted the bodies with stones and sank them in the lake we would no longer want to drink the water. And if we laid them among the rocks behind camp, the simplest course, they would be there in plain sight, exposing those who still lived to the horrible temptation of cannibalism in the final extremes of hunger.

I finally concluded that the bodies would have to be burned on the campfire. I would do the job at night, with Theinhaus, Koeten, or Vanstone helping me. It sounds unreal now and I realize we could not have done it. It was a fantastic, hunger-begotten plan, but at the time it seemed logical enough.

All through our stay we had carried out one reconnaissance trip after another, in every directon, in the hope of finding some clue that would guide us to the weather station on Nichicun. In that event, the stronger of us might be able to reach it on foot and send help back for the others.

These exploratory trips were rugged business, too. Whoever made them had to climb endless hills, slog across bogs and tundra, wade waist-deep in icy streams, sleep without a bag and with no shelter except a bough lean-to—and go without food until he was back at camp!

You see, each time men went out they carried three tins of food—almost half of what we had left—and agreed to open them only if they were unable to rejoin us. And each time the parties staggered painfully back into camp and returned the tins unopened. I shall never cease to marvel at the courage and decency of those men.

Toward the end of September we knew there was no hope for us unless we could find our way to Nichicun soon. The last reconnaissance trip was made by Theinhaus and Vanstone. They trudged off to the northwest one morning in a freezing rain, looking like animated mummies in their ragged clothes. They came back at dark the second night in terrible condition, drenched, cold, and exhausted, and fell into their bags more dead than alive. It had been the worst trip yet, but they brought word that sent hope rocketing in all of us.

From the top of a low mountain to the north they had sighted an arm of a big lake that they were sure was Nichicun. If they were right we knew at last where we were. The outline of our lake—indicating it was Patamisk—the lay of the country around it, and the lakes we had sighted to the north all supported their report. That would put us less than 10 miles south of the lower end of Nichicun, and some of us might still force ourselves to walk that far. When we reached Nichicun 50 miles of foot travel would still lie between us and the weather station, an impossible distance in our condition, but we could reduce it by building a raft and crossing the lake.

So we agreed on a desperate and agonizing plan. We would split the party and make the try. Abel and Koeten were beyond traveling and one man would have to stay behind with them. Since Levesque would be of little use without an interpreter, we'd have to keep him and Everitt together. Vanstone's boots were about gone. So we settled it. He would stay with Koeten and Abel. Theinhaus, Levesque, Everitt, and I would try to get through to the big lake. If we reached it and found it was not Nichicun we would return to camp. (That was a promise I know now we could never have kept.)

The weather was so bad we'd have to carry a shelter. We'd take the tent, leaving our bags behind. From the bags the three in camp would rig a cover on the half-chinked walls of the Indian structure. We would leave them the gun—only 12 shells remained—since without it they could not keep alive until help came. Since we'd have no way of hunting food, we'd take the bulk of the remaining rations, leaving behind four tins of fruit juice. Our share consisted of a handful of dry beans and three tins of beef. That would have to do for the four of us. It was a forlorn outlook, but we had nothing to lose.

When morning came I sent Levesque, Everitt, and Vanstone ahead to hunt and meet Theinhaus and me at the north end of our lake. There Vanstone would leave us and come back to camp with the gun.

It was a bleak, cold morning, with rain and snow falling. Theinhaus and I took down the tent and rolled it, shook hands with Abel and Koeten, and trudged away, not looking back. It had been a solemn, almost wordless parting and I did not expect to see either of them alive again.

Theinhaus and I had walked less than a quarter mile when I found I could not carry the wet tent. Without it we'd face nobody knew how many shelterless nights. It was a grim decision, but the tent was too heavy for either of us and we had no choice. We left it in an open place where Vanstone could find it easily, and went wearily on.

We reached the north end of our lake shortly after noon and found Everitt, Levesque, and Vanstone awaiting us. They had a fire going and they had good news. They had shot a partridge!

We discussed the disposition of the bird at length. It was desperately needed back at camp—but to the four men who were to march north it might make the difference between success and failure, and on that the lives of all seven depended. So in the end it was agreed we should take it.

I hated to say good-by to Vanstone. From the start he had been one of the best members of our team, carrying out every order cheerfully and volunteering for the hardest work. I watched him walk away with tears in my eyes.

The four of us walked steadily in wind and gloom until dark, and by that time our light loads—an ax, three paddles, two flare cartridges, 30 feet of rope for the raft we were to build, and our three precious tins of beef—had become an almost unbearable burden. We halted for the night at the spot where Theinhaus and Vanstone had camped on their last trip, built a fire, and laid up a bough shelter. We cooked and ate the partridge that evening. The portions were small but it was the best meal we'd had in many days.

We needed it. It snowed hard all night and the wind blew a gale. We lay huddled in the open lean-to, half frozen in our wet clothes, sleepless and terribly discouraged. It seemed as if morning would never come.

At daylight we warmed and spooned out the partridge broth, then slogged north once more, stumbling along like drunken men. That forenoon Levesque's legs started to give out. He could carry nothing, but Everitt called up some final reserve of strength and took Levesque's load, and we plodded painfully on.

We hoped that day's march would take us to the lower end of Nichicun. I realized the party would have to split again, for this evidently would be Levesque's last day on his feet. We'd have to leave him on the shore of the lake with Everitt while Theinhaus and I attempted the crossing on the raft—and Nichicun is 20 miles long!

The day was endless. We stumbled through deep gullies, crawled up hills, waded streams, staggered across one muskeg after another. Levesque complained frequently that his hands were cold, finally pulling a pair of socks over his gloves, and I knew the end was not far away for him.

Shortly after noon we reached the hill from which Theinhaus and Vanstone had sighted what they believed to be Lake Nichicun. We could see the distant water, gloomy and forbidding under gray storm clouds. It looked right for Nichicun. "We'll know tomorrow," we agreed.

Levesque could no longer keep up and we halted more and more often for brief rests. About 3 o'clock we heard the sudden hum of a plane. It grew louder and louder. "My God, he's coming over us!" somebody cried. We could see the ship, a big R.C.A.F. Lancaster, bearing down no more than 200 feet above the trees. I fumbled in my pack for our flares and fired one directly in front of him. The star shell streaked skyward, a faint spark in the daylight, and the plane thundered away. We waited numbly while its drone died out in the south, and no one said anything. In my whole life I have never known another minute of heartbreak and despair to match that one.

Less than 15 minutes later the impossible happened again. We heard him coming back. Again, as he roared by almost overhead, we sent a Very flare—our last—at him unseen. But somehow it didn't seem quite so bad that time. We hardly expected to draw his attention.

We heard aircraft to the south again toward dark but did not believe they were searching for us. We could not know that things had turned in our favor at last. R.C.A.F. Search and Rescue, which had called off the hunt earlier, had resumed it at the urging of our families and friends. And it had abandoned it again when our radio signals were no longer heard. Then, toward the end of September, Canada's minister of mines and technical surveys, George Prudham, had visited the iron properties at Fort Chimo. Mining men there had urged that another attempt be made to find us. Prudham put the wheels in motion and on October 1—the morning the four of us left the camp on Lake Emmanuel—the search planes took to the air again.

We had dragged ourselves to a hilltop when oncoming darkness halted our march that afternoon, still short of the big lake. Reluctantly we opened and ate one of our three small tins of beef, knowing we could go no farther without it. We kept a fire going and lay under a flimsy bough shelter that night, lashed by snow and a bitter wind. Nobody slept at all. It seemed we would never be able to sleep again. There was no breakfast next morning, not even partridge broth. Theinhaus and I set out at daybreak, without loads, leaving Levesque behind with Everitt. We intended to climb the hills in front of us and find out whether the lake was Nichicun.

We staggered to the crest of the last hill about 8 a.m. and looked down on a big, empty lake—but not big enough or dotted with sufficient islands. We stood staring at each other, stunned and wordless, aware that this was the end. There was nothing to do but go back to Everitt and Levesque, tell them the truth, and make ready for the march back to the three we had left.

We could never have made it, of course. Levesque could not walk now and we would not have abandoned him while he lived. By the time he no longer needed us, we'd be too far gone to travel, and death would soon follow. By then the three back at camp would have died too, and the bush would keep forever the secret of what had happened to us, for when the ice went out of Lake Emmanuel in the spring, the Norseman's waterlogged and ice-sprung floats would almost certainly carry it to the bottom.

Theinhaus and I broke the news to Levesque and Everitt, and the four of us decided first of all to try to scrape together a meal of frozen berries and reindeer moss. We were crawling around on hands and knees on the snowy hillside when we heard a plane coming from the south.

It was low, almost at treetop height, and it set us wild. There on the open hillside, with a fire still burning where we had spent the night, we'd have a chance of being seen. Theinhaus stumbled toward the fire to build up a smudge. Everitt and I ran for the crest of the hill, slipping and staggering, and I whipped off my shirt to make a signal flag. Even Levesque tottered to his feet and stood waving his arms like a grotesque human windmill.

As the plane came on I identified it as an R.C.A.F. Canso amphibian. It roared over the brink of the hill, barely clearing the trees. We kept on waving, and I saw Theinhaus piling the evergreen branches of our lean-to onto the fire.

The plane lumbered on a quarter mile while we waited in an agony of suspense. Then it came around in a wide turn and headed back, straight at us. We'd been found! The date was October 3, our 40th day in the bush.

This time a loudspeaker in the belly of the Canso shouted a message, "Stand by for a parachute drop!" The parcel came away and the orange chute blossomed and floated down. We ran to pick it up but the metal canister had hit a rock and the lid was jammed. There was an ax back at the fire and we stumbled that way. While we pried at the cover the plane came back and we heard the loudspeaker again: "Stay by your fire. We'll land on the lake and send a walking party in."

In the canister were chocolate and biscuits, dehydrated meat and salt, mittens and socks and moccasins. We ate the salt first of all!

When the food was gone I started slowly south to meet the walking party. The man in charge, Flying Officer Gary Williamson of Vancouver, B. C., was a bit ahead of the others. He and I met on an open hillside and he was within hailing distance before I saw him. I had not known until then that my eyes were giving out.

I suppose Williamson and I should have done something dramatic, but we didn't. All we did was shake hands and say "Hello." I guess we couldn't think of anything else.

I asked for a cigarette, and then I remembered Abel and Koeten and Vanstone. "What about the others?" I mumbled. "There are three more of us, back at our camp."

"They were found yesterday afternoon," Williamson told me. "They're on the way out now."

It turned out that the Lancaster which had missed us the day before had spotted our Norseman on Lake Emmanuel about an hour after flying over us. Unable to land on water, Squadron Leader Jack Woods had called in a Canso by radio. Abel and Koeten were huddled by the fire when the Lancaster came over, and Vanstone was half a mile away, searching for berries. Somehow he found the energy to run back toward camp, shouting wildly and waving his arms. He saw the two invalids dancing around the fire, hugging and kissing each other, while the plane circled overhead. He thought, "They look awful and I look awful, so I'm not hugging anybody." But he hugged them anyway.

Then the Canso came in and put down on the lake. When its pilot, Wilfred, came ashore in a portable boat, he reports, Abel met him and kissed him with a cigarette still in his mouth. But the three men refused to be taken out that day. Vanstone put it simply: "We want to be sure the four others are found." They spent their last night in the bush warm and well fed. Rescue had come for Koeten on his seventh wedding anniversary.

The alarm was already out for us. While Theinhaus and I had been making that last desperate trek across the hills next morning—only to find we were nowhere near Nichicun—nine planes were winging north from the R.C.A.F. base at Bagotville to search for us around Lake Emmanuel.

Levesque had to be carried half a mile to the plane. When we got there the crew had a steaming meal ready for us—milk, soup, and steaks. Real food was too much for me, and it came up about as fast as it went down. But that no longer mattered. I'd plenty of time to learn to eat again. Ahead were soft beds, medical care, showers, shaves, smokes, our families, home—all the things we had dreamed and talked about for so long.

The Canso lifted for the return flight and in minutes the heart-breaking miles we had trudged in those two final days were behind us and we were over Lake Emmanuel. The Norseman was gone. They had brought in gas and flown her out. I caught a last glimpse of our little clearing, empty, covered with new snow, no sign of life around it. It was hard to believe we had not dreamed those terrible weeks.

A reception awaited us at Bagotville that a movie queen would have envied, with a hushed crowd of about 200 clustered around the air station. There were reporters, press photographers, television men, and radio technicians. Flash bulbs started popping and microphones were shoved in front of us almost the instant we stepped out of the Canso. We hadn't realized what big news we'd be to a world that had waited 40 days for word of us.

There was an ambulance waiting, too, but only Levesque needed it. Theinhaus even managed a little jig on the landing platform as he stepped out.

It surprised me to find that the air-force doctors rated me in about as bad shape as Levesque. They ordered the two of us to bed at the base hospital and put us on a special diet, but pronounced me well at the end of three days and turned me out. Levesque was hospitalized only a little longer. Everitt also spent the week-end at the base, but as a walking patient.

We were all happy when the doctors said none of us were "bushed." In Canada the term means a man is bush-queer—off his rocker from living too long by himself in the woods, overwhelmed mentally by the immensity and loneliness of the country. That had not happened to any of us.

Vanstone, Abel, Koeten, and Theinhaus flew on to Montreal that same Saturday afternoon. Newspapermen who made the flight with them said it was easy to pick them out among the 47 passengers on the big airliner. They unwrapped sandwiches and peeled oranges all the way!

In the end none of us showed any lasting effects from our ordeal. I walked with a cane for a couple of months, but we all came out of it surprisingly well. Theinhaus and Koeten were back in Europe in a few days. Vanstone headed back to Toronto and school and his girl. Abel went home at once, as did Everitt, Levesque, and I when we were well enough.

Long before you read this we will all be back at our normal pursuits. But the bush will never look quite the same to any of us again, and we'll never wonder how the condemned feel when a last-minute reprieve comes through.

Look at Those Bass!

J. Harvey Jeffries

February 1955

"I go back," says Author Jeffries. "I cradle my plugcasting reel in my
left hand on each retrieve, guiding the line onto the reel with my thumb
and forefinger. My father started me baitcasting at six before reels
had refinements like line guides. He was a country doctor and infected
me with the only fever he couldn't cure—fishin' fever. I was born in
Ford, Kentucky, and later lived in Chevrolet! But Louisville has been
'home' since 1922. I got my BA from Louisville University and my MBA
from Harvard Business School in 1932. I worked for Jewel Tea Co., Inc.
until 1942 and then for Brown & Williamson Tobacco Corp.
until I retired in 1970 as Director of Marketing Research. For twenty-five
years I belonged to a unique association that fished the last week in
April and added a new member annually. Homer Circle dubbed us The
APES (April Piscatorial Endeavor Society). We fished all over the South
and Southwest. Billy Burns, also a member, still fishes for big bass whenever
he can get away from his two bluegrass farms. And, oh, yes, I still fly
fish occasionally on the Beaverkill Trout Club waters."

The dock was still some 200 yards ahead as we entered the channel. I cut the
motor, eased our respectable string of bass over the side, and began readying
tackle for our departure. It had been fun, these last two days. We'd been fishing
Dale Hollow Reservoir, that fabulous smallmouth lake on the Kentucky-Tennes-
see border.

Ferd, in the bow, called out, "Looks as if someone's in trouble at the dock—
must have a motor overboard." Intent on my own task, I didn't look up, but I
jumped with Ferd's terse, "It's fish. Look at those bass!"

It was fish—an almost unbelievable catch of smallmouth bass being lifted over
the side of the dock.

And so I first saw Billy Burns and was privileged to meet and know Kentucky's top black-bass fisherman.

Once in a great while a new or unexploited body of water will flare into
brilliance like a nova star—producing prize fish with regularity. And so it is with
Dale Hollow, created when U.S. government engineers built a power and
flood-control dam across the Obey River. Its deep, cool, clear waters seem
ideally suited for smallmouths. It's more than a guess to say that somewhere
in Dale Hollow's sparkling waters swims a new world-record smallmouth. In
fact, that's one reason that compels me to fish those waters so often.*

Wherever you find such fishing you'll hear tales of extraordinary fishermen.
Many of the tales are untrue, of course, and many are apocryphal, yarns that
you'll hear everywhere of things that never actually happened anywhere.

But the ones about Billy Burns are true. He has probably hooked and landed
more really big bass than any fisherman ever to wet a line in Dale. On many dif-

*The author was prophetic. On July 9, 1955, just five months after this story
appeared in OUTDOOR LIFE, David L. Hayes of Elizabethtown, Ky., caught a
smallmouth bass weighing 11 lbs. 15 oz. in Dale Hollow Lake that still stands as
the world record.—Ed.

ferent occasions Burns has brought in eight-fish strings of black bass averaging better than five pounds per fish. One such string, of smallmouths, averaged 6 pounds 5 ounces per bass.

And on March 10, 1950, fishing only from noon until dark, off a point in the Jolly Creek area of Dale Hollow, Burns took seven bass weighing as follows: 8 pounds 8 ounces; 8 pounds 6 ounces; 8 pounds 4 ounces; 7 pounds 15 ounces; 7 pounds 12 ounces; 7 pounds 10 ounces; 7 pounds 3 ounces— a total weight of 55 pounds 10 ounces, or an average of 7 pounds 15 ounces per fish.

Billy Burns lives in Lexington, in the center of the famed Bluegrass area of Kentucky, a Mecca for bass fishermen. Here, about 1810, watchmaker George Snyder built the first multiplying casting reel.

In this same general area E. H. Peckinpaugh developed the first cork-bodied bass bug; and most of those safe, efficient, fishing boats on our Great Lakes of the South today are patterned after boats engineered by fishermen of the Bluegrass area. It's a region steeped in the tradition of bass fishing, and Burns is giving that tradition a boost.

He has the scientific approach. I asked him early in our acquaintanceship, "Billy, how come you catch so many more big bass than other fishermen do?" When he replied, "I fish for big fish," I glanced at him, expecting a smile. He was dead serious, and later I came to know exactly what he meant. Burns is constantly experimenting to locate big bass and find out what will interest them.

Take his Dale Hollow discovery, for instance. On one of Tennessee's wonderfully promising days in late March, he and I were fishing Dale Hollow just after a cloudburst dumped five inches of rain in 24 hours and turned the lake—usually crystal-clear— a definite saffron color. Only the jig fishermen were doing anything with the Hollow's big bass. We weren't interested in jigging, so we decided to run the 20 miles to the headwaters of the lake and fish the Obey River itself for wall-eyes. As we fished through that lazy, early-spring day with the sun warming our backs, Billy started talking in his quiet, almost shy way about his first limit string of Dale Hollow's lunker bass.

Fishing alone—as he usually does when his college-age son, Bobby, can't get away to be with him—Billy was casting a point with a heavy, deep-running plug. To sink the wide-lipped plug even deeper, he was retrieving at an extremely rapid rate. All at once the plug hit an underwater tree stump, bounced up—and Billy was fast to a smallmouth which, when boated, weighed over six pounds.

Billy anchored his boat and continued casting and retrieving in the same fast manner, bumping the plug off the bottom and through the bushy stumps. He hooked and landed his limit of those overgrown bass before the day was over.

A few days later Burns proved to himself that the first catch was no accident by catching four more big ones off the same point with the same tactics. And in the months that followed, fishing every minute he could be away from his tobacco farm, he discovered another point on the lake where he could catch those monster smallmouths.

Billy was totally unprepared for the furor which followed his fabulous catches. First excitement and admiration—then ugly rumors. Burns was using wing nets or gill nets, some said. Others suspected he was snatching fish off the rocky points with gang hooks, or hand-grabbing them in the headwaters of the Obey.

All who knew Burns as the true sportsman that he is—the man who coached the basketball team from tiny Midway, Kentucky, to the state championship in 1937 and to whom fair play is almost a fetish—tried to stop the wild stories. But they persisted to such an extent that on February 19, 1949, Tennessee game wardens asked Burns to show them how he was catching the big fish.

Billy, hurt and angered, refused to take the officers into his boat. He did tell them which point he'd fish that day. The officers watched through glasses from a bluff above it and saw him hook and boat four bass weighing from 5 to 7½ pounds each.

Late that afternoon Burns "discovered" his third hot spot for lunkers, and in the next two years he found five more.

With the same scientific approach used to increase the yield on his tobacco farm—and in formulating basketball plays until he retired from coaching in 1944—Billy studied the how and why of his record catches.

He noted that almost all his big bass were coming off much flatter-shelving points than the steep ones previously favored. But he couldn't understand why, of two almost identical points, one produced big bass and the other gave up only small fish. Then, in the fall of 1951, a drought and a heavy demand on Dale Hollow's power facilities left the reservoir unusually low. Billy Burns walked the exposed land on those points and found his answer.

In profile, every big-fish point sloped gently for 40 to 50 feet under the normal waterline, then dipped sharply—just as though a stream had cut its way across. Billy's big bass came from these ravines, whereas all the unrewarding points sloped smoothly.

Bushes six to ten feet tall lined each side of the ravines, bushes formed by sprouts from tree stumps left after the timber was cleared from the area to be flooded. Burns was bouncing his plug through these bushes on his big-fish points.

"But don't you lose an awful lot of plugs that way?" I asked.

"I did at first," said Billy. "Used to buy 'em by the dozen, but now I have a system which works pretty well—two identical casting outfits. I fish with one until it's hung, then I turn to the second. When it too snags, I pull the boat close and use my plug knocker. That way I don't scare the fish in the hole so often, and I don't lose many plugs."

Billy also found out at low water why big fish could be taken off one point only by casting out and retrieving toward shore, while another point produced only when approached from the side or by casting in toward the point from a boat out in the lake. The lure had to get into the "dip" to produce.

During this day together Billy mentioned that he didn't catch as many big fish now as he did several years ago.

"Fewer fish?" I asked.

"Oh, no, there're undoubtedly more big bass in Dale now than ever before. I'm just getting too old to take it," he said. I thought that a rather odd statement from a man I'd judge to be in his middle 40's. I didn't realize its significance until we were on the way back to the dock—with our limit of wall-eyes, thanks to Billy's knowledge of where the high water had hidden the riffles of the river bottom.

A couple of miles short of the dock Billy shut off the 10-horse motor and we drifted in to a gently sloping point. It was late afternoon; the sun had set, and storm clouds covered the sky. It was spitting rain.

"Here's a really good point, not one of my secret five, but a 'big' one nevertheless. We aren't likely to catch bass in this muddy water, but I'll show you how it's done." He pulled the boat 100 feet off the point, then turned and cast out into the lake. The heavy plug sailed out farther than I could cast—and I've done a bit of plugging. Then Billy brought the lure in literally as fast as he could reel, and every 10 feet or so of retrieve he'd rear back and pump the lure to send it into a fast dive.

I fished with him for some 15 minutes, and then I knew what Burns meant about not taking it any more. My light, sporty reel froze with the unaccustomed strain, but not before my arms were dead tired and I was ready to say uncle.

Billy uses a stiff-action rod and the heaviest fresh-water reel he can buy; he has fitted a star-drag mechanism to the reel. He showed me two lures, utterly different in action from the deep-traveling plug he fishes most often, which he has found successful. One is a spinner-and-bucktail combination. The other, a locally made shad-minnow imitation with a very "tight" action under a fast retrive, weighs more than an ounce.

I put aside my rod and reel and picked up the camera. If the growing darkness would permit, I wanted a picture of Burns in action. How he powered those long casts; how fast he really did retrieve the plug, and especially I wanted a picture of that two-handed jerk, he gave the rod at every six turns or so of the reel handle.

I ran out the roll in the camera and was reaching for the gadget bag and more film when Billy said, "Got him!"

Sure enough he was fast to a fish—a heavy one, from the way Billy was giving line.

Feverishly I worked at reloading the camera. If it was a smallmouth, he was almost sure to jump—and I wanted to be ready. Almost immediately Burns yelled, "He's coming up. Here's your picture!" I turned, and the finest small-mouth I've ever seen on the end of a line burst from the water, turned completely over, and headed back down. My hands were trembling. I had trouble completing the camera-loading job. But I was too late anyway. The smallmouth didn't jump again.

Burns played it masterfully. As soon as he felt it was solidly hooked he picked up the paddle and—sculling with his left hand—started slowly for deep water. He kept a constant, moderate pressure on the fish. Frequently he gave line.

Billy says playing a big fish with the paddle, so to speak, makes double sense—wears him out faster and gets him into deeper water, where there's less danger of snagging the line on an underwater rock or stump.

He almost never uses a landing net. He says a net in the boat tempts him to try and land a big bass before it's completely played out. Smallmouths especially—because of their tremendous power and fight—are often lost at the net.

It was nine minutes by my watch before that bass came in to the boat on his side and Burns felt it was licked. He reached down, gripped it by the lower jaw —thumb outside its mouth, fingers inside—and lifted it in.

On the official scales at the dock five minutes later, the smallmouth weighed seven pounds four ounces. Burns had delivered—even in that cloudburst-mud-died water.

I'm a tobacco-company executive, not a writer, but the things I learned about G. L. (Goldman Luther) Burns were too interesting to pass up. Grads of Tran-sylvania College, Lexington, Kentucky, will tell you he was an outstanding athlete there from 1923 to 1926, playing football, basketball, baseball, and tennis. And photographic evidence of his prowess as a fisherman hangs on the wall of a Dale Hollow fishing camp. But Billy himself is not one to parade his accomplishments. He fishes only because he's happy doing it, and what he does—basketball coach-ing, tobacco farming, fishing, or whatever—he tries to do exceedingly well.

He usually fishes alone, and comes and goes quietly. Get him to talk, though, and he modestly says anyone who'll fish the Hollow as carefully as he does can bring back the same kind of catches.

Typically, Burns hasn't stopped experimenting. On my latest trip with Billy the water was quite low, exposing some of the sprouts that are slowly decaying underwater. Burns, during drought levels, is cutting fresh bushes and wiring them on the old stumps around his favorite points.

A Tiger Has Killed

Jack O'Connor

November 1955

Jack O'Connor made his first tiger hunt in 1955, and his first story, "This Terror of Asia," ran in October. Some say there isn't much to shooting a tiger, but the October story belies them. Jack hunted with Lee Sproul, and the first week they heard tigers roar and saw tiger tracks, but no tigers. Then on a night deer hunt by jeep they caught the briefest glimpse of baleful green eyes in a spotlight. Another day, they sat in trees while beaters sought to drive a tiger out, but it slipped away at the side. After a night in a machan, O'Connor reluctantly took a shot at a cat so badly spotlighted he couldn't distinguish stripes from bush shadows. It got away with a flesh wound. Finally, with boys in trees as "stops" on either side of a gulch, elephants drove another cat toward O'Connor and Sproul standing fifty yards apart. The cat came out on Sproul's side and he got it. Now read Part 2.

Anyone who has ever been in the Salt River Valley of Arizona has a pretty good notion what the tiger country near Kashipur, in northern India, looks like. Actually a man who has grown up in any of the irrigated valleys of the West could go to the land around Kashipur and imagine he was home. When I first saw it I was struck by its resemblance to the country around Phoenix when I was a kid, or to the flat, irrigated valleys of Utah and southern Idaho.

Near Kashipur there are big feathery trees, most of which are figs but which at a distance look like the great cottonwoods of the irrigated Southwest. And there are fields of sugar cane and golden wheat stubble and green row crops, and narrow dusty country lanes and little mud-and-wattle villages that look not unlike the adobe and ocotillo huts of Mexico. And there are little wandering creeks and shallow rivers, big patches of reeds along the banks, and occasional patches of jungle, the way there used to be a few acres of mesquite forest along the river-banks in southern Arizona years ago.

The jungles may be small, but spotted axis deer live in them, and so do monkeys and peacocks and jungle fowl and beautiful little long-tailed parakeets, as green as jade is green, and little birds so incredibly blue they seem fragments of some distant magic sky. And beyond the yellow of the reeds and the pale straw of the stubble fields and the green of trees and hedgerows, blue serrated foothills rise; and beyond them, remote and delicate, often sensed rather than seen, are the great Himalayas.

It is a thickly populated country, a land of many villages. Often one little group of huts is so close to the next that a man with a strong voice can make himself heard from one village to the next. It is a land of many noises, great and small—the lowing of the creamy, humpbacked sacred cattle of India, the barking of dogs, the cackling of hens, the bleating of goats, the shrill babble of children, the singing of women at work. Children drive herds of water buffaloes and cattle to graze in the grass and in the jungles. Peasant farmers harvest their grain with sickles not much more efficient than pocketknives.

But when I first saw this country, I was bitter with disappointment. Tigers here? Preposterous! A man might as well look for a tiger among the flower beds of some American suburban home. Tigers among all these people, tigers in the midst of these farms and right next door to the villages? Don't make me laugh!

In northern India tigers may be hunted in the national forests only the last two weeks each month. When we landed at Kashipur we had just completed 14 days of hunting in the foothills of the Himalayas. My companion, Lee Sproul, had shot a tiger. I had seen the eyes of another by spotlight and one night, shooting from a tree by flashlight at a tiger behind a bush, I had scratched its cheek with a .375 Magnum bullet. Lee and I had sat through dreary nights in machans. We had driven with men and with elephants. We had prowled the high-grass country at night on elephantback with spotlight. Still I had no tiger.

Two weeks in supposedly fine tiger country, and I was as without a trophy as if I had done my tiger hunting in New York's Central Park. My amigo Herb Klein had hunted a couple of weeks near Nagpur, India, and had shot five tigers. Another friend, Prince Abdorreza Pahlavi of Iran, in still another part of India, had taken eight in the same length of time. I had come more than halfway around the world for a tiger and I might as well have stayed at home to shoot woodchucks.

So now the three of us—Lee Sproul, our outfitter A. D. Mukerji, and I—were driving through this alleged tiger country in our asthmatic jeep after a night in a government resthouse in Kashipur. Bullock carts loaded with wheat straw or sugar cane turned creaking off the dusty roads to let us by. Village dogs yapped at us. Scrubby chickens fled cackling from our path.

We were going to meet the three faithful elephants that had made the long trek down from the foothills, where we had used them for driving. If by some remote chance there happened to be a tiger in this improbable place, it was absolutely necessary that elephants be used. The cover was too thick for humans.

But fat chance! I had about as much faith in finding a tiger there as I had of seeing my Aunt Gertrude go riding by on a white horse playing Lady Godiva and wearing nothing but pink tights and a blond wig.

Then suddenly, in the dust, beside the road, I saw great round tracks—or pug marks, to use the correct Anglo-Indian term.

"Stop," I yelled. "Tiger tracks!"

The jeep wheezed and clattered to a stop. While we were inspecting the tracks an excited native came running up and began to chatter Hindustani to Mukerji.

"What does he say?" I asked.

"He says if we're hunting tigers to come and shoot one out of his cane field. He says a big one (possibly the one that made this track) killed a bullock last night and dragged it into the cane. Now when anyone goes near it, it growls and the men are afraid."

"What did I tell you?" said Mukerji. "Lots of tigers."

And there were, as improbable as it may sound. Down from the foothills, along with the elephants and their pilots or mahouts (pronounced ma-hoots), had come our crew of shikaris (native scouts and hunters), as well as other mysterious characters who scratched the elephants' tummies and performed other obscure chores. When we joined them they were all jumping with excitement.

"Tell the Old Sahib (pronounced s.o.b.) that he's sure to get his tiger," they chorused. "There are tigers everywhere. We're up to our hips in tigers!"

When we boiled it down, we found that after their arrival the afternoon before, they had discovered tracks in the dusty little roads of a tigress and two cubs and of a middle-size male tiger, all of whom lived in a big cane patch. There was another male, they said, that made his headquarters not far from the riverbank. Down in the reeds and the high grass of the riverbank lurked the largest tiger of them all. To judge from the signs they made with their hands, his pug marks were only slightly smaller than those of a bull elephant. And then upstream a couple of miles there lived an ornery old lady tiger who had somehow lost her cubs.

All told, about nine tigers lived along the river bottom there right among the farms. It was a chummy arrangement and for the tigers a very convenient one. During the day they'd bed down in the reeds beside the stream, and when night fell they'd go hunting. Now and then they killed an axis deer in a patch of jungle, and occasionally they'd devour a hog deer out in the short-grass flats.

But mostly they simply ate cattle, so many that the native Indians felt that they were in the chips if they could bring more than half their calves to maturity. Tigers were to be endured—like flies, drought, typhoid, children, mosquitoes, and other catastrophes. Old Shere the Tiger was to them as natural as rain and stars and sunsets, as much to be expected as the hot dry winds of April and May and the torrential monsoon rains of late June and July.

Now and then a farmer would come face to face with a tiger when he went early to his field, or some children after birds' nests would report that they had blundered into Old Stripes in his bed and had been growled at. Always the villagers would see tiger tracks in the roads and in the fields and practically every day some tiger would take a cow or a buffalo.

For the most part such an arrangement is almost friendly. The people leave the tigers alone and the tigers leave the people alone. Of course the tigers take their toll of cattle but that's only to be expected, as the way of a tiger with a cow, like the way of man with a maid, has been going on since the world began.

But now and then a sport from town or some local shikari takes a poke at a tiger, usually with buckshot fired from some rusty old Spanish single-barreled shotgun. Sometimes he actually kills the tiger, but more often he wounds it. Many times the magnificent creature slinks away, to die of infection and to be found only when the vultures drop to the carcass, but very often the tigers are crippled or slowed down by the wounds, so they are not powerful enough to kill cattle or fleet enough to catch deer. Then they turn man-eater. When we were hunting in the Kashipur area three man-eaters were said to be within a radius of 30 miles.

We were really in tiger country now! In order to get our quarry located, we bought a supply of buffalo calves and staked them out in spots where tigers were likely to pass. Almost every morning a shikari would come peddling up to our resthouse on a bicycle and announce dramatically, "A tiger has killed!"

But we were to discover that even in this odd and excellent tiger country there is many a slip between tiger and rug. Take the lady tiger and her two cubs in the cane patch, for example:

The very first night, she walked out of the field, spied one of our calves, killed it, and dragged it back into the cane to feed her half-grown young. The circling vultures told us where the kill lay, and that she was still on it, or so near that the birds were afraid to come down. We built two machans by a lane through the cane, perched upon them, sent the elephants in to drive. Did we see any of the three tigers we knew were there? We did not! If we'd had a dozen elephants we might have pushed some out. As it was, the wise old gal and her cubs simply sneaked around our elephants. The next night she killed another one of our calves.

And there was the case of a the big male tiger in the patch of jungle.

It looked as if getting him would be a cinch. All the villagers could tell us where he lived, when he had killed last, which path he usually took to his night's hunting. Our shikaris tied a calf out. The tiger killed it. The fact that the vultures were perched hungrily in trees in the middle of that little patch of jungle showed us where the tiger was.

It all looked very easy. Tigers are used to the noise of the natives, and when they bed down for the day they stay put. Our men went about preparing for the drive as nonchalantly as if they were building extra bleachers for the world series. They tied two native beds called charpoys upside down in trees to serve as machans. They put sheets of newspaper on bushes so that they would flutter and frighten the tiger to keep him on the desired line of retreat. The men who were to serve as lookouts or "stops" climbed their trees with shouts of glee. It was like boy-scout day at the county fair.

Finally, when all was set, Mukerji and I climbed into one machan (the one where the tiger was most likely to pass, since I still had not shot a tiger), while Lee and an Anglo-Indian named Joe Hardy, who'd joined our party as a guide, climbed into another.

Then the drive began, and the little jungle became suddenly hushed and quiet. This was it. This was drama! The three elephants formed a line and worked the place over, patch by patch. Every time they'd come to a particularly thick bit the line would halt and one of the elephants would go into it, knock down shrubs, shake trees. All was quiet except for the crash of underbrush, the occasional crack of a limb.

Nearer and nearer came the slow, relentless crash of the elephants.

Then one of the stops high in a tree yelled, "The tiger is coming. I see him ahead of the elephants!" Then another cried, "The tiger tried to sneak out, but saw a paper and turned back."

I had a fairly good field of view of 35 or 40 yards. The elephants were about 75 yards away now and my heart was in my throat. Old Stripes was on his way and he was—at long last—my meat.

Then all at once, to my right where Lee's machan was located, I heard the sharp blast of his .35 Whelen and looked up to see a tiger sprawl on the ground for an instant and then get up and take off.

In a zoo a tiger looks orange-yellow. See one in the shade and he likewise looks quite orange. But see a big wild tiger in the sunlight and he's bright red. And so it was with this tiger. He had tumbled at the shot, but in an instant he was up and galloping through the brush and tall grass like a scarlet streak.

Lee took another crack at him and so did Joe. From our machan Mukerji let fly with both barrels of a shotgun loaded with 12 gauge ball. By the time I could duck around him, the tiger's front end was disappearing into another patch of jungle, but I swung the crosshairs in the scope on the .375 Magnum ahead of the fleeting cat and blasted off with the same results.

Poor Lee! He felt as low as a man caught pilfering funds for the orphans' home. His machan, where the tiger was not supposed to pass, had been too close to the brush. The elephants were almost upon him, so he had decided that the tiger had slipped out or that it was my time to get the shot. Then all at once the big cat had burst out of the brush within 20 feet of him, traveling like a turpentined tom. Lee had only time to throw his scope-sighted .35 Whelen down between his legs and shoot when it seemed to be pointed in the right direction.

We scrambled down out of the trees and ran to the spot where the tiger had disappeared. A few drops of blood that looked as if they'd come from a muscle wound glittered red on the yellow grass, and I discovered where my .375 bullet had plowed through the brush.

The elephants were lumbering up when suddenly Lee wheeled and yelled, "There it is!" Apparently the tiger had gone into the first dense patch it could find and had lain down, because later the sign told us that Lee had indeed seen the tiger and that it was probably only scratched, possibly along the flank.

But nevertheless we mounted our elephants, and while we covered the ground in front our shikaris tracked . . . and tracked . . . and tracked. All that afternoon we stayed on the looping trail of the tiger. Sometimes we could see a little blood, and occasionally we found where he had laid down to rest. Then there might be a puddle of blood the size of a dollar. The feeling grew that his wound was superficial. But we didn't want to give up as long as there was any chance we might come upon him.

As the day wore on it became hotter and hotter and Lee and I got thirstier and thirstier. The animal's trail wound back and forth across a clean, cool-looking little stream that was shaded by lovely jungle trees, by tall grass and reeds. Now and then the boys would pile off the elephants and fill up with water. They had never heard of germs and water-borne diseases. Mukerji had, as he is an educated man, but he is an Indian and to a great extent immune to the frightful ailments that seem to lie in wait for the unwary American or European in any unboiled water in India.

Lee and I drooled at sight of the voluptuous water but we knew that dysentery would get us if we drank it. So we simply suffered.

Once a shikari reported a cobra. Another time we flushed out a wild sow and a litter of young, and once we flushed a leopard (which in India is always called a panther). But we didn't want to shoot the sow and couldn't have shot the leopard. Finally the tiger's wound stopped bleeding. We gave up and went back to the jeep, where some boiled water awaited us.

Almost every day tigers killed our baits, and almost every day we drove. But nothing happened. We scared the daylights out of generations of monkeys, moved a good many axis deer, wild boar, and peafowl. But tigers? Not a one.

The big tiger that lived down by the river was a particularly irritating character. Our shikaris staked out so many buffalo calves that he couldn't stir from his reed patch without running into one. But he'd just pass them by.

One morning a shikari came to gather the calves that had been quaking all night with the acrid smell of tiger in their noses. He heard the tiger's heavy tread in the reeds to his left. Presently he heard the great beast taking a bath in the little creek, grunting and splashing like a fat old man. Finally he heard the tiger go off about 50 yards and lie down.

The shikari was so certain he knew where the tiger had bedded that we tried a drive. I was perched in a tree overlooking a road the cat would have to cross, but I saw no tiger. A magnificent wild boar, the largest I saw in India, came trotting by, and later a couple of little hog deer sneaked past, heads down and almost crawling.

Time passed. The elephants belonged to some bush-league maharaja. He wanted them back, as he was throwing a shoot for some butter-and-egg men from New Delhi. We stalled the maharaja, crossed the palms of the elephant men. Came the time when we had but two more days to hunt, as the maharaja had threatened something very drastic and oriental unless he got his elephants back soon. If someone had offered me a few rupees that morning for my chance at a tiger, I probably would have sold out.

For breakfast Lee and I had watery oatmeal flavored with gray Indian sugar and diluted with pale blue boiled milk from a starving humpbacked cow. We drank a cup of ersatz powdered coffee and then tried to kill the taste with the wonderful Indian oranges which were both food and drink to us.

Then we heard excited yells outside the resthouse. Mukerji burst in. "The big tiger has killed!" he said, beaming. "The one by the reed bed!"

To me it seemed like an omen. Surely the fates couldn't dangle another tiger in front of my face and then jerk it away. . . .

We really prepared for this drive, and I was delighted to find that the terrain looked like the best for us and the worst for the tiger of any we'd tried in India. The grass the tiger would come out of was tall—just about as high as a tiger's back—but there was a good tree for a machan and I could shoot down. The belt of high reeds by the creek where the vultures told us the tiger lay was narrow enough so that it would be beaten nicely by three elephants.

So this was it.

To make sure there'd be no slip-up Mukerji had loaded the three elephants with all manner of odd local characters. He had armed some with shotguns they were to shoot off to add to the noise and thus help move the tiger.

Tensely I waited for the elephants to do their job, but the beasts came all the way to the machan without moving anything except a few peafowl and a couple of hog deer. I was sick with disappointment.

Then Mukerji and the mahouts had a big argument. Mukerji wanted them to drive again, closer to the creek. The mahouts said it was unnecessary—that if a tiger had been there it would have moved. Not knowing anything about it, I was nevertheless inclined to agree with them.

Finally Mukerji got them to try again. Once more the three lumbering elephants came through the reeds, but this time farther to the left. Again the whooping and the hollering. Again the shotguns, fired off to move the tiger. Again the swish of elephants.

All at once I saw something big and red and round above the grass in front of the elephants. It couldn't be the great massive head of a big he-tiger, but it was. And then the great beast was loping through the grass, quartering but coming gradually closer. At times he was just about out of sight, but at the top of his bounds I could see him well, a massive male tiger shining red in the sun—red as a new copper penny, red as an Irish setter, red as blood.

My first two shots went right over the top of his back because I shot at him on the top of his bound, but on the third shot I made myself shoot a bit ahead and low into the grass. I heard the bullet go thunk and I knew I'd hit him hard and solid, probably in the rib cage. He staggered for a moment then and slowed, but didn't go down. He was dead on his feet, though I didn't know it. Careless of the elephants, he turned and staggered back toward the reeds that so long had sheltered him. He went into the reeds and down into the nullah where ran the cool little stream where he had drunk so often after killing.

But his lungs were full of blood, and he couldn't make it up the far bank. Suddenly I heard the death cry of the mighty tiger. I had never heard it but I knew what it was. It made my breath catch and tears come. It was part roar, part shriek, part lament. Then he collapsed and fell over backward, dead.

I scrambled down off the machan and ran to the spot where my great trophy had fallen. Already the elephants had come up, and some of the beaters had gathered around it. He lay there striped and beautiful, orange-red and black. He was as large as a small horse, and between the ears he was wider than the shoulders of a big man. As I stood there looking at the great gorgeous cat crumpled in death, I was a little sad and half-embarrassed. I'd have his hide tanned and his head mounted. I'd spend the rest of my life with him, yet I hardly knew him.

We measured him later—properly, since tiger measurements don't tell much less the job's done right. A man might say he killed a 10-foot tiger, meaning that's what the tape read after the animal was skinned and the hide stretched. Actually, his 10 feet would shrink to less than eight according to the "official" method of measuring big cats.

That is to lay the beast on his side, drive a peg in at the nose and one in at the end of the last tail bone, then roll the carcass away and measure the distance between the two pegs—not from center to center—with a steel tape. (Some people measure from peg to peg with the animal still in place, but obviously to lay the tape "over the curves" as it's called, adds maybe eight inches to the reading.)

Correctly measured, my Indian tiger went nine feet nine and was distinctly larger and heavier than my African lion, which my outfitter Don Ker said was the longest he'd ever measured (nine feet seven).

In his book The Tigers of Trengganu, Lt. Col. A. Locke says he thinks the standard for Indian tigers can best be set by the "Bachelor of Powalgarh," which figures in the late Jim Corbett's classic Man Eaters of Kumaon. Locke calls the Bachelor, hunted season after season by sportsmen because of its great size, "truly a king among tigers" but adds that when measured by Corbett and his sister it went, not 12 feet but 10 feet seven inches over curves.

"This animal," Locke concludes, "would probably have been about 10 feet if measured between pegs. I doubt very much whether so experienced a sportsman as Corbett would have regarded this tiger as an exceptional specimen had it not been unusually big even for India."

Getting back to my old he-tiger of Kashipur, he was one big tiger, as you can tell from looking at his photo. I think he's the biggest tiger I've ever seen a picture of.

It didn't take me long to find the bullet hole. It was a bit high, a trifle too far back, but a good solid lung shot nevertheless. With a hit like that from a 270-grain, soft-point bullet from a .375 Magnum he should have gone down in a hurry. He didn't. Tigers are tough, and if I ever shoot another I'll use the lion medicine of Syd Downey, the African white hunter—a .416 or a .470 soft point.

Now that the tiger was dead we were all a little drunk with excitement. The mahouts and shikaris whooped and yelled. One of the shikaris who'd been fasting to bring me luck, and whom I called Dopey the Dwarf because of his resemblance to the Disney character, became hysterical and wept. He said that if he died now he'd die happy because his poor old gentleman (me) had shot that wonderful tiger, the largest, fattest, finest tiger ever to live in northern India.

And so we put him on an elephant and we all rode in triumph through the villages to the jeep. The people cheered, the dogs barked, and the bullocks hitched to a cart in a wedding party smelled the tiger and ran away. The scared little brown bride got thrown out on the ground, and for a moment it looked as if an international incident was in the making. But when Lee and I passed around five-rupee banknotes, the people bowed and said the American sahibs weren't so bad after all.

And that night we had two more drinks than usual before dinner. Even the curry tasted good!

The Gamest Fish of All

Roderick Haig-Brown

March 1956

Roderick Haig-Brown is known as one of the world's ten most famous fishermen. Born in England in 1908, he emigrated to Canada when he was seventeen and worked variously as a logger, trapper, guide and fisherman, and came to know the salmon and trout he writes about with such authority. Haig-Brown now lives in Campbell River, British Columbia, where he writes and fishes when not acting as provincial magistrate and judge of Family and Children's Court. Among his many books are *A River Never Sleeps, Fisherman's Winter, Fisherman's Spring* (*Summer* and *Fall*, too) and *Saltwater Summer*. For the last he received the Canadian Governor General's citation for literature. Other awards include the Crandall Conservation Trophy and a National Award in Letters from the University of Alberta. And he has written other OUTDOOR LIFE stories.

The fighting qualities of gamefish are always a matter for lively discussion among fishermen. The talk can lead to pious exaggeration, extravagant prose, written and spoken, and tales calculated to scare the boldest child away from water of any kind. It may even develop into sharp debate and shattered friendships or, in extreme cases, to physical violence, all of which are far from the ideals of the gentle sport.

North American disputes seldom attain the vitriolic heights of those periodically revived between fictional Salmo S. Stuffinton, Lt. Col. (Ret.), and E. Lucius Upanasdic, Comdr. R.N. (Ret.) in the correspondence columns of British sport magazines. But when equally fictional Cyrus K. Bass of America's Midwest clashes with Joe Ironhead of the Pacific Coast, things can get pretty hot.

I think it's a pity that we fishermen have allowed ourselves to get into the habit of using the word "fight" so freely in connection with our sport and our quarry. Our sense of humor has slipped so far that we see nothing ridiculous in the idea of a 200-pound man "fighting" a two-pound trout or bass. We talk about "battles" with 10-pound salmon and delight in words like "lunkers" and "tackle busters." Some of us even call our fish "ferocious sluggers," and "savage warriors," "racing broncos" as though the spirit shown by Joe Louis, Genghis Khan, or a fire-breathing stallion stirred under their scales.

Yes, I know; it's all a matter of proportion—just a convention of extravagance long ago sanctified by habit and usage. Every fisherman knows how to discount it and come up with the right answers. But it is a misleading convention which tends to obscure the real delights of the sport by distorting them, and to promote argument that disturbs the peace of the brotherhood.

The truth is that a two-pound fish does not fight a 200-pound angler. It fights the clinging hook and the restraint of the two-pound-test line, and even then the noblest and most exciting part of the fish's reaction is flight, not fight. The fisherman's pleasure is in the power, speed, and acrobatics of the flight, not in any ferocity of attack or fear for his own safety, as the excitable convention would have us believe. His skill is in yielding to flight, in guiding it where it can do least damage to his tackle, and in using it to tire the fish until it can be controlled and led to beach or net.

If one thinks in terms of speed, strength, and activity rather than of ferocity and pugnacity, it becomes easier to sort out and evaluate the ramifications of dispute. It becomes clear at once that the relative strength of tackle, the conditions of waters in which fish live, and, above all, the condition of the individual fish itself are immensely important and may easily outweigh differences between species.

Over and above these factors are the personal preferences and prejudices of the angler. Nearly all of us are inclined to favor the gamest fish of our youthful memories. Some of us are more impressed by a fish that jumps a lot than by one that runs fast or seems determined to seek out snags and weeds. Others give credit to a strong, sulky fish, or one that makes many short rushes instead of one or two long ones. Still others feel that everything depends on a few quick, uncontrollable moments immediately after the strike. A select few well-known anglers, insisting that nothing matters after the strike, make a practice of disdainfully handing their rods to friends or guides as soon as they have set the hook.

I'm far from immune to preferences and prejudices. I love salmon and trout practically to the exclusion of other fish. I admire a fast, top-of-the-water fish that takes off the moment he feels the hook and jumps at least once before I can collect my wits. And I believe that the most fascinating part of fishing is the strike and all that leads up to it, rather than the playing of a fish after it's hooked. But I shall try to be fair in the comments I am going to make.

The most important single factor responsible for the performance of a gamefish is likely to be the fish's physical condition. A fish that is full of roe or milt, or one that is recovering from recent spawning activity, cannot be expected to show the speed and violent motion it would have had a few months earlier or will have a few months later. Obviously, then, it is unfair to compare performances among fish without taking this into account. Generally speaking, a fish that has never spawned will be stronger and more active than a fish of similar size that has spawned.

A fish hooked in a fast stream has every chance to perform better than one hooked in a lake or a quiet pool. A fish that has spent all its life in a stream or lake will take better and quicker advantage of obstructions than will a migratory fish. A fish hooked in a shallow stretch is likely to run faster and farther than one hooked in deep water. A fish so wary that an angler must use extremely light tackle is bound to be exciting and difficult to land, even though he may not be as active as one that is easier to fool.

A fish hooked on a fly has a better chance to show his quality than one hooked on larger or heavier bait. The position of the hook's hold makes a difference; a lightly hooked fish always seems to jump quicker and oftener than one that is solidly hooked. A soft-mouthed fish like a grayling can be as difficult to handle as a much more active fish that has a tough mouth. And, to make comparisons still harder, individual fish of the same species, hooked under apparently identical conditions, can vary more in performance than two fish of different species.

I have the greatest respect for the brown trout. He's the remembered fish of my youth, and has taught me more about fly fishing than any other fish. Of all the trouts and salmons, he is the most exacting in the conditions he sets as to tackle, and he is the most determined in seeking the shelter of weeds and snags when he feels the hook.

Often it is necessary to go after brown trout with a fly hook less than a quarter of an inch long and with a leader that breaks at less than a one-pound strain. Feeding between two familiar weed beds or within a few feet of some favorite tangle of brush and pilings, a good brown trout is a formidable problem on such gear. It is as likely to fool an angler and break his gear as is a more forthright, vigorous fish hooked in open water.

The best chance I've had of comparing brown trout with other fish was in South America two or three years ago. Browns were often side by side in streams with rainbows, eastern brook trout, and landlocked salmon. They were noticeably slower and less active than either rainbows or salmon, though superior to the brooks. Yet I remember one brown that must have jumped at least a dozen times, so rapidly that he seemed to be tailwalking across the river. I also remember two or three others, big fish, that jumped right into the air as they took my fly in fast water.

A cutthroat trout is rather like a brown of comparable size, though usually stronger and more inclined to jump. Searun cutthroats have fooled me by running and jumping until I was convinced they were rainbows. But they lose this vigor soon after entering fresh water, and then are rather slow and sullen performers and grudging jumpers, though still powerful. They seldom give in as easily and completely as do brown and brook trout.

I think it's safe to say that rainbows, whether landlocked in lakes, resident in streams, or fresh-run steelheads returning from the sea, are incomparably the fastest and most spectacular performers of all trout. If a fish tears off line from the moment he feels the hook and jumps two or three times in his first run, he's usually a rainbow. If his second run is almost as far as his first, he continues to jump, and persistently refuses to lie on his side and be drawn to net or beach, he's not only a rainbow but probably a virgin fish or one that has just come in from the sea.

Even among rainbows, there is wide variation in performance. An unspawned Kamloops trout weighing three or four pounds and in its third or fourth summer is the fastest and most acrobatic lake fish I know. The best river rainbows, in such streams as Oregon's McKenzie and British Columbia's Skagit, are just as good, and in addition take full advantage of all natural hazards.

But a spawner, even though well recovered, is much less impressive. Large winter steelheads, which usually enter rivers within three or four months of spawning time, are progressively less active as the season draws on. The brightest March fish, fresh in from the sea, will be slow and tame compared to a November or December fish of the same size, and may even be inferior to a recovered kelt on its way downstream in May.

Best of all, and possibly the most brilliant fish that swims, is the true summer steelhead which enters a river nine or 10 months before spawning time. A fresh-run 10-pounder, preferably hooked on a dry fly in shallow water, is usually beyond control for several minutes after the hook is set.

Steelheads, though they are true trout, are nearer salmon than trout in life history, habits, and performance. I've never caught an Atlantic salmon and a steelhead in the same river, so for me a comparison between the two is more difficult than others I'm making. But it seems to me that the two fish are strictly comparable. An early-season Atlantic salmon is as good as a summer steelhead; a late-season salmon is often no better than a winter steelhead. An Atlantic salmon has the important advantage of commonly running much bigger, and perhaps that's enough to hold for him his title of supremacy among fresh-water gamefish.

Pacific salmons usually are caught in salt rather than fresh water, which makes comparison still harder. All may be caught on rod and line at some time or another, and all perform well, but only two species, the chinook (king tyee, or spring), and the silver (coho), are caught regularly enough to be counted among well-known gamefish. For size and power, chinooks are in a class by themselves —30 and 40-pounders are common and 50 and 60-pounders may reasonably be hoped for.

When a big chinook takes off on his first run there's no argument about who is in charge. It takes strong tackle to stop or to turn him within 100 yards. When he thrashes on the surface, as he usually does at some stage, it's a sight to impress the calmest angler. And when an early-season fish, just down from the north, takes off in a series of crashing jumps, it is a picture of strength and beauty to be remembered a lifetime.

The chinook tends to swim deep, applying his power deliberately and doggedly, often sulkily, rather than spectacularly. The silver runs on top of the water and out in the air and, like a rainbow trout, takes off the moment he feels the hook. He's much smaller than the chinook, averaging eight or 10 pounds and rarely reaching 20 pounds. But on fair tackle a run of a 100 yards with half a dozen jumps is nothing for him, and he often will repeat the performance as soon as the line is recovered.

The Florida bonefish is usually considered the fastest of salt-water gamefish. It will run 200 or 300 yards across the tide flats so fast that a cheap reel will freeze. But I have known friends come to silvers straight from bonefish and insist that silvers are just as fast and far more exciting because they jump—not once, but several times. I've seen them jump into and over boats; I saw one that jumped into a lady's lap, flipped overboard, and broke the line before the echoes of her screams died away.

Both chinooks and silvers can be caught in rivers, and when they first run in they are really fine gamefish. The chinook can seldom be persuaded to take a fly, but his power is increased by the current and his performance takes on new proportions in narrow waters—especially to an angler who is fishing from his feet instead of from a boat. This is true of only the freshest fish and for only a week or two after the run begins. Maturity comes rapidly, and the fish turn sulky and slow. They have strength and weight, but no zip.

The silvers remain the better fish. They often take small flies with wild freedom, and will tear away from a strike with the sudden violence of summer steelheads. Even an October cock, bright-red and hook-jawed, will run 100 yards or more and jump as though the air was as familiar as water.

I've found the chars—eastern brook trout, Dolly Vardens (including arctic chars), and lake chars—less inclined to jump than even brown trout, and considerably slower than salmons and rainbows. But they are good fish, and sea-run Dolly Vardens in top condition can be very strong indeed. I imagine the same is true of sea-run eastern brooks, though I have never caught them.

I have caught Atlantic (Sebago or landlocked) salmon only in South America, but they were large and in excellent condition. With one exception, I found them inclined to make short, fast runs that rarely took out much backing, but the runs were repeated many times. They jumped suddenly and excitingly, often from shallow water and usually on very short line at the start of the run.

They were far from being as fast or as spectacular as steelheads or sea-run Atlantic salmon, but it was difficult to tire them because of the shortness of their runs. An active fish on a short line is far more likely to break tackle than one that puts on his best show at a distance. I thought them very good fish indeed, and exceptionally beautiful both in and out of water.

Pike and bass, especially bass, often strike suddenly and very hard. Of all fresh-water fish they can most truly be said to have fierce and angry qualities. They are savage head shakers when hooked, and smallmouths put fury and fight into their jumps. Despite this, I've never found them as fast nor as exciting as trouts and salmons, and their performances have none of the grace and beauty of jumping steelheads or salmons.

In the end, it remains a matter of individual preference or prejudice. The moments of true hazard, in my experience, come immediately after the strike, before the fisherman has had time to steady himself, and again at the very end, when the tired fish is on a short line near the net.

The fish that most regularly throws me off balance at the start, no matter how well prepared I think I am, is the summer steelhead. The strike, the run, and the first jump seem crowded into a single second, often with a change of direction and another, sometimes disastrous, jump while I'm still fumbling for control.

Of the finishers, all the rainbows and the salmons rate highly. But sheer weight counts for a lot on a short line, especially when the fisherman is doing his own netting or gaffing. I think it must always be true that the heaviest fish, whether chinooks, Atlantic salmon, or winter steelheads, are likely to produce the most dramatic moments.

There will always be plenty of room for argument. Conditions, tackle, and individual fish vary, and so do the moods of fishermen. Under its own ideal conditions, every fish I've mentioned is a worthy gamefish, and at one time or another every one has proved too hot for me to handle.

Dalls of the Yukon

Charles Elliott

January 1959

Charlie Elliott has grappled with nature most of his life. He even farmed
for a while. He has hunted and fished in all corners of North America,
starting in the river swamps of Covington, Georgia. He went to the
Forestry School at University of Georgia when he wasn't fishing on the
Oconee River. He worked for the U.S. Forest Service in Montana and on
two occasions for the National Park Service. In Georgia he was variously
District Forester, Director of the Parks Department, Commissoner of
Natural Resources, and, finally, Director of the New Game and Fish
Commission until 1948. He is the author of a dozen books on the
outdoors, his latest being *Care of Game Meat and Trophies.*

The ridge crest was jagged and rocky, and it pitched down the mountain at a
hazardous angle for three quarters of a mile before it leveled off. I plastered
myself against its rim and glanced at Louis Brown, who had clawed his way to a
perch beside me.

"You can fall off this place," I whispered, "in three directions."

"Well—just don't fall," he replied, "and don't move a pebble if you want a
shot at that ram down there."

"We'd save bullets," I said, "by dropping a rock on him."

"Start crawling," Lou instructed.

I've done a lot of plain and fancy stalking in my time, but no approach to a
game animal has ever measured up to that crawl. We couldn't stand, or even
squat on our haunches without being spotted by the sheep. And crawling down
that precipitous drop on our bellies was impossible. There wasn't any way but on
our backs to negotiate that first almost-vertical, quarter mile. I inched down, with
my rifle balanced between my lap and knees. Then suddenly my elbow dislodged
a stone the size of an egg, but I fielded it on the first bounce.

"Good catch. That could have started a slide big enough to bury the critter,"
Lou commented dryly.

We continued downward in this crawfish fashion, and half an hour and one
dislocated vertebra later, we reached the last rocky outcropping that hid us from
the ram. He stood in a narrow gap about 250 yards below, majestically surveying
his wild domain. For the twentieth time, I studied his head through my glass.
From the spread and set of his horns, we knew they were slightly less than 40
inches, but his crown was exquisitely carved—all the way to its light-brown tips.
With time running out, I knew that this was the ram I wanted.

"Think you can hit him from here?" Lou asked, softly.

"If I miss after this stalk," I said, "I'll use the second shell on me."

This was the dramatic climax of my finest hunt. The time was last August, and
I was here expressly for the purpose of bringing to the readers of OUTDOOR
LIFE a report on the hunting possibilities in this virtually uncharted wilderness
near the Arctic Circle.

For three weeks we'd scoured the massive, unnamed mountain ranges on the
black arctic side of the Mackenzie Mountains in Canada's Yukon Territory. We
were looking for a record Dall sheep head, but hadn't found it. For the better

part of 21 days, I'd crawled on my belly along the dizzy slopes, peering into canyons so rugged and vast that I had to push back from the edge to catch my breath. I'd been 200 yards or less from 18 rams, and had even passed up two or three with horns an inch or so longer than this one I now surveyed from the perch of an eagle. I'd also turned down others with badly broomed horns, and many sheep smaller than the one below us. Still I hadn't seen that massive head we'd traveled more than 4,000 miles to find.

My three hunting companions were business men and ranchers from California. They were also top sportsmen, and I considered it my privilege to hunt with them. We'd combed an area of several hundred square miles and had glassed hundreds of white sheep, including ewes and lambs, and we'd left behind some rugged days with mountains that stood on end and majestic valleys I'm sure no sportsman had even seen much less hunted in before.

John Harness, who's hunted all over North America and made two trips to Africa, took the ram with the longest curl—a shapely 41-incher. Bill Boone, a veteran of hunts in Canada, Alaska, and Africa—as well as our Western states —nailed one about the size of the ram standing below us. So did Paul Sloan, whose hunts have taken him to Mexico, Canada, Africa, and many times to the Southwest. I was the only one who hadn't scored.

We were hunting in one of the last great wilderness areas of North America. From the northernmost highway in the Yukon Territory, a gravel road running east and west between Keno Hill, Mayo Landing and Dawson—famous old town of gold-rush days—the earth reaches out in a rugged and desolate pattern for 400 miles to the rim of the Arctic Ocean. Some of the Yukon River's headwaters rise here, then head westward across Alaska, but most of the watersheds feed their nameless creeks and rivers northward off the bleak ranges and eventually into the Mackenzie River and the Arctic River.

Only a few of the mountains, rivers, and creeks have names. Some of the country was mapped a few years ago by such sketchy methods as triangulation and key points. A couple of survey teams went through on horseback, but most of the contour data was gathered by survey crews in helicopters.

For 10 days before we flew out of Dawson on a charter plane to meet him, our outfitter, Louis Brown, had made his way north from Mayo Landing with the packstring for 250 winding miles into the heart of the hunting territory assigned to him by the Yukon Game Department. Lou has hunted and trapped this country for 25 years—10 as a commercial outfitter—but there were tremendous chunks of his 12,000 square miles of upended terrain just south of the Arctic Circle where even he had never left a boot print.

Two and a half hours of flying over the endless, unpeopled ranges convinced me that we were one of the most isolated hunting parties on the continent.

We found Lou Brown waiting at an isolated lake on Wind River, where he and the plane's pilot had agreed in advance to meet. From the moment I laid eyes on Lou, I was impressed. He's a handsome, powerfully built Canadian in his middle 40's. Originally from Alberta, he came into the country as a young man, lured by the spell of the far northland. At Great Slave Lake, in Northwest Territories, he failed to find work, but met another adventurer building a boat to float the MacKenzie River 1,000 miles to its mouth. Lou helped him complete his boat, and together they made the two-month trip to the Arctic Ocean. Lou left his companion at Ft. McPherson, came up the Peel River to the Bonnet Plume, and crossed the rugged mountain range afoot to Mayo Landing. He's lived there ever since, except for two years he spent trapping in the Bonnet Plume country.

Many times you can judge a man by his horses. Most of the string of pack and saddle horses we had were bred and raised by our outfitter. There were no squealers, biters, or kickers in the bunch. They were mountain-wise and sure-footed in a country where one misstep on the trailless slopes might spell disaster. Lou was as gentle with his Indian guides as he was with his horses, and I never heard him raise his voice, even in the tight places.

To do the cooking for our party, he'd brought along Vic (Frenchy) Poirier. Originally from Quebec, Frenchy spent some time in Alberta, and landed finally at Mayo where he did a stretch in the Keno mines before opening a little restaurant. He'd closed down his eating establishment to come on this hunting trip. Rugged and handsome, Frenchy knew guns, and could handle a rifle or a horse. And with the simple iron stove in the cook tent, he baked bread and turned out a brand of meals you'd expect at home.

Four Indians from the Loucheux tribe completed our party. They were Bob Martin, Paul Sloan's guide; Doc Johnny, chief guide and Bill Boone's shadow; Jimmy Davis, horse wrangler, woodcutter, and handy man around camp; and Paul Germain. Paul, assigned to me, had that pleasing, inscrutable, and ageless countenance of so many Indians. I asked him how old he was.

"Dunno," he said. "Sometimes 45, sometimes 55—maybe."

It took me only one afternoon to discover that Paul Germain had the sharpest eyes of any man I've ever known. We were on a mountainside above our first Wind River camp, and he called my attention to a white dot high on a distant slope.

"Sheep," he said.

I found the dot through my 8X binoculars.

"Just another white rock," I replied.

The guide nodded, but kept looking. I was glassing another slope when he touched my arm and pointed to the dot again.

"Sheep."

I swung the glasses, and sure enough, my "rock" had moved and was standing broadside so I could make out neck, legs, and body.

"Ram," he said.

I believed him, and we climbed to get a better look at the horns. From the valley, where we tied our horses, the ram didn't look too far away. But five hours afoot on the almost vertical moss patches and rockslides, gave me my first appreciation of the area's tremendous distances. I fell winded on my belly, and we crawled to a rim overlooking a ragged canyon.

From the creek bottom we'd spotted only one; now we saw three rams grazing on the sparse grass. Two were small. The third had a fair curl on one side, but his other horn ended in a jagged break. Lou told me later that he's seen many sheep break off their horns by jabbing the ends into rock cracks and twisting until the points snap off. Then they further broom the ragged edge by rubbing it against rough boulders. This happens, Lou figures, when the horns grow too long, the curl extending past the ram's eye and obstructing his vision at certain angles.

The sheep were grazing away from us now, and I thought I made my guide understand that we should get close enough for pictures. We crawled over the canyon rim, pulled ourselves up the other side of the slot by handholds, and snaked along on our bellies across the rocky hillside. We paused to watch one of the rams lie down.

Since we'd run out of boulders and brush to hid behind, we stood up and walked directly toward the rams. The largest, which was lying down, scrambled to his feet, and Paul grabbed my arm.

"Shoot! He run!"

I continued to saunter along and the rams walked slowly in front of us until they stood on the skyline.

"Shoot!" the Indian pleaded.

I took a picture and continued my slow advance, pausing now and then until I was about 100 feet away. The ram highest on the mountain got a little jittery and turned as if to leave.

"Baaa-a-a," I said.

That snapped him to attention, we strolled another 10 feet closer, and I took one last picture as all three stepped beyond the crest of the mountain.

On our way back, with my knees about to break in two, I could hear my guide behind me, muttering to himself. "We see sheep on mountain. Climb to top. Only take picture. Holy smoke."

That wasn't the last climb we made for sheep without burning powder. I learned the hard way that 8X glasses simply aren't strong enough for this kind of stalking. We could see sheep on the mountain and tell they were rams, yet we had no idea whether we were looking at a world-record head. So we had to climb until we were close enough to study a head, and then either go after it or turn it down. Lou kept a 20X telescope in his saddlebag and used it every day, and Paul Sloan had brought his own 20X spotting scope, which saved him and his guide plenty of footwork. But Paul Germain and I climbed and climbed, often for six or seven hours, until we were close enough to check a head with my binoculars.

Then we hunted two days with Bill Boone and Doc Johnny. The first day, the four of us stalked three sheep through a rough canyon, and climbed a slanting break in the canyon wall, coming within 100 yards of some fair rams.

The second day, we carried the spotting scope, set it up in a rocky creek bed, and picked out a ram close under the rim of a tremendous ridge flanking the valley. We tied our horses in a willow clump, packed guns, glasses, scope, lunch, and cameras, and started the climb. The route we chose ran along the crest of a steep ridge, and after five hours we were close enough to peep through a crack in the mountain wall. Now we could see two good heads instead of just the one we'd first seen. One ram was lying down, his rump toward the cold wind blowing up the mountain. The other, 200 yards to the left, was standing, staring suspiciously in our direction.

"You want him?" Bill asked.

I told him we still had plenty of time and I'd rather do more looking for a larger trophy. While we stood whispering, the ram turned and walked uphill from the craggy point, giving us a rear view of his complete curl. That decided my hunting partner. He moved to get a better shooting position over the rock. The ram, evidently seeing the movement, broke into a trot, climbing to the right.

By now he was almost 500 yards away. Bill, using a .300 Weatherby Magnum, touched off a marvelous shot for the distance, but the 150-grain handloaded Nosler bullet struck a bit low. The sheep stumbled, then went up the slope on three legs. Bill spilled two more shots at him before the ram dodged behind a rock.

"Wish I'd missed altogether," Bill said, "Can't leave a winged sheep in these hills."

We'd been without water all day, so we dropped into a gut of canyon, where a trickle of icy liquid ran from under a rock. From that point we made a dizzy climb across the slope, over acres of shale where the footing was uncertain and a misstep would have sent us crashing into the valley. We skirted towering stone pillars which looked so shaky that a hard wind might topple them.

"Ever have earthquakes here?" I asked Doc Johnny.

"Plenty earthquakes," he said.

For my own peace of mind, I didn't pursue the subject further. Another hour or two of this kind of climbing put us on a sawtooth, windy backbone between two immense valleys. Working our way along the crest, we saw three rams before we spotted Bill's wounded animal standing on a rim with his front foot up.

It was a roof-top descent over shale, but Doc Johnny and Bill went after him, down one of the vertical slots.

We lost sight of the hunters, but saw the ram work slowly downhill at an angle. Just as he turned across a slope, we saw him stumble. A moment later the echo of a rifle shot drifted to us. The ram fell, but even with a leg out of commission, managed to cross a steep canyon and lie down on its far rim. Through the glasses, we could tell he was watching the men, though we still hadn't seen them. After half an hour, the ram got to its feet again, practically crawled across a slanted bench, and went out of sight over a rocky wall.

Bill and Doc Johnny stayed with him. They were at least another three quarters of an hour picking their way over a steep rockslide, finally crawling to where we'd last seen the ram. There, Bill lay on his belly, trying to get as comfortable as possible, and after a long wait, squeezed off a shot. Through the glasses, I watched him push back to his knees, and shove his hunting cap back. His guide stood up, and we knew it was all over. My hunting partner had made a successful all-out effort and retrieved his cripple. He and Doc Johnny were past midnight getting to camp.

During the next two weeks, I gradually learned to identify sheep with my naked eye. I simply picked out a pattern of white dots on a mountain, and if the pattern remained the same, I knew it was a rock. If it shifted, we glassed the slope for rams. If the bunch contained some sheep about half the size of others, we knew we were looking at ewes and lambs.

I also learned that even in top sheep country, good heads come hard. To be certain you don't pass up any records, you have to get close enough to look them all over. The tremendous distances sometimes made this a real chore. One indication of a good head is the size of the sheep. But many times, after we'd climbed to look at an especially large animal, we'd find one perfect curl and the other horn broomed to a stub.

My guide and I had a couple of days when we saw no sheep. At our third camp on Bourbon Creek (Bill Boone and Frenchy gave the stream its name), we saw two big rams on the mountain. We left camp early and climbed all day to a high peak overlooking Bonnet Plume River. We followed the crest for miles, searching out the hidden nooks on both sides. The mountain was marked with sheep tracks, and dozens of beds. Much of the sign was fresh, and though our expectations ran high all day, we didn't see a single sheep.

That same day, John Harness and Paul Sloan, hunting a dozen miles away, stumbled onto a mineral lick with more than 30 Dalls. Paul got a fleeting shot at a ram that Lou was sure would go 43 to 45 inches, but the animal was too far away and Paul only knocked a few grains of dust into its hide. John and I rode back to the lick next day. We found 16 sheep there, with only one small ram. The big bunch had moved on.

It seemed to me that with only 10 or a dozen hunters going into the 12,000 square miles each fall, every mountain would be covered with sheep. Lou said that wolves take a terrible toll when the sheep bog down in deep snow and the packs can race across the top. Other sheep are killed by temperatures of 60 and 70 below, and by snowslides. Lou has found skeletons at the base of many a slope.

We left Bourbon Creek, rode through a long, timbered flat to Bonnet Plume River, then upstream eight miles before we found a spot where the water was spread over gravel bars and was shallow enough to cross with our packstring. Twenty miles from Bourbon Creek, we made our fourth camp on a high bluff. Paul Sloan set up his spotting scope, and when John Harness and I returned from a three-day fly camp 20 miles away on Pops Creek, Paul not only had collected a good trophy, but had spotted a band of rams in one of the high valleys across the river. Lou and John made an 18-hour expedition and, near sundown, John took the best ram of our safari, the 41-incher with a wide curl.

They saw other good rams in the vicinity, and next morning Lou, Doc Johnny, and I packed a horse with grub, a tarpaulin, and our sleeping bags and crossed the Bonnet Plume again in search of a big head.

We arrived at the head of the valley in late afternoon, searched out a couple of canyons, found only one slightly better-than-average head, several small rams, and a flock of ewes and lambs. It was almost dark when we got back to our horses in a downpour. We climbed into soggy saddles and rode down the creek until darkness caught us in a clump of willows and aspen.

"This," I stated, "is stark, raw wilderness."

"She's sure raw and stark tonight," Lou answered good-naturedly through the sodden darkness.

I've seldom faced the prospect of a drearier night, but what I didn't count on was the skill and ingenuity of those two men. We tied the horses, then Lou swung his ax while I dragged brush to make a clearing in the stream-side willows. Doc Johnny soon located a couple of sound, dry aspen poles, chopped them into splinters, and built a roaring fire that turned raindrops to steam and warmed the air under the tarp we'd pitched.

Doc Johnny hung a slab of sheep ribs over the fire to broil and we unloaded the horses, leaving on their saddles and pack saddles to keep them warm. By the time we'd spread our sleeping bags and brewed a pot of tea, the ribs were golden brown and dripping with rich juices. I've never had more of a sense of well-being on any hunt than I had that night.

It rained all night, and slowed to a drizzle when we got up at dawn. While we cooked breakfast, the clouds lifted; at the head of the valley we could see the tall peaks covered with snow.

"It's a question," Lou said," "of whether we should keep looking for the rams in this valley, or try the next one over."

I thought about my three hunting partners waiting in camp for me to finish hunting sheep so we could move into grizzly and caribou country upriver. I thought how the snowline would move farther down the mountain each day until the whole upended world was smothered in white. Most of all I thought how, after three weeks of grueling hunting, I still didn't have the outsize trophy I wanted. I made my decision.

"If we don't find the rams in this valley this morning, let's go after that largest head we saw on the mountain yesterday afternoon."

We rode up-valley again until the rocks began to punch up through the sphagnum moss; we hobbled our horses and left them to graze on the lush grass. Our glasses showed two rams looking down on us, and not another sheep. We began the long climb up the canyon which would lead us to the head of the valley, and put us on top to stalk along the backbone of the ridge above the rams.

That's when I went down that quarter of a mile of rocky crest on my back, leaving bits of shirt wool and patches of skin. And now Lou and I sprawled only 250 yards above the largest sheep. For the last time I covered his crown inch by inch with my variable Bausch & Lomb sighting scope set on 8X. He was the ram I wanted. I got settled down to touch one off from my .300 Magnum, custom-built for me by T. C. Kennon of Atlanta, Ga.

"He's straight downhill," Lou whispered. "Better hold a little low."

I held low and that was where my bullet hit—in the chest cavity. The ram staggered and half turned, as if wondering where the standard .300 Magnum Silvertip had come from. My next shot was a little wild, hitting the ram in the rib cage and going completely through his body, only staggering him. A shoulder shot tumbled him off the sharp ridge, and he rolled almost half a mile down the treacherous slope before jamming against a rocky projection.

"Well, that's that." My words sounded rather abrupt, even in my own ears. Lou looked at me with his quiet, searching gaze.

"What I mean is," I said, "that's the end of the roughest, toughest, wildest, and finest sheep hunt I ever had."

Stag Line

Bill Rae

January 1959

This space might better have been given over to another wapiti story, "High, Wide and Handsome," by Fred C. Mercer (Jan. 1960). His Montana elk at the time was the biggest ever killed by a known hunter (it has been displaced by an older trophy since turned up by the Boone and Crockett Club). It also won the coveted Sagamore Hill Award. But I'd like readers to know just how an eastern dude felt going over Deer Creek Pass, the beauty of the whole adventure. Besides, I guess an editor should expose his writing to the criticisms of writers. Turnabout is fair play. I didn't sign my name to more than half a dozen of the things I wrote for OUTDOOR LIFE in my twenty-two years of editorship, but this was a memorable experience. I've been over Deer Creek twice since, but I confess it never got to be like falling off a log. (Don't use that expression!)

Like hundreds of hunters before us, Chuck Cooley and I had sworn not to shave until I got the elk for which I had traveled from 42nd Street in New York City to the Thorofare in northwestern Wyoming. Twelve days of our hunt had already gone. As I worked my fingers glumly through the matting on my face, Charlie Elliott spoke up.

"Boss, you shore are goin' to be a sensation walkin' down Fourth Avenue next week with that set of muttonchops if we don't fix it for you to kill an elk mighty soon," he said. "You look like you just stepped off a whaling ship."

"Don't worry," I answered. "I'm going back to New York with an elk if I have to stay here all winter."

Chuck, my salty-tongued guide, grinned until the wrinkles around his eyes ran down into his beard like rivulets into a forest. "You know," he said, "if we don't get out of this everlovin' country pretty soon you might do just that anyway."

We knew that was no joke, even though Charlie drooled like a cow moose in a wallow as Chuck said it. We were hunting in the headwaters of the Yellowstone River in one of the last remaining wilderness areas in the United States. Here in the Thorofare, locked in by the ramparts of the Continental Divide and the Absaroka range, great herds of elk work out of the high country down toward the winter refuge in Jackson Hole at this time of year. At the same time, mule deer travel in great numbers the other way through the timber to the high passes in the Absarokas and thence to the South Fork of the Shoshone, where the snows aren't so deep.

Hence the name Thorofare.

But now we had a mystery on our hands. Something had happened to this two-way traffic. There were no elk, or none to speak of. Our beards testified to that. And since it was just a couple of days short of November 1, it behooved us to find them, collect our trophies, and head for Deer Creek Pass and civilization before the snows blocked our exit through the two-mile-high passageway. Once the snows came in earnest, we might just as well resign ourselves to spending the winter in Hammett Cabin.

Hammett Cabin was built, not for dudes like us who practically asked to get snowed in, but for trappers or wayfarers unfortunate enough to get themselves waylaid by winter in the 9,000-foot high valley of Thorofare Creek, whose walls of mountains and ridges soar upward another 2,000 or 3,000 feet. There is never a lock on the door of Hammett Cabin, and the cabin is always well stocked. The only obligation is to leave something in place of what you take for the next fellow —whether food or lantern fuel, soap or fresh-cut firewood.

It was comfortable enough now in the cabin, two-hours' ride by horseback from Bridger Lake. Kenny Hill, a short-order cook in Cody during the winter, was serving up hot biscuits and elk meat with white sauce (the meat from a previous hunt) to a whiskered group of dudes and guides. (I remember once he whipped up a raspberry cake with chocolate frosting.) The amateurs were Elliott, Southern field editor for OUTDOOR LIFE, Bob Hogg, Atlanta businessman, and myself. The professionals, besides Hill, were Cooley, Frank Lasater, and Don Wildon, guides, and Freddie Zinn, tough young horse wrangler.

All of the latter hail from Cody, Wyoming, which owes its name to the famous scout, hunter, and showman, Buffalo Bill Cody. In fact, our outfitter, Max Wilde of the Lazy Bar F Ranch in Valley, Wyoming, was himself one of Buffalo Bill's scouts. A few days before our arrival, Max had got himself into a rope tangle with a horse while putting out bear baits for our hunt in the Thorofare and all but had his arm torn out of its socket. Unable to come with us, he'd hand-picked these men to herd us through the same wilderness Colonel Cody had hunted in his heyday.

Outside in the night were the 30-odd horses that had carried us and the camp into the Thorofare. Now and again one of those browsing near the cabin snorted or shook his bell. Beyond, coyotes howled, one answering another, far into the distance. Above the cabin the wind soughed in the spruce and fir. But all these sounds only heightened the cheerfulness of the cabin, until the conversation turned to winter. Then Frank Lasater told of the winter he had trapped into the Thorofare and found two horses, little more than skin and bones, standing deep in the snow chewing the bark off the logs of Hammett Cabin. They were too far gone to save.

Just the presence of Lasater on this hunt underscored our gamble. Frank, an old-time mountain man with eyes the distant blue of the sky, was an outfitter himself, but his hunting parties, like those of all the other outfitters, had departed and he was helping out the injured Max Wilde by serving as a guide for us. In other words, their regular season was over. And now in our straits, he took charge. "We've got two more days to get elk for Bill and Charlie," he said, "and we'll be lucky if the snows don't hit us while we're doing it. We've been up and down every creek within hunting radius of this cabin and haven't had any luck. Now suddenly today I got me an idea."

The idea of hunting in the Thorofare in late October was that of the aforementioned Charles Elliott, the working stiff's Clark Gable, who was squiring me on my first big-game hunt. Charlie has hunted in the Thorofare for 20 years, and is an aged-in-the-woods friend of both Max and Frank. For the past 10 years, his ambition has been to get snowed into the Thorofare for the entire winter.

But right now he had something more important on his mind—to see that I got an elk. He had written me lyrics on what magnificent game country this was— elk, deer, bear, moose and, yes, even sheep, but most of all elk. The Thorofare, he assured me, fairly swarmed with elk, that noble American stag which only the encyclopedias seem to call the wapiti. But now the noble stag was letting him down. He chewed his cigar in a circle of gloom.

We'd seen everything else. Antelope stared at us from the plains as we approached Cody, and lit out for the horizon only when we stopped the car. (They've learned the shooting doesn't start until the car stops.) We saw more of them when we made the 45-mile trip from Cody to the Wilde ranch in Valley.

After we'd crossed the South Fork of the Shoshone and scaled the heights into Deer Creek Canyon, the first thing I saw, when I dared look down, was a brace of Rocky Mountain sheep.

Weary hours later, when we finally reached Hammett Cabin, a bull and a cow moose watched us placidly from one of the network of beaver ponds laced together by Thorofare Creek. Some days later, when we sought to change our luck by riding down to Bridger Lake for some fishing, we cut a fresh beartrail and my horse nearly climbed out from under me when he got the scent. That same trip I looked down the lake and in a space of half a mile saw six separate moose feeding in the water.

On another occasion, two bulls knocked their horns sportively and hollowly in a little park in the timber not 20 yards from us. A special permit is required to hunt moose in the Thorofare, and not many are drawn. Thus, for the most part unmolested, the moose are bold and brash. On our return trip this day, two more bulls, a young one and an old one, eyed us arrogantly as we rode within feet of them. Chuck kept grunting tauntingly at them, and you could almost read the evil in their minds as they pivoted to watch us.

"What do you do," I asked Chuck, "if they rush you?"

"You ride like hell," said Chuck. "They got good early speed, but a horse will beat 'em out in the long run."

"I hope I'm still with the horse," I said, "but just suppose one of them's good for the distance. What do you do then?"

"You shoot him," said Chuck, "in self-defense. But be sure you hit him—and be sure you can convince the game warden it was self-defense. If you can't, you might as well miss."

It was on this day, too, that Charlie rolled a coyote, the only one I actually saw, though I listened to whole choirs of them every night. Deer were a common sight, and a story in themselves. As for fish, we quickly caught our limits of two and three-pound Yellowstone cutthroats both in Bridger Lake and a nearby bend of the Yellowstone River (See "Elk on the Side," November, 1955, OUTDOOR LIFE.) And as our horses splashed toward the river, we startled a flock of feeding mallards.

As a matter of fact, we even saw an elk the morning of our first hunt, a pretty good-size one, too. But it had a narrow beam, like a V, and we didn't give it a second thought as a trophy as it watched us from the edge of the timber across the meadow. (As the days passed, that beam grew broader in imagination.) The only thing we didn't see, in fact, was a buffalo, and I wasn't sure we wouldn't meet one of those in Deer Creek Canyon that first day out of Valley.

To understand, you have to picture Deer Creek Canyon. From Max Wilde's ranch, a mile above sea level, it's a ride of 11 miles to Deer Creek Pass and, in that stretch, the trail climbs upward another mile. So when you reached that windblasted pass across the Divide your altitude is 11,000 feet. Since it's another 17 miles to Hammett Cabin, that first day's ride is something that stays with you a long time, especially if the last time you rode a horse was in the C.M.T.C. at Fort Ethan Allen, Vermont, in 1925.

Yet that last 17 miles is like a canter in the park after you traverse the canyon. In places the trail is little more than an edging on vertical walls, and if you dare look down you can just make out the ribbon of the creek, 1,000 feet below. To add spice, the horses like to walk on the edge of the trail with a sort of casting-off movement of their outside hoofs.

Toward noon, we rode down a series of switchbacks to the bed of the creek where it rushes through the cool timber, and ate our lunch in a nest of huge boulders. It was a great relief. Casually, and hopefully, I asked if we were going to continue to travel at this lower level.

"Why, boy," said Charlie, "that was just a little old rise of ground. Now we climb."

At this point, Chuck Cooley got to reminiscing about the time a stray bison from Yellowstone Park ran headon into a party of hunters he was guiding. The packhorses in the lead turned tail and tore back through their own string, scattering guides and dudes alike and smashing their packs against rock and tree. It came the turn of a stubby little mule to face this strange, humpbacked, hangheaded monster with horns of the devil. For a moment, she planted all four feet in the trail and dared the creature to come on.

The bison came on.

The mule swapped ends and shot back over the trail like the hot blast from a jet engine, flattening everything in her way.

"We had a husband and wife among the dudes," said Chuck, "and after that damn mule near bowled me over, she shoot through on the inside of them like oversquoze toothpaste, and the horses pawed the air and showed the whites of their eyes like the devil had blowed his breath on 'em. I'm tellin' you I thought the whole shebang was going to wind up in the bottom of the canyon. That mule came to a stop up a draw, trembling like the ague and lookin' back to see if what she saw was true. I wasn't no better.

"Lucky for us the buffalo was as scared as the mule by all the commotion, and it took off the other way. But it took two hours to calm down that string, repack all the gear, and head back in the right direction. That's what makes this old horse here, Croppy, so jittery. He's never got over it. You have to watch him close. Let him see a tree stump, or you pull out a handkerchief, and he'll get so jumpy he'll spook the whole outfit before you know it."

We soon had an illustration. We began climbing after lunch, as Charlie said we would, and as we neared Deer Creek Pass we began to see the snow that had fallen lightly, the night we hit Cody. Here the storm had been heavier, and the snow had stuck. Where the trail turned away from the sun, stretches of ice appeared and soon only patches of slide rock showed through the blanket of white.

When we surmounted a series of dizzy switchbacks and the trail leveled off again, the horses were up to their hocks in snow.

We were really riding high now. The long train of packhorses stretched out ahead of us with Chuck Cooley in the lead. They rounded the butte guarding the pass and, except for a couple of stragglers, were shut off from view. Kenny Hill and the other guides followed, and the dudes brought up the rear. With that 1,000-foot-off below, I leaned my weight toward the canyon wall.

Suddenly there was a lot of yelling, and the horses came around that butte running right for us! I felt my hair rise. Charlie and I had just reached a 90° angle in the trail, like the corner of a room only not quite so straight up and down. It was a steep draw and we headed our horses far enough up it to get out of the trail.

I expected a buffalo to come charging around the butte. Instead, Chuck appeared bellowing curses punctuated by whoa after whoa. Kenny Hill went into action waving his arms and matching Chuck curse for curse. His flailing arms, and probably his red hair, turned the lead horses. Then Kenny whipped out a slingshot he carried to keep the packstring on the prod and stung the end horse on the rump a couple of times to keep him moving back toward Chuck.

The other horses began to retreat, and soon were following Chuck docilely again toward the Thorofare, only this time he led them up over the steep butte instead of by the trail.

I turned my horse, Major, back onto the trail but he was now heading back toward the Valley. I took a deep breath and reined him the other way. Half-way around I said to Charlie, "How much room have I got?"

Charlie looked down at the horse's hoofs on the brink of the canyon.

"You got plenty of room—"

I brought the horse the rest of the way around.

"—a good six inches," he finished.

I did it once more in the middle of the night. When I woke myself up, I was halfway to the bottom of the canyon.

When we topped the butte and began to descend the gentler slopes of the Thorofare, we discovered why the horses had spooked. The Pass was belly-deep in drifted snow. Chuck had wrestled his horse through all right, but the lead pack-horse bogged down halfway across and then began to flounder. It turned back and panicked the horses behind it. It was like a chain reaction, and Croppy's buffalo couldn't have done a more effective job. Like Croppy, I'd always remember it.

But Deer Creek was forgotten during the next 12 days, and we became more familiar with the clear, icy streams which feed into Thorofare Creek as it gathers its forces to join the Yellowstone River—Butte Creek, Pass Creek, Scatter Creek, Hidden Creek, Open Creek, and others without name. All these creeks—a deceptive term considering the swathes they cut—have their own canyons, ridges, and mountain spurs. On a map, and probably, too, from a point high in the sky, this watershed resembles a gigantic well-tree platter, only much more ramified.

Consider just one—Hidden Creek. It lies in Blind Basin, so-called because, except for a spiraling corridorlike trail between two mountains, it is walled in on all sides by rimrock soaring 1,000 feet. The day we assaulted Blind Basin the sunless trail was icy and my horse, Colonel (not a promotion; a different horse) twice slipped to his knees. With no place to go, except over the edge, I stuck with the horse—and it proved to be well worth it.

Blind Basin is 12 or 14 miles long, and is threaded by the coolest and clearest stream I've ever known. That's Hidden Creek, which bores through the mountain wall and pours into the Thorofare in a great waterfall. The valley is like a Shangri-La. I've seen its like in moving pictures, but never believed anything like it actually existed. It was almost a profanation that the only reminder of civilization we had in the Thorofare, a highflying airplane, passed over us the day we hunted Blind Basin.

The rimrock looked like the ruined walls of great lost cities, like many Angkor Vats perched 1,000 feet above us. Below were the forests of spruce and the lovely sloping parks in which we hoped to find elk. From this magnificent retreat a world-record trophy came years ago. We had pinned our hopes on it, too—but no elk bugle was to shatter the cathedral atmosphere of beauty and stillness.

So now with November upon us, we were worried about Deer Creek Pass again, worried we wouldn't get our trophies in time to cross it before the snows buried it completely. There had been one other storm, a few days after we reached the Thorofare. Its snow was gone from the sunny ridges, but still lay on the cold slopes and in scattered patches in the timber.

It helped Walter Griffin, one of our original party who had had to return to his business in Jacksonville, Fla., to get a magnificent mule deer. (See "Blood and Snow," December, 1955, OUTDOOR LIFE.) And it helped Chuck and me to dog another big buck for two days—only to have me miss him completely, unbelievably and noisily.

Those were the events leading up to the bull-session at Hammett Cabin which opened this story. So when Frank Lasater said he had an idea about the elk, we listened. That morning Bob Hogg and his guide, Don Wildon, had journeyed beyond the Yellowstone River to hunt the high country there, unsuccessfully— and then on the way back to the cabin, incredibly, had walked right into a couple of elk jousting in an open valley. It was a good six-pointer Bob shot. But Don talked us out of going there. They had seen no concentration of elk.

"Don's right," said Frank. "We ought to go the other way. We've only had a couple of storms and there's not more than a foot of snow on those peaks. It's been a lot milder than we expected. The way I see it, the elk started down from the high country with the snow, but when the weather softened up they went back above timberline. I think we'll find them up at the head of the Thorofare. I don't think the big herds ever came down."

Nothing else seemed to make sense, so Frank, Charlie, Chuck, and I agreed to take out next morning with a couple of tents, a packhorse apiece, set up a jack-camp at Butte Creek, and then hunt the high ridges around Woody and Bruin Creeks. It would be a long haul, so we'd leave early. The rest would stay at Hammett Cabin, pick up Bob's elk, do some fishing, and meet us with the rest of the outfit at Butte Creek in a couple of days.

Next day, we stopped at Butte Creek only long enough to put up one of the tents and throw our gear inside. In midafternoon, Charlie and Frank turned up Woody Creek while Chuck and I rode on to Bruin Creek, where eventually we wrestled the horses up the flank of a steep ridge until the timber ran out at 11,000 feet. We tied the horses in some gnarled whitebark pine, last vestiges of timber, and sprawled out to look the country over.

Our mystery was quickly solved. First I spotted a herd of at least 50 elk, and then Chuck picked up two more herds of about the same size before I glassed my second bunch and nearly rolled off the ridge in excitement. In short order, we figured we'd seen about 250 elk. Frank Lasater had called it. The elk were only now on the move.

"Hell," said Chuck, as he glassed the peaks and ridges around us, "this is like hunting sheep. I've never seen elk so high this late in the season."

There was only one thing wrong in this picture and, after our first enthusiasm, it sank in. The nearest herd was the first one I'd seen, and that was high on the slope of a ridge separated from us by a deep canyon. We'd have to drop down half a mile, cross a nameless tributary creek, and climb another half a mile even if we were to take the shortest route without trying to conceal ourselves. And it was already late in the afternoon.

Chuck started grimly for the horses. "Let's go," he said.

"We'll never make it," I said emptily.

"You want an elk don't you?" said Chuck. "At least we can try."

Suddenly a whistle cut the air. It sounded something like a bo'sun's pipe. It was so near it startled me, and I expected to see Charlie or Frank walk over the crest of the ridge. Chuck flattened me with a downward sweep of his hands. Slowly he crawled to the ridge crest and looked over; then he motioned me up the steep pitch. Keeping me low, he pointed toward some alpine conifers on the reverse slope of the ridge.

"See 'em!" he breathed jubilantly.

There in a shallow basin below us were elk—20, 30, 40? I couldn't tell in the quick look he allowed me. We were at the top of the ridge, and it was as if we were on one slope of a roof and the elk on the other. They were some distance from us, heading for the top, and the way they were quartering they'd be a lot farther from us by the time they reached it.

Chuck backed down till he could run bent over without being seen by the elk, and motioned peremptorily for me to follow. Running at a stoop is hard work anyway; doing it all at 11,000 feet is murder. Any exertion sucks the breath out of your lungs until you're left gasping. A couple of times I fell because of the steep pitch. Chuck did once, too, but my heaving pleas to wait a minute fell on deaf ears.

When we'd run like a couple of lopsided sauguses for a quarter of a mile, and crawled like snakes another 200 yards, he stopped suddenly and I collapsed behind him, sucking in great gobs of air and trembling from exertion. The slope had eased off and we were coming to a level topping. Just at that moment the first of the elk topped the rise and was angling slightly away from us. Then they came—spikes, calves, cows, and bulls, in single file.

Chuck was wedged up against me. "Don't move a finger," he whispered in my ear, "and they won't scare. Think you're part of the scenery, and don't shoot until I tell you."

There was nothing between us and the elk, not even a blade of grass. We lay right out in the open, flat on the shale. Maybe 100 yards from us the elk moved slowly, serenely, one behind the other like the clay figures in a shooting gallery. Fortunately, the wind was blowing toward us. In our tearing run, I'd sunk to my knees once long enough to jack a cartridge into the chamber of my Winchester 70. I tightened as a good-size bull came over the rise. Chuck restrained me.

"I saw a bigger one down in there," he whispered.

I was glad to wait. My breath was coming more normally now and my shakes subsiding. I swept my eye along the line of elk parading before us and counted 19 of them. Many of them stared right at us and went on unperturbed.

Only one calf was disturbed by the sight of us. It broke into an alarmed trot and caught up with a cow. It looked back as if to say, "Look, Ma, there's something there." But Ma must have said, "Don't look and it won't be there."

Now on the rise appeared a big rack. Slowly the elk materialized, and Chuck gripped my shoulder. "Get ready," he said. "This is the one."

I waited. It seemed an eternity before the bull carried those big antlers to the point nearest us, a little more than 100 yards away. I held the sights on its shoulder, took a deep breath, slowly let out half of it, clamped down on the rest of it, and squeezed the trigger.

The elk went down with incredible suddenness, crashing heavily to the ground, just exactly as if someone had pulled a rug out from under it. Chuck pounded me and I babbled some inanity.

"A beautiful six-pointer," Chuck crowed, "—and now we gotta get out of here. It'll be dark soon."

All we could do was rough-dress it. We'd have to come back for it the next day. It was getting dark as we took the long walk back to the clump of pines where we'd left the horses, and by the time we'd traveled the long ridge to the point where we could begin the half a mile descent to the valley it was pitch dark.

Slanting down a steep ridge through timber in utter blackness is like running full tilt through a back yard strung with clotheslines at night. The horses get through the trees all right but more often than not there's a barrier of invisible branches just about head high—to the horseman. Spice is added when you're not sure whether there's any edge to the trail or anything between you and the bottom 2,500 feet below.

After being jammed against tree trunks a couple of times, and almost decapitated a couple more, I got off to walk. This was worse. I nearly stepped off into space.

"Grab the horse's tail," Chuck suggested. "About 15 years ago I was guiding a bunch of big-league ballplayers, Boston Red Sox they were, and we got into a fix like this. One of those guys grabbed the horse's tail, sat right down in the snow, and let that horse drag him all the way to the bottom on the seat of his pants."

"Don't tell me his name," I said. "He might be one of my heroes."

"Of course," said Chuck, "I think you're better off ridin'. The horse can see better than you can. You learn to trust your horse."

So I trusted him, but, even so, when we reached Butte Creek, where Charlie and Frank had put up the other tent and had a hot supper waiting for us, I had lost every button on my jacket, both pockets were torn, and I had a big right-angle gap in the knee of my pants.

"Where's the wildcat you tangled with?" Frank asked.

There was jubilation that night. Charlie and Frank had come upon elk on one of the lower slopes and Charlie had quickly got the meat bull he'd wanted. So we set out next morning with the four packhorses to fetch the meat. (It takes two horses to carry one elk.) After we'd quartered Charlie's bull, Frank returned to Butte Creek, but Charlie decided to come along with us and take pictures to record the event.

When we finally reached my elk, Charlie said, "Hey, you guys weren't kidding when you said you were hunting sheep." He'd taken two pictures when it began to snow, and in short order a blizzard plastered us with white. The camera, useless anyway, was forgotten and we worked furiously to cut the elk up for the haul to Butte Creek.

"Mr. Elliott," said Chuck, between cussing out a dull blade and sweeping snowflakes from his eyes, "it looks like you got your wish. Lucky we got plenty of meat."

A couple of hours later as we struggled along the skyhigh ridge leading back to the valley, the snow suddenly let up, but it was plain there was plenty more where that came from. Still later, as we rode through the valley, Charlie suddenly stopped and pointed to an opening in the timber above us. A couple of elk walked into the little park. Then more followed and in short order we counted 72 of them working their way through the spruce. They were still coming when we finally moved on toward the cabin.

"They're on their way to Jackson Hole now, sure enough," said Charlie. When we told Frank later, he said shortly, "If they're in such a helluva hurry to get out of the country, we ought to be, too."

Saturday morning, while the rest of the hands rounded up the horses scattered between Hammett Cabin and Butte Creek, Frank packed them as fast as they brought them in, and sent part of the string on its way with Chuck and Bob Hogg. And when they finally came up with a couple of saddle horses, Frank packed Charlie and me on our way. We eventually caught up with Chuck and Bob at Deer Creek Pass, and as we started down the zigzag trail into the canyon, the wind chilled our bones and whipped the horses' tails between their legs.

But the snow held off. With only 11 more miles to go, it was plain Charlie wasn't going to spend this winter in the Thorofare, either. In fact, he didn't get his wish to be snowed in until nearly four years later—and, of all places, it was at my home just 35 miles outside of New York City.

Brown Bears Do Attack

Ralph W. Young

August 1959

Ralph W. Young is a veteran Alaska guide who writes with the polish of an English professor about one of the world's roughest jobs—steering sportsmen in range of big game. He was born in Milton, Pennsylvania, and raised in Oregon and Washington, but moved to Alaska forty-five years ago, hunting for sport and working as a commercial fisherman, trapper and seal hunter before he became a full-time guide and outfitter. Many of his clients are after Alaska brown bears, and he has been in on the kill of hundreds of them. Yet he's generally friendly toward brownies and dedicated to their preservation. "I talk to them in their own language," he says, "and we usually understand one another. Once, though, I had a brownie sniff me as I lay dozing in the sun on a creek bank. I couldn't think of a single appropriate remark."

A few months ago, there appeared in this magazine a well-written and convincing article about brown bears ("Do Brown Bears Attack?" November, 1958, OUTDOOR LIFE). This article interested me considerably, because, like its author, Earl J. Fleming, I live and work in Alaska. Unlike Mr. Fleming, however, I have never "interviewed" many bears, but I have had a few bears make solid attempts to interview me. On the basis of such experiences, I have drawn some conclusions that are very different from Mr. Fleming's.

The one conclusion of his I differ with most of all was summed up in these words: "Any bear possibly will charge if sufficiently provoked or disturbed. (But) I believe that most bears accused of charging were not actually charging at all."

It was the lure of the big brown bears that brought me to Alaska, and it's the bears that have kept me here. I started hunting the bears in the Kodiak area in 1932, and I suppose it was inevitable that I would take up guiding hunters as a profession. Since 1946, I've been at it on a full-time basis. I figure I've spent more than 2,000 days in the field with the bears—hunting, photographing, and observing their behavior—and I'm still learning about them.

I've guided more sportsmen than I can remember; the number certainly goes into three figures. Most of my hunters have come from Texas, New York, or Wisconsin, but I've had a smattering from nearly every state east of the Mississippi River, as well as from Oregon, Washington, and California. I've had clients from as far away as Austria, Germany, Switzerland, Italy, and Brazil.

Many of my hunters are world-famous sportsmen. They include men like Jack O'Connor and Warren Page, both winners of the Weatherby Big Game Trophy; Carl Goehringer of New Jersey; A. C. Gilbert of New Haven, and Bob Johnson, the Band-Aid man.

I have guided members of the Explorers Club, the Adventurers Club, the Shikar-Safari Club, and the Camp Fire Club of America. My clients have been corporation presidents, businessmen, teen-age kids, women, salesmen, farmers, doctors, lawyers, and airline pilots. One was a service-station attendant, another a barber, and one a genuine baron.

I'm acquainted with half a dozen sportsmen who, though they have hunted big game all over the world, still consider the Alaska brown bear the most dangerous animal on earth to hunt or photograph. On the other hand, I know just as many men with vast hunting experience who don't rate the brownie so highly. Only last fall, for example, I guided a chap from Wisconsin who referred to the brownie he killed as an "overgrown field mouse." He made this profound observation on the basis of having seen exactly 19 bears on a single hunt.

My own attitude toward the brownie is one of tremendous respect and admiration. I base my opinion on the thousands of brown bears I've seen, and on the several hundred brownie kills I've been in on. I firmly believe that no animal is more dangerous to hunt than these mighty monarchs of the northern wilderness.

To begin with, the Alaska brown bear has tremendous size, strength, and tenacity of life. And though attaining about twice the size of an African lion or a tiger, the brownie is just as quick and agile as either of these beasts. A brownie in full possession of its faculties, and making a determined attack, can cover 100 feet in a bit less than two seconds. This statement sounds fantastic, but it's true.

A charging brownie is one of the most dramatic and chilling spectacles nature has to offer. As often as not, bears start their attacks with no preliminary warning, and invariably at close range. Nor do they charge in the classic storybook manner—erect on their hind legs, paws extended to engulf the hapless victim in an apocryphal bear hug. A bear standing on its hind feet is as harmless as a man doing a handstand. A bear charges on all four feet, in great leaping bounds, very reminiscent of a huge, eager dog chasing a cat. When a brown bear charges, it's a life-and-death matter. Nothing short of death will stop the animal. The bear kills you, or you kill the bear. It's that elemental. On the several occasions I've faced charging brownies, I have never had time to get in more than one hastily aimed shot, and the only thing I've seen in my sights is blurred hair.

The single factor—above all others—that makes the Alaska brownie so dangerous to hunt is the complete unpredictability of its behavior. No one, no matter how much he has hunted, nor how much he thinks he knows about bears, can always correctly predict how any brownie will react to any given situation. Every bear is an individualist. Some are cowardly; some are brave. There are foolish bears and smart bears. Most bears panic at the scent of man; a few are indifferent and even contemptuous of man's close presence. Most unpredictable and volatile of all are females with cubs. During the years, I've seen so many bears do so many things that I take nothing for granted when hunting them. It's one of the reasons my wife is not a widow.

Several years ago one of my dudes shot a brown bear late in the evening at the head of a timbered cove. I sent him down the creek to watch our skiff while I skinned out the trophy. Halfway through the operation I looked up and spotted a small male brownie watching me from the edge of the woods, 100 yards away. Sitting on his broad rump, he was evidently greatly interested in what I was doing. While I worked, I kept close watch on my unwanted visitor.

After completing the job, I had to walk to within 35 yards of the bear to wash my hands and clean the skinning knife. The animal made no move to give ground. Then, with the pelt lashed to my packboard, I moved downstream 200 yards and looked back.

The brownie had walked along behind me, picked up the still-warm carcass in his mouth, and was carrying it back to the woods to eat. The whole area must have reeked with man scent and the smell of death, yet the bear was completely indifferent to all this. I can find nothing in the rule book on bears to cover this behavior.

Do brown bears attack? Of course they do. I'll go so far as to say that a wounded brown bear will almost always attack if it gets the chance and is physically able to. Every year, in the normal course of guiding hunters, I trail several wounded brown bears. It's a disagreeable job, and if I didn't get paid for it I wouldn't do it. There are people who enjoy living dangerously; it just happens I'm not one of them.

Although following up a wounded brownie in thick cover is hazardous, it isn't exactly suicidal provided the tracker knows his business and maintains control of the situation. The tracker has one tremendous advantage—the bear doesn't know it's being followed. So long as the hunter keeps this advantage, the odds are overwhelmingly on his side. If, however, the bear locates the man before the man finds the bear, and if the range is short, it's a toss-up who will come out of the fracas alive.

In any situation, Alaska brown bears are most impressive animals. And meeting one that is thoroughly aroused, in the gloom of a southeastern Alaska rain forest, is an unforgettable experience. The bear always looks twice as large as it really is, and has the nightmarish, malevolent look of some prehistoric creature. Each time I finish the job of trailing down a wounded brown bear I feel weak and limp. Sometimes the reaction is so strong that I vomit. I guess I'm no hero.

Will a brown bear attack without apparent provocation? My answer is an unequivocal "Yes." At least three times I have been charged by brownies that had no provocation except that we happened to be in the same area at the same time. In none of the three cases were we hunting the animals that attacked us.

The first unprovoked attack I experienced was in the summer of 1950. I was guiding Dr. Sterling Bunnell of San Francisco, and we were photographing bears on Admiralty Island. One fine, bright day we set up our camera in a likely looking place alongside a salmon stream, and settled down to wait. In due time a medium-size brownie appeared downstream, too far away to photograph. He picked up a dead salmon, ate it, and, moving downstream, finally disappeared around a bend in the creek. I thought we'd seen the last of him. However, in the usual unpredictable manner of the species, the brownie—unknown to us—turned and traveled in our direction through the thick cover bordering the creek. Next time we saw him he was coming out of the woods directly opposite our blind, and hardly 60 feet away. The doctor swung his camera over to get the picture, and I automatically covered the bear with my .375 Magnum. The brownie saw our movements and although he was only a few feet from cover, chose instead to attack. He covered half the distance between us in two mighty bounds before I dropped him with a shoulder shot.

Maybe the bear was just bluffing—but suppose he wasn't! It's about the same situation as if a hoodlum shoved a .45 into your belly and demanded your money. He might be bluffing, but how can you be sure?

In September 1957, I was guiding Lee Doerr of Cedarburg, Wisconsin, on a brown-bear hunt. Lee had made it very plain that he wanted a large, trophy-size brownie or no bear at all. The first day we went afield we walked up a creek on the southern end of Admiralty Island where salmon were plentiful and bears numerous. Right from the start we began seeing bears—small bears and medium-size bears—but nothing that interested us. The farther upstream we went, the more plentiful were the bears. Finally we came to a mean stretch of water where the creek broke up into many rivulets. Hundreds of salmon were stranded in the shallows, and the area was laced with big trees that had blown down in a recent storm. It was just the sort of place bears love to feed, and precisely where an experienced hunter dreads to meet a brownie. We moved through this jungle with extreme caution, and were nearly in the clear.

Suddenly, to our left, we heard a tremendous splashing, and out of a hidden backwash came three bears—a sow and two cubs. They all ran up the far bank, and the two cubs jumped over a log into the woods. The female made as if to follow them, then suddenly swapped ends.

Uttering a series of coughing roars, she came straight at us from a distance of 100 feet. So unexpected was the attack, and so rapid the action, that I think she might have made it to us if she hadn't been forced to cover part of the distance through three feet of water. Lee and I both hit her fair in the chest, and dropped her at a distance of about 35 feet.

If ever there was an unprovoked attack, this was it. The bear had no broken teeth that might have pained her, she was unwounded, her cubs weren't threatened, and the avenue of escape was clear. And for our part, with a limit of one brownie to the license, we had no desire to kill her. Yet we had no choice. This sow meant business. She definitely was not bluffing.

A year later almost to the day, I had another experience with a brown bear—this time a near-fatal one. I was hunting with Jerry Kron of Mount Kisco, New York, a well-known scouter, and a salesman for a Rochester photo-supply company. Again this was on Admiralty Island.

We really shouldn't have been hunting that day. It had been raining hard for 36 hours and all the streams were at flood stage. The creek we were on was so high that we could wade it on only a few of the shallower riffles. So we spent most of our time struggling through the almost impenetrable thickets of devil thorn, blueberry, and alders that line the banks of any Admiralty Island salmon stream. Fish were scarce, and on our slow progress up the creek we never saw a track or fresh bear sign. Finally we decided there was no point going farther, and started across a point of land to strike another stream, which we intended to follow back to tidewater.

In a few minutes we found ourselves in the midst of one of the worst jungles I've ever seen. The brush was higher than our heads, and we actually had to force our way through it. Visibility was practically zero in any direction.

Presently I saw a raven fly up out of the brush ahead, perch in a dead hemlock, and begin croaking dismally. Ravens acting this way often indicate the presence of a bear. I climbed up on a spruce log several feet in diameter to look around. I huffed and snorted, trying to get any bear that might be in the area to answer me. Nothing happened. The only sound or movement in that dismal, dripping jungle was the raven still perched in the tree. I checked my rifle to be sure the sights were clear, and jumped down off the log. Jerry was directly behind me. I had taken perhaps six steps when I heard something come crashing through the brush in our direction.

As soon as I saw the brute, I pressed the trigger. That was the luckiest shot of my career. The 270-grain bullet passed through the brownie's neck and lodged in the spine for an instantaneous kill. It died just nine measured feet from where I stood. Jerry said the animal went back two feet after I shot. If so, I killed the bear at a range of about seven feet.

We carefully examined this brownie for signs of old or fresh wounds, but found none. It was a perfectly healthy specimen. The only possible reason it could have had for attacking was that we happened to be in the same patch of brush. Furthermore, it must have charged without knowing what manner of creature it was attacking.

It's always startling to meet a brownie at such close range. Years ago I guided a well-nourished gentleman from a small country in central Europe. All the brownies we saw up to one eventful day were mild-mannered, inoffensive, and small. My client wasn't impressed. He enjoyed relating his experiences hunting such exotic game as wild boars, European brown bears, tigers, leopards, and Indian buffaloes. He made it quite plain that he didn't consider the Alaska brown bear in the same class as any of those horrendous beasts from the other side of the Atlantic. Since my hunting experience has been confined to a very small portion of North America, I didn't presume to debate the point.

One afternoon toward the end of the hunt, after another unsuccessful day afield, we were wading down a salmon stream. We came to a large spruce that had fallen across the creek, and were about to crawl over it when a brownie—a really big one—rose up on the other side of the log directly opposite us. I've never been so close to a live brownie before or since. I believe I could have touched the animal.

Both my client and I had our rifles slung on our backs, and were absolutely at the mercy of the bear. In a crisp, firm voice my companion said, "Attention!" I've never figured out whether he was talking to the bear, to me, or to himself. In any case, it was the most superfluous remark I've ever heard.

The brownie glared at us for what seemed a long while. Suddenly it snapped its jaws, making a sound like a steel trap springing shut. It roared once, leaped up on the creek bank, and disappeared into the jungle.

It took my dude a while to recover from this experience. He was visibly shaken, and had trouble lighting a cigarette. Finally he remarked, "I zink zoom day one of zese bears kill you, no?"

I doubt if there's a professional brown-bear guide in Alaska who has handled as many as 20 hunters who hasn't faced at least one bona fide attack by a brownie. I'm acquainted with four guides, ex-guides rather, who were seriously mauled by brown bears.

Allen Hasselborg told me he'd been charged no fewer than 12 times during his career. His crippled right arm was a reminder of one encounter that had a near-tragic finale.

Hardy Trefzger had his arm nearly bitten off and was practically scalped by a bear that he'd been photographing. This bear attacked the moment it saw Hardy, and without the least provocation.

Ed Younkey and Lee Ellis were both severely mauled by wounded bears, and both consider themselves fortunate to be alive today.

Then there's the classic case of Frank Barnes. Barnes was a guide, and also the mayor of Wrangell, Alaska. Thus he was a well-known and respected man locally. One fall he took a party of sportsmen up the Stikene River to hunt waterfowl. They left their cabin in the morning and were hiking toward a lake where they hoped for a good day's sport, when one of the party discovered he'd forgotten an essential piece of equipment. Barnes volunteered to go back to the cabin for it. A short while later a single shot was heard from the direction Frank had disappeared. His companions waited a reasonable time, and then went back to investigate.

They found the guide wedged so tightly into the crotch of a tree that he had to be chopped out. He'd been fearfully mauled, and his face had been bitten off and was lying in the trail. Incredibly, Barnes was still alive and rational. He kept repeating, "She got me! She got me—" He died four hours later in spite of the efforts of his friends to get him to a hospital where expert medical care might have saved his life.

Of course no one will ever know exactly what happened that day in the gloomy rain forests of the Stikene River. Undoubtedly, however, this was another authentic case of a brown bear making an unprovoked attack. Frank was carrying only a shotgun at the time, and being an experienced hunter would never have shot at a bear with such a weapon except under extreme duress. Probably he met a sow with cubs, and she charged the moment she saw or smelled him, as they sometimes will.

I hope no one gets the impression that I'm trying to build a case against the bears. The only reason I live in Alaska is that there are brown bears here. I consider them the grandest and most interesting animals on earth. I'm dedicated to their preservation. So long as Alaska brown bears live, there'll be at least one creature in North America that cannot be tagged, branded, taxed, or deprived of life, liberty, and the pursuit of happiness without a fight.

I'll go on guiding bear hunters as long as there are bears and hunters and so long as I'm physically able. I have a premonition that somewhere out on Admiralty, Baranof, or Chicagof Island, there's a brownie—perhaps yet unborn—that has my number on him. Someday we'll meet, and it will be one for the bears. It isn't a thing I worry about.

My Last Grizzly

Dan Ludington
as told to James Doherty

November 1959

A few years before this story, 1955, William R. Waddell, who had never seen
a bear in 20 years of hunting, killed a 540-pound black bear in the
Adirondacks ("New York's Biggest Bear," by William R. Waddell as told to
Ted Janes, May 1956). It was not only New York's biggest, but still is tied
for 53rd in *Records of North American Big Game.* As if that weren't
enough, it was killed with a three-barrel gun, a 12-gauge double with .32/40
rifle barrel underneath. The rifle killed the bear. The Hollenbach—later the
Three Barrel—Gun Company made rifles, shotguns and the three-barrel gun,
or drilling as it is called in Europe, where such guns are popular and still
made. The Three-Barrel Gun Co. operated in Moundsville, W. Va., from the
1890's until 1918–1920, when it failed because of the high cost of
production.

I should have cut and run clear out of Alaska that snowy October morning
nearly 10 years ago when Jerry Luebke kicked open the door of my lodge at
Summit Lake. Unfortunately, my crystal ball wasn't working. I hadn't seen the
big guy in weeks, and anyway I'd always pictured fate as a frowner, which Jerry
certainly was not. He was a grinning giant in a size 44 wolfskin parka—an old
friend with whom I'd shared many a campfire.

Now, 10 years is usually enough time to take the edge off the memory of any
run-of-the-mine day. For me, however, this was to be no ordinary day. Jerry's
first words—delivered after my two kids, Milton, then four years old, and Rendy,
two, had been shooed off his knee—come to me as clearly now as they did a
decade ago.

"I hate to tell you this, Dan," he said laconically, "but you and Maxine are
about to have visitors. If not today, then tonight for sure."

As foreman of the Alaska Road Commission camp at Paxson, a wide spot in
the Richardson Highway about 150 miles southeast of Fairbanks, Jerry was a
sort of ambulatory newspaper for 20 or more roadhouse operators who, like
myself, depended on highway traffic for a living. If he said visitors were on the
way, I could believe it.

My place, Moochigan Lodge, sat on the edge of Summit Lake, a stone's throw
from the highway and nine miles north of Jerry's homestead at Paxson.

"Why the sad face?" I asked. "After all, a little late-season business would be
the next best thing to an early spring." I meant it, too. The summer of 1949 had
come and gone like a running deer. Worse yet, it promised to be a long, cold
winter.

"It's nobody you know," Jerry replied. "I'm talking about that old sow grizzly
that's been raising cain around Paxson for the past couple of weeks. The one with
the cub. You've probably heard about 'em already."

This was some of the best grizzly country in Alaska. We knew it and so did
swarms of sportsmen who regularly made our lodge their hunting headquarters.

Here, the Richardson Highway bisected a panorama of low, brush-covered
hills laced with blueberry thickets. Fishing was excellent in dozens of nearby

287

lakes and streams. Annually, the caribou herds drifting past provided a ready source of meat for lean-bellied predators.

But a killing frost had denuded blueberry bushes for miles around in mid-August that year, and reports of marauding bears had been only too common. Indian summer had been frozen in its tracks, and the area's population of big game had grown hungrier and more ill-tempered with each passing week.

"Anyway," Jerry continued, "the sow and her cub have moved up to your neck of the woods. They're hungry, Dan. They've been prowling the old fish camps, and the sow's a big one. She's buffalo-colored and mean." A recital of the grizzly's depredations followed.

According to Jerry, the sow and her cub had been busier around Paxson than a colony of beavers. Garbage cans, ever a favorite target, had been ransacked nightly and a number of food caches violated.

It wasn't until Jerry told of actually being chased by the grizzly, however, that I became alarmed. With Maxine hanging on every word, he recounted an incident that had taken place the previous evening.

Dusk was coming on, and Jerry had been working in the clearing behind his cabin at the edge of the road commission camp. Suddenly, with no more warning than a sneeze, the sow had charged from a nearby clump of brush.

From her position on the back porch, the big fellow's wife screamed a warning. Jerry looked up, found himself cut off from the cabin, and legged it for the camp bunkhouse. He'd won the race by a whisker.

I digested the tale in silence, then shrugged in a poor attempt to conceal my misgivings. But Maxine wasn't fooled.

"I just thought of something," she exclaimed. "Dan killed a caribou last week. The meat is hanging outside the kitchen door right now, like an invitation to supper."

I had to grin, remembering the day not too many years before when I'd suggested to Maxine that she learn to hunt. Just then she was outguessing her teacher.

"And the wind, Dan," she continued excitedly. "It's been in the north since yesterday. The old sow is bound to have caught the scent. She'll be here about dark like Jerry says. Wait and see."

"Maybe," I said, "and maybe not. Anyhow, with this fresh snow on the ground the two of them shouldn't be hard to track."

Jerry nodded agreement. Without a word, Maxine crossed the room and plucked my .401 Winchester autoloader off its pegs. That model was discontinued in 1936, but I had mine rebuilt around 1939. If my wife was worried as she handed me the rifle, she didn't show it.

Throughout my 22 years in Alaska I'd killed my share of bears, and I guess Maxine had confidence in my ability. It still gets me when I realize how she was forced to revise her thinking before dark.

It was snowing lightly when Jerry and I left the roadhouse. We climbed into his pickup and headed south along Richardson Highway. I remember turning in my seat as we rounded the first curve. Maxine was waving good-by from the roadhouse door.

"Last report I had," Jerry said, "the sow and her cub were poking around near Fish Creek. Might be a good place to start looking." Then, as an afterthought, "Dan, that old devil will go about 800 pounds, and she's just itching for trouble. How about postponing this deal? I'll take tomorrow off and we'll make a hunt of it."

I shook my head. Jerry's recent, narrow escape had convinced me of something that made killing the bear quickly imperative. It was my guess that the animal was nursing an old wound.

I told Jerry that in my opinion someone armed with a small-caliber rifle had taken a shot at the sow. As her wound festered, her temper had followed suit until she became hostile and constituted a real menace.

In all the years I'd been in Alaska, and while acting as a big-game guide, I'd never heard of a healthy bear charging a human being. As a rule, the average bear—any variety, any size—is sociable enough when left alone. Though he'll go out of his way to keep your scent in the wind, the odds are long he's not looking for more than a nodding acquaintance. On occasion, I'd even run bears out of my way with rocks and sticks, or just an ear-splitting, banshee yell.

Though he shared my suspicions about the sow, Jerry made one last attempt to stall off my search. Again I rejected any delay. While he eased the truck through the snow, I strained my eyes for bear sign.

Funny, I thought, how a first snowfall can change the look of a countryside. Yesterday the brush had seemed visibly thin, like a blanket of twisted wire laid across the hills. Today, it was thickly padded with the white down payment of an early winter.

We'd gone a little over a mile when I signaled for a halt. Near the mouth of a small culvert that ran beneath the highway I'd spotted a welter of tracks.

"Could be some trucker stopped for water," Jerry said, "but let's have a look."

He pulled the truck off the road and we climbed out. From 20 feet away you could read the sign like a book. The footprints were big and comparatively fresh. The telltale cub tracks were right there beside the big ones. Following them toward the low ridge that paralleled the road would be easy.

I felt a surge of excitement as I climbed to the top of the pickup, and, between the intermittent flurries, scanned the white slope with my binoculars. I remembered other winters when I'd hunted and trapped these hills alone. Every dip and rise in the landscape was back-of-the-hand familiar.

Right now, however, my quarry was at least one ridge away. The glasses revealed no sign of life on the nearest hillside.

I jumped to the ground. Without a word, Jerry climbed into the truck, backed it farther off the highway, then pocketed the key.

"What's the big idea?" I asked.

He shrugged, and the wolfskin parka wrinkled comically around his neck.

"I'll climb to the top of the ridge with you and have a look around," he said. "Might see something moving on the other side."

The bears had broken a wide trail, and walking was easy. A light snow was still falling, and I judged the temperature to be a comfortable 10°.

On the summit of the ridge we came across droppings to which the snow had already begun to adhere. This, and the amount of snow that had collected in the tracks, convinced us the sow and her cub had a good three-hour head start. Their trail angled slightly across the valley below, then rose again to the next low ridge about half a mile away.

By now, Jerry's conscience had begun to get the best of him. His road-clearing gang faced a long, tough day, and more snow was definitely on the way. With a final warning about watching my step, he waved good-by and started back the way we had come. I continued on.

Within minutes, the snow began to thicken noticeably. An hour or two of this and the trail would be obliterated. I picked up the pace.

By now, however, something else had begun to disturb me. Beyond the shadow of a doubt, the sow and her offspring were headed for my lodge. Mentally, I projected their route. By nightfall, it would bring the pair to my back door and the ripening caribou meat that even now must be wafting its mouth-watering scent across the hills.

By the time I'd panted to the second ridgetop, the valley beyond was curtained completely by the snow. It fell in long, sullen waves from the lowering sky and all but hid the line of brush about 10 yards below the ridge crest where the tracks ended.

I stopped and thought the matter over carefully. The chances were good that a mile or more still separated me from the two grizzlies. The tracks were filling up. The snow made the binoculars useless, and plunging blindly into the brush was out of the question.

The sow was man-wise and mean. In all likelihood she was still traveling. On the other hand, she might have caught my scent and doubled back under cover of the storm to stalk me.

Later—while mulling things over in a hospital bed—I would conclude that this moment of hesitation probably saved my life. Had I turned back, the sow would have nailed me from behind, unseen. Plunging ahead would no doubt have proved equally fatal.

At any rate, I was standing there, cold and undecided—my binoculars in one hand, my rifle in the other—when the sow exploded like a four-footed thunderclap from the line of brush not 30 feet away. Her deep-throated roar ripped through the silence on the ridge. Instinctively, I let the binoculars fall on the strap around my neck, swung my rifle in the grizzly's direction, and yanked the trigger. In the split second that should have preceded the blast, I glimpsed the sow's crazy red eyes and the hair standing ramrod straight along her back. Then I experienced the sickest, most all-gone moment in my life.

For the first time since I'd bought the .401 back in 1932, the autoloader failed to fire. Instead of its usual, death-dealing bellow, the rifle responded to my trigger pull with a dry, harmless click. Desperately, I pumped another shell into the chamber just as 800 pounds of rock-hard, crazy-mad grizzly slammed me to the ground.

Luckily, my binoculars broke the force of the sow's first swipe at my chest, made with a right paw the size of a football. But despite the protection of the glasses and four or five layers of heavy clothing, her claws laid open my chest as neatly as a surgeon's knife—and I didn't feel a thing. As I staggered backward, I managed to crack the sow a solid blow on the nose with the butt of my rifle. She snapped viciously at the weapon, but I hung on. It was my only hope, and I knew it.

Then I was on the ground, and from my worm's-eye view the bear looked as big as a mountain. Methodically, she began making mincemeat of my left arm, and when I yelled in pain she snapped at my head.

In the years since, I've relived that moment 1,000 times in my dreams. Without fail, the memory of the grating sound the sow's teeth made across my skull is enough to awaken me in a cold sweat. And always I wake up kicking, just as I was kicking when it happened.

By now, though only a few seconds had elapsed since the bear struck me, I felt as if I'd been flat on my back for an eternity. And while I kicked and screamed and cursed, I kept thinking what a lousy way this was to die. I thought of Maxine and the kids—Maxine with another baby on the way and me in hock to my blood-soaked eyebrows. The more I thought of it the harder I kept digging my size 12 boots in the sow's belly.

Then, as if annoyed at the time it was taking to put me away, the grizzly bit through my face from the center of my nose to my right temple. The blurred image of her on-coming fangs was the last thing I ever saw through my right eye.

The pain inside my head mushroomed to killing proportions, and I fought frantically to retain consciousness. The temptation to drop my rifle and grab my head was almost overpowering. But I was staking my dwindling chances on the gun—and finally my opportunity came.

Annoyed at my incessant kicking, the sow, which had transferred her attentions from my head to my left leg, eventually backed off and grabbed my right leg above the offending boot. In that single, redeeming instant, I pointed the rifle at her broad chest and pulled the trigger.

I saw the hair blow straight up on the grizzly's back as 250 grains of lead crashed completely through her. She dropped my foot and reared upward a few inches, her forepaws off the ground. Her death roar and that of the rifle sounded almost as one. She flopped on her belly at my feet—lifeless.

I fell back in the snow. It seemed terribly quiet all of a sudden, though my ears still rang. Then the realization began to sink in. The bear was dead. I'd won. I was alive!

I said it over and over to myself, five, maybe six times, I couldn't believe my luck. Like a fighter on the verge of being knocked out, I'd thrown a desperation haymaker and connected.

A moment later, reality in the form of a 100-foot-high wall of pain put things back in sharp focus. When the spasm passed, I staggered to my feet.

Now that it was all over I was scared. Thank God, I thought, Maxine can't see me now.

I put my right hand on top of my head. My scalp was literally in ribbons. A large piece of skin was draped across my good eye, and I eased it upward gently. It promptly tumbled down again, triggering a fresh flow of blood. I ripped off what was left of my undershirt and wrapped it around my head. With only my right arm usable, it took a bit of doing.

The grizzly had given my left arm a thorough going over. I surveyed the mess impersonally, as if it belonged to someone else. One glance convinced me that even if I made it to a doctor, the shredded arm would have to come off.

As a souvenir of the blow that knocked me down, I had three deep claw cuts across my chest. I remember marveling at their neatness. Six inches higher and the swipe would have been fatal.

But it was my lacerated left leg that concerned me most. It was on fire with pain, and I faced a long hike back to the highway. Just above my left ankle the blood was pouring from a big hole where the bear had got in some of her final licks.

I cautiously shifted my weight to the leg. The bone appeared to be intact, but movement was sheer agony. I groaned—both in pain and at the thought of the distance I had to travel.

Suddenly, I noticed I'd begun to shake. That's right, I thought, go ahead and panic—panic like a damned tenderfoot, out here in the middle of God-only-knows-where, and you've had it.

Then, from force of habit, perhaps, I leaned down to pick up my rifle. That was stupid. I awoke, probably only moments later, with my face buried in the snow, smothering.

That did it. Time was running out. I lurched to my feet, and, without so much as a backward glance at my dead attacker, went reeling down the trail.

My attention focused on only four things during the next terrible hour and a half. The first was a snappy debate with myself about the wisdom of taking a shortcut to the highway. I abandoned the notion quickly in favor of returning the way I'd come. At least one person knew the route I had taken and would look for me along the trail if I failed to show up.

And I recall seeing the brush move along the trail and imagining it was the cub. You're an orphan now, little guy, I said to myself. Old Man Winter will get you, sure as hell.

Next, somewhere along the way, I looked down at my right hand and saw it still clutched the rifle. Angrily, I flung it into a snowbank. Packing all that extra weight, I thought. How dumb can you get?

Finally, I remember something flopping against my left cheek. Reaching across with my right hand I tried to brush it away. It was my mangled left ear, hanging by a thread of skin to the side of my head. Gingerly, I tucked it back beneath my blood-soaked turban. Doctors can do wonders nowadays, I thought. Ten to one they'll sew it back on.

A pain-racked eternity later, I staggered onto the highway at the exact spot where I'd left it. Luck was with me.

As I slumped to the ground, a freight truck was braking to a stop at the culvert. The driver, Lewis Clarke, was an old friend.

While he loaded me into the cab I mumbled details of my scrap with the grizzly. Louie kept saying something that sounded like "Good God," and shaking his head. We finally got going north, in the direction of my lodge. I insisted we roll right past. I didn't want Maxine and the kids to see me like this. Anyway, the nearest doctor was at Big Delta Air Force Base 70 miles north, where the Richardson Highway joins the Alaska Highway.

The trip was a confused blur in my pain-occupied mind. I recall that we stopped at a roadhouse well beyond mine, and Louie passed the word ahead to the Army Alaska Arctic Training Center, which also occupied the base and ran the hospital. He called Maxine also and told her I'd been hurt. She promised to go at once to Fairbanks where I was eventually to be taken.

An Army ambulance met our truck some miles south of the Big Delta intersection. At the base I was given sedatives and first aid, then placed in another ambulance that headed for the hospital in Fairbanks in a blinding snowstorm.

In the 50 miles between the towns, the ambulance got stuck four times in king-size drifts. It was early evening before Dr. William Smith of the Fairbanks Medical and Surgical Clinic got me on his table.

In the hours that followed he took more than 200 stitches in my face, scalp, chest, arm, and leg. He managed to save the arm I'd given up for lost, and to reattach my ear. My right eye, however, was beyond repair.

Ten days later, I was bound for Seattle and a succession of operations spread out over a period of six months. I was fitted with a plastic right eye. Today, 10 years later, I'm still trying to get used to it.

I've regained complete use of my injured arm and leg. The leg, by the way, gets a workout every morning. Immediately after rising I kick the head of a huge bear rug that decorates the floor of my bedroom.

Jerry Luebke made me a present of my ex-assailant's hide. The day after my epic one-rounder in the wilderness, he returned to the ridge, skinned out the grizzly, and recovered my rifle. As we suspected, the sow had been wounded once before—with a slug from a .25/20.

I can only theorize about the failure of my first shot. About a year after the battle, I went back to the scene and found the cartridge that had misfired. The primer was dented, but not deeply enough to ignite the charge.

I had taken the rifle from a warm room into the cold. It's possible that lubrication in the trigger spring mechanism congealed with the change in temperature. Also, some snow may have got into the warm breech and later have frozen. Either situation would have been enough to prevent the spring from sending the firing pin forward with sufficient force to fire the cartridge.

That grizzly, incidentally, was the last I've taken from that day to this. I'm now cook and camp manager for a contractor building storage tanks in Adak, and I don't do much hunting—just a little bird shooting now and again. The loss of my right eye makes it necessary for me to shoot left-handed, and that's no good for bears.

Ray Bergman Says Goodbye

Ray Bergman

March 1960

Ray Bergman sold his first story to OUTDOOR LIFE in 1927; he became angling editor of the magazine in 1934. In all, the great angler-writer-teacher wrote more than three hundred articles and stories for OUTDOOR LIFE. This was the last piece he wrote, marking his retirement at sixty-eight. He had told me he was tired and wanted to fish for a while without writing about it and worrying about deadlines as he had for twenty-six years. "Those were happy years, Bill," he said, "but, you know, the column I could write in a day or two in those years now takes me almost a month to do. First, I want to rest, and then I want to do one more book." Ray did the fishing and fully expected to do an occasional story for OUTDOOR LIFE. He never did. He started on the book, but it was only a start. To his wife, Grace, who typed all his manuscripts and was his constant companion in travel, he said one day: "I can't do it, Grace. I wanted to so much, but I can't do it." The greatest of all angling editors died February 17, 1967, at seventy-five, in Nyack, New York.

My angling column has been in each issue of OUTDOOR LIFE for 26 years. I wrote monthly features and a column about fishing for 12 years before I became OUTDOOR LIFE's angling editor. I am getting along in years. The time has come when I need to take a rest from the steady demands of writing to meet deadlines each month. For this reason I have resigned as angling editor.

It was a tough decision to make. Since joining the OUTDOOR LIFE staff in March of 1934 I have written for it exclusively. The association has been a happy one. Hence, I want to make it plain that, while this is my last monthly angling column, it is not necessarily the last story I will write for the magazine. I merely want to be free from a regular schedule.

I started writing simply because I loved fishing and wanted to share what I learned from my endless experiments with fishing tackle and tactics. Rather like a person airing his ideas through a letter to the editor, I typed out my first fishing story in 1921 and mailed it to the old Forest and Stream magazine. The story was published, and I have been writing similar stories ever since. All my writing has followed the same basic concept: to give the reader factual information gained and tested by my own practical experience, and to make it as interesting as my writing ability would allow.

I have been fishing as long as I can remember. As a child I fished with my father on the Hudson River, which runs by my home town of Nyack, New York. By the time I was 10 years of age I was using a bicycle to pedal to lakes and streams near Nyack to fish for trout, bass, pickerel, and panfish. Eventually I was seeking more distant waters by train and in an early vintage automobile with blowout-prone tires mounted on those frustrating clincher rims.

Though fishing has been my main interest, I have also written a few articles about hunting. At the age of 10, I acquired a .22 rifle (a brass-bore Hamilton) by selling magazine subscriptions. I was in the woods and hills as much as I was on the water, and I brought many a squirrel and rabbit home to add to the family larder.

I have only one painful recollection of my days as a boy hunter. This happened when I was 11.

Father had a double-barreled, muzzle-loading, 12 gauge shotgun. He didn't object to my hunts with the .22 rifle, but he had forbidden me to use the shotgun. This created a desire in me to fire that gun the first chance I got.

Before long the opportunity came. Father was at work in the city and mother had taken a later train to go shopping there. Neither would be home until 6 p.m. It was a splendid setup.

That day I played hooky. I gathered up the shotgun, the powder horn, a bag of shot, and the necessary firing caps. Making sure that none of the neighbors saw me, I sneaked into the woods.

I charged the old muzzle-loader with powder and shot, and began scanning the trees for squirrels. I saw one, drew a bead on it, and pulled the trigger. The next thing I knew I was flat on my back. I had put in too big a powder charge and had held the gun too loosely. Besides, I was just a small child. The tremendous recoil bruised my armpit and badly injured my right hand.

I got the gun home and put it back where it belonged, but I knew I was in for some questioning. I could get away with the bruised armpit, but I couldn't hide the injured hand.

I am sorry to say that I lied about the hand. I told my parents I'd hurt it by falling. I was guilty of further treachery at school, where I showed my injured hand and was excused from the laborious written work by classmates were doing. I represented myself as a partial invalid for as long as I could. Perhaps my punishment for these boyhood deceits came through a loss of solid enthusiasm for shotguns, which some outdoorsmen cherish as I do my fine fly rods.

I was also a trapper during my youth and early manhood. Trapping season came at a time when there wasn't any fishing. It gave me an extra excuse to explore the woods and waters. I always inspected the trout waters near my traplines regularly during the closed fishing season—just to spy on the brook trout. This helped a lot when the fishing season opened. I knew just where to fish and how to approach the good spots without frightening the trout.

I was the proprietor of a sporting-goods store in Nyack when I was in my early 20's, but I still ran a trapline in season. I often got up at 3 a.m. to run my lines before I opened the store. Routine haul from my traps at this time was a few muskrats and skunks each week, but one morning I made what I considered a bonanza catch on my eight-trap brook line. In one trap was a star-black skunk, a premium-pelt animal with only a small patch of white on its head. In another was a very dark and large northern mink, and in the last was the largest muskrat I'd ever caught. They were all bonus-price furs.

I delayed getting back to the store until the last minute before I should open it for the commuters to pick up their papers. I wanted people on the streets to admire my catch.

I stalked slowly and proudly into town at the right moment—and drove a stream of pedestrians off the sidewalk as if I'd been playing a fire hose ahead of me. Skunk trappers forget how skunks smell to persons unaccustomed to the odor. My trek through town disrupted Nyack so that incident was headlined on the front page of our local paper.

It took a serious illness to get me started writing seriously. In April my doctor recommended a six to eight-month recuperation period in the woods. We didn't have enough money to consider such a thing, but God and good fortune came to our aid. A friend connected us with a couple in the Adirondack mountains of northern New York who had a cabin for rent at a very low fee. A family rented our own home furnished, which carried the expenses of both, as well as supplying a moderate surplus.

It was a marvelous seven months. All I did was fish and hunt. I wrote a two-part article about it that was accepted by Forest and Stream with a request for more.

Following my wilderness recuperation, I took a job with the fine old-fishing-tackle firm of William Mills & Son of New York. After some 10 years on that job I started a one-man tackle business of my own, doing most of my business through mail order. I have been in some phase of the fishing-tackle business all of my adult life.

Between fishing for sport and working with fishing tackle, I naturally acquired a large store of knowledge of fishing subjects. I drew on this information to write four successful books—*Just Fishing, Trout, Fresh Water Bass,* and *With Fly, Plug and Bait.* My book *Trout,* which went through 13 printings after its first publication in 1938, was later revised to include a section on spinning tackle.

I remember 1932 as a banner year. I had taken leave of absence from William Mills & Son. By that time I had been writing and selling stories and articles for about 10 years. My wife and I had saved enough to finance a long fishing trip.

We began our fishing in the Catskills of New York state, then to the Adirondacks in the same state—all familiar territory. Then we went to New Brunswick, Canada. All this fishing was mostly for trout and salmon, although we also took some bass and northern pike. Next we made a long trek west to Lake of the Woods in Ontario, Canada, for muskies. Ernie Calvert, now deceased, gave us expert instructions on how to catch these giant members of the pike family. We also got well acquainted with northern pike.

We went from Ontario to Wisconsin, getting a variety of fishing. Then we drove down to North Carolina, where we fished for channel bass off the island of Ocracoke. Later we spent considerable time fishing in the bayous of Mississippi and Louisiana. After that we headed north, expecting to fish the Ozarks in Arkansas and Missouri, but at Little Rock winter struck so suddenly and hard we started home.

An ice storm plagued us for miles. By the time we reached Virginia a blizzard had taken over. We decided to keep going. We didn't make many miles that day but we managed to reach a town in northern Virginia about dark where we spent the night.

Next morning we got up before daylight. It was bitter cold and the roads were snowy, icy, and slippery. Before we reached Harrisburg, Pennsylvania, in late afternoon we'd worn out two sets of tire chains. We bought another pair that didn't fit well. We had about 200 miles to go. Being young, we decided to make for home.

The road was treacherous, the cold intense, hovering around 10°. The car was a five-year-old Model A Ford. It had no heater. The new chains got messed up within 30 miles. I took them off and we made out better without them.

We just had to keep going on. There wasn't much else to do. This was before the days of motels scattered all along the highways. There were few cars on the road.

Our own home in Nyack had been closed for months, so we went to the home of my wife's parents. How wonderful were the warm greetings, the warm house, the hot tea and food. It was a perfect ending to our first long fishing adventure.

Since then we have fished in all the good fishing states, as well as many of the Canadian provinces.

Throughout the years there have been some fishing experiences that I remember more vividly than others, and some friends who through their knowledge and helpfulness taught me many of the secrets of successful fishing.

One of the first was an Adirondack guide named Chan Wescott, long since deceased. He put me to many subtle tests before he decided I was worth helping.

Then he started giving me advice on where and how to fish. He taught me much about wet-fly and bait fishing, and I was a proud young man when one day he told me I was a good fisherman. It was an honor to be accepted on even terms by those old-time Adirondack guides.

The late J. D. (Don) Bell, who was a lawyer in Hillsdale, N. Y., was the source of much inspiration and help in dry-fly fishing. Gruff, tender-hearted Dan was older than I by about 18 years, yet he could wear me out on the stream until he reached the age of 70 and keep up with me until he became 80.

One of the English setters that was Don Bell's constant companion was forever exposing the brawny, thunderous man for the soft touch that he really was. It was common practice for this setter to splash into the trout pool Dan was stalking and swim nonchalantly through the hole before the lawyer could make his first cast. Don would bellow threats at the top of his great voice, promising punishments too terrible to relate. The dog, knowing full well that all would be forgiven, would swim till it tired of the game.

Don had a weakness for dogs and dry-fly fishing. He never fished for anything but trout, and to my knowledge he never fished with anything but dry flies. I learned much of what I know about dry-fly fishing from him.

I must confess that to me the trouts are the most enjoyable fish to catch. I like them all: the rainbow as the best and most spectacular fighter, the brook trout for beauty and dogged battle, and the brown for its seeming intelligence and its first spirited runs when hooked.

I also love to catch black bass, and I must say that a smallmouth bass of equal size in the same type of water can put a rainbow in a questionable spot as to which is the better fighter.

In some waters I have found the largemouth bass a very good fighter, but as a rule it doesn't have the staying power of either the smallmouth or the rainbow trout. Largemouths make up for this by their gameness in striking surface lures.

Trout and bass have held first place in my heart all through the years, but that doesn't mean I haven't greatly enjoyed fishing for all the other fresh-water fish. Muskies, steelheads, and salmon have all had a part in giving me plenty of thrills. I like fishing for pike and pickerel.

I have never been enthusiastic about walleyes (pike-perch) though I have fished for them plenty. If they run large, they'll give you a fair fight, but on the whole I think a yellow perch of equal size is as active as a walleye.

I believe the valiant fight of the common sunfish or its close relative the blue-gill is as good a resistance as that shown by a trout or bass of comparable size and maturity. However, it seems to me that sunfish show less intelligence in trying to escape. They simply tug and pull hard, mostly in a circular movement, whereas a trout or bass will leap and roll and tangle your line in snags.

If I had a flair for fiction, I might claim that I was charged by a huge rainbow trout I hooked while wading the Ausable River of upstate New York about 25 years ago. The fish took a dry fly I cast to the Slide Rock Pool and made a powerful run upstream. I was using a light 3X leader and standing hip-deep in the strong current, so there was nothing I could do but let the trout run. I saw him for the first time as he raced downstream and leaped high in the air within five feet of me. There was no mistaking the identity or size of the fish. It was a rainbow trout that would certainly have weighed more than 15 pounds, probably as much as 20.

This great fish took my line far downstream then, and I thought I'd lost him when the line went slack. A second later he was curving the slack line toward me on a sizzling upstream run. This time he was headed straight for me, and he never changed course. He struck the leg I was awkwardly balanced on with such force that I was upended in the water. The trout's mouth must have been open, for my waders were slashed as if his teeth had hung in them momentarily. Perhaps he was trying to knock off the dry fly that was stuck in his jaw.

Needless to say, the monster rainbow broke off as I floundered in the water. I dropped the rod in the tumble and only managed to retrieve it because the loose line looped around my leg.

There have been many interesting experiences in my years of fishing. Once, for example, some disgruntled anglers at Cranberry Lake, New York, decided to have me arrested as a game hog.

We were fishing where Brandy Brook flows into Cranberry Lake. On this particular evening the brook trout there were exceptionally wary. Only those fly fishermen who knew all the tricks for this water were catching any. I was one of those in the know, having been well coached by an old guide of the area.

There were eight anglers at the inlet, and this made the short stretch of shore rather crowded. Among the anglers who couldn't catch any fish was a party of three generally disliked by the local residents and an old saw filer who was on the job of sharpening saws for the Syracuse University forestry students who had a camp at the flow of another brook.

I had caught all the fish I wanted and so had my partner. I was about ready to head for our nearby tent when it occurred to me that the saw filer fishing close to me hadn't caught a fish. He had mentioned that he'd promised the boys at the forestry camp a feed of trout.

I decided to teach him how to get these "flow" trout. It was difficult because of the darkness (night fishing was legal then) but he finally got the knack. Eventually the old saw filer got his limit of brook trout.

In the meantime the three disliked big shots from the village had heard my voice in the dark and all the splashing of the saw filer's catch. They hadn't caught a fish.

Irritated by the sounds of our success, the three luckless men decided to send one of their party to town to get the game warden. They were sure I was exceeding the bag limit.

The game warden was routed out of bed and hauled six miles by boat to investigate. Our catch was strictly legal, but the sleepless warden arrested one of the three soreheads for fishing without a license. I must confess that this amused me.

Before a dam put an end to long float trips on the White River in the Ozarks, my wife and I enjoyed many wonderful days on that river. We fished it so much that Jim Owen of Branson, Missouri, included our home town on a sign post in one of the restaurants. The sign showed the mileage to St. Louis, Tulsa, and other large towns within a reasonable distance of the river. Jim added Nyack—over 1,200 miles distant—to the list. Jim Owen introduced me to the Ozarks, something for which I have ever been grateful.

My wife and I have had many excellent guides. We remember them all with fondness. We have also had a few poor ones.

There is one thing I wish to press home to you about this guiding business. When a man is hired as a guide his responsibility is to see that the angler he's guiding gets the best possible service. The guide should always place the angler in the best available spot for catching fish. If fishing from a boat or canoe, the craft should be anchored or held in a place that gives the advantage to the sportsman who's paying the bill. The guide should not fish at all unless the paying sportsman asks him to.

I have found the guides in the north country the most considerate of their clients. We have never had one of them who'd think of fishing himself without being coaxed to do so. In this respect the Canadian guides have been outstanding.

I recall with amusement the heroic struggle described by a fisherman who lugged a big northern pike into the lobby of a resort hotel on the Canadian shore of Lake Erie. It had taken every grain of this man's strength and cunning to subdue the whopper he displayed before admiring hotel guests.

I was dressed for dinner and substantially changed in appearance as I stood listening to this story. The talkative angler didn't recognize me. I had met him on the lake that day and given him the big pike to keep him from coming in fishless. I didn't bother to tell the crowd that the fish they were ogling had been boated after a rather dull tug o' war against the spring of my fly rod.

I have fished in some dangerous situations due to the weather, but somehow the most memorable was a windy day in Wisconsin. This wind was raging at 60 to 70 miles an hour. Trees were toppling all over the woods, some of them dropping dangerously close to the cabin where we were staying. My wife stayed indoors and so did the owners. I went out to enjoy the play of the wind and got a great kick out of watching three nearby trees gradually succumb and fall. Not that I wanted the trees to be destroyed, but nothing could be done about that and it was definitely exciting to be out in the blow and to see things happen. The entire lake looked like the froth on a glass of beer. One couldn't possibly fish it and any small boat on it would have been capsized instantly or blown against the shore.

In the middle afternoon I became a bit bored watching the play of the elements. I was about to go inside and read a book when I remembered a protected creek that ran into the lake close to our cabin. It was well guarded against the wind by banks and staunch trees. A state road culvert was at the upper end.

I decided to investigate. I took a spinning outfit and a small box of lures and was partially blown to the edge of the stream. The reasonably calm section was short, not more than 150 feet long.

The wind was strong there, too, but most of it whizzed over my head and didn't disturb the creek much. I hooked two small muskies in this stretch and was about to fish it again, having reached the culvert end. Then I heard a splash that seemed to come from the culvert.

My first cast sent the lure well inside the tunnel, perhaps a distance of 15 to 20 feet. Because the current was coming toward me and I hadn't seen the lure hit, I started reeling quickly. A few seconds later I had hooked a fair muskie, the only decent fish we caught during our stay.

I wish I could name all of the fine folk who have helped in one way or another along the road to my retirement. I trust that they will accept my sincere thanks for their generous aid in this general way.

Some of you may wonder what I'm going to do now that I've resigned from OUTDOOR LIFE. Candidly, I'm going to rest and do nothing except exactly what I feel like doing. What I feel like doing is some more fishing in a lazy, indolent way. I also hope to assemble all the notes I've made through the years. Then I'll write again when the urge comes to do so. Farewell for the present. I wish you all health, long life, and many tight lines.

—RAY BERGMAN

Easy Does It

Robert Traver

August 1960

Robert Traver is the pen name of John D. Voelker, justice of the Michigan
Supreme Court whose first novel in 1958, *Anatomy of a Murder*, was a Book
of the Month Club selection and on best-seller lists for more than a year. It
was also made into a motion picture starring James Stewart and Joseph N.
Welch, previously a star in the McCarthy hearings. After the novel's
publication, Traver was quoted as saying, "If you could have showed me a
place where trout fishing was in season all the time, I'm sure I would never
have written another book." Soon thereafter his fifth book, *Trout Madness*,
appeared, from which this story is an excerpt. Traver, a native of Ishpeming
in Michigan's upper peninsula, retired in 1960 to devote more time to
writing.

I heard the rhythmic whine and whish of his fly line before I saw him.

It was late afternoon, and I was sitting on the edge of a flood-blasted high
gravel bank overlooking a wide bend in the Big Escanaba River, leaning against
one of a whispering stand of white pines, sipping a tepid can of beer and waiting
for the evening rise. The sun was curving down, and half of the river was already
in shadow. Whish sang the music of the unseen fly line, and I leaned forward
craning to glimpse the sturdy fisherman who had penetrated to such a remote
stretch on one of my favorite trout streams.

Then he rounded the bend below me, wading up over his waist, breasting the
deep, powerful current, inching along, a tottering old fisherman supporting and
pushing himself along with a long-handled landing net which also served as a
wading staff. As I sat watching, a good trout rose between us. The old man saw
it, too, and paused and braced himself against the current. He then paid out his
line—false-casting to dry the fly and at the same time extend his line—and then,
when I had about concluded he would never release the thing, whished out and
delivered a beautiful curling upstream dry-fly cast. The fish rose and took the fly
almost as it landed and I leaned forward watching the old fisherman as he
expertly gathered in his slack, like a man harvesting grapes. He then suddenly
whipped out his long-handled net and scooped in the fish as it passed him on its
downstream run. It was a spanking beauty, and I sat chewing my lip with envy.

The old fisherman held up his glistening fish and admired it and then creeled
it. He then seemed to spend an interminable time selecting and tying on a new
fly. He carried a little magnifying glass through which he peered at his fly boxes
like a scientist bending over his retorts. In the meantime two more nice fish and
risen between us, a circumstance which would have normally spurred me into
action—not there, indeed, for this was now the old man's stretch—but I was held
riveted to the spot by the sheer artistry and pluck of the old man's performance.

The ritual of choosing and tying on the fly completed, it must have taken him
another five or 10 minutes to push and maneuver himself against the urgent river
to assume his chosen casting position for the lower rising trout. Again there was
the expert, careful, painstaking cast; again the obedient take on the first float;

Copyright © Robert Traver 1960

299

and again the sudden deft netting of the fish on its first down-stream run. I thought the tottering old gentleman would surely founder and drown as he fought up through even deeper water to try for the third trout. He seemed to teeter in the current, like a wavering tight-rope walker, and I restrained an impulse to shout a warning. Even I, a relative adolescent, had never dared wade up through this particular deep bend. But the old man didn't drown, and he calmly took the trout—again in as impressive a display of quiet fishing artistry as I had ever seen.

Here, I told myself, was a real fly fisherman, cool, deliberate, cagey, who for all the disabilities of his years could plainly fish rings around me and all the rest of my eager fishing pals. His performance was an illustrated lecture on one of the hardest of fundamentals for fishermen to learn; easy does it. But my heart went out to him as he continued to struggle manfully against the insistent current to reach still a new rise opposite and a little above me. On he came, like a man shackled by nightmare, still using his landing net as a staff. When he had fought his way opposite me, I couldn't resist offering my nickel's worth of comment.

"Nice job of fishin'," I said, with all the foolhardy aplomb of the winner of a local dance marathon undertaking to compliment Nijinsky.

He glanced quickly up at me—one keen, appraising, wrinkled glance—and then away, as though I were a squirrel scolding and chattering on a bough. "Hm," he sniffed, that was all; just "hm."

"Wouldn't it be a lot easier," I said, still filled with concern and still determined to take the fatal plunge, "wouldn't it be a lot easier if you fished downstream?"

The effect of this remark was as though I had deliberately impaled the old man with my fly or thrown a rock at his rising trout. His whole body seemed to shudder and recoil; then he stood stock still and sighted me through his glasses, adjusting them, as though at last discovering that I was not a foolish squirrel but rather some new species of buzzing and pestiferous insect. "Harrumph," he snorted. "Listen, young fella," he said, "I'd sooner sit on my prat on the public dock at Lake Michigamme and plunk night crawlers for bass than ever fish a wet fly!"

Thus shrivelled, I sat there red-faced and watched him teeter and struggle out of sight around the bend above. On the way, he paused and took two more lovely trout.

This exchange of pleasantries between trout fishermen took place some 15 years ago. Since then my anonymous old dry-fly purist has doubtless been gathered into the place where the meadows are always green and the trout always rising; but the lesson of our brief meeting was well learned. Ever since then my fellow fishermen may have at their trout from baloons or diving bells, for my part, without dredging up a single comment from me. And while I still fish the ignominious wet fly just as avidly as the lowly plunkers plunk for bass at Lake Michigamme, I have since learned that when dry-fly fishing is in season (alas, it frequently isn't in our chilly and temperamental northern waters) it is the most thrilling and rewarding—and exacting—of all methods of taking the fighting trout.

There was that enchanted day on the Yellow Dog when I learned once and for all the invaluable lesson of the short, accurate, dry-fly upstream cast. I've never forgotten it.

It was about noon when I pulled out of the stream at the ruins of the old logging dam and fought my way to the top of the shattered old dam through the inevitable tangle of alders. There I sat and drank in the view, looking far up and down the sparkling and dancing Yellow Dog River, enjoying the comparatively cool breeze, and waiting for Carroll to join me for our noonday sandwich. I could still see evidences of the old dam lying jumbled all about me; great square, rusty, hand-forged spikes still protruding from the rotting timbers. I reflected that the nearly forgotten white pine lumberjacks were giants in their day, while today's so-called "lumberjacks" are merely unhappy mosquito-bitten mechanics caught far away from home.

The remote Yellow Dog River is a fabulous little rockingchair stream; as wilful and turbulent and wenchy as a handsome native dancer; the kind of seductive trout stream that keeps fishermen misty-eyed and mumbling to themselves trying to fathom its tempestuous moods and to realize its promise. But few are the fishermen that ever solve or subdue it. Its virtually unending series of shallow pockets and pools, gravelly riffles and rapids, wild chutes and quiet glides, offers a bewildering variety of fishing and harbors some of the loveliest trout in Michigan. The only problem is to get on to them.

This particular day Carroll Rushton and I had been slugging away at the problem since shortly after sunup. I still didn't know how he was doing, but I ruefully knew that I, at least, was still several thousand light years away from the solution. Fishing mostly downstream, I had caught or pricked scores of dancy, spittin' little trout. Out of desperation and low pride I had finally kept several seven and eight-inchers for the fry pan (we had planned our usual stream-side trout fry to augment our sandwiches). But I hadn't so much as seen a decent rising trout much less raised one to the fly. Mostly I had fished downstream wet or occasionally slack-line dry because of the difficulty of making a decently controlled upstream cast in the brushy, unkempt little stream. I was getting a trifle despondent and anxious for Carroll to join me so that I could lay the sly preliminary groundwork for a move on to other more fishable if less fabulous trout waters. And I needed his vote.

But where was Carroll? I looked at my big silver watch, the kind that strikes the hour and the quarter hours, and saw that it was past 12:30. A couple of partridge in the woods back of me suddenly decided to get into the time act, and began to beat their tom-toms, starting in their slow, deliberate rhythmic fashion, and concluding in a crescendo of rapidly fluttering wings. Out of boredom more than hunger, I fished out my sandwich and ate it; then I filled and tamped and lit my pipe and just sat there looking down the glittering serpentine course of the river waiting for tardy Carroll to join me. When Old Big Ben struck one, I knocked out my pipe and ground out the embers and moved slowly downriver along the heavily wooded bank in quest of the missing fisherman.

One-fifteen chimed; then 1:30; then I began to get a little worried. Where was my man? Carroll was usually prompt in meeting at the agreed time and place. And this was pretty wild and woolly country. So I got back away from the insistent noise of the stream on a little rise of ground so that I might better both see or hear him if he was in trouble. Still no Carroll. Big Ben tinkled 1:45 and I was just about to vent one of my blood-curdling shouts when through a thin grove of dappled poplars I saw a man plodding slowly up the river. I craned to look. Yes, it was Carroll all right; the Old Fox himself. But what was he doing? I peered more closely. Of all things, he was fighting a fish, and a good one, too, judging from the bow in his rod. Feeling like a wallflower at a prom, I shook my head in envy and admiration as I watched him creel this handsome specimen. He always carries an old-fashioned rigid wicker creel about the size of a pack basket, so there was no way to judge whether this was his sole catch of the day.

I was just about to shout a greeting and try to lure him elsewhere when I saw him tie on another fly and continue fishing. Hm. Fishing must be fairly good. But where were the long, whistling dry-fly casts for which he was locally famous? I quietly moved closer to the river. The Old Fox was intent as a real fox, stalking, squinting, inching—and delicately casting out not more than 15 feet of line! As I watched him, he rose and got on to a respectable trout—a 10–11 incher, at least

301

—and released it before my incredulous eyes. Then I saw him change flies again and stealthily inch a few more feet upstream. He paused below a modest riffle and, still working the short line, rose and was fast to a lovely trout on his first cast. He postured and turned like a marionette during the whirling fight. His net sagged under this specimen, and I stood there entranced while he fumbled in his creel, as though counting, and then unhooked and released this spanking fish! He then lit a cigarette and suddenly quit the stream—almost walking into me stealthily spying on him.

"Ah, good morning Mister Bear," he said drily.

"You Old Fox," I said accusingly. "You sly, deceitful, rum-soaked, double-dealing—er—foxy Old Fox—what have you been up to now? I saw you release those fish. Have you finally completely blown your top?"

"Spying on me, were you?" Carroll grew mock indignant. "Creeping up on me unbeknownst and ferreting out my trade secrets, were you? Well, if you must know I threw the first one back because he was too small—I've already put back many bigger ones—and the last one because I discovered I already had my limit. I had merely lost count. But how'd you do, Izaak Walton, Junior?"

I swallowed hard and ignored this barb. "Lemme see 'em," I demanded.

"Sure, sure," Carroll answered loftily. "The proof of the pudding gathers no moss." He hefted his heavy pack basket off his shoulder and poured out a torrent of big trout upon the ferns—perhaps the loveliest catch I have ever seen, at least outside of Canada.

I sank to my knees in an unfamiliar attitude of prayer and stared at them in awe. Fifteen glistening trout they were—mixed browns, rainbows, and brooks—and all of them $2 fish, that is, 15 inches or over. (My regular trout pals and I have worked out a standing wager on our fishing. We each pay the winner a dollar for the longest trout over 12 inches. The loser's ante jumps to two bucks a head if the longest fish goes 15 inches or over. The net result of this is good; we find ourselves more and more frequently returning a lot of legal-size trout we might otherwise have kept.) I shook my head. "My heavenly days," I murmured, a defeated and broken man, corroded with envy.

"How'd you do?" Carroll repeated sweetly, plunging the needle farther.

Reaching in my sweat-dampened pocket I fished out my answer—two wrinkled dollar bills—and bleakly handed them to him. "Kept four dwarfed grandchildren of your smallest fish," I said. "But how did you do it?" I went on, incredulously. "What'd you use, man—Parisian postcards?"

"Oh, I used only one fly," Carroll answered, stifling a yawn, as offensively modest as a man who'd just swum the English Channel with one arm tied behind his back—and then refused to be photographed.

"You lying fox—I just saw you change flies twice."

"Don't be hasty, chum—I only used one fly pattern—but I put on a fresh fly after every fish. Today they were temperance trout—they wanted them strictly dry. I kept nothing under 15 inches. Boy oh boy, what a day, what a stream."

"But what fly was it?" I demanded. "Confess, damn it!"

Carroll shrugged and widened his hands and bowed his head in mock surrender. "You've caught me, pal—it was the little Betty McNault—No. 16."

The Betty McNault (I have seen it also variously spelled McNall and McNoll) is a dainty little hackled hair fly, tied and appearing much like a minor variant of that old reliable, the Royal Coachman. It is a tremendously versatile fly; one that can be fished either wet or dry. Oddly enough, like so many effective flies, it looks like no natural fly I've ever seen floating on a stream. Carroll always carried oodles of them, in all smaller sizes, but the No. 16 is far and away his favorite—especially, as I wryly discovered, for stalking big trout upstream in the tumbling and fuming Yellow Dog.

"Nobody but a magician can manage an accurate long cast in these brambles," Carroll finally relented and explained between mouthfuls of sandwich. "All you can accomplish is to put the fish down in those very intervening places where you might otherwise have a Chinaman's chance to take them—the ones lying there right before your patrician and alcoholic nose. So what do you do? You get disgusted and stubborn and careless and try to fish downstream and, in these clear waters, only manage to scare the pants off of every decent trout within 50 feet. You've thoughtfully been herding the big ones down to me all morning. And all you get are the Junior Leaguers. But don't you see—in these noisy, tumbling waters, from below you can almost walk up and pet these fish. Do you follow me, my disconsolate friend?"

"Yes, sir," I answered meekly.

"Therefore," he went on, "if you would only muster the wit and the patience to try, you will find that you can float a dainty cast directly over their suspected lies. And you don't miss nearly as many fish as on the imperceptibly delayed strike involved in long upstream casts on these fast shallow waters." Carroll paused. "But enough of this pompous lecturing. Class is dismissed. Get going, now, while I clean out these fish. Here, take half a dozen of these virgin Bettys."

I took the flies humbly and followed instructions—and in little over half an hour had taken six trout between 10 and 15 inches. I had also raised several more, one a spaniel. They were really on the prod that day, though needless to say the Yellow Dog doesn't always deliver that way. But it is a rare day when Carroll Rushton doesn't dredge up a companion Old Fox to enable him to relieve me of one or two of those officially engraved likenesses of George Washington so thoughtfully provided by the U. S. Mint.

In fact, between them, Carroll Rushton and Tommy Cole have perhaps taught me most of what I was ever able to absorb about the mysteries of fly fishing for trout. Carroll it was who initiated me into the roll cast, perhaps the only department of the sport in which I might excel him. Both he and Tommy are slow, deliberate, undramatic fishermen, almost sleepily casual performers, true disciples of the all-important easy does it. More than being excellent fishermen, they are philosophers who fish. Both have fly fished for many years and both are battle-scarred Old Foxes of the stream who possess to an astonishing degree diabolical "fish sense" and fishing dexterity.

The only thing Carroll hasn't been able to impart to me, unfortunately, is perhaps the most important thing. It is this: how in the bloomin' blazes does he know where the favorite lies of the big trout are? Ah, there's the rub! That, alas, is one of the fascinating mysteries of fishing; here is an instinct, a secret sense, that no fisherman can ever divulge to another—even if he would. And so, to this day, I continue to pay him tribute regularly in damp $1 and $2 installments (I hope my wife never reads this). But I have grown philosophical about it all—I now regard it as money well spent, a payment more in the nature of a deserved tuition, so to speak, to be able to study at the casting elbow of the Old Fox himself.

New Record Whitetail: A Five-Year Stalk

Al Dawson

August 1963

This story has some fantastic angles. The nontypical whitetail deer killed by Del Austin not only had the biggest rack ever recorded by the Pope and Young Club (bow-hunting records), but at the time also the biggest ever recorded by the Boone and Crockett Club for a known hunter (bow or rifle). Still, it was third in the *Records of North American Big Game* behind two heads listed No. 1 and No. 2 for years. They were Texas bucks, remarkably similar and owned by the Lone Star Brewery Co., but who killed them, where and when were not known. However, the late Grancel Fitz told me then it was believed that the two old Texas racks, like the Nebraska racks mentioned in this story, were from one buck, and it was so determined. It was also determined that the now one Texas buck was killed in 1892 in Brady, Texas, by Jeff Benson, and it is now No. 1 in the records with Austin's buck No. 2.

The first time I saw the deer I made myself a promise. I'd hunt him until I hung that strange and magnificent rack on my wall, no matter how long it took, unless another hunter killed him first. I didn't guess then that I was taking on a five-year assignment and the most fascinating outdoor quest of my life. Before I was through, I'd have a liberal education in the almost incredible wariness and stealth by which a big whitetail buck survives the hunting seasons.

I met him first in October, 1958. I was hunting in my favorite area, on the farm of a friend, Dan Thomas, along the Platte River south of Shelton, Nebraska, 30 miles northwest of my home in Hastings where I worked as a salesman for a meat-packing house. I was carrying a 57-pound bow and three arrows. I'm 36, took up bowhunting seven years ago, and have not used a gun for deer since.

I had crossed a cornfield, on the watch for fresh sign, and had stopped at a fence to look over an adjoining alfalfa field and the timbered river bottoms beyond. Ready to move on, I saw a band of five or six whitetails break out of the timber and run straight for me. The lead buck was tremendous. I had seen nothing like him.

His rack was big and massive, and was the queerest, most deformed set of deer antlers I had ever looked at. There were heavy, spraggly points, long and short, growing from the main beams in all directions. Strangest of all, he had two long prongs curving out and down on either side of his head between eye and ear. They extended below his jaws, giving him an odd, lop-eared appearance.

I knew I was looking at a dream trophy, a nontypical whitetail big enough to go well up on the record list, with antlers the like of which I could never hope to see again. At that, I didn't realize how good he really was.

A deer trail crossed the fence where I was standing, but I was in the open. So I risked a couple of careful steps back and sank down on one knee in a clump of weeds, an arrow nocked and ready.

The buck was 50 or 60 yards away, still coming like the wind, when he suddenly swerved. I had the wind, and to this day I don't know what alerted him, unless he had seen movement when I backed up or didn't like the looks of the weeds that hid me.

He cleared the fence 70 yards from me and stopped looking directly at me. I knew he wouldn't come closer, and I couldn't resist a shot. But the arrow sailed under him. He whirled and ran, leading his bunch in a big circle back into the bottoms.

I retrieved my arrow and started to follow his track. But I knew it was useless, so I went back to my car. I had no interest in any other deer that morning.

Then and there I named him Mossy Horns. I know it sounds corny, but with that irregular rack and those two long tines on each side of his face, it fitted him. I vowed I'd keep after him until that wonderful head was mine.

I knew I'd have a lot of competition. I was not the first hunter who had seen him, nor would I be the last. Stories had circulated in that neighborhood for two or three years, among bowmen and gun hunters, of a big buck with an unusual rack. I had heard them but had discounted them as tall tales. Now that I had seen him, I realized none of the stories had done him justice.

I hunted the river bottoms along Dan's farm until the bow season closed after Christmas. I had half a dozen chances at lesser deer, but on each occasion the memory of that freak rack kept me from shooting. If I filled my license I'd be through. If I waited, I might get another chance at him. I saw him twice more, but at a distance both times, and then the season ended.

I had hunted alone that fall, but when the 1959 season opened, Gene Halloran, a retired farmer, and Charley Marlowe, a Hastings advertising executive and the only member of our Oregon Trail Bowhunters Club who had killed a deer with bow up to that time, joined me. I never like to wish partners bad luck, but I couldn't help hoping neither of them would get the buck I was after.

By that time Dan had his own reasons for wanting the big deer killed. Two years before Dan had planted 50 young spruces for a windbreak about 30 yards from his house. For some reason, the big buck had taken either a marked liking or dislike to them. He tore them apart with his antlers and hoofs and killed every one. There was no question what deer had done it, either, for he left his tracks all over the place; no other whitetail in those parts could have made them.

The Platte bottoms in that area are covered with a dense mixture of cotton-woods, brush, willow tangles, weeds, and grass, and are dotted with countless islands, some small and easy to get to, others big and surrounded by deep water. Many places that can be reached early in the fall become inaccessible later when the sloughs and channels are half-frozen. A belt of wild country with farmland on either side and the shallow river winding through the center, those bottoms are a deer hunter's dream.

Halloran, Marlowe, and I built tree blinds in half a dozen places, nailing up small platforms 10 to 20 feet from the ground, depending on the trees we put them in and the height and thickness of the surrounding brush. Such blinds are a big help to the bowhunter, since they get him up where deer are not likely to smell or notice him. In the kind of country we hunt, they are close to essential. The cover is so dense it is almost impossible to stalk deer. We have to figure their routes and habits from their tracks and then wait them out.

Unless alerted by movement, whitetails rarely look up. They are used to danger on the ground and look for trouble at that level. They don't pay much attention to a platform or a motionless hunter waiting overhead. Getting into a tree above them often means the difference between a long shot and a shot at good bow range—or no shot at all.

For all our preparations and many hours of hunting, the long archery season was slipping by without our glimpsing the big buck. I was resigning myself to the fact that he had moved out of the area or might even be dead. We'd had no word of a hunter taking him, but there are always poachers as well as natural misfortunes.

Marlowe finally got a good doe and quit hunting. Gene and I kept at it, but I had about given up hope of Mossy Horns. Then, one November evening, I saw him coming extremely cautiously down a slough 150 yards away. Unless he changed course, he'd walk past me beyond range. He stopped twice at the edge of thickets to watch and test the wind. So far as I could tell, his antlers were identical with those he'd carried a year before. I concluded I had learned something many hunters don't know. Apparently nontypical whitetails remain in that category all their lives, growing a rack substantially the same shape each year.

I waited until he was beyond me, with a thick screen of brush between us, and then started the most careful stalk I'd ever made. A hard wind was blowing, and he was heading into it. By keeping off to one side with brush between us, maybe I could close in for a shot.

I tiptoed after him for half a mile. He stopped several times, and each time I waited. Three times he rubbed his antlers vigorously against a bush, and while he was doing so I sneaked closer. I had him in range twice, but there was too much brush in the way.

Finally he stopped again, at the border of a thicket, alternately standing quiet and alert, then fighting a bush with his hard and polished antlers. I inched in until I was 25 yards away and was slipping around a willow clump to shoot when a dry twig broke under my feet.

The buck didn't look, stomp, or snort. He went out of sight in the brush in one crashing bound. Well, I reflected, no deer lives to reach that size without learning all there is to know about avoiding danger.

I saw him once more that year, on the last evening of the season, as I was coming up from the bottoms at dusk. The light was almost gone, but I made out the white throat patch of a deer, and then the huge antlers of Mossy Horns took shape in the gathering dark. He was standing in the open, out of range, calmly watching me. I stopped to stare at him, and when I moved he whirled, and his upflung flag waved derisively, then faded out of sight at the far side of the field.

"O.K., Mossy," I muttered under my breath. "Next year it will be different." It would have been, too, but for a piece of typical deer-hunter impatience and a blunder on my part.

That fall of 1960, our hunting party grew to four. Del Austin, a warehouse manager from Hastings and an enthusiastic convert to bowhunting, joined Marlowe, Halloran, and me.

I had kept track of the big deer all summer. Dan saw him about every three or four weeks, never far from his hangout on the Platte bottoms, and when the season opened on September 10, we all believed we had his habits figured out.

There was one particular spot in which I had faith, the corner of a cornfield bordering the bottoms. I had found his fresh tracks there three or four times toward the end of summer and concluded it was one of his regular crossing places. So I built a blind in a nearby cottonwood and resolved to stay in it until he came along.

I waited in that blind every chance I got for seven weeks, growing more and more impatient. Then, one cool afternoon toward the end of October, two bucks strolled out into the corn 200 yards down the fence. They were far from matching the deer I wanted, but they were good whitetails and I yielded to temptation. As soon as they were out of sight in the corn, I climbed down and started after them. I was pussy-footing down a corn row 70 yards from the tree when something made me look back. Mossy Horns was standing under my platform looking hard in my direction. Apparently, he wasn't sure what I was, but he walked slowly away until he got my scent, and that was that.

About a week later, Charley Marlowe was in a tree blind when four deer walked past him at good range. He drove an arrow into a young buck, and it ran out into the corn and dropped. Before Charley could climb down, the big deer stepped out of the brush 30 yards away, stood broadside, blew a couple of times, and ran back toward the river. Marlowe's license was filled, but he admitted afterward he was glad when the deer skedaddled. "A man can stand just so much temptation," he told us with a dry grin.

Before that season ended, I had another chance. I was back at my stand in the cottonwood, and my wife Velma, who has bowhunted as long as I have, was in a smaller tree about 50 yards away. We waited all afternoon, and dusk was deepening when I started to climb down. Just then I heard a twig break, and there was the big buck, head lifted, ears pointed ahead, taking short mincing steps. I had never seen an animal more alert.

I froze and let him walk under my tree and beyond it. Then I drove my arrow at his shoulder. I heard it hit, a good solid thunk, and he flinched and bolted. There was a woven-wire fence nailed to the tree Velma was in, and he crashed into it so hard he almost toppled her off her platform. Then he was gone.

We could find no blood, and by then the light was so poor we decided to go up to Dan's house, kill half an hour over a cup of coffee, and come back with a flashlight. That was as long a 30 minutes as I can remember.

We found the feathered end of my arrow not far from where the deer had crashed into the fence, but that was all we found. There was no blood or any other hint of what had happened. I was haunted the rest of that season by worry that I might have killed him—that he might have crawled into a thicket to die without our ever finding his magnificent rack. The last week I filled my license with a 160-pound, three-point (Western count) buck, my third deer and the first with a bow.

Nothing happened the next summer to relieve my fears that I had killed Mossy Horns. For the first summer in three years Dan failed to see him, and we resigned ourselves to the likelihood that if my arrow had not finished him, time had. From the size of his rack when I first saw him in 1958, we concluded he'd be at least eight years old.

The next season didn't have quite its usual appeal for me, and as it went along and my luck stayed bad, I felt less and less enthusiasm. Charley and Del each killed a nice doe—Del's first deer—and my wife got a four-pointer. Gene was laid up temporarily from a heart attack. I kept on hunting alone, but my heart wasn't in it.

The season was three quarters over and snow was piled in deep drifts on the bottoms before I got a chance at a deer. Late on a bitterly cold afternoon, I was back in the same tree where I had shot at the big buck when I spotted a button buck coming through the willows 100 yards away. Then a bigger one walked into sight behind him, and bringing up the rear was the deer I had given up seeing again.

My heart did a somersault. He was walking warily and craftily, turning his head from side to side to work that enormous rack quietly through the brush. It looked no different from when I had seen it last, except that it seemed bigger. The tangle of stubby point stood out like overgrown thumbs, and the down-curving prongs on either side of his head were at least a foot long. In spite of the icy wind, I started to sweat.

The two lead bucks turned out toward the corn, but the big fellow stayed in the willows. Halfway between the brush and the field, the smaller bucks tried to get through a deep snowbank but couldn't, and they finally turned away from me to go around it. Now the big deer followed. It was as if he remembered that cottonwood of mine and was avoiding it.

While the three were picking their way through a clump of trees at the far end of the cornfield, half a dozen does came out of the willows single file, walked under my platform within six yards of me, and started to feed. The two smaller bucks came down along the edge of the field and joined them, but Mossy Horns hung back in the timber. It was almost dark before he ventured into the corn, and then he stayed well out of range.

That was the only time during the 1961 season that any hunter laid eyes on him, but at least we knew he was still in the area. I gave him up finally, and filled with a four-pointer.

Dan had a field of milo that he didn't get around to harvesting that fall. A herd of whitetails fed there all winter, the big buck among them, and early in the spring, on the bottoms not far from that field, Dan had the rare luck to find his shed antlers lying close together. Next to the head itself, that was about as good a tropy as a man could ask for. The tips of several points were missing, but one down tine measured 11 inches, the other 13 (one still carried a ring of dried velvet), and the rack was the most impressive any of us had ever seen. I had proof now of every claim I had made about this deer for four years.

The story of that find has an interesting sequel. Last spring, some six months after Mossy Horns was finally killed, we learned that Max Wilkie, a farmer living about two miles from Dan, had found another set of shed antlers from this same buck four or five years before. The down-swept tine on the left side is broken off about three inches from the main beam on this set, and the right one is short, but from the shape and points there is no question that the rack belonged to a younger Mossy Horns.

In the summer of 1962, I decided that if I couldn't get to the big buck, I'd try bringing him to me. I spent weeks cutting deer trails through the heavy brush of the bottoms, in places where I had seen him most often, and building tree blinds overlooking them. Then, a month before the open season, I cleared out to give him and the other whitetails a chance to get used to them.

Two other partners joined us that fall, Kenny Whitesel, a farmer living near Hastings and one of Nebraska's top bowhunters, and Charley Marlowe's 16-year-old son Chad. That made six in the party, and each of us had his heart set on Mossy Horns. I was beginning to worry on one score. Would his head still be the trophy it had been in the past? Unless we were wrong, he was not less than nine now, and bucks carry poor racks in their declining years.

I got the answer to my doubts before the season was many weeks old. A new interstate highway, I-80, was being built through our hunting grounds on the north side of the Platte, and the north channel had been temporarily dammed. Walking the dry river bed one afternoon, I saw unmistakable tracks where the big buck had gone up the bank into an alfalfa field. I tracked him to a willow-grown island, jumped him, and got a good look at his antlers as he crashed away. They looked as big as ever.

I avoided that island from then on, not wanting to drive him out of his bedding area, and I also shunned the trails he was using. I saw him twice the next week. The first evening I was in a tree where a runway crossed a big slough. Just before dusk, four or five does walked under the tree, and then a four-point buck followed, stopping beneath me to rub his antlers on a bush. The big deer showed up right after that, but he moved off without coming close enough for a shot. The next time he was even more cautious, sneaking out to the edge of the brush downwind from me and then vanishing quietly.

Seeing no more of him for a week, I searched the river bed again, found his tracks on a trail he had not used before, and built a new blind. I had a hunch it was now or never. Bowhunting season would close November 2 for nine days while riflemen took the field. Mossy Horns had grown to a legend in that neighborhood now. A lot of hunters wanted him, and I doubted he'd survive the gun season.

An hour before dark, my first evening in the new blind, I saw him slip out of thick willows on an island and head my way. He crossed the dry channel, entered the brush below the bank on my side, and came on until he was only 15 yards from me. I had deer scent sprinkled around the base of the tree, the wind was in my favor, and I was sure it was all over but the shooting.

The deer had other ideas. He stopped in brush so thick I could barely make out his outline. Nothing that has happened to me in a lifetime of hunting shook me up the way the next 10 minutes did. They seemed like 10 hours. Neither of us moved a muscle. Although a deer is not likely to look up of his own accord, he is almost sure to detect the slightest motion, even in a tree overhead. Finally the buck turned, bounded up on top of the bank, still in thickets where no arrow could get through, and started to walk around my tree. The wind had died, and everything was so quiet I was afraid he'd hear my pounding heart.

He halted where a fence came down to the river, not 20 feet from my platform, and I wanted to try for him the way a strangling man wants air, but I knew better. If I muffed this chance, I couldn't hope for another.

He tortured me for another 10 minutes, finally clearing the fence and walking out into a field of alfalfa. He was 45 yards from me when he stepped out of the brush, and I sent my arrow at him instantly. It sang just over his back and whacked into the ground beyond him. He was back in the thicket in one long jump.

We were hunting every possible minute now, knowing the bow season would soon recess. On the last afternoon in October, Halloran, Whitesel, and I got to Dan's place early, hurried to the bottoms, and chose our stands. Del Austin and Charley Marlowe left Hastings after work, knowing they'd have less than an hour to hunt but counting that worth the trip.

Del had planned to use one of my blinds but couldn't afford to waste time looking for it. So he put up a small, portable platform he'd brought, a rig that could quickly be hung in a tree. Before he climbed up on it, he poured buck lure around the tree and trimmed away some zillow tops that might interfere with his shooting.

There was only room to stand on the platform, and Del hadn't hung it quite level. His legs ached and he couldn't change position, but he stuck it out as long as there was enough light for shooting. At last he gave up, clipped his arrow back in the bow quiver and took out a cigarette before climbing down.

As he opened his lighter, he heard a crashing 50 yards upwind, and then the biggest deer he'd ever seen broke out of thick brush. In the fading light, Del could not see the horns clearly enough to identify the buck, but he realized that this was a buster whitetail and that its guard was down, maybe because of the deer scent around the tree. That can be a powerful attraction for a buck at the peak of the rut.

The deer came at a dead run, stopping once and half turning as if looking for something, then coming again. He skidded to a stop, broadside, 20 yards from the tree, and Del drove a broadhead in behind his front leg. The buck whirled, plowed into the brush, and was gone. Del heard him stop briefly 40 yards away, and then walk on through the dry leaves.

Marlowe, Halloran, Whitesel, and I got back to Dan's about dark. We waited an hour, then started out with flashlights to look for Del. We met him halfway to the river, listened to his story, and went back with him to search for the deer. He was still not sure it was Mossy Horns, but from his description I had very little doubt.

We found the trail easily. There was a lot of blood and before we had followed it far we found the broken arrow, snapped off 10 inches above the head. That meant a hard hit with deep penetration. We trailed the deer through brush and slough grass for three hours, and by then our lights were giving out and the blood sign was down to a few drops or a smear every 30 to 40 yards. At last we lost it altogether. Del tied his handkerchief on a bush to mark the place, and we went home to wait for morning.

I didn't sleep much, and at daylight I was back. I picked up the trail and had followed it another 100 yards when I heard Del and Dan coming. We spread out, and the next time I saw Del he was crouched down with his bow at full draw. But after a few seconds he eased off and motioned for me to circle in from the other side. Then I saw the deer lying in a clump of willows, antlers tangled in the brush. One look was all I needed. Del had killed the buck I had hunted for the past five years.

The signs of age were plain on him. He was gray around the face, his loins were sunken, and he carried hardly an ounce of fat. From what I know of meat animals, I estimated he was 60 pounds lighter than he'd been in his prime two or three years before, but still he dressed out at 240. His rack was less massive than the shed one Dan had found, but it was still a terrific trophy. He was as stout-hearted as ever, too. Del's arrow had done a clean and thorough job, yet he had run nearly a quarter of a mile after he was hit.

Measured by Glenn St. Charles of Seattle, an official measurer for the Pope and Young and Boone and Crockett clubs, his rack scored 277⅜ points. The Pope and Young Club is concerned with recording trophy game shot by bowmen, and this deer's antlers exceed its existing record of 186¾ for a non-typical white-tail by nearly 100 points. Even more impressive than that, his rack is the third biggest recorded for a nontypical whitetail and the biggest ever claimed by a hunter. The two top heads in this category score 286 and 284⅜. But the late Grancel Fitz, writing in the most recent edition of Records of North American Big Game, published by the Boone and Crockett Club in 1958, said of them: "In the nontypical whitetail class we know nothing of the two very old and strikingly similar specimens which stand at the top, except that they are Texas bucks from the old-time Buckhorn Saloon collection in San Antonio . . . But both of these remarkably symmetrical freaks are far ahead of any other trophies in their class." And certainly Mossy Horns was way ahead of the next buck on the nontypical whitetail list, shot in British Columbia in 1905 and scoring 245⅞.

We could find no sign of my shot of two falls before, even when we dressed him, and the only guess we could make was that my arrow had struck one of the down-pointing tines alongside the buck's neck and broken its head off without drawing blood.

We dragged him across the bottoms to the edge of the fields, and I stayed with him while Del and Dan went back after Del's car. I had a lot to think about—all the miles I had tracked him, the many times I had seen him, the shots I'd had and missed. Until the previous night, I had always kidded myself that I'd be the hunter to down him. I suppose because I had hunted him longer than anyone else and thought I had earned the right. I won't say I wasn't jealous of Del's good luck, for I'm afraid I was. But at the same time, next to taking that tremendous rack myself, nothing could have pleased me more than having it fall to a hunting partner, a fellow bowhunter, and a sportsman who deserved it on every count.

Turning that angle over in my mind, I felt better. And then I had another happy thought. The big buck had left plenty of sons there on the Platte bottoms. Some of them were bound to turn out big, and somewhere among them there might even be a nontypical rack something like his.

This Happened to Me

For years OUTDOOR LIFE's feature "This Happened to Me" placed No. 1 in the monthly reader survey. It was "most seen" and "most read" of all material in the magazine. Of course, one can't miss it and the reading isn't heavy, but let's give credit where credit's due.

These true tales are contributed by readers and translated into sketches by OUTDOOR LIFE's artists. The feature first appeared in June 1940 and was drawn, as it was for the next twenty years, by Frank Hubbard. Hubbard was succeeded by Carl Pfeufer and he in turn by Sam Glanzman. Now a fourth artist is drawing it.

The tales came to us in letters, yellowed news clippings, scrawls on butcher paper, and typewritten notes, and even manuscripts running up to ten pages. The artists translated the adventures into sketches and associate editors wrote the captions in carefully counted words.

Hubbard was as talented with the canoe paddle and cane pole as with pen and brush, and once made a canoe trip down the Kentucky River with his brother Harlan, a painter. He did sports cartoons and sketches for the *Cincinnati Post* before moving on to New York and a career as an illustrator and etcher.

Hubbard once sent the staff a "This Happened to Me" postcard while he was vacationing at Lake Sunapee, N.H. He had wandered over to Bellows Falls, Vt., and was arrested by a jeepful of soldiers for making sketches too near the Bellows Falls power station. Fortunately, one of the soldiers was an OUTDOOR LIFE reader.

313

This Happened to Me!

A TRUE TALE, TOLD IN PICTURES

STRANGER IN A PORCUPINE DEN

By ROY WOODBRIDGE, Ottawa, Canada

This Happened to Me!

A TRUE TALE, TOLD IN PICTURES
RODEO ON A TRAPLINE
By ARTHUR S. ERWIN, Wadsworth, Nev.

RUNNING MY WYOMING TRAPLINE, I FOUND A LARGE BOBCAT WITH A FOOT IN EACH OF TWO TRAPS...

THERE AREN'T ENOUGH MEN IN WYOMING TO TIE ANOTHER BOBCAT ONTO THAT HORSE AND MAKE ME GET ON WITH HIM!

315

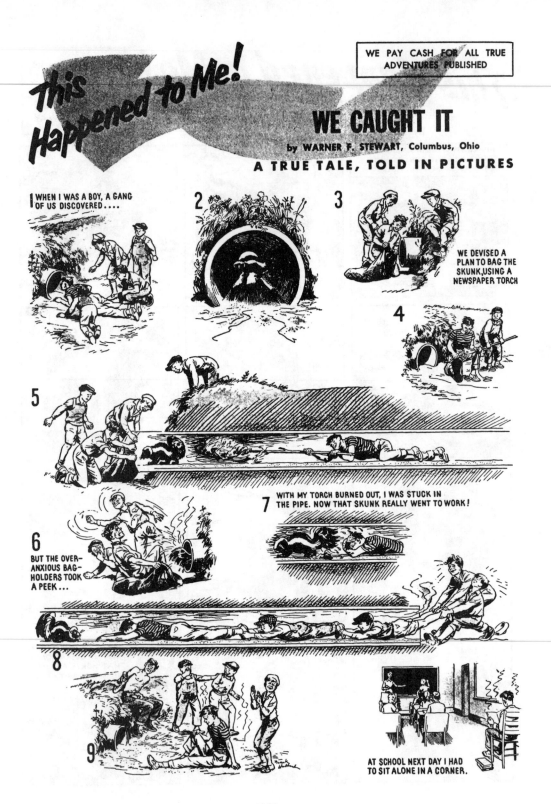

This Happened to Me!

WE CAUGHT IT

by WARNER F. STEWART, Columbus, Ohio

A TRUE TALE, TOLD IN PICTURES

1 WHEN I WAS A BOY, A GANG OF US DISCOVERED....

2

3 WE DEVISED A PLAN TO BAG THE SKUNK, USING A NEWSPAPER TORCH

4

5

7 WITH MY TORCH BURNED OUT, I WAS STUCK IN THE PIPE. NOW THAT SKUNK REALLY WENT TO WORK!

6 BUT THE OVER-ANXIOUS BAG-HOLDERS TOOK A PEEK...

8

9

AT SCHOOL NEXT DAY I HAD TO SIT ALONE IN A CORNER.

This Happened to Me!

FLIRTING WITH TROUBLE

by BILL GEEGAN, Bangor, Maine

A TRUE TALE, TOLD IN PICTURES

1. JIM BISHOP, TRAPPER, GUIDE, AND FAMILY FRIEND, TOOK ME HUNTING WITH HIM YEARS AGO IN NORTHERN MAINE, WHERE HE HAD A CABIN. TO TRY MOOSE-CALLING, WE TOOK COVER AND JIM SOUNDED OFF

2. THEN I TOOK MY TURN AT IT AND JIM SAID I DID PRETTY GOOD. BUT THERE WAS NO RESPONSE...

3. SO WE HIKED ON. CROSSING AN ALMOST TREE-LESS BURNED-OVER AREA NEAR HIS CABIN, JIM UNLOADED THE RIFLE. I HAPPENED TO LOOK BACK...

4. "RUN FOR IT, SON!"

5.

6. "THIS TREE WON'T HOLD. WE GOTTA GET THE GUN OFF THE GROUND. GIMME YOUR BANDANNA"

7. JIM MADE A LINE WITH HAND-KERCHIEFS AND HIS BELT, AND TIED ON A SNELLED HOOK FROM HIS HATBAND

8. AFTER HALF A DOZEN TRIES, HE FINALLY GOT THE HOOK CAUGHT, UNDER THE LEVER

9. JIM GOT A CARTRIDGE (HIS LAST) IN THE GUN FAST, AND BLASTED AWAY. HIS FOOT SLIPPED AS HE FIRED, BUT THE BULLET KNOCKED OFF THE MOOSE'S LEFT ANTLER AND FRIGHTENED HIM OFF.

317

This Happened to Me!

KILLER FOILED
by LOUIS ANDERSON, Petaluma, California

A TRUE TALE, TOLD IN PICTURES

THREE OF US IN TWO BOATS, ONE TOWING THE OTHER, WERE ON OUR WAY TO FISH OFF BODEGA ROCK, NORTH OF SAN FRANCISCO BAY, WHEN · · · SUDDENLY WE SAW A HUGE DORSAL FIN STICKING THREE FEET OUT OF THE WATER AND MOVING SLOWLY

2 THE FIN DISAPPEARED, THEN THE BOAT CANTED SHARPLY AND A GRINDING NOISE CAME FROM BENEATH IT

3 A MOMENT LATER A KILLER WHALE BURST OUT OF THE WATER, AND, GRASPING THE BOAT IN ITS JAWS, SHOOK IT AS A DOG SHAKES A BONE

4 VAN TRIED TO BEAT THE MONSTER OFF WITH AN OAR · · ·

5 THEN REVERSED IT AND POKED WITH THE HANDLE. IT SANK INTO THE HUGE EYE ABOUT 10 INCHES

6 THE KILLER BACKED OFF THEN, AND WATER STARTED POURING INTO THE BOAT

7 AND WAS UP TO THE SEATS BY THE TIME WE BEACHED

8 STEWART ROWED THE SOUND BOAT TO THE COAST GUARD STATION AND REPORTED THE INCIDENT. THEY FLEW VAN AND ME OFF THE ROCK BY HELICOPTER

9 THE DAMAGED BOAT, LATER RECOVERED, HAD TOOTH MARKS ON THE GUNWALE WITH A SPREAD OF 16 INCHES—THE DISTANCE FROM ONE SIDE OF THE KILLER'S MOUTH TO THE OTHER.

This Happened to Me!

Coil of Terror
A TRUE TALE by Wayne Brown, Fairbanks, Alaska

WE PAY CASH FOR ALL TRUE ADVENTURES PUBLISHED

One morning my brother Frank and I went duck hunting on Florida's Lake Bradford. Leaving our car, we separated, hid in shoreline brush

I soon bagged my ducks, and then decided to lie down for a short snooze while waiting for Frank

I awoke after awhile and, turning my head lazily, I was suddenly frozen with terror—a huge rattlesnake was coiled and ready to strike not two feet away!

I knew if I reached for my gun, or tried to roll away, he'd hit me. How could I escape?

Then Frank appeared. He saw the snake, but he couldn't shoot without hitting me

Circling carefully, he came to within six feet of me, slowly raised his gun

One shot blasted the snake's head off. It was the closest call I have ever had

This Happened to Me!

Prisoners of a Well

A TRUE TALE by T. Corrigan Mishou, Bangor, Maine

WE PAY CASH FOR ALL TRUE ADVENTURES PUBLISHED

With my son, a friend, and my old English setter, I was hunting woodcock on an abandoned Maine farm

When the aging dog, Pippa, vanished, I thought of the area's unused wells

Sure enough. Led by muffled barking, we found her—in icy water 15 feet down

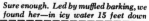

The boys took off for rope from our jeep a mile away, but I doubted Pippa would last

I had to help. Foolishly, I inched down the well to hold her head up

Water, measured with pole I'd tossed in, was over my head. I couldn't stand in it

Nor could I climb the slick, wet sides. Pippa's fix was also mine

I fought to hold on. We were about done when, an hour later, the boys arrived with a rope

I managed to loop it around Pippa. Then I climbed up it and we hauled her out, exhausted but alive

This Happened to Me!

Trapper Trapped

A TRUE TALE by James Leach, La Follette, Tenn.

I approached one of my coon sets in Tacket Creek region of Tennessee, unaware that I had trapped a large bobcat

When I got within reach, the cat leaped, hit my shoulder, and knocked me over a crevice between the cliff and ledge I was on

I fell feet first into the crevice, wedging myself down about seven feet

The fall broke my right arm. I couldn't defend myself against the screaming cat

It clawed at my face and neck. I knew my only chance lay in finding some way to reach my gun

I twisted my body enough to draw the .22 handgun with my left hand

I was losing a lot of blood from the mauling, but I managed a killing shot

I fired shots until help came. I was hospitalized for 18 days, but, thank God, I was saved from slow death

This Happened to Me!

Bayonet Charge

A TRUE TALE by Cecil McGraw, as told to Sock Clay, Portsmouth, Ohio

I was moving cautiously along a low ridge in southern Ohio, looking for a squirrel that I could hear cutting in a nearby tree

As I eased over a rotten log a horde of angry yellow jackets suddenly swarmed up from the ground and covered me all over

There seemed to be thousands of the insects. They got into my eyes, clothes, and shoes and under my hat and kept stinging

I ran downhill through heavy brush, but the faster I ran the more they stung me

The Little Scioto River was nearby; I made a dash for it and dived in

I stayed under a long time, but when I came up they were still there—and mad

I went down again and this time swam a few yards underwater. The tactic worked

As I pulled myself out I was shaking and nauseated, but I finally made . . .

. . . it back to my truck. I had over 100 stings and was ill from them for a week

THIS HAPPENED TO ME

Backseat Bully

A TRUE TALE
By Herbert H.
Brusman
Adams, Oregon

Working for New York Conservation Dept., we trapped problem black bears in the Adirondacks

After knocking out a 400-pounder with a new drug, we loaded the bear in my station wagon

Driving alone, I headed for a new home for the bear. As a biologist, I'd done this before . . . but something was wrong

The bear was awake! I had to think fast: keep the bear off balance or he'd kill me. The car bucked as I hit the gas

I swerved the car from roadside to roadside as the bear tried to get at me. He struck the sides of the car, nearly overturning it

I saw a dirt road I knew and careened down it. The growls and snapping teeth sounded determined

I saw an opening near a river, hit the brakes, and leaped out. I got on the roof as the bear smashed the seats, windows

After the bruin exited from the rear window, it rolled in dirt and ambled off. The next bear will be hog-tied!

THIS HAPPENED TO ME

Tarpon I Didn't Want

A TRUE TALE
By
Lamar Underwood,
New York, New York

My friend Tom and I were tarpon fishing in Parismania River, Costa Rica. We used separate, guided boats to photograph each other playing fish. Suddenly Tom yelled that he had hooked a big one

I laid down my rod, and reached for my camera; Tom was 50 yards away

As I picked up the camera, Tom yelled, "Look out!" I was shocked to see his line sawing through the water right at me, only about five feet from my boat

In one incredible leap, the tarpon soared through the air, twisting and turning. He hit me broadside, his head landing on my right foot, his body and tail hitting me head-on. The collision knocked me right out of the boat

As I surfaced, the fish was still thrashing wildly in the boat. My guide desperately tried to avoid it

Had he landed the fish, Tom would have released it. Instead, it died in the boat. I had a broken foot, and spent weeks on crutches

The Mystery Beasts

Ted Janes

July 1964

I consider this one of Outdoor Life's best articles, evidence in itself that one great writer replaced another when Ted Janes succeeded Arthur Grahame as Eastern field editor in 1962. Janes had hunted and fished from Hudson's Bay to Florida and written about his outdoor experiences since 1930. And he had served as an editor of four outdoor magazines before settling in with us. He was born and still lives in Westfield, Mass., where he is trustee and former president of the Public Library. He was educated at Deerfield Academy, Williams College and Cape Cod, where he says he still takes "summer courses" in striped bass fishing. He's the author of more than a dozen books (his latest, *I Remember Cape Cod*, Stephen Greene Press, 1974) and winner of a Freedoms Foundation Award for an article on Plymouth, Mass. His first story for Outdoor Life was "Wardens Make Good Guides" (August 1940).

Each year, in the Northeastern United States, a few hunters have the unexpected opportunity to shoot strange, wolfish animals which are later variously labeled, depending upon who does the identifying. Frequently, there is violent disagreement among the sportsmen, taxidermists, old guides, and trappers called in to inspect these animals. Invariably, local newspapers dub such a critter a "Mystery Beast." Usually, the state conservation department sends a biologist to examine the corpus delicti, but in most cases his findings are not accepted and the affair ends in more argument and acrimonious letters to the editor.

Such incidents have been increasing in frequency of late, with the result that mystery beasts are sighted or shot in several Northeastern states each year. Just what are these controversial critters and what is the source of the wide diseagreement concerning them?

Outdoor Life assigned me to find the answers to these questions, and in trying to do so I have talked or corresponded with state and federal game biologists, hunters, trappers, taxidermists, veterinarians, naturalists, and ecologists throughout the Northeast. I learned, in part at least, the answer to the second question very quickly. The disagreement concerning these animals stems largely from a confusing combination of fact and fiction, which becomes increasingly involved the more one delves into the subject. However, out of this confusion, certain facts emerge which serve to shed light upon the situation and help to place these incidents in their proper perspective.

First, it is certain that many of these mystery beasts are plain, ordinary dogs. Some are stray, deer-chasing, farm or household pets. Individuals of practically every breed will roam the countryside hunting if given the opportunity. It isn't hard for hunters to recognize a setter, a spaniel, a beagle, or even a collie encountered in the woods, but when we come to shepherd-type dogs or crosses thereof, it is a different story.

Some police dogs, to all but the trained observer, closely resemble timber wolves. It is not surprising that hunters, coming upon such an animal loping along on the trail of a deer, are sometimes entirely certain that they are seeing a wolf, especially if the sighting takes place deep in the forest and far from human habitation. But distance from civilization means little. Deer-running dogs of this type will often cover 25 miles in a day and be home to lie in front of the fireplace at night.

Some of these dogs are wild, whelped and raised in the woods, or they are homeless dogs which have reverted to the wild. In appearance, cunning, and viciousness, many resemble wolves far more than dogs. Several years ago, such a dog in Maine, known as the Sangerville Monster, terrorized an entire township. When he was finally killed on the Piscataquis River ice, an observer described him as the fiercest-looking animal he had ever seen. Certainly a hunter shooting this vicious and destructive wild dog—a huge mongrel of the shepherd type— might well have supposed he had bagged a wolf.

Woods-roaming dogs—both pets and dogs gone wild—have increased greatly in numbers during recent years and are making serious inroads into whitetail deer herds from Maine to West Virginia. Many are the mystery beasts of the North-east. However, to the trained scientist there are skeletal, dental, and other features which definitely prove they are dogs.

An increasingly large number of these animals are coyotes, which have been expanding their former range. Just as the beaver, opossum, porcupine, and black bear have moved into areas from which they had long been absent or in which they had never occurred before, so the coyote has been gradually infiltrating the Northeastern United States over the past 50 years.

Coyotes made their first known appearance in this general area in New York State in 1912. Having expanded their range eastward from Ontario along the Canadian border, they then crossed the ice-bound St. Lawrence River. This was Canis latrans thamnos, largest of the species, which ranged eastward from Minnesota and western Ontario and is now known as the Northeastern coyote. It is about the size of, and somewhat resembles, a German shepherd dog.

It was not until 1925 that the first of these animals was shot in New York by a hunter at the town of Belmont Center in Franklin County, about 14 miles south of the Quebec border.

Who was this hunter? What were the circumstances under which he shot the coyote? No one seems to recall, although there must have been quite a to-do in the town when he came home lugging this strange trophy.

Little more was heard from New York's coyotes until the 1930's when another specimen was shot at Belmont Center, this time by a game protector. By the 30's coyotes had also been reported some 200 miles south around the Luther Forest Preserve below Saratoga and at Vischer Ferry on the Mohawk River. Here we can begin to name names. The first coyote shot in this area was bagged by a Jack Hallren of Wayville, and it was taken to the Saratoga County Court House where the late Fred Streever, outdoor writer and hound man, was called in to help identify it.

Later Streever recalled, "It needed only the briefest examination to show that this was no dog, nor fox, but in all surface appearances had the same general appearance of coyotes which I had shot during big-game hunts in the West and Mexico."

During the next several years, Streever and his companions killed over a dozen coyotes ahead of hounds in the Saratoga region and, later, over a dozen more in the Stony Creek area in Warren County. Meanwhile, reports came in with increasing frequency of coyotes in widely separated parts of the state—from the Adirondacks and the Catskills, from Jefferson, Clinton, and St. Lawrence counties. These crafty and prolific immigrants from farther West flourished in their new homes. It is also said that these early settlers were given an assist by coyotes brought in as pets from the West, and later set free or allowed to escape. More and more hunters began to see coyotes and more and more coyotes were shot.

From the first, there was confusion. For a time, some wildlife authorites stubbornly insisted that these animals were not coyotes but wild dogs. Some hunters as stubbornly maintained they were timber wolves. Eventually, the weight of proof became so overwhelming that both game men and most hunters agreed that coyotes had become a definite part of the New York outdoor scene. But even today some confusion still exists.

One reason for this may be the variations in color phases from gray to brown and from dark to light which exist between individuals of different areas. In a restaurant near Northville, I even saw a mounted cream-colored coyote which had been shot in the vicinity a few years ago.

"A fellow over in Broadalbin got this one's mate," the counter man told me, "and he's as dark as she is light."

Another factor is the size of these animals, which are considerably larger than their Western cousins. They were always the largest of the 19 species and subspecies of Canis latrans, and they have grown even larger here in the Northeast on an abundant diet of snowshoe hares and deer. Out West, coyotes average from 25 to 30 pounds but Eastern specimens weighing up to 50 pounds or more are not uncommon.

Still another source of confusion is terminology. In the West, coyotes are often called prairie wolves and in the Midwest brush wolves. This latter name has caught on to some extent in the East, and to many hunters a wolf is a wolf is a wolf.

By the late 1940's, coyotes had become well established in New York and had spread throughout the northern half of the state from the Hudson River to Lake Ontario. Biologists and game-management personnel now had ample opportunity to study this new resident and to learn much about his adaptation to Eastern ways.

The coniferous northern forests, and the wooded stream valleys and sub-marginal farmlands of fringe areas, have all proved to be ideal habitat for these former dwellers of the plains. Their diet consists of all kinds of fish, flesh, and fowl—dead or alive—as well as fruits in season. The chief food is rabbits—which coyotes can catch easily. They also eat a few deer and birds, and occasionally a pig, turkey, lamb, or chicken.

Coyotes can and do kill deer, especially in winter when they can run their victims down in the snow and hamstring them just as wolves do. But many of the deer they eat are dead or starving, or crippled by hunters and would have died anyway. Sometimes coyotes hunt alone or in pairs, sometimes in small packs.

Through the years, coyotes have learned to live with man and have increased in numbers. Actually, it was civilization which paved the way for the expansion of coyote range. Loggers and farmers, opening up the country, created the sort of habitat these one-time plains animals like best, and the extermination of their chief enemy, the timber wolf, from portions of its range set the stage for their spread into the Northeast.

Coyotes are full of guile but are not as crafty as the wolf, according to veteran trappers. They are, however, adept in avoiding snares and steel traps and one state trapper, Ed Maunton, figured that it took about 30 man-hours of hard work to trap one coyote.

"They cover a lot of territory in their hunting," Maunton declared, "and it may be days or even a week before they return to a certain area. You've got to wait 'em out, and even then you won't get 'em all. The ones you don't catch smarten up fast."

Trapping is probably the best way to control coyotes, although it is a losing battle. A good example of this is the average of 20 coyotes a month trapped for some years within the city limits of Los Angeles without noticeably reducing the population.

Coyotes mate in February and their five to seven pups are born in April in a den excavated by the parents or in an abandoned fox burrow. The male helps feed the young when they are weaned at about six weeks. The family stays together until fall when the young pups leave home. Their chief enemies during this growing-up period are eagles and horned owls. Grown coyotes will not attack man but they will fight viciously if disturbed by other animals, and there are records of their slugging it out on equal terms with the Canada lynx and the bobcat.

That coyotes are not very destructive to deer herds is proved by the fact that there are many more deer today in the Adirondacks than there were before the brush wolves appeared upon the scene. But even before coyotes gained a foothold in New York, sportsmen demanded that a bounty be placed upon them—in spite of the fact that the bounty system has never been successful in controlling any animal anywhere in the country. Many states have placed bounties on coyotes since Missouri initiated the program in 1825. Millions of dollars have been paid out, but there are probably more coyotes today than ever before. From 1936 to 1946, for example, Michigan paid over $300,000 in bounties on 23,000 coyotes, only to find that these animals had increased one and a half times during this period. But bounties seem to be the first idea which comes to laymen's minds, and sometimes for criminal reasons, as we shall see.

In any event, a bounty of $100 was set in New York. In the late 1920's the bounty was raised to $300, with the result that three coyotes killed in Orleans County brought their captors the tidy sum of $900. These animals were sent to the late Professor A. A. Allen at Cornell University.

As soon as news of this profitable venture spread, large numbers of persons, including a detachment of State Police, took up coyote hunting practically as a business. Because Dr. Allen feared that unscrupulous bounty hunters might import coyotes into the state, he sponsored a bill making it unlawful to own or import destructive wild animals without a permit. This bill was introduced into the legislature, passed, and signed into law by Gov. Alfred E. Smith just a month after the three Orleans coyotes arrived in Professor Allen's laboratory.

The good professor had reason for being suspicious. In a Midwestern state, a small but steady income accrued to one enterprising individual who for several years staked out his shepherd bitch in coyote country and then brought the resulting pups in for a bounty of $25 a head. A Far Western state learned that it had paid bounties on hundreds of coyotes killed in a neighboring state where the bounty was lower. Other similar cases of fraud are numerous.

As time went by, bounties in New York were lowered and eventually discarded over much of the state, but even today several counties continue to pay bounties averaging $25. Biologists, as a group, oppose bounties, but the system persists.

Poisoning as a control measure has proved even less successful than trapping, and much more dangerous. Strychnine was the agent originally employed, and it resulted in the death of valuable wildlife. Today its place has been taken by 1080, a far deadlier poison. Indiscriminate use of it has destroyed deer, birds, dogs, sheep, and cattle—but not many coyotes, which early learned to avoid it.

Meanwhile, despite hunting, trapping, and poison, coyotes continued to flourish in New York and gradually began to spread into neighboring states. The first specimen seen in Vermont was shot in the mid-1940's at Orleans. During the 1950's they increased considerably but now, according to Commissioner George W. Davis, the coyote population appears to have become stabilized.

"We don't feel that coyotes pose any threat to our deer herd," he states. "Sure, they take an occasional fawn or snowbound deer, but they'd much rather kill rabbits."

There is no bounty on coyotes in Vermont.

A coyote was shot at Holden, New Hampshire, some years ago but they are still not plentiful in the state. In 1937 a coyote was trapped near Edinburg in Penobscot County, Maine, and since then several others have been killed in various parts of the Pine Tree State, the latest in a place known as Lower Enchanted Township in Somerset County. A coyote was shot in Massachusetts in 1957 and another in Connecticut in 1958. Recently there have been other sightings in both states.

In 1958, Laurence Pringle, a graduate student at the University of Massachusetts, carried on a special predator study during which he trapped three female coyotes on the Quabbin Reservation. He reported that there were two others that he did not catch, and that there were several sightings of coyotes on the reservation during the spring and summer of 1959. A 31-pound female was shot near Grafton that year and another coyote was shot at Leyden in 1961.

The brush wolves made their first appearance in Pennsylvania in the early 1960's, and several are said to have been shot by deer hunters in the northern part of the state in recent years. From the foregoing it can be seen that coyotes have definitely established themselves in New York and Vermont and are gradually extending their range throughout New England and other parts of the Northeast. In some localities they are common enough to have become old hat; in others they are still rare enough to cause confusion and inspire letters to the editor.

In some cases, mystery beasts are coydogs, a cross between coyotes and dogs. These two animals are not naturally compatible, and the brush wolves will frequently kill domestic dogs, except females in heat. At one time there was scientific disagreement on whether or not coyotes and dogs could breed, but it has now been proved that they can and do. The various mixtures of coyote and dog resulting from these matings further confuse the identification process.

Henry S. Carson, Maine game biologist, says, "Even with the best of reference materials, it is not possible to make positive identifications in all cases. A simple technique that will work 100 percent of the time has yet to be devised."

In 1960 an event occurred which may well have significant results in this search for better techniques. In that year a group of hunters tracking down deer-killing predators in Corbin Park near Newport, New Hampshire, came upon fresh gravel scattered upon the snow at the entrance to an old fox den. The hunters heard whimpering cries and dug into the den, where they found five recently born puppies. This litter was turned over to the State Fish and Game Department, which still has three of the animals. The mother, incidentally, was never caught and apparently left the area.

Studies of these specimens have been conducted via funds supplied by Harvard University, the National Academy of Science, and Sigma XI. In 1963 the National Science Foundation approved a $38,000 grant to Miss Barbara Lawrence, Curator of Mammals, Museum of Comparative Zoology at Harvard University, to continue these studies for three more years. Miss Lawrence will make chromosome comparisons of bone marrow from the specimens with dogs, wolves, coyotes, and coydogs. Her results will be checked against those of Dr. Murray L. Johnson, Puget Sound University, Washington, who—under a separate grant—is working on species identification through variations in blood proteins.

At the same time, Walter and Helenette Silver, New Hampshire Fish and Game Department biologists, will continue to conduct growth and behavior studies and breeding experiments with these animals. To date they have raised three litters from the original stock—two from a brother-sister mating, and one from a cross with a wild female dog. Neither Miss Lawrence nor the Silvers have published any findings as yet, but these studies should advance identification techniques.

Meanwhile an interesting pattern has already emerged which shows a definite relationship between coyote populations and the incidence of coydogs. This pattern has been seen in New York and Vermont and is emerging in other New England states.

A study made by Greenleaf Chase and Earl Westervelt, of the New York Conservation Department, shows that in the Adirondack region, where coyotes are most abundant, practically all wild canids trapped or shot are either wild dogs or full-blooded coyotes. Very few coydogs are found. This was not true in the 1940's, when coyotes were estalbishing themselves. Then coydogs were present in greater numbers.

The same situation holds true in Vermont. According to state biologist Roger Seamans, during the 1950's both coyotes and coydogs were killed in the northern section of the state. But today coyotes dominate in remote areas where they are most plentiful. This pattern is also developing in Maine and New Hampshire.

To Seamans and several other authorities, this pattern indicates that coyotes infiltrating a new area will settle for dogs as mates as long as there are not enough coyotes of the opposite sex. When a sufficient number of coyotes is present to provide mates, they prefer to breed with their own kind. When coyotes mate with dogs, incidentally, they are likely to select those breeds which most nearly resemble themselves—shepherds and mongrels with shepherd blood.

One thing these mystery beasts almost surely are not is timber wolves, despite a great deal of popular fancy to the contrary. Dr. William J. Hamilton, Emeritus Professor of Zoology at Cornell University, states flatly, "There are no timber wolves in the Northeast."

There are several reasons for the persistence of the wolf myth. One, as I have pointed out, stems from nomenclature—prairie wolf and brush wolf as alternative names for the coyote. In fact, in Mexican Indian language coyote means "little yellow wolf." Another reason, also mentioned, is the undeniably wolfish appearance of large coyotes, coydogs, and wild dogs. And, finally, part of the persistence of the myth is wishful thinking.

From earliest times, wolves have been surrounded by an aura of romantic legend. We are a pioneering people, and while wolves remain, the frontier is not dead. Illusion dies hard, and it is somehow reassuring to populate our wilderness areas with elemental things like wolves as an antidote to our atomic civilization. And so the hopeful rumor of wolves in our forests persists. Some hunters will even hint darkly that state conservation department officials are fully aware that wolf packs are aprowl in local woodlands, but that they are keeping the information to themselves to prevent unfavorable publicity. Parents wouldn't allow children to attend summer camps, vacationists would shun the area, and the recreation business would go to pot.

Others demand defiantly, "If there are coyotes in the Northeastern United States, why not wolves?"

The answer is that for the past 50 years or so our Northeastern terrain has been entirely unsuitable to support these animals. It is a simple matter of ecology, the relation of a species to its environment. A century ago the great pine forests of Maine and New York were being cut down by the westward-moving loggers, and when they disappeared the wolves disappeared with them. Not all at once, but gradually. They had already been driven from Massachusetts, New Hampshire, and Vermont by encroaching civilization. Unlike the coyote, wolves have been unable to adapt themselves to life with man.

While the country remains primitive, inhabited by only a few settlers, wolves can survive by depredations upon sheep and cattle. But as soon as land is cleared and towns spring up, wolves are forced to leave. They have always thrived best where food was superabundant—near the great caribou herds of the North, the vast bison concentrations of the plains, and the cattle ranges of the West. Everywhere today these natural food supplies are decreasing and everywhere wolves are becoming scarcer. There are no wolf packs left in southern Quebec and southern Ontario to expand into New York and New England as the coyote has done. Instead, their Canadian range has been constricted to ever-shrinking areas of the far north where remnants of the once numerous packs are struggling for survival.

Wolves are much larger animals than coyotes. A king-size coyote might weigh up to 60 pounds, but wolves average from 75 to 110 pounds. However, it is true that coydogs and some dogs may tip the beam at 90 pounds or more, so size is not always a significant factor in distinguishing wolves from their wild cousins. Neither is color. Wolves vary from black through gray to brownish white, but so do coydogs, dogs, and, to a lesser extent, coyotes. These factors also confuse the issue and lead to the false label wolf being pinned on other wild canids. The important point, however, is the fact that wolves cannot and do not live in the Northeastern United States. Only trained biologists can make accurate identifications of the dogs, coyotes, and hybrids which do inhabit this area, and sometimes even they are wrong.

To sum up, coyotes in considerable numbers are present in the Northeast and are continuing to expand their range. However, in time their populations become stablized in each new area. They pose no serious threat to the region's deer herds and may even be beneficial in helping to maintain nature's balance. Where there are coyotes there will be coydogs, especially in fringe areas, but their numbers will never be great and their effect upon deer populations will also be negligible. Most numerous and most dangerous of all are wild dogs, which continue to take a sickening toll of deer annually.

These are the mystery beasts of the Northeast. The only wolves in this region are the ones who walk on two legs.

The Illusion That Kills—
A Thing Called Early Blur

Frank Woolner

November 1965

A combination of normal mental and physical circumstances can lead one hunter to kill another. It's called Early Blur. There is a safeguard against it. It's a color known as fluorescent blaze orange. Two brothers linked these recent discoveries and launched a powerful hunter-safety campaign. Now sixteen states make it mandatory to use the color in big-game hunting, seven advise it and others are moving toward it. The accident toll has dropped some sixty percent, it is said, since the campaign's inception. For one, Georgia required the color in 1974 and enjoyed its first big-game hunting season without fatality in history. One of the brothers is Frank Woolner, editor of the *Salt Water Sportsman*, rod and gun editor of the *Worcester Evening Gazette* for nearly twenty years, author of ten books on the outdoors—and author of this story.

For the sake of hypothesis, let's assume that you are an experienced big-game hunter with a roomful of trophies, have spent thousands of hours in the woods, and have a proper scorn for imbeciles who mistake human beings for game.

Now picture yourself on opening morning of the deer season. You're tired, perhaps, after a long predawn motor trip into the back country, but thrilled at the prospect of a new and wonderful adventure.

Blue shadows lie under the black growth. First light touches the birches. It's cold, but a multitude of deer tracks frozen into an abandoned tote road offer mute promise. You're going to see a deer and, once again, you're going to score on opening day.

Then, later, just as it always has been, there is the almost imperceptible blur of movement and dark, indefinable color at a brushy swamp edge. Instinctively, you check the wind. It's right. You freeze and wait. The shadows in the swamp are frustrating, but you know that a deer is there like another shadow in the cover. You want that deer, and all of the old magic of the hunt sets your heart pounding.

A tick of alien sound mars the all-pervading hum of the wilderness. Another! You do not move your head, but only your eyes. Deer mistake color and form, but they never miss movement. You hardly dare to breathe.

Then, slowly, as though materializing out of the morning mist and the play of shadows, a great buck takes shape. Like so many other bucks you have seen over the years, this one has a heavy, bull-like neck. His head is down, surely savoring the track of a doe. His branching antlers are indistinct against the tangle of brush, but he's the deer you wanted, the deer you expected to see.

You raise your rifle, center iron sights behind the shoulder, and squeeze off. The shot resounds in the hushed woodlands, and the deer is gone.

Down of course, and you feel a mingling of satisfaction and guilt at the ease with which this kill was made. You reload, slowly, even though the hunt is ended, and walk forward.

A man is sprawled on his back, vacant eyes bulging at the sky, a gaping hole in his chest and blood still spurting. You have killed him. There is no circumvention of the nightmare. The man is dead. You see at a glance that first-aid is useless.

You may suffer near mental collapse or an immediate heart attack. You may break down and weep uncontrollably, retch, smash your rifle against the nearest tree.

Worst of all, next to the impossible, horrible fact that a man lies dead, is the terrible conviction that your own mind has crumbled—that you no longer have the moral right to associate with normal human beings.

Perhaps you'll run. More likely, you'll stumble out of the woods, notify the proper authorities, offer no defense, and prepare to suffer the consequences. These, depending upon the laws of the state involved, may be considerable.

Can this happen to you, or to me? Indeed it can!

Most horrifying of all the facts in the man-mistaken-for-game category of shooting accidents is proof that, given a reasonably well-defined combination of normal physical and mental factors, any intelligent human being, expert or tyro, man or woman, can see a deer where no deer exists!

Fortunately for hunters, there is an existing safeguard, one that may almost completely eliminate mistaken-for-game hunting accidents in the future. Only the average sportsman's reluctance to accept a major break-through in the field of firearms safety can roadblock this advance.

During a 90-day series of tests at Fort Devens, Massachusetts, in 1959, technicians of the Massachusetts Division of Fisheries and Game, vision experts of the American Optical Company, and several thousands of United States Strategic Army Command troops proved that fluorescent blaze orange was the color most likely to insure safety for a deer hunter.

Fluorescent blaze orange was declared best after exhaustive tests proved that it is the only color easily detected by persons with normal vision and by those with varying degrees of color deficiency; that fluorescent blaze orange is so completely out of place in nature that it is both immediately apparent and most unlikely to be mistaken for any color in the natural scheme, and that the fluorescents appear most brilliant during the accident-prone hours of dawn and dusk or when heavy shadow destroys much of the available light.

The tests at Fort Devens also found that standard yellow can be seen as white at certain hours of the day, particularly at dawn and dusk. Any qualified vision expert, incidentally, can prove that a square of yellow material, at a certain distance from the eye, automatically appears white. I've had this worked on me, and it's an unsettling experience.

On the basis of the 1959 tests, Massachusetts, in 1962, enacted a law which made mandatory the wearing of 200 square inches of fluorescent red or orange material about the head and shoulders during the deer season.

Red was added at the insistence of one legislator who remained unconvinced that the tests had proved anything new. Although fluorescent red is an adequate safeguard when viewed by humans with normal color vision, there are certain deficients who see it as a particularly dull hue.

At any rate, the mandatory wearing of fluorescent orange or red brought Massachusetts through three successive deer-hunting seasons without a single casualty in the mistaken-for-game category. No Bay State shooting season on record, prior to 1972, had been able to boast a comparable safety record. In 1959, four victims were mistaken for game, three were wounded and one was killed. In 1960, two men were mistaken for game, but the accidents were not fatal. In 1961, two men were mistaken for game, one was killed.

This rather stunning success had not been lost upon states which, annually, still find it necessary to list a grim total of human fatalities alongside the deer kill.

Many, however, continue to endorse the wait-and-see approach, and many are influenced by sportsmen who are sure that big-game animals are spooked by the brilliant fluorescents. (The various deer are not.)

Although all of the armed services of the United States, civil aviation, and many police organizations have now adopted fluorescent orange as the most vivid and visible of colors, a considerable segment of the outdoor press has maintained a seemingly logical opposition to the mandatory wearing of color for protection. It is based on these conclusions: that any hunter who shoots another human being does so because he is trigger-happy or drunk or both; that the killer in the woods is mentally retarded or immature, and that education in the handling of firearms is the only solution to a vexing problem.

No one, least of all the proponents of fluorescent blaze orange as insurance against hasty shooting, denies that education is sorely needed. Nor is the average sportsman opposed to regulations which would bar from the woodlands all mental cases or drunks.

Unfortunately, the grim records that tell of mistaken-for-game tragedies rarely place the shooter in any abnormal category. He is no easily detected, accident-prone citizen. He is not an alcoholic, a lunatic, or even a jumpy, nervous individual—although all of these have been found guilty. In fact, until very recently, the perfectly normal mental and physical combination of circumstances that occasionally lead one hunter to kill another have been unknown.

Two research psychologists at Harvard University found the answer while, as so often happens in the field of pure research, they were searching for facts far removed from the annual spectacle of the hunting accident. Moreover, Harvard's Dr. Jerome S. Bruner and Dr. Mary Potter did not, at the time, associate their findings with hunter-safety.

Jack Woolner, audio-visual aids superintendent of the Massachusetts Division of Fisheries and Game—the man who, together with Dr. Oscar Richards of the American Optical Company, had launched the Fort Devens color study in 1959—was mildly interested when he read about a certain research project dealing with human perception at Harvard's new Center for Cognitive Studies.

Jack, incidentally, is 45 and my brother. I'm four years older, a rod-and-gun columnist for the Worcester *Evening Gazette*, and editor of the *Salt Water Sportsman* magazine in Boston, Massachusetts. Jack has also become a television personality specializing in outdoor subjects, and his shows have won three awards during the past four years.

Quite suddenly, Jack knew that Harvard's research had explained, almost without question of doubt, one of the major reasons why hunters sometimes mistake other hunters for game.

Jack had previously discussed with Dr. Leonard Mead, Professor of Psychology at Tufts Univeristy, the possibility that people have the ability to "see" objects they want to see.

Dr. Mead cited experiments which seemed to prove that any normal person, under certain conditions, is subject to a strange variety of wide-awake hallucination.

It might be, he thought, entirely within the realm of possibility to conjure up a deer out of the play of light and shadow in a woodland. However, Dr. Mead suggested, it would be logical to assume that the illusion could be blocked by something unnatural, such as an unusual color, that would ruin the initial hypothesis.

Now, studying an article by Dr. Jerome S. Bruner, titled "How We Learn & How We Remember," in the November, 1963, issue of the *Harvard Alumni Bulletin,* Jack suspected that Drs. Bruner and Potter had explained the phenomenon completely and in detail.

Curiously, at about the same time that color safety studies got under way at

Fort Devens in 1959, Harvard's new Center for Cognitive Studies came into being. Although worlds apart at that time, one of the first research projects launched at this seat of learning was destined to complement and explain the success of the Fort Devens color findings.

Drs. Bruner and Potter were involved in the study of perception, including the ability of the human eye to recognize various objects. "Perception itself," Dr. Bruner wrote, "is a magnificent achievement and yet, withal, visual perception is extraordinarily stupid. We see a bend in a stick in the water, though we know perfectly well that when we take the stick out it is not bent, and when we put it back in it still looks bent."

Studying the subtleties of perception, these researchers rigged a slide projector and displayed transparencies on a screen. Subjects first saw a picture that was hopelessly blurred, then, over a period of two minutes, the image gradually was brought into sharp focus. Observers were asked to identify the picture as soon as it became recognizable.

"After a certain amount of clearing up of blur," Dr. Bruner wrote, "the subject recognized the picture." However, it was apparent that recognition came well beyond the point when anyone walking into the room would effect immediate recognition.

"There was apparently something about living in early blur with the picture that prevented recognition of it."

This was a challenging finding. To establish its existence beyond question of doubt, two groups of undergraduates were shown identical pictures. The first group watched each slide change slowly from hopeless blur to a middling point of focus, then the projector was turned off and the subjects wrote their guesses about the substance of the picture. Only 25 percent proved to be correct.

The second group was shown the same pictures, but in reverse. They started in medium blur and went back out of focus. Seventy-five percent of this group, unhampered by the strange effect of early blur—because it came last, rather than first—shortly recognized the picture. Drs. Potter and Bruner became convinced that their earlier hypothesis was correct.

"It soon became apparent to us what was happening. There is an interesting thing about low-grade information. Low-grade information tempts us with hypotheses. The interesting thing about an hypothesis is that, generally speaking, there is usually enough information around to confirm it partly."

Pursuing the experiment, a new and rather shocking by-product of early blur was discovered. Some of the undergraduates suffered a genuine variety of hallucination in which they "recognized" the picture before it became very clear, then continued to "see" that which they had willed themselves to see—after full focus had been attained!

One slide depicted a red and silver fire hydrant of a type common in Boston. Subjects often had a tendency to see this as two wine glasses on a table covered with a damask tablecloth. As the picture became clearer, they would, Dr. Bruner reports, "dig themselves in deeper and deeper" with a description of the glasses and table—until they reached a point that got to be called the "My God!" reaction.

"From the suddenness with which the thing would break through, it was quite clear that there had been a great deal of interference because of the confirmation of hypotheses that were near misses—the most dangerous thing in perception— the near miss in which a person says, 'Ah, I got it! This is good enough!' "

The severity of this hallucination, prompted by early blur and the mind of the subject, is attested to by the fact that some subjects were unable to reach the "My God!" reaction until the picture was in full focus.

Dr. Bruner, himself, admits to mistaking a photograph of a bicycle rack he had used on hundreds of occasions for a painting by Renoir, and to elaborating on the masterpiece for a full 40 seconds following the point of complete clarity.

Harvard's Center for Cognitive Studies duly recorded the results of this interesting experiment, then progressed to other phases of research in the field of perception. No one appears to have evaluated the tremendous importance of this knowledge to the hunter.

But Jack Woolner, reading Dr. Bruner's article in the *Alumni Bulletin*, saw beyond the projection booth in a Harvard laboratory. Jack was completing his own hypothesis. Might not a sportsman, his mind attuned to the hunt, his every sense groping for a deer, suffer a like illusion? More than any other individual, the big-game hunter often works in a world of early blur. His is the first, pale hour of dawn in the wilderness, and the last blue wash of gathering twilight. He stalks his quarry in the gloom of black growth and in the big cedar swamps where, even at midday, broken shadows and splotchy patches of sunlight confuse vision.

Ask any veteran of the backwoods whether he's ever seen a deer, only to find, after careful stalking, that the "deer" was a curiously shaped stump or the silhouette of a bush against the sky? Invariably, the answer is yes.

Dr. May Potter, who looks more like a pretty, red-headed undergraduate than an erudite research fellow, declares quite categorically that hunters can be victimized by early hour blur in the woodlands. The desire to see a deer, implemented by sound, color, movement, and poor visibility, can set the stage almost as unerringly as that slide projector at Harvard.

The gunner who wears clothing of a color that merges into the woodland shadows or who—worse—is clad in garments of gray or brown is, in Dr. Potter's opinion, "continually giving off deer clues."

Now, in order for early blur to accomplish its potentially deadly work in the woods, there must be some "clue" upon which human perception can build an hypothesis. It may be a rounded leaf that looks like a buck's ear, a twisted alder that resembles antlers, perhaps a patch of brown or gray that could be the hide of an animal.

That momentous initial clue may, on the other hand, be the curve of a man's shoulder glimpsed through a latticework of brush, the tawny gleam of light reflected from a gunstock, or the white flash of a carelessly employed handkerchief.

Make no mistake, a healthy mind can do the rest. Under the insidious influence of early blur, it has been proved possible for any normal, intelligent human being to build the image of a deer.

Fortunately, Drs. Potter and Bruner also proved that the illusion can be handicapped or dispelled by providing alternative clues. It was found that the subject, when given a list of four alternative guesses about the picture (including the right answer), did much better, even though three of the four were entirely plausible, but false suggestions.

In this case, Dr. Bruner wrote, the subject "stays wide open, or, as one famous coach puts it, he stays loose as ashes. He is able to go back among alternatives and is less likely to get stuck."

The illusion could also be dispelled, and Dr. Potter is certain of this, by the presence of completely incompatible clues. It follows that a hunter wearing fluorescent blaze orange could not be mistaken for a deer because the color offers no possible clue upon which to base a "near miss hypothesis." Indeed, since the fiery fluorescent is unlike anything in nature, it simply has to shout "Man-made!"

One of the arguments employed by those who oppose the mandatory use of color as a hunter-safety measure is the established fact that hunting is a safe sport. It is. In fact, one of America's great insurance companies place the hunter-accident rate a few points lower than the accident rate of a church social!

Nonetheless, men are mistaken for deer and are shot. Maine recorded 10 such accidents, three of them fatal, in 1964, and Maine got off relatively easy by comparison with other states.

It is worth noting that there is no known instance of a mistaken-for-game accident where the victim was wearing fluorescent blaze orange, and many thousands of sportsmen have been wearing fluorescent garments during the past three years.

Hypothesis? No, fact. Fluorescent blaze orange shatters a dangerous illusion before it can take shape. The color is so startlingly vivid that it dispels all "deer clues."

There are today, almost certainly, a few living sportsmen in Massachusetts who would be dead and buried were it not for the law which has compelled them to wear this attention-commanding material during the past three big-game hunting seasons in that state. Harvard's Center for Cognitive Studies has provided the explanation.

Want a final hypothesis? Within the foreseeable future, those who worked on the Fort Devens tests in 1959, together with Dr. Mead of Tufts, Drs. Bruner and Potter of Harvard, and a host of psychologists, may well be credited with the most important contribution to hunter-safety since the invention of firearms.

How to Shoot the Bird of Peace

Nord Riley

July 1966

From Spain comes "The Life of Riley" by our author. "Born Wyndmere, North Dakota, in time to see Kaiser hang in effigy between town's two general stores. Caught first fish at six, and shot first bird on wing at eleven. Been fishing and shooting ever since. Went to University of Chicago, worked on San Francisco Chronicle, quit to go to Mexico to learn to write. Caught a fish so titanic I lived off bragging about it in print for some time (first story sold was to OUTDOOR LIFE: 'The Devil's Own Fish,' May 1939). Wrote for magazines in California until captured by Selective Service in 1942. Won first place with rifle at Fort MacArthur, but was so blind in one eye Army decided I wasn't fit to be shot at. Kept me on as camp newspaper editor. Began short stories after war, gradually killing off *Satevepost*, *Collier's American Magazine* and some others. *Cosmopolitan, This Week, MacLean's* survived me. Wrote a good many TV shows—G.E. Theatre, Ford Theatre, Dobie Gillis, My Favorite Husband, etc. Ashamed of the lot. A play made it for a while, thanks to Tom Ewell and Joan Fontaine, and then died of mutiny among other things. In 1969 took my wife and three daughters to Europe for a year. Still there. I'm doing a book, I think."

The most popular gamebird in the United States lives in town, dresses like a clergyman, has a reputation for piety and nonviolence, sings hymns, and has scriptural credits that range from Genesis to John. Heeding the New Testament injunction to love his enemy, he builds his nest in the hunter's back-yard tree and from there seduces the man's family by dropping empty egg-shells on his children and cooing at his wife. He sits with sparrows on telephone wires. He is a delicate quarter-pounder with pink feet and the facial expression of a nun. He runs like an old lady and in the air gives off squeaking sounds as though he hadn't been up for some time and needed oiling.

Since he looks exactly like his wife, he seems above carnality, and yet the millions that are shot each year are replaced and added to by a female whose slatternly nest never has more than two eggs in it. No other gamebird comes to the table so often and in worse condition. He is utterly ignored by most cookbooks. With wine and cloves he is superlative, but he is usually fried. Eating him fried is like feeding on mummies.

He is the mourning dove.

He is also a fraud and an imposter. With an image resting on the work done for Noah during the high water by his Old World relative, the turtledove, and on his jobs as an artist's model to symbolize purity, peace, and hand soap, he has lobbied himself through 40 percent of the country's state legislatures as a songbird in need of legal guarantees against loss of life and limb. It's just one man's opinion, but I don't think he can sing. He can't even chirp. He keens. In graveside tones, he fills the suburbs from morn till night with a dirge of singular tedium.

Having spent my early years in North Dakota, a state under the impression that a dove is a songbird, and having been confirmed in a church whose altar paintings had a limit of doves in them, I still—25 years later—feel funny when I shoot a dove. I get the feeling I've just bagged the chaplain.

No one, not even a resident of a state in which doves are fair game, is immune to the bird's reputation and appearance. A man taking up hunting for the first time should never start on doves. They'll ruin him. In recent years, I've persuaded three men to give hunting a whirl. It is testimony to my dull wit that I started them all on doves. None ever hunted again. The dove's gray, fragile gentility, his sweet face, and his familiarity took their toll on my friends' enthusiasm. And what really did them in was executing the wounded.

Jim Vance, a crony of mine for many years, joined a recent hunt. He'd never fired a shotgun before. He appeared to have a natural accuracy and was doing well until he trudged across a plowed field to Leroy Younggren, a veteran gunner. In his right hand, Vance cradled a wounded dove. He held it out to Leroy and said, "What do I do now?"

"Stomp on him," said Leroy, his mind on a bird coming in from the south.

"Stomp on him?"

"Either that or wring his neck."

Vance stroked the bird's brow and adjusted a ruffled feather as he weighed the alternatives. "I'll stomp him," he mumbled.

It was a bum decision. Stomping a dove in soft plowing is hopeless. After a few minutes, he shambled over to me. He was obviously shaken; the bird was disheveled. "I stomped the little fellow knee-deep," said Vance, "and every time I looked down, there he was looking back up."

"Do what I do," I told him. "Push in his forehead."

Vance fell back. "You're kidding!"

I explained that it is a harsh fact of hunting that wounded creatures must be dispatched with swift mercy. "A dove has a skull like a peanut shell. Push it in, and it's all over."

Very probably, we'd already lost Vance when I told him that, but when he tried to push in the forehead of his dove we lost him forever. It was plain bad luck; not one bird in 100 is like his was—an elderly cock with a skull like a filbert.

Since I left North Dakota and came to California, I've spent every September 1—excepting those of the war years—hunting mourning doves and their plumper cousins, the whitewings. A quarter of a century of this has given me a chance to weigh the dove against the classic gamebirds of our land, the ducks, geese, pheasants, sharptails, and quail. I believe the dove deserves to be rated No. 1. No other bird gives a hunter such a wonderful run for his money or provides so much sport, adventure, conviviality, and great eating. It's time to unfrock the masquerader.

It is difficult for a man accustomed to quail to believe that a bird residing in his blue gum, balancing on his antenna, eating his boysenberries, and moaning incessantly is a legitimate gamebird. He doesn't believe it until he finds the dove out in the country and tries to hold a gun on him. Then it becomes clear that la dolce vita has no effect on the fowl's native skills as a flyer.

The mourning dove is a master aviator. That slim body, long-tailed and scimitar-winged, is an artist's idea of grace. It's for going 70 miles per hour. It's for sideslipping, banking, corkscrewing, weaving and diving.

That ought to be enough, but the dove has another aerial antic—a flight of such eccentricity of speed that he appears to be drunk. A quail, a sharptail, a Hungarian partridge, or a pheasant jumps up, ascends to 20 feet, and wings off in a straight line at constant speed. Not a dove; there's nothing stodgy and reliable about him. He flies at 200 feet or at two, and his inconstancy kills you.

One of the most common and rewarding September spectacles is that of a single dove sprinting, stalling, darting, and turning as he weaves his way across 80 acres and through the shot patterns of a dozen hunters and then, with the bravado of a bullfighter, drops to earth and calmly eats his morning cereal. It's not unusual to hear hunters shout and clap at such a performance. He is very hard to hit, this bird, and he is missed more than any other.

A word about his meekness. Is there, in the entire country, another gamebird that, upon espying a skirmish line of armed men ahead, neither ascends as does a duck nor darts into a bush as does a quail, but insists upon charging? A dove doesn't avoid danger; he simply revs up and plunges through.

That sweet face of his is a swindle, too, as much a swindle as that of the pheasant, which has the meanest-looking countenance of all the gamebirds. The pheasant also struts and beats his chest. But who is it that, when the going gets tough, sends his women up to attract fire and then pulls his head down and runs like a thief?

For years, it was my whim to shoot doves with a single-shot, full-choke 12 gauge. It was light, fit me well, and, having but one round in it, made me take more care in shooting. Once (and only once) when doves were coming straight at me—favorite shot—I dropped 10 with 11 shots. Then, one sunny, 115° afternoon outside Indio, California, the forearm fell off that old Iver Johnson. I lashed it back onto the barrel with black friction tape. That done, I missed the next 17 birds. I was pondering whether to use the 18th shell on myself when Leroy Younggren, lounging in the shade of the next telephone pole, heard my oaths.

"You're starting to shoot funny," he said. "Are you having your usual sunstroke?"

September 1 on the Southwest deserts is generally the hottest day of the year. I am a middle-aged blond with skin that in many ways resembles cellophane. It's watertight but translucent. Sunlight comes right on through it and cooks me internally, much as a roast is cooked in one of those new infrared ovens. At one point, I turn magenta and begin to see a variety of spots—exploding stars, mainly—some of which I shoot at.

I checked my vision by staring at the ground. "No stars," I told Leroy.

"Gnats?"

At times when heat waves are bad and perspiration is heavy, I mistake a nearby gnat for a faraway dove and bang away at it. On this afternoon, a breeze had blown away my halo of insects. I walked over to Leroy. He is six feet four and thin enough to stand in the shade of a telephone pole and have enough left over for a guest.

"I'd better find out what's wrong quick," I said. "I'm running out of shells."

"Here comes one," he said. "Let me see what you're doing."

When the dove was in position, I fired. He flew on. Leroy sighed. "Ah, Riley, you do need constant care, don't you?" He reached over and, with his dampened forefinger, tapped down a shred of friction tape sticking up from my barrel. I had been using it as my front sight.

After that, I switched to my Winchester pump with a variable choke. Heeding the advice of those experts who insist that anything tighter than a modified boring is a waste of both opportunity and shells, I set mine at improved cylinder. With heavy shot, I found it uncommonly good on geese.

But when I turned it on doves, my average of two shells per bird sank to four to one. Three years ago, it slumped suddenly to six to one, but that was the year my pith helmet was loose. My first shot jarred it down over my eyes, and I found myself getting off my second shot in complete darkness. Last fall, I went back to full choke, and once again doves fell. Anyone else would have known better than to fire at them with an open boring.

Though he is classed as an upland gamebird—and I suppose he is, because he can't swim—the dove differs importantly from quail, pheasants, grouse, and partridge. They are ground dwellers, live out their entire lives within a mile of home, are fast on their feet, prefer hiding to flying, and get dizzy at altitudes of more than 100 feet. A dove resides in a tree, walks as though his feet hurt, and takes to the air at the slighest provocation. High or low, near or far, he loves to fly, and in this respect he resembles nothing quite so much as a teal in a Prince Albert.

Like waterfowl, the dove follows aerial tracks in going out to eat and drink. This habit of his provides some of the most exhilarating pass-shooting a man can find. The trouble is, though, that a dove is also the smallest of upland game birds, with a body the size of a lemon and a neck like a wet macaroni. If he had a brain bigger than a grape seed, he'd have a headache. At 150 feet, which is a common distance in pass-shooting, a bird this size often flies right through the pattern of an improved-cylinder boring.

Jump-shooting doves from weed patches and stubble fields is also good, though prostrating, sport, and here again a tight choke is best. Doves don't hold for man or beast; they cut out with a rusty, quaillike clatter.

A fruitful dove hunt depends upon more than a full choke. There are several key requirements. The first is to hunt on the opening day of the season, which in California is usually September 1. There are millions of doves around then. But a week later, because of the hostilities and a drop in temperature, most of them are in Mexico. The second requirement is to go where the doves are. Doves are everywhere, but concentrations of them are confined to certain areas, and the extra hours of driving it may take to reach these areas are worth it.

Our group goes 200 miles from the Los Angeles precincts, where most of us live, to the Mexican border section of the Imperial Valley. The veterans of this group have been making the trip for 30 years, but—well as they know those flat, fertile fields—they always send down a reconnaissance party a day ahead of the opening, for scouting is the third necessity for success with doves. Crops rotate, dove tastes are fickle. What was kafir corn last fall is now plowing; doves that swarmed over a field in the past have deserted it for one that seems identical.

In sum, if a hunter will make the effort to go to where the doves are the day before the season opens, locate a field the birds are using, be there at dawn, and fire at them with a full-choke gun, he'll have a great time.

The best explanation of the dove's preeminent popularity is quite simple: he provides the ordinary hunter with something to shoot at. In many regions, good duck hunting is available only to those who belong to costly clubs, and the daily limit may be as low as two. Many farmers charge for hunting pheasants on their land, and a reasonably good shot can, in California and other states, get his limit of two cocks with two shells. Quail prefer private property. Grouse are scarce.

But our gray and melancholy groaner is around by the millions. Because he loves to fly, and because he has no game refuges, he is the one bird the ordinary hunter can readily get a shot at. Thousands of dove hunters do their shooting from country roads.

Though the limits on doves—37 in Arizona, for example—read like those for ducks in the 1900's, and though most hunters seem to limit out on opening day, the dove isn't going the way of the auk and bison. He is more than keeping up. In California, the daily limit was recently hiked from 10 to 12. This seems impossible for a bird that lays but two eggs (a bobwhite lays 15). Here again, the bird is deceitful. She lays two eggs all right, but in some areas she does it four times a year. And when her daughters are six weeks old, they lay their first two eggs. Add to this dogged reproductiveness the fact that perhaps half the dove population lives in the suburbs, thus remaining safe from crows, magpies and other rural egg fanciers, and it becomes clear that hunters can shoot doves with a clear conscience.

Another captivating thing about doves is that they are cheap and fairly comfortable to hunt. Most dove hunters appear to have been dressed by the Salvation Army. I, for example, am annually mistaken for a bleached bracero. All the dove hunter needs is enough clothes to keep from being arrested, a gun, and lots of cheap, lowbase 7½'s and 8's. No boat, no hip boots, no thermal underwear, no camouflaged jacket, no waterproof pants, no handwarmer. For decoys he uses the bodies of the fallen, for a blind the shade of a tree.

This is also a sport for the old, the sedentary, and the ramshackle. Our group includes two recent coronary victims, both of whom shoot from camp stools and send out either a dog or a relative to pick up the dead.

For many of the ink-stained wretches who toil in cities, the opening of dove season has become a social event. It provides the first blast of the hunting year, and, since dove hunting is no good after the opening, everybody shows up for the opening. Our little posse runs to about 25 men, none of whom see each other except on the first two or three days of September. Edgar Bergen flies down. Chill Wills and Cannonball Taylor drive down together. Rip Torn flies out from New York.

Our most treasured member is the sales manager of a brewery. He brings down several kegs of medical supplies—on tap—for our dispensary, a room of the motel set aside for the sunstruck, the parched, and the neurotics like me who insist they have holes in their patterns. When all of us and the thousands of other groups hit the fields together, the result is rather like an armed uprising during Mardi Gras.

Once the birds are bagged, ignorance and stubbornness take over. Everyone I know insists on cleaning his birds soon after he shoots them. This almost always at about 10 a.m., when the temperature is 110°. The hunters have been up since four, they've fired at least 50 rounds, they are sore in the shoulder, hot, and thirsty. Yet they all have this compulsion to pluck and draw. Somewhere, somehow, they have been persuaded that, unless a dove is immediately shorn of the feathers that protected him and relieved of the organs that made him work, he won't be fit to eat a few hours later.

I suspect that women, either high-school hygiene teachers or wives, are to blame. Women know nothing about game and hate to cook it, but they are hell on germs, ptomaine, and meat that isn't bright red. Men, who seldom cook, tend to take their wives' word on culinary matters. In my opinion, the man who sits out in the scorching, fly-ridden air and cleans doves is a misguided, unwholesome litterbug. The birds are going to be tougher, the chances of decay may may well be greater and the hunter leaves on his host's field a fetid mess of feathers, feet, heads, and entrails. A sane sportsman would get out of the sun, return to his quarters, put his doves in a cool place, and have a glass of beer. Both parties will be improved.

A week in the refrigerator does wonders for doves—they all grow tender, and none spoil. I've brought home hundreds, left them intact in the icebox for a week. and never lost a bird to spoilage. Cleaning a chilled dove is infinitely less distasteful than cleaning a hot, fresh one. Viscera and feathers go into the garbage can. No flies, no odor, no litter. That's sanitary.

Should you pluck or skin? I say skin. Most people pluck. Because of my age and physical dilapidation, I no longer fistfight about it; I have subsided to a roar. I have noted that none of the pluckers cook; they just pluck. I cook—30 or 40 doves a year. To give the pluckers a fair roll, I've cooked doves with their skins on and their skins off. It's no contest.

There are three sound reasons for skinning doves: 1) it's faster and easier; 2) doves are often too gamy in taste for many people, and the gamy taste is in the skin; 3) if the dove is cooked in a liquid, as he should be, the skin is unappetizing to many a diner's eye. I have a dreary hunch that those who pluck also fry. God forgive them.

Around our house in Manhattan Beach, California, are a good many cookbooks. The general ones all have sections dealing with quail, pheasants, grouse, ducks, geese, and even mudhens, but they utterly ignore the commonest gamebird in the country. Even some of the cookbooks devoted exclusively to game omit doves. Harry Botsford's commendable Fish and Game Cook Book has dozens of good recipes for everything from woodcock to squirrels but not one for the mourning dove.

Confronted with a dozen unfamiliar, maroon-breasted little bodies and unable to find any directions for cooking them, most women become irritable and fry. This bit of inside information I gathered by interviewing the wives of my hunting companions. From them I got some pretty emotional statements, one of which—"I hate doves!"—was unanimous. Another—"I cooked them once and, so help me, never again!"—was very popular, too. All declared, one way or another, that doves were tough and strong. And, indicating the depths of their desperation, most of them asked me how I cook mine.

Well, madam, the recipe that has worked well around here for 20 years isn't at all complicated. First you leave the doves in the refrigerator for a week, then you skin them. That done, you melt between an eighth and a quarter of a pound of butter (a good oil will do, too) in a heavy skillet. Add to this a couple tablespoons of finely chopped onion and a chopped clove of garlic. Flour and season the doves lightly and brown them, keeping the heat low to prevent burning the butter and blackening the onions.

When the doves are a light brown, transfer them to a Dutch oven or covered casserole dish. Into the skillet pour a cup of claret or Burgundy, swirl it around, and, with a spoon, pry loose all the stuff that has struck to the bottom. Pour this, plus a cup of hot water, over the doves. Add three or four cloves, a two-inch slice of orange peel, a pinch of nutmeg, and cover.

Put the vessel in the oven at 300° or on top of the stove over a low fire. Cook for 45 minutes or more, adding more hooch as the need arises. Cooked this way, all the doves will be tender, moist, delicious, and not gamy. Figure two or three doves each for the ladies and three or four for the bucks. My wife, who loves game, prefers doves cooked this way to any bird in the business.

I Had to Have Moose

Olive A. Fredrickson

May 1967

In the summer of 1966, Ben East had been put in touch with a story possibility at Horsefly, British Columbia, and I had got wind of one at Lonesome Lake and still another at Vanderhoof, B.C. I asked him to look into those, too. On a B.C. map the three points form roughly a triangle. It was an epic trip during which he drove six thousand miles in four weeks. The Horsefly story didn't pan out, but Lonesome Lake yielded up two yarns by Jack Turner and Vanderhoof two more, one being this story by Olive Fredrickson, the first of a series of five, as it turned out. The series drew rave responses from readers and the upshot was that East and Olive Fredrickson collaborated on a book, *The Silence of the North* (Crown, New York, 1972), that I have no hesitation in calling the most gripping tale since Eric Collier's *Three Against the Wilderness*.

The canoe was a 30-foot dugout that the Indians had "given" me. They'd be along in the fall to claim payment in potatoes.

It had been hollowed out from a big cottonwood with a hand ax, but the tree wasn't straight to begin with, and the canoe had inherited the character of its parent. Otherwise the Indians would not have parted with it. As a result it was not only heavy and unwieldy but also so cranky you hardly dared to look over the side unless your hair was parted in the middle.

I was in the stern, paddling. My six-year-old daughter Olive was wedged firmly in the bow. Between us were Vala, five, and the baby, Louis, two. We were going moose hunting, and since there was no one to leave the children with, we'd have to go as a family.

We weren't hunting for fun. It was early summer, and the crop of vegetables I had planted in our garden was growing, but there was nothing ready for use yet, and we were out of food.

The moose season wouldn't open until fall, but at that time British Columbia game regulations allowed a prospector to get a permit and kill a moose any time he needed one for food. I was not a prospector and, anyway, I had no way to go into town for the permit unless I walked 27 miles each way. But my babies and I were as hungry as any prospector would ever be, and we had to have something to eat. I was sure the good Lord would forgive me, and I hoped the game warden would too, if he found out about it.

So one hot, windless July day—shortly before my twenty-eighth birthday—when fly season was getting real bad, I called the youngsters together.

"We've got to go try to kill a moose," I said. I knew the moose would be coming down to the river on that kind of day to rid themselves of flies and mosquitoes.

I had never shot a moose, but necessity is the mother of a lot of new experiences, and I decided I could do it all right if I got the chance. I got Olive and Louis and Vala ready, loaded them into the big clumsy canoe, and poked four shells into my old .30/30 Winchester Model 94. I jacked one into the chamber, put the hammer on half cock, and started upstream against the quiet current of the Stuart River.

It was a little more than a year after the June day in 1928 when a neighbor, Jack Hamilton, had come to our lonely homestead 40 miles down the Stuart from Fort St. James, in the mountain country of central British Columbia. He had a telegram for me from the Royal Canadian Mounted Police at Edmonton, and had to break the news that my husband, Walter Reamer, a trapper, had drowned in Leland Lake on the Alberta-Northwest Territories border. Walter's canoe had tipped over in a heavy windstorm.

That was almost 40 years ago, but I still remember raising my hand to my eyes to wipe away the fog that suddenly clouded them and Hamilton leading me to a chair by the kitchen table.

"You'd better sit down, Mrs. Reamer," he said.

I looked around at my three children. Olive, then only five years old, stood wide-eyed, not quite taking it all in. Vala was playing with her little white kitten, and Louis lay on his back, reaching for his toes. What was to become of them and me?

Olive leaned her head against my skirt and began to cry softly for her daddy, and I felt a lump in my chest that made it hard to breathe. But that was not the time for tears. If I cried, I'd do it out of the children's sight.

"Will you be all right?" Jack Hamilton asked before he left.

"I'll be all right," I told him firmly.

All right? I wondered. I was 26 and a homesteader-trapper's widow with three little children, 160 acres of brush-grown land, almost none of it cleared, a small log house—and precious little else.

That was just before the start of the great depression, the period that Canadians of my generation still call the dirty thirties. There was no allowance for dependent children then. I knew I could get a small sum of relief money each month, maybe about $12 for the four of us, but I did not dare to ask for it.

Olive and Louis had been born in Canada, but Vala had been born in the United States, as had I. I was afraid that if I appealed for help, Vala or I or both of us might be sent back to that country. In the very first hours of my grief and loneliness, I vowed I'd never let that happen, no matter what. It was the four of us alone now, to fight the world of privation and hunger, but at least we'd stay together.

My father had been a trapper, and my mother had died when I was eight. We had been a happy family, but always poor folk with no money to speak of. And after I married Walter, his trapline didn't bring in much. I had never known anything but a hard life, but now I was thankful for it. I knew I was more up to the hardships that lay ahead than most women would be.

I don't think I looked the part. Please don't get the idea that I was a backwoods frump, untidy and slovenly. I was small, five feet two, and weighed 112, all good solid muscle. And if I do say it, when I had the proper clothes on and was out dancing, I could compete with the best of them in looks.

There were a lot of moose around our homestead, some deer, black bears, wolves, rabbits, grouse, fox, mink, and muskrat. I decided I'd become a hunter and trapper on my own.

We had a little money on hand to buy food with. We had no horses, but I dug potatoes, raked hay—did whatever I could for our few neighbors to pay for the use of a team. By the next spring, I had managed to clear the brush and trees from a few acres of good land.

Olive was housekeeper, cook, and baby-sitter while I worked outside. I planted a vegetable garden and started a hay meadow. I hunted grouse and rabbits, and neighbors helped out the first winter by giving us moose meat. We managed to eke out a living. It was all hard work, day in and day out, dragging myself off to bed when dark came and crawling out at daylight to begin another day. But at least my babies and I had something to eat.

Then, in July of 1929, our food gave out. I couldn't bring myself to go deeper in debt to my neighbors, and in desperation I decided on the out-of-season moose hunt. With the few odds and ends we had left, we could make out on moose meat until the garden stuff started to ripen.

We hadn't gone far up the Stuart in the cranky dugout before I began to see moose tracks along shore and worn moose paths leading down to the river. Then we rounded a bend, and a big cow moose was standing out on a grassy point, dunking her ungainly head and coming up with mouthfuls of weeds.

I didn't want to kill a cow and maybe leave a calf to starve, but I don't think I was ever more tempted in my life than I was right then. That big animal meant meat enough to last us the rest of the summer, and by canning it, I could keep every pound from spoiling. I paddled quietly ahead, whispered warnings to the kids to sit still and keep quiet. The closer I got, the more I wanted that moose. She finally saw us and looked our way while I wrestled with my conscience.

I'll never know what the outcome would have been, for about the time I was getting near enough to shoot, Olive let out a squeal of pure delight, and I saw a little red-brown calf raise up out of the tall grass. That settled it.

The children all talked at once, and the cow grunted to her youngster and waded out, ready to swim the river. We were only 200 feet away at that point, and all of a sudden she decided she didn't like us there. Her ears went back, the hair on her shoulders stood up, and her grunts took on a very unfriendly tone. I stuck my paddle into the mud and waited, wondering just what I'd do if she came for us.

There was no chance I could maneuver that cumbersome dugout out of her way. But I quieted the youngsters with a sharp warning, and after a minute the cow led her calf into deep water and they struck out for the opposite side of the river. I sighed with relief when they waded ashore and walked up a moose trail out of sight.

A half mile farther up the river we landed. I took Louis piggyback and carried my gun, and the four of us walked very quietly over a grassy point where I thought moose might be feeding. We didn't see any, and now the kids began to complain that they were getting awful hungry. I was hungry, too. We sat down on the bank to rest, and I saw a good rainbow trout swimming in shallow water.

I always carried a few flies and fishhooks in my hatband, and I tied a fly to a length of string and threw it out, using the string as a handline. The trout took the fly on about the fifth toss, and I hauled it in. I fished a little longer and caught two squawfish, and we hit back to the canoe.

I built a fire and broiled the rainbow and one of the squawfish on sticks. The kids divided the trout, and I ate the squawfish. As a rule squawfish have a muddy flavor, and I had really caught those two for dog food. But that one tasted all right to me.

A little farther up the Stuart, we came on two yearling mule deer with stubby spikes of antlers in the velvet. They watched us from a cut bank but spooked and disappeared into the brush soon after I saw them. A little later the same thing happened with two bull moose. They saw us and ran into the willows while I was reaching for my gun. I was so disappointed and discouraged I wanted to bawl.

That made four moose we had seen, counting the calf, without getting a shot, and I decided that killing one was going to be a lot harder than I had thought. And my arms were so tired from paddling the heavy dugout that they felt ready to drop out of the sockets.

I had brought a .22 along, as well as the .30/30, and a little while after that I used it to shoot a grouse that was watching us from the bank.

I had about given up all hope of getting a moose and was ready to turn back for the long paddle home when I saw what looked like the back of one, standing almost submerged in the shade of some cottonwoods up ahead. I shushed the kids and eased the canoe on for a better look, and sure enough, I was looking at a young bull, probably a yearling. Just a dandy size for what I wanted.

He was feeding, pulling up weeds from the bottom and putting his head completely under each time he went down for a mouthful. I paddled as close as I dared, and warned Olive and Vala to put their hands over their ears and keep down as low as they could, for I had to shoot over their heads.

I put the front bead of the Winchester just behind his shoulder, at the top of the water, and when he raised his head I let him have it. He went down with a great splash, and I told the kids they could raise up and look.

Luckily for us, the young bull did not die right away there in deep, muddy water. I don't know how I'd ever have gotten him ashore for dressing. When I got close with the dugout he was trying to drag himself out on the bank. My shot had broken his back. I crowded him with the canoe, feeling sorry for him all the while, and as soon as I had him all the way on dry land I finished him with a head shot.

I had always hated to kill anything, and by that time I was close to tears. Then I saw Olive leaning against a tree, crying her heart out, and Vala and Louis with their faces all screwed up in tears, and I felt worse than ever. But I reminded myself that it had to be done to feed the children, and I wiped my eyes and explained to them as best I could. About that time a porcupine came waddling along, and that took their minds off the moose.

Dressing a moose, even a yearling bull, is no fun. I went at it now, and it was about as hard a job as I had ever tackled. The kids tried to help but only succeeded in getting in the way. And while I worked, I couldn't help worrying about my out-of-season kill. What would happen if I were found out? Would the game warden be as understanding as I hoped?

When the job was done, I built a small fire to boil the partridge I'd shot and a few pieces of moose meat for our supper, giving Louis the broth in his bottle. I felt better after I ate, and I loaded the meat into the dugout and started home. But it was full dark now, and I was so tired that I soon decided not to go on.

We went ashore, spread out a piece of canvas, part under and part over us, and tried to sleep. The mosquitoes wouldn't let us, and I finally gave up. I sat over the children the rest of the night, switching mosquitoes off with a willow branch. Daylight came about 4 o'clock, and we got on the way.

I'll never forget that early-morning trip back to our place. My hands were black with mosquitoes the whole way, and the torment was almost too much.

Joel Hammond, a neighbor, had given me some flour he'd made by grinding his own wheat in a hand mill, and the first thing I did was build a fire and make a batch of hot cakes. The flour was coarse and sort of dusty, but with moose steak and greens fried in moose fat, those cakes made a real good meal. Then I went to work canning meat.

That was the only moose I ever killed out of season. When hunting season rolled around that fall I got a homesteader's free permit and went after our winter's supply of meat. It came even harder that time.

The first one I tried for I wounded with a shot that must have cut through the tip of his lungs. He got away in thick brush, and I took our dog Chum and followed him. Chum drove him back into the river, and he swam across and stood wheezing and coughing on the opposite side, too far off for me to use my only remaining shell on him. Chum swam the river in pursuit, and started to fight him in shallow water.

Another neighbor, Ross Finley, who lived on the quarter section next to ours, heard me shoot and came up to lend a hand. He loaded Olive and me into our dugout, and we paddled across to where the dog was badgering the moose. When we got close, Finley used my last shell but missed.

The bull, fighting mad by now, came for the canoe, throwing his head this way and that. I was scared stiff, for I couldn't swim a stroke and neither could Olive. I knew that one blow from the moose's antlers would roll the dugout over like a pulpwood bolt.

I had the bow paddle, and I moved pretty fast, but at that the moose didn't miss us by a foot as I swung the canoe away from him. He was in deep water now, and Chum was riding on his shoulders and biting at the back of his neck. The dog took the bull's attention for a second or two, and I reached down and grabbed Finley's .22, which was lying in the bottom of the dugout.

I shot the moose right at the butt of the ear, with the gun almost touching him. He sank quietly out of sight, leaving Chum floating in the water. The dog was so worn out from the ruckus that we had to help him ashore.

We tried hard to locate the dead moose. But the current had carried it down-river, and it was days before we found it. The carcass was lying in shallow water at the mouth of a creek, the meat spoiled.

There were plenty more around, however. We could hear them fighting at night, grunting and snorting, and sometimes their horns would clash with a noise as loud as an ax hitting a hollow log. In the early mornings I saw as many as five at one time along the weedy river shore. I waited and picked the one I wanted, and that time I killed him with no trouble.

The Stuart was full of ducks and geese that fall, and there were grouse every-where I went in the woods. I had plenty of ammunition for the .22 and always a few .30/30 shells around, I canned everything I killed and no longer worried about a meat shortage. Life was beginning to sort itself out.

A few unmarried men came around and tried to shine up to me, but I wasn't interested. All I wanted was to get more land cleared and buy a cow or two and a team of horses of my own. The young homestead widow was proving to herself that she could take care of her family and make the grade.

But before the winter was over I had another crisis. By February most of our food was gone, except for the canned meat and a few cans of vegetables. We had used the last of the hand-ground flour that Joel Hammond had given me and were desperately in need of groceries. I had no money, but I decided to walk the 27 miles to Vanderhoof, on the Prince George-Prince Rupert railroad, and try to get the supplies we needed on credit. I knew I could pay for them with potatoes the next fall, for by that time I had enough land cleared to grow a bigger potato crop than we needed for ourselves.

I left the three children with the George Vinsons, neighbors a mile and a half downriver, and started out on a cold, wintry morning. I had a road to follow, but only a few teams and sleighs had traveled it, and the walking was hard, in deep snow. Two miles out of Vanderhoof I finally hitched a ride.

I didn't have any luck getting credit against my potato crop. Those were hard times, and I guess the merchants couldn't afford much generosity. I tried first to buy rubbers for myself and the kids. We needed them very badly, and they were the cheapest footgear available. But the store turned me down.

A kindly woman who ran a restaurant did well by me, however. She gave me a good dinner, and when I put her down for 50 pounds of potatoes, she just smiled and shoved a chocolate bar into my pocket. I saw to it that she got the potatoes when the time came anyway.

Another storekeeper told me that he couldn't let me have things on credit, but he gave me $2 in cash and told me to do the best I could with it. I knew where part of it was going—for the oatmeal and sugar I had promised Louis and Vala and Olive when I got home. But I couldn't see any way to pay for another meal for myself or a room for the night, and I walked around Vanderhoof thinking of how wet and cold our feet would be in the slush of the spring thaw.

I was about as heartbroken as I've ever been in my life.

Finally I decided to make another attempt. Some of my neighbors on the Stuart River traded at a store at Finmoore, 19 miles east of Vanderhoof. I also had a friend there, Mrs. John Holter. I'd walk the railroad track to Finmoore and try my luck there. At the time I didn't know how far it was, and I expected a hike of only 10 miles or so.

It was about dark when I started. The railroad ties were crusted with ice, and the walking was very bad. My clothes were hardly enough for the cold night, either: denim overalls, men's work socks, Indian moccasins, and an old wool sweater with the elbows out, worn under a denim jacket.

I had never been brave in the dark, any time or any place, and I can't tell you what an ordeal that walk was. All I could think of were the hobos I had heard stories about, the railroad bums, and I was afraid of every shadow.

I got to the lonely little station at Hulatt, 15 miles from Vanderhoof, at midnight and asked the stationmaster if I could rest until daylight. I lay down on the floor by the big potbellied stove. It was warm and cozy, and I was worn out. I started to drift off to sleep, but then I began to worry about the children and the likelihood that if I was later in getting home than I had promised, they might come back to the house and get into trouble starting a fire. Things were hard enough without having the place burned down. I got up and trudged away along the track once more.

It was 2 o'clock in the morning when I reached the Holter place. Mrs. Holter fixed me a sandwich and a cup of hot milk, and I fell into bed. She shook me awake at 9 o'clock, as I had told her to. Those scant seven hours were all the sleep I had in more than 36.

Mrs. Holter loaned me another $2, and I went to the general store and struck it rich. The proprietor, Percy Moore, stared at me in disbelief when I poured out my hard-luck story.

"You've walked from the Stuart River since yesterday morning?" he asked in amazement. "That's forty-six miles!"

"No, forty-four," I corrected him. "I got a ride the last two miles into Vanderhoof." Then I added, "I've got fourteen more to walk home before dark tonight, too."

The first thing he let me have, on credit, was the three pairs of rubbers we needed so desperately. Then he took care of my grocery list. Eight pounds of oatmeal, three of rice, five of beans, five of sugar and—for a bonus—a three-pound pail of strawberry jam.

I plodded away from Finmoore at 10 o'clock that morning with almost 30 pounds in a packsack on my back.

Three inches of wet snow had fallen that morning, and the 14-mile walk seemed endless, each mile longer than the one before. My pack got heavier and heavier, and sometime in the afternoon I began to stumble and fall. I was so tired by that time, and my back ached so cruelly from the weight of the pack, that I wanted to lie there in the snow and go to sleep.

But I knew better. After each fall, I'd drive myself back to my feet and stagger on.

To this day I do not know when it was that I reached our place, but it was long after dark. Chum met me in the yard, and no human being was ever more glad to fumble at the latch of his own door.

I slid out of the pack, pulled off my wet moccasins and socks, and rolled into bed with my clothes on. The last thing I remember was calling the dog up to lie at my feet for warmth. The children awakened me at noon the next day, fed me breakfast, and rubbed some of the soreness out of my swollen legs and feet.

Next fall, when I harvested my potato crop, I paid off my debt to Percy Moore in full, except for one item. There was no way to pay him, ever, for his kindness to me when I was broke and had three hungry children at home.

I was to make many more trips to Finmoore in the years before I left the Stuart, for I did most of my trading at his store. And when times got better, he and his wife and daughter Ruth often came out and bought vegetables and eggs from me. I remember walking back to his place the next year, carrying six dressed chickens, selling them for 50¢ apiece, spending the money for food and packing it home. Three dollars bought quite a heavy load in those days.

How It Feels to Die

Dr. Judd Grindell

November 1967

In another story, "New Light on Snakebite," by Nelson Wadsworth (March 1969), Dr. Clifford C. Snyder laid down these rules for field treatment: Avoid exertion. Kill snake for identification if possible. Apply flat tourniquet between bite and heart, loose enough to insert finger. It's safe for one hour. Sterilize fang wounds with alcoholic sponges. With scalpel or knife sterilized in flame make incision connecting both fang marks and extending ¼ inch beyond each puncture. Cut only through skin and fat. No cross incisions. Finger-squeeze venom gently twenty or thirty minutes. No oral suction. If ice available, put in cloth and apply to bite area, but no more than an hour. Move ice away gradually. Quick removal results in sudden uptake of venom. Antivenin can be used in field only if package instructions are followed and required skin test for allergy has proved negative. Get victim to hospital or doctor as quickly as possible.

The elk hunt had been a good one even though we had taken no trophies. The time was September, 1953, and we were camped in northwestern Wyoming, in the high country between Jackson Lake and Two Ocean Pass about 10 miles south of Yellowstone National Park.

My two companions were Dr. Lyle French, a neurosurgeon from Minneapolis, Minnesota; and my brother Jack, an army captain and a legal assistant in the Adjutant General's office, then stationed at Camp Carson, Colorado. Our outfitter was Ted Adams.

None of us had the slightest inkling that Lyle and Jack were about to see me face a most horrible ordeal.

Elk were plentiful, and we had seen several fine racks that would have been easy to take with a rifle. But we had been using bows, and that's another matter.

I have hunted with a bow for the past 32 years, and I greatly prefer it to any other method—for the wonderful challenges it presents and for the high quality of sportsmanship it demands. In my book, the hunter who takes a good trophy with a bow has met his game on even terms, and that's how I like it. Most bowhunters don't feel too unhappy about missing a shot. They know they've at least had the keen delight of stealing to within a few yards or even a few feet of an animal.

We'd had the usual minor frustrations on this hunt. I missed one fairly decent shot at an elk. Jack used all his arrows one forenoon in a vain attempt to take a big mule deer, then had a fine bull elk walk nonchalantly out in front of him and start grazing while he watched helplessly.

"But I had a wonderful morning anyway," he told us later in camp.

We killed a deer for camp venison, and then we were joined by Fred Bear, the widely known Michigan bowhunter, who brought along an antelope he had killed east of the mountains. So we lived high on wild meat, which I rate the best of all, and enjoyed every single minute.

But time was running out, and on September 20 Jack and Lyle and I packed out and headed east for the antelope country around Gillette.

We got to the little town of Recluse, 40 miles north of Gillette, the next afternoon. One of our elk guides had given us a letter of introduction to a rancher there, Mayne Lester. Mayne invited us to stay overnight at the ranch and start our antelope hunt the next morning and when he told us what the prospects were, he didn't have to twist our arms.

We turned in early and were roused at daylight by a cheery banging on our bedroom door. Half an hour later we sat down to an old-fashioned ranch break-fast—plates heaped with eggs and fried potatoes, plus toast, coffee, jam, and honey.

Our host was too busy to hunt, but he gave us detailed information on the lay of the ranch (it covered 13 square miles, or more than 8,000 acres) and how to hunt it. Because it's extremely difficult to get within bow range of antelope in the open country they inhabit, we were falling back on rifles for this hunt.

We spent the first couple of hours in a four-section area without seeing game, then crossed the highway and entered a nine-section chunk of arid ranch land.

Lyle saw an antelope and started after it. Jack and I walked up a rolling, sage-covered hill about a mile from the road and sat down on a rock outcrop to rest and use our binoculars to scan a wide valley.

We didn't know it, but we were very close to bad trouble.

Within four or five minutes we spotted a pair of ears that appeared to be an antelope's sticking up out of the sage a quarter of a mile away. We studied the situation and agreed that Jack should try the stalk. By making a big circle, he could keep out of the animal's sight and come up behind it with the wind in his face.

Jack walked away, and I lay down behind the outcrop to watch through the binoculars. The animal was so well hidden in the sage that, even though I knew exactly where it was, it disappeared completely whenever it lowered its ears.

For a long time, nothing happened. Then, suddenly, the "antelope" raised its head and looked back in the direction from which Jack was approaching, and I saw that it was a doe mule deer. She got to her feet, listened and looked for a moment, and went rocketing off. The game was over, so I stood up to signal Jack.

Without the slightest warning, something struck me sharply on the back of my right leg just below the knee. I looked down and saw a four-foot prairie rattle-snake, its fangs tangled in my pants and still embedded in my flesh, twisting and thrashing to get loose. I reached down and—all in one swift motion—grabbed the snake behind the head, drew the fangs out, and threw it as far as I could.

Up to that minute I hadn't given rattlers too much thought, though I knew they inhabited the area. That's the wrong attitude to take anywhere in snake country.

I felt no real pain, such as many snakebite victims describe. The strike was like the whiplash of a branch against my leg. It was accompanied by two sharp but not very painful pricks, as if I had been jabbed mildly with a pair of hypodermic needles. In effect, that was what had happened.

But though the bite didn't hurt much, I knew, even as I pulled the rattler's fangs out of my leg and flung him away, that I had been seriously bitten by a snake that causes much terrible suffering and a few deaths each year.

Dr. French, off somewhere after an antelope, was probably two or three miles away by now. Jack was out of sight across the valley, and because of a strong wind there was no chance he could hear me if I shouted. Right then, I was entirely on my own.

My immediate thought was of first aid. I knew exactly what needed to be done, for I was a 40-year-old physician and surgeon with a general practice at Siren in northwestern Wisconsin. (A bad accident with a horse on another elk hunt 10 years later forced me into early retirement, and my wife Arline and I live now on

Totagatic Flowage, a beautiful north-country lake between Spooner and Superior, Wisconsin.)

Though I knew what to do, I couldn't do it. I realized with a sudden shock that I had no snakebite kit and no hunting knife or other sharp instrument with which to cut into the bite.

I didn't even have anything that would serve as an effective tourniquet. (My boots were the laceless pull-on kind, I was wearing no belt, and because the day was very hot my underwear consisted only of shorts.)

And there was no way to resort to mouth suction, since the bite was out of reach behind my knee.

For an experienced and, I had always believed, a reasonably sensible doctor, I had got myself into a sorry predicament. The only first aid I could manage was to lock my hands around the leg and use both thumbs for compression just above the bite.

Jack finally came into sight half a mile away, and I signaled him frantically. But he thought I was trying to show him the location of his quarry.

It was a long time before he got close enough to realize that I was pointing to my bared leg and yelling "Snakebite! Snakebite!" at the top of my voice. He ran the rest of the way so fast that when he got to me he could barely talk.

Just as he started toward me, I glanced at the spot where I had thrown the snake, to see what had become of it. It was no longer there. You can imagine the jolt I got when I saw it only a few feet away, crawling slowly but steadily straight at me.

I could hardly believe my eyes. I'm sure that the rattler was not coming back to attack me. In all likelihood it had a hole under the rock outcrop and was bent on returning to that retreat.

The outcrop formed a flat shelf a foot or two above the ground. Apparently the snake had been lying there and had stayed motionless and silent while Jack and I walked up and sat down only a few feet away. Not even when I lay behind the rock, no more than a foot or two away from it, did the snake move or rattle. And because of its natural camouflage I failed to see it.

It was only when I got to my feet that the rattler finally lashed out. Had it been lying on the ground instead of on the rock shelf, it would have hit my boot and probably done me no harm.

Whatever its intentions were now, however, I wanted nothing more to do with it. I brought up the rifle and blew the snake almost in half. Then I resumed the handlock above the bite.

Jack panted up then, but when I asked him for his hunting knife, he gave me a blank look. He wasn't carrying one, either.

I knew that cutting was essential, to drain the wound and remove part of the venom, but we still had no way to do it. Jack and I had hunted together since we were 13 and had cleaned plenty of game in the field. This was the first time in our memory that either of us had been without a knife.

Jack was wearing laced boots, however, so we could at least make a tourniquet. We tied one of the boot thongs in place above the bite, tightening it just enough to impede the circulation of lymph, and Jack fired three spaced-out shots to let Lyle know that we were in serious trouble. He repeated that signal two or three times and then hurried off to find our partner.

Alone once more, I lay there and faced the fact that I might die.

"Well," I remember thinking, "what better place, with the sun and wind in your face?"

There was even a certain element of justice in it. We'd been hunting wild things, and a wild thing had struck me down.

I still felt no pain from the bite itself, but now I became aware that my scalp, lips, tongue, and hands were getting numb and that speech was becoming difficult. That meant the venom was spreading through my body.

Next I looked off into the distance, and everything I saw was doubled, as when you look through the range finder of an unfocused camera. Only by the greatest effort could I make the two images coincide. In the next few minutes even that became impossible, and my vision faded gradually into a series of crazily unrelated and momentary images.

My ordeal was beginning. Though I had never treated a case of snakebite, I knew enough about it to realize that what was coming would be one of the most terrible experiences a human being can endure. It is matched, in my opinion, only by the agony of severe and extensive burns.

Once the general symptoms appeared, they progressed with frightening swiftness. The numbness and tingling and weakness grew worse. I remembered that I must loosen the tourniquet for 20 or 30 seconds at regular intervals, but the third time I did that I realized that each loosening was followed by an increasing wave of weakness and a strange sensation of floating. It was as if invisible hands were pushing me sideways. It all resulted from the release of more venom into the circulation.

There is some question in medical circles on the benefits of first-aid procedures in snakebite, especially the use of a tourniquet for construction. A few doctors have suggested that it might be better to omit both cutting and constriction. But I am sure that Jack's bootlace saved my life in the first 90 minutes after I was bitten. And I strongly advise that the victim of any such mishap take first-aid measures at once if possible.

Next I became aware of nausea and a deep pain in my abdomen, which was relieved by a session of violent vomiting. For two or three minutes I felt a little better, but then the floating-away sensation returned, and this time it was accompanied by a roaring, rushing sound in my ears. I knew what that meant. My blood pressure was falling into the critical range. I was going into shock.

If so, I thought to myself, I must have a fast, "thready" pulse. I mustered strength to try to check it. My hands waved weakly and without much coordination but finally settled in the right position. I could feel nothing. My fingers were too numb to detect a pulse.

That bit of activity had called for tremendous effort, and somehow the tourniquet had slipped loose. I could expect a real jolt now. I tightened and tied the lace again—and just in time. The roaring and the illusion of floating came once more, much louder and faster, and I realized that my chances for survival were growing slim.

In my years as a doctor I had seen a lot of life begin and a lot of life end. I delivered some 4,000 babies before retiring from practice, and I had spent almost four years overseas as an army doctor in World War II.

But now, for the first time, I knew firsthand how it feels to die.

Fragments of thought went through my mind, as apparently happens in the closing minutes of life:

This must be what it's like . . . just peaceful floating away and the most delicious tiredness . . . what of Arline and the three girls . . . fine wife, wonderful kids . . . they need you . . . too tired, can't . . . you're a quitter, you can try.

I fought back then, in flashes of unbelievably clear and lightning-fast thinking —resisting the feeling of drifting off, refusing to be pushed into the oblivion that was waiting for me.

Then stomach pain racked me once more, and I vomited again. I noticed that my mind cleared briefly each time that happened. The effort of retching was raising my blood pressure for a minute, giving my brain more oxygen.

I decided to try breathing deeply. But I kept vomiting, and deliberately drawing in deep breaths became too much of an effort.

Then I heard footsteps, and Lyle French was bending over me. He had a knife. "Turn a little," he said gently.

I did, but nothing happened, and I realized that he was hesitant about making the needed cuts through the fang punctures. Sick as I was, it struck me as odd that such a small thing should give pause to a surgeon who was used to performing the most intricate brain surgery.

Later, when the whole thing was over with, I asked Lyle about that moment.

"That was the first time in my life I ever had to cut into flesh while the patient was conscious," he told me with a smile. "And I confess I didn't like the idea."

But at last I felt severe pain in my leg, grinding and burning. I could measure the length of each cut and feel the knife rip out. I asked Lyle if the incisions were bleeding.

"Yes, good flow," he replied.

Furious roaring again, even faster now . . . pain in abdomen worse . . . whole leg numb and heavy . . . trying to see Lyle's face . . . no use . . . balancing on a tightrope . . . going to fall off . . . vomit and vomit and vomit.

And then, on top of everything else, I suffered the misery and embarrassment of diarrhea.

I was hardly aware that Jack had left. He hiked quickly down to the car and raced back to the ranch to summon a doctor from Gillette. I lost track of time but finally heard voices all around me—Jack's and Lyle's and a stranger's, then a girl's. I understood dimly that the doctor and a nurse from Gillette had arrived.

I heard someone mention antivenin, and the doctor said, "I'll put part above the bite, where the leg is swelling, and the rest higher up." Then to his nurse, "Mix up that other vial right away."

I felt pain as the needle near the wound went in but none from the rest of the shots, and I didn't even know when the second vial was injected.

The antivenin took effect far quicker than the venom itself had—and with equally dramatic results:

More vicious vomiting . . . taste of bile . . . bitter . . . can't see . . . roaring and floating are back . . . somebody's opening my eyes with fingers . . . remember to breathe . . . pain in belly more and more severe . . . more diarrhea . . . wish I could see Jack . . . I touch him in a blinding, dazzling cloud . . . can't hold arm up . . . floating away faster and faster . . . this is curtains.

If the phrase "more dead than alive" was ever justified, I guess it applied to me at the point.

Then, in the midst of it all, there was a sudden lurch, and the dizzying sense of motion was gone, the roaring in my ears subsided, and I came back to reality— lying on the ground in the sagebrush. I could hear better, and the intervals between vomitings were longer.

I heard the young doctor (it was many hours before I learned his name—Dr. R. V. Plehn) ask about blood in my vomit. When somebody answered that there was none, he said quietly, "He may have a chance then."

As they made ready to start for the hospital, I was suddenly sure that I could survive the trip, just as I had been sure, only a short time before, that to move me at all meant certain death. But I had to try twice to get out a very weak, "O.K., Jack."

Somehow a car had been driven up on the hillside, and I was laid on the back seat. The 40-mile ride to Campbell County Memorial Hospital in Gillette was fast, but was also something I'd just as soon forget.

Thirst began—not ordinary thirst but a burning, cottony clogging of my mouth

355

and throat. Lyle gave me water from a canteen, but I was unable to swallow. My chest cramped so that I could hardly breathe, and I asked to have all the car windows opened. The rush of wind on my face gave me some relief, but I remember vomiting two or three times, and feeling dirty and ashamed. My mind seemed clearer, but still I saw everything outside the car window only as a gray fog.

"Nearly there, Judd," I heard Lyle say. "Hang tough!"

Then we stopped, there were more voices, and someone said, "Bring the bed right out to the car." I felt myself lying between cool, soft sheets and being rolled down the hospital corridor.

I was aware of an intense and increasing craving for sweetened fluids, reflecting my dehydration and lowered blood-sugar level caused by the vomiting and diarrhea. If I am ever called upon to treat a snakebite of this type having these symptoms, I'd take special care to supply additional sugar and fluids. I tried to tell one of the nurses walking beside me how terribly I wanted a cold sweet drink, but I couldn't speak.

Next I was aware of new pain, sharp and intense, developing in my lower abdomen. It was as if I were being pulled apart. I sensed that another doctor—he proved to be an older associate of Dr. Plehn—had come into the room, and I heard him exclaim, "My God, look at that swelling!"

My eyes were pried open again, and I tried to let the doctors know that I could hear what they said, but it was no go. The torture in my belly grew, and my whole abdominal wall became as rigid as a board. Every breath was a fight against pain and knotted muscles, and for the second time I knew what it is like to die.

But I was too tired and had suffered too much to care. Dying would bring relief.

At last, five hours after the snake struck me, I passed out.

It was six hours before I regained consciousness. During that time, Jack went on a mission that saved my life.

I was given the hospital's third and last vial of antivenin. There was no more in Gillette, but Jack located two vials in Billings, Montana, and the Montana State Highway Patrol rushed them south. Jack met the patrol car and brought the vials the rest of the way, and I got them at once. I'm sure that without them I would have died in that venom-induced coma.

I returned to the world of awareness to hear my doctors discussing the "optimum level for amputation." Should they take my leg off below the knee or above, and how far?

I tried to let them know that I was against the whole idea, but it was half an hour before I could open my eyes, roll my head, and move an arm enough to alert a nurse to the fact that I was conscious. An hour after that I got my first look at the bitten leg.

There is no adequate way to describe the consequences of such a snakebite as I had received. My whole leg looked more like an elephant's than a man's, both in size and in color. It was slate gray with patches of pink. And neither foot nor ankle was discernible—swelling had engulfed everything clear to the base of my toes.

I have been asked since whether the severity of my experience might have been caused by the penetration of a vein by one of the snake's fangs. This would have introduced venom directly into the blood. For obvious reasons, such bites have grave consequences.

But I don't think that happened in my case. It was 20 minutes after the bite before I felt the first effects of the spreading poison. If a vein had been punctured, the general symptoms would have appeared almost at once.

I believe that, instead, I got an abnormally large dose of venom in comparison to the size of the snake—probably almost the entire contents of his poison sacs —as a result of his hanging on and struggling to free himself. Before I got his half-inch-long fangs out of my leg, he must have pumped in far more than he would have delivered with one lightning-fast stroke.

I wasn't going to part with that leg if it could be avoided. As I pointed out to Jack and Lyle, I thought I might have quite a few years left after recovering from this thing, and I contemplated spending some of that time at the same kind of activity that had got me into this fix. For that, an artificial leg would hardly do.

We did some judicious pin-sticking in the swollen leg and learned that fairly normal sensation was still scattered over most of it. The amputation was postponed, and in the end it proved unnecessary.

In fact, in view of the severity of swelling and general symptoms, and the very close call I'd had, the final outcome was a most fortunate one. That rattler did me no permanent damage.

I left the hospital at the end of 10 days, and we headed for my home. The arrangements for the drive were a bit strange. I was settled comfortably on pillows laid across the back seat, but a bulky and highly unusual looking leg protruded out of a rear window. I rode all the way to Wisconsin that way, too.

But right then I was the most thankful hunter in the whole U.S.A.—and I still am.

Wolves Don't Live by Rules

Frank Glaser
as told to Jim Rearden

March 1968

Frank Glaser drew on the experiences of forty years of trapping and hunting in the wilds of Alaska for this and the many other stories he and Jim Rearden did for OUTDOOR LIFE. At the time, he was living in Fairbanks and had recently retired as predator-control agent for the U.S. Fish and Wildlife Service, a job he held for eighteen years in such stations as Fairbanks, Nunivak, Kotsebue, Noatak, Nome, and Anchorage. He had roamed the territory since 1915.

Jim Rearden is an authority on Alaska's wildlife. He has been head of the Department of Wildlife Management at the University of Alaska; a biologist with the Department of Fish and Game; a registered big-game guide, and now, for the second time, member of the Board of Fish and Game. He has written more than twenty-five stories for OUTDOOR LIFE and is now outdoor editor for *Alaska* magazine.

It was a cold clear March day at Savage River on the north slope of the Alaska Range. I was sitting on a hill watching a muskeg flat on which several hundred scattered caribou were feeding. A quarter-mile below me, a coal ledge jutted from the 15-foot-high river bank, and a yellow seepage from it smeared the blue-white river ice. Five caribou stood licking at the stain.

I was looking for wolves, and idly I glanced at the five caribou from time to time as I swung my binoculars to scan the snow-covered land. After an hour of careful watching I saw a lone gray wolf trotting across the flat. Soon three others single-filed down the river to my left. Then another appeared on my right, picking its way upstream.

The five wolves were converging on the caribou at the coal seep.

The wolf on the flat trotted to the edge of the bank above the unsuspecting caribou and peeked over at them. Then it backed off to lie down and wait. The group of three wolves left the creek and disappeared into the spruces below me. I lost track of the fifth wolf.

I watched the five caribou. After about 10 minutes a gray wolf streaked out of the timber and grabbed a big cow by the flank. The remaining four caribou scattered as the frantic cow skidded and staggered, trying to shake the clinging wolf. She tried to jump from the slick ice to the bank but immediately fell, floundering on her side, the tenacious wolf still clamped firmly to her flank. Three of the other wolves appeared and swarmed over her, chopping and slashing.

And then, incredibly, she pulled free. All of the animals skidded on the slick ice, but the frantic cow made it to the bank, humped her way to the top, and hooked her front legs over. The wolf on the bank met her head-on, sinking his teeth into her nose. He hung on as the two of them rolled and flopped down the steep slope to the river ice.

A red stain spread across the ice as the five wolves killed the cow and started to eat.

Another March found me on the same hill, again watching scattered caribou and looking for wolves. Below, on the open flat, a lone cow was feeding. Three wolves, trotting single-file with heads and tails down, started to cross the flat half a mile downwind of the caribou.

When they caught its scent, one of them, a big gray, immediately lay down in the snow while the others turned and loped into a nearby draw. After his partners had been gone a few minutes, the big gray wolf openly ran to within 100 yards of the caribou, sat down in plain sight, and started to howl.

The caribou stopped eating and curiously stared at him. She even walked toward the wolf, occasionally bounding nervously into the air. The two other wolves came into sight behind her, sliding along on their bellies like cats stalking a bird. Frequently they raised up and peeked ahead to see how close they were.

The caribou remained intent on the performing wolf in front of her. The gray wolf howled, trotted back and forth, and gradually worked closer and closer to the nervous but fascinated caribou. When the wolf was within 40 yards, it sat and howled continuously.

One of the stalking animals dashed from behind a knoll about 30 feet from the caribou, grabbed the animal's flank, and hung on. The two other wolves joined it in seconds, and the three of them quickly pulled her down.

There you have two common daytime hunting techniques used by wolves. I have seen as many as six wolves play the decoy game—they're very good at it. Sometimes, however, wolves simply run their prey down.

One April, again at Savage River, I saw a cow moose on the skyline, running and continually looking behind her. Five wolves soon showed up on her trail. I grabbed my rifle and ran up to an open sidehill from which I thought I might be able to take part.

The moose ran into a dense patch of spruces, the wolves right behind her. After a while she came into the open, with the wolves jumping and biting at her and then leaping back as she tried to strike them with her hoofs. They were too far away for me to interfere, so I sat and watched through binoculars.

She made a game fight of it. As the wolves slashed at her, leaping in and dodging back, she stood on her hind legs time and again, running at them, pawing and striking with her front hoofs. But finally the wolves simply pulled her down.

When I got there, they had eaten a few pounds of the hindquarters and had left. That animal was slashed and bitten all over the body, and pieces of hide as big as a man's hand had been peeled off. The moose was heavy with calf. I have seen pregnant caribou cows killed the same way.

As a private trapper and a government wolf hunter, I have observed wolves in Alaska since the late 1920's, when—for the first time in this century—they became common in Alaska's interior. The more I learn about wolves, the less I like to generalize about their hunting methods and other habits—wildlife doesn't live by rules.

I have read many incorrect statements about wolves. Two in particular that many people believe are that all the wolves in a region join forces each night to hunt, and that wolves invariably hamstring big-game prey.

Actually, wolf "packs" are almost always family groups, sometimes containing as many as two or three generations. However, during breeding season, when different families combine, I have often seen groups of 30 to 45 wolves.

At Savage River I was awakened early one March morning by the howling of several bands of wolves. I got up, dashed out with a rifle and binoculars, and located three bunches.

As I watched, all three came together on a big flat. I'd guess that there were three or four families.

Suddenly all of those wolves appeared to pile on one wolf, and the growling and yipping carried for miles in the still, cold air.

I saw how I could get within rifle range by working through some timber. As I hurried along I pictured in my mind six or seven dead wolves and a bunch of crippled ones, and I figured that a lot of hides and bounty money were going to come my way pretty easily.

But my dreams were shattered when I got within rifle range. All the wolves had left but two, and those two were mated. Not one injured wolf could I see. In the years since, I have found that wolves seldom seriously injure one another when fighting.

The largest bunch of wolves I have ever seen numbered 52. I had a good 45 minutes to count them. Fifty were black, and two were gray. The peculiar thing about these wolves was that they were together in October. Ordinarily the big packs form only during breeding season in February or March.

Except during breeding season, strange wolves are not welcomed into a family. I once watched, for some time, a pair of wolves that had a den with a bunch of pups in it. The family group also contained four other adult wolves, which might have been brothers and sisters, parents, or even grandparents of the mated pair.

One day—when all six adults were lying about, sleeping after a night of hunting —a big gray wolf, strange to the group, showed up on a ridge and trotted casually toward the den.

One of the adults saw the stranger when he was 100 yards away and immediately ran toward him. The five others were right behind. The first wolf struck the stranger with a shoulder, knocking him over. Before he could recover, all six of them had him, holding him from all sides.

There was no snapping and letting go as you see in a dog fight—each of the six simply grabbed the visitor and hung on, stretching the wolf out and banging him against the ground.

After perhaps 30 seconds of this, they all suddenly let go and stood back. The strange wolf got to its feet, hobbled down the ridge a few hundred yards, and lay down. I didn't see him in the area again.

Wolves are doglike in much of their social behavior, and it isn't difficult to take advantage of some of their habits.

When I first started to trap on Savage River in 1924, I noticed that my sled dogs refused to pass up the few scattered clumps of grass that were exposed on the high wind-blown ridges. They simply had to lift a leg to every clump, and they'd go far out of their path to reach one of these "signposts."

The next summer, I planted about 70 clumps of high grass on the ridges I trapped. I dug holes about six inches to the south of each clump and set spikes there to which I could fasten traps. When winter came and trapping started, I simply set the traps in the holes and covered them with dry dirt.

Wolves, like my dogs, would get the urge to raise their legs to these isolated clumps to leave their sign. As they did so, they stepped into my traps.

These were efficient wolf sets, and I also caught many foxes in them. An occasional wolverine or lynx would visit these clumps of grass, too, and I'd have their skins in my cache by spring.

I love the sound of a howling wolf, and after hearing it for years I found that I could imitate it. Often in the 1930's, on quiet evenings at my trapping cabin at Savage River, I would step outside and howl. If wolves were around, they usually answered, and they would frequently howl for hours as I dropped off to sleep.

I have called many wolves to within rifle range. Pups are especially easy to call.

Once, my calling had quite an effect on a superstitious Eskimo. On that occasion I had been sent to Golovin, on the Seward Peninsula, to try to take some wolves that had been killing the Eskimos' reindeer.

One morning I awoke and heard wolves howling near where the deer were grazing. An Eskimo herder and I went up on a ridge and counted nine wolves about two miles from us.

Soon a lone wolf howled behind us. I answered him, and he called back. We talked back and forth for some time before I spotted him with my binoculars. He was working his way across a big flat. As I watched him, he'd howl when I did and then come closer.

We lost sight of him in some low hills, but I kept howling occasionally. Finally he trotted into sight out of a ravine about 50 yards away, went up on a high snowdrift, and looked around, trying to find the "wolf" he had been talking with. It was an easy shot.

For the rest of my stay there, that Eskimo herder was half afraid of me, and he passed his uneasiness on to other Eskimos in the area.

I have often watched wolves hunting and killing moose and caribou in the daytime. But more often I have heard them killing caribou at night and have seen the kills the following day.

In my experience, February through April are months during which wolves seem to kill the most big game. The wolf's breeding season starts in February, and family groups merge then as the unpaired young wolves select mates. When these large groups join forces, they make heavy kills.

When wolves and caribou were numerous at Savage River in the 1930's, I could sense when there was going to be a big kill. As dark came on, there would be a lot of howling; I've heard as many as four separate packs within a few miles of my cabin. After the preliminary howling, all would be quiet, and I could almost feel the tension in the hills.

When the evening kill was made, usually around 10 or 11 o'clock, howling would start again. At that time I'd usually be reading or finishing up a day's skinning. Often the howling continued for hours after I went to bed. This seemed to be especially true on dark moonless nights.

I often investigated on the day after such a kill. Ravens would be flying around the dead caribou, so they were easy to locate. I'd find from one to 15 carcasses.

When attacked by wolves at night, a caribou herd crowds together instead of scattering and running. It's easy for wolves to catch the terrified animals and slash open their flanks. The caribou's paunch falls out, he steps on it and drags himself a way, and then he drops.

Almost invariably, all the animals killed in one herd will be within a few hundred feet of one another.

I think that the wolf is the brainiest animal in Alaska. He learns well, and he learns fast. A good example of this braininess is his reaction to being shot at from a small airplane.

In the early 1950's, wolves existed in large numbers on the arctic slope north of the Brooks Range. Caribou were just recovering from a bad slump then, so the U. S. Fish and Wildlife Service, for which I worked as a predator agent, organized a wolf hunt with small planes from Umiat on the Colville River.

There are no trees in the area, so we could fly low with ski-equipped planes and kill wolves with shotguns loaded with buckshot, a technique that some bounty hunters and some sportsmen still use in Alaska.

Normally we searched for wolves at an altitude of about 400 feet. When we found a bunch, we'd make a circle a mile or so away, drop to within 40 or 50 feet of the ground, and then come in on them.

The wolves usually ran straight away in single file. We'd fly on their left, and the gunner would shoot out the right side of the plane, often at ranges of 20 or 30 feet.

Usually the first pass at a bunch of wolves was easy, and shooting was simple. But the second pass was another story. By then the surviving wolves would have learned a lesson. Many of them would weave back and forth, at a dead run away from the plane, when we got within a couple of hundred yards.

Occasionally a really smart wolf would learn to dodge left every time the plane got close, so that he would be under the plane and out of the gunner's sight.

We buzzed one wolf that stopped on the edge of a high rim. The terrain forced us to come at him from above, and each time we neared he dropped off the rim and out of sight. When we were directly above him, he would be hard to find and even harder to hit. I fired eight or nine shots at that wolf as we made pass after pass over him for at least half an hour. Finally my pilot made a dangerous approach from below and pushed the animal into the open, where I got him with a clear shot.

The belief that wolves always take sick, crippled, or otherwise misfit animals doesn't always hold true. A wolf will take what is available, and he doesn't go out of his way to kill the weak. Wolves commonly kill stragglers, but though some of these animals are weak, others are not.

A wolf's teeth—the uppers fit on the outside of the lowers—work like a pair of shears. His jaw muscles are extremely powerful.

At one time, I had in harness a number of dogs that were three-quarters wolf. Their teeth were quite similar to those of wolves. They could hold a frozen rib of a moose or caribou in their front paws, feed it into the sides of their mouths, slice it off into quarter-inch pieces, and then grind the pieces into pulp.

A wolf can crack bones that even a grizzly bear can't break.

Some people are said to "wolf" food, and the word is appropriate in that context. I have opened the stomach of hundreds of wolves and have commonly found fist-size chunks of meat there. The bitch wolf feeds her weaned pups by regurgitating such chunks—I've often seen these pieces around wolf dens.

I think that wolves are unusual in their awareness of man. Even in wilderness areas, where they have little or no contact with humans, wolves have a pretty definite reaction to an encounter with man.

It has also been my experience that the wolf is the only animal able to recognize a motionless man for what he is. A bear, moose, caribou, or any other animal I know about in Alaska cannot recognize a motionless man by sight alone, especially if the man's silhouette is broken by a rock, log, or tree. But a wolf can.

Several times—when I have been absolutely motionless and wearing dull clothing, with the wind in my favor and my outline broken—wolves have approached, looked at me for a moment, and then whirled and run.

I don't regard the wolf as a coward, as do many people. Actually he's very brave.

I once watched two wolves drive a large grizzly from their kill. Another time, I saw a family of wolves drive three grizzlies from their den.

On still another occasion, in Mount McKinley National Park, I was watching a family of wolves feed on several caribou they had killed. They would sleep, feed a bit, and then sleep some more. Eventually a big dark grizzly ambled up the river bar, feeding on roots and whatever else he could find. Suddenly he got the scent of the dead caribou, whirled, and sat up, leaning into the wind. A moment later he took off at a run toward the carcass of the wolf-killed caribou.

Six wolves were lying near the dead caribou, and when that bear plunged into their midst, they scattered in every direction. One big gray ran off a few hundred yards, stopped, and howled. Four of the others gathered around her, and then the five of them trotted off.

The last wolf was a big black. He stood watching as the others filed off.

The bear sprawled across one of the carcasses, watching the wolves leave. Then the black wolf walked, stiff-legged, from behind the bear. As he neared, the bear glanced around but didn't move. The wolf walked as if he were on eggs—his tail straight out, his head straight—almost like a pointer on a hot scent.

When the wolf was about 10 feet from the grizzly, he leaped in and bit the bear's back, hard.

I clearly heard the bear roar as he lurched over backward, reaching for the wolf. The wolf lit out downhill, with the bear hot on his tail. The bear gained, finally getting so close that he'd have had the wolf in another jump if the wolf—his tail held low and his hind legs spread—hadn't made an abrupt turn.

It was a beautiful maneuver. The bear actually rolled over in his attempt to make the turn. He was as mad as a hornet when he picked himself up. He turned, walked back to the meat, and found the wolf already there.

The wolf backed off when the bear arrived, and then he lay down about 20 feet from the grizzly. But soon he circled, tiptoed close again, leaped, and bit, and once more the bear chased him down the hill.

The wolf tired of the game after about half an hour, and he trotted off in the direction the other wolves had gone.

It's my opinion that the wolf has been called a coward because he is so shy of man and because he commonly hunts in a large group with the odds in his favor. But these facts demonstrate his intelligence to me.

A wolf can become lonely, I believe, if kept away from others of its kind. And a female wolf has pretty strong maternal feelings toward almost any pup. I used these traits to make $50 when a dollar was worth something.

It was spring at Fairbanks, and I was approached by a man named Van Bebber, who made a business of keeping and feeding sled dogs for people. A couple of months earlier, Van Bebber had acquired a three-year-old female gray wolf from a trader up on the Tanana River. The wolf was in a cage when he got it, and he had released it in a stout pen with 10 to 12-foot walls.

Van Bebber had a buyer willing to pay $200 for the wolf, but he had been unable to catch her and put a collar and chain on her. She was so violent when he tried force that he was afraid she would kill herself.

Since I drove wolf-dogs and was a trapper, Van Bebber reasoned that I was an expert on wolves. He offered me $50 if I could put a chain and collar on the wolf without hurting her.

It became obvious that the wolf was terrified of Van Bebber, so I asked him to leave. Then I took a three or four-month-old pup of his, put it on a chain, sat down in the middle of the pen, and started petting the pup.

I spent the afternoon there. Once in a while I released the pup, and it would run over to the wolf. She would smell it, it would try to play with her, and she would respond halfheartedly.

While petting the pup I would howl like a wolf, and soon the female was answering me, with a real low howl. By that evening I'd had my hands on the wolf two or three times. But each time, she leaped back stiff-legged and her mane came up.

Next day I went into the pen with a choke collar in each pocket of my coat, plus a chain. I figured that if I could slip the collar over her head, I could snap the chain into it afterward.

She circled me one way and then the other, fast and nervously. Again I howled and used the pup as bait, and I got my hands on her. Twice I almost had the collar on her, but she leaped back.

The third day, the wolf was noticeably tamer and very fond of the pup. She obviously had looked forward to our return—her actions said so when we came in.

It was almost anticlimactic when I slipped the collar over her head and, a little later, snapped the chain into it.

The wolf's cruelty is not exaggerated.

One September day, I noticed a bull moose standing in the river near my cabin. The next day, he was lying on the bank with his head on the ground. I went over to see what was wrong with him and found that, though he was alive, he couldn't lift his head. Wolves had eaten 25 or 30 pounds of meat from one of his hindquarters. The suffering animal had been standing in water, trying to cool the feverish leg, when I had first seen him.

I shot the moose to end his suffering. Then I followed his back-trail to see what had happened. Five wolves had run and pestered him until he became exhausted and fell. They had eaten what they wanted and then had left—or perhaps they left because they heard my dogs barking or smelled my cabin.

Twice since then, I have found moose in similar conditions, both times in deep snow with a light crust that had supported the wolves but not the moose.

When wolves make a kill and are hungry, they'll usually drink some hot blood and then eat the hams. Sometimes they'll eat the tongue. A large number of wolves may eat an entire animal except for the skull and the very largest bones —and even these will often be cracked open so that the wolves can get the marrow.

There are a great many variables in the relationship between wolves and big game. Some wolves are much faster than others. The speed of big-game animals, even those within the same species, varies greatly.

It takes a large number of wolves to pull down a mature bull moose that has hard antlers and good footing. But two or three wolves can finish off the biggest bull that ever lived if he is antlerless and is caught in deep and crusted snow.

An animal in advanced pregnancy is vulnerable to wolf predation anytime. But the same animal at another time of the year might be able to run circles around the wolf, for the wolf is actually a relatively slow runner.

Because caribou are night-blind, one of any age or sex is highly vulnerable on dark nights. During daylight, however, practically any adult caribou can outrun wolves if he sees them in time. Wolves know this and hunt accordingly.

In the North, wolves depend more upon caribou for food than upon any other species of big game. Wolves exert strong influence on the caribou herds, especially young caribou.

In June 1940 in McKinley Park, Harold Herning, a park ranger, and I were eating lunch on a little hill overlooking a fork in the Teklanika River. In the V of the fork were 350 or so caribou, mostly cows, yearlings, and calves.

For several months previously, we had been observing a family of six wolves led by a small black female. Now, as we watched, these wolves trotted up the river and, upon smelling the caribou, dashed over the bank toward them. The caribou fled.

The little black female was much faster than the other wolves. She soon left them behind. Some 40 or 50 two and three-week-old calves bunched up and dropped behind the main body of caribou, and the black wolf was soon among them.

She grabbed one calf by the middle of the back, reared up, shook it, flung it aside, and continued the chase. She bowled over the next calf with her shoulder. Before it could get up, she grasped its back, shook the animal three or four times, and dropped it. The third one was also knocked over.

The fourth calf happened to be in soft ground, on which a wolf is clumsy. The black female hit the calf, knocking it down, but at the same time she stumbled and rolled end over end herself. The calf was the first to get to its feet, and as it started to run, it accidentally bumped into the just-recovering wolf, knocking her flat.

That angered the wolf, and after half a dozen jumps she caught the calf by the back and raised it high in the air, shaking it. Then she slammed the calf down, put both of her front paws on it, and actually bit out large chunks, tossing them aside as fast as she could.

The wolves didn't eat any of those calves. Each had bites through the backbone and into the lungs and heart.

Despite his savageness, however, I admire the wolf. He's a fascinating animal, and I'd hate to see him disappear.

Alaska has taken some steps toward making the wolf big game (see "I Say Make Wolves Big Game!" OUTDOOR LIFE, January 1968), thereby reducing the danger of the animal's being wiped out in our 49th state.

The wolf is a trophy of which any sportsman can be proud. But my guess is that there won't be many wolves taken by trophy hunters. These fine animals are just too smart for that.

Heaven Is a Steelhead

Joe Brooks

October 1968

This was Joe Brooks's first story as OUTDOOR LIFE's fishing editor, but he had contributed regularly since June 1953, when we ran "The Big Hole," the Montana trout stream he called "the best I ever fished." He began trout fishing in Maryland and eventually quit the family insurance business in Baltimore to fish, and write about fishing, waters the world over. He was a director of the OWAA, ran the Metropolitan Miami Fishing Tournament for three years and starred on ABC's American Sportsman TV series. He was honored by Trout Unlimited for his work in conservation and was a founder of the Brotherhood of the Jungle Cock (dedicated to teaching boys). An all-tackle man as well as an all-round athlete, Brooks pioneered with the fly rod in salt water and landed seventy species on flies (including a 148-pound 8-ounce tarpon). He wrote ten fishing books, the last *Trout Fishing*, just before his death in 1972 at the age of seventy.

Bill McGuire was into a fish. It streaked across the pool so fast I thought it was going to climb the trees on the far bank. Then it made a dogleg to the right, skittered five feet across the surface, and sank from sight. But it came right out again in an arching leap and headed upstream, still showing plenty of power and speed—a big, going fish if ever there was one.

Bill reeled fast, to keep the line tight. Then the fish came to the top, slowed, swirled, and dropped downstream, still facing into the current but slanting to the right, and with hard sweeps of its tail gained a couple of feet.

These were rough tactics. This steelhead was hard to hold.

Then the fish surged forward a few feet. Bill swept his rod in toward our bank, pulling the fish our way and getting it out of the current, reeled fast, and had the trout coming. Things looked good.

But then that fighting steelhead pulled out all the reserves, shooting toward the tail of the pool and again jumping clear. That effort tired the fish, however, and Bill followed it downstream, easing toward the bank as he went. He got the fish coming good and skidded it up onto the sloping beach.

"About eighteen pounds," Bill said, lifting the steelhead by the gill cover. "What a fish!"

The small bullet-shaped head was made for boring into heavy currents. The body was thick, deep, and strong-looking. An overall sheen of silver spoke of months in the sea, but the flared gill covers showed a faint blush of crimson, and there was a crimson slash along each side from gill cover to tail.

"He's traveled two hundred miles from the salt," Bill said. "He's beginning to get back his rainbow colors."

Bill took the hook out and put the fish back into the river.

"Go on upstream and spawn," he said. "And thanks for the memory."

That fine fish was the heaviest of eight steelheads Bill landed that day on the Babine River in northern British Columbia. All were taken on flies.

The steelhead, one of the greatest of all gamefish, is almost entirely confined to the coastal waters of western North America. In some places rainbows that run upstream out of lakes to spawn are also called steelheads. But the true owner of that name is the rainbow that goes to the salt and then comes into coastal rivers.

Here is an extremely strong fish that makes amazingly long runs, breasts mighty currents, soars up and over falls, thrashes through rocky shallows—moving relentlessly upstream in answer to the hereditary urge to spawn in the waters of his origin, waters that often are hundreds of miles from the sea. A few spawning steelheads die. But many survive and work their way back to the salt. There they fatten again in the sea's bounteous larder and regain strength so that they can return to the river and spawn once again.

From late August to mid-March (and even later in some rivers) the steelhead hordes enter rivers all along the West Coast from California to Alaska. Like waves beating on the shore, come the steelhead hordes. Then they hurry upstream, heading inexorably for the spawning beds.

There are summer steelheads and winter steelheads. The summer runs occur from late May through October, the winter runs from December or January to about mid-March.

On the Babine River, where I watched Bill McGuire take those eight steelheads, the best period is the last two weeks of September and all of October. But winter comes early this far north, and icy blasts sometimes send late fishermen out of there on the run.

Part of the thrill of steelhead fishing in the Babine is the wildness and splendor of that country—the dank smell of the forests, the racing rapids, the "feel" of a land that demands the best from every man. It is stern, remote, and wonderful.

In late September and through October—at the peak of the river's steelhead run—the landscape takes on a holiday look. The mountains shove up stands of lodge-pole pine, whose dark green provides a rich backdrop for the flamelike oranges of the aspens and poplars. The mountainsides appear to be dotted with lighted candles.

All of those trees seem to rank up and march down the slopes to the lakeshores, leaving occasional grassy, open spaces in which moose feed.

And along the shorelines you get an eyeful of rising trout.

The same rivers that harbor steelheads are also used by Pacific salmon, which spawn there and die. In the Babine you see sockeye, humpback, chinook, and coho salmon, all bound upstream to perform the last act of their lives. Many of the salmon, already half dead, are blotched with whitish fungus. Gaunt and sunken-eyed, the salmon dig out spawning beds and go about the act of spawning.

The sockeyes are bright red along the body, with greenish head and tail. Their beaklike mouths are studded with sharp teeth. The backs of the males show a decided hump, another manifestation of the spawning phenomenon.

Along the shore, spawned-out and dead fish lie rotting and from them rises a heavy odor. But the smell is more pungent than unpleasant, so you soon forget it as you fish.

Perched on the fish carcasses are the ever-hungry gulls, mewing and crying, pecking and pulling at the flesh. Sharing the spoils are dozens of bald eagles, in there getting their share or perched on log jams and trees along the river.

All are part of nature's cycle.

It is sometimes hard to get your offering to a steelhead before a salmon or one of the river's resident rainbow or Dolly Varden trout grabs it. If we did hook a spawning salmon, we tried to shake the hook out. If unsuccessful, we carefully released the salmon, hoping that it would live long enough to make its contribution to the future of its species.

Insurance man Moses Nunnally and I had flown from our homes in Richmond,

Virginia, to Seattle, Washington, where we'd met Bill McGuire. Bill is director of research and development for Eddie Bauer Outfitters of Seattle, and he knows the Northwest thoroughly.

In Bill's car we headed for the Canadian border, which we crossed near Sumas, Washington, and picked up the Trans-Canada Highway. At the town of Cache Creek, British Columbia, we turned onto Highway 97 and continued north to Prince George. From there we headed westward on Highway 16.

Five miles south of the town of Smithers we took off on a dirt road. Forty-five miles later we reached Babine Lake. Ejnar Madsen and Jim Clark, owners of Norlakes Lodge, were waiting at a dock with a launch, in which we rode to camp, located 20 miles down the 115-mile-long lake.

The Babine River, which we were going to fish, slips out of the lake some four miles below the lodge, at the Indian village of Babine. The river is wide up there, with long, shallow stretches. Then it narrows and runs faster as it nears a weir three miles downstream. Below the weir it rattles along through breathtaking country for 20 miles and on into an almost impenetrable canyon. It then enters the great Skeena River, main artery for steelheads coming inland from the ocean. The Kispiox and the Babine are two of the Skeena's most famous tributary rivers.

From start to finish the Babine runs for about 60 miles, in a generally westward direction.

The Babine's steelheads average 15 pounds, but many are considerably heavier —the females as big as 15 pounds, some males to 35.

The biggest steelhead reported from the Babine was a 47½-pound fish taken in a net by the Babine Indians. The largest ever taken on rod and reel went 31¼ pounds and was caught on bait by Wendell Henderson of Kelseyville, California. Several other anglers have taken Babine steelheads to 30 pounds, and fish estimated to have been in the 40-pound class have been lost.

The Babine's largest fly-caught steelhead weighed 26 pounds and was taken by Jim Sharp of San Francisco, California, in 1958.

One day Jack Albright of Bellevue, Washington, representative for a ski-clothing manufacturer, and I took the biggest steelheads we'd ever caught on flies. The fish were hooked in the same pool and within a few minutes of one another.

Jack and I had gone downstream several miles below the weir and had stopped to fish a fine-looking pool. It was about 600 feet long and 125 feet wide, with a good current throughout. I fished the head of the pool while Jack waded in a couple of hundred feet downstream from me.

He had just got into position when I saw him wave and point to the opposite bank. On the sandbar at the head of the pool, we had seen within 10 feet of one another the tracks of wolves, moose, and grizzlies. Right away I thought, grizzly!

But it was a moose that Jack had spotted, a majestic animal whose antler spread must have been at least 55 inches. Eventually the bull turned and faded into the dense underbrush.

The moose was a good omen. Jack and I were into fish right away.

I made a short cast across-current, heard a splash, and got a strike that made me jump. That steelhead must have been lying just below the surface.

It was a good fish, and he zipped off downstream as if he were going to tear Jack's legs off. But he jumped half-way between Jack and me and fell back with a thump, tossing the water far and wide. Then he made a run of about 100 feet, stopped, and hung there.

I edged to shore, keeping a tight line, and walked downstream, reeling as I went. Then the fish raced upstream, fresh and flying, and jumped right opposite me. I got a good look at him, and I knew that this was the biggest steelhead I'd ever had on. Jack saw him, too, and came running.

368

I finally beached that fish, which weighed 20 pounds.

Back we went to our fishing, and now it was Jack who got the action. He gave a whoop, and I jerked my head around in time to see a tremendous steelhead in the air. It fell back with a splash and tore the surface to shreds as it steamed for the far bank. Then, just as suddenly, it turned, rushed right back at Jack, and came out of the water only 15 feet from him.

I could see that this steelhead was bigger than the one I had just landed.

Jack stayed with that big, strong fish for 15 minutes. Finally he got it into the shallows, where its color blazed up and seemed to tint the water with crimson and pink sparks. The fish was fat and round-looking, its weight riding the length of the body into the tail—a powerful fish from a mighty breed.

Jack skidded the steelhead onto shore. The scales said 25 pounds—a skookum (might good) steelhead for sure.

We had released all of our other fish, except a couple that we'd eaten, so Jack and I both felt that we could be excused for keeping these two for mounting. They were the sleekest-looking steelheads I've ever seen—fine products of a great river.

The Babine was loaded with big fish. The next day, I fished the pool below the weir with another of the camp's guests, Don Ives, a machine salesman from Seattle. I was about 200 feet below Don when he hooked a fish so big that if I hadn't seen the crimson on its sides during a jump, I'd have thought that it was a chinook salmon. The fish streaked downstream with a definite goal in mind, maybe the salt.

Don raced past me in pursuit of the great fish and disappeared around a point. Twenty minutes later he came trudging back.

"He took me down through the next two pools," Don told me. "He got into a pocket behind a rock, and I got most of my line back. Then the hook pulled out. That fish must have been forty pounds."

I could well agree. That was certainly the biggest steelhead I'd ever seen. And Don's reel handle was bent to about a 40° angle from the pressure that had been put on it.

In many steelhead rivers you can occasionally take fish, especially summer-run fish, on dry flies and by skating spiders; or you can take them on flies fished just under the surface. But all of us at the Babine camp tried this kind of fishing at one time or another without luck.

Most of us used a sinking-float line, the first 30 feet of which sinks while the rest floats. With such a line you can make very long casts and put the sinking section out where the fish are. It will go down quickly and allow leader and fly to work in the holding water. The floating section is easily mended, or flipped upstream, letting you keep the fly out there and drifting freely. And the sinker-floater is much easier to retrieve and pick up than is a conventional sinking line.

Moses Nunnally, though he is an old hand at fly casting, had never fished this kind of line before.

"Couldn't I do just as well with a floater?" he asked.

I explained that the fish were holding deep in the riffles and pools and didn't seem to want to come up to take. Now and then they moved up a foot or so, but most of the time they nosed down and picked up a fly as it slid along the rocks on the bottom.

I'd guess 85 percent of all steelheads taken on flies are caught by the users of sinking lines, lines that get the fly right down to the fish. Many anglers use a line that sinks in its entirety, but an old steelheader's trick is to splice a sinking head to a monofilament line or to a level nylon floating line. By using a very heavy head—a 333-grain shooting head, for instance—and splicing a nylon running line to it, you get an outfit with which you can easily make casts of 125 feet. The light nylon will float and so won't be pulled by the current as would a heavier line.

However, the new combination sinking-floating lines, now made by a number of fly-line manufacturers, eliminate the troublesome job of splicing two lines together. The new lines also eliminate another problem—possible weak spots at the splices.

Moses' first cast with the sinker-floater on the Babine was a good one of about 85 feet. But as soon as the fly and line landed, the current grabbed the line and put a big belly in it. I knew that consequently the fly was rushing across the pool far too fast.

"Mend your line," I said hastily. "Flip the floating part upstream so the water won't pull on it and drag the fly away from the fish."

In any steelhead river having a fairly stiff current, the heavy push of water will quickly belly a line and pull leader and fly out of the lies of fish. I told Moses to throw a slack-line cast (a serpentine toss) and then to mend the floating part of the line. That way, the fly floats freely for a longer distance, straight down-current, out where the fish are.

I explained that some fishermen make a cast and feed the shooting line out of their hands or let it run out of the shooting basket (we used shooting baskets on the Babine) so that the fly gets down and works along the bottom.

"After the fly has finished the downstream float and the current starts to pull it across the pool," I told him, "let it go, keeping the rod tip high and imparting no action to the fly. It'll work across the pool and come to a stop directly below you.

"A steelhead may hit at any part of a float—sometimes as soon as the fly lands, sometimes when it's out in the current—or he might follow it across-current and hit on the swing. Most of them do hit on the last part of the swing or just when the fly stops moving and hangs in the current."

"That's what he did!" yelled Moses, who was following my instructions religiously. "I've got one!"

He raised his rod tip, and 30 feet out from us a steelhead took to the air. It was a good, deep-bodied fish, and it fought a great fight. Moses finally beached the trout, which weighed 14 pounds even.

"Not bad," I said. "Two casts and one steelhead."

Some steelheaders bring the line in as soon as the fly's cross-current swing is complete. Others retrieve the fly upstream for several feet, jerking it as they do so, before bringing it in for the next cast. On the Babine I have got hits from steelheads on those slow, foot-long jerks, so I stick with that kind of retrieve wherever I try for steelheads.

Or the Babine, as elsewhere, to get the best float with a sinking line you have to judge the water's depth and force.

Sometimes the current is so great and the water so deep that, even with a sinking line, you must cast well upstream so that the line has time to get down before it reaches the place where you know or suspect the fish are lying. On the other hand, the fish may be holding where the water is shallow and the current relatively slow. In that case you have to toss the line and fly a bit downstream so that the line won't sink too much and catch on rocks.

Moses raised another point that day.

"I've always thought that the longer the leader, the better your chances for fish," he said. "But we're using short leaders."

"When you use a sinking line," I said, "the leader should be no longer than six feet. A ten or twelve-foot leader such as we use in most trout fishing would only defeat the purpose of the sinking line. The heavy line would go down, all right, but the current would force the long, light leader—and the fly—up toward the surface and out of bounds for deep-lying fish. The short leader keeps the fly down where you want it, only inches from the bottom."

(In any big steelhead river, long casts are usually needed. For that reason, as well as for ease in handling the sinking lines, I advise steelheaders to use a 9 or 9½-foot fly rod. With such a stick you can throw either the WF-9-F/S or the slightly heavier WF-10-F/S line. The number in each line designation classifies the weight of the first 30 feet of the line. The designation WF-9-F/S means that the line is a weight-forward floater-sinker in which the first 30 feet weigh 250 grains, thus making the line a No. 9 according to standards set by the American Fishing Tackle Manufacturers Association. The WF-10-F/S is the same type of line but has a 30-foot weight of 300 grains. I like the lighter of those two lines for fairly shallow water and the heavier one for deeper water. The No. 10 line sinks faster and makes long throws a little easier.)

On my first trip to the Babine, Bill McGuire had handed me a shooting basket and insisted that I use it. As I said earlier, most steelhead rivers demand extra-long casts—throws of 80 to 100 feet. To handle that much line while wading, it is almost essential to use a shooting basket.

If you don't, you must loop the shooting line in the fingers of your free hand, and the long coils often drag in the water, twist in the wind, or become entangled and bunch up against the rod's first guide, spoiling what could have been a fine throw.

With the shooting basket strapped around your waist just above your belt, you can strip in line so that it lies in neat coils in the basket. When you make the next cast, the line slips out freely and easily.

"When you're ready to retrieve," Bill had told me, "tuck your rod under your arm, and use both hands to strip the line into the basket in front of you. You can use a lot more line this way than if you tried to hold it in your hand."

I did as he said, and it was a pleasure on the next throw to see the line's heavy head go out and then to look down into the basket and see coil after coil disappear.

Best fly patterns for steelheads very according to the river being fished, and they are used both weighted and unweighted. In general, the best patterns, especially for winter steelheads and during late runs in big rivers such as the Babine, show some pink, red, or orange, along with some white. These flies are tied to imitate salmon eggs, on which steelheads feed heavily.

On the Babine we used all the color combinations just mentioned. We started with No. 4 and No. 6 hooks but eventually went to 1/0 because we found that these bigger hooks bit better into the mouths of big steelheads.

Our favorite pattern was the Babine Special, first tied by Bill McGuire. It has an orange body with a pinched-in center, a white hackle, and no tail. Its design is very simple, but that was the fly we all came to depend on.

Rex Palmer of Seattle ties another good one. It has an orange body, white hackle and a green tag. He calls it the Palmer Special.

As far as I have been able to discover, no one has ever taken a steelhead from the Babine on a dry fly. Next time I'm there, I intend to put in some time trying to do just that.

Breakfast at Midnight

Jay Mellon

July 1969

To most hunters the supreme challenge is to shoot all four species of North American sheep. How, then, about James R. "Jay" Mellon II of Pittsburgh and Nairobi who can boast of scoring a super slam of all *thirteen species* of the world's sheep? That was our story, "The Thirteenth Ram," in OUTDOOR LIFE for February 1972 in which Mellon related how he reached this pinnacle by shooting the rare bharal, or blue sheep, at sixteen thousand feet in India's Himalayas. No wonder Jack O'Connor says of him that, although only thirty-one, Jay Mellon has probably collected a greater number of big-game animals than any man that ever lived, "some of which I have never even heard of." Mellon was awarded the Weatherby big-game trophy in 1972. Of his three stories for OUTDOOR LIFE the following is my favorite.

It fills me with delight to recall the events of an epic hunt when they are still fresh in my mind. As I write this story, hardly a month has passed since the shooting of the largest Marco Polo sheep taken in half a century. The early snow may now cover its bones, which lie at the base of a glacial moraine on the Great Pamir Range of Afghanistan amid some of Asia's most awesome scenery.

Rising over 20,000 feet, a line of gigantic peaks, eternally snow-covered, forms the main chain of a long east-west range. From these peaks broad stony valleys studded with sapphire-blue lakes and marked with the sparsest grasses slope gently northward to the Panja River. These valleys are known as pamirs, or pastures, and one in particular is called Tuli Boi by the Kirghiz shepherds who live there. This valley and the pamirs that lie adjacent to it are the haunts of Ovis ammon poli, probably the world's most coveted hunting trophy.

Wonders are many in the natural world, but few compare with this giant white sheep of the pamirs. An old ram stands over 40 inches at the shoulder and carries superbly curled horns, which are longer, on the whole, than those of any other beast on earth. Despite his 250 pounds, he gallops over the most jagged moraines with a regal, almost floating, ease; and Prince Demidoff, who hunted Ovis poli earlier in the century, marveled at how "His fine sturdy body all seems to point to and culminate in support of his massive horns, which he always carries with pride and dignity."

Little need be said about the strange but familiar history of this animal: how its long curling horns aroused the wonder of Marco Polo, a 13th-century traveler following the caravan route to China; how for centuries it was thought to be mythical, like the unicorn, until a British adventurer sent its horns to England in 1834. Since then, very few of these sheep have been shot—first, because in summertime the rams live at 16,000 feet in a land so rugged that it looks like the face of the moon, and second, because only a sliver of their range falls outside Communist territory.

Ten years ago Ovis poli could still be hunted in the Hunza district of Pakistan by consent of the native ruler. But political pressure (which has ruined much of the world's best shooting) recently forced the closure of Hunza to foreigners. Today, these sheep can be hunted in only one small area outside Communist territory. This is the narrow Wakhan Corridor of Afghanistan, where in August 1959 our ambassador, Henry Byroade, shot the first two Marco Polo sheep taken by an American since the Morden-Clark Expedition, over 30 years before. In August 1967 Texan George Landreth killed a Marco Polo in the Wakhan (see "Greatest Trophy of All," OUTDOOR LIFE, October 1968).

Sooner or later most big-game hunters get tired of lowland shooting and develop a strong preference for mountain game. At 26, I have reached this stage. Originally I came from Pittsburgh, Pennsylvania, but I've lived in Africa for over five years. Hunting takes up much of my time, and I've collected many wildlife specimens for museums. Five times in the last year I turned my back on the comforts of home in Nairobi and set out on the high road to sheep country. I took many fine rams on those hunts, and I returned to mountain shooting each time with greater fanaticism.

Of course it was inevitable that my passion for collecting Asian sheep should one day boil over into a stab at Ovis poli. Yet the decision to hunt him, when it came, was largely haphazard. I had given it little thought in advance and, beyond a few inquiries by mail, had taken no steps to arrange a hunt.

Then one day, as I was poring over pictures of these sheep in some old hunting books, a sudden rush of madness came over me and I knew all at once that I had to have this colossal trophy. I got on the next plane and flew to Afghanistan. There, I obtained shooting permits from the government and scheduled a hunt to begin in six weeks. In Kabul, the fledgling tourist organization agreed to furnish tents, gear, and a few untrained servants—mostly city men from the lowlands. They also offered to supply tinned food and several canisters of oxygen (in case of severe altitude sickness). For the rest, we would live off the land. My permit allowed for five sheep at $6,000 each. Not exactly a rummage sale, I admit, but I didn't argue.

Once away from Kabul, my predicament was like that of a presidential candidate: I needed a running mate—someone to share the trials that lay ahead. I began casting about for one in the home museums. At one point I envisioned a little ad, which might have run like this: *WANTED: A cheerful fanatic who expects the worst and will probably get it.*

Fortunately I had friends at Pittsburgh's Carnegie Museum, which wanted a Marco Polo sheep group. Among these friends was Dr. Arthur Twomey, director of education at the museum, who had collected birds with my father in Central America, with my grandfather on a haphazard cruise across the South Pacific, and with me on many African expeditions.

"Would you share the ups and downs of one more wild goose chase?" I asked Arthur.

I was certain what the answer would be.

We met in Kabul in early September. Arthur had arrived beforehand to make a lecture film on the Afghan people and the city forts and monuments. But we had little time for puttering around the ruins. Snow falls early in the Great Pamirs, and the sheep ranges are considered inaccessible after September. We therefore hurried to Faizabad by air, having sent our gear and servants ahead in a truck. The government assigned us a personable young headman named Sefad Mir, who also served as interpreter. Mir quickly arranged with the local governor for us to use a mud-walled guest house. He also cooked up a tasty shish kebab with rice and produced the most delicious watermelons we had ever eaten.

Faizabad is still completely rural. Turbaned merchants shout the virtues of their wares from tiny cubicles along the dusty streets. Women wear long black veils, and the cry of the muezzin still summons worshippers to prayer five times daily. Almost every building is made of mud, and I remember thinking as we left the city that a flood or rainstorm could wash the whole of it away while we were gone.

It was a grueling drive to the Wakhan. All day we bounced over frightful tracks, caught up at times in a slow-moving stream of laden mules, donkeys, and fat-tailed sheep. For many hours we followed the course of a river, crossing and recrossing it on the most terrifying bridges. They were so rickety that every time we traversed one safely I muttered, "God is good." My plans to film one of us driving over such a bridge quickly foundered when Arthur said, "I'll make the movie; you can be W. C. Fields."

On the second day, we reached Qala Panja and were quartered in a wooden house built for the present Afghan king's first Marco Polo sheep hunt. Already we were hemmed in on three sides by the enormous sweeping mountain ranges of central Asia. Directly before us the Great Pamirs rose to 20,000 feet, a single east-west range bracketed by the Wakhan and the Panja rivers, which flow together a few miles away to form the Oxus. To the south, on the far side of a steep glaciated range, lay Pakistan. And northward, across the Oxus, we could see the watchtowers and collective farms of Russia. Sharing common borders with China, Pakistan, and the Soviet Union, this narrow strip of Afghan territory is still, in some sense, a crossroads of the world, as it was in ancient times when it formed the main caravan route to Peking.

Next morning, mules and horses were furnished by the local governor and we started off up the Wakhan River toward Babatangi. To our regular retinue of guides, camp servants, and mule drivers the governor had added a few soldiers, allegedly to protect us from brigands, but actually to make sure we didn't wander over the border and provoke an incident with the Russians. For part of the trek my horse was led by one of these soldiers, a handsome turbaned musketeer who drank sour milk from a goat-skin and shooed away the curious as we passed through villages. He would have looked at home among the characters of James A. Michener's novel, *Caravans*.

By evening we arrived, sunburned and saddle-sore, in Babatangi village and made camp under the towering south wall of the Great Pamirs. Looking up, Arthur and I could see the challenge that awaited us. From 9,500 feet the trail led steeply up to 16,000 feet and to Marco Polo haunts, if not to the certain game itself. As night came I took pills for altitude sickness, checked the pressure in our oxygen canisters, and dozed off dreaming of adventures to come.

I was shaken awake at dawn by the protracted thunder of an avalanche on the Pakistan side of the corridor. Arthur was already up, and when breakfast had been gulped and the animals loaded we set out on the "horror climb," as we later called it. All morning our mules and horses slipped and scrambled up the steep slopes, dislodging little landslides. Following with the heaviest loads was a herd of panting, slobbering yaks, which often lay down in open revolt, unmindful of the floggings and beatings that followed.

We lunched in a meadow at 14,000 feet. Everyone felt weak from our sudden rise in altitude. Also, Arthur was suffering from headache and I from nausea. We tried to eat watermelons but had lost our appetite and only nibbled on them. I needed all my strength just to get back into the saddle.

Later, as we were crossing the 16,000-foot Sari Gez Pass, Sefad Mir gave me a strange warning.

"Watch your horse," he said. "If he starts to tremble, let him rest at once or he will die."

Horses apparently die often when carrying loads at over 14,000 feet, and yaks should really be used. So I kept a nervous eye on my mount as we were crossing the pass and didn't notice for a while that I myself had started to tremble. The

Afghans were very much surprised when I suddenly sprang from the saddle and lay down.

Having crossed over to the northern face of the Great Pamirs, we camped that night at 14,500 feet, everyone exulting that the horror climb was behind us. Arthur and I inhaled oxygen for several minutes and were relieved when all the symptoms of mountain sickness—headache, weakness, and stomach upset—quickly vanished. Our morale spurted higher still when Sefad Mir announced that the local shepherds had seen Ovis poli on the hills above our camp and that many could be found in nearby Tuli Boi Valley.

By noon the next day we had reached Tuli Boi and had made camp beside some stone shepherd huts at 13,700 feet. While Arthur studied the curved, knotted horns of 30 ibex feeding on the valley wall just above camp, Sefad Mir and I went into one of the stone huts and learned that the Kirghiz man who lived there was sharing his home with a moody and unpredictable lodger.

"Yes," the shepherd said, pointing to some deep claw marks on the rafters, "I share this hut with a bear. He sleeps here all winter but has to be out by May when I come up from the low country. In October, I leave and he moves in again."

Naturally I appreciate that good fences make good neighbors, so I said that I was sure the bear would live up to his treaty obligations but that I would sleep somewhere else just in case he showed up early.

Arthur and I had finished supper and were sitting at the table wrapped up like Eskimos when Sefad Mir barged in and asked when he should wake us.

"Just wake us when you usually get up on a hunt like this," I said innocently.

He nodded and left. Arthur and I crawled into our sleeping bags and had just dozed off when Mir came in again, hung a lantern on the tent pole, and pushed a bowl of porridge into my hands.

"What the hell are you doing here?" I muttered.

"Breakfast time, Sir," said Mir cheerfully. "Here's your porridge, Dr. Twomey."

"Porridge!" we yelled. "It's midnight, you fool!"

"Of course," he answered, still unruffled, "but that's when we eat breakfast here."

And so it was for the next 14 days: breakfast at midnight.

By 1:30 a.m. we were riding our yaks up the Tuli Boi Valley between towering peaks that were ghostly white in the starlight. Our thermometer read 18°, and I was suffering, for the airline had lost my down clothing and I had only light sweaters and native garments to wear.

Seven hours later we had reached the end of Tuli Boi Valley and were riding in the morning sun across grassy downs at 16,000 feet. Sefad Mir walked cautiously in front of the yaks and peeked over each little rise before we crossed it. Suddenly he signaled, and we slipped to the ground.

From behind a boulder Arthur and I caught sight of our first Ovis poli—two old rams that were standing on a ridge in the sun. Their huge horns and noble carriage made such a picture that I am still under the spell of my impressions, and doubtless always will be. For a long time no one spoke. We just stared incredulously through our glasses, dumbfounded at the animals' beauty.

About one ram, there could be no argument. I knew at once that we would either shoot him or never live it down. Mir, who had taken many Marco Polos, said its horns would measure 60 inches, and no one disputed his claim. So the stalk began.

By using hills and depressions for cover we made an easy approach to within 170 yards of the rams. It was now just a question of who should fire, and Arthur and I had a polite little argument in which each of us proposed that the other should do the honors, like Alfonse and Gaston motioning each other through a door. But I was the more insistent, and my friend finally agreed to shoot. I was relieved, quite frankly, because Arthur was over 60 and I was afraid that our next opportunity might require more climbing than he was capable of. I needn't have worried.

Sefad Mir and I lay on the ground holding our ears as Arthur took aim with his .300 Weatherby Magnum. Boom!

The ram sprang up and made a last frantic rush downhill. But death was already in him. When he fell, the second sheep, a smaller animal with 52 to 54-inch horns, stopped beside him to look back. I lifted my Model 70 Winchester .300 Magnum and rested the crosswires on the ram's chest, but I didn't shoot. I have never regretted this decision.

Our first Marco Polo measured 57 inches, and we were delighted. His horns were superbly curled, almost perfect in their symmetry, and not at all broomed off. We hoped, of course, to find a better ram in time. But for the moment, we could relax.

For the next eight days we enjoyed some of the most difficult and interesting hunting that either of us has known. Not a day went by when Marco Polos were not seen, but the old rams were incredibly wary and all but impossible to stalk. They stayed at the uppermost end of the valley and did most of their grazing by night. Often, just at daybreak, we would see them trooping in single file up onto a steep moraine or across the ice itself. Invariably they bedded down in some utterly impregnable spot—each ram facing a different way, the wind wrong, and no cover at all for a stalk.

Sometimes at dawn we would surprise a herd while it was grazing. But if the sheep saw us at the same instant we saw them (which was often), they would rush together and stand looking at us in such a tight cluster that no one dared shoot for fear of hitting the wrong one, or maybe even two with a single shot. On those occasions when everything went right and I got a ram in my sights, he was always too small. This was, after all, the hunt of a lifetime, and to settle for a ram in the low 50's, when there were 60-inchers about would simply have been a betrayal of standards.

There were other problems too. We had both arrived in the Pamirs with severe colds and could only keep them in check with massive doses of antibiotics. In addition, Arthur had dysentery and a streptococcus infection in his throat, and I had a sharp bronchial cough that sounded like the overture to a case of pneumonia. Each night, we pilfered the medicine chest like raccoons rummaging in a trash barrel. And, though our own needs were considerable, we also had to care for the servants, who came to us every day with headaches, dysentery, altitude sickness, nausea, and infected fingers. We'd dip into our dwindling stock of pills and hand out the precious medicine, which I still suspect was then sold to the local people. Acromycin became so dear that every time I gave some away it was like watching my own blood spill into the sink. One night we cut the last capsule in two and washed the halves down with a toast to luck.

As the weather got steadily colder, my thin sweaters and native clothing, which were inadequate in the best of times, became a source of torment. It was inevitable that I would go down to warmer country before long, either by my own free will or feet first. I remember promising myself each night as I rode, numb and shivering, up the valley that we would decamp for Kabul that very day.

"Never again!" I swore. But by evening I had always relented.

Thus we played out our desperate game of hide-and-seek with the rams of Tuli Boi. Our patience and fortitude were all but gone when suddenly one morning fortune relented.

Arthur and I had eaten breakfast at midnight and had left camp when the yaks were saddled. At dawn we parted company where the valley splits into two branches. Arthur headed eastward up a side valley while I continued southward toward the top of the range. We had decided that I would take the two shikaris, since I had not yet shot my ram. Arthur was a perfect cavalier and agreed to hunt with the dishwasher and the cook.

Little need be said about my own adventures that morning: how the shikaris spooked a large herd of rams in the semidarkness; how my yak Flying A, who was noted (even among yaks) for his leaden sloth, rebelled and tried to roll on me; and how all morning long the sheep made fools of us and we saw only rear ends disappearing over hilltops. Instead, let's take up the thread of Arthur's adventures.

It was just getting light when the cook spotted two huge rams walking up Arthur's little valley, but off to one side and out of range. Because the wind was still blowing downhill, everyone agreed to let the sheep move out ahead before following them. In less than an hour the three men set out, with Arthur leading. But things quickly went wrong. The sheep disappeared in some broken ground ahead, and Arthur had to proceed with extreme caution. He wasted an hour, expecting to jump the rams at any moment. He knew that the wind would change around 8 o'clock and start blowing up the valley. Time was a real problem.

Up where the valley ended was a grassy basin, toward which glaciers descended from several directions. Arthur, puffing and blowing, reached the edge of this basin and peeked over a boulder. His heart could ill afford to miss a beat just then, but I'm sure it did. There were the rams, and not just the two, but also seven others. Arthur swung his spotting scope from ram to ram, completely stupefied by the size of their horns, which on several of the animals turned sharply down at the points and were clearly over 60 inches long. The rams lay on the grass in a line, all eyes and ears for trouble, each one chewing his cud with a slow grinding motion. The whole herd was staring fixedly downhill, looking straight at Arthur. He couldn't crawl closer. It was a 400-yard shot or nothing.

Arthur was still deliberating about which ram to shoot at when a light breeze began to blow against the back of his head. The wind had changed. Panic swept over everyone. Arthur scooped up his .300 Weatherby, leaned it on a rock, aimed. Too late!

The closest ram got the scent and sprang up, as if hit by a bullet. The whole herd then rose and rushed together into a cluster. With the sheep milling at 400 yards, Arthur couldn't chance a shot. His spirits sank to their lowest point in his 50 years of hunting.

But luck had not deserted him. One old ram suddenly broke away in panic from the herd and raced diagonally up a rockslide, away from Arthur. There was no way to tell whether he was the largest, but no one cared. He was enormous, and his horns were obviously a good half a foot longer than those of our first sheep.

The range (which we later measured) was about 525 yards when Arthur fired. The ram, still running fast, looked pretty small even in a 9X scope. Arthur swung the crosshairs several yards ahead of his target and let fly. There was no puff of dust, but the ram didn't flinch. He just kept running over the rocks with a gliding, effortless gait. Arthur fired again, this time at 600 yards and more from honest rage than from any reasonable expectations. A puff of dust rose behind the big sheep.

But Arthur was determined. He had just cranked in a third shell when the cook and the dishwasher began to cheer. The old ram had stopped and was staggering. A second later, he fell dead. The first bullet had lodged in his lungs.

Later that morning I found Arthur sitting silently beside his prize, like a crusader who had found the Holy Grail. An old man who had long since despaired of ever seeing one of these great sheep had conquered hunting's highest peak.

"How big?" I asked excitedly.

"What do you think?" said Arthur, grinning like a devil.

"Well, it might make forty inches, Professor," I answered teasingly. Actually, my guess was 60.

Arthur handed me the steep tape, and I measured both horns several times. The longest went 64½ inches. The other was 64. Both horns had a base circumference of 16¼, and they measured 44½ inches tip to tip. The circumference of both spirals was 19½ inches.

Arthur's ram was the largest recorded wild sheep of any kind taken in about half a century. Arthur skinned it whole for a life-size mount, which will be displayed in a diorama at the Carnegie Museum. Then we rode back to camp, still somewhat dazed by events, and deeply conscious that a great moment in hunting annals had just passed.

Of course I wanted to stay longer in Tull Boi Valley and hunt for the ram of my dreams. But events conspired against my success. In the days after Arthur's triumph sheep were scarce in the valley, and our daily hunts turned up almost nothing. By then, Chris Klineburger of Jonas Bros. Taxidermists of Seattle, and Bill Picher, a California orange grower, had arrived in camp, suffering from altitude sickness. We hunted together for two days but had no luck.

On the third day, Picher's condition turned into pulmonary edema. That evening, despite our desperate efforts to save him, he died. Further hunting was therefore unthinkable. Arthur and I set out at once with Chris, and we brought the body to Kabul in a record three days. Since then, the 20,000-foot peak at the head of Tuli Boi Valley has become Mt. Picher.

And so I returned from the unique experience of a Marco Polo sheep hunt without having fired a shot. I had passed up several rams, and I am happy with that decision. Like bridge, trophy hunting is contractual by nature. You set yourself a goal and try to reach it. If you can't, it is better to leave with nothing than to settle for a poor head that will irk you every time you see it hanging on the wall. And besides, there's always next year and the chance to hunt again.

It is a great consolation that in this sport a man with patience and willpower eventually gets what he wants. We hunters can take comfort from a little poem that proudly proclaims:

> He knew the troubles of tracking,
> The business of camps and kits,
> And the pleasure that pays
> For the pain of all,
> The ultimate shot that hits.

My next Marco Polo sheep hunt has already been scheduled.

The Henry Poolman Story

J. S. Barrett

April 1970

The proceeds from this story are being turned over by the author to an educational fund for Henry Poolman's daughter. The fund was set up by the East Africa Professional Hunters Association, of which Poolman was a member. Harry L. Tennison of Fort Worth, Texas, president of Game Conservation International, is joint trustee. Of the story, the author has this to say: "This is a story I never expected to write. When you finish reading it, I think you will know why. In the three years since the affair, however, so many inaccurate versions have been told, including one badly garbled account in a national magazine, that I have decided it is time to set the record straight. So I have put it down here exactly as it took place during our hunt in Kenya."

The lion came at us fast. I saw Henry Poolman knocked aside, and the next thing I remember was looking down at the great cat's head. He had my left forearm between his jaws and was crunching down on bone.

My rifle was in my right hand, and I belted him hard with the barrel — a futile, instinctive blow that had no effect. His swift, savage rush carried me to the ground. If I live 100 years, I'll never forget his huge head and black mane only inches from my face. His eyes blazed like yellow fire. Although it takes time to tell it, it was over in seconds, but the details are branded indelibly in my mind.

We hadn't started out after a lion that morning. We wanted buffalo, and my wife Jean, Poolman, and I had left camp before daylight with two black trackers and gun bearers, Gatia and David.

Our camp was at the foot of Mt. Kilimanjaro in excellent Kenya game country midway between Tsavo National Park and the Masai Amboseli Game Reserve. We had been on safari three weeks, and that was the last day.

It had been an exciting hunt, and we had taken some splendid animals, including a rogue elephant that came as an unexpected bonus and carried almost 100 pounds of ivory on each side.

I'm a retired manufacturing executive from Buffalo, New York, 57 years old, with a wife and three grown sons. I have hunted at every opportunity for the last 20 years, mostly for ducks, upland birds, deer, and elk.

My hunting started when I moved to Boise, Idaho, in 1949 with my family. There's great duck shooting around there, and the bug bit me. From that, I went on to big game. We lived at Boise for several years, and by the time we left I had done well on deer and elk and had livened things up by killing a bear and a bobcat or two.

In the spring of 1966 an invitation came along that was more than Jean and I could resist. We were spending an evening with friends, Steve Spaulding and his wife Belle. Steve is in his late 50's, an executive with the Buffalo Aeronautical Corporation. A year or so before, he and Belle had had a very successful hunt in Kenya.

"We're going back," Steve said out of the blue that night. "How would you two like to join us?"

It didn't take long for Jean and me to accept, and Steve started to make the arrangements with the Nairobi safari firm of Ker, Downey and Selby. We booked a hunt to start March 1, 1967, and were assigned four top-grade hunting blocks and two of the best white hunters in the business, Henry Poolman and Terry Mathews.

Much as I enjoy hunting, I have never been greatly interested in trophies, and I did not want to start an African collection. That problem was solved when the Buffalo Museum of Natural Sciences, where I had contacts, asked us to convert the hunt into a quasi-scientific project by bringing back bird and animal specimens for their East African collection. The museum would arrange the necessary permits for anything not covered by our licenses.

The four of us flew to Nairobi via Zurich the last week in February. We put in two or three days getting acquainted with our professional hunters and shopping for safari clothing. Jean and I also visited Nairobi National Park for our first look at Africa's teeming wildlife. We saw a geat variety of game within 15 minutes of downtown.

We left Nairobi on the morning of March 1 for our first camp in dry hilly country near the south end of Lake Rudolph in the Northern Frontier District. Our group consisted of 30 in all. There were Steve and Belle, Jean and I, Poolman and Mathews, and 24 safari hands, who would serve as skinners, trackers, and gun bearers and staff the commissary department. The blacks were all natives of Kenya, mostly from the Kikuyu tribe.

The Spauldings had Terry as their white hunter, and they rode north with him. Jean and I would hunt with Henry, and we were together in his car. Both vehicles had four-wheel drive and would be used as hunting cars.

It was quickly apparent that Jean and I had drawn a fine professional hunter. Thirty-six years old, Poolman stood about 6 feet 2 and weighed 220 or better, without an ounce of fat. He knew African game as well as a man can. He was tireless at following an animal, a crack rifle shot, cool and sure in a pinch. If he had a fault, it was contempt for danger to himself. His right thigh had been badly scarred in an encounter with a lion a few years before.

A Nairobi paper would call him, after his death, "A great bull of a man," and the description fitted in its most complimentary sense.

When he was not off on safari, his home was on a fine farm at Naro Moru, north of Nairobi, where he lived with his wife and their daughter Adelaide, then five years old.

We reached the native town of Baragoi — consisting of a mission school, a small store, and a cluster of mud huts — on the second day and set up camp on the banks of a dry wash just outside the three-mile protected zone around the town.

The area was good game country, especially for various antelopes, and teemed with birds. In the next few days we took oryx, gerenuk, and Grevey's zebra and got a head start on our bird collection.

Terry Mathews is an authority on the birds of East Africa, and he had borrowed two excellent bird skinners from the Nairobi National Museum to accompany us. The variety and number of birds was amazing, and we soon had the two skinners busy from sunup until after dark every day preparing study skins. Terry took care of the labeling and helped with the skinning.

Before the safari ended, we collected more than 300 birds, representing 230 species and ranging from hummingbirds to vultures and marabou storks. Except for the larger kinds, they were shot with a .410 shotgun or with a .22 rifle firing cartridges loaded with No. 12 "dust" shot. Out of the 300 bird specimens, only three couldn't be used because they were mutilated.

Before we left Nairobi we had heard of a rhino that was bothering herdsmen on a ranch near Rumuruti, about 150 miles south of Baragoi. When we were offered a permit to kill it, we jumped at the chance. Rhinos are becoming scarce in Kenya and getting a permit to take one is far from easy. If we shot this one, we knew it would provide a specimen of major importance for the Buffalo museum. The day is not far away, in my judgment, when no hunter will be allowed to kill one.

We drove south to the Milner ranch at Rumuruti and set up our tents in the front yard. We were given the use of the guest-house bathroom facilities, a real luxury on safari. For the next few days we lived like kings. We were invited to hunt on neighboring ranches, and we met many new friends.

Steve and I caught up with the renegade rhino the first morning. We came on it at 30 yards when it was browsing in shoulder-high bush. I was carrying a .458 Magnum Winchester Model 70, Steve had a .470 Holland and Holland double. Both were loaded with 500-grain full-metal-case bullets.

The rhino whirled to face us but changed its mind, swung broadside, and pounded across in front of us, hidden by thick brush. When it broke into the open we fired together, and that huge ungainly brute actually turned a somersault. Its head dropped, the horn dug into the ground, and the massive body flipped heels over applecart.

One bullet had gone through the heart. The other had entered the neck, had passed through the brain, and had come out the forehead, nicking the rear horn. It had been an easy kill, but a rhino is a rhino, and we were able to send the skin back to the museum for a full body mount.

We took impala, gazelle, water bucks, and more birds at that camp. Lions were bothering a herd of prize Santa Gertrudis cattle on a neighboring ranch, and we put out baits. But there were no takers.

We left at the end of five days, stopped in Nairobi to drop off our trophies with Major W.G. Raw, managing director of the Rowland Ward establishment there, and replenished our supply of film. Then we drove south 200 miles to two hunting blocks at the foot of Kilimanjaro.

We camped on a small creek about 30 miles north of Rombo, a Masai manyetta — the usual collection of mud huts. Because the Masai are herdsmen, the village was in the form of a circular kraal enclosed by a boma of thornbush. Goats were kept in it, and the cattle were driven inside at night for protection from lions, leopards, and hyenas.

We hoped to take buffalo, fringe-eared oryx, reedbuck, eland, and lesser kudu. We got a bonus, too. On our first trip past Rombo we were stopped by a native game warden. He spoke no English, but Henry was fluent in Swahili, and talk flew back and forth between them. Finally Henry turned to me with a broad grin.

"Bloody elephant is tearing up their corn patches and storage huts," he explained. "The blighter has to be shot, and he's offering us the chance. What do you say?"

I said yes in a hurry. A chance at an elephant was something I had not even thought about.

Early the next morning the game warden and his assistant led Henry and me out to a waterhole and showed us the dishpan-size tracks of the renegade bull. The hunt turned out to be a long hard walk. The country was dust dry, and as the sun climbed, the day got very hot. We followed the tracks for seven hours. When we finally overtook him, he was standing in an open place at the edge of a clump of trees, 200 yards ahead.

The stalk was easy. Brush hid us the first 150 yards but then thinned out. At the edge of cover, hardly more than 40 yards away from the bull, Henry gave me a sharp order: "Take him now. He's seen us."

I was carrying the .458 Winchester with solid bullets. Henry had emphasized that the fatal shot on an elephant is in the earhole, a spot on the side of the head just in front of the external ear and marked by a fold of skin. A bullet there goes into the brain and kills instantly.

I thought I knew what to look for, but the massive gray brute was backlighted by the sun and the side of his head was in shadow. I made out a dark patch that I took for the earhole and put my 500-grain solid into it. The elephant didn't flinch. I tried again in the same place; he whirled and ran.

I got another chance and shot for the spine but didn't quite hit it. The bull was getting away, wounded, and Henry did what a white hunter is supposed to do. He fired his .470 and broke a hind leg.

I learned something then. An elephant can't travel on three legs. This one pitched forward so hard that he drove his tusks into the ground and lay helpless on his huge belly. I ran in to about 10 feet, and that time I found the earhole. He died without a struggle.

He was a very good elephant — one tusk weighed 99 pounds, the other 96 — but I'll never kill another. That bull had to be destroyed, and if we had not done it the game warden would have. But that huge majestic animal was too awesome in death for me to want to kill another. And when I learned that the Masai do not eat elephant meat, and that the great carcass must go to the hyenas and vultures, I felt worse.

Steve was taking some good animals, including a buffalo that made the record book. A few days after I shot the elephant, I had the luck to come upon a big bull eland. I went after him with my 7 mm. bolt-action Brno, got two quick shots as he ran off, and hit him both times with 173-grain bullets. The first one broke a shoulder and should have put him down, but we had to follow him a mile before we got close enough to finish him off. He had 29¾-inch horns, good enough to put him on the Rowland Ward record list.

We come finally to the morning of March 21, last day of the hunt. I was still without a buffalo. Jean and Henry and I got up at 3:30. At daybreak we were 55 miles from camp. We had seen buffalo there, but no good bulls.

We had made a small change in arrangements that day, a change that was to have unbelievable consequences.

Ethia, one of the two old and experienced trackers and gun bearers who regularly went with Henry and me, had eaten too much meat from Steve's buffalo the night before and was too sick to hunt that morning.

Henry replaced him with David, a young native Kenyan in his 20's, who was just getting started as a gun bearer. He was mission-educated and spoke some English but had gained very little safari experience. What was coming was to prove tragically too much for him. Gatia, our other experienced hand, went with us.

We parked the hunting car at the foot of a hill that offered a lookout, and Henry and I started to climb it. Henry reached the crest while I was only halfway up. He took one quick look, wheeled, and came back with a wide grin on his face.

"How would you like a lion?" he asked. "There's a bloody good one over there. Black mane and all. You're in luck, maybe."

We hurried back to the hunting car and drove around the hill to the foot of a low ridge where we'd have scattered clumps of brush to cover our stalk. We left Jean there in the car.

I took my Czech Brno rifle because of the excellent Weaver scope. I wanted that scope for the lion. The rifle was loaded with 173-grain softpoints.

Henry carried his .470 double, and Gatia followed us with the .458. Both were loaded with solids. Henry had given David my Browning over-and-under 12 gauge shotgun to carry. It was loaded with buckshot in both barrels and would be used as a back-up gun at close quarters if trouble came.

We got within 125 yards of the lion without difficulty. From there, the ridge was open, grown up with short yellow grass and strewn with boulders. There was no cover to crawl through, and the lion saw us coming. He was standing broadside, an arrogant, magnificent cat, and I didn't need to be told not to wait any longer. But just as I was ready to shoot, he started to run.

I've had buck fever many times in my life, and I've had it hard, but so far it had not bothered me once on that African hunt. I believe, however, that it hit me then. Certainly I didn't make as good a shot as I'm capable of. The lion was behind a bush before I could fire. When he came into sight again, he hesitated, and I got his shoulder in the scope and touched off.

"High," Henry barked, and with that, the lion really ran.

I sent two more fast shots after him before he went over the ridge, but he showed no effect, and I was sure I had missed. Then Gatia and David, higher on the slope, started to yell in Swahili.

"He's down," Henry translated. "You clobbered him! Come on."

We climbed the ridge and crossed it quietly. The lion was lying on his belly with back toward us not more than 20 yards away. I had a strong feeling that he was not dead. His position seemed wrong somehow.

A year later, when I finally got a look at his skull, I learned all that will ever be known about what my bullets had done. One of them had broken his lower right jaw.

It seems unlikely that a broken jawbone alone would have stopped him, and if he had lain down to ambush us, he had picked a poor spot. I'll always believe that one of my shots hit him in the body, possibly in the lungs, and prevented him from running off. But we'll never be sure. In the end, hyenas would tear him apart before he could be skinned.

We went halfway down to him, and I stopped and started to bring my rifle up for another shot. Just then Henry said, "Congratulations!" over his shoulder, and in that same instant, I saw the great maned head turn. The lion looked back at us and rolled as if to regain his feet. Then Poolman sprang in front of me to put himself between his client and danger and blotted the cat out of my sight.

It all happened in a fraction of a second, and I'll never be clear on one point. I seem to recall that I fired from the hip as the cat rolled and before Henry leaped between us, but I can't be sure. Gatia unloaded all the guns before he put them in the hunting car after it was all over, but when I asked him later whether mine had an empty case in the chamber, he could not remember.

Henry had been at my right and a step or two ahead. He and the two gun bearers were nearer to the lion than I was, and the lion could have gotten to them easier, but for some reason, he singled me out for his attack. Because I was the one who had hurt him in the first place? I'll never know.

In any case, he had his sights set on me and what he did was typical lion behavior. John Kingsley-Heath, the Nairobi white hunter who was so savagely mauled by a wounded lion in 1961 said something about that. In his story "A Lion Mangled Me," Outdoor Life, March 1963, he wrote: "Once simba picks his victim he stays with it. A wounded leopard will rush from one member of a party to another, biting each in turn, leaving one and running for the next. A lion takes time to finish what he begins."

I heard two shots from Henry's .470, so close together they blurred into each other. Next I saw him bowled aside and his rifle go sailing through the air. He fell flat on his back at my right, and a crazy flicker of thought ran through my mind: "When we get back to camp tonight, I'll razz you plenty for lying there on your fanny while a lion grabs your client!"

I can only conclude that I had not yet had time to be scared. Looking back, I believe the lion was half dead at that point and running blindly for me. Henry had probably hit him both times. By then the lion probably had three bullets in him, maybe four, but he was still 400 pounds of deadly fury.

The cat carried me backward six or eight feet as I fell. I landed on my side, lying across him, with my left forearm clamped in his jaws. I felt no pain, but I was aware of his teeth crunching through my wrist bones.

I did the wrong thing. I grabbed his lower jaw with my right hand to keep him from closing his mouth, but I recall thinking, "He'll bite your fingers off." I yanked my hand away so fast I cut the skin on the inside of my fingers on his front teeth.

Then I saw Gatia dodging in with the Winchester. He shoved the muzzle between the lion's body and mine and drove two shots into the cat's spine. The gun was so close that I felt the two blasts and the jolting hammer blows that went through the body of the lion. But the jaws did not relax on my wrist, and I screamed, "Shoot him again!"

The third shot did it. I felt the jaws loosen, and the heavy muscular body go slack. I had trouble getting my hand and watch strap untangled from his teeth. When I did pull free, I could not see my hand. It was turned back, and the ends of the broken arm bones protruded from the bloody stub that had been my wrist. Luckily the lion's teeth had frayed but not severed the artery. I remember mumbling to myself, "Well, at least I've got a stump left." Then I rolled to my knees and looked around.

What I saw was sheer horror.

When the lion smashed into me, I had heard a shot and a muffled cry and saw Poolman throw up both arms and topple backward. Now he was lying a few feet away. His chest and shirt front were a mass of blood.

What had happened was almost too fantastic and dreadful to believe. As the lion knocked him off his feet and streaked past him, Henry had twisted around and grabbed the tail in a last-ditch attempt to keep the lion from getting at me. The lion's rush pulled him part way to his feet and into line with young gun bearer David. At that instant, David fired a load of buckshot at point-blank range. The buckshot did not touch the lion, but it smashed into Henry's chest and killed him instantly.

I crawled over to Henry, felt for pulse, and listened for his breathing. He was dead.

From the hunting car at the foot of the ridge, Jean had heard the lion roar — none of us remembered hearing that, but she did. She heard the shots, saw my hat fly off and Henry falling backward. She came running up the slope and took charge, cool and capable.

David was hysterical, but she pulled him together and sent him hurrying down to the car for our medical kit. She washed my arm, poured on antiseptics, bound the hand back into place as best she could, and gave me a couple of codeine tablets.

I was in shock by then, and I have no clear recollection of what happened next. I felt no pain, but I do remember a deadly fatigue. Some people who have heard the story have asked whether we did the right thing. I don't know. The decision was of necessity made by Gatia and David, and in the shock and horror of what had happened, I believe they did the best they could.

I didn't really lose consciousness completely, but I must have almost blacked out on my feet. The next I remember, we were jolting along in the car with Jean supporting me and Gatia at the wheel.

"Where's Henry?" I mumbled.

"Back there with David," she told me.

The two blacks had talked the thing over in Swahili. Henry had been a big man, between 220 and 240, and it was 300 yards to the hunting car. They decided against trying to carry the body that distance. Maybe they didn't want to remove it until the police came. Instead they moved it to the shade of a nearby tree, and David stayed to keep hyenas and vultures away. Gatia, who had had very little experience at driving, undertook the long, rough trip back to camp. Jean couldn't handle four-wheel drive.

Gatia tried to drive as fast as he could. A little man, about 5 feet 2, he could not see over the front fender, and he hit rock after rock. The bumps were terrible, and I kept yelling, "Pa'le, pa'le," thinking it was the Swahili word for slow. Actually it meant, "Just then." I should have been saying, "Po'le, po'le." Gatia kept pouring on coal, and we kept hitting rocks.

Steve and Terry had gone out that morning to make a round of leopard baits. They wouldn't be back, and that meant there would be nobody at camp who could operate the radio. But a young couple from Texas, Ron and Mary Cauble, were trapping and studying baboons near us as part of a research project on primate behavior. We headed for their camp.

My wristwatch had stopped at 5:41 when the lion bit into it. It was three hours later when we reached the Caubles. Those three hours were awful.

Ron and Mary took over. She contacted the Ker, Downey and Selby headquarters in Nairobi on the radio, and then Ron left to bring in Henry's body. He picked up a couple of Kenyan military police on the way.

There was an emergency landing strip and a first-aid station manned by a competent Indian intern at Oloitokitok a few miles from our camp, and I was driven there immediately. The safari firm had an aircraft and a doctor on the way at once, and everything humanly possible was done for me. At 1 o'clock that afternoon, about seven hours after the lion attacked, I was in the Nairobi Hospital.

Ron Cauble went out next morning to have a look at the lion. He found most of it devoured by hyenas. The only thing he could salvage was the skull, and when he brought it to my home many months later, I learned that one of my bullets had broken the lower jaw on the right side. I had fired at the right side of the running lion. Henry fired from ahead.

The unlucky David was arrested, and the Kenya police authorities made a painstaking investigation. In the end, Henry's death was ruled entirely accidental, and the young gun bearer was exonerated. It was, however, an accident that in all likelihood would not have happened with an older and more experienced man such as Ethia.

My Browning was held by the police for a time, but I got it back through the safari firm after four months.

I spent 18 days in the hospital, and then flew home. My wrist healed surprisingly well, and although my fingers will always be a bit numb, I have recovered about three-fourths of the use of my hand.

I said in the beginning that I'll never forget that agonizing minute as the lion grabbed me and bore me to the ground. I will never forget, either, the sight of Henry Poolman springing in front of me to take the attack on himself. I'll always figure he saved my life at the cost of his own. He was one of the best, that man Poolman.

My Toughest Patrol

Don D. Ellis

December 1970

When Don Ellis speaks of his "toughest patrol" he means his toughest in his twenty-seven years as a game warden in the mountains of British Columbia, first out of Kamloops for fifteen years and then out of Kelowna for eleven more. The only relief he and his partner enjoyed in eighteen days of freezing ordeals was a couple of brief encounters with mountain lions, their favorite quarry. OUTDOOR LIFE readers may recall an earlier yarn by Ellis, "Hound Man's Dream," November 1967, in which in one chase three lions are brought to bay in the same tree. Ellis was to write another story called "The Cougar Does Attack," in September 1971.

Charley Shuttleworth and I were out on the snow-covered ice of Adams Lake when we noticed ravens feeding on the shore a mile or so away. Two of our cougar hounds were pulling our loaded sled. We had a third hound along, but she was a strong-minded female that wouldn't work in harness and so ran free.

The bitch saw the ravens about the same time we did, and since the wind was blowing from them to us, she probably got scent of what was going on as well. She hit for shore on a beeline. The two dogs that were hauling the sled took one look at her and cocked their ears. Immediately, they lit out after her with the sled swinging and lurching along behind.

Even in harness, dogs can usually outrun a man on snowshoes without half trying. Our dogs all were out of sight before Charley and I reached the shore of the lake, but the two that were hitched to the sled didn't get far. The bank was steep, and it was grown up with trees and brush. Before the harnessed pair got to the top, the sled hung up. The two dogs were fighting when we got there.

We broke it up, pulled the harnesses off, and let them go. The third hound was already long gone on a fresh cougar track. We found the cat's kill, a medium-size deer, where the ravens had been feeding. Then we took out after the dogs up a very steep mountainside.

The cougar, a big tom, was too full of deer meat for much of a run. They put him up a tall pine in less than a mile, and the rest was easy. Charley and I got his pelt off and were back at the lake in a couple of hours, ready to put the two dogs back in harness and go on our way. It had been a very easy cougar hunt, almost too easy to be interesting. But before the trip was finished we'd have one of another kind.

We had an assignment that was nothing out of the ordinary. At the outset it hadn't sounded especially difficult, but it was to lead to 18 days of the hardest travel and bush camping that came my way in the 27 years I worked as a game warden in the mountain country of British Columbia. In short, it was my toughest patrol.

"I want an elk count in the Adams Lake and Tumtum Lake country," Inspector Robert Robertson had told Shuttleworth and me. "We've got to decide whether to open the season next fall. I expect it will take you about two weeks."

Robertson, now retired, lives on Shuswap Lake 60 miles from Kamloops. Shuttleworth has been dead for several years. I have been retired since 1965 but am still living at Kelowna, where I was stationed during my last 16 years on the job.

When Inspector Robertson sent Shuttleworth and me on the elk count in the winter of 1942, I was working out of Kamloops and Charley was too. I was a game warden; he was a predatory-animal hunter. Charley was part Okanagan Indian, and he was one of the best woodsmen and partners I have ever traveled with.

Game counts were a routine part of our job. The time to make them was in the dead of winter when elk, moose, and deer were bunched together and tracks indicated their numbers even if we didn't see the animals themselves.

The elk count involved a hike of 150 to 200 miles. There was two feet of soft, light snow in the woods. That meant a man would sink almost halfway to his knees at every step, but we were accustomed to winter foot travel and hard going, and we made our preparations without any misgivings.

We kept our supplies as light as we could. We took flour for bannock, pancake flour, dry beans and peas, dried onions, plenty of salt and tea, and enough salt pork to grease the fryingpan for any game we killed — no canned goods at all.

Our equipment consisted of sleeping bags, a change of clothing apiece in case we got wet, extra socks, a warm coat for each of us, and a 12 x 12 piece of light canvas for a leanto tent. When we drove away from Kamloops in a truck during the last week in January, our packsacks weighed around 60 pounds apiece.

"I'd like you to pick off any cougars you come across," the inspector had told us, so we took our three cougar hounds along. That suited Charley and me. Cougar hunting was a recognized part of our jobs and also had been a favorite sport with both of us for many years. We were going into good country for the big cats. Almost certainly we'd have the opportunity for a hunt or two.

We could drive the first 60 miles to Skwaam or Agate Bay near the south end of Adams Lake. The rest of the trip would be on snowshoes.

At Agate Bay we got an unexpected lift. We arranged to leave our truck at a hunting-and-fishing camp there. The owner, Fred La Fave, was very much interested in our trip since he hoped our elk census would turn up enough animals to justify an open season. He offered to make us a sled for our outfit with a pair of homemade skis for runners.

I had two sets of dog harness. With the hounds pulling the sled wherever the terrain permitted and especially on the ice of Adams Lake, it would be far easier than carrying the entire load in our packs.

La Fave put the sled together, and the next morning we loaded it, hitched up the two dogs that were willing to work, strapped on our snowshoes, and headed north up the lake. It's about 30 miles from Agate Bay to the north end, where the Adams River comes in.

The temperature that morning was 10° below zero. Before we got back to Agate Bay, La Fave had five days of 40°-below weather at his place, and I'm sure it was no warmer where we were. We were lucky on one score. The weather stayed clear, and there were no snowstorms.

We got a foretaste of what was ahead about an hour after we left La Fave's camp. Charley Shuttleworth never liked to travel on ice, especially out in the middle of a lake, which is the safest place of all. He insisted on keeping close to shore, where there is always danger from thin ice and airholes, often hidden under deep snow drifted against the bank.

We were plodding along with the two hounds pulling like a pair of Eskimo huskies when my partner crashed through without warning. The ice under the snow simply gave way and dropped him to his armpits in the bitterly cold water. He had a light pack on his back and snowshoes on his feet, and he was wearing heavy clothing. There was little chance that he could get out without help.

Back at La Fave's camp I had happened to see a rope with a hondo on the end and had asked to borrow it for the trip. I'd had no idea then what we might need it for, but I knew from experience that it would be a handy item to have along. Now the rope was coiled on top of the loaded sled. I grabbed it up and shook out a loop.

I had done a little calf-roping in my younger days before going to work for the Game Branch. (I came out to British Columbia from my birthplace in Wales in 1910, when I was 11.) I knew what to do, but I was out of practice, and the question was whether I could do it before Charley lost his grip on the edge of the ice and went under.

We were lucky. My loop settled over his head on the first throw and he worked it down under his arms. I stayed back from the airhole and pulled. With help from the rope, Charley clawed his way out, snowshoes and all.

In the sharp cold, his wet clothing froze as hard as armor in minutes, but we got ashore and I built a roaring fire. When he was thawed and dry enough to travel again, we went back on the ice, but we went up the middle of the lake, a mile or so from shore.

It was the next afternoon, at the mouth of the Momich River about seven miles from the north end of Adams Lake, that we saw the ravens that touched off the hunt for the big cougar. There wasn't a lot of daylight left when we got back to the lake with our dogs and the cat's pelt. Then we spotted an abandoned trapper's cabin on the shore and decided to stop for the night.

In the cabin was a good stove of the kind we called airtight heaters. There was also four feet of snow on the roof and a few pack rats inside the place.

Once we got a fire going, it was warm and comfortable. We made coffee, and just as I started to drink my first cup, I happened to look up at the roof. The ridgepole was bent like a strung bow under the weight of all that snow.

"I'm getting out of here," I blurted out as I dived for my packsack.

"This cabin has been here for years," Charlie retorted. "It's not going to fall in right now."

"Maybe not," I told him, "but I'm pulling stakes."

In the Canadian Army during the First World War, I was buried alive in an unfinished dugout with 21 other soldiers. We were waiting to go over the top at 5 a.m. and the Germans started to shell us. We dived into the dugout for shelter and we were down at the bottom when one of our own tanks clattered over the mouth of it and caved it in. Seven of us got out alive.

I was left with a case of shock that lasted for 10 years after the war. I was also left with a lifelong dread of being trapped in a situation of that kind again. The idea of staying in that old cabin if the roof might fall in on us was more than I could endure.

I grabbed my pack and snowshoes, and out I went. I moved so fast that I convinced Charley, and he came scrambling out behind me. He was no more than through the door when the sagging ridgepole let go with a groan and then a crack like a pistol shot. The roof came crashing down in a cloud of snow.

Coming on the heels of Charley's dunking, that cave-in made both of us wonder about our luck on the rest of the trip.

"Trouble comes in threes," I reminded my partner. "What do you suppose is going to happen tomorrow?"

We fixed up our square of canvas for a leanto, built a good fire, and cooked supper. We didn't get a great deal of sleep that night, however. Dry firewood was hard to find after dark, and we spent half the night collecting enough to keep the fire going.

Before we left camp the following morning, we loaded a supply of cougar meat onto the sled for dog food. We had counted on shooting grouse for the dogs and ourselves, and also on finding cougar-killed deer that we could feed to them and maybe eat a steak or two ourselves, but we'd had no luck with either. The buck the cougar had killed was too far gone. I had shot a coyote the day before we killed the cougar, and the dogs ate most of it. By that time, the dogs were hungry enough to eat just about anything.

It didn't take us long after leaving the site of the caved-in cabin to find out what our next streak of luck would be like. We had traveled only a couple of hours when we saw black open water ahead and realized that our route to the upper end of Adams Lake was blocked. The water was probably kept open by the current of the Adams River that runs the length of the lake.

Adams Lake is deep, and the shore is steep on both sides. There's no real beach, so it's very difficult to walk along the shore. We climbed the bank and dragged our sled up behind us, but there were too many big rocks and windfalls for hiking.

We were on the west side of the lake. Ahead, on the opposite side, we knew there was a trail. It wasn't a good trail, but we could use it if we could cross the open water.

We were debating about backtracking in the hope of finding safe ice to cross on, and that's when we saw the boat.

It wasn't much of a boat. It was only 10 feet long, a leaky derelict overturned on the shore. We learned later that it had gone adrift from La Fave's camp some time before. Probably it had been carried up the lake by the wind. We found a set of oars with it, but no oarlocks. At some time in the past, somebody had stuck old files in the gunwales on each side to serve as oarlocks. We had to make-do with them.

The lake was calm in the still cold of the winter day, and it wasn't a long row, only about a mile. It was a case of risk it or turn back and abandon the whole project. So we loaded three dogs and our whole outfit into that old tub and started across.

We had about three inches of freeboard, and when we were halfway to the east shore, a breeze came up. Then we started to take water. Ice previously frozen in the bow had broken out, and that action had opened a hole.

There was a lard can rolling around in the bottom of the boat, and Charley started to bail. About that time, the hounds decided things weren't going right. They abandoned ship one at a time, jumping over and all but capsizing us. Somewhat to our surprise, considering the bitter cold of the water, they made it to shore.

With the weight of the dogs gone, we had six inches of freeboard and the boat didn't leak quite so badly. But then one of the oarlock files came out and fell overboard. I drove my hand ax into the gunwale to replace it and kept on rowing. Somehow we made it to the bank. By then the boat was nearly full of water. Another 50 feet and we would have swamped. Charley and I were wet and shivering in spite of the exertion of rowing and bailing, and our clothes were sheathed in ice.

We got a fire going and called it a day. Our three hounds didn't return to our camp until 6 o'clock the next morning. I suppose they had found a cougar track. They probably treed the cat and stayed at the tree all night but gave up at daylight when we failed to appear. Charley and I were not interested in cougar hunting just then.

We got a start at first light that morning, and noon found us at the head of Adams Lake. On the way, we saw two timber wolves and a band of moose.

An old logging road ran north from the head of the lake. It wound in and out along the Adams River some 40 miles to Tumtum Lake. We boiled tea and ate lunch. Then we headed up that old road. The snow was a lot deeper than it had been on the ice. There was a thin crust that didn't hold us up, and it made hard footing for the dogs.

We covered only eight miles that day, and when we came to a trapper's cabin we holed up. That one was in use, and the trapper had kept the snow shoveled off the roof. He was out on his line, but it was the custom of the country to move in and make yourself at home under those conditions so we knew we'd be welcome to use the place overnight. There was a good stove, and after our few nights of siwashing in our leanto tent that cabin seemed as cozy as home.

That night, however, turned out to be another one that allowed us little sleep. It was a bright moonlight night, still and very cold, and wolves started howling in the brush around us shortly after dark. That set our hounds to baying, and we howled back at the wolves, hoping to bring them in close enough for a shot. Although wolves and dogs exchanged insults most of the time until daylight, the wolves stayed back in the brush in typical fashion and we never caught a glimpse of them. In the morning, tracks showed that they had skulked to within 100 yards of the cabin, but they were too wary to come closer.

We were in first-class game country. There are moose, deer, elk, goats, and black and grizzly bears in the high country between Adams and Tumtum lakes. We began to look for elk tracks, leaving the trail and circling back into the hills to do it. We soon found out that the elk were not wintering in that area. There were only a few tracks, and they all led north toward Tumtum. There we would probably find whatever elk we were going to find.

At the south end of Tumtum Lake, just above the place where the Adams River flows out of it, but on the opposite shore, we found another unused cabin and spent the night there. The next morning we unloaded the sled, put everything into our packsacks, and struck out northwest into the hills on a 50-mile circle that would take us around the headwaters of the Adams. The six days that followed were as hard a grind as I can recall.

We had not cut down the weight of our packs very much, and 50 to 60 pounds is a heavy load for a man on snowshoes, especially on soft snow where he sinks a foot at every step. We took turns breaking trail and slogged along hour after hour. The dogs walked in our tracks. Ordinarily, cougar hounds do plenty of ranging, but travel was so hard that our hounds were content to tag along behind us.

We finished each day bone tired and siwashed at night in our leanto, warm and comfortable in spite of the far-below-zero cold. A leanto tent, made from a square of canvas, can be a surprisingly good shelter even in the dead of winter if you know how to fix it up. It's far better than an unheated cabin.

To make such a shelter, you look for two trees about six feet apart and fasten a pole between them at head height. Then lean one end of four or five other poles on the crosspiece for rafters and ram the low end of each rafter into the snow. With the 12 x 12 canvas draped on this slanting frame, the ends of the canvas will hang down on each side, forming windbreaks. By standing small evergreens along the two sides and kicking or shoveling snow onto the canvas all around the bottom, you have an open-faced tent, windproof on three sides. A snowshoe is a satisfactory shovel.

For a bed I always started by putting down two six-inch-thick logs for sides without clearing the snow away and then filled the space between them with springy fir branches overlapped like shingles. With the snow underneath, they make a soft mattress and also keep the cold from coming up from below. The two logs stop drafts from the sides.

The fire should be built about four feet out from the open face of the leanto, using long chunks of wood as big as you can drag. By putting the ends of the logs within reach of your bed you can reach out with your ax and shove more wood into the fire without leaving your bed. Heat from a fire arranged that way reflects from the inside of the sloping canvas, and you get no smoke under the leanto.

We were beginning to run low on grub. Our flour for bannock was about gone, and small game seemed hard to find. But we shot enough snowshoe rabbits and squirrels to get us by, and Charley and I fared better than the dogs. They were really hungry.

In the rough country 15 miles north of Tumtum Lake, we swung south, back toward the Adams River and home. But home was many hard miles away.

We had found fewer elk than we expected. We had seen a total of only 32. From those sightings and from tracks and other sign, we concluded that there were hardly more than 80 in all in the Tumtum district.

We were traveling on the ice of Adams Lake once more when we found fresh cougar tracks for the second time on that trip.

Two of the cats had come down off the bank. Then they had padded along on the ice for a way but had then turned back to shore and headed up a canyon. We figured them for a female and her grown youngster.

We turned the hounds loose, and they went out of hearing in a hurry. A short distance up the canyon, we found where the cougars had killed and fed on a deer. Not far from the kill we jumped six deer that had stayed bedded right there while the cats ate, proving something I learned long ago. Deer are not much afraid of a cougar. Unless he is stalking them, the deer are likely to pay very little attention to him.

That deer behavior may result in part because a cougar kills a deer quickly. He makes so little commotion that others 50 or 100 yards away often do not know what is happening. Once one of the big cats makes its final spring at either a deer or young moose, the victim is almost sure to be dead in two or three jumps.

One thing I am certain of. Cougars do not chase deer out of the country, as hunters so often claim. The two animals have lived together for many centuries and are accustomed to each other.

Charley and I followed the hounds back into the hills. In half an hour we heard them barking treed. When we got there, they had the two cougars up in a couple of trees less than 100 feet apart.

We easily shot the husky young tom, but the old female was behaving like no cougar either of us had ever seen. When dogs put a cougar up a tree, the cat usually crouches on a limb and looks down without much show of resentment except for an occasional low snarl. That one appeared to be in a frenzy of rage. She was growling and biting at the branches around her. At the shot that brought the young tom down, she sailed off her perch like a giant flying squirrel, landed in a cloud of snow, and lit out.

The hounds overtook her in a couple of hundred yards, and she climbed again. But when she saw Charley and me coming, she jumped and ran once more.

She did that four times in all. The last time, she picked a tall fir and went up too high to jump, but she was still in a very bad temper. The ground under the tree was littered with small branches she had bitten off as she climbed. When we arrived on the scene, she was still snarling and snapping at the twigs around her.

"There's something wrong with that cougar," I told Charley. "She'd make short work of a hound if she stopped to fight on the ground."

"The way she's acting, she'd make short work of three hounds," he agreed.

We brought her down and looked her over. It didn't take long to discover the probable reason for her meanness. She had a scar running across her head from ear to ear just above the eyes. When we examined her closely we found that her skull had been broken at some time in the past. Although the injury had healed, a piece of the skull still floated loose, held in place only by the skin. The only explanation we could think of was that she had fallen over a cliff, something neither of us had ever known to happen to a cougar.

I suppose it had left her with a permanent headache. It was no wonder that she had a grudge against the world.

Charley and I pelted the two cats and were back on the ice about an hour after our dogs had taken the tracks.

We came out and made our report to Inspector Robertson. On the strength of it, the Game Branch decided on an elk season in the Tumtum district the following fall, but the kill totaled only two bulls. I'm still not sure how much of the poor showing was because of the small herd and how much was because of the difficulty of getting in and out of that country. I confess I'd have thought twice before I went elk hunting in some of the places Shuttleworth and I had seen.

While I was writing this story, I laid out a map and retraced the route Charley and I took, and measured the distance we traveled. I found out that we had covered over 175 miles in those 18 days.

Four nights, we slept in cabins. The rest of the time, we sheltered under our canvas leanto. Except for the one cabin where a trapper was wintering (and we never saw him), we did not find an occupied human habitation all the while we were away.

I have a snowmobile now. If Shuttleworth and I had been able to use one apiece, we could have made the same trip easily in two or three days. More likely for a game count of that kind today a helicopter would be used, and a single day of flying can do the whole job.

I often tell my wife I was born 50 years too soon, but actually, I liked the old ways better.

Old Paint

Larry Dablemont

July, 1972

This was Dablemont's first magazine submission and it was a ten-strike. It was picked up from OUTDOOR LIFE and reprinted in Dutton's *Best Sports Stories — 1973*. Outdoors in the Ozarks has been his life. He was graduated from University of Missouri with a degree in Wildlife Management, was chief naturalist for Arkansas Parks and, when he moved from Houston, Mo., to Harrison, Ark., seasonal naturalist at Buffalo National River in 1974. He is an editor for *Fins & Feathers* magazine, and freelances for several others, having done several other pieces for OUTDOOR LIFE since his debut. He raises Labradors and writes a column for *Gun Dog* magazine. "Old Paint" led to his first book, *The Authentic American John-boat*, published by David McKay. He lives near Harrison with his wife Gloria and their three daughters.

Old Paint has been put out to pasture. The aging johnboat lies beneath a sycamore tree on Missouri's Big Piney River at the mouth of Hog Creek. The boat, a relic of my boyhood, is now a decaying playground for young mink and a resting place for a kingfisher that adds noise and color to the eddy beneath the big white bluff.

The bright, shiny canoes that have tended to replace johnboats for Ozark floatfishing and hunting owe their regional popularity to wooden pioneers like Old Paint. We had some times together, Old Paint and I. Whenever I see the green johnboat there beneath its tree, the sight brings back a flood of memories about the years when I was growing up in the vicinity of Houston, Missouri.

I was 11 years old in 1958, the year that my father, Farrel Dablemont, built the flat-bottomed craft. Dad said from the start that the boat was the best of the many like it that he had made. I helped give the johnboat its first coat of paint — a dull green to blend with the river. In the years ahead, many more coats of paint would be applied to hide accumulated scars and patches.

Dad and I finished the boat in time for the duck season in late October, when autumn leaves lay bright and thick along the river, and the fall chill was beginning to give way to the cold winds of an Ozark winter. We took Old Paint (the boat didn't receive its name until years later) on its maiden voyage early on the first Saturday of the duck season.

The morning air was crisp enough to raise fog from the surface of the Big Piney. I sat in the front of the boat, just behind our on-board blind of willow and oak boughs. Dad, his old '97 Winchester pump gun beside him, paddled the boat through the quiet eddies and dodged the rocks when we hit rapids.

I was too young for a gun, but I was thrilled just to see wildlife along the beautiful Big Piney and ride the rough water in the new boat.

We drifted quietly beneath the bluffs and overhanging sycamores while we listened to the sounds of the river — kingfishers stuttering and squirrels barking, and more rapids roaring just around the bend. Old Paint responded easily to each silent stroke of Dad's paddle.

We hadn't gone far when Dad spotted a lone mallard feeding among some fallen leaves in the quiet shallows along the bank. I watched through the blind as we floated closer to the unsuspecting mallard.

With a powerful stroke of the paddle, Dad quickly turned the boat sideways. He dropped his paddle and then reached for his gun as the startled mallard took off. The gun roared, and the greenhead folded and dropped. At that moment, a big fox squirrel darted from the water's edge and scampered to the high branches of a big maple.

Dad usually passed up squirrels if he thought that the shot would alarm ducks farther downriver. But this time my father had already fired once, so he shot the squirrel. The dead bushytail fell to a fork in the tree, about 20 feet above the ground.

My family has always relished wildmeat, and Dad was never one to waste game. He climbed the tree to retrieve the squirrel while I watched from below.

Dad is a big man, standing six feet two inches; in those days he weighed 200 pounds. The branch he was standing on moved a little when he reached for the squirrel, and Dad lost his footing. He grabbed for a limb and then crashed to the ground while I watched in stunned silence.

Dad landed hard on some big tree roots that stuck out from the bank. He rolled onto the water, and at first I thought he was dead. With strength beyond that of an 11-year-old, I pulled my father from the water and then helped him to crawl up the bank to level ground. He rolled on his back and gasped with pain. His face was covered with blood from a cut over his eye, and he was spitting still more blood. Years have not dulled my memory of that moment.

Dad must have known that I was ready to panic, but he managed to calm me down and sent me to a nearby road for help. I found the road, and a passing motorist stopped, took charge, and rushed Dad to a doctor.

That afternoon, a friend of the family took me back to the river to get our boat and equipment. He let me out on the highway so I could fetch the boat and float it downstream to a farm road where the craft could be taken out. I didn't stay long at the scene of Dad's accident, but I can still remember the dried blood on the leaves where he had lain. Otherwise, the river was calm and peaceful, and the day had warmed considerably.

I paddled Old Paint for the first time then, with Dad's shotgun beside me. I remember thinking that the first trip in the new boat might have been the last for Dad. As it turned out, Dad didn't use the new boat again until the next spring. He was laid up several weeks with three broken ribs and a punctured lung, plus some minor injuries. But some good times were to come with Old Paint.

To a family that lived with the river as mine did, johnboats were tools of the trade. Dad's father, Fred Dablemont, had raised four sons on the Big Piney, six miles from Houston and deep in the south-central Missouri Ozarks. The Dablemonts lived the lives of rivermen, trapping in the winter, selling fish and bullfrogs in the summer, and guiding parties of hunters and fishermen year-round. Grandpa was active on the Big Piney until a few months before his death in 1970, at the age of 74.

Rivermen depended on sturdy, stable, and easy-to-handle boats, and Grandpa made the best. Like boatbuilders in other parts of the Ozarks, Grandpa had his own special pattern for his products; he called them "sharpshooters." The name johnboat apparently was coined by someone other than the men who first built such boats. The craft might just about as easily have been known as pirogues, or even as wooden canoes. The large 20-foot johnboats were developed for big Ozark rivers like the Current, White, and Gasconade. But on smaller streams such as the Piney, shorter boats were better. Grandpa's sharpshooters were usually 14 feet long, not built for motors, but designed to be handled with a stout sassafras paddle. My family grew up with the home-built boats and could do things with a boat paddle that I've never seen equalled.

Besides the boats that they made for their own use, Grandpa and his sons sold their johnboats, as many as 25 of them in a summer, to aspiring floaters in three states. The going rate for Grandpa's johnboats was $25 apiece in the 1920's and 30's. Dad sold his first johnboats in the 1950's for $35 each. In the 1960's, the price went up to $50 because of increasing lumber costs.

Transportation was limited in the early days, and the Dablemonts didn't haul their boats back upstream by road after a float trip. If Grandpa or his sons took a party on a float trip one day, they ran the boat back upriver the next day. They could go upstream over a riffle just deep enough for the boat.

There was no such thing as switching sides with a boat paddle. The Dablemonts would paddle from one side all day, maneuvering the boat for miles without a sound and without lifting the paddle from the water.

The wooden boats could be operated so quietly that it was easy to stack some tree limbs on the bow, arrange some branches to hide the boat's occupants, and sneak up on a flock of ducks, a watering deer, or any other wildlife.

The johnboats were tough and maneuverable, as well as quiet. The craft could take hard knocks and could slide easily over rocks. The high-floating boats were practically impossible to swamp, and they responded to the lightest touch of the paddle.

The metal boats and canoes of recent years are lighter than old-fashioned johnboats, and the modern craft are fine for joyriding. But when it comes to landing a 40-pound flathead catfish on a trotline in the middle of the night, or running a trapline on a rough river in zero-degree weather, a man doesn't want a canoe; and when a successful duck-hunting or floatfishing trip depends on silence and the best possible concealment, a man doesn't want aluminum, or so Grandpa always said. Grandpa and Dad made their boats sleek, strong, and dependable. Old Paint was no exception.

The spring after Dad's accident, we took the boat to the Ginseng Eddy, one of the most beautiful spots on the Piney. Three big, deep eddies were filled with several species of fish. I was there practically every day, usually late in the evening when the high ridge shadowed the river and everything was quiet and peaceful. Alone, I would maneuver Old Paint through those eddies, fishing my favorite spots for bass, bluegill, and goggle-eye (rock bass).

I learned to handle a boat well that summer, though I still lacked the strength to do many things that would come later. I also learned that the river was important not only to me but also to the other forms of life that seemed so busy while I relaxed in the middle of the stream, waiting for a strike. A family of young mink regularly showed up at the base of the big bluff, playfully chasing one another or eyeing the brood of wood ducks that hurriedly followed their anxious mother to the cover of the opposite bank. A kingfisher was always nearby, sounding upset about something, but always ready to plunge to the river in search of an easy meal. And on rare occasions, I could see a big old smallmouth bass that lurked in the depths and was just too smart to catch. That was a summer for learning, and appreciating.

By the next fall, in 1959, I had a gun of my own to carry — a single-shot Iver Johnson. The ducks and squirrels were thick on the river that year. Dad and I hunted quite often then with Dad's Cousin Charley. We had some memorable hunts, but the one that we'll all remember occurred in December on the last weekend of the season. The river was high and treacherous, and the temperature was blue-cold — somewhere in the low 20's. Ice was everywhere — hanging from limbs that dipped into the water, lying in sheets along the surface of the quiet backwater areas, and even encrusted on the blades of the boat paddles.

At 10 a.m. we headed into a long stretch of water with Cousin Charley handling the boat. Around a bend, a fallen tree jutted across the river, and the current slammed into the log headon with a roar. Water splashed up and poured over the downed trunk. Charley could have avoided the log easily enough by cutting out of the current and into the dead water, but when he applied power to the paddle, the blade caught between two large rocks and then snapped off.

We hit the tree seconds later. Old Paint leaned, and water poured in ever the side. I went overboard and under the water for a moment, still clutching my precious shotgun. But Dad, who had leaped from the boat with his own gun a second earlier, grabbed me and hauled me to the bank. Shocked and numbed by the cold, I watched Dad return to the chest-deep current to help Charley pull Old Paint away from the log. If the boat had sunk in the fast water close to the log, the two men couldn't have dragged the craft free of the tremendous current.

None of our equipment had been dumped. Old Paint had remained precariously upright, though the boat was nearly filled with water. We had lost only one thing: Charley's new Winchester automatic shotgun!

Dad ordered me to run up and down the bank to keep my blood circulating. Every movement was torture; my clothes had instantly turned stiff with ice, and the cold both numbed me and burned me at the same time.

Fortunately we had dry matches, but the wood was damp. Dad and Charley poured the powder from several shells onto the gravel bar and then dug dead leaves and twigs from drift-piles. The powder was touched off, and the flash ignited the leaves at once; small twigs dried and slowly began to burn. We gradually built the small blaze into a bonfire and then we stripped. Charley returned to the icy current in his insulated underwear and began searching for his gun. On the third dive, he came up with his gun and a grin that defied the cold water.

Our clothes dried slowly as we stood, half-naked before the blaze, roasting on one side and freezing on the other. Eventually, we got underway again.

A few months later, and suddenly it was spring again. Old Paint and I went into the floatfishing business. We had a grand old time, taking people on float trips and making 75¢ an hour for the services of the two of us. As a river guide, I began to gain valuable experience. I didn't have a great many clients, but business picked up as word got around.

Some of my clients got wet. One fellow jumped from the boat when a water snake dropped from an overhanging limb; another man was swept overboard by a low branch that he had failed to duck. I didn't have the strength yet to be a top-notch guide, but Old Paint helped me by staying upright.

Several years rolled past, and Old Paint and I kept on floating. I didn't go to Houston High School parties or to other social affairs, because I preferred the river, running trotlines in the company of Old Paint and a cousin who became my fishing partner.

Old Paint and I were working the entire river from mouth to source by then. In 1962, when I turned 15, one of my floatfishing clients, a lady fisherman who was as green at the sport as a spring sapling, hooked into the big smallmouth that I had been still trying to catch in the Ginseng Eddy. Old Fighter, as we called the fish, must have had some anxious moments at the end of the lady's line. But in the end, the bass took my client's plug back with him to the depths of the Ginseng Eddy. The lady didn't cry as I expected her to do. Instead, she was ecstatic merely because she had seen the fish and had fought him awhile. I learned something about sportsmanship that day.

I had another client that summer whom I remember well. He came down from the University of Missouri, and though I don't recall his name, I'll always remember his advice. When I told the man about the river — the fish, the bullfrogs, and the great blue heron — he told me that I should become something called a naturalist. Though I didn't know what a naturalist was, I soon found out, and the desire to become a naturalist was the force that helped a poor country boy to get a college degree. I later became Chief Naturalist for Arkansas State Parks, and an outdoor columnist for the *Arkansas Gazette*.

By my last year in high school, Old Paint was getting along in years, for a johnboat. The wooden boat was getting water-soaked and heavy, and though we had newer johnboats by then, Old Paint remained my favorite.

That spring, I moved Old Paint to a big eddy on the upper end of the Piney at the mouth of Hog Creek, where I did a lot of trotlining for big flatheads.

I dedicated my efforts to the rugged sport for one month that summer and I was rewarded with catfish weighing 10, 15, 18, 24, and 26 pounds. All of the big cats came from below the big white bluff that towers over the eddy.

I let my floatfishing business taper off that summer, and I tried some plugfishing. We caught some big bass at Hog Creek, and one largemouth weighed nearly eight pounds.

But I left Old Paint at Hog Creek just a little too long, and inconsiderate floaters shot holes in the aging boat. I brought Old Paint home for repair, patching the holes and a crack in one side, and then added a fourth coat of drab green paint. Dad, who saw little reason to put more effort into the old boat since we had better ones, gave it the name that still sticks in my mind.

"Not much left of this boat but patches and old paint," Dad sighed, examining the boat and shaking his head.

Soon afterward, I enrolled at the School of the Ozarks, and I was away from Big Piney the first time in my life. In 1967, I began studying wildlife management at the University of Missouri. My quest for a formal education claimed me for five days a week, but come Friday evening, I'd hitchhike home to refresh and relax my mind on the river — fishing, hunting, or just floating in the old johnboat. Old Paint was beginning to leak a little, but it still floated high and responded well to each stroke of the paddle.

In 1969, my third year of college, disaster struck. I arrived early one Friday afternoon for an early-spring camping trip, but Dad had rented Old Paint to a St. Louis man who was floating the river with two sons. The floaters were expected to return before dark, but as so often happens in the Ozarks, storm clouds turned the sunny day to gray, and darkness came early. The torrent of rain that followed raised the river slowly for two hours, before the storm ended as quickly as it had begun.

Dad and I were worried about the floaters, and we went to the take-out point. I hiked upriver in search of the party. I had often sat out storms in caves along the river, but these floaters were inexperienced and unfamiliar with the Big Piney.

The man and his sons could have passed the take-out point, for the river had become higher and much faster. Or the party could have swamped the boat in the swift current. I returned by dark, sure that the people were in trouble. By then the Piney was rolling nearly five feet above normal and was still rising.

Dad hurried back to check at the hotel, but there had been no word from the floaters. We notified the authorities and began organizing a search party. But the St. Louis man finally called from a farmhouse four miles below the scheduled take-out point that he and his sons had missed in the storm.

The search was called off, and we hurried to the river to bring back the wet and weary floaters. In his haste to find safety, the man had pulled the boat up onto the bank until it was solidly out of the current, but he hadn't tied the line. The fishermen had then left the boat and their supplies, fishing equipment, a rifle, and an expensive watch. I hurried to the place where Old Paint had been abandoned. Wet grasses soaked me to the waist, and I was sure that the rising river had swept the johnboat away.

I stood in the darkness and listened to the roar of the swollen Big Piney; the water was 10 feet above normal. The rest of the countryside was silent, as though in fear of the angry river. That night I said good-bye to an old friend of a boat, for I knew the johnboat wouldn't survive the raging stream. The St. Louis man was heartbroken over loss of his equipment, and left his address, in case anything might be recovered.

A week after the flood, a friend and I returned to the Piney in a newer boat. We floated the lower end; I suppose I hoped that some miracle might have spared Old Paint from the flood.

The river was down by then, but the water was still high enough for easy floating, and the fishing was good. But I still couldn't get Old Paint out of my mind. Nearly every stretch of water reminded me of things that had happened in the years of my boyhood: the place where I shot my first woodchuck; the riffle where the big buck crossed the river in front of me two summers ago; an eddy where I camped and caught a big catfish on a trotline.

Suddenly, we arrived at the gravelbar where Dad, Charley, and I had swamped on the duck hunt nearly 10 years before. I glanced toward the willows where I had helped Dad and his cousin gather driftwood and leaves to build the life-saving fire on that cold December day.

Way back in the thick willows, I glimpsed a flash of green. I quickly reversed my paddle stroke, backing the boat to the bar. I plunged through the willows, and stopped below Old Paint.

The boat was perched on top of a 10-foot-high heap of debris. The bow of the johnboat pointed downstream as though the craft were ready and raring to float. I climbed onto the drift, and I was amazed to find all of the equipment that the St. Louis man had abandoned the week before during that stormy night. I could imagine how happy he would be to recover his gear. But he couldn't be happier than I was.

That summer, I retired Old Paint to the eddy at the mouth of Hog Creek for limited use during the remainder of its days. The johnboat had lasted about twice as long as our other boats. Because of my sentimental attachment to Old Paint, the craft had been painted, patched, and treated with wood preservative each year since Dad had built it.

I have gone back to the eddy often, but Old Paint is now beyond much use for any rugged floating. Next spring, the high waters of the Piney will take the boat away, and the summer drifts along the river will contain pieces of the johnboat that has become a part of the Piney to me.

A boat is a boat, I guess — nothing more than boards and paint, and memories. Boards and paint are destined to rot away, but memories become priceless with age.

I'll remember my boyhood on the Big Piney, and a johnboat that we called Old Paint. And I guess that I'll just never feel completely comfortable in a canoe.

Hunt for a Man-Killer

Raymond R. Lyons

November 1972

John Cartier, Midwest field editor for OUTDOOR LIFE, and a veteran hunter and fisherman, read this story by Ray Lyons and was so impressed that a year later, when he decided to hunt mule deer, wrote to Lyons for a booking. The outfitter worked him into a late-season hunt with three others to be guided by himself, his son Tad and son-in-law, all of Collbran, Colorado. It was deer hunting new to Cartier, requiring four-wheel drive, horseback and foot-slogging in the snow to reach the hunting area 9,000 feet up and 11 miles from the nearest good road. But he saw bucks bigger than he had ever seen before, got a good trophy himself, as did the other three, and was as happy with his choice of Lyons as were the authorities for whom Lyons tracked down the man-killer of this story.

Sunday, July 25, 1971, began like any other summer Sunday in the quiet mountain village of Collbran, Colorado, where I operate a guiding-and-outfitting business. I was trimming a wild-rose hedge in my yard. Bear hunting didn't cross my mind, since our bear seasons are closed in the summer. If somebody had walked up to me and said that within moments I'd be organizing the most important bear hunt of my life, I'd have thought he was crazy.

The sudden change from relaxation to serious business came when my daughter Shirley saw me in the yard.

"Gosh, Dad," she exclaimed, "I thought you had gone trout fishing. Some man just phoned. He sounded shook up. He wants you to call back right away. I wrote his number down."

I dialed the number and found myself talking with Glenn Rogers, a regional manager for the Colorado Division of Game, Fish and Parks. That's when I first thought of bears. Several times in the past Glenn had asked to use my dogs to go after stock-killing bears. But I wasn't at all prepared for the shocking story he blurted out.

"It's a real mess this time, Ray," he began. "We've got a man-killing bear to deal with. It happened about two o'clock this morning in a private campground north of Grand Lake. A big bear walked up to a man's tent, ripped it wide open, and attacked. The man didn't have a chance. He was killed on the spot and then carried fifty yards before the bear left him. Can you take your hounds and go after the bear? We don't want any more deaths."

I'd made my decision before Rogers asked the question. I told him it would take a couple of hours for me to get organized. He said he'd phone back and tell me exactly where to go.

I immediately called my oldest son, George. He was working on a rush irrigation project at a nearby ranch and couldn't get away. My second son, Raymond Jr., was at home, and he volunteered instantly. We call him Tad. He's only 16, but he's a veteran of many bear hunts and is very able with the hounds.

I figured I needed one more man, and I knew who. I called Warren Bruton, a 29-year-old woodsman who operates a guide service for deer and elk hunters from his ranch near Molina. Warren told me he had a few matters to clear up, but he would be ready to roll by noon.

Right after that, Glenn Rogers called back and told me that accommodations, meals, and more manpower would be supplied by the National Parks Service and the Colorado Game, Fish and Parks Department. I learned that the tragedy had occurred near the western edge of Rocky Mountain National Park in the north-central part of the state. We were to go directly to the park.

Tad, Warren, and I were on our way about 1 o'clock. Our four-wheel-drive pickup was loaded with my 10 hounds, sleeping bags, and a change of clothes for each of us. Collbran is in the west-central part of the state, so we had to drive at least five hours through the mountains. It wasn't until we were rolling down the highway that I developed the first twinges of anxiety about the coming hunt.

Going after a black bear with hounds offers just about all the excitement a man could want, but running down a killer bear differs from a sporting chase. A bear doesn't turn killer without reason. A known man-killer obviously has little fear of man, and hunting one can be dangerous.

I recalled an incident that still makes my hair crawl. Several years ago my hounds tracked a mean male, and they finally spotted him from a distance of 250 yards. I could tell by the wild tonguing. Normally a bear will run when dogs attack. This one didn't run one step. He was ready to tear the whole world apart right on the spot.

I was sitting on my horse, waiting to see which way the bear would run. I couldn't see the bear, but from the sounds the dogs made I knew they were charging in straight at the animal. Right after that, the furious howls of courageous fighting changed to yelps of terror. I leaped from my horse, hit the ground running, and lit out downhill. It took only seconds for me to reach the scene, but when I got there the fight was all over and the bear was gone.

Two dogs lay dead. Two more were writhing on the ground. Another's back was nearly broken, and one had an eye knocked far back into his head.

Such experiences have taught me that you never know what a really angry bear will do. I was also concerned because I'd never dealt with a man-killer before.

Several other things also contributed to my mounting tension. I was unfamiliar with the country where the fatal attack had occurred. And I didn't like the idea of so many people being involved in the hunt. What if something went wrong and an inexperienced hunter got killed?

I was aware that the tragedy was being splashed over the front pages of newspapers and was bulletin news on radio and TV. I was on the spot because I was the one who had to get the bear.

I was born 54 years ago at the winter headquarters of my father's cattle ranch near Grand Junction, Colorado. While growing up around cow camps, I met many old-time bear hunters. I was still very young when I decided that a bear hunt is the best of all adventures.

During the next few years I acquired some dogs and took many scoldings for "fooling with houn' dawgs." My father believed that running hounds is the first step toward the poor house. I was 14 when I helped dad wrangle horses and pack out venison for some visiting deer hunters. I have served as a guide or outfitter every year since — except 1944, when I was piloting B-17's over Germany during World War II.

After the war I accepted a job with the U.S. Fish and Wildlife Service as a predatory-animal control agent. I acquired another pack of hounds, and I used them to track down many troublesome bears. Incidentally, all the bears in Colorado are black bears.

Eventually I returned with my family to the valley where I had grown up. I bought a ranch and tried raising cattle, but I was too interested in hunting. I sold the ranch in 1957 and went into full-time guiding and outfitting. My sideline specialty was assisting stockmen in tracking and killing bears that were menacing livestock. It was through this activity that I became known to personnel in the state Game, Fish and Parks Department.

It was nothing very new for me to be called out on a bear hunt. I guess that nearly 400 black bears have been killed over my dogs by myself and other hunters.

Tad, Warren, and I had trouble with the truck three times during the drive across the mountains, and it was dusk when we arrived at the edge of the park and spotted a park-department patrol car. Its driver had been alerted to watch for us. He escorted us 11 miles to the Holzwarth Neversummer Ranch, a dude ranch near the scene of the tragedy. A dozen or more National Park Service personnel and state game men were waiting for us. John Holzwarth III, part owner of the ranch, was present to provide information on the attack and describe the surrounding terrain.

Knowledge of the terrain was very important, but at the moment, I was much more interested in the details of the killing. The story was told by Bert McLaren, a National Park Service official who was in overall charge of the hunt.

"The man's name was John Richardson," he began. "He was a thirty-one-year-old resident of Denver. He was camping on ranch property with his brother-in-law and several other relatives. Most of the members of the group were asleep in a bus-type camper. Richardson was spending the night in a tent pitched close to the camper. That was the situation about two a.m. last night.

"According to reports we received, the bear attacked his victim without apparent reason. He clawed open the tent and went after Richardson without warning. Nobody knows how long the fight between the man and bear went on before Richardson's terrified yells awakened people in the camper."

McLaren then told us that the victim's brother-in-law had looked frantically for a weapon. The only thing he could put his hands on immediately was a heavy frying pan. He rushed outside, but it was too dark to see much, so he ran back and turned on the lights of the camper.

Then he spotted the bear carrying Richardson into nearby timber. He went wild, rushed headlong at the bear, and beat the animal on the head with the frying pan. The bear dropped his victim and started toward the second man but didn't attack him.

As soon as the man with the skillet backed off, the bear picked up Richardson, who was already dead, and dragged him through a barbed-wire fence. The would-be rescuer rushed in and beat the bear on the head again. That's when the bear dropped his victim and walked off into the timber.

Paul Gilbert, district manager for the Game, Fish and Parks Department, then told us that he had horses and men ready for the hunt. He also said that live traps had been set for the bear. The most disappointing news was that a heavy rain had fallen late that afternoon. All scent had been washed away.

With a Geological Survey map and excellent verbal descriptions by John Holzwarth, I was able to get the lay of the land well in mind.

Holzwarth's Neversummer Ranch sprawls over the more-level part of a north-south valley between two high mountain ranges. The ranch buildings are located in meadows bordered by lodgepole pines. The pines fade into balsam and spruce on the higher elevations. The peaks, up to 12,000 feet, are barren rock, swept clean by storms. Tiny streams splash down narrow canyons to a small river on the floor of the mile-wide Kawuneeche Valley.

Baker Creek Basin is in the Neversummer Mountains just west of the ranch, and it bottoms out at the attack site. The areas immediately adjoining Baker Creek are relatively free of timber, but they're edged by dense forest, willow swamps, and deadfalls. That type of terrain is good black-bear country. There was little doubt in my mind that our bear was in the mountains west of the meadows.

"We'll hunt the basin first," I told the group. "It's close to the kill site, there's good cover, and there's no reason in the world the bear should go any farther. The map shows ridges surrounding the basin, so my plan is simple. In the morning Tad will take one group of men and dogs up the ridge on the north side of the basin. Warren will take another group and some dogs up the south side. They'll spot armed men about half a mile apart at points where they can see and hear for long distances.

"I'll start in with the rest of my hounds at the attack site. Hopefully my dogs will get on the bear's trail and jump him. After that, anything can happen. If he runs, one of the men on stand may be able to get a shot at him. If he stops and fights, it'll be up to me unless some of the other hunters can close in on the fight before I get there. That's why it's important for Tad, Warren, and me to keep in contact at all times with walkie-talkies."

There wasn't much chance that we'd kill an innocent bear. Richardson's brother-in-law had gotten a good look at the bear during his attack with the skillet. He told us the bear was a very large adult black with a dark-brown coat. Brown bear hairs had been found on the fence through which the victim had been dragged.

Bert McLaren reminded us not to shoot the bear in the head if we could avoid it. The biologists wanted to examine the animal's brain for signs of rabies. Some of the men felt that the bear was almost certainly rabid.

I had reservations about that idea. A rabid animal will attack any living thing it can catch. And a black bear is lightning fast. Our bear had paid little attention to Richardson's brother-in-law, even though the man had beaten him with a skillet. It didn't add up. The bear could have killed the second man in a flash, but he didn't. Richardson, for some reason, was the bear's chosen victim.

I got my first real break when the hunters assembled near the ranch house at 6 a.m. the next morning. Somebody reported that a bear had raided a garbage container at the lodge during the night. I rushed there and found two clear paw prints in sandy ground. They were huge. The garbage container was made of heavy-gauge welded sheet metal. Full, it must have weighed almost 700 pounds. The lid had been torn loose, and the container had been moved several feet.

It takes a big bear to exert that kind of strength, and a bear that size will not condone the presence of another large male in his area. I was convinced that the damage had been done by the man-killer.

I put our plans into action at once. Tad and his group used four-wheel-drive vehicles to go up an old jeep road along the north rim of Baker Creek Basin. Warren and his party had to walk to their positions along the ridge on the southern edge of the 1,000-acre basin. The last man in each group was stationed at timberline. The hunt started when Tad and Warren reported by walkie-talkie that their men were positioned.

Gary Bicknell, head wrangler for the ranch stables, was waiting to move out with me. This was the first time I'd seen him, but he struck me as a good man to have around. We had two horses to ride, Moon for him and Utah for me. Gary had a .30/30 Winchester, and he said he knew how to use it. I wore a .45 caliber single-action Colt revolver in a belt holster, and I also had my .30/30 lever-action carbine.

I turned Old Joe, my strike dog, loose on the smoking-hot trail. He had the scent line dead to rights for several hundred yards, so I unleashed two more dogs. Then they all lost the trail.

I was sure the bear would head west toward the basin, so I circled that way. We wasted an hour because I couldn't believe my theory was wrong, but the hounds just couldn't find any scent where I thought it should be, so we headed back toward where the bear had raided the garbage container. I leashed all the dogs so that Old Joe could work out the scent at the point where they had overrun the line.

He found it again and then turned east up a horse trail that was worn deep into the turf. There I found part of a fresh bear print. Old Joe was in full cry, so I let Bullet and Ruff loose. In seconds trail music rang out over the entire valley as the dogs lit out toward the mountain slopes to the east. When I realized what was happening, I groaned. I'd deployed a couple dozen men on the western slopes, and it was now obvious that the bear had gone into mountains on the opposite side of the valley.

The race went up a steep slope, over benches, across ridges. The voices of the dogs came through loud and clear when they crossed high ground but faded as they dipped under rims or went into the timber. The bear ran into some of the roughest country on the side of the mountain. Then he made a decision.

Some bears will climb a tree when pursued for a few miles. Some will stop and fight and then run again. Some will stop and fight to the finish. Others will leave the country if they can. When your dogs have run a bear a few miles, you learn what he's going to do. This one had decided to stay on the mountain and fight and run in spurts. My job was to get there while the dogs were fighting the bear so that I could get a shot.

The chase went back and forth across the face of the mountain. Gary and I punished our horses in an almost straight-up climb. Each time we stopped to listen to the dogs, Gary told me that horses couldn't be ridden up those rugged slopes. And each time he said that, I gave Utah a good thump in the ribs and we climbed another 100 yards or so. The last time I did that, the dogs were fighting and howling about 300 yards above us. We didn't get far, though. Fallen timber blocked our way.

"We'll split," I yelled to Gary. "Take your horse around this stuff, and try to get level with the fight. Then come in from the north. I'll circle around and come in from the south. Be careful."

I managed to go only a short distance before I had to stop and tie Utah to a spruce. I ran, jumped, and clawed my way closer to the madhouse of fighting and roaring above me. When I had closed the distance to 60 yards, I got my first glimpse of swirling dust, darting dogs, and a very large, enraged, brown-colored black bear.

A long opening through the spruces gave me a chance for my first shot. I fired the .30/30 in a hurry when the dogs fell back for a split second. I think the bullet missed the bear. He showed no shock, shudder, or other response.

To my complete surprise, the rifle jammed when I tried to lever another cartridge into the chamber. It had never jammed before. I know now that the jam was caused by a defective handload. I lowered the rifle, pulled out my Colt, and raced ahead.

I ran in close to get a clear second shot and fired from about 15 yards. Fur flew from the animal's rib cage just behind his shoulder. He whirled and started climbing a big Englemann spruce.

I moved in closer in order to get out from under the branches of other trees that blocked my view of the climbing bear. I was about 20 feet from the big spruce when I fired several rapid shots with the Colt. I saw each one strike home in the rib area. I couldn't believe it when the killer kept climbing. I moved almost under the tree to fire again. I had to shoot through his stomach to get the bullet into his lung area.

The big spruce was bare of branches for the first 20 feet. The bear was reaching for the lowest branches when I hit him with the last shot from the revolver. I figured he was almost dead, but then a frightening thought flashed into my mind. The Colt was empty, and I had no more cartridges for it. My rifle was jammed.

Just then the fear-crazed killer started back down the tree. He seemed to slide down the trunk in slow motion, and his claws cut long grooves in the bark. When he reached the ground 15 feet from me, Joe, Bullet, and Ruff were all over him in a second. The dogs were swatted aside, and the infuriated bear was staring at me with the reddest and most hate-filled eyes I've ever seen. Undoubtedly he was going to charge.

"You goofed, Ray," I thought. "Now it's your turn to find out what a man-bear fight is like."

There was no use in running. I knew the bear would be on top of me in one jump. I thought of using my rifle as a club, but it seemed a puny weapon.

Then I yanked the lever of that rifle with all the strength I had. Something gave, and I thought I'd broken the lever. Then I realized that I had ejected the fired cartridge case. I slammed the next round into the chamber of the .30/30 just as the bear lunged at me.

There was no time to aim. I snapped off the shot at point-blank range. The bullet smashed into the top of the bear's shoulder, and he dropped instantly.

When I calmed down I realized that the revolver shots had done much damage. Lung shots kill because the animal drowns in its own blood, but if a large artery or vein isn't cut, death may not come for several minutes. That's just what happened in this case. I shudder even now — a big bear can kill a man in seconds. Later examination showed that the final rifle bullet had stopped the charge cold by breaking the bear's spine.

About 20 men helped to get the bear down the mountain. The carcass was then taken to Colorado State University, where several rabies tests on brain tissue all proved negative. Three veterinarians examined the bear's skinned skull and found recent bruise marks on the nose and around the eyes, almost certainly inflicted by the frying pan wielded by the victim's brother-in-law.

The brown bear hair taken from the barbed-wire fence matched the dead bear's hair perfectly. The animal weighed 306 pounds and was in perfect physical condition. He measured six feet from nose to tail. There was no doubt that he was the right bear. The man-killer was dead.

Pheasant from the Butt

Nord Riley

March 1975

This is Nord Riley's second appearance. A biographical sketch appears with the first story, "How to Shoot the Bird of Peace." He has gone on to do many more stories for OUTDOOR LIFE, and in one of them, "Hunting with Father," he describes his attitude toward hunting. "Many people," he says, "ask why civilized men love to hunt. I know why I do. For one thing, I am not all that civilized. My family has been hunting for 3,500,000 years, and it is in my deoxyribonucleic acid. For another thing I was born amid guns in a land feathered with sporty, toothsome birds to a father who took me hunting with him. I haven't got over it. Nothing turns me on like the sight of ducks flying or quail running." Here's how he feels about driven pheasants.

Foul weather harassed us all the way from Dublin to Tullamore in the center of Ireland, but with the red-haired lady from Cork at the wheel of her tiny automobile we hurtled through the gates of the Charleville Estate with eight minutes to spare. We stopped outside a building where about 20 people were clustered in the rain. A tall, lean man in tweeds detached himself from the group and hastened to us on a stiff leg. He peered at me through spectacles flecked with water.

"You're the American chap?"

"Yes."

"Major Hutton-Bury. How do you do? It's getting on ten o'clock. Take one of these, will you?"

He thrust slips of paper at me. I drew one, and he moved off. My slip read: Charleville 6,8,1,3,5,7,2,4. I asked the red-haired lady what it all meant. The Irish Tourist Board had sent Kate Nielson, a pretty, competent young woman, to look after me on my first driven bird shoot.

"It's your butt list," she said. "Each of the numbers indicates which butt you'll be shooting from at each of the eight stations." Squinting through the downpour, she added: "I say, the Major is anxious to start. You'll want to change clothes. Could you manage in the car? While I dash inside?"

On an occasion as posh as this was said to be, I hadn't expected to have to change my pants in a car — oh, a Rolls, maybe, but not a Fiat 600.

I was a little worried whether I was dressed right. I knew that my normal attire in the fields of North Dakota, California, and Arizona — odd bits left over from recent wars and hand-me-downs from my children — would get me ejected and I didn't own the tweed knickers, jacket, and long stockings that the upper-class Irish and Englishmen wear for shooting. But as an American I figured I might get by in my old tweed jacket, dark wool pants, tattersall shirt, and tie — a costume that would have got me arrested as a sex deviate in North Dakota.

I needn't have worried. The weather was so rotten, cold, and wet that everyone's outfit was covered with raingear. I wore my son's discarded ski jacket (a vivid seagreen job), a canvas cartridge belt, and knee-high rubber boots.

Kate came out so swollen in sweaters and parka that I mistook her for a wintering Tibetan. A small covered wagon drawn by a sodden ass pulled up. The vintage Irishman inside put down his reins and took the two boxes of shells I was holding.

"You'll not be wanting to carry that great weight around with you," he said.

Isn't that nice, I thought, an ammunition carrier.

Major Hutton-Bury marched right out in front of us.

"Do come along now!" he shouted, and with a punctuality I'd never before witnessed in Ireland he led us off to the first covert. We were eight guns, several wives, a boy or two, and some dogs. The clever ones had umbrellas.

I walked in ignorance. All I knew about driven bird shoots had been absorbed from movie scenes of the British aristocracy at play. These affairs were staged on huge estates, generally a nobleman's. Gamekeepers reared thousands of birds that beaters drove over the guns. The bag ran into many hundreds a day, and the birds cost far too much money, especially if you like to eat what you kill. No matter how many birds you shot on one of these shootups, you always wound up with two, His Lordship putting the rest on the market. Twas a sport of kings — George V and George VI banged away with great accuracy and delight — and pedigreed rich men.

But now in Ireland seven estates had been opened up for ordinary mortals with cash. For $100 to $200 a day almost anyone could have a fling at driven bird shooting. I was at Charleville on the outskirts of Tulamore in County Offaly. Not far away was Durrow Abbey, where Michael Williams, maker of a famous Irish liqueur, will put you up in one of his spare bedrooms for a weekend for something more than $300. This fee includes a driven shoot on Saturday, rough shooting on Sunday, bed, board, drinks, and that traditional brace of pheasants.

The Major led us to the first station, a spot so close to the building we'd just left that I felt we must still be in the back yard. The covert resembled no pheasant grounds I'd ever hunted. A swath about 60 feet wide had been cut through tall timber. The undergrowth was thick. Our group began splitting into twos and threes. The redhead and I shuffled around like lost tourists.

"What number are you?" inquired a comely woman in a blue quilted parka.

"Hello. Six."

"There." She pointed to an undistinguished patch of wet grass and shrub directly behind us. In the rain I had failed to see the marker. I must say I had been looking for something a bit more sumptuous than a bare lath with a piece of damp paper stuck to it.

"You're the American."

"Yes."

"Mrs. Hutton-Bury. Dreadful weather."

"We ran through snow getting here from Dublin this morning."

"Snow? Did you really? How annoying for you. How annoying for all of us. The birds won't like this, you know. They loathe having to get about in the wet like waterfowl."

"How many do you have?"

"Fifteen hundred. But whether they'll fly in this rain we shan't know for a while, shall we?"

"Mrs. Button-Bury . . ."

"HUTton-Bury."

"Mrs. Hutton-Bury, is there any special drill for these shoots? I've never been on one before."

That shook her up a good deal. Worry fretted the moist, noble brow. "Never shot at all, do you mean?"

"No, no, I've plugged a few of these critters here in Ireland and in the States, but it has been what you people call walk-up or rough shooting. Never with beaters. Or umbrellas."

"Oh, dear!" She shot a thin-lipped look at Kate for having brought out this tatty novice. Time was short, however, and she rallied.

"The birds come out very quickly. You have something under three seconds to get your gun up and fire."

"Three seconds. Not so bad."

"Unless you are rather agile your second shot may well be behind you. Now, what you must never, NEVER do is bring your gun about like this." She made an arc with her arm as though following a low-flying pheasant from the wood in front to the wood behind. "That would make it a bit dicey for the chap next to you, wouldn't it?"

I said I could see that it would lead to nervousness in the butts.

"And of course you mustn't shoot at low birds coming from the wood."

"Might bag a beater?"

"Quite."

"Do I shoot hens?"

"Shoot everything that doesn't belong to Lord Rathdonnell on your right or Captain St. Lawrence there on your left."

Major Hutton-Bury had chivied everyone into positions about 30 yards apart along one side of the swath. I peered down the line. Under the low, leaking clouds it was not a chic spectacle, not a sight to strike envy in the breast of the Duke of Edinburgh, not at all like the magazine photos of smartly caparisoned aristocrats amid glowing autumn foliage under blue skies. The trees were leafless and somber. Some shooters huddled under their wives' umbrellas; others hunched on their shooting sticks.

I stood with my female assistant beside my lath, a suave figure in an odious green jacket, my $100 Spanish double-barrel hung over my arm. Above the sound of the wind and the rain came the tumult of the beaters as they shouted and whacked the brush with sticks.

Men rose from their shooting sticks. Womenfolk retreated. Dogs whined. I was filled with excitement and unease. Any minute now I was going to have to shoot a pheasant, and I knew damned well I couldn't. I was about to make an ass of myself.

"I do think you might load," said Mrs. Hutton-Bury, who had decided to stay beside me. Kate had retired to a bush from which she was to count the bodies, if any.

With no confidence whatever I put two shells into my gun. I didn't doubt *them*. They were light English loads — 1 1/16 ounces of No. 6's — that I knew from experience to be reliable and effective. I doubted my gun. The rules of Irish gun clubs state: "Double-barrel guns only to be used; repeater guns, if carried, may only be loaded with two cartridges." (Grasp *that* sentence, and you're on your way to understanding the Irish.)

All my life I'd shot pump guns. For Irish shooting I'd had to buy a double-barrel — a light, solid 12-gauge made by Aguirre and Aranzabal of Spain. The first season with the new gun I'd shot better than I'd expected. This season I couldn't hit my hat with it.

The problem developed when we came back to Ireland after a year in Spain and Austria. My two daughters, Katie and Jan, wanted to get back to the convent school on Dublin Bay where, as the only Protestants in the place, they were treated as pets. I wanted to get back to what I think is the pleasantest bird shooting in Europe and the British Isles.

I'd gone straight to County Donegal to shoot grouse where I'd shot birds before. Out on the heathered moors with my broad-backed ghillie John Brown, a man who spoke English slowly because his normal language was Irish, and led by that incomparable bitch, Flash, I missed every grouse that rose. Once, when I missed an easy pair, I hurled the gun 20 feet into a mound of drying peat and swore I'd never shoot the damned thing again.

I did, though. I took it out to Counties Galway and Clare for the opening of the pheasant season in November. In that serene region, with good Irish friends to tell me what I was doing wrong, I couldn't hit a pheasant, not one. I thought I might need medical attention, but mostly I thought I'd better send for my old Winchester Model 12 residing in a closet in Manhattan Beach, California.

There hadn't been time for that, and here I was, standing in the rain with two women, veteran upper-class Irish guns on each side of me, beaters herding pheasants toward me, and armed with a gun I couldn't shoot.

Pheasants began to come out of the dark, dripping wood like projectiles from hidden cannons. One of them entered my bailiwick at a height of 40 feet. The time had come. I let go at him. He crashed at Kate's feet.

No one said a word. Mrs. Hutton-Bury seemed relieved. I remained impassive except for a swelling of the veins in my temples from stifling a Tarzan cry. I'd finally hit one.

Up and down the line guns blazed as pheasants came out of the trees in goodly numbers. In a complete reversal of form, I couldn't miss. A bird fell every time I shot, and I got to feeling pretty exultant. Presently, though, I realized that accuracy isn't the only necessity in driven bird shooting. There is one other: speed in reloading. Being a righthander who has to shoot from the left shoulder because of a bad right eye, I reload a double-barrel with all the dexterity of a bear cub wearing boxing gloves. Pheasants sailed overhead as I switched the gun from left to right hand to break it open.

"No ejectors?" asked Mrs. Hutton-Bury between clenched teeth.

"Nope, extractors," I said, plucking away at empty shells with my fingernails. "This gun cost me only forty pounds."

"Mmmm."

After extracting the empties, I had to pry two shells loose from my wet cartridge belt. Mrs. Hutton-Bury couldn't stand it any longer.

"Oh, do let me help!" she cried, and thrust two shells into my hand. From that time on, this kind and gentle woman, the lady of the manor, was my reloader.

Most birds came out too low, but there were more than enough high ones, and I banged away until I spotted the beaters, wet men and boys in dark clothes thrashing the undergrowth as they advanced. They came up to the far side of the swath and gazed across at us. They looked as sodden and miserable as we did.

The Major marched out in front of us to signal the end of the drive.

"You did rather well, it seems to me," she said. "I counted eight."

Mrs. Hutton-Bury left to help her husband. Kate and I picked up. By that I mean Kate pointed at each dead bird, and I picked up. The gamekeeper's assistants were retrieving too. The donkey and the covered wagon came by, and we turned our pheasants over to the ancient Celt inside. He hung them up by the necks from a frame made for that purpose. Fifteen had been shot.

Our little band folded shooting sticks, got under umbrellas, lowered their heads to the gale, and trudged off to Station 2. Butt 8 was at the end of the line. I had trees to my right; to my left was Captain Purdon. Major Hutton-Bury dropped by.

"I daresay the birds will be coming out rather low in this weather. Let them through. Not much sport really."

The gamekeeper moved his beaters about like a general. From one covert to another was often several hundred yards. Yet we seldom had to wait long in the rain and wind before the first birds showed up. Some flew out high from the timber, but a good many took to their heels as the beaters bore down on them. Some ran out into the open, had a look at the armed group facing them, and dashed back. I saw some that simply couldn't make up their minds who was worse, the silent guy with the gun or the boisterous one with the stick. Their indecision saved their lives, for they flew at the last moment and were too low to be shot without danger to the beaters.

At Station 2 there weren't many birds, in the air or afoot. A cock flew midway between Captain Purdon and me. He shot it neatly. Two hens were cleverer: they left by flying through the trees on my right. They flew like ruffed grouse, showing a lot of agility for pheasants. I missed one but hit the other with my second barrel. She didn't fall but was obviously jolted. I ran into the trees and saw her descend into a green field a quarter-mile away. I stood there wondering what the procedure was for lost birds.

"You're not to worry," said a voice beside me. "She's down in the turnips. I have me eye on her." It was a drenched young man put there by the gamekeeper to mark such birds.

"A wounded pheasant's damned hard to find," I said.

"Ah, it is, it is, for the man alone, but we have the dogs, do you see?"

That was all at Station 2: my bird in the turnips and four or five others plugged by the other guns. We picked up, opened the umbrellas, and made off through the wet grass and the storm to the next station. The rain fell heavier, the wind blew harder, and it was very cold. I suspect we looked more like a band of refugees than a party of sportsmen who'd paid over $100 each for the privilege.

At no station after the first were there as many pheasants. I shot two or three usually.

Easy shots, for the rain slowed the birds, and they came at me in the way I like best, overhead. Had the weather been clear they would have come out of the trees much higher and much faster, and would have been a real challenge.

While going from one cover to another we passed a castle, a good-looking pile that had not been wrecked by age or Cromwell. A fellow gun plodding beside me told me that the Hutton-Burys usually served lunch for the shooting party in the castle.

Remarkable place to eat, really," he said. "Excellent service, the kitchen being a good furlong from the dining room. Servant in top form couldn't make the run in less than five minutes. Ended up putting in a kind of tram line."

We wouldn't be eating in the castle today. Its roof leaked.

The Major announced a schedule change. Instead of shooting the customary six stations before lunch and two after, we would skip the last two.

"Damned nonsense to go on, eh?" he said. "Everyone's miserable."

Like most of the others, Station 6 was between two stands of trees, but with a difference: the distance between them was much greater, allowing the wind a better swipe at us. I was soaked. Even duck hunting in North Dakota in November hadn't made me this cold. The beaters, poor devils, had been slowed down, and we had to wait a long time for them to get into position. I became curious about the gentleman to my left. He sat out in the open on his stick, dressed in tweeds and without raingear. I inquired if he weren't cold.

Not too bad, actually. You see. I'm inside layers of tweeds. They're awfully good at soaking up the wet, but I've become so bloody heavy. Must weigh two stone more than when I started."

The first pheasant out of the wood was his, a damp cock pushing through the rain. He fired twice without rising from his stick.The cock was not hit.

"Damned odd," said the tweeded man. "Couldn't get my arms up."

My final chance came moments later when two cocks approached at a height of 40 or 50 feet. Like my neighbor I had a sensation of having become inoperable, of having solidified. Yet in the most astounding accident of the day both birds fell.

"J-j-j-jolly good!" cried the redhead from Cork, tottering out of the bushes, the coldest woman I have ever seen. "God, could I use a drink!"

We were rescued by car and carried back to the manor house, a sprawling building with central heating. In a downstairs john I stripped to my goosepimples. I was wet everywhere. I wrung out my shorts and hung them on a radiator. The magnificent sweater my wife had made for me had the weight of the sheep from which it came — and also its odor. I'd brought a change of trousers and jacket, but I had no replacement for my shirt or necktie. I joined the lords and ladies soaking wet from the waist up, with a tendency to steam.

My fellow guns, dried out and rehabilitated, were hard to recognize. Kate showed up in garments borrowed from our hostess. We had the bonhomie that infects people who have survived an ordeal together. Whisky flowed. Mrs. Hutton-Bury, charming reloader, introduced me as Dead-Eye Dick. One splendid fellow told me he had watched me all day and I had missed only once. Of 53 birds shot, I'd dropped 17. Top gun.

I saw no reason to tell them of the booby prizes I'd won in Donegal and Clare. Or that shooting wet, driven pheasants doesn't compare with the variety and the exhilarating surprises of field shooting in the corn and stubble of North Dakota.

But I went into the dining room to Mrs. Hutton-Bury's curry feeling better than I had all fall.

Billabong Buff

Jim Carmichel

June 1975

I have been asked how Jim Carmichel came to be chosen to succeed Jack O'Connor as Shooting Editor of OUTDOOR LIFE and would like to bestow the credit where it is due. Jack was seventy in 1972 and was ready to ease up himself. My own retirement was imminent and names were being thrown at me the way basketballs are thrown at the hoop. I took time out from the heat for a field trip with Charlie Elliott, our Southern Field Editor living in Georgia, and happened to mention my dilemma. It was then that I heard the name Jim Carmichel for the first time. Charlie had been keeping a close eye on gun articles appearing under Carmichel's name and had met him when Jim was with the Tennessee Game and Fish Commission. "He really knows his stuff," Elliott said. "You can't miss with him." The rest is history. That's the way the basketball bounces.

My tired and sweat-soaked companion, Fred Huntington, had no way of knowing it then, but his decision to go back to the truck for a rest while I went ahead to check on a couple of wallows may very well have cost him some of the most spectacular motion-picture footage ever made of a charging water buffalo.

But I have to admit that it sure looked as though Fred had the right idea. The tropical sun was at its zenith, and the humidity fairly steamed out of the mushy landscape. If one stayed in the shade and sat very still, life was just manageable. But we were slogging through billabongs after buffalo (billabong is the Australian term for a lagoon or rain-filled floodplain), and the rivulet of sweat that began behind my ears and cascaded between my shoulder blades had long since plastered my shirt and walking shorts to my skin.

It was early February, and we were hunting the giant Asian buffalo in Australia's wild "top end." Because the Island Continent lies below the equator, summer comes there when it's winter in North America. It was midsummer and the height of the tropical monsoon season. The coastal areas of the vast Northern Territory, Australia's northernmost district, had become a sea of tepid, adobe-colored water.

Ordinarily you would hunt buffalo there during the cooler and dryer winter months, but Fred, his wife Barbara, and I were on our way home from a sheep hunt in Iran. During our stopover in Australia, the chance to hunt the big buffalo was too alluring to pass up. The Huntingtons live in Oroville, California, where Fred is the top man at RCBS, the well-known makers of rifle and pistol reloading equipment. He wanted to stop by some of the larger Australian cities to see his distributors.

Fred had hunted buffalo in Australia a couple of years before and had such an exciting hunt that he suggested I try for one of the huge black bulls while he made a movie of the action.

As every schoolboy knows, Australia is the home of an absolutely mind-boggling assortment of wild creatures. Everything from frogs that kill dogs to ants that build bridges can be found there, and the hunting is fabulous.

Much of Australia's hunting has in one way or another been profit-motivated. Kangaroos provided the leather for countless pairs of American baseball shoes. The dingo, a wild dog, was relentlessly pursued to protect the vast Australian sheep industry. And rabbits, a foreigner to the Down Under country until a few were accidentally released over a century ago multiplied in such numbers that in some areas a farmer's survival was a matter of man against bunny.

For sheer size, however, nothing on the continent challenges the huge Australian buffalo. Like the rabbits, buffalo are not true natives but were introduced back in the 1800's. Asian water buffalo were brought to the steamy shores of Northern Australia to be used for plowing and other farm chores. These natives of the tropics were better able to survive in their new home than were the farmers who sought to conquer the Northern Territory. As the farms closed down, the buffalo were released into the wild and, like the rabbits, reproduced in enormous numbers.

Coal black, weighing upwards of a ton, and carrying a set of rearward-curving horns that can span over six feet, the Australian buffalo is a rugged customer and a worthy opponent for any sportsman. For sheer man-stopping orneriness he is not quite the equal of his cousin, the African Cape buffalo, but Australian buffalo maim and kill enough chaps to keep you looking over your shoulder when you think a buffalo might be in the neighborhood.

Our guide told us that when the pods of a local palm tree get overripe and rather alcoholic, they are eaten by the buffalo, and for a while the woods are full of crazy-drunk, mean-tempered beasts that charge everyone and everything that happens along.

These Asian buffalo, contrary to some opinions, are not just descendants of domestic work animals. The draft animals brought to Australia were themselves only one or two generations removed from the wild Indian buffalo. Thus the Australian variety has not "gone" wild but merely has reverted to its natural state, with all the cunning and sense of self-preservation of any wild game animal.

In one day's hunting I got to within shooting distance of a half-dozen or so, but after they decided what I was and what I was up to they charged off, snorting and flailing their tails, into the dense brush. Their behavior reminds me of the Cape buffalo I've hunted in Africa: curious enough to stand and watch you approach but capable of a quick disappearing act when they catch human scent or otherwise sense danger.

When Fred hunted in Australia a couple of years before, he bagged a huge bull with horns measuring several inches over six feet. Then, as on our recent trip together, he was guided by Don McGregor, the master of Patonga Lodge and one of the best-known fishing-and-hunting guides in the Northern Territory.

Don's hunting concession includes exclusive access to some 1,100 square miles of government-owned wilderness land, and each year he is granted a quota of buffalo that may be bagged by his clients. In addition to buffalo, Don offers hunting for waterfowl, wild boar, and dingo — and some fantastic fishing.

The local barramundi, a basslike tacklebuster, is the most delicious fish I've ever tasted. The cost of eight days of hunting with Don is 1,000 Australian dollars (about $1,300 U.S.) for one hunter. For a party of three the cost is reduced to about $700 per hunter. This includes everything: guiding, food and lodging, and trophy preparation. There are no license fees or other incidental costs.

Getting a rifle into Australia involves more red tape than Fred Huntington and I thought it was worth, so with a promise from Don that I could use his rifles, we shipped our two .280's home from Iran. As it turned out, Don is a rifle nut of the first water and handloads his own ammunition. The rifle he had ready for my hunt was a Czech-made Brno bolt gun in .30/06 caliber and topped off with a 4X scope. Ordinarily McGregor favors the .375 Holland and Holland for the big buffs, but for the moment the '06 was all he had to offer. I was soon to find out first-hand why Don prefers the big bone-crushing magnums.

McGregor's Patonga Hunting Lodge is about 150 air miles east of Darwin, near Jim Jim Creek (a "creek" that would equal a major river in most parts of the world) and not far from the Woolwonga Aboriginal Reservation. During the dry winter months Patonga can be reached by road, but in summer the daily cloudbursts change the roadbeds into surging rivers and the lodge is surrounded by water. The only way in then is by air and boat.

At the beginning of the wet season Don parks vehicles on high ground in different parts of his hunting territory so he'll have some transportation when the rising water changes the gently rolling landscape into islands. Outboard boats are then used to commute from island to island.

I got an idea of how this works when the Huntingtons and I flew from Darwin to a bush strip near the Jim Jim by charter plane and were met by Don. We had only about a three-mile drive before the road dipped into a mile-wide stream. There we put our gear into a boat, crossed the swollen creek, and transferred our stuff into another truck. From there we drove to Patonga.

Before Don opened his hunting lodge a dozen years ago, he had been a crocodile hunter whose bare-handed exploits made him a legend before he was 30. It's hard to find a book on modern Australian hunting that doesn't mention his adventures.

Besides Don, his wife Sandy, and their son Rodney, the lodge is staffed by Mick, a very pleasant young aborigine who speaks with a crisp British accent and is the son of the legendary Yorky Billy, the Australian counterpart of Buffalo Bill Cody.

On the day of our arrival Mick was checking out the buffalo herds and trying to locate some trophy bulls. Buffalo are great swimmers and move from island to island with such ease that finding them at any given time is largely a matter of luck. That evening Mick said he had seen an especially good bull on an island 15 to 20 miles away, but the animal was not with a herd and would probably be hard to find again. However, Mick had followed the bull a good part of the day and could tell Don approximately where the old buff's mud and wallows were. During the heat of the day buffalo like to take their ease in cool mud wallows; if you can find the wallows you can usually find the buffs. Luckily Don had a truck parked on the island where Mick had spotted the bull. That might save us miles of walking — provided the bull didn't decide to swim to another area.

Next morning, over a hearty breakfast, Don set me straight on what we were in for. I had the false notion that wet-season hunting was a series of island-hopping jaunts and that the game could be spotted from a boat. This might be true in some instances, but the island on which Mick had spotted the big bull was at least 20 miles across and densely covered with palms, palmettos, and hardwoods. The truck would be helpful only for getting us to the general area where the big bull was last seen. But from then on, we would be wading billabongs and churning through mudflats.

The trip to the island was an hour-long boat ride through a forest in which bright-blossomed vines slowed our progress and spider webs as big as 10 feet across caught our faces. Toward the end of our trip we cruised above a roadbed, now under three feet of water, and even passed a stilt-legged grocery store and tourist shop, each bearing signs "Closed for the rain."

Don's truck was parked on a paved road that led down a long grade and simply disappeared into 10-mile-wide Jim Jim Creek. By then the sun was high and the air was becoming slightly hazy with its burden of humidity.

During the next hour or so we spotted eight or nine small herds and some fine buffs, but they would charge into the bush as soon as we got within 100 yards or so. Most were cows and calves, and the only mature bulls were on the smallish side.

I must admit that I was beginning to hope that we would spot a shootable bull not too far from the road. As morning gave way to midday, the temperature soared and the atmosphere turned to live steam. The prospect of a long hike in that climate was not particularly appealing to me.

For a moment I thought I was in luck when we came across a fine old bull that was inclined to stand his ground as we drove to within 100 yards of him. With Fred's movie camera whirring in the background, I got my first good look at a trophy-size Asian-buffalo bull. The horns were as black as his hide and grew straight out from his head for a foot or more before beginning a rearward sweep. They were as wide as those on any of the mounted heads I'd seen back in Darwin, but this bull was not the one we wanted — the one Mick had spotted earlier.

After we got under way again, another bull broke out of the cover, dashed across the road, and crashed into some thick brush not more than 50 yards ahead.

"Am I seeing things, Don, or was that a *red* buffalo?" I asked.

"You're not seeing things. That bull has traits of albinism. Let's get out and see if we can find him. If we get another look be sure to notice his nose. It will be as pink as a baby's foot."

Don eased the truck to a stop under a low tree, and we slipped out and fancy-footed our way around the patch of dense growth into which the bull had disappeared. A moment later the animal crashed out of the brush, galloped halfway across a grassy clearing, then skidded to a stop and spun around to face us. For an instant it looked as though he was about to have a go at us, but his curiosity had gotten the best of him, and he only wanted another look. His nose was pink, just as Don had predicted.

An hour later we came to the swampy lowland where Mick had spotted the big bull the day before.

"There are four or five wallows within a mile or two of here," said Don. "We'll move slowly and check them out one by one. If we jump him you'll have to shoot fast because in this cover he'll vanish in a second."

Fred wore knee-high rubber boots, but — like Don — I was barefoot, and as we moved through the swamp the warm black muck oozed between my toes and brought back memories of stalking bullfrogs in farm ponds.

We followed a circular route of about three miles and found three or four spots where our quarry had been rolling in the mud, but there was no sign of him. It looked as though we had missed him entirely, but Don said we could check a couple of other wallows. At that point Fred elected to head back for the truck and wait for us.

Don and I had not gone much more than a quarter-mile when he suddenly stooped low to get a better look under some trees ahead.

"There he is," he hissed. "He's asleep in that mudhole ahead."

I looked where Don was pointing but could see only a dark hulk glistening with slime and so deep in the wallow that I couldn't even make out which end was which. An instant later, though, all doubt was gone. With a throaty bellow the bull heaved his bulk out of the hole and stood snorting at us with his head down.

He was facing us head-on, so I centered his chest with the crosshairs and pressed the trigger. It was a good shot. It *had* to be — the range was 50 yards at most, and through the scope the target looked as big as a truck.

When the 180-grain slug hit him he only gave a slight twitch and then charged us. My second shot, meant more to stop the charge than to kill, caught him near the joint of his right shoulder and caused him to swerve and angle by us a few yards to our right. My third shot, rapid-fired into the same shoulder, seemed to have no more effect than the first two, but before he had gone another 20 steps his legs collapsed and his giant bulk crashed into the ground.

Don's preference for the .375 H & H was by then easily understandable. My first shot into the bull's heart was the bullet that killed him, but he could have done some very unpleasant things before he fell. The shoulder shot turned him just enough to save us, but the '06 just didn't have as much punch as I would have liked.

Don and I were struggling to roll the bull over to check where my shots had hit when Fred came dashing up.

"What's all the shooting about?"

"Well, old buddy, it's like this," Don answered. "If you'd been here three minutes ago..."

"Never mind that," I interrupted. "Just help roll this big fellow over, and we'll carve out some dinner steaks."

Greatest Mule Deer of Them All

Doug Burris, Jr.

December 1975

> In September 1975, OUTDOOR LIFE carried a story in which six top Western guides revealed, as the title said, "Ways to Get the Biggest Bucks." Three months later this story appeared, "The Greatest Mule Deer of Them All," about the deer killed by Doug Burris, Jr. in 1972 which is the present World Record. Burris and his friends call their annual quests "poor-boy hunts," no guides and no outfitters. Yet the guides would have no quarrel with them. Their approach is the same. Everything planned to the smallest detail. Burris even bought a copy of the Boone and Crockett Club's *Records of North American Big Game*, 1964 edition, to check where most of the big heads were coming from.

I was walking the edge of a small canyon in Colorado's San Juan National Forest when a rifle roared half a mile or so ahead of me. Till then I'd figured on stillhunting to a plateau covered with scattered oak brush 400 yards north of me. A clump of brush there would have been a fine place to take a stand.

When I heard the shot I decided to get to a vantage point on the plateau as fast as I could, so I took off at a dead run. I was almost on the plateau when I noticed movement in the oak brush and aspens on the other side of the canyon. I slammed to a stop and stared at the biggest deer I had ever seen. His body was enormous, and his rack seemed large enough for an elk.

He wasn't running flat out, but I knew I had to shoot in a hurry. The range was about 250 yards. The buck was moving up the canyon and away from me when I found him in my Leupold 3X-to-9X scope, I put the crosshairs on his back and touched off my Sako .264. He went down in his tracks. My big-game handloads consist of 125-grain Nosler bullets backed with 66.5 grains of No. 4831 powder. It's a very potent load.

I watched him for a while to make sure he wasn't going to get up, and then I ran down a side canyon and up the other side of the big one to the fallen buck. When I ran my hands over the huge 18-point rack, I knew the antlers were very good. I was sure the deer would score high in the Boone and Crockett Club's record book.

If someone could have told me that my 1969 Colorado buck wasn't even good enough to make the minimum score for listing in the record book, I wouldn't have believed him. That's the way it turned out, but a still bigger deer was ranging the same stretch of country.

I'm 37. My wife and I live in Seguin, Texas, with our 17-year-old son and two daughters, aged 15 and eight. I'm a construction superintendent with an outfit that builds shopping centers, high-rise office buildings, and similar units.

Except for 3½ years spent in the U.S. Air Force, I've lived in Texas all my life. I began hunting when I was seven. My dad got me started and taught me to be a good hunter. I killed my first Texas whitetail when I was 13, and I've been nuts about deer hunting ever since. Though many of our Texas deer are so small we call them jackrabbits, we do have some large whitetails in the southern brush country. Some of those bucks field-dress at 200 pounds or a bit more, and some have exceptional antlers. Many years of hunting brush-country deer gave me trophy-hunting fever.

I have always wanted to hunt Dall or Stone sheep in Alaska or British Columbia, but I've never had the money or the time. I finally decided that the next-best thing was to stay with deer and hunt trophy antlers.

My interest in camping had a lot to do with that first mule-deer hunt in Colorado in 1969. My friends and I have several four-wheel-drive vehicles and an assortment of camping gear. Charlie Fuller of Floresville, and Jack Smith of San Antonio, do a lot of hunting with me. Jack is my age. He's a carpenter. Charlie, a few years younger, has a fertilizer-application operation. Both like to hunt deer the way I do, and they like to camp. Early in 1969 we decided to hunt in the mountains where we could camp on public land and do without guides and outfitters. We call it a "poor-boy hunt."

I did quite a bit of research on trophy mule deer before we chose the San Juan National Forest. From what I'd read in OUTDOOR LIFE and other outdoor magazines, I knew that many giant bucks were taken not too far from the Four Corners, where Utah, Arizona, New Mexico, and Colorado touch.

I also bought a copy of the 1964 edition of the Boone and Crockett Club's book "Records of North American Big Game." Study of the section on mule-deer trophies backed up my contention that southwestern Colorado would be a good place to go. We knew there were better bets, such as the Jicarilla Apache Reservation in New Mexico, but we couldn't get permits, and we wanted to go into country where we could camp on public land. We eventually drove to Cortez, Colorado, and hunted northeast of town.

The three of us all got bucks that first year, and my big buck had a rack that measured 41 inches across the outside spread. Each antler had "cheater" points extending horizontally from the outside curves of the main beams. Though the rack had a very unusual spread, the tines weren't very long, and that's why my trophy didn't make the record book.

When I killed the deer, I didn't know much about official scoring systems for big game, but I did know that where there was one grandote (a Mexican term we use for big bucks) there should be more. We didn't need a better reason to head back into the same area. We've never been sorry.

The second year, I got a buck with a 33-inch outside spread. The third year, I was lucky enough to come up with another good deer. Every season I've hunted in those mountains, except one, I've taken a buck with an outside antler spread of 30 inches or better, and other members of my party have taken very good bucks too. Many hunters in the area kill deer with spreads as narrow as 12 inches. Every fall I pass up many deer to get the best one I can find.

Most of the men in our group hunt that way. We all love the mountains, and we like to hunt hard from dawn to dark. We don't want to miss one minute of hunting on these trips. None of us will take a small buck unless time is running out on the last day.

I don't want to imply that we're trophy crazy. Much of our pleasure derives from the planning and preparation that goes into our hunts and the talkfests that go on for months after each trip. We make the most of camp life too. I'm usually the cook because I enjoy it. We come into camp each evening, warm up by our wood stove in the cooktent, swap stories about what happened during the day, and take our time over meals while we plan the next day's hunt. Then we sack out early enough for a good rest so that we can do it all over again.

We go back into the Cortez area each year because it has proved itself, and because our camping gear is suited to that kind of country. We're not equipped to backpack into remote areas or pack in with horses.

Our cooktent, which also serves as a community area, is a 14 x 16-foot wall tent. We have 9 x 12 Coleman sleeping tents. Everybody contributes something to our outfit. We found out during our first trip that it's best to take plenty of blankets and raingear.

On the front end of our trailer is mounted a large box in which we pack all our food and some other items. If the weather is warm during our hunt, we have all our venison butchered, wrapped, and quick-frozen in Cortez. We pack the meat and dry ice in the box for our trip home. If the weather is cold, we hang our field-dressed deer from a game pole and then haul them home whole for butchering there. Either way, the venison we put in our freezers provides delicious meals far into the winter.

We make our trips from Texas to Colorado with two 4WD's. The big unit is my three-quarter-ton Dodge Power Wagon equipped with a winch. Behind the Dodge we tow a Jeep on a 20-foot trailer. We usually ride in the wagon and pack the Jeep and the trailer with our gear.

Our average cost per man totals about $155, and that includes Colorado's nonresident deer license ($50). A big chunk of the rest of each man's expenses goes for gas. We drive straight through from Texas. That takes 20 to 24 hours, depending on driving conditions. We use the Jeep each day to put men out in hunting areas, so we burn a lot of gas. We bring plenty of steaks and a normal supply of groceries such as beans, potatoes, flour, canned goods, breakfast mixes.

We plan to arrive in our hunting area the Thursday before the Saturday opener of the deer season, which is always in late October. It takes two days to set up camp, get organized, and do a little scouting. We figure on hunting three to five days, but we do not set up a hard-and-fast schedule.

As few as two men have gone to Colorado with me and as many as eight, but everything seems to go along smoothest with about four in the party. In 1972, the year I shot the world-record mule deer, there were four of us. Jack Smith went along, but Charlie Fuller couldn't get away. Robbie Roe and Bruce Winters were my other partners. I knew them through my job, and we had done a lot of hunting together.

We drove up into Colorado and camped in the same spot I'd picked out four years earlier. I knew the hunting country fairly well by that time, and I had selected five specific areas that seemed to hold the most deer and the biggest bucks. They're all laced with relatively thick oak brush, some aspens, and a few pines. Thick oak brush is the key to success. If you've got tangles of that stuff and lots of them, you're going to find deer.

The oak-brush areas most attractive to deer run to broken terrain in the form of canyons and side canyons, plateaus, and mesas. The best technique for hunting that kind of terrain is a combination of stillhunting and standing. I like to stillhunt the plateaus and small canyons. I've learned that deer work the small finger canyons and get down into the very bottoms of them. They range back and forth through the canyons, often go up on the mesas and plateaus.

That's why the combination of hunting techniques works so well. When I'm still hunting I often spot deer ahead of me or across a canyon or draw. If I take a stand on a good vantage point I may have deer working toward me.

The problem is that deer may use one area today and vacate it tomorrow. So I choose an area and hunt it out. If deer are there, I stick with it; if they aren't I move to the next area. That isn't hard to do, because the San Juan country is mostly rolling terrain, and the altitude is only about 8,500 feet where we hunt.

Our first day of hunting in 1972 began in typical fashion. We checked the wind direction before dawn and decided on the areas each man would hunt. Then we piled into the Jeep and headed up a mountain two-track. I dropped Robbie off first and then Bruce. A few miles farther on, Jack got out of the vehicle. Dawn wasn't much more than a dull-gray promise in the eastern sky. The black void above us was spitting drizzle.

"Robbie and Bruce will walk back to camp whenever they feel like it," I told Jack. "You want me to pick you up at a set time, or do you want to hunt all day in the rain?"

"I'll meet you right here at dark," Jack answered.

I knew he'd say something like that. Jack likes to hunt as much as I do.

We all saw many deer that day, but all the bucks were small. None of us fired a shot.

But I came very close to filling my tag on the second day of the hunt. It drizzled again, and I just ambled along till 10 o'clock. Then I got real serious about my stillhunting. I don't know why, but the really big bucks in that area seem to move mostly from 10 in the morning till about 1 in the afternoon.

About noon I spotted a deer in thick oak brush 200 yards ahead. We were both on a plateau. The animal was a big one, so I assumed he was a buck, and I started moving in on him. My stalking was quiet because everything was wet, but I couldn't close the distance very fast in that thick brush, and the deer kept moving away from me as he browsed.

At one point I saw part of his rack, just enough to know the antlers were in the trophy class. The excitement ended when I tried to cut him off at the edge of the plateau. When I got there, he was gone. I'll never know whether that buck sensed my presence or went off on a predetermined course.

When Jack and I got back to camp two bucks were on the game pole. Robbie had nailed a five-pointer with his 7-mm Remington Magnum rifle equipped with a Leupold scope. Bruce's deer was also a five-pointer, but the antlers were heavier. Bruce collected his venison with a Winchester Model 70 .30/06 rigged with a Leupold scope.

When we awoke the third morning, the dad-gummed drizzle was still with us. I suited up in my Browning raingear and filled my pockets with dried fruits and jerky. I knew it would be another long day before I could bake myself beside the wood stove in the cooktent. I dropped Jack off on the trail and then drove on and parked near the area I had hunted the day before.

A slight breeze was coming down off the mountain, so I decided to stillhunt into it and get farther back into rougher country. About 9 o'clock I started into a 400-yard-wide canyon and began working up toward one rim. I was about three-quarters of the way to the top when I spotted two bucks feeding in a clearing 1,000 yards away in the canyon. I stopped and watched them for several minutes because I was astonished that I could see their racks from such a great distance with the naked eye.

Then I looked at them through my Bausch & Lomb 7 x 35 binoculars. Both were definitely in the trophy class. It was fairly late in our hunt, so I decided it was best to cash in on one of them. I'd make the stalk and decide which rack was best when I got within range.

I eased on through the oak brush for about 200 yards and busted out a doe. She pushed on ahead of me. I didn't think she would spook the bucks, but I watched them for several minutes to make sure. They continued feeding away from me up the slope. I could keep them in sight at this point because they were still in a clearing.

I eased back into some cover and stalked ahead for about 45 minutes while the drizzle came on stronger and stronger. During that time I didn't see the bucks, because they had moved into a patch of brush, but I was pretty sure they were still nearby. I would have seen them if they had moved out on that slope. There was a 75-yard-wide opening at the top of the canyon, and I would have seen or heard them if they had run back toward me or along the canyon bottom.

An additional 30 minutes passed before I decided I couldn't be more than 200 yards from the deer, but I still couldn't see them — the patch of brush was up to 10 feet tall. Then I busted out a doe again. She crashed along toward the bucks. I figured they'd spook, so I took of at a dead run for an opening 20 yards ahead of me. If I was going to do any good, I had to shoot in a hurry.

Just as I broke into the opening, three deer ran into view. Two were the bucks I'd been stalking; the third was still bigger. He was lagging behind, and even in the split-second I had to shoot, I knew he had the best rack by far.

My handloaded Nosler 125-grain bullet flew 300 yards, ripped into the buck's heart-lung area, and blew up. He stumbled, hit the ground, and lay still.

When I examined the antlers — six unbelievably massive tines on the right side and five on the left — I knew I had killed the finest trophy buck I'd ever seen, but I had no idea that he was the best typical mule deer ever taken. The enormous body of the deer concerned me most at the moment.

Normally we can drive a vehicle close to our kills and then drag the deer out to the 4WD. But I was way back in rough country, and we couldn't approach with a vehicle. It would have been impossible for me to drag that deer very far by myself.

I decided to hike out to the Jeep and drive back to camp for help. Since Robbie and Bruce had already killed their bucks, the odds were they would be in camp. They were.

We went back to my deer, dressed and quartered it, and packed the quarters and the head out to the vehicle. When we returned to camp we found Jack waiting for us. He needed some help with a heavy-antlered five-pointer he'd killed with his .270 Weatherby Magnum. By the time we got that buck out, the day and the hunt were finished.

When I got home I took my buck's head and cape to taxidermist Ed Schlier in San Antonio for mounting. He's an official measurer for the Boone and Crockett Club, so we rough-scored the green antlers. Our preliminary figures indicated my buck would be among the top 10 listed in the typical-mule-deer category. That was exhilarating, but I didn't think much more about it till one night several months later when my phone rang at 1 a.m.

"Doug," Ed blurted out, "I think your buck may be the best typical mule deer ever taken. I scored the antlers this evening, and I couldn't believe it when I came up with a total score of two-hundred twenty-six! That's nine better than the previous world-record typical mule deer. I've been double-checking my figures for hours, but they always come out the same. If they hold up with Boone and Crockett officials, you've got a new world record. I figured that news was worth waking you up."

It sure was, but it was just the beginning.

The North American Big Game Award Program — jointly sponsored by the Boone and Crockett Club and National Rifle Association — requires that any big-game trophy likely to win an award must be rescored by a panel of judges. Accordingly, I sent the mounted head off to the program headquarters in Washington, DC.

In February 1974 the program coordinator phoned me and invited me to attend the Fifteenth North American Big Game Awards meeting on March 24 in Atlanta, Georgia. I guessed my buck had proven good enough to win some kind of award, but I was too busy to go to Atlanta.

That was my position till I received several more calls from other program officials. They told me that if I missed the awards meeting, I would very much regret it later, so I scraped together some cash, cancelled several appointments, and flew to Atlanta.

At the banquet I was presented with the award for the best typical mule deer taken during the most recent three-year award period. I also received official recognition for taking a new world record. In addition I won the Sagamore Hill Award, which is given only to hunters whose outstanding trophies are of great distinction. This award is the highest given by the Boone and Crockett Club. Only one may be given during any big-game-award period, and only 10 have been presented during the club's history.

I was stunned. When I think about it, even today, I'm still stunned.

Twist's Last Morning

David Michael Duffey

October 1976

Dave Duffey became OUTDOOR LIFE's dog editor in July 1959. A Wisconsin native, Duffey was graduated from Lawrence College in Appleton, where he took a course in genetics and heredity to prepare himself for dog breeding and training. He has been reporter and columnist for the Appleton *Post-Crescent*, the Milwaukee *Sentinel,* and the Green Bay *Press-Gazette*. He holds the first dog-training permit issued to a Wisconsin resident. He has written five books on bird hunting, hunting dogs and their training, and has been a warden and guide. He has entered and placed dogs in AKC retriever trials, has judged such events and gunned in pointing dog trials, and has managed both commercial and private game farms in Wisconsin.

There is a bad side to owning, training, and breeding good gundogs. None live forever, and Seairup Twist was no exception, much as I wish it could have been otherwise.

The bare essentials about this white-and-black Pointer bitch are that she was whelped March 28, 1963, by Seairup's Tyson Ariel out of Seair Nell. I found her dead and stiff in her kennel compartment on the bitter minus-18° morning of January 8, 1976, just two hours before I sat down to write these words. She was with me for nearly 13 of the almost 17 years I've been writing OUTDOOR LIFE's Hunting Dogs department.

I first laid eyes on Twist (named for a then-popular dance) in September 1963 when Don Johnson, a Dousman, Wisconsin, real-estate man and bird-dog fancier, showed me a litter of Pointer pups. Johnson let the pack out of their pen to romp across the fields. As the 5½-month-old youngsters shagged stink birds, Johnson said, "Would you want to see anything prettier? I'd like you to take that sturdy liver male home with you. These pups are a double-cross back to Seairup, Dr. George Oehler's champion, and that pup is the image of his both-sides granddaddy."

But my eye was taken by a lithe, easy-moving bitch of good size. She was already exhibiting the smooth gait that would be a pleasure to watch when she'd flow across open country, flying to what she quickly learned were birdy objectives. I told Johnson how she attracted me, and his response was generous: "Hell! Take 'em *both* home. I got more here than I'll ever use or get rid of."

So I brought home not one but two well-bred pups, neither of which I really needed. I wound up keeping Twist and trading off the male pointer.

Throughout Twist's lifetime, when she was shot over she went with her birds. I never broke her steady to shot. As a rule, Pointers need all the edge they can get in reaching downed birds if they are to complete retrieves, and few dogs that are shot over a lot retain their training-acquired steadiness unless their masters are sticklers for form. She was not perfect, not a super-dog. But her off days were few and far between. She required no formal, by-rote training in any aspect of her work. She found, picked up, and brought back the first bird of every species she encountered. She had heart and endurance enough to shrug off injury in the field.

Twist was one of those rare pointing dogs that can pin a ruffed grouse and keep it there until the man shooting over them moves up to within gun range to flush, eliminating the need to poke-shoot at a bumped or wild-flushing bird. She also became an expert on woodcock.

Grouse and woodcock make up the bulk of the hunting I do in Wisconsin, but Twist was to do the job on southern Illinois and Missouri bobwhites, Saskatchewan sharptails and Hungarian partridge, Montana sage chickens and sharptails, and Nebraska prairie chickens. And when a pointing dog was called for, she helped fill the bag on released pheasants, chukars, and quail at shooting preserves.

Her last quail hunt came in her 11th season. Melting snow was on the ground in Missouri. Late in the day, after we had busted up a covey, she came down hard on point in a pasture — a highly unlikely spot for a quail. No one else would walk in to honor her "find." But I did. Old Twist never lied to me, and the intensity of her point gave off sparks reminiscent of her glory days. I stomped a tight-sitting bob out of the wet grass, and I am glad now that I did not miss that tough shot. It was Twist's last quail.

When we headed in that night, she walked alongside me, wet and shaking, pacing as a fatigued dog does, with head and tail low.

But in the following fall she seemed to be rejuvenated. Within the limits age and aches impose, she danced and pranced when let out of the kennel, and she even managed to struggle up into the back of the van. I had not the heart to leave her at home.

However, I was sad and apprehensive. Like terminal-cancer patients, old dogs seem to shed the lethargy and pain of years shortly before the end comes. It is a deceptive thing, a gloomy prospect.

As snow and cold closed in, Twist became more reclusive, staying curled in the straw of her kennel box, whining softly and often howling, and only sampling the food that was always available.

Then this morning dawned. Twist's life ended sometime between the late-afternoon feeding and watering and the morning exercise, clean-up, and watering — probably in that chill just before dawn.

A dog who never had to be carried out of the field was cradled in my arms as I carried her out of the kennel.

Many men dream themselves fortunate to have found and enjoyed one good bird dog in their hunting lifetimes. Because of my interests and work, I have had fine gundogs before Twist and I look forward to enjoying others after her passing. But on this, the day of her death, I know she will always be one to remember. Wherever she is, may the autumn sun melt the frost early, the birds hold tight under her points, and the man she is hunting for show his appreciation by shooting well.

The Leap

Jerry Gibbs

November 1977

Gerald M. Gibbs was a schoolteacher who became the Jerry Gibbs OUTDOOR LIFE
readers have known, since his first story appeared in May 1973, as fishing editor
succeeding the late Joe Brooks. Gibbs, a graduate of Fairleigh Dickinson University,
taught for a year at Sussex (New Jersey) High School before entering the magazine
field. At the time of his appointment, Gibbs was co-editor of *True's Fishing Yearbook*
and assistant outdoor editor of *True Magazine*. Previously he had headed the Outdoor
Group of magazines at Davis Publications. He is both a writer and a photographer and
his many fishing and hunting stories have appeared in outdoor and travel-adventure
magazines nationally. He served for three years in the U.S. Navy. He lives in Vermont.

He's coming up! The fish might be a salmon, a bass, a tarpon, or a trout. It doesn't
matter. The emotion is the same.

You can see your line stretching straight, and rising. You can feel the way the fish is
moving, and you know the explosion will occur in moments. When he's in the air your
eyes will focus on his head — the gill covers spread wide, mouth open — and you will look
frantically for your fly lure while the rest of the fish's body locks into view. He will do
impossible things in a thrashing blur, and all the time you are hoping, pleading, praying
that the hook will hold, you will marvel at his jumps and his total commitment to gaining
his freedom.

To me, the leap of a gamefish is the most thrilling thing in all sportfishing. The strike is
electrifying, yes, but the leap gives a fisherman wings.

At 5 o'clock one afternoon I was with two veteran anglers who had fished the world's
finest waters. It had been a long, hard day of tagging sharks off Long Island's Montauk
Point. We were weary, and our ribs and guts were sore from being hammered by rod
butts. We were ready to quit when a triple hookup rattled our reels. The man who had on
what seemed to be the largest shark coasted, applying no pressure, while we brought in
the two smaller ones — a dusky and a blue — and speared home the spaghetti tags and
clipped the wire leaders. Then we started on the big one. The moment the shark felt
pressure he went wild. There was a short spurt and a sudden explosion as 400 pounds of
mako came up. Because nothing had disturbed him he had stayed near the boat, and he
went up and up to what seemed to be 30 feet but which probably was closer to 15. At the
top of his leap he made the mako's typical head-over-tail flip, crashed flat back in, and
was up and out five times before we could go to work on him.

Why do some fish jump like this while others fight their battles deep below the
surface? Opinions differ widely, and no one knows for sure. But some key elements
appear to be highly influential in determining whether a fish leaps or not. One of them is
the biological makeup of the fish.

Take the bluegill and the largemouth bass, for example. Both are of the sunfish family,
but only the largemouth is a significant jumper. To understand why, examine the tail of
each. The largemouth's tail is proportionately larger than the bluegill's and its muscu-
lature is more highly developed. The bluegill is a proportionately deeper fish than the
largemouth, and it uses its wide side in resisting capture, just as a deep-bodied permit does.

Consider the tail shapes and sizes of the great salmonid jumpers. They are broad,
chisel-shaped appendages that enable salmon and trout to release sudden spurts of power

for their leaps. The tails of midwater predators such as tunas, jacks, and bluefish, on the other hand, are designed more for speed. The tuna's tail is unique in that it is not flexible. It is designed for extremely high sustained speed. To use it, the tuna vibrates it at unbelievable speed. As a result, the tuna is a bulldog. When you have finished with one you know it in your back, your arms and legs, and every fiber of your body. But the tuna does not jump. The tarpon does.

It is the tarpon's magnificent leaping capability that makes anglers devote lifetimes to pursuing him. The tarpon doesn't have the wedge-shaped tail of the trout or salmon. It is somewhat forked, but it is also flexible. Besides body configuration, tarpon are used to coming up to the surface. The silver king possesses a unique primitive lung arrangement that permits him to gulp air as he rolls. The air is passed from throat to swim bladder through a tubelike organ. Tarpon leap most spectacularly in shallow water, where they are traditionally sought. When hooked in deeper water, some tarpon jump only once or not at all, preferring to slug it out below the surface.

Nature has equipped northern pike and muskellunge with long, snakelike bodies that undulate through water. They lack the ability to make the sudden snaps that shoot more torpedo-shaped fish into the air. Pike and muskies often make true jumps when hooked on light tackle; otherwise they thrash and twist on the surface rather than jump entirely clear of it. Young northerns and muskellunge are more likely to jump than older ones, and that is true of many species.

It is easy to understand why a hooked fish leaps. He is seeking escape from the unyielding pressure that holds him captive. Airborne, his frantic thrashings are much more likely to expel the hook than the same movements underwater. Sailfish, for example, fish of the boundless high seas, panic at constraint and zoom through the surface with awesome violence, their swordlike bills slashing frantically.

But fish also jump when totally unrestrained. The salmons and some trout learn early to jump away from their enemies. Salmon must leap over obstacles, such as falls, en route to spawning grounds. An Atlantic salmon, once he has returned to the stream of his birth, will hold for days or weeks in lies before spawning. Sometimes, in these gentler currents, he will jump free. He is not eating, not fighting, not escaping from anything, so why should he leap? The theories are endless. Perhaps a sea-run fish in prime condition, a fish used to the freedom of the sea, may feel cramped and become restless in a constraining river. He leaps.

No one who has caught one questions an Atlantic salmon's ability to leap when hooked on a fly. What is strange is his steadfast refusal to jump when hooked on a spoon or spinner. Such metal lures don't inhibit trout, however.

One summer when I was fishing a fast run in Montana's Jefferson River, I was sure I had struck into a hard-fighting rainbow trout. A bright flash and glint of airborne silver made me shout in surprise, for the river was best known for its big brown trout. The fish went down, then shot through the surface again. There was deep water to my right and left, and I couldn't move to a better position to fight the fish. The fight slowly brought him closer, and for the first time I saw that it was a good-size brown trout.

I've taken browns from time to time that have given as fine an aerial performance as any rainbow. Yet normally brown trout — especially the larger ones — are deep fighters inclined to foul a fine leader in tangled underwater jungles. What makes some of them jump? I think it has something to do with water quality — both pH factor and swiftness of current. Plenty of oxygen in the water seems to make all fish far more active than they are otherwise.

Though I have kept no records, I am quite sure that smallmouth bass hard-muscled from bucking swift currents are better jumpers than the same species that inhabit marginal lake water. They fight harder, and they take advantage of current. You can't just follow them as you wish if you are wading deep, and sometimes it seems as if they are diabolically aware of it.

And so it may be said that the ecological niche filled by a fish has something to do with its ability as a jumper. I have caught rainbow trout that were feeding heavily during a dense flight of mayflies. Most of these trout catapulted into the air after they snapped my flies. Most of the brown trout that jumped for me had also been feeding at the surface. But trout used to feeding on minnows or other bottom life usually have responded best to deep-swimming streamers. They do most of their fighting below the surface. So do many other gamefish that rarely, if ever, jump — walleyes, perch, catfish, bonefish, flounder, shellcrackers, and permit.

The first time I fished for Arctic char I was prepared for anything. I had heard that these fish jump as spectacularly as Atlantic salmon. In northern Quebec, I balanced on a midstream rock casting a white curly-tail jig upcurrent. The fish that hit did so in a fiery flash in shallow, clear water. Throbbing strongly, it fought an upcurrent battle, then suddenly turned and ran downstream. There was no way I could check him with the four-pound-test line I was using. I would like to tell you how, silhouetted against the setting sun, he smashed through the surface. But he didn't. Quite some time later, water in my boots, shins barked from jumping boulders, I beached a lovely red Arctic that had fought like a charging rhino but had not jumped. Not once.

All right, I thought. Char are good, but they're not Atlantics. But the next day I caught silver char, far from the sea yet still without redness that heralds the approaching spawn. They jumped. They leaped in the fast water, churned through foamy runs, and leaped again. They were wonderful.

Closeness to the time of spawning seems to affect the jumping impulses of other fish too. Cutthroats, cohos, even chinook will jump just before or soon after entering many West Coast rivers on late-season spawning runs. Then they stop jumping. The closer to spawning time it is the less these fish break the surface. Even late-running steelhead or Atlantic salmon may not give quite the spectacular leaping fight that they do when running in summer. And in very early spring when the water temperature is in the low 40's, steelhead will not leap the way they do later.

What makes the whole picture even more confusing is fish that jump only sometimes. When I first started to fool around with snook in the backwaters around mangrove islands near the Everglades, I knew several things about the species. I knew what I could catch them on sometimes, that they were good to eat, and that they jumped pretty well before cutting off my lines. Then a friend took me to some channels in more open water. He told me that snook don't jump. Right away my faith was shattered. Probably there weren't any snook in the place, I thought. But there were, and we caught them on small white bucktail jigs sweetened with live bait shrimp. The snook we hooked fought strongly and boiled on the surface, but my pal was right. They didn't jump.

Well, barracuda don't always jump either, and neither do the pikes and the rainbows. And how do you explain why Spanish mackerel may jump freely to feed or to escape from enemies yet refuse to go into the air when hooked. I can't, but I'm not worried about it. I know that some of the fish I hook will leap at least some of the time. What more could I ask?

Danger Stalks Their Jobs

Amos Burg and Ben East

April 1979

Amos Burg, an Alaska outdoor writer, photographer, and adventurer, revels in the outdoors, says Ben East, his co-author of this story of tragedy. He grew up in Oregon, but at sixteen signed on a tramp steamer for a long voyage to Japan and Europe. Back in the States, he traveled alone by canoe over the Lewis and Clark route, then down the Mississippi to New Orleans. He went back to school to study zoology and journalism. To sea again on a tanker to Alaska, where he filmed the caribou migrations, and with his partner paddled 2,000 miles down the Yukon. He made twenty-five films for the Encyclopaedia Britannica and a dozen more for the National Geographic Society. In 1954 he joined the newly formed Alaska Department of Fish and Game to set up a division of education and information, and still contributes to the department publication.

Hosea Sarber was one of the most diligent and effective game wardens the Alaska Territory had ever had. An ace woodsman and crack rifle shot, tireless, fearless, impartial, and persistent, he was as respected as any man in the territory. But only by the law-abiding. Violators of game and fish laws hated and feared him.

In 1948, after 13 years in the Petersburg area, Sarber was transferred to Ketchikan and promoted to assistant district agent for predator control in southeastern Alaska. Wolves were making murderous inroads in the Sitka blacktail deer population on a number of islands that shelter the Inside Passage there. Sarber's assignment was to reduce wolf numbers. He did the job so well that the deer began to thrive again.

But Hosea was also interested in wildlife protection. He continued to do enforcement work — and to make enemies.

In late July of 1952 he left Petersburg in the patrol boat Black Bear to check suspected commercial fishing violations at Kuiu Island. With him was an assistant, Doyle Cisne. He left Cisne with the boat in the Bay of Pillars and went on to Rowan Bay, several miles to the north, in an outboard-powered skiff. He did not come back. Searchers found the skiff on the beach. Sarber's gun and binoculars were in the boat but he was not. An intensive week-long search by boat, aircraft, and on foot failed to turn up any trace of him.

Three things could have happened. A bear could have made a surprise attack, killed him and dragged him off. But Hosea knew bears as well as any man in Alaska, and neither his superiors nor friends believed that had happened. He could have leaned over the side or stern of his skiff, perhaps to clear kelp from the propeller, suffered a heart attack, and fallen into the sea. But that theory was doubted by those who knew him. The most likely explanation seemed to be that the men he had gone to check on had shot him and buried or sunk his body.

That theory got support 26 years later when it was rumored that a prisoner at the Lemon Creek Correctional Facility at Juneau let the word out that he knew who had killed Sarber. The FBI entered the case and asked questions, but nothing came of the investigation.

The disappearance of Hosea Sarber remains one of the unsolved mysteries of the Alaska wilderness. So far as the record shows, he was the first man engaged in game-and-fish work in Alaska to die in the performance of his job. But he was far from the last.

In the 28 years since Sarber's empty skiff was found on that lonely beach, no fewer than 29 fish-and-wildlife researchers or protection officers have lost their lives in accidents connected with their jobs. Many more, probably at least twice as many, have missed death by little more than the thickness of a hair.

There are no statistics on which to base a factual comparison, but that appalling record makes it seem likely that the men who study Alaska's fish and wildlife or enforce the laws that protect those resources hold the most dangerous jobs in the state.

The tragedies that have claimed or come close to claiming the lives of Alaska's fish-and-game men fall into four basic categories: Aircraft crashes; drowning, often but not always as a result of a swamped boat; exposure to severe weather or cold water, and bear attacks, suspected more often than proved. Finally, there are those cases like that of Hosea Sarber where the cause of death cannot be learned — cases that will remain unanswered riddles.

The most shocking plane accident occurred in September of 1954, in connection with a fish-and-wildlife-service aerial stream survey on Admiralty Island. Four fishery workers, a secretary, and a pilot were conducting the survey, in the King Salmon Bay area, flying a two-engine Grumman Goose. Because the 42-year-old pilot, Robert Meek, was among those who died, the precise cause of the crash was never learned. But experienced Alaska flyers believed that the plane was flying low over dense forest when both engines failed.

The crash happened in late afternoon. The Grumman plowed headlong into the trees, tearing off an engine and a wing, and wreckage was scattered for more than 200 yards.

Three of the four fisheries men, George Kelez, Dick Shuman and Larry Kolhoen, and secretary Patte Bedwell died instantly. They ranged in age from 25 to 45. The pilot suffered head, chest, and leg injuries and died later that night.

By what those who saw the wreckage called a miracle, the sixth man survived, despite broken ribs, deep body and head gashes, and severe hip damage. He was Gus Helsinger, a fisheries biologist.

Despite his condition, Helsinger wrapped the pilot in a sleeping bag, moved him under a wing of the aircraft and then began an agonizing trip, half walk, half crawl, through thick timber to the beach.

There fate came to his aid. C. L. Anderson, director of the Alaska Department of Fisheries and Game, was on a flight from Sitka to Juneau with a veteran bush pilot. Helsinger heard the small plane coming, whipped off his shirt, and waved it from the open beach. He was seen and picked up.

The search party that was sent out before dark that night could not locate the wreck. The men camped a few miles away, and hope for the life of Meek burned dimly through the night. But when the searchers finally found the Grumman, after daylight, they found five dead persons with it.

In July of 1970 James Erickson, a 27-year-old senior Dall-sheep investigator, and Gerald Fisher, an experienced pilot of the U.S. Fish and Wildlife Service, were making a sheep survey in a remote area of the rugged Brooks Range.

Aerial counts of mountain game are always risky, for the pilot has to fly close to the ground and slowly, often over mountain barriers 4,000 to 5,000 feet high. Veteran researchers rarely undertake more than 3½ hours a day of this grueling work, sometimes because that is all the good light they have, sometimes because both pilot and observer are too tired to continue.

Erickson and Fisher were flying in Tatuk Creek Canyon, a cleft in the mountains wide enough to turn their Super Cub in, but there were sheer walls on either side and a ridge at the head that rose too high and steeply for the Cub to climb over.

Fisher undertook a turn and the little aircraft went into a stall spin, plummeted to the ground, and exploded in flames. The pilot and observer died instantly.

Over the years, other pilots have died in airplane crashes. Lee Larson, Lester Barozza, Robert Lawler, Harold Wright and Jonathon Ward, for example, died making aerial salmon counts, planting fish, and inspecting nets. Spencer Linderman was killed in an air crash while on a mountain goat survey at Cherno Glacier in 1975, and it was an aerial caribou survey that claimed the lives of two conservation officers, Leroy Bohuslov and Gary Wohfeil, in the Alaska Range in March of 1965.

So runs the record of aircraft mishaps in the roadless areas of Alaska. Unfortunately, the record of other mishaps is equally grim.

Paul Kissner, a 22-year-old fish-and-game technician, did not die from the mauling a brown bear gave him on Admiralty Island in July of 1967, but he spent three weeks in the hospital, a year in out-patient therapy, and was left with a stiff leg and nightmare memories he will carry to his grave.

Kissner and Bruce Millenback, a fellow researcher, were surveying Dolly Varden streams in the Hood Bay area. They were hiking across the side of a steep mountain, through thick tangles of undergrowth. Hoping to find a better route, Kissner slipped out of his pack and laid it on the ground. In it was their only firearm, a .44 Magnum handgun. The brown bears of Admiralty were not yet on the salmon streams, so the men had left their rifles in camp.

While Millenback waited with the pack, Kissner pulled himself up a vertical cliff by clutching vines growing in the crevices and then fought his way into thick alders. He had gone about 100 yards when he heard, just ahead, a savage noise, like the grunting of an angry hog. The young technician realized he was almost face to face with a brown bear.

He jumped behind the alder clump and yelled for his partner to fire the .44 in hope of scaring the bear off. Millenback, however, did not hear his partner's shouts.

The bear came in a savage rush. Kissner could not see it in the brush, but he could keep track of it by the noise it made as it crashed through. It broke out of the clump he was hiding behind, grabbed him by a thigh and shook him like a terrier shaking a rat. When it dropped him he rolled backward and plunged over a 20-foot cliff. It was his only hope of escape.

He landed face down on a narrow ledge, and to his horror the bear tumbled after him and grabbed him again, this time in the buttocks.

Up to now the man had felt no pain. The shock that often goes with an attack by a big carnivore apparently had left him numb. But the bear's teeth in his buttocks hurt like blazes, and when it also bit deep under his arms and in his back — he was holding his hands over his face to protect his head and throat — the pain became excruciating.

What Kissner did next he knew might mean death, but it was his only hope. He rolled off the ledge and plunged down an almost verticle avalanche chute for 300 feet, bumping from one rock to the next. At the end he shot into space and dropped 20 feet down. Deep snow at the bottom of the cliff cushioned his fall.

But again to his horror, the bear came tumbling after him head over paws and crashed into the snow with its muzzle almost touching him.

Apparently the brownie did not like what had happened. He sat up, looking dazed, shook his head as if to clear it, got to his feet, and walked into the brush without looking at Kissner.

Kissner wrapped his T-shirt around his thigh, which was bleeding badly, and then tightened his belt around the upper leg. He tried to yell for Millenback, but was too weak to make more than a low mumble of sound. It took his partner 20 minutes to find him.

Millenback packed Kissner's right leg in snow, stuck sticks in the snow to keep the injured man from rolling over the cliff beside him, and started a fast five-mile hike to the sportfish station on the shore of Admiralty for help. He made it in time with one minute to spare. The radiophone in the fish-and-game protection office in Juneau shut down at 5 o'clock. It was 4:59 when Millenback's call came through. A helicopter carrying Dr. Henry Akiyama was airborne and on the way in minutes.

On his snow-covered ledge Paul Kissner was waiting in agonized fear that the bear would return. He had made up his mind that if that happened, he would push himself off the ledge and risk a second fall of 300 feet to avoid being mauled to death. But the bear did not return.

The helicopter landed a half mile from him and two rescuers hiked in and lashed him on a stretcher. Then the chopper flew in, its blades barely clearing the cliff where he lay, lifted him, and raced for the hospital at Juneau. The next summer Kissner was back on the trails of Admiralty, going about his job as usual.

Of the unexplained deaths, the most disastrous for the U.S. Fish and Wildlife Service occurred in the Brooks Range.

Clarence Rhode had worked for the service for 23 years, since he was 22. Working up through the ranks, he was named regional director in 1948. Widely known and highly respected as a fish-and-wildlife administrator, not only in Alaska but in conservation circles throughout the country, he took an active hand in establishing the Arctic National Wildlife Range.

On August 20, 1958, Rhode took off from the Fairbanks airport in a Grumman Goose with his son Jack and wildlife agent Stanley Fredericksen for a flight into the Brooks Range to survey game and cache a supply of fuel for a light plane that had been assigned to curb illegal hunting in that area.

The last radio message from the Grumman came at 4:25 that afternoon. The plane was then on Chandalar Lake. In midafternoon a day later it was seen heading west over the lake. It faded to a distant speck in the sky — and vanished forever from human sight.

To this day, more than 20 years later, what happened to the men remains unknown.

An entirely different kind of arctic mishap cost marine mammal biologist John Burns and his Eskimo helper, Tony Koezuma, a five-day ordeal on the ice of Bering Sea and came very close to claiming their lives.

Engaged in marine mammal research and based at Nome, where Koezuma had lived for eight years since moving there with other King Island Eskimos, the two men readied their skin kayaks on the morning of Saturday, November 28, 1964, for a one-day research hunt for seals.

The temperature was 18 below and both men were dressed for the cold. Each carried a rifle, and the kayaks carried two small sleds. For a noon snack the two hunters had sandwiches and a thermos of coffee.

The morning was clear and completely windless, but Bering Sea winds are tricky in November. Burns and Koezuma crossed a half-mile open lead, landed on solid ice on the far side, and started their hunt. By 10 o'clock in the morning the wind was blowing 40 knots out of the north, and the lead had widened to three miles. Because of broken ice, they could not recross in the kayaks to get back to the beach.

They lashed the skin boats together and lay down in them to get what sleep they could. The boats were resting on rubbery ice, bobbing up and down with the seas that rolled under them. At daybreak the wind was gusting to 60 knots.

The ice was moving offshore now, and before the day was over the men were beyond sight of land. The sandwiches and coffee were gone and the men had nothing to eat on Sunday or Monday.

The ice was drifting toward the west, so the two walked steadily east to maintain their position relative to the shore, dragging their kayaks on the small sleds. On Monday they walked for 20 hours, rested for four hours, and began another 20 hours of trudging over the endless ice.

The air search that had been underway since Sunday, covering an area of 16,000 square miles, paid off Wednesday. The pilot of a light plane spotted two black specks moving across the ice and radioed for a helicopter. Burns and Koezuma were rescued.

Alaska's fish-and-game men have had too many close calls to keep track of, but a few of the stories are worth relating. Weighing, measuring, and tagging polar bears off Barrow in March of 1969, biologist Jack Lentfer overtook a sow and dropped her with a tranquilizing drug from a dart gun. But when he walked up to her, she rolled to her feet and came for him. The dart had frozen and she was far from immobilized. She had lain down only because she was tired from the long chase by helicopter.

Lentfer made tracks for the chopper, but when he looked back he saw he was losing ground fast. His partner, Lee Miller, was waiting at the aircraft with a .338 Winchester and Lentfer yelled for him to use it. Miller put a warning shot into the ice but had to kill the bear with a second when she kept coming.

Obviously, being a fish-and-wildlife researcher, or a protection officer, in Alaska is not the same as holding such a job in any of the other 49 states.

A number of years ago, shortly after Alaska gained statehood, one of the authors of this story was getting together material for a report on the consequences of political interference in game-and-fish affairs. A deeply concerned employee of the fish-and-game department who had supplied inside information in confidence had this to say of the men in the ranks with whom he worked:

"With very few exceptions they are able, dedicated, and hard working. They are so absorbed in their jobs that you'd have to hold their heads under water for 10 minutes before they'd realize they were wet."

Nobody has paid a more richly deserved tribute to the fish-and-wildlife men of Alaska.

Alaska can be proud of them and the rest of the country owes them its gratitude.

Doggone!

Joel M. Vance

April 1979

Joel Vance, forty-eight, is a graduate of the University of Missouri School of Journalism and a veteran of thirteen years on daily newspapers. He won the Excellence in Craft Award of the Outdoor Writers Association of America in 1980 and has been on the board of directors of the OWAA. He has twice won awards contests for his articles for the *Missouri Conservationist*. He is the author of the Outdoor Life/Dutton *Upland Bird Hunting* and of a collection of humorous short stories, *Grandma and The Buck Deer*, published by Winchester Press. This story, he says, reflects his wry love of the bird dog, his two Brittanies in particular. He and Marty, his wife of twenty-seven years, have five children. They own forty acres near Jefferson City, with a cabin and a small lake — and no telephone.

Fine sporting art is prone to show feathery-tailed bird dogs staunch on apprehensive game-birds. Tweedy gentlemen cradling elegant double-barreled shotguns approach from the background.

Thus the artist captures the quintessential thrill of the bird hunt. He has, you would conclude, summed it all up in his frozen tableau.

Not quite, I hasten to interject. A victim, as it were, of 25 years of bird hunting, I maintain there are many memorable moments of the hunt that somehow have been overlooked by those who wield pig bristle and carving knives.

When have you seen a painting of a pointer eating his master's lunch just before his master trudges into view as hungry as a junkyard rat? Who has captured the rapture of a setter rolling in a fresh cowflop? What artist portrays a stylish Brittany relieving himself on the shell vest of his master's former best friend? Who details the exquisite style of a German shorthair going through a short-tempered farmer's chickenyard like a canine mowing machine?

Fess up — you've never seen any art like that. Whoever modeled for the Mona Lisa might have had skin that looked like an artillery impact area, but that's not the way she came out on canvas.

But if you've bird hunted at all, you have seen the dark side of the dog, the side not seen on calendars.

Someone should write about the egg-suckers of the world, the beasts for whom the term "underdog" was coined. Sometimes the dog who does graceless things is an excellent hunter, but often he is a squarehead who couldn't smell a cock pheasant if it were busy ripping off the end of his nose. Underdogs. Who sticks up for a hunting dog whose most memorable moment was when he vomited on the back seat of his owner's new Blazer?

Well, I have no intention of defending dogs whose names are Lucky or Ace but should be Trouble or Stupid. But I can't help feeling sympathy, if not downright affection, for dogs that go around with little rain clouds over their dense skulls.

Campfire talk often turns to the triumphs of long-past dogs, but those tales of glory quickly fade — "my dog can outdo your dog" stories get boring fast. The tales that grip the crowd, that elicit hearty laughter and inspire counter-tales are those that concern not the gilt-edged pointers and retrievers of yesteryear but the time your hunting buddy's dog ate all of the day's bag of birds.

Tell one such story in a group of hunters and you'll hear half a hundred more. Everyone knows someone who has a retriever that insists on eating the first duck of the day and then will perform flawlessly the rest of the time.

A friend of mine had a retriever that never ate ducks, but ate everything else, including long-dead animals and, once, a bloated carp. It was a disgusting trait on the face of it, made even more so when the dog invariably threw up the carrion at some point on the long road home.

Regurgitation is a fairly common theme. Sad to report, my own Brittany, a paragon of dogdom whose faults, if any, are sins of omission rather than commission, who is a candidate for dog sainthood, who huddles close to me in the long, cold nights in a tiny tent not because he is cold but because he loves me and wishes me to be warm, on his very first auto trip threw up partially-digested foodstuff in such quantities that there had to be more of it than there was dog.

In case it has escaped your notice, there are two ends to a dog. I know a man who left his dog in his car overnight while he slept in a motel room and dreamed of a fine hunt-to-be. The dog fell victim to Montezuma's Revenge, virulently so, and when you consider that a bird dog is a bottomless gut, able to create as much waste as a troop of circus elephants, you can imagine what the car looked like in the grim, gray light of morn.

The dog-left-in-the-car figures in many a tale of canine catastrophe. Retrievers are eminently sensible dogs, almost human in intelligence (though that may not be any commendation), but the best of them have their erratic days.

I have a friend (large and short-tempered, so he will remain nameless) who left his dog in the car. Now, dogs are prey to nearly every human foible, but frustration is the one that nearly always leads to disaster. The frustrated dog is a bomb with the fuse lit. This one took out his aggravation on the inside of his master's automobile. He turned the headliner into confetti, chopped the seat cushions into material suitable for a high jump pit, and, frosting on the cake, somehow opened an entire case of shotgun shells and scattered them through the wreckage.

The two Brittanies I have had shared an inexplicable passion for shredding expensive foam sleeping pads. One pad belonged to an acquaintance who, unreasonably, expected me to explain why my dog would do such an idiotic thing.

No one understands why dogs do ridiculous things. The hunter who was horrified when his dog ate the inside of his car was entranced when a bird dog owned by a quail-hunting partner caught a goat.

The two men were hunting when a peculiar sound caught their ear. It resembled a mewling child, in considerable distress.

Apparently it was something that had happened before, for the dog's owner suddenly cried, "I know what that is!" and sprinted through the cedars and broom sedge. When my friend puffed uphill to the scene, he found a tethered, bleating, gnawed-on-goat rolling its eyes wildly . . . and his companion taking a wild swing at the dog with an exquisite Model 21 double barrel.

The dog ducked and the gun hit a rock and flew into pieces. "You wouldn't believe what he did to his Model 21!, and he could have shot himself in the belly with both barrels!" my friend said, awestruck. The trigger guard was twisted, the stock splintered, and the gun wouldn't go back together. Nor did it ever shoot accurately again.

The dog, slightly chastened, hunted only quail the rest of the day.

Moving tributes have been written to dogs, encomiums that make you wonder how members of the same species so praised can defile bedspreads, chase rabbits, bust covies, and dig holes in the neighbor's lawn big enough to hide Mount Rushmore.

Sen. George Vest, the late Missouri lawyer, eclipsed Patrick Henry, William Jennings Bryan, and Howard Cosell when he delivered a eulogy — in court — for a hound named Drum. Vest represented Drum's owner, who was seeking damages from a fellow who had succumbed to the temptation that often plagues those carrying guns when a dog misbehaves. The fellow had shot poor old Drum, sending him to that great sheep pasture in the sky, for Drum's alleged trespass was an excessive predilection for chewing ewes.

Vest talked of the nobility of the dog, his loyalty and faithfulness unto the death of his master, and brought forth tears — as well as a judgement for damages — from the jury. There now is a stone dog in Warrensburg, Missouri, where Drum was immortalized, and that staunch statue has just about the same skull configuration as that of a dog, now defunct, who belonged to a quail-hunting buddy of mine.

"Old Tramp is dead," my friend mourned. "I think I'll have his shock collar preserved in plastic."

The shock collar is a dog trainer's equivalent to human electroshock therapy. It is an electronic leash that enables the trainer to jolt bad manners out of a misbehaving dog at a distance the dog didn't believe possible. The psychological shock of knowing how far is far enough to escape punishment is supposed to cure a dog of delinquency. But almost every dog learns that he only gets the jugular jolt if the collar is on and, if it isn't he can chase rabbits, bust coveys, play deaf, and do all the things he enjoys and his owner doesn't.

So the dog owner, who already has laid out enough cash to finance the takeover of a medium-size Latin American country, now has to buy a dummy collar so the dog won't know when he's wearing the hot one.

There are people who train dogs and there are people who think they train dogs. The dog of a friend of mine was an unruly sort, prone to pouncing on quail coveys like a great roan leopard just as his master got not quite within gunshot (either of the quail or the dog).

A shock collar was the last resort. The proverbial 2x4 had not made a dent, except in the wood. My friend fitted a shock collar to his Irish companion and they set forth to do battle with small gallinaceous birds.

The dog quested masterfully, finally locking on a point so classic it could have been painted by Lynn Bogue Hunt. My acquaintance hit the go-button and jolted that dog out of a canine reverie as deep as hypnosis. The dog yipped, surged forward, and flushed a 20-bird covey into the middle of next week. "Great Jeezley!" shouted a fellow hunter. "Why did you do that?"

"Well," muttered my embarrassed friend, who too often had been the butt of bad dog jokes, "he looked like he was gonna break point...."

The common barnyard chicken sprints noisily through many a bird-dog story, victim of feather shock, reason for hunter mortification and dog disgrace. If you haven't owned a dog that got seriously involved with a chicken, you know someone who has. Someone who never will forget the dark moment. Because you won't let him.

An outdoor writer I know, possessed by a very large but gentle-mouthed black Lab, watched in humiliation as the dog chased down a fleeing chicken in front of the farmer and proudly bore it back to his owner. Seeking to deliver some sort of esoteric object lesson, my friend grabbed the ruffled chicken from his dog's mouth and clubbed the dog with it... and killed the chicken.

"Whyncha come back next week and bring your dog," the farmer said laconically. "We was fixin' to butcher chickens then anyway."

The ultimate chicken joke involved the late Don Wooldridge, a superb wildlife photographer, not quite as adept at dog discipline.

Don had an immense Lab named Mike, usually a paragon of good dog behavior — except during thunderstorms when he tended to rip doors off their hinges as he tried to find a hiding place.

Wooldridge and Jim Keefe decided to do a bit of hunting and cruised the countryside looking for a likely spot. Finally they spied a nice family farm and stopped to ask permission. Luckily, there was no one home to witness what followed.

"It had been raining," Keefe recalls. "The instant Don opened the car door, Mike surged out, charged into the barnyard, and began grabbing chickens."

Poultry panic ensued. Feathers filled the air like snow in a Montana nor'wester. Wooldridge chased down his burly black dog, grabbed the animal, and slipped in the muck of the barnyard. It was a muck composed of rainwater and all the other substances that make a soggy barnyard no place to lie down.

The dog and the man rolled over and over in the slime and then a group of curious cows, attracted by the commotion, sloshed over and began butting the wrestlers. Wooldridge cried out to Keefe for help and Keefe did the only thing possible under the circumstances. He leaned against the car and laughed until his stomach hurt.

Although it was chickens and not barnyard essence that attracted Mike, there is something about a cowpie that exerts irresistible charm on a dog. To a bird dog, a cowpie is a Kohinoor diamond, a bovine bouquet absolutely shimmering with glorious fragrance. There is nothing quite so discouraging to a hunter as sending out a white dog and getting back a green one.

Poor Lucky or Happy cannot figure why, when he knows how lovely he smells, Daddy is getting all red in the face and saying Those Words to him.

However redolent cowpies are, they still have a hint of the sweet country about them, a certain acrid charm that reminds one of the family farm, Mom, and apple pies. Not so with carrion. Nothing about carrion evokes haymows, wood stoves, and girls named Cindy Belle. Not to the hunter.

But Dog, using that marvelous nose so bragged about by his owner in rural watering holes, can find something dead so far away he needs a bus ticket to get there and will lower his shoulder into it as eagerly as a National Football League linebacker blindsides a hapless quarterback.

Almost as inflammatory to dog sensibilities as old dead things are those things newly deceased. Of course, it is part of his heritage to seek out the fallen birds his master shoots.

But the wolf is never very far below the silky surface of the most souful-eyed Brittany. There lurks beneath the velvet hide of my loving Brit a ravening predator, ever ready to do battle with fellow dogs that challenge his right to possess steaming game guts.

Chip attacked a rather large setter named Jake in a South Dakota ravine when I rinsed prairie grouse blood off my hands in a tiny stream. Jake's only sin was being there when the scent of blood rose into the hot prairie wind. What followed was a re-enactment of King Kong vs. Godzilla.

You quickly learn not to reach into a dog fight. Many people you meet who have one hand have learned this lesson the hard way. I once broke up a fight between Chip and a bird dog (over guts) by pouring beer down the setter's nose. Apparently he had no taste for fine lager. This time the dogs' enthusiasm for mayhem cooled when they toppled into the pool and discovered they could not chew and breathe underwater.

So the hunting dog lollops his way through life, often giving his master occasion for rejoicing — quivering points, impossible retrieves, supernormal field skills — only to temper that joy with a trick so dumb it could have been pulled by a cocker spaniel.

Yon pointer, locked on a bird bevy so intently you couldn't disturb him with cannonfire, will hold the birds mesmerized until the hunter ambles up and leisurely doubles off the rise, and at that moment the hunter wouldn't take a million dollars for Ol' Rex.

But that same dog later on will antagonize a herd of grazing cattle and, as they galumph after him, seek refuge behind his fuddled master and both of them will scamper under a fence just ahead of 14,000 pounds of hoofed fury.

Ask any bird hunter what it is that draws him to the fields year after year and he'll fumble for words and finally stammer:

"Aw, gee, I don't know . . . gosh, it's, well, I guess . . . I guess I just like to see the dogs work!"

Uh-huh . . .

Deer Camp

John D. Randolph

October 1979

It was hard to decide whether to pick this story by Randolph, editor of *Fly Fisherman* and a lifelong whitetail deer hunter living in Vermont, or another one by him about a different kind of deer camp called "The Stump Sitters" (February 1979). Inspired by a couple of Wisconsin hunters, the group made it a rule its members had to stay on their stands at least ten hours a day, observing and studying whitetails in their natural habitat. The Stump Sitters now are an organization with more than 7,000 members, says Randolph, and are destroying some cherished myths about whitetails. They have things to say about deer behavior and hunting that have not been said before. A hard choice, but I have to stay with this one.

If someone were to ask me where I most want to be tomorrow, I would say deer camp. I wouldn't make that choice lightly or from inexperience, for I've had many special hideouts, and I've seen and felt many wonderful things. I've known sunlit spots in favorite rooms. I've heard doves coo softly as the sun rose and squalls scudded across far-off Caribbean islands. I've heard bull elk bugle across high valleys in the Rockies, and I've felt the pitch and heave of ships and boats when the sea was clean and free and spoke with a roar that made you feel small.

All this was fine — I wouldn't change it — but nothing ever felt or smelled so good as deer camp on the night before the hunt. Nothing brings me quite the same warm comfort as thoughts of hunts past or deer camps to come. Everyone needs a good spot, and every hunter has one at deer camp.

I can recall my first trip to deer camp. It was an important trip — although I couldn't know it at the time — for all the others would be judged by that one. The camp was a 100-year-old schoolhouse that sat on the north slope of a great mountain in western Massachusetts. It was the night before deer season, a time of tall imaginings and grand expectations for all schoolboys of the region.

We rode into camp that night by Jeep. To this day, I can remember the smell of the Jeep, packed with guns and wool hunting clothes and home-cooked food. We bucked over ledges, along abandoned dirt roads, and through mud holes. There was always the chance of mucking down to the axle. The trip was a grand adventure in the night, with the pot-of-gold camp at the end.

Warming the old building was the first order of business. Mice scurried in the cold dark as my father groped for matches in the cupboard. As soon as the kerosene lamps were lit, the camp became cheerful, and when the fireplace finally roared and snapped with hemlock and then oak, camp became home.

Everyone pitches in at deer camp, each man to his own talents. Why some men make better fire makers and others better cooks, I do not know. Each boy or veteran seems to find his own style and practice it without direction. There was venison that first night for all of us, and homemade breads and pies too. The venison sizzled and filled the camp with magic smells. We ate by the light of the fireplace, and the men told deer stories. I just listened by the fire, with the shadows of men and boys playing on the walls. Outside, a moon played across cold December hills. In bed, I listened as the embers died, and the old cast-iron stove cooled and snapped. I lay under an old buffalo robe, the legacy of bygone sleigh riders, and felt the cold creep into the schoolroom. I could not sleep but imagined great-racked bucks browsing through leafless hardwoods on the mountain.

Then suddenly my father was jogging my shoulder in the dark, and I heard a match scratch. Breakfast was in the making.

I will take deer-camp memories such as this, and a myriad of others, to camp with my son and my companions this season. And a million others will make their first-morning preparations, talk about their grand dreams, in a million places; it's all the same. Each deer-camp gang has favorite stories and favorite spots and a history of its own, but each is part of the great clan, kin to all others in deer country.

Last year I opened Pennsylvania's deer season at Camp Quicktime, and it was like going back to the old schoolhouse.

Like so many deer camps, Camp Quicktime began as a hunter's dream. It all started with a pitched tent in a clearing near Tioga Junction, Pennsylvania. The tent became a permanent structure, a boar's nest for deer hunters Bob Schumann of Karrsville, New Jersey; Eastern Airlines pilot Alan Schock of Mt. Bethel, Pennsylvania; Lyall "Bucky" Mayberry of Woodglen, New Jersey; and Carl Helm of Riegelsville, Pennsylvania. A second generation of deer hunters, the Mayberry boys, Mike and Glen, and young Mark Schumann and John Schock, grew into membership as the structure of the camp took shape.

You walk in the front door, and there's a gun rack at your right, each station holding a rifle. You see a handmade .58-caliber Hawken; the hunters take their rifles seriously. The bunkroom is a nest of rough-cut bunkracks with ladders here and there to reach sleeping lofts and the high bunks. Clothing and equipment is thrown, hung, piled, and scattered everywhere. A locker-room smell is mixed with odors of damp wool, food, and the sweet smell of gun oil, boot leather, and sleeping bags.

Deer camps are built around stoves, and Camp Quicktime is named for its stove, which sits in the food parlor. Men may not cook a meal all year at home, but let deer camp call and a million gourmet cooks are born overnight. It's a secret carefully kept from women — and don't you dare tell it — but the best meals of a hunter's life are eaten at deer camp.

Across the kitchen from the old woodstove is the map. The names of good places have a familiar ring: The Baseball Field, The Oil Can Stand, Old Bridge, The Spring Stand, The Buck Tree. This is the magic geography. These are the spots where hunting things have happened.

Looking at the map and talking about the places in it that first night at Camp Quicktime excited me so I couldn't sleep. The camp would average about 90 percent hunter success, someone said. The bucks were not large, but the deer herd was healthy. Everyone would see whitetails the next day, and most of the hunters would drag bucks off the mountain.

I crawled into my sleeping bag and lay there thinking, imagining how the racked buck would appear just after it became legal to shoot in the hardwood patches above camp. I dozed briefly and glimpsed the great buck as he hooked a tree, pawed and blew steam through his nostrils in the cold morning air. The great buck, sensing something, froze, inhaled, deeply, and blew loudly through his nostrils. His tail went up, then down briefly, and he whirled, bounded over a blowdown, and was gone. Through a haze of sleep, I heard pans in the kitchen. It was time.

We ate steaming eggs, and the plans were made. I was given the Oil Can Stand, since it was easy to find and had a reputation as a buck run. The great basin below the ridgeline would be covered by standers. Al took down his handmade Hawken, hefted it briefly and handed it to me. The Hawken balanced solidly on the palm of my hand, and its front sight-blade and rear sight eased into a perfect sight picture when I shouldered it. The rifle felt good, the way a Garrison rod feels in your hand the first time you grasp it. Al would use the rifle that morning for the first time. We couldn't know the opportunity that he would have with it on the hillside just above camp.

On the camp porch the first cold breath of air made me gasp. The figures moving ahead of me were silent, dark, and faceless. You don't talk at such moments because you are thinking out the hunt, the walk to the stand, and the things that will happen to you alone in the woods. I climbed the ridge to where two old roads joined and an oil can hung from a tree limb.

I stood in the black woods by the oil can, and I made my ears see for me as the trees dripped and the other hunters moved uphill to their stands. Until light crept into the hemlocks, I would have to rely only on my ears to detect the tiny noises of hooves. It was always eerie — this early-morning standing — so totally alone in the chill darkness with only ears to sense with. Soon the outlines of trees and then branches became clear. Across the valley, and from a hundred valleys as far as sound would carry, cracks and booms of rifles announced Opening Day. The noise went on for 10 minutes before a slight tapping noise stopped my breath. The tiny noise electrified me more than a rifle shot. I knew a deer was there — I could feel it — before my eyes separated its shape from the hemlock gloom.

The deer was tip-toeing, aware that something had changed in the woods. The smell of man was everywhere, and the deer was sneaking and testing the wind. I put my scope on the animal but could see no antlers in the gray. The deer caught a whiff of man smell, and her flag began to lift. She walked stiff-legged, looking back at me all the while. Then she bounded back down the mountain.

Fifteen minutes later I spotted three deer sneaking across the ridge above me. They had winded me, but I figured if I sneaked up the road I could intercept them. I had gone maybe 100 yards up the road when I spotted Bucky dragging a deer toward me. He had taken the first buck with one shot. We talked briefly, and he headed toward camp.

As I sneaked up the road, I heard a shot perhaps 400 yards uphill to my left. I stopped for one-half hour, then continued uphill. Glen Mayberry was grunting and hauling a 150-pound six-pointer at the edge of a small alder run as I topped the first ridge. It wasn't 7:30 yet, but both Mayberrys had taken bucks, both brought down cleanly with one shot. Glen started to explain how he'd taken the buck, but the sharp crack of a nearby rifle ended the discussion. Glen continued dragging the buck downhill. I sneaked along the road toward the top of the mountain.

I could hear what I guessed to be groups of two and three deer to my left and right. Then four does trotted nervously through the oaks. They kept looking back, as though a hunter were following them. I watched them with my tiny 8X binoculars and studied their backtrail, hoping to spot a buck sneaking and holding back. The does continued through the oaks and were gone. Fifteen minutes later, six more deer trotted into the oaks above me. They winded me and broke, flags popping through the hardwoods. I could see no horns, but now there were deer running everywhere back and forth through the hardwoods.

Crack! The sound of a rifle shot sounded so close that I looked for deer and the hunter both at once. I eased 15 yards to the edge of a ridgeline and saw the hunter stooped over something in a small stand of pines just below the lip of the ridge. It was Carl Helm, dressing a buck that had jumped above him along the ridge. Carl said the buck had burst by him at full speed, breaking briefly into view in the softwoods. Carl had snap-shot just once and taken the buck in that fleeting instant. So far, our camp's score was three shots: three bucks. Alan's prediction that most of us would take a buck that first morning was beginning to haunt me. Whitetails were thick, but I had yet to see a horn.

During every hunt, a depressing midday moment follows the tense moments of morning, when the stillness of dawn erupts with the staccato of gunfire, and whitetails dash crazily through the woods. By midmorning, the deer sense the presence and the intent of the hunters and begin to tiptoe and test the air and look. Then the tempo of the hunt changes. You feel the tension ease and the panic go out of the deer, and you wonder if the glimpse of the buck horns you had earlier was the climax of your day.

I munched a sandwich and listened to the wind sough through the pines high on the basin rim. Three does eased through the oaks below me, then a fourth, fifth, and sixth trotted aimlessly across. The afternoon slipped away.

I began to shiver, and as my eyes searched the woods below, I felt the cold creep into my hands and feet, then up my legs. When the cold began to get the upper hand, I eased off the ridge toward camp, moving slowly, with each foot searching out a twig-free spot in the leaves.

I was about 200 yards above the Oil Can Stand when I spotted the movement of a deer below me. It was the twitch of an ear that betrayed the whitetail. It was listening to me, and my stopping for a moment caused the deer to flick an ear in hopes of detecting another sound. I did not move for 15 minutes, and the duel of silence finally unnerved the deer.

When the deer moved again, I could see two deer, both moving patches of brown in the dusky gloom of the thick hemlocks. Even in the gloom, I could discern a large patch of white, moving ghostlike with the patches of deerhair brown among the trees. The whiteness of the thing riveted my attention and made me shiver. The moving white thing was much larger than the lifted-tail and buttocks area of a normal whitetail. And to make things more perplexing, I could have sworn I'd seen horns. Had I seen an apparition, the ghost of a whitetail buck? Or was I creating my own apparition after a long day among antlerless deer on the mountainside?

If I could sneak downhill along the old road, treading noiselessly among the damp leaves, the wind would be just right for a circle below the deer. I just might be able to cut them off.

What I had seen kept bothering me as I sneaked downhill and quartered back uphill toward the path of the deer. There! A movement just ahead and above me. I swept the movement with my hunting glasses. Al Schock moved toward me out of the dark trees.

"Did you see him?" Schock asked softly as he approached with his Hawken cradled across an arm.

"See what?"

"The white buck. I had him right there — probably could have shot him."

"Why didn't you, then?"

"Brush — just a little brush. I wanted to make sure with the Hawken. I'll get him tomorrow or the next day. He's almost pure white."

The woods dripped and began to turn black as we ambled down to the brook and across the meadow to camp. A chill, damp wind blowing from the south carried the smell of rain and the aroma of wood smoke and cooking food. As we approached the porch, easy laughter drifted out and curled around the camp. The stories of the day were in progress while food sizzled on the Quicktime stove. Al would arrange a meeting with the white buck the next day — I was sure of that. But it didn't matter then. The return to deer camp each evening is a reunion. Tonight the white buck would be a hunting tale, a dream, and tomorrow's grand adventure. Next year the camp's map will have a new feature — The White Buck Stand — and in a decade someone will probably ask, "Do you remember the day Al shot the white buck?"

The All-Time No. 1 Whitetail

Ron Schara

November 1979

Dr. Watson probably would have classified this as one of Sherlock Holmes's greatest cases, and Holmes probably would have got most of his clues from Ron Schara, Outdoor Editor for the Minneapolis *Tribune*. A native of Postville, Iowa, and graduate of Iowa State University in 1968, Schara edited the South Dakota *Conservation Digest* before joining the *Tribune* in 1968. He has written two books, *Muskie Mania* and *Ron Schara's Minnesota Fishing Guide*. In 1977 he conducted the first Tribune Fishing Fair and Clinic for 3,000 persons. He is married and has two daughters. Schara's story is based on several interviews with Jim Jordan before his death, Jordan's written record of the hunt and talks with Jordan's widow.

Jim Jordan stared at the fresh deer tracks in the snow. Three, maybe four deer had recently shuffled by, he figured. But one set of hoof marks caught his eye. The snow-molded hoofs were huge; the toes splayed outward like the legs of an overloaded chair.

Jordan cradled a .25/20-caliber Winchester in his arms and took a deep breath of cold morning air. If the tracks were any indication, he had crossed paths with a huge whitetail buck. Jordan peered at the tracks again. He had never seen such massive hoofs. He knew he had to follow the inviting track. That decision launched him on a bizarre deer hunt that really lasted for 64 years.

The tracks Jim Jordan followed on a November morning in 1914 were made by the world-record whitetail buck. But for more than six decades, a series of strange twists of fate kept Jordan from being recognized as the man who shot the great buck.

The current edition of North American Big Game, the record book, states that the name of the hunter who took the world-record typical whitetail is unknown. The record book also states that the location was Sandstone, Minnesota, which has turned out to be a mistake. For more than 60 years, about the only thing known about the No. 1 set of antlers was that they were discovered at a rummage sale in Sandstone. When Jordan heard of that discovery, he knew that the record really belonged in his name. He had written down the story of the hunt the day the record buck was killed and he remembered vividly. But events made him give up hope of being listed in the records.

Several years ago, I wrote a column for the Minneapolis Tribune pointing out the mystery of the world-record antlers. Later, I got a call from a reader who said that the hunter might be an elderly man who lived near the St. Croix River, which flows between Minnesota and Wisconsin. I looked the man up; his name was Jim Jordan. I wrote about the story he told me in the Tribune in 1977, and that attracted the attention of officials of the North American Big Game Awards Program, now administered jointly by the Boone and Crockett Club Association. They investigated, and in December of 1978, the Boone and Crockett Big Game Committee recognized Jordan as the man who shot the record buck.

The story begins on November 20, 1914, a clear, sunny morning in northwestern Wisconsin, a morning that dawned on six inches of new snow over the vast stretches of Wisconsin's woods. Jordan, who lived on a small farm near the little town of Danbury, woke up particularly early. He looked out and liked what he saw: his farmyard freshly covered with snow. It was the opening day of Wisconsin's deer season, an event that Jordan never missed. He was 22 years old, a woodsman, logger, and trapper, and he loved deer hunting most of all.

Jordan hopped out of bed, dressed quickly, and hustled out to the barn to harness his horse to a buggy. He wanted to be ready when Egus Davis rode up. Davis arrived on schedule, unsaddled his horse, and threw his gear into Jordan's buggy. Together, the two quickly headed into Danbury, bought their 50¢ deer licenses, and turned the horse and buggy southward toward the Yellow River. When they arrived where they wanted to hunt, Jordan tied his buggy horse, and the two hunters headed into the aspen timber on foot. They had hunted in the familiar woodlands during previous deer seasons. Today, they planned to hunt together rather than split up; Davis discovered that in the rush to open the deer season, he'd forgotten his hunting knife.

As Jordan anticipated, the hunting conditions were ideal, thanks to the new snow. Quietly, softly, the two trudged toward the Yellow River. They hadn't walked far when Jordan spotted a doe, raised his rifle, and fired. The big doe fell. Davis was elated by the quick success. He suggested that they drag the doe back over the short distance to the horse and buggy. But Jordan was impatient. He handed his hunting knife to his friend. "Here's my knife. You can have the doe, but you also can take the deer back by yourself. I want to keep going," he told his hunting partner. Davis nodded his approval, and Jordan, minus his hunting knife, headed off by himself. He hadn't gone far when, up ahead in the virgin snow, he spied a string of pockmarks meandering through the aspen thicket. From a distance, he knew the tracks had been made by deer, and he knew they were fresh because of the overnight snowfall.

His attention was drawn immediately to the set of supersize hoof-prints. He couldn't resist the temptation to follow. He checked his Winchester lever-action rifle one more time; it was loaded, but the magazine wasn't full. The buck that made those imprints in the snow might not be far away. He quickened his pace. The fresh deer tracks wandered southward for a few hundred yards and then turned back north toward Danbury and closer to the Soo Line railroad tracks that roughly paralleled the course of the Yellow River. Jordan continued until the deer trail led toward an opening, the railroad right-of-way. The wandering deer — there were three or four sets of tracks, including the giant buck — had probably crossed the railroad and continued, he thought to himself.

Suddenly, Jordan heard the familiar whistle of an oncoming Soo Line freight train. He paused near the open swath in the aspen. A quick glance at the trail told him the deer had not crossed the tracks. The fresh sign ambled along the grassy strip between the tracks and the timber's edge. He had a good, clear view, north and south, on his side of the railroad bed. Still, he couldn't spot the deer that had made the tracks he had been dogging. The train whistled again, still a long way down the track.

Suddenly, just ahead, Jordan saw movement — heads raised up out of the heavy, tall grass along the railroad tracks. The bedded deer were alerted by the oncoming train. There were three deer or four, Jordan wasn't sure. His eyes were already glued to the third one that appeared above the snow-laden clumps of grass less than 100 yards away. It was a huge buck.

Jordan didn't hesitate. He quickly shouldered his .25-caliber Winchester and steadied the iron sights on the big buck's neck. The deer remained motionless, listening for the train, and unaware of Jordan's presence. The buck was poised, head high, his enormous head ornament shining in the sunlight of the cloud-free morning. Jordan squeezed the trigger.

The rifle bucked but Jordan's eyes never left the huge deer. The does bounded for the jungle of aspen. The buck went in the opposite direction. Jordan fired again, then again. Once more, and that was the last cartridge in the rifle. The speeding buck disappeared.

Jordan was quite sure he'd hit the buck once if not twice. What's more, tracking conditions were still ideal. He figured he'd catch up with that buck again, sooner or later. Sooner, probably, if the animal was seriously wounded.

He quickly picked up the buck's trail. Anxiously, he followed the buck's bounding footprints, looking for blood. Then he remembered his empty rifle. He paused and dug frantically in his coat pockets for more ammunition. He had, he discovered, only one more cartridge. His last shot would have to be fired at close range.

Jordan continued to follow the buck's trail. He found blood, not much, but some. He trudged on. The buck seemed to be heading toward the Yellow River. Jordan didn't mind at all, for the river flowed not far from his farmstead. Suddenly, about 150 yards away, he caught a glimpse of the giant whitetail. He raised his rifle, then lowered it. With only one shot left, he decided to wait for a closer shot.

The whitetail headed for the river where it turned west. Jordan was not far behind. He now saw the buck most of the time as it stumbled toward the river. At the river's edge, the buck stopped, his massive head and neck arched low above the ground. Jordan continued to close the distance between them. Suddenly, the buck plunged into the shallow river, struggled against the current, and stepped out on the far bank. By that time, Jordan had also reached the river's edge. Again alerted, the mighty whitetail raised his head and looked back.

"He looked right at me," Jordan told me years later. "I aimed at the backbone this time because he was such a big deer; I didn't think my rifle could bring him down if I didn't hit him there." Indeed, Jordan's Model 1892 Winchester, firing the pipsqueak .25/20 cartridge, was really inadequate for deer hunting.

Jordan fired his last shot; the huge whitetail collapsed.

Jordan rushed across the shallow river, oblivious to the icy water that poured into his hunting boots. The buck hadn't moved. For the first time, Jordan could take a close look at the marvelous whitetail. Never had he seen such a set of antlers. Never had he seen such a heavy deer. He reached for his hunting knife, then he remembered. He had loaned it to Egus Davis.

No problem, Jordan thought. If his calculations were correct, he wasn't much more than a quarter-mile from his farm. He'd walk back to find Davis and get his knife.

David had already returned to the farm with the horse and buggy and the doe. Jordan told of his hunting luck. Then he and Davis hurried back toward the river where the big buck had fallen. But when they arrived, there was no buck in sight.

"The buck must have flopped one more time and slid into the river," Jordan explained. "I went down to the bend of the river and there he was, hung up on a big rock. I waded out in water waist deep to get to him. Later, it took a whole bunch of us to pull him home. I can't remember if he weighed just a little over 400 or just under 400 pounds."

The news of Jordan's mammoth whitetail spread quickly. Neighbors and town folk rode out to take a look. One of them was George Van Castle, who lived in Webster, about 10 miles south of Danbury. He worked on the Soo Line Railroad, but he also did taxidermy work in his spare time. He greatly admired Jordan's trophy and offered to mount the head for $5. Jordan accepted. He'd seen plenty of big bucks, but none as big as his. Van Castle picked up the unskinned head and caught the Soo Line south to his home in Webster. Jordan didn't know it then, but he would not see his prized whitetail trophy again for more than 50 years.

Shortly after Van Castle agreed to mount the head, his wife became sick and died. Troubled by the loss of his wife, Van Castle decided to move to Hinckley, Minnesota. But he never told Jordan, who waited for months but heard no word about his mounted trophy. Finally, he made a trip to Webster, where he learned that Van Castle had gone to Hinckley, and so had his mounted whitetail.

Jordan considered making the trip from Danbury to Hinckley to reclaim his deer, but such a trek was not easy. Although the towns were only 25 miles apart, they were separated by a long bridgeless stretch of the St. Croix River. Time passed. Eventually, a new bridge across the St. Croix connected Danbury and Hinckley. But by that time, Van Castle had married again and moved to Florida.

"I never heard from Van Castle again," Jordan recalled. He gave up all hope of seeing his whitetail trophy again. He and his wife, Lena, moved to a small acreage near Hinckley, along the Minnesota side of the St. Croix. He was not a young man any more, and life had not been easy. Still, he hadn't lost his interest in deer hunting. He shot his share of good bucks. Their many racks hung from the rafters of the Jordans' home, and he could easily tell when, where, and how each had been taken. He started collecting deer antlers as a hobby. That hobby led to still another twist of fate.

One day in 1964, a Minnesotan by the name of Robert Ludwig was strolling down Main Street in Sandstone, a small town about eight miles from Hinckley. Ludwig was a shirt-tail relative of Jordan's, and he also collected antlers. He came to a rummage sale on a vacant corner lot. The goods — dishes, antiques, furniture — were the usual assortment. One item, however, caught his eye. It was an old, dusty, decrepit, mounted deer head. Ludwig looked it over. The mothy head had been stuffed with yellowed newspapers and homemade plaster, and it had been sewed up with twine. But the antlers were magnificent. Ludwig couldn't believe their size. The rack, massive and perfectly shaped with five equal points on a side, was larger than any he had collected.

Ludwig paid $3 for the head and took it home. His wife was less than overjoyed at his bargain. The mount was beyond repair, but the antlers were huge.

Ludwig, a forester for Minnesota's Department of Natural Resources, became curious about his $3 antlers. He obtained an official form for measuring typical whitetail racks and measured the huge rack himself. He wasn't sure what the total point score meant, but he sent his results to a St. Paul naturalist, Bernie Fashingbauer, an official measurer for the Boone and Crockett awards program.

Fashingbauer thought Ludwig's measurements must be wrong. If they were right, the rack qualified as a new world-record typical whitetail buck. He contacted Ludwig and arranged to see the big rack and to take his own set of measurements: an unbelievable score of 206⅝, a world record.

The score was submitted to Boone and Crockett officials, who asked for measuring by a panel of experts. The experts came up with the same score. Ludwig had indeed found the new world-record typical whitetail rack. He couldn't wait to tell his friends and relatives — particularly Jim Jordan, since Jordan was also interested in big antlers.

Jordan looked at the record rack when Ludwig showed it to him. He was stunned. It was the same rack he had lost 50 years ago to Van Castle, the taxidermist.

Ecstatic about the discovery, Jordan had a picture taken of himself with the record antlers. He showed it to old friends who had seen the head five decades ago. They agreed it looked like the same buck. Ludwig, however, disagreed. Four years later, in 1968, he sold the record head for $1,500 to Charles T. Arnold, a deer antler collector from Nashua, New Hampshire. Arnold still owns the record rack, which has since been remounted and refurbished with a new cape.

So Jordan was separated from his trophy, although he continued to insist it was the same buck he killed in 1914. He also insisted he wasn't interested in any of the money Ludwig received for selling the world-record head.

"I just want to set the record straight," Jordan told me in the fall of 1977. Of course, the record eventually was set straight when the Boone and Crockett Club credited Jordan with killing the world-record whitetail buck. But the long hunting adventure took one more bizarre twist when the announcement was made in December 1978.

Jordan never heard it. Less than two months before his record claim was officially accepted, Jordan died at the age of 86.

THE 64-YEAR DEER HUNT IN BRIEF

1914 — Jim Jordan shoots an enormous whitetail buck on November 20. George Van Castle offers to mount the head for $5. Jordan agrees, and Van Castle takes the unskinned head to his home in Webster, Wisconsin.

Later, Van Castle moves to Hinckley, Minnesota, but does not inform Jordan.

Years later, Jordan visits Hinckley to see Van Castle, but the taxidermist has moved to Florida.

1964 — Robert Ludwig, a distant relative of Jordan, buys the Van Castle mount for $3 at a rummage sale in Sandstone, Minnesota. The cape has deteriorated. Ludwig shows the trophy to Jordan, who is sure that it came from the buck he shot in 1914.

Ludwig measures the rack and sends the Boone and Crockett form to Bernie Fashingbauer, an official B & C measurer, who measures the antlers again at 206⅝ points — a world record. The rack, later measured by a B & C committee, is officially recognized as the No. 1 typical whitetail, hunter "unknown."

1968 — Ludwig sells the rack to Charles T. Arnold of Nashua, New Hampshire, a collector of antlers. Arnold still owns the trophy, which he is refurbishing with a new cape.

1977 — As a result of a story by Ron Schara in the Minneapolis *Tribune,* the Boone and Crockett Club begins investigating Jim Jordan's claim.

1978 — The club officially recognizes Jordan as the man who shot the world-record typical whitetail. Jordan died two months before the recognition.

The Teeming Desert

Byron W. Dalrymple

August 1980

Byron Dalrymple's first story for OUTDOOR LIFE was "Run, Perch, Run" (April 1945). At the time he said his postwar objectives were a cabin in the wilderness, plenty of outdoor sports, and time to write about them. As a band musician, he'd found that traveling gave him the chance to fish in nearly all the states. So what happened? In the past 40 years he has written something like 3,500 articles for several magazines and last fall Outdoor Life Books published his 20th book, *Hunting for the Pot/Fishing for the Pan*. He is a professional photographer and has produced several films on outdoor subjects. He has a ranch in Texas where he tests fishing and hunting equipment, and a couple of bass lakes of his own. He has lived his dream, obviously, but he still doesn't explain where he found all that time.

Dawn leaps suddenly across the vast sweep of cactus and thornbrush that fans northward from the Mexican border at Laredo, Texas. In minutes the glow becomes harsh and probes every spiked shrub and spined cactus clump, laying black shadows at their feet.

We sat atop a high knoll, a wintering Yankee friend and I, listening to a distant coyote wailing and yapping his coded signature, signing off until evening. We stared out over the landscape. There was not a tree in sight, unless a person counted dwarfed mesquites, huisache and retamas.

Nothing stirred. I had brought the Northern friend here, to what Texans call the brush country, so that he might see and feel the presence of the unique place where tomorrow we would begin a deer hunt, with intermittent hours also spent with quail.

He sat quietly as the light grew and rushed uninhibited over the landscape. He raised a binocular and swept it impatiently across the drab vista. He really didn't need to speak, because I knew already what he was going to say, having heard it many times from first-time visitors to the southwestern deserts.

"What an utterly barren place," he finally muttered. "You can't be serious. *Deer* in *that? And quail?* I simply can't believe it!"

It was the classic response. The word "desert" invariably conjures in the average mind a picture of a barren, heat-struck land, dust dry, awaiting the unwary with a tangled shield of vicious spines and spikes, bereft of all but the most specialized creatures. The truth, little known to the average outdoorsman, is that the southwestern deserts of the United States and northern Mexico are home to the most amazing variety, and often abundance, of wildlife found anywhere on the continent.

I smiled inwardly, thinking that within the next several days the Yankee would change his opinion. In the very country we were scanning dwell some of America's largest whitetail deer. In fact, the brush country counties of southern Texas have produced almost all that state's record whitetail heads, and Texas stands second among the states in whitetail records.

I was remembering experiences in the expanse before us, and also in other deserts — of southern New Mexico, Arizona, more of the same south of the border. I'd seen several species of deer, quail, doves and pigeons, predators, rabbits, rodents, even waterfowl, and a welter of nongame species. Indeed, far from being barren, our southwestern deserts teem with wildlife.

I could dimly see, not far from the knoll on which we sat, an old camphouse nestled in the brush. Out of it, a few years ago, I hunted often. The "wet" years were most memorable. A wet year in any of the U.S. desert country is one during which an area gets 10 to 15 inches of rainfall instead of the usual 3 to 6. When that occurs, the desert erupts. Nowhere on the continent are there such astonishing population bursts of birds and small animals. One year, just for fun, five of us, hunting blue quail, declared a 200-yard circle around the old camphouse a refuge inviolate to shooting. We loved to hear birds talking. We estimated, by counting coveys as carefully as possible, that some 300 scaled, or blue, quail resided within that 200-yard circle!

Each day we hunted only an hour or so outside the circle, because that was all the time we needed to kill a 12-bird limit. Possession limit was 36 birds. We decided to harvest them because a massive die-off was certain. We took the 180 birds legally allowed within a mile of the camphouse, and we never got off the *senderos,* or ranch trails.

Some of these high-cycle desert eruptions are unbelievable. During the late 1950s all across the Southwest ample rainfall brought prodigious quail production — blues, bobwhites in the few areas where they occur, Gambel's, Mearns, valley quail. One preseason day I drove along a 15-mile stretch of side road through cattle-ranch country 50-odd miles south of San Antonio. Two others were with me. There were both bobs and blues in this region. Both sides of the road were bordered with vast brush country ranches. Quail coveys swarmed out on and along the highway, apparently picking gravel.

We counted as best we could and decided we'd seen 900 quail in that 15-mile stretch — and we were of course seeing only birds that lived near the road. There must have been hundreds of thousands scattered throughout the brush and cactus. Cottontails seemed almost as plentiful. That fall during a deer hunt in the same area I shot cottontails for the camp pot several times early in the morning. I'd start from camp and walk a *sendero,* and in 30 minutes have 10 or a dozen. It made no difference which way from camp I hunted.

Such population explosions of prey species in the desert are always accompanied by a lagging but similar skyrocketing of predator populations, especially of bobcats, gray and desert foxes, and coyotes. And they are invariably followed by awesome forage-creature die-offs, and in turn by a drastic matching decline of the predators. The astonishing fecundity of our deserts in the "good" years, however striking, does not have the sustained drama of the region's amazing wildlife variety.

Why and how so many species were able eons ago to colonize the deserts is both intriguing and perplexing. One might presume that the hot, dry climate, the tough, thorny vegetation, the meager water supply, would have discouraged exploration and settlement by wildlife. The average hunter thinks of the verdant northern forests, eastern woodlands, western mountains as the prime American wildlife ranges. Fact is, none of those is even in the running for variety or abundance.

Some common species, such as the whitetail deer, the cottontail, and the bobcat, are animals whose massive colonizations over vast areas of the continent are well known. They are cases illustrative of ability to adapt also to the deserts. But many desert dwellers are found nowhere else. And in some instances — the bobcat is a prime example — those also found elsewhere are at their highest population levels in the desert, even in dry times.

The wild cats are a classic example both of adaptation to and evolution in the desert. The southwestern arid regions are, surprisingly, the hub of the continental distribution of all but one of the North American wild cat species. Until its virtual extirpation, the jaguar roamed here in modest numbers. Here also was the original center of the continent's cougar population, now worn thin by habitat destruction and human population pressure. The handsome ocelot, until a few years ago when its hide became excessively valuable, was still not rare in northern Mexico. A few remain in impenetrable chaparral thickets of extreme southern Texas.

The beautifully marked house cat-size margay, unknown even to most southwestern outdoorsmen, was once fairly common, at least below the Rio Grande. The low-slung, long-tailed, slender and unspotted jaguarundi (the reddish eyra cat is actually a color phase and not a different cat) remains, in remnant, endangered. Few modern sportsmen ever see this awesomely secretive cat, which weighs possibly 15 pounds. Bob Snow, a tough desert hunter who worked for years for the Texas game department and later guided hunts with his dog packs for jaguar and lions in the backcountry of Mexico, told me once of witnessing a startling display by a jaguarundi. A mourning dove skimmed the low brush, and suddenly the lean cat shot upward out of cover and with one deft swipe of claws plucked the bird from the air.

I remember, on trips into the brush with the Burnham brothers, renowned callers and call makers, nights when we brought in half a dozen bobcats in as many half-mile-apart stands. In both Arizona and Texas I have had bobcats come to a call from behind or to one side, and have turned in broad daylight, to find the quizzical cat sitting on its haunches staring at me. Even with severe hide-hunting pressures of late, the bobcat populations of the southwestern deserts remain higher than anywhere else over their immense range. Only the lynx, of all the cats of North America, is missing from the southwestern United States and of the cats noted, only the bobcat and lion range elsewhere within the country.

Deer are the most prominent big game — and the most incongruous desert dwellers. How vividly I recall my amazement at my first sight of a trophy whitetail buck bounding over prickly pear clumps and plunging through crackling thornbrush!

Curiously, too, deer are present in more distinctive subspecies forms in deserts of the southwestern United States than over any other comparable area of the continent, except possibly extreme southern Mexico and Central America. The Texas whitetail subspecies forms the largest single deer herd on the continent. A tiny oasis of another whitetail subspecies, the diminutive "flagtail," or Carmen Mountains whitetail, exists in far western Texas, in a few individual mountain ranges of Brewster and adjacent counties, and south into Mexico.

The first one I ever shot, a young buck, weighed 45 pounds field-dressed. The largest I've taken weighed 80. In the Big Bend country where this snug-racked little deer ranges, it is surrounded at low elevations by abundant desert mule deer, and in the foothills of its desert mountains by scattered, larger Texas whitetails. In this scenic sweep of desert and mountains, I have hunted deer, chiefly mule deer, for 18 straight seasons without a first-day blank. I have counted, while four-wheeling along trails on a huge ranch there, as many as 200 mule deer in one day. A few years ago I bagged three kinds of deer in three days — desert mule deer, Texas and Carmen Mountains whitetails.

Farther west, in southwestern New Mexico and southeastern Arizona, lives the well-known Coues, or Arizona, whitetail, a subspecies with its own category in Boone and Crockett records. In desert settings on westward across Arizona, into California, and below the border, the mule deer has reached its greatest number of tangent races — in addition to the desert mule deer, the burro deer, the Inyo mule deer and several other subspecies.

The deserts are the quail capital of the continent, the focal point of both variety and abundance. In a thin strip of eastern New Mexico along the Texas border are both bobs and blues (scaled quail). Once, when quail here were on a high cycle, three of us flushed two coveys simultaneously, a shotgun range apart. I was in the center, swung on a bird — and saw two fall, one beyond my intended target. The flushed coveys had crossed in flight, and I picked up one bobwhite and one blue.

In southeastern Arizona one fall, three of us tried to bag three kinds of quail in one day, and we succeeded. These were the beautiful Mearns, the males reminiscent in build and speckling of miniature guinea hens, the blue, and the handsomely plumed Gambel's. To be sure, the Mearns is a bird of the grass and oak zone above the desert floor, but it still is a product of the southwestern desert regions.

The valley quail, close relative of the Gambel's, fills its place in the arid portions of southern California and ranges the length of Baja. It can by no means tolerate, however, the bleak conditions the doughty Gambel's seems not only to make do in but to enjoy and thrive in. Look sometime in your travels at the utterly barren country — truthfully so in patches — south of Lordsburg, New Mexico. Here earth dried until it cracks sustains in many places practically nothing except creosote brush and hummocks of the most viciously thorned dwarf mesquite. Yet some of the best Gambel's quail hunting I've ever experienced was here.

In southern Arizona, on a large area closed to hunting, state and federal personnel are attempting to bring back the once-abundant masked bobwhite, a rare and endangered bird even in Mexico. This quail was a victim years ago of overgrazing.

There are, below the border, a welter of unusual quail species — barred quail, Douglas quail, singing quail, tree quail. And hidden away in southern Texas, its range covering only a few counties, is a race of scaled quail, the chestnut-bellied blue, of which even some natives are unaware. In a few of my secret hunting locations these richly embossed, elegant blues share the range with abundant bobwhites. Guessing which may flush next lends a tang to hunting.

The deserts are also the focal region for those sun-loving birds, the doves and pigeons. Mourning doves of two subspecies nest and winter here. This is the continental center of whitewing dove production. Those who have yet to experience a truly tremendous white-wing dove flight, nowadays possible only below the border, have missed what is the closest approximation in our age to what the passenger pigeon flights must have been like. I've shot south of McAllen, Texas, and Reynosa, Tamaulipas, when for four solid hours these colonial birds, some flying out to feed and others returning, simply covered the sky.

Occasionally along desert foothills one sees bandtail pigeons, and along the border there are scattered redbilled pigeons, handsome big mulberry-colored birds. A bit farther south into Mexico they are abundant, and the shooting is sensational. There are also, on both sides of the border, nongame ground doves, Inca doves, white-fronted doves. And then if you want to experience a shoot for the rarest desert game bird of the lot, in the worst tangle of spines you will ever see, go to the southern tip of Texas, where the delicious drab-colored, noisy, pheasant-like chachalaca is still on the game list. You can also find it below the border. On either side, you'll find it among impenetrable thorns, which it seems to love, and some of the finest rattlesnake producing country on the continent.

Yet all of this barely scratches the spiny desert surface. On peak cycles, jackrabbit swarm — blacktail jacks, antelope jacks, the rare white-sided jacks of southern New Mexico. There are several kinds of cottontails. Gray foxes, diminutive swift foxes and the ubiquitous coyote revel in rabbit prolificity. Pack rats, kangaroo rats, a host of small ground squirrels, mice of numerous species, and other rodents are staples of predator diet. The big gray wolves once here are now almost certainly extinct. The red wolf, persecuted mercilessly and now with its blood heavily diluted by coyote hybridization, is on the verge of extinction, but once was abundant.

Four kinds of skunks, badgers, scattered raccoons, big-eyed nocturnal ringtail cats, armadillos, an occasional opossum, bats galore, almost unbelievably in a few places porcupines, in Arizona coatimundis, and in scattered locations where water flows permanently, even beavers — these add to the welter of desert wildlife. The nongame bird species, resident and wintering, number in the hundreds. Hawks and eagles appear in winter, often in astonishing numbers. The desert handsomely feeds them. The roadrunner is a kind of desert ambassador. I never see one without recalling the quaint Mexican tale about its tracks. Roadrunners have four toes, two pointing ahead, two back. This, the legend has it, keeps enemies from following. Who could tell from its tracks which way it went?

Among the larger animals, the javelina is a classic desert dweller, indeed molded by this thorny land. Pronghorns are present in suitable places, both the southern subspecies and the rare desert antelope of Arizona and Sonora. Curiously, black bear studies in Arizona have shown some of that state's best bear range to be in desert terrain, where in good fruit producing years the animals gorge on prickly pear tunas. Of all the desert big game, the desert bighorn, awesomely harassed by human pressures ever since early Spaniards ate their first one, is the regal representative.

Perhaps to the desert tenderfoot the presence of waterfowl and shorebirds might seem strange. Vividly I recall years ago shooting jacksnipe around a ranch tank near Tucson. I've done it often in the Texas brush. Some of the best duck hunting in the Southwest goes mostly begging each season; desert tanks swarm with almost every U.S. species. Shorebirds such as willets and yellowlegs send their liquid calls across the cactus patches.

In camp, we had our feet up, the Yankee friend and I, sipping red whiskey, smelling the pungent mesquite coals mixed with the delicate scents of broiling quail and venison backstrap. He was excited about his find — half a dozen arrowheads.

We were discussing the ancient history of the arid lands sweeping across the Southwest from the Gulf of Mexico to the Pacific, the fact that the deserts were once among the most heavily settled centers of Indian civilizations. "Lo, the poor Indian," the Yankee murmured, smiling and lifting his glass. "I begin to understand now. Where else did he ever have it so good?"

'Last Gobbler

Bruce Brady

April 1981

Bruce Brady was graduated from Lawrenceville School in New Jersey (1953), received a BA Degree from the University of Mississippi, majoring in English and journalism, and subsequently an LLB Degree from the University Law School. He actively practiced law for ten years before becoming involved in outdoor writing. A correspondence with Jack O'Connor about handloading brought the suggestion that he "try his hand at an outdoor piece." He wrote a story on night fishing for bass in 1968, unsolicited, and I bought it without knowing its origin. Next he worked as a regional stringer for Charlie Elliott and then, just before I retired in 1973, I hired him as Mid-South field editor. Five years later he left OUTDOOR LIFE to freelance. Now, in 1982, I learn he has just rejoined the magazine as an editor at large. Welcome home.

It was 3:00 a.m. when Price Shurley's alarm clock awoke him on the morning of April 8, 1969. Taking care not to disturb his wife, he eased out of bed, slipped into his camouflage coveralls, and double-checked his equipment. Assured his callers, headnet, shells, and knife were in their proper pockets, he shouldered his old Browning 12-gauge automatic and stepped out onto the porch, closing the door behind him.

Outside it was dead calm. As was his custom, he looked up into the predawn sky. Overhead the stars sparkled brightly, bringing him promise of turkey gobbling and another beautiful spring day in the Mississippi woods.

At 3:15 a.m. Shurley joined a hunting companion for breakfast at a McComb cafe. After a hearty breakfast they began the 11-mile drive to some woods in Amite County where the morning's hunt would take place. Shurley had scouted the woods a number of times to locate turkeys and to study their movements. Two afternoons before he had made a blind of natural vegetation on a low ridge where he anticipated the turkeys would move after they came off the roost. Shurley planned to position his companion in this blind.

At 4:45 a.m. the two men stepped from the truck and began the three-quarter-mile hike that would take them to the hunting area. In due course the blind was located and Shurley's friend took his seat. Shurley then continued on for a safe distance before sitting down with his back to a large pine.

About 5:50 a.m. Shurley began to *putt* occasionally with his diaphragm mouth caller. Two hens answered his calls, and at about 6:45 a.m. they flew off their roosts to the ground. Shurley attempted to call them up, hoping that a silent gobbler would be present when they came into view.

After about 15 minutes of intermittent calling, Shurley looked around and saw his companion approaching. He motioned to reveal his position, then looked back in the direction he expected the turkeys to appear. Shurley's companion had indeed seen the movement, but to him it looked exactly like a gobbler's head, and he shouldered his gun for the shot. When Shurley glanced back a moment later, he looked into the muzzle of a 12-gauge shotgun loaded with three-inch magnum shells at a range of 22 yards. He waved again, but it was too late. The gun roared, sending a load of No. 6 shot crashing into Shurley's face.

"It was a terrible hunting accident," recalls J. E. Thornhill Jr. of McComb, Mississippi, who was a close friend of Price Shurley. "It always is when one friend shoots another. Price survived somehow, but he was totally blind for the rest of his life."

Thornhill believes the accident would have killed a lesser man. Shurley was a powerful specimen, standing six-feet five inches and weighing more than 250 pounds.

"He looked as though he could play defensive end for the Pittsburgh Steelers," says Thornhill.

Price Shurley worked as a locomotive engineer for the Illinois Central Railroad, but he was better known for his hunting and fishing abilities. He was generally acknowledged to be one of the finest turkey hunters in south Mississippi. Stories of his calling ability and hunting prowess were legion. He was 50 years old at the time of the accident.

He hunted all Mississippi game from deer to doves, but turkey hunting was his first love. He was also expert at hand-grabbing big catfish. It is said that Price Shurley had an uncanny sense of touch for big fish. Once he had located a catfish in a hollow log or up under a washed-out riverbank, he could take a twig and, by feeling the fish, estimate within ounces what the catfish would weigh when he finally wrestled it out of its lair.

"Because he was such a successful hunter and hand-grabber," Thornhill recalls, "he was sometimes labeled as an outlaw by those who were jealous of his success. But in all my years afield with Price, I never saw him 'outlaw' any game."

Shurley had always been a happy, sociable man, but after he lost his sight he became brooding and morose. Eventually he began hand-grabbing again, for it is touch and not sight that is important in this unique sport. On fishing trips he seemed to come out of his shell and revert to the old Price again. But when spring came and the scent of blooming dogwood filled the air Price Shurley really hurt.

"I guess there were just too many old gobblers in his mind for him to accept the fact that he had bagged his last one," Thornhill reckons.

He recalls a day when he paid Price a visit. They sat on the porch and enjoyed a good talk about bygone days they had shared in the field.

"It was dusk and I was about to leave when Price asked me to stay a minute longer," Thornhill remembers. "He went inside and returned with his old Browning autoloader in his hands. He said it was too good a turkey gun not to be in the field and he wanted to pass it along to me. I insisted on paying him for his shotgun. Driving home that evening I realized that Price had finally accepted the fact that he could never bag another gobbler. When I got home I put my gun in the rack, and I've used Price's Browning since that day."

Thornhill and other friends occasionally took Shurley with them on late afternoon rides through the big woods, where they would stop and listen for turkeys to gobble as they flew up to roost at twilight.

"I could never tell from Price's reaction whether these outings helped or hurt him," Thornhill recalls. "I do know that he liked to give advice to hunters who were having problems with smart gobblers. He listened carefully as the hunter told him about it. He would ask countless questions about the way the birds reacted to various calls and about the lay of the land. Then he would suggest a series of calls to try, or encourage a change in the position of the hunter's blind. He always expected a report on how this advice had worked. I could sense his mental involvement and the pleasure he got from the tales I told him about smart turkeys I tried to work."

Thornhill recalls that Shurley's physical adjustment to blindness was rapid. "When Price had his sight he was an amazing woodsman," he said. "He used all his senses, and I learned a great deal from him when we were in the field together. I suppose being blind served to sharpen his already remarkable remaining senses. He could identify men by the sound of their walk and women by the scent of the cosmetics and perfume they used."

Thornhill considered taking Shurley along on a hunt so that he could listen to the calling and gobbling, but when he considered how tough it is to negotiate turkey woods where speed is often critical, he was afraid it would be too difficult for Price. He decided that if he ever roosted a bird alongside a road, he would invite Price to come along, but that perfect situation never seemed to appear.

Then about three years after the accident the spring turkey season rolled around. Halfway through the season Thornhill located a good gobbling turkey and tried to call him into range. This old tom resisted his most enticing calls for six days straight.

"Finally, I asked Price for advice," Thornhill told me. "I told him everything I could remember about each hunt, recalling as many specific details as possible. He listened intently, quizzing me when I failed to make some point clear. While we talked, I remembered how his eyes used to sparkle when we plotted against an old boss gobbler.

"At last he settled back in his chair and said, 'There's some obstacle between you and your turkey — a fence, a thicket, a creek. There is some spot of ground there that he chooses not to cross. You have two options — come in from another direction or make him overcome his fear.'

"A creek wound through those woods, and I told Price I had never been able to get a gobbler to fly across a creek. A big grin spread across his face, and he said, 'Well, that's one difference between you and me. I never had that problem.'

"I wanted that gobbler badly, but I wanted even more to see if Price could call him across the creek, so without really considering the consequences, I told him I would pick him up at 4:00 a.m. He would do the calling and I would do the shooting.

"At first he made no reply. He just sat there behind those dark glasses. Then I detected the trace of a smile and he said he would be ready."

At dawn the two men were half a mile into the deep woods. They stood in silence as the sounds of a new day grew louder. Then way across the bottom an owl hooted and the old turkey gobbled from his roost tree in reply. Arm in arm, the hunters moved forward 300 yards while the turkey continued to gobble.

Thornhill helped Shurley take his seat at the base of a big tree. While he cut branches and fashioned a blind, Shurley raked away ground litter where they would sit side by side. As Thornhill sat down at his friend's left side, the turkey gobbled from the ground. He was off the roost.

"Price put his mouth caller into place and began making a series of excited clucks, and the turkey answered immediately, as I knew he would," Thornhill recalled. "Then for the next half hour Price and the bird exchanged calls. We could course the bird easily because he was so vocal, and I knew he was nearing the creek where he had stopped each day to gobble and strut for another hour. I whispered this information to Price, but he only replied 'Sit still.'"

The gobbler did in fact stop at the creek, which was 80 yards or so away in front of the blind. He strutted and gobbled on the far side of the stream, walking back and forth over a 50-yard area. The tom raged and gobbled for 30 minutes, but Shurley made no reply. Thornhill strained his eyes for a glimpse of the turkey.

"And then the gobbler hushed, and I began to wonder if he had crossed the creek and was coming in or if he had found some hens and was moving away," Thornhill said. "I was about to tell Price to call again when the turkey gobbled some distance away from his strutting area. Instantly Price began a call I had never heard before. It was a series of loud and broken cackles with some shrill whines and excited putts thrown in.

"The tom answered with a double gobble, and then we heard his heavy wings beating. I didn't see him, but I could hear him as he flew across the creek and pitched in 75 yards or so off to our left front. I figured the turkey would come in from the left on Price's side of the blind, but it wasn't until I put my finger on the safety that it occurred to me to pass the shotgun to Price. He was making some soft clucks and purrs when I silently pushed the gun across his lap. 'You kill him,' I whispered. 'I'll help you kill him, Price.'"

When Shurley moved his hands to the smooth-worn stock of the Browning he whispered, "This is my gun." It was; it was Price's old turkey gun.

"By this time, my heart was in my throat," Thornhill says. "Having that gobbler on our side of the creek was thrilling, but what we were about to try had me breathing so hard I was afraid the turkey would hear me. All this time Price sat there like a man made of stone."

Minutes passed before the turkey gobbled again. They could tell he was 50 or 60 yards away now, but still out of sight. Luckily, he was still off to the left where the barrel of Price's gun pointed as it lay across his lap. Thornhill said a silent prayer that the bird would hold his course.

"And then he gobbled again loud enough to knock off your hat, and Price let go a loud cackle right back at him, much louder than I would have dared to call," Thornhill continued. "The turkey answered with a quick gobble, and Price countered with another cackle, to which the turkey double gobbled. Price had blown that turkey's mind, and I knew then it was only a matter of time before he came up. I prayed he would come in so Price could get a shot.

"We could hear the heavy drone of his strut and the rasping of his wing tips as they dragged the ground. He was moving slightly to the left again, and I looked past the tip of Price's nose in an effort to see him.

"Then, suddenly, he appeared. He was in a full strut and every bit as big and beautiful as I knew he would be. His head was a flaming red with wattles as big as buckshot. His beard was a black stripe down his bronze breast. My heart was pounding as I whispered, 'There he is,' and Price silently slipped off the safety."

The turkey stood motionless for several seconds and then moved slowly forward. When he stopped he was no more than 40 yards away. The turkey's head was behind the trunk of a big pine. Thornhill whispered to Price to shoulder his gun, which he did in one fluid motion.

With the fingers of his right hand, Thornhill touched Price's right elbow and pushed gently. Price responded, and the muzzle of the gun moved to the left. Thornhill looked down the side of the barrel and whispered, "Up — up some more," and he saw the barrel settle on the half-hidden gobbler.

"Right there," I whispered, and Price froze the gun in place. "From where I sat I was looking down the side of the barrel. As strong as Price Shurley was, I knew in my heart that he would hold the gun steady for as long as it might take to get the shot."

Probably only seconds passed, but it dragged like hours while the two men sat waiting. The thought crossed Thornhill's mind that Price had to kill this turkey. He hadn't considered what failure might do to his friend. Now it came to him that the next moment might destroy Price Shurley. A miss now might accomplish what a magnum load of No. 6's had failed to do on another turkey hunt.

Finally the gobbler stepped out, but he was partly screened by underbrush. He angled slightly to the left again, and again Thornhill pressed Price's elbow. The muzzle inched to the left, and then the turkey stepped clear of the brush.

"Shoot," Thornhill whispered, and the Browning roared.

"Price held the gun," Thornhill reflects, "but the good Lord must have been with him, because the turkey went down with feathers flying."

Thornhill sprang to his feet, dancing and yelling, "You got him, Price! You did it!" But when he looked down at Shurley, he was just sitting there with the shotgun across his lap.

"I always went straight to my turkeys," Price said quietly.

Thornhill turned and ran to the fallen gobbler. He was a fine turkey with a 9½-inch beard and long, hooked spurs. He carried him back to the blind man and placed the great bird across his legs.

Price's fingers worked their way to the spurs first, and he ran his thumb and index finger over them. Then he stroked the heavy beard and felt the tips of the wings, which had been worn blunt by strutting. He hefted the turkey and guessed the big tom's weight at 20 pounds.

"I couldn't tell from the way Price reacted to the kill how he felt about it all," Thornhill remembers. "I didn't know what I should say, so I didn't say anything. Price came to his feet, so I picked up the turkey and the gun and we started back to the truck. He took hold of my right forearm and we slowly worked our way out of the woods.

"On the ride home Price was quiet, and I understood. I knew he was thinking about everything that had taken place that morning and that he would come to some conclusion about what it all meant to him. I was worried sick that it had all been a tragic mistake, and that killing the tom would prevent Price from coming to terms with his blindness.

"We must have been about halfway home when a grin crossed Price's face, and he said, 'I knew we would take him when he double gobbled on our side of the creek.'

"Relief swept over me, and we began to talk about every call Price had made, every answer the turkey had given, and every touch I had made on Price's elbow. All the tension vanished, and we laughed and congratulated each other on our million-to-one shot hunt.

"We were almost home when Price asked, 'He's still in the bed of the truck, ain't he?' I glanced around and assured him the turkey was there. 'Good,' he said with a smile. 'A turkey isn't yours for sure till you close the oven door.'"

The two men showed that turkey all over the county and told the story of the hunt 100 times. And that hunt remained the high point of Price Shurley's life for the rest of his days. He died in 1976 of natural causes not related to his hunting accident.

"It was a crazy idea, and we didn't set out to do it," J. E. Thornhill told me. "I don't think we could have done it again, but we did it that time, Price and me. And if I take a thousand turkeys before I am done, none of them will ever mean as much to me as Price Shurley's last gobbler."

Record Book Bear the Hard Way

Creig M. Sharp as told to John Cartier

May 1981

John O. Cartier, a graduate of Michigan State U., left a job as plant manager of a railroad equipment factory to become field editor for OUTDOOR LIFE in 1965, but well before that had sold more than 100 feature stories to a variety of men's magazines as a hobby. Since then, he has traveled the breadth of the U.S. and from Alaska to Mexico gathering material for his own stories and for ghosted yarns by others. His latest book, *Hunting North American Waterfowl*, follows books on deer hunting and trophy hunting, all published by Outdoor Life Books. He is a native of Ludington, Michigan, where he lives with his wife Bernice and son Jack.

The huge brown bear was ambling out of an alder patch when Gary Grinde and I spotted him only 80 yards away. We were near the top of a snow-covered mountain above Karluk Lake on Kodiak Island, Alaska. He was unaware of us, and I had a wide-open shot.

My .340 Magnum's magazine was full of 250-grain Nosler loads. I put the crosswires of my 3X-to-9X Redfield scope, set at 6X, low on the bear's left shoulder and sent the slug on its way.

That moment, on April 28, 1977, marked the beginning of a physical ordeal almost too horrible to describe. Its results put me in hospitals for almost a year, subjected me to 26 operations, and left me with injuries that will remind me forever that a brown bear is one of the most powerful animals on earth.

When my bullet hit the bruin, it knocked him flat on his back. He roared with a ferocity that echoed across the mountain, and his legs thrashed in the air. Then he sat up so violently he flipped himself onto his stomach.

I tried to shoot again as fast as I could, but my rifle jammed. The cartridge extractor had slipped over the rim of the fired case, and the case was still in the chamber. While the bear was going through his contortions, I pushed the other cartridges down into the magazine and slammed the bolt shut. When I reefed back on the bolt handle, the spent casing came partway out of the chamber. I pulled it out with my fingers, tossed it into the snow, and chambered a fresh round just as the bear completed his somersault.

He apparently lost control of his movements and began rolling and sliding down the steep slope. I put another slug into him just before he pitched over a 200-foot drop-off.

"You hit him hard both shots," Gary said. "He isn't going far, but let's be damn careful."

We ran to the edge of the drop-off and looked over. There was no sign of the bear, but we figured he must have fallen directly into a patch of alders about 300 yards in diameter. We eased downhill, rifles ready. There was a good chance that the bear was still in the alders, so we stayed well out from the trees as we began circling the patch.

On the far side we found a blood trail with splatters up to three feet wide leading over a hill. The hairs on the back of my neck stood erect when I realized what our discovery meant. Though the bear was wounded, he had enough strength left to make an uphill escape, or was it really an escape? Could he be leading us into thick cover where he could easily circle around and attack from the rear?

We took a 10-minute break and tried to decide what to do. It was then about 5 o'clock in the evening. Though it was cloudy and dreary, we knew the long Alaskan day would give us two more hours of daylight. I was angry with myself for not killing the bear with my first shot, and I was mad about my rifle jamming, but I had no thought of leaving a wounded animal.

Gary didn't even hint at giving up, so we carefully followed the blood sign. It led us along a trail of destruction, proof of the enormous strength of the animal.

The bear had smashed through alder stands by breaking trees up to six inches in diameter. His fury was so great that he uprooted some aspens and left others smashed and splattered with blood. The knowledge that the bear was far from dead left me with a hollow feeling in the pit of my stomach.

At 7 o'clock, after staying on the trail for more than 2½ miles, we decided our venture was getting too risky to go on. Dusk was coming on, and a light drizzle began.

We were at the top of a steep descent that led down to the lake where we had beached our boat. I started down the slope first, and I was about 10 yards ahead of Gary when a vicious roar and a rushing sound shattered the stillness. It came from a thicket of alders behind me and to the left. My nerves had been tuned so finely for so long that I reacted like a coiled spring. As I began whirling around, I saw the bear making a full-speed charge from less than 20 yards away, but I was moving so quickly I figured I had enough time to put a bullet into his head.

In that instant my right foot snagged in underbrush. My coordination was ruined before I could shoulder my rifle. I didn't have time to become terrified, and I remember thinking that the bear was charging so rapidly he would overshoot me. That hope faded as fast as it started. The bear braked, skidded, and then crashed into me. He clamped his jaws around my left thigh and yanked me off the ground like a rag doll. He began shaking me, and I prayed, "Please God, don't let him kill me!"

Deadly adventures weren't new to me. I was born in Beaumont, California, in August 1943. My father was in the Air Force, so I was raised all over the Pacific Coast and the Far East. I had close contact with weapons and war, and I put in a lot of combat time in Vietnam after I joined the Navy. I was stationed in Alaska twice, and that had a direct bearing on my enthusiasm for hunting. The mountains and rivers and exceptional hunting and fishing captivated me so much that I promised myself I'd spend the rest of my life in Alaska.

When I made the brown bear hunt I was a Navy chief in charge of recruiting in Alaska. Gary was a U.S. Army sergeant. The third member of our group was Kent Whisnant, also a Navy chief. We were all in our 30s. At the time I was engaged to be married. My fiancée Kathy had just finished her reign as Miss Alaska. My partners and I planned a two-week hunt, and we based in a Forest Service cabin on the shore of Karluk Lake.

We took a four-man rubber raft and a four-horsepower outboard motor with us when we left Anchorage on April 26. I said goodbye to Kathy just before we left. We flew to Kodiak on Western Airlines and then made the hour flight to Karluk Lake on a chartered twin-engine aircraft. The lake is about a mile wide and 11 miles long. Our cabin was at one end of the lake, near the Karluk River, which drains it.

For the first two and a half days we hunted on the slope across the lake by glassing the hillsides with a spotting scope. We saw bears, but none close enough to stalk.

About 4 p.m. of the third day Gary and I returned to our observation point. Kent stayed at the cabin because he wasn't feeling well. We had just settled down with the spotting scope when two bears walked into view 2,000 feet up the mountain and about 300 yards apart. One was the big blond-shouldered animal we had spotted once before. The other was cinnamon-colored and smaller, but both were in the trophy class and both were near the tree line.

We started climbing, but when we got up to the slope where the bears had been they were nowhere in sight. We skirted around the mountain for a mile and a half, then sat down to rest. A few minutes later, the cinnamon-colored bear walked out of the alder patch at almost point-blank range. His sudden appearance was so startling that neither of us said a word. I simply signaled Gary that I was going to shoot, and then I touched off. But as I said, I didn't put the bear down, and that got me into the trouble that followed.

When the bear clamped his jaws around my left thigh, swung me off my feet, and began shaking me, I did not feel any pain. But I went wild with rage and fright. I began screaming and swearing at the bear, and as soon as I did he dropped me on my back. I rolled into a ball to protect my face and vital organs, still clutching my rifle, but the bear picked me up and flipped me over onto my back. Then he came for my face.

His head looked enormous. His jaws were open, and my own blood was running out of his mouth. His foul breath was the rottenest thing I've ever smelled. It was so sickening that I could hardly breathe. As he leaned over to rip my face off, I instinctively jammed my rifle into his mouth. He bit down on the stock near the floorplate and tried to yank it away from me, but I had a grip on the fore-end and pistol grip, and he couldn't pull it away, though he lifted me off the ground. The bear's teeth broke the stock almost in two in front of the magazine well. Finally, he let go and pulled back for a fresh attack, but the rifle's sling snagged on his teeth. He clamped down on the heavy leather sling and yanked with such force that both sling swivels sheared off, but I kept my hold on the rifle.

By that time, Gary was on the scene, screaming at the bear and shooting. He fired three 250-grain Silvertip bullets into the bear with his Model 77 Ruger .358 Winchester. After his third shot, he accidentally tripped the floorplate of his rifle, and the three remaining cartridges spilled out onto the ground.

Then the bear turned away from me and lunged toward Gary but didn't attack him. He wheeled around and bolted downhill, running over me as he left. When he hit me, I went tumbling and came to rest in a sitting position. I was so mad I leveled my broken rifle as best I could and fired a wild shot. The slug exploded dirt and snow off his left rump when it hit him, and it knocked him down. He got up immediately and crashed into some alders 100 yards away.

We reloaded our rifles as fast as we could in case the bear came charging back. Then Gary said, "How bad are you hurt? Can you get up?"

As I tried to move I saw that my right foot hung free and was flopping about.

"Broken right leg," I said through gritted teeth. "Check my left leg, I think he tore it up pretty good."

"For sure," Gary said. "It's bleeding bad. Watch for the damn bear while I give you first aid."

He took off his jacket and shirt, and then his underwear top and bound it tightly around my left leg to stop the bleeding from several holes where the bear's teeth had punctured my flesh. Then he splinted my right leg with broken branches secured with parachute cord. Gary stared at me and said, "You're really busted up. I've got to get you to a hospital."

I didn't have much doubt that he would do just that, if there was any possible way it could be done. Gary was an experienced Vietnam combat veteran. He had been in many situations where a man can't survive unless he pushes to his physical limits and beyond.

Gary tried a fireman's carry to get me down the mountain, but it was too steep and slippery. I had terrible pains shooting through my legs. Each time Gary fell I also crashed down, and each time I hit the ground the pain became so intense I almost passed out.

We decided it would be better if I tried sliding down the slope on my rear. It was a tortuous trip, especially when I came to deadfalls and snags. I used my hands to lift my legs over or around obstacles while Gary watched for the bear. It wasn't far down to the beach. We made it in 45 minutes, but our boat was about three miles down the shoreline. The weather couldn't have been worse. Freezing rain was pouring down, the strong wind was getting stronger, and it was pitch black.

Gary covered me with his shirt and coat, left both rifles, and then ran down the beach toward the boat. Though he was gone about an hour, it didn't seem long to me. I didn't learn until later that he had all kinds of problems before he got back to me. He almost ran into another bear. He reacted by jumping into the lake and swimming around the bear. After he got the boat going, he hit a rock and broke the motor's shear pin. He tried rowing, but the high wind made progress impossible. Luckily he found a small nail in one of his pockets, which he fashioned into a makeshift shear pin.

The wind was roaring now, and white-capped waves were rolling more than four feet high. Some of the swells splashed into our boat, and we took on water from a small hole in the bottom. I was resigned to swamping at any moment. Finally, we saw a pinpoint of light far in the distance. Kent had put a lantern near a window so we could home in on it.

When we got to the beach Gary ran to the cabin to get Kent's help and found him in bed extremely ill with flu. But as soon as Kent learned what happened he leaped out of his sack and ran to the boat with Gary. Both carried me into the cabin, put pressure bandages on my left thigh and cut off my right boot. The bottom of my right foot was demolished. It was a mass of torn flesh surrounding a gaping hole in my instep.

I was now engulfed with a feeling of helplessness. My shivering was uncontrollable, and the throbbing pains in my legs were close to intolerable. Gary and Kent changed all my clothes, put me inside two sleeping bags, and fed me hot coffee and soup. Nothing more could be done for me until I could get medical help. Gary knew the only way to get it was to head down the Karluk River and keep going until he found somebody with two-way radio contact to the outside.

Going downriver meant using the boat, and it was loaded with ice and had a hole in its bottom. Gary and Kent carried the boat into the cabin, still inflated. By the time they got it thawed out and dried so that a patch would stick, it was 4:30 in the morning. Then Gary went downriver about eight miles to Portage Campground. There he found a fisherman who showed him a trail that led overland eight miles to Larsen Bay.

Though Gary had already been through an enormous physical ordeal, he came up with still another act of courage and ran that trail. At Larsen Bay he found a commercial fisherman who took him by skiff to a nearby village. There he used a two-way radio to contact the Coast Guard Air Rescue Service. Within moments a helicopter carrying two doctors took off.

Meanwhile, Kent stayed up and poured fluids down me. Each time I'd begin sinking into deep shock he'd bring me out of it by talking and insisting I pay attention. I'm sure that both of my friends saved my life several times.

The helicopter arrived about noon. It took me to the air station dispensary in Kodiak. I was then flown to Elmendorf Air Force Base hospital in Anchorage. X-rays taken of my right foot showed bullet fragments and told an astonishing story. Though we had assumed that the bear had demolished my foot, it turned out that one of the three bullets Gary had fired into the bear had plowed through the animal and into my foot. It entered through my instep and then went straight up my leg for nine inches, smashing every bone it hit.

The first doctor that checked the damage wanted to amputate, but in a military hospital two doctors have to agree that such surgery is necessary. They decided to wait for three days to see if any feeling returned to my foot. It did, so the doctors began a long series of operations to repair the damage.

I was in the Air Force hospital for four months, then I was sent to Bremerton Naval Hospital in Washington state where I stayed for six months. After that I was in and out of hospitals for short stays during the next three years. I had the final operation on my right leg in February 1980. Its use is now fully restored.

After I left the dispensary in Kodiak, Gary hired an air taxi and went back after the bear. He and the pilot found it only 150 yards from where I'd lain on the beach. I often wonder if he was still alive while I was there. The odds are that the animal was dead because Gary found six bullet wounds when he skinned it. The bear had been hit twice in the left shoulder (my first shots) and once each in the right lung, neck, and left lung (Gary's shots), plus my final shot which ripped through the left rump.

The skull officially scored 29, and it tied for the 2nd Award at the last North American Big Game Awards Program sponsored by the Boone and Crockett Club and the National Rifle Association. My trophy now ties for 86th place among the 263 Alaskan brown bears in the record book. I had the bear mounted life size and standing erect, and the mount is now on display in the Federal Building near my home in Anchorage.

There's no way I could have made it back to good health as soon as I did without the nursing care given by my bride Kathy. We were married on May 14, a little more than two weeks after my ordeal. My injuries weren't enough to change our plans — I went to the altar in a wheelchair.

Index